FROM THE SCULPTOR'S STUDIO

LAURENCE KING

First published in Great Britain
in 2021 by Laurence King Publishing
an imprint of The Orion Publishing Group Ltd
Carmelite House, 50 Victoria Embankment
London EC4Y 0DZ

An Hachette UK Company

10 9 8 7 6 5 4 3 2 1

A CIP catalogue record for this book is
available from the British Library.

ISBN 978 1 91394 759 0

Design by Alexandre Coco
Printed in China by C&C Offset Printing Co Ltd

Laurence King Publishing is committed to ethical
and sustainable production. We are proud participants
in The Book Chain Project® bookchainproject.com

BOOK CHAIN PROJECT

www.laurenceking.com
www.orionbooks.co.uk

FRONT COVER:
Anish Kapoor
Mother as a Mountain, 1985

Wood, gesso and pigment
140 x 275 x 105 cm
(55 ⅛ x 108¼ x 41⅜ in)
© Anish Kapoor. All rights
reserved, DACS 2021

BACK COVER:
Fiona Banner
aka The Vanity Press
Harrier, 2010

BAE Sea Harrier aircraft, paint
7.6 × 14.2 × 3.71 m
(24 ft 11¼ in × 46 ft 7⅛ in ×
12 ft 2⅛ in)
Photo: © Tate, Andrew
Dunkley and Sam Drake ©
The artist; courtesy the artist
and Frith Street Gallery,
London (see page 16)

FROM THE SCULPTOR'S STUDIO

Conversations with Twenty Seminal Artists

Ina Cole

Laurence King Publishing

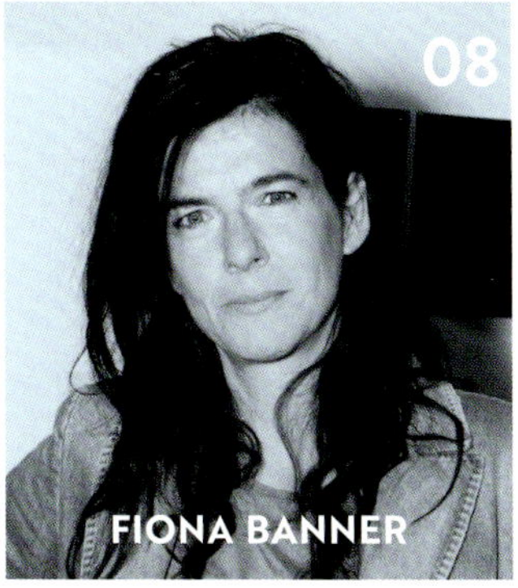

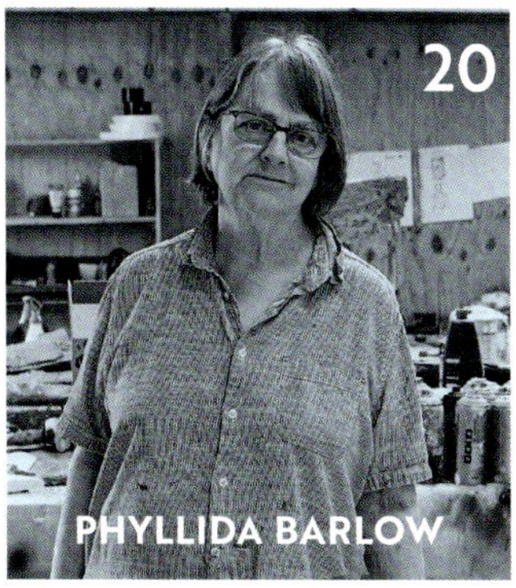

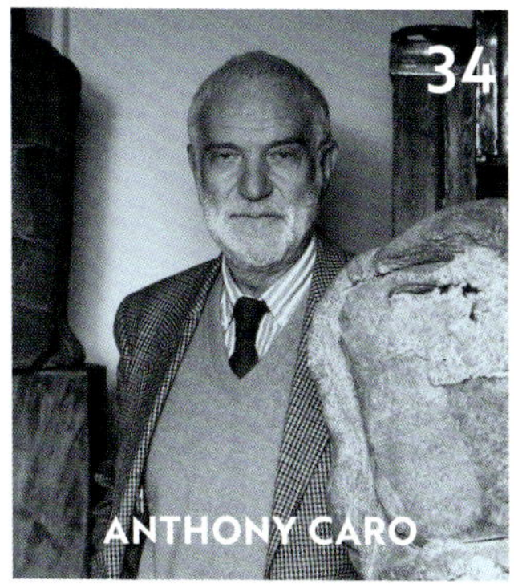

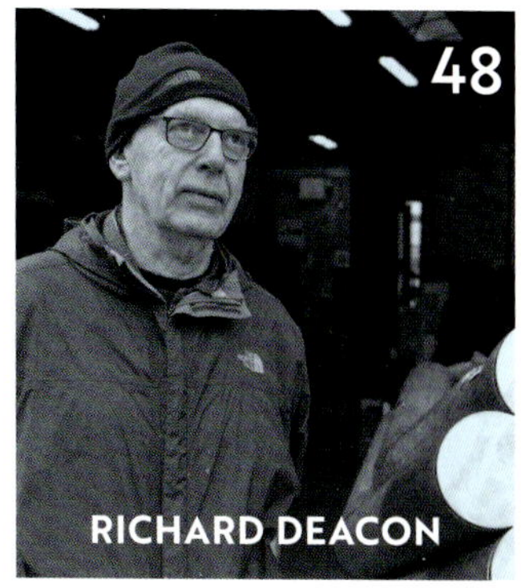

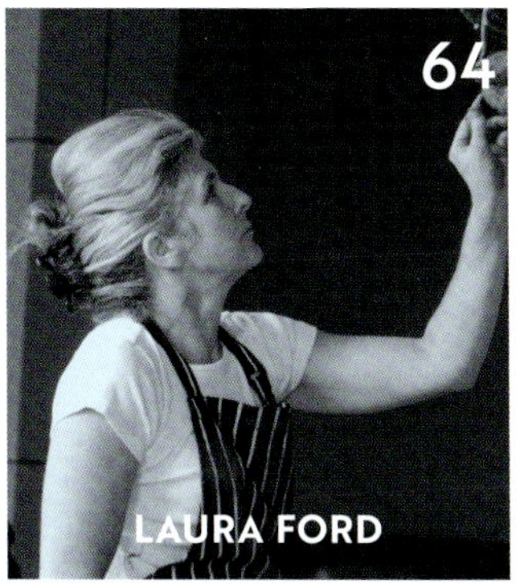

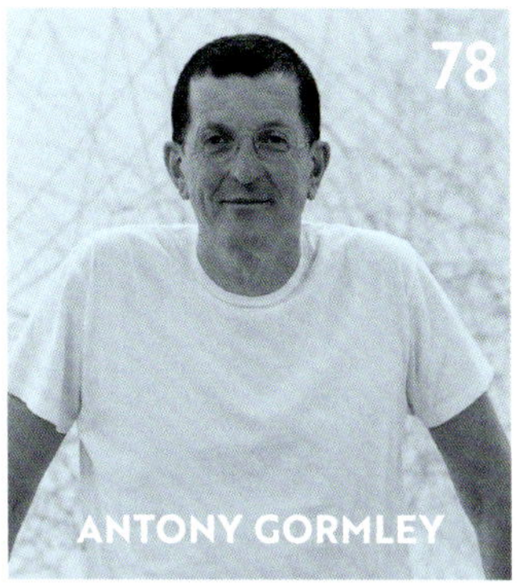

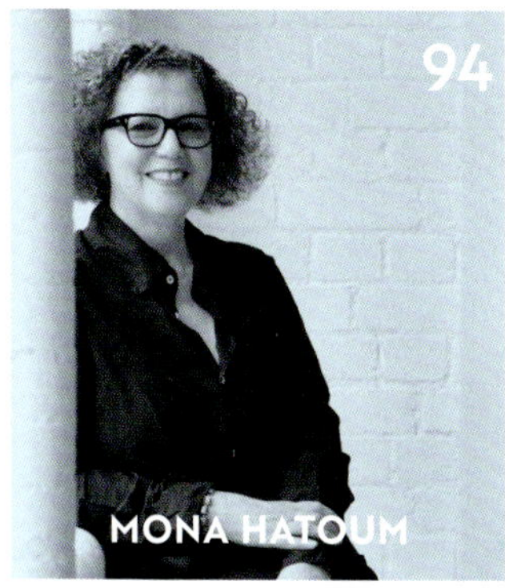

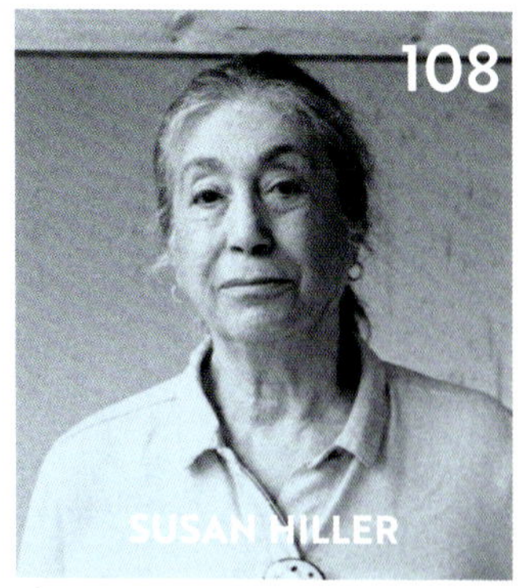

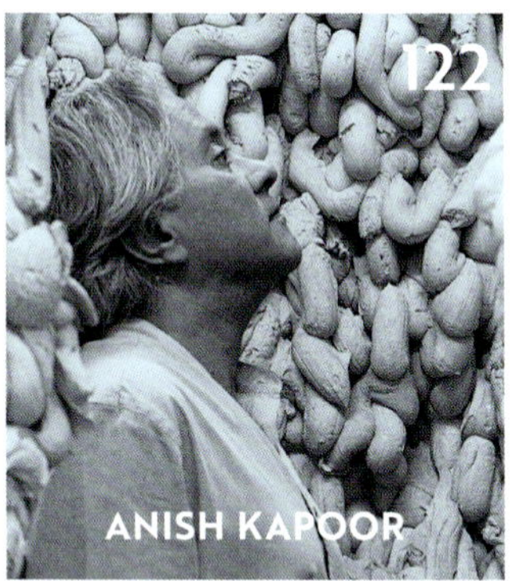

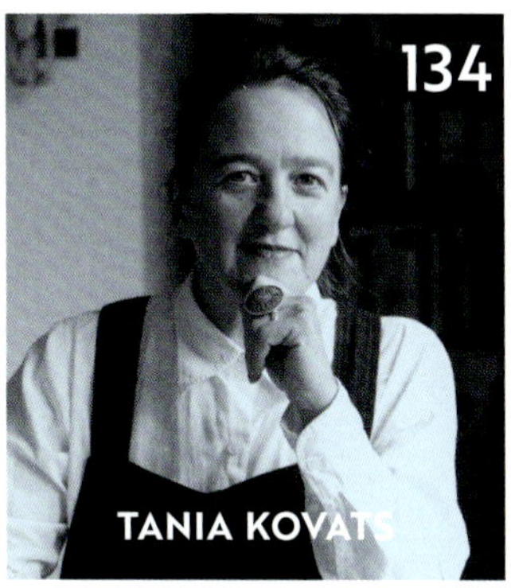

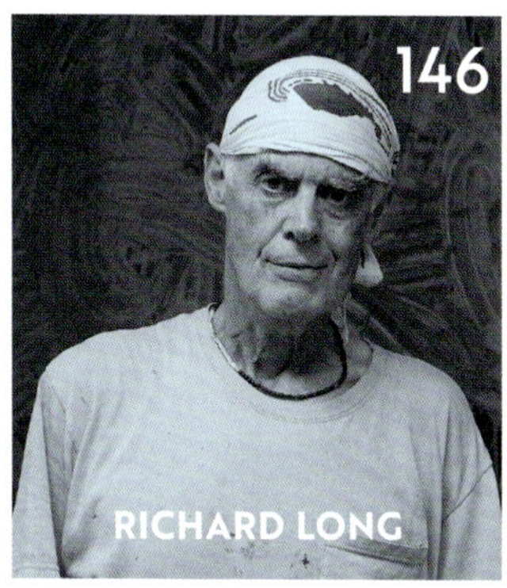

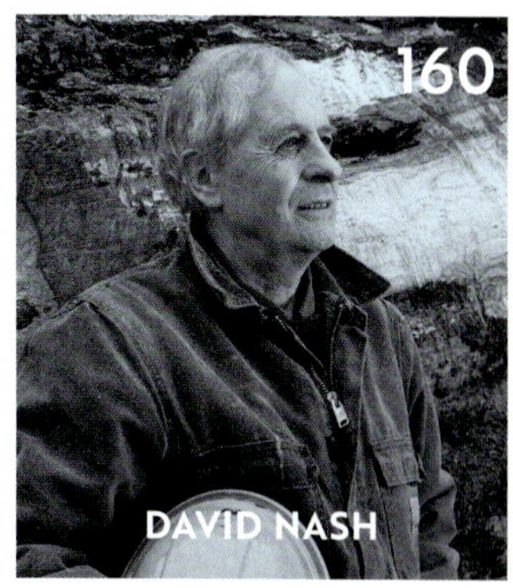

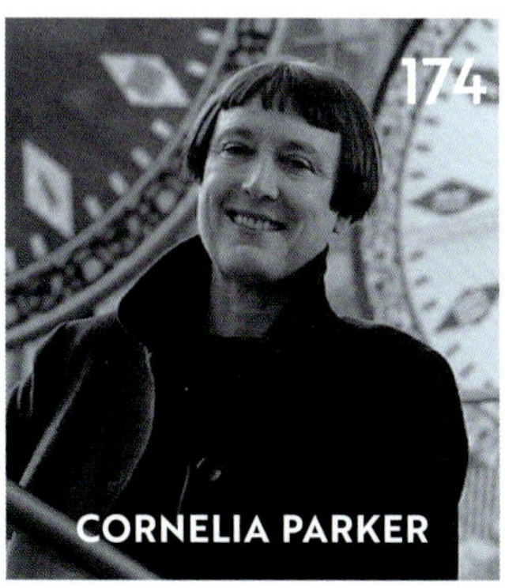

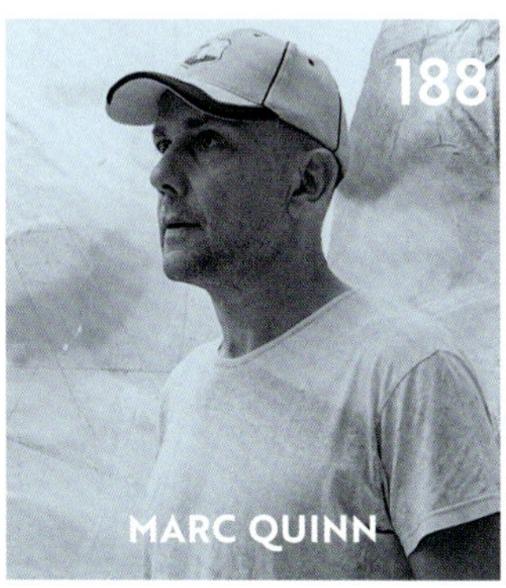

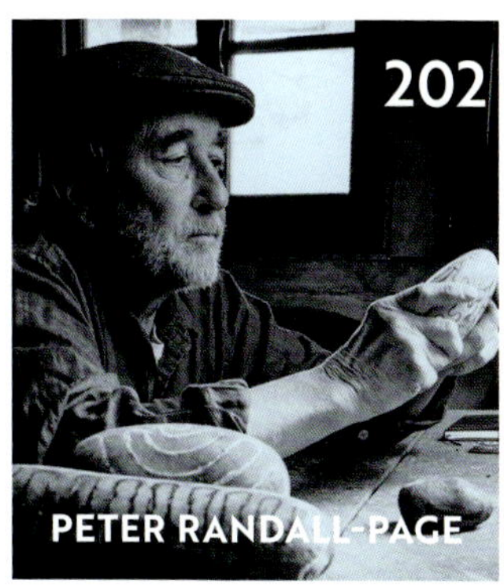

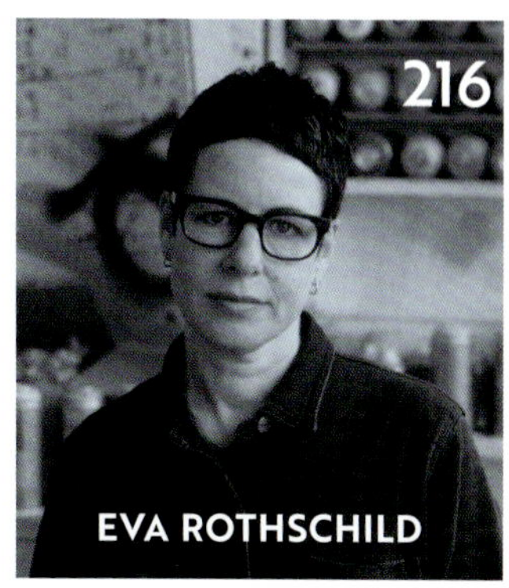

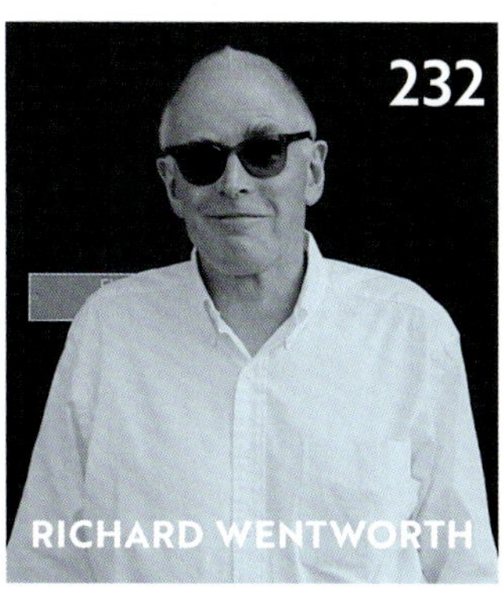

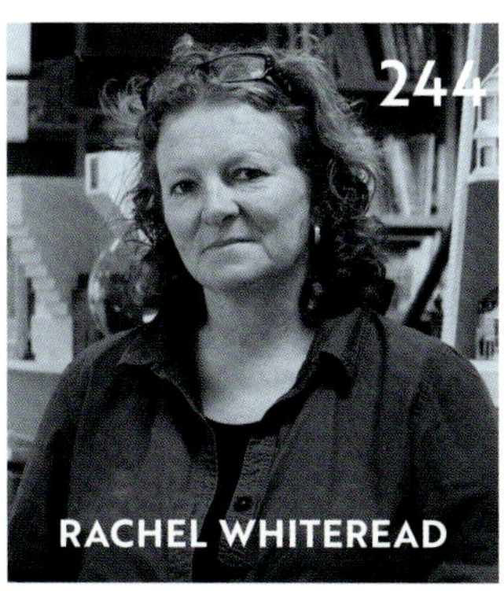

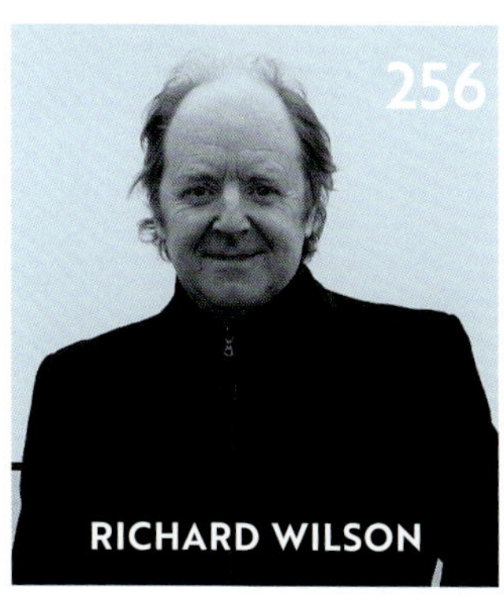

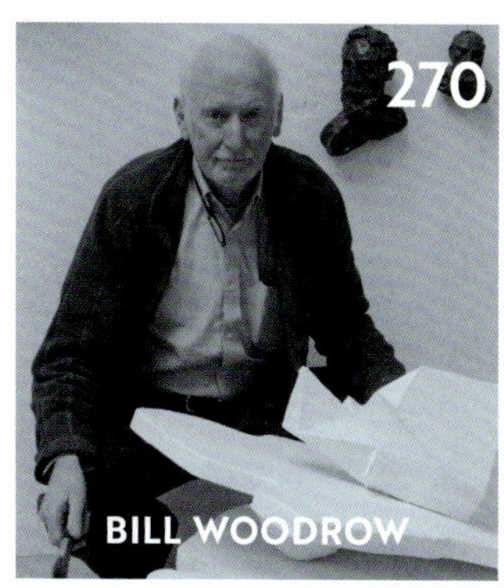

INTRODUCTION

From the Sculptor's Studio has originated from edited transcripts of recorded conversations that I conducted with 20 contemporary artists: Fiona Banner, Phyllida Barlow, Anthony Caro, Richard Deacon, Laura Ford, Antony Gormley, Mona Hatoum, Susan Hiller, Anish Kapoor, Tania Kovats, Richard Long, David Nash, Cornelia Parker, Marc Quinn, Peter Randall-Page, Eva Rothschild, Richard Wentworth, Rachel Whiteread, Richard Wilson and Bill Woodrow. These artists are credited with some of the most ground-breaking works of the late twentieth and early twenty-first centuries, and the texts offer a window into their practice, going behind the scenes to reveal how many of the artworks were created. Process is, in itself, an adventure, through which new discoveries are realized. Hence, each interview serves as a conduit for the artist to reflect on their influences and methods, thereby uncovering illuminating, and often unexpected, insights into modes of production and engagement. The intention is not to impose prescribed concepts; rather, it is to propose an open approach that allows the voice of the artist, the source, to shine through and elucidate the act of making.

Through these conversations, *From the Sculptor's Studio* sets out to explore and build upon Britain's sculptural legacy, which traces its modernist roots to the 1930s. Since then, the practice of sculpture has undergone many pivotal innovations, while art history of the period remains subject to vigorous debate. The 'meaning' of a work of art changes when viewed through the prism of history, and so, inevitably, that meaning can become distorted, even neutralized. Such is the fate of intention: it is continuously redefined. Once a work leaves the studio, it assumes a life of its own, inviting interpretation to become a touchstone against which human sentiment can be measured, or a carrier for the sociopolitical concerns of an era. Indeed, the inherent ambiguity of an artwork is part of its purpose. Yet, when intention dissolves through the process of re-evaluation, it does not necessarily indicate a more enlightened, or truthful, viewpoint has been reached. Artists are, after all, the key interpreters of their practice and, when navigating an exhibition, the viewer, generally speaking, has a desire to know what the artist, not the historian, was actually thinking. By utilizing recorded conversations, therefore, distortion of the facts can be somewhat mitigated, as the makers' ideas are fully articulated in their own words.

The cultural and social legacies of the past clearly filter and shape individual and collective responses to both the present and the future. And, although the interviews, in part, forge a discussion on how past influences continue to direct individual enquiry, they simultaneously highlight the substantial variables found within contemporary acts of making. Since the late twentieth century the practice of sculpture has become increasingly plural, thereby opening the door to new possibilities and a greater merging of disciplines. *From the Sculptor's Studio* uncovers a diversity of working methods, through the use of materials that range from the organic and degradable to products of high-tech engineering. Some artists turn outwards, to unbounded nature; others turn inwards, to their own bodies. There are those who rely on science and technology, or multi-disciplinary teams of experts, in the realization of a work. Likewise, while the studio is still a place in which to experiment and refine, there are those artists who pursue a more nomadic approach to making. Of course, there are also those who oscillate between different approaches, and who choose to situate themselves within multiple disparate settings.

By claiming an ever-increasing vocabulary of materials and methods, artists are forging paths where none previously existed. Some create an immersive experience that entices the viewer into an environment, in which the transformation of physical space triggers the transformation of emotional and cerebral space. And, by becoming a participant or witness, the viewer emerges from that experience temporarily altered, through having undergone a transitory physical and mental separation from the norm. For others, the aesthetic autonomy of the artwork is absolute, initiating an enriching alliance between viewer and object. As an independent form, filled with alchemical energy, the artwork can make the same claim on space as a human body and, by occupying the space of sculpture, the mind is freed to establish connections that can be immensely powerful and challenging. In *From the Sculptor's Studio*, the artists reflect on how, through the development of their own practice, these profound ways of seeing are both generated and sustained.

Society remains predisposed towards the transitional object – one that has the potential to evoke memory and emotion – and on this point, sculpture's intrinsic purpose is clear. Throughout history, objects have acquired meaning peripheral to their inanimate reality through the beliefs and ideologies imposed upon them. Society continues to be bound by old traditions: by the spirit of the tribe, by a host of beliefs, superstitions and taboos. Feeling compelled to fix one's attention onto an object that appears to inhabit some other realm is a primal concern and, still, engenders a sense of personal aspiration or enlightenment. Sculpture can serve to fulfil this impulse, as it is an experiential language. Being able to walk around, or into, a work of art provides a moment of stasis in a world of perpetual motion – a pause, or an opportunity for contemplation. By bringing together a wide range of contemporary approaches, *From the Sculptor's Studio* affirms the artwork's enduring capacity to inspire reverie, curiosity, shock, awe and, even, fear. Whether as an independent form, or as a succession of encounters, it holds up a candid and unflinching mirror that exposes all of life's facets, nuances and, above all, paradoxes.

Ina Cole

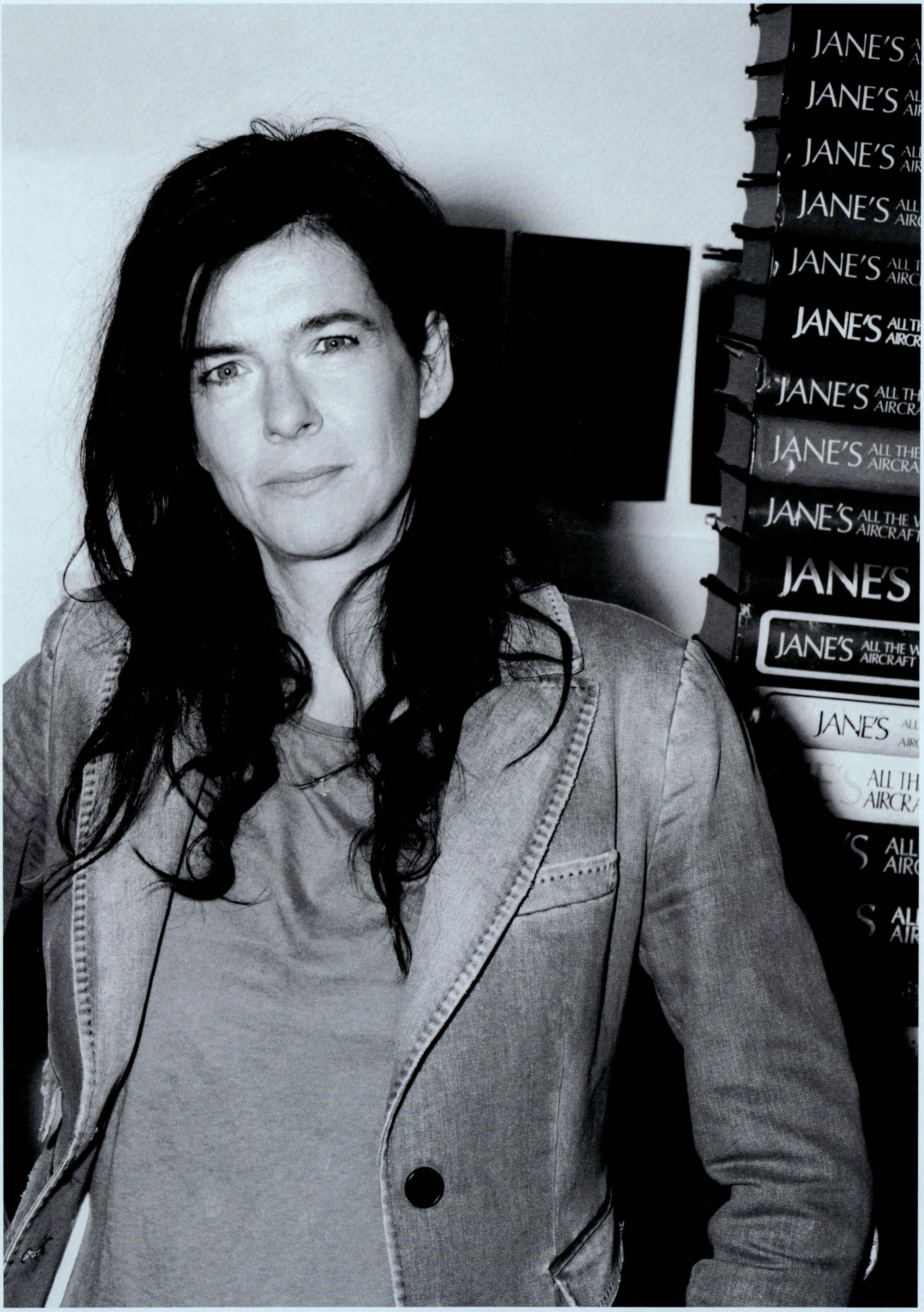
JANE'S
JANE'S
JANE'S
JANE'S
JANE'S
JANE'S
JANE'S
JANE'S
JANE'S
JANE'S
JANE'S
JANE'S

FIONA BANNER

Born 1966, Liverpool, Merseyside

For Fiona Banner aka The Vanity Press publishing is, in itself, a performative act through which notions of authorship and copyright can be questioned, and her work is concerned with how language and history become appropriated and mythologized by society. She established The Vanity Press in 1997 on publication of a 1000-page wordscape book, *The Nam*, comprising a frame-by-frame transcript of Hollywood films about the Vietnam War. Her work often develops from obscure sources, including the books of Fred T. Jane, founder of the annual publication *Jane's All the World's Aircraft*, while *Darkness Stack* and *Breathing Bag* reference Joseph Conrad's seminal novella *Heart of Darkness*. Banner's projects pose uncomfortable questions about society's responses to the forces of power and conflict, as seen in *1066*, her panoramic wall drawing examining the Battle of Hastings. By the same token, *Harrier and Jaguar*, a challenging commission for Tate Britain's Duveen Galleries, in London, rendered her concerns at a monumental scale.

Ina Cole: You established The Vanity Press in 1997 with the publication of *The Nam*. In 2009 you registered yourself as a publication under your own name and ISBN (International Standard Book Number). Looking back, what provided the impetus for this?

Fiona Banner aka The Vanity Press: I'm interested in making art that moves around in different ways to the art object *per se*, and how a book can become legitimate, transferable or moveable currency. All art is a form of vanity publishing. Registering myself as a publication was a way of playing with the myth of biography and the need to describe ourselves and our lives. It was also a riff on the absurdity, impossibility or conceit of that. Am I a publication, a fiction or a period of time? It's a joke, but a performance as well, so very considered. Later, I started working under the name Fiona Banner aka The Vanity Press, which seemed natural, as I collaborate a lot. It's an acknowledgement that it's not just me.

IC: Your practice draws upon the physical dimension of language and the manner in which meaning becomes manipulated through time. How did this evolve into the making of sculpture?

FB: I never really set out to make sculpture; it's simply that ideas and texts sometimes find form in a sculptural way. The relationship between spoken and written language, and sculptural form, acknowledges that words are an extension of our physical selves. *Full Stops* (1998), my first sculptures, came from several years of using straightforward writing as a medium. My work had suddenly lost content; language fell away, and I was just left with punctuation. So, those pieces represent language stripped of content – a crisis. Feeling lost, or empty, isn't a vacuum; it's a physical experience, and I wanted to make physical that sense, which is how the sculptures of massively blown-up full stops happened. They characterize uncertainty by using blankness as content. Turning a negative, a breath in or a pause, into a positive, or emptiness into tangible shapes, seemed like a way to proceed.

IC: Many of your earlier text pieces retell sequences from entire Hollywood war films and make a statement on how events are fictionalized and mythologized. In *Mythologies* (1957), the French essayist Roland Barthes famously wrote about myth as a system of communication with an unlimited mass of signifiers. He identified a problem in that intentions can become naturalized; in other words, myth abolishes the complexity of human acts. There's a curious parallel with his concept and *The Nam* (1997).

FB: Myth is important in structuring belief. Just look at the grandiose mythologies out there in politics today. I made *The Nam* because I'd seen those Vietnam films, and got simultaneously repelled and seduced by how they retell a conflict that was televised when I was a tiny kid. *The Nam* is absurd and unwieldy, as much a sculpture as a book. It doesn't disappear in the hand in the way a book is supposed to; it challenges its own ability to be consumed as a book. How history is mythologized, eroticized, gendered and consumed is as relevant now as it was when I made *The Nam*. We create lineage and understanding, even though we know it's fabricated and politicized. In a sense I'm reflective, yet on the other hand I'm a dumb consumer. I worked with those Hollywood films not only because they're brilliant, but because I got completely drawn into their mythological space, before reflecting on them politically.

IC: *1066* (2010) is an immersive wall drawing about the Battle of Hastings. It makes reference to the Bayeux Tapestry, which stands as a primary historical document of this event. In *1066*, is the shape and flexibility of the letters, in terms of typographic structure, as important as their meaning?

FB: They're inseparable. There's always a question around how language can and might exist. I wanted *1066* to have a sense of space, not only in the here and now, but historical, or even oral, space. It's overwritten several times, partly as a natural circumstance of planning the layout as I went along, and partly as a

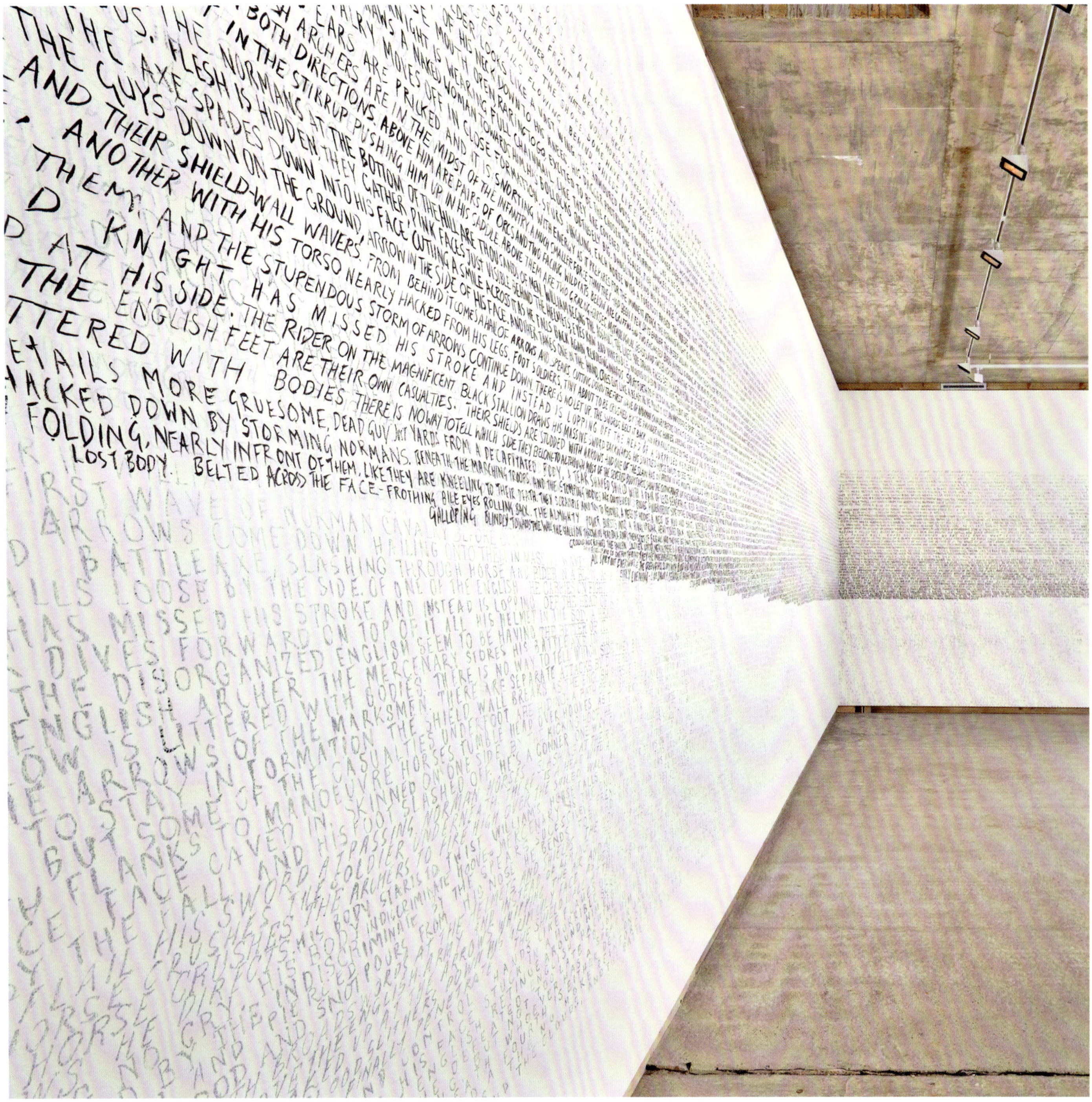

Fiona Banner
aka The Vanity Press
1066, 2010 (detail)

Indian ink on wall
2150 × 400 cm
(70 ft 6½ in × 13 ft 1½ in)
Installation view:
Frith Street Gallery,
London, 2010–11

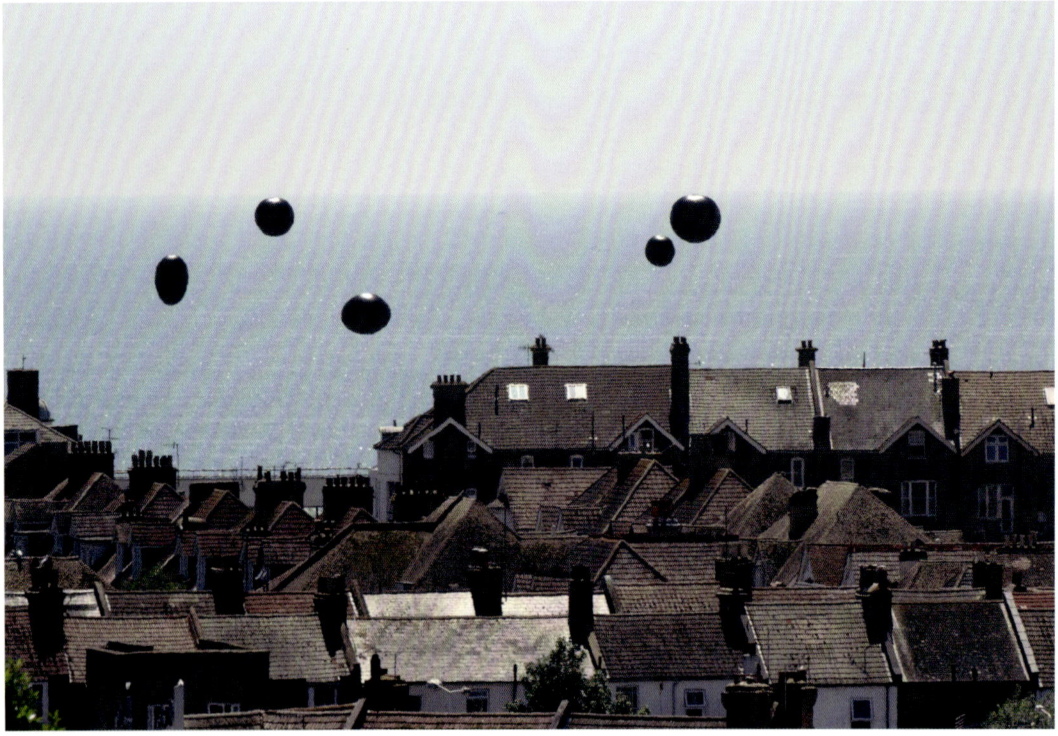

←
Fiona Banner aka The Vanity Press
Buoys Boys, 2016

Full Stop inflatables (Onyx, Bookman, Capitalist, Didot, Courier) Sculptural performance, De La Warr Pavilion, Bexhill-on-Sea, 2016–17

way of one documentary overwriting another. I could have continually rewritten it and the story would be told differently each time. The victor writes the history. It's an incredibly slanted view, not even-handed at all. In *1066* the slanted writing and layers of text aren't contained in a rectangle; it's like naïvely looking for a truth, which is also layered and, in the end, impossible to find. In the absence of a major film about the battle, I based the text on the Bayeux Tapestry. This is, in itself, a bit like a storyboard, and still considered a primary historical document of the conflict. When I first saw the Bayeux Tapestry I was shocked at its brutality. Looking closely, I noticed the horses going into battle have huge erections, which is funny given the tapestry was stitched by nuns in defeated Sussex.

IC: You've had a long interest in Joseph Conrad's novella *Heart of Darkness* (1902), resulting in *Darkness Stack* (2016), and a kinetic work *Breathing Bag* (2016) that bears the inscription 'Mistah Kurtz – He Not Dead', a subverted reference to Conrad's main protagonist in the novella. *Heart of Darkness* transcends its era to stay continually relevant, but what drew you towards it?

FB: It has stayed relevant; it's a lens for different ages. My first awareness of *Heart of Darkness* was through the film *Apocalypse Now*, and, more recently, I came across Orson Welles's unmade film script for *Heart of Darkness*. Conrad's narrative is dense, and also lyrical. It feels more like a painting than a text when you're reading it, engorged with ideas around the hero and the anti-hero. I produced a work using Welles's script, with actor Brian Cox, and this became the world première of Welles's *Heart of Darkness* (Artangel, 2012). The script refers to now: late capitalism, greed, abuse of power, white supremacy, disgust with society, disenfranchisement, but our constant need

→
Fiona Banner
aka The Vanity Press
The Man and
Mistah Kurtz, 2018

Merlin helicopter tail blades, bespoke plastic bags and paint
177 × 40 cm
(69¾ × 15¾ in)

↓
Fiona Banner
aka The Vanity Press
Falcon 59400 pt, 2019

Pneumatic ship's fender
3.3 × 6.5 m
(10 ft 10 in × 21 ft 3⅞ in)
Installation view:
Frith Street Gallery,
London, 2019–20

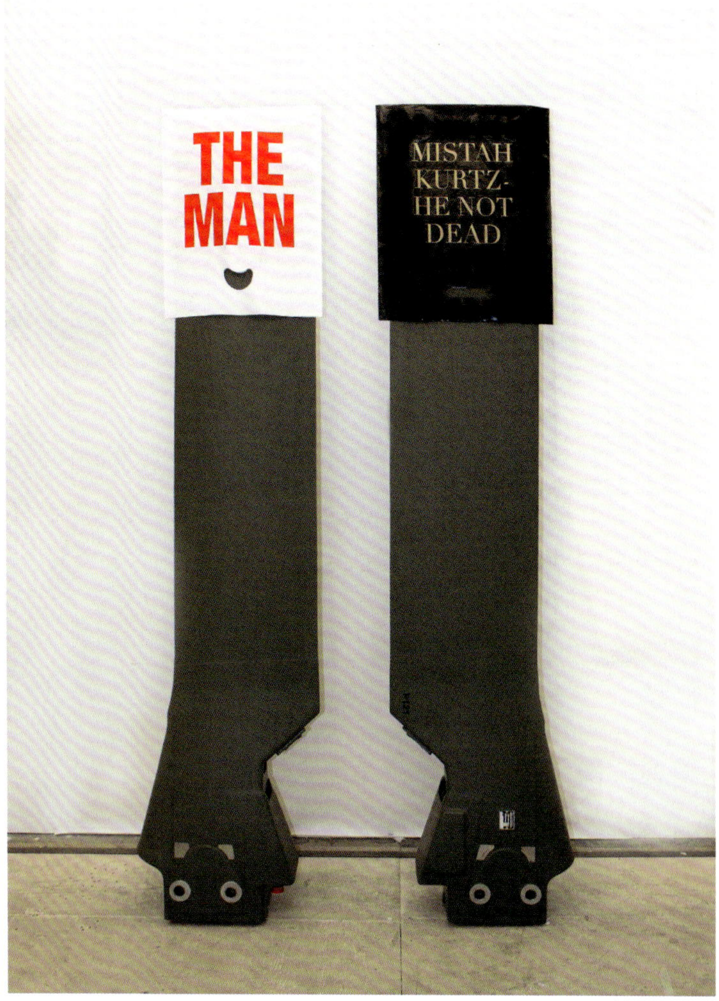

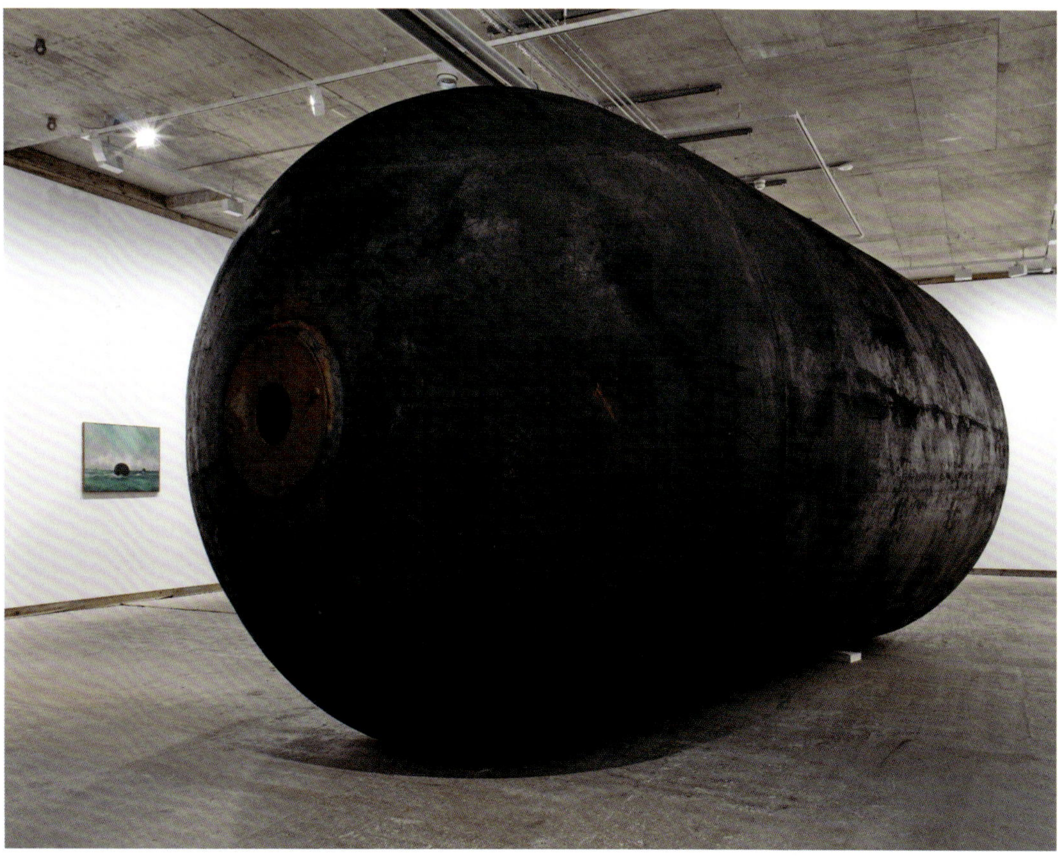

for more. All of this conflates in Conrad's novel. Then I published a luxury magazine, an alluring and worrying version of *Heart of Darkness* set in the City of London, which mirrors our insatiable desire for luxury and consumption.

I've always made bags for my publications. It's a nod to how they are mobilized. *Breathing Bag* twists the famous phrase, 'Mistah Kurtz – He Dead', to 'Mistah Kurtz – He Not Dead'. The ubiquity of the supremo baddie is that there's always another one. 'Mistah Kurtz – He Not Dead' is a grandiose statement, inscribed in gold onto a lowly plastic bag. This becomes a sculpture because it has air pumped in and out of it, as if it's breathing. It's imbued with a strange feeling of urgency and narrative, as the breathing speeds up then stops, so it develops a bizarre presence. *Breathing Bag* uses an Arduino, a mini computer with a specially devised programme, that sits behind a wall, with a mini fan attached to it. I most enjoy my work when it appears super full of itself, but it's a joke as well. We take art incredibly seriously. It's a dubious and overblown, yet crucial, enterprise. So, the vulnerability and fetishistic nature of the sculptural object is always a key driver for me.

IC: The deflation of the art object, actual or metaphorical, is pertinent to both *Buoys Boys* (2016) and *Falcon 59400 pt* (2019). *Buoys Boys* are five helium-filled inflatables that have travelled across the English Channel. They echo the form of full stops in different typefaces, while *Falcon*, a ship's fender, was the centrepiece of an exhibition at Frith Street Gallery in London (2019–20).

FB: *Falcon 59400 pt* is a rubber inflatable, so it collapses when the air gets sucked out of it and becomes a non-object. There's a general mood in my work around freight and movement, and the currency of these apparently fixed uber-objects, which are also transient, both functional and non-functional, as they're on exhibition and then packed away. They have a slippery context in life and their meaning is open to interpretation, which also links to intellectual freight, copyright and ownership. The initial concept for *Buoys Boys* – first shown at the De La Warr Pavilion in Bexhill-on-Sea, East Sussex (2016) – was for them to be sited in the water, but, in the end, they floated above it instead. The word 'channel' is interesting: it could refer to a channel of communication, or to a fluid, transient space, as well as a barrier, or block.

This idea informed the making of *Falcon*, which both resembles, and becomes a stand-in for, the full stop from the font Falcon. So, if that font was blown up to a point size of 59400, it would be as large as the ship's fender. *Falcon* is uber-present, and a void as well. It has a role as a super muscular divider which stops ships from colliding, but it's also an absent space keeping things apart, and this, in turn, relates to the role of the full stop in language. In a wider context, the Frith Street Gallery exhibition referred to a period of suspended animation, in the way we're floundering around issues on climate change, Brexit and our identity as an island. There's a lot of mistrust around the use and misuse of language.

IC: A preoccupation with aircraft is also central to your practice. *1909–2011* (2010) records a century of military aircraft using volumes of Fred T. Jane's *All the World's Aircraft*, collected over many years. How did you come by all these books, and why did you decide to construct a precariously high tower from them?

FB: The title of that work changes every year; it's a tower that gets added to, so it becomes increasing unwieldy. Fred T. Jane began *All the World's Aircraft* in 1909, and, over the years, they illustrated some extraordinary aeroplanes that went into pre-production but were never made. At first, I just had a couple of his books. The content is fascinating and the graphics are cool, so I decided to make a work from them. I never quite understood their enigma but came to think it was due to their transsexual nature: they're called Jane's yet contain incredibly macho content. The fact they're stuck with that incongruous name creates a funny tension. I then accumulated more of them, even though they're quite hard to find. An American collector once offered me the full collection, which is when I realized I was actually more interested in the act of collecting and didn't want them as a library.

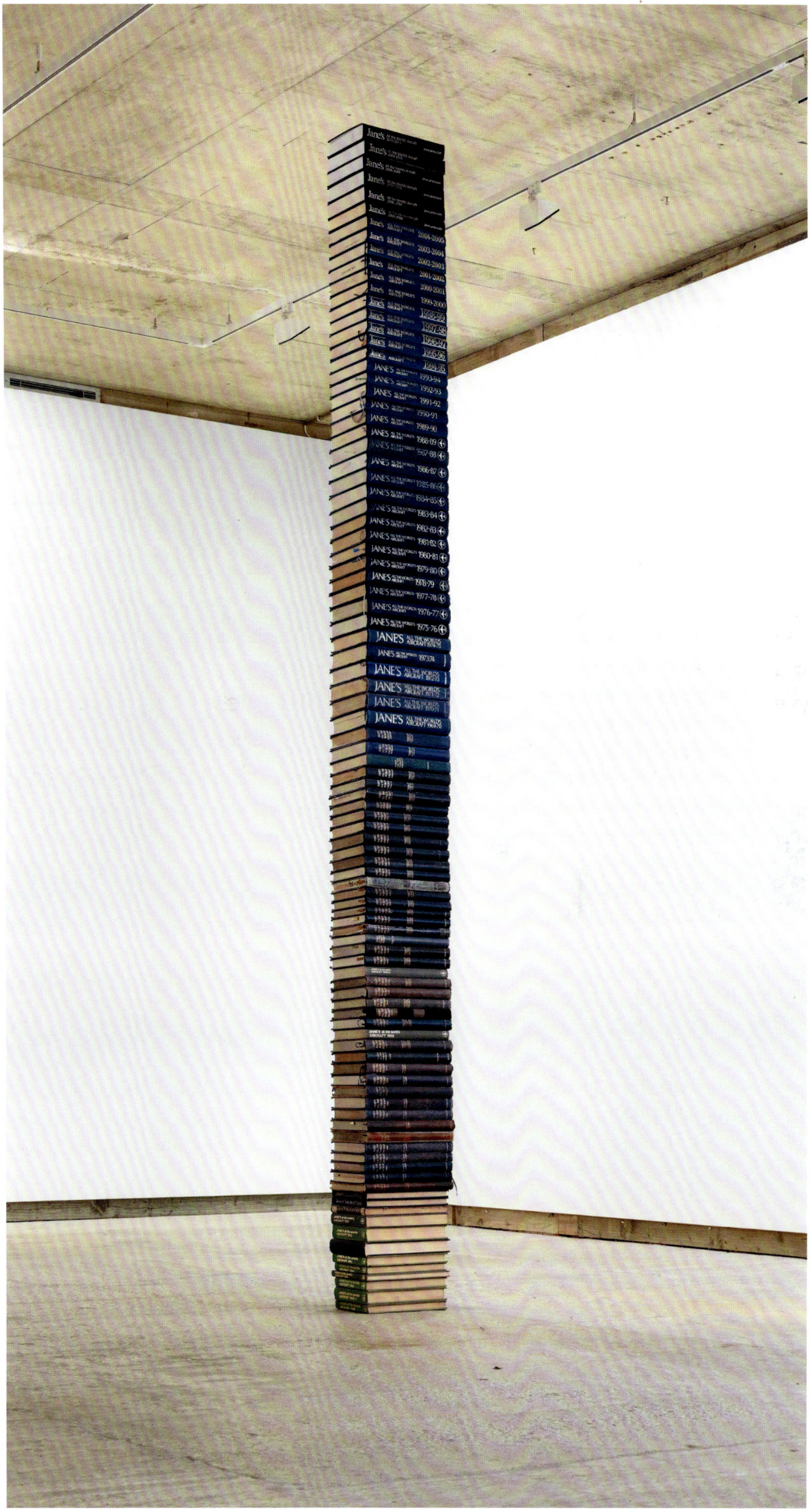

Fiona Banner
aka The Vanity Press
1909-2011, 2010

97 *Jane's All the World's Aircraft* books
22 × 35 × 375 cm
(8¾ in × 13¾ in × 12 ft 3⅝ in)
Installation view:
Frith Street Gallery,
London, 2010–11

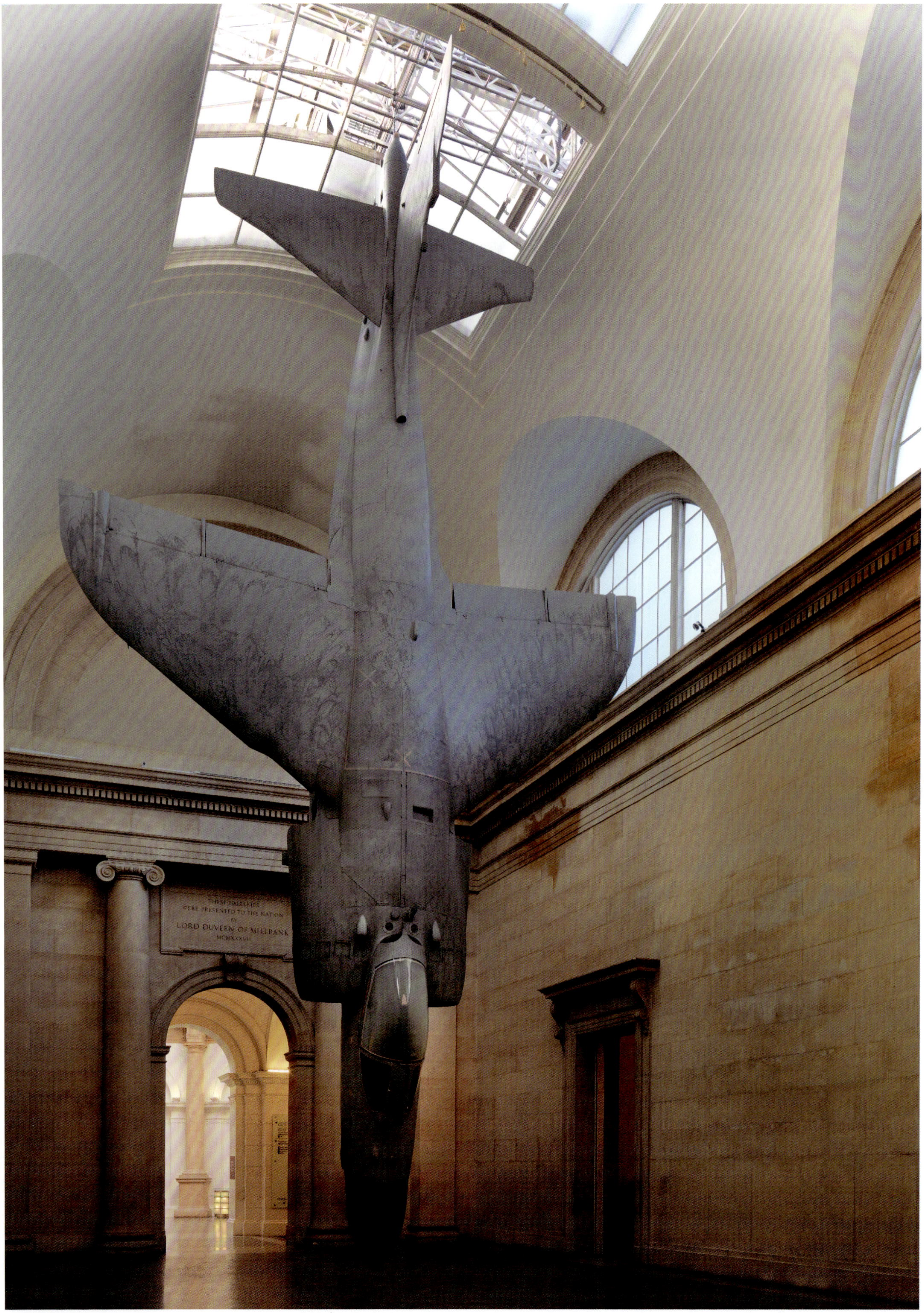
WERE PRESENTED TO THE NATION
BY
LORD DUVEEN OF MILLBANK

←
Fiona Banner
aka The Vanity Press
Harrier, 2010

BAE Sea Harrier aircraft, paint
7.6 × 14.2 × 3.71 m
(24 ft 11¼ in × 46 ft 7⅛ in × 12 ft 2⅛ in)
Installation view:
Tate Britain, London, 2010

→
Fiona Banner
aka The Vanity Press
Parade, 2006

177 kit model planes
and nylon wire
Installation view:
The Power Plant,
Toronto, 2007

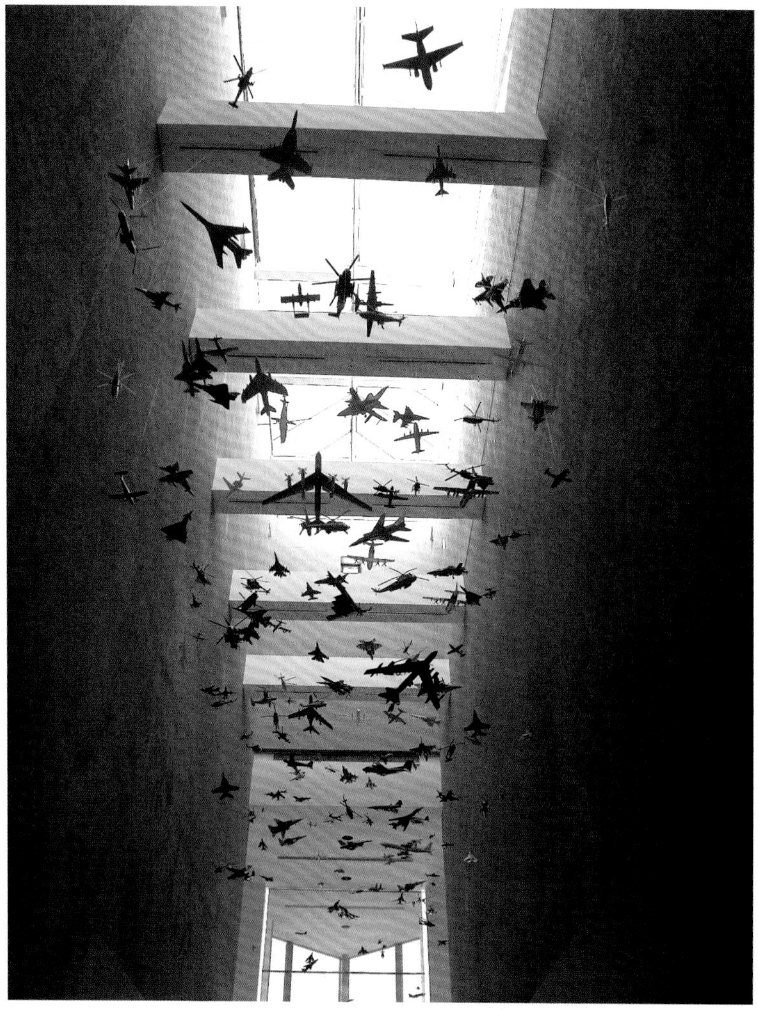

I ended up making the simplest piece I could think of; the sculptural equivalent of a list, which is a stack. This stack can also be seen as representing a passage of time that starts with the beginning of flight, as you can see the typographic changes through the decades on the spines of the books. Building a stack this high is precarious. I had many attempts and it kept falling down, so it became wedged and propped. The volumes are heavy, and building a tower became an ephemeral, uncertain process. There's also a fragile, vertiginous element, as when you're standing underneath it sways slightly.

IC: *Harrier and Jaguar* was a commission for Tate Britain's Duveen Galleries in 2010. Visually, these two aircraft are supreme entities, but you stripped them of their power, in that *Harrier* hung nose down from the ceiling, while *Jaguar* lay inert on the floor. What did you mean when you said they represent the opposite of language?

FB: They represent the opposite of communication, or what happens when it breaks down. *Harrier and Jaguar* were decommissioned aircraft I bought from the Ministry of Defence. We celebrate conflict in a way we don't really like to think about. Intellectually, we all loathe war, but there's an odd celebration around it that goes far beyond supporting the troops. As an island, Britain's investment in the military exceeds what seems proportionate. The Duveen Galleries, in the heart of Tate Britain, provided a good place for a discussion on how aesthetics and power coexist, and our dodgy relationship with that duality as a society. I wanted two planes that were contemporary; the Harrier had gone from being an extraordinary phenomenon in the Falklands to virtual obsolescence, while the Jaguar had performed in the first Desert Storm and Bosnia, amongst other conflicts. Both had a violent history. *Harrier and Jaguar* has been melted down and exists as ingots, stamped and stacked on pallets as a reduced currency, or reduced to a currency. I wanted to erase the heroic image of those aircraft, as they're so potent in terms of their history and previous life. If *Harrier and Jaguar* had been kept whole and sold on for further display, it would have been a completely different project. Having pushed their fetishistic nature – through stripping and polishing and turning them into incredible vanitas – then doing the opposite in order to store them, felt really good. I also particularly liked the fact they were named after two predatory, but quite beautiful animals. I was quite specific about getting those two planes.

IC: The names of military aircraft often refer to animals at the top of the food chain and, consequently, the survival of the fittest. Do you think our elevation of these objects reflects an inherent aspiration to conquer and control?

FB: We're animals too, right? *All the World's Fighter Planes* (1999–2009) is a compilation of newspaper clippings I collected, representing every type of fighter aircraft in the world. The text on the cover references all their names, which frequently come from nature – Chinook, Tiger, Puma, Eagle. In another work, *Chinook* (2014), two sets of helicopter blades whizz and whirr around, avoiding collision, in a theatre of conflict and contradiction. There's something incredibly primitive about all these planes. As much as they're technologically overpowering, they feel like dinosaurs, in that they reference all-powerful nature, yet reveal the primitive aspect of ourselves.

IC: *Tornado* (2010) is a suspended bell cast from the fuselage of a jet fighter. Bells are traditionally used to assemble communities of people for significant events. Their function is universal, but their symbolism varies across cultures. What were your considerations when fusing these potentially clashing elements to create this perfect form?

FB: I like the word 'clashing'; I want to make objects that require completion, and some resistance in terms of understanding is important. Bells do bring people together, and they're also about dispersal and departure. One way or another they mark time. As *Tornado* is untuned the sound is a simple reflection of its form. Just before making it, I remembered a bell my grandfather had in his flat when I was a kid. I used to climb up on a chair to ring it, which was really exciting. I was always utterly shocked by how this physical object became transformed into a sound that was so much bigger than me; it felt like a very sculptural experience. It turns out the bell had come from a warship, which I didn't know at the time.

The idea of creating a bell from a Tornado – a plane with a horrendous but oddly exhilarating sound – made sense, even if they seem like opposites. Not that the bell is passive and the aeroplane aggressive *per se*. It's just physical engagement with the bell is important, particularly in a gallery where there's such a formal relationship to art. The bell invites you in and, if you engage with it, that moment is published by a vast sound.

Fiona Banner
aka The Vanity Press
Tornado, 2010

Aluminium from a
Tornado fighter ZE728,
rope, steel fixings
158.5 × 158.5 cm
(62⅜ × 62⅜ in)
Installation view:
Frith Street Gallery,
London, 2010–11

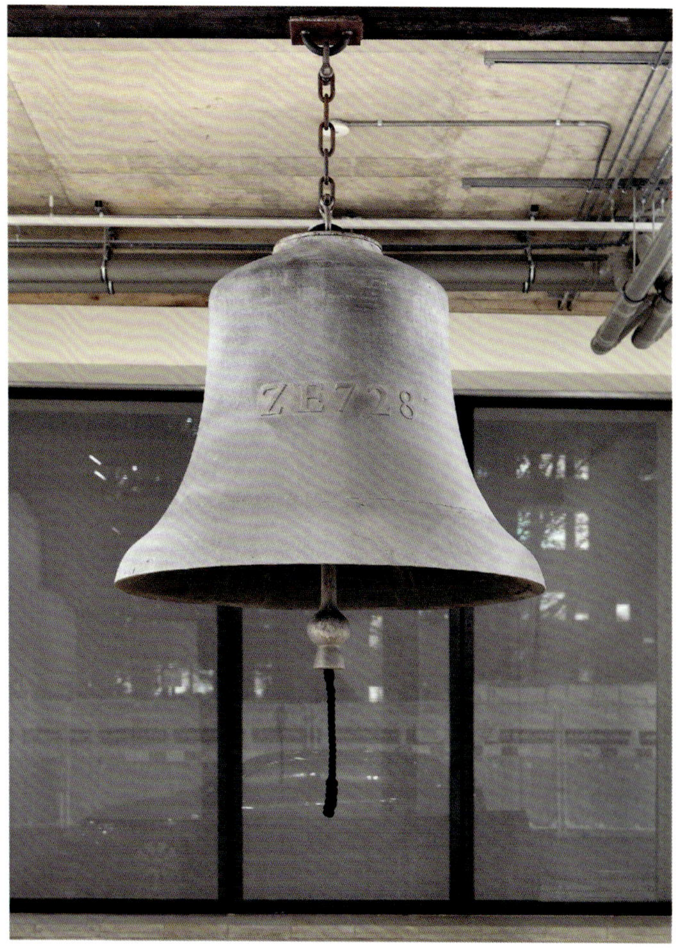

IC: You've recalled another childhood memory of walking in the Welsh mountains, as a fighter jet suddenly tore through the sky overhead. Why did this early experience inform your practice to such an extent?

FB: It's to do with the complicated relationship between beauty and violence. I remember walking through a calm, pastoral scene with my family when a man-made force of nature, an unbelievably gripping and devastating intervention, literally knocked the words right out of us. Yet it was really beautiful, and the contrast of that moment has stayed with me. It became a good metaphor for this clash of sensibilities between the emotional and the intellectual. It's why I used that particular memory with *Harrier and Jaguar* to create such a highly staged scenario at Tate Britain, as it's a space to reconsider and critique aesthetics. Of course, there's no answer, but the opportunity to put the question out became available and that was my response. We discuss work intellectually because the strategies of logic can be helpfully employed in that way, but there are many different reasons for making a work, and referencing memories is just one of them. We have a desire to impose history or linearity, even though events really just happen. If you reflect on it, there are a zillion reasons why people do something. It's a web, not a line.

Interviewed in 2010 and 2020

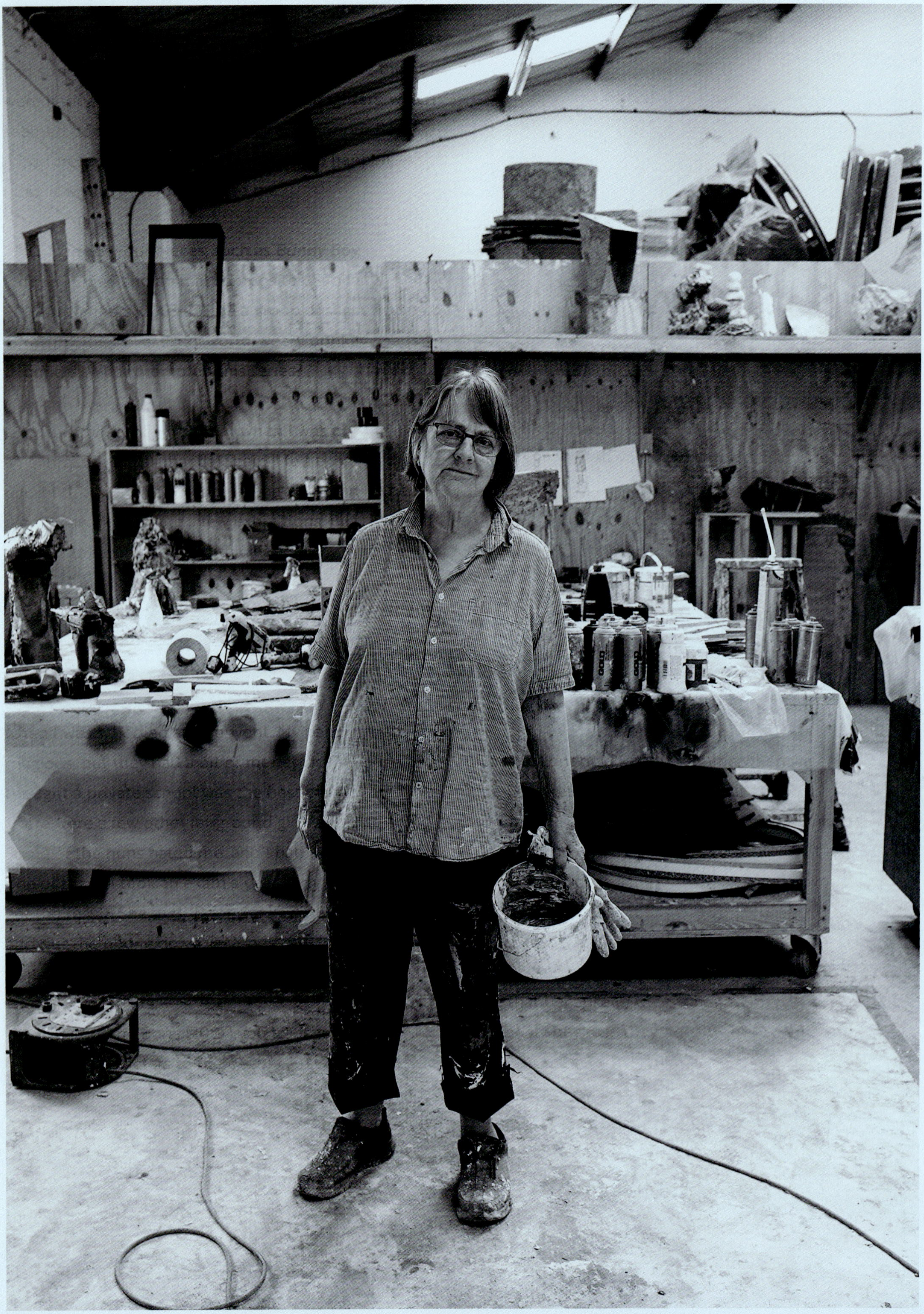

PHYLLIDA BARLOW

Born 1944, Newcastle upon Tyne, Northumberland

Phyllida Barlow's practice is one of production and deconstruction, and she uses everyday materials that are often discarded or recycled for new projects. Her methods involve crushing, wrapping, stretching, stacking and rolling, and the malleability of her materials is important since many of these projects are configured *in situ*. Barlow's skill in courting accident and chance remains unsurpassed, and installations often overspill the architecture that contains them. Upright, fallen and suspended structures are juxtaposed to exude an all-encompassing theatricality, and the frequent application of bright colour contributes to their sense of unbounded energy. Multiple scenarios exist simultaneously, and viewers are enticed into thrillingly close proximity, even though the structures can appear on the point of collapse. Conversely, smaller sculptures have a leaner appearance, offering greater restraint. Of human scale and beguilingly tilted, they encourage a more intimate, contemplative experience of form.

Ina Cole: You're a great-great-grandchild of Charles Darwin, and you inherited his complete published letters. What do they reveal about his ideas, and did this ancestral connection impact on your family home when you were a child?

Phyllida Barlow: Darwin's letters are wonderful to dip into. I cherish them. He had exceptional contacts globally who fed his curiosity about what constituted the living world and how, in the end, we're all one and the same. There's no differentiation between the animal and botanical world and us. That, to me, is remarkable. However, his shyness and reluctance to reveal a radical idea caused him to prevaricate, and this shyness is a family characteristic I feel great empathy towards.

After the death of his beloved daughter Annie, certain aspects of religion no longer held any validity for him. Darwin lived in an age of conflict between enlightenment and conventionality, and was stuck in the middle, paralyzed. His position on religion greatly influenced my father, who was an atheist. My mother was rigorous about the Darwin connection, advising me not to talk about it because it would be easier to make my way without that as leverage. This had a great impact on me, especially when going to Chelsea College of Art in the 1960s, which had a socialist approach to education. Anything that smacked of a privileged upbringing was more of a hindrance, and I became quite inhibited about the association.

IC: When you studied at Chelsea, George Fullard was one of the most important teachers there. How did he influence your perception of what sculpture could be?

PB: George Fullard, among others, was able to impart that the act of making was, in itself, an adventure. You didn't have to imitate, or be dominated by, the idealisms of the past when sculpture had a historical narrative, monumentalized and celebrated individuals or was dominated by the plinth. A sculpture that falls over or breaks is just as exciting as one that reveals itself perfectly formed. All the acts of making in the world are there to be plundered and contain within themselves the potential to be transferred to the studio and adapted. I learnt casting, modelling, armature building, carving, welding and construction, the core aspects of sculpture as a twentieth-century discipline. Yet George taught us that sculpture wasn't merely about a set of rules. Many elements in my work – towers, stacks and rounded, broken or gridded forms – have all been there from that early time, but continue to be explored in unlimited ways.

IC: You also studied at Slade School of Fine Art and later returned to become one of its most influential teachers, a position you held until 2009. Have you now been granted new freedoms or did the structure of a teaching position – and the cross-fertilization of ideas with your students – aid the progression of your own practice?

PB: I had to earn a living and there was no choice. In the mid-1960s, through the Coldstream and Summerson Reports, the reassessment of art education as a force for good meant, for a time, art schools became patrons to younger artists. That's now been swept away, but I was one of the fortunate ones who benefited from being invited to teach, and the payment was a kind of patronage. The artist was still held in romantic awe. I wasn't expected to do anything other than share my way of thinking creatively for the benefit of students. However, it was a short window of opportunity that couldn't be sustained; hence, the role of art schools came under the scrutiny of subsequent governments. Yet there was a fertility which has been hard to emulate since. It's a fascinating saga, and I think education is in a harsh place at the moment.

IC: Early on, you were inspired by Arte Povera's preoccupation with non-traditional techniques. Did you begin to use materials sourced from the everyday to counteract the fact that sculpture can command its position so authoritatively within a space?

PB: *Tent* (1967) was created in direct response to Arte Povera, in a basement studio where I lived after leaving the Slade. It was a complete break from my earlier

Phyllida Barlow
untitled (series of 10), 1965

Plaster and acrylic paint
Each object approx.
40 × 30 × 30 cm
(15¾ × 11¾ × 11¾ in)

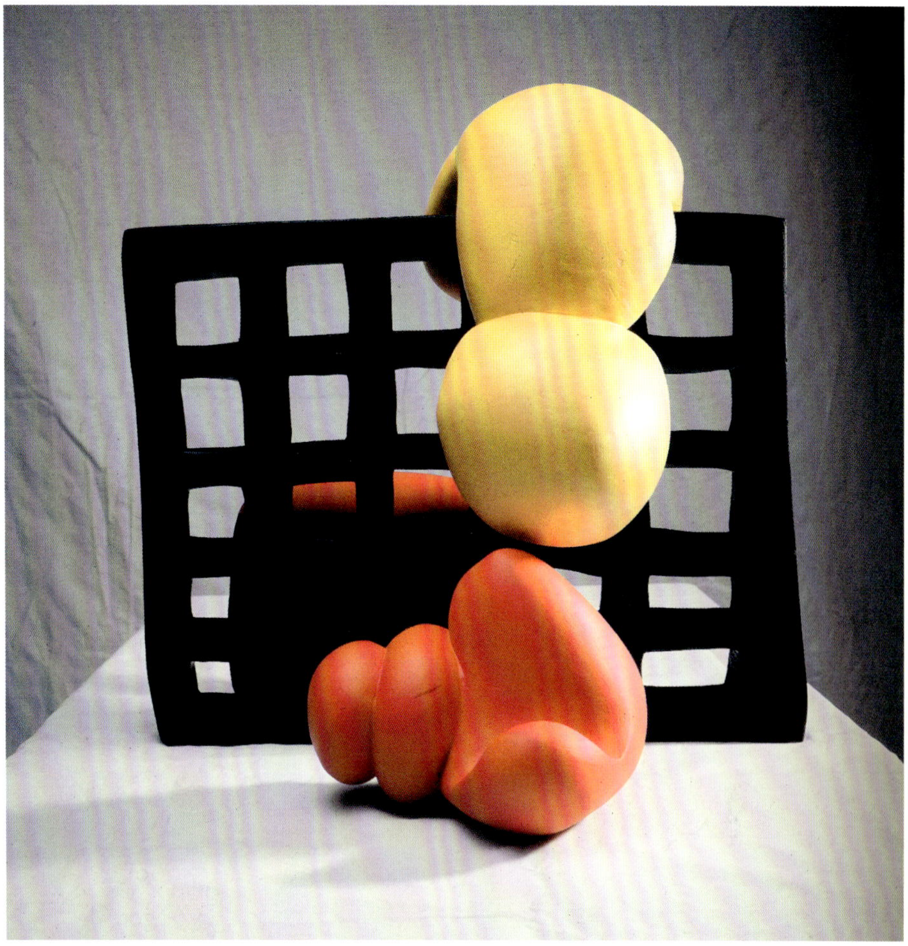

works, which were semi-figurative, organic shapes heavily modelled from clay, placed in conjunction with geometric forms. *Tent* offered a way to rethink the use of paint and surface and examine assemblage and an interior. It was made on loose wooden structures with canvas slung over, heavily painted, layer upon layer. Held within the structure was a cast fibreglass floor piece with pebbles, marbles and ping-pong balls. *Tent* wasn't rooted in sculpture as monument. It was expressive of a more intimate experience, both in terms of its surface and how you engaged with it – or peered into it.

However, it provoked absolute hostility and never went on exhibition. It was difficult to know what it was as an object, but I had to trust myself and balance that with a critical attitude, which is a difficult juggling act. I was so excited by the simplicity of how *Tent* came about, and by the sheer delight in transforming canvas into a strange, theatrically painted surface. I instinctively knew *Tent* was unusual. Then I came across Eva Hesse just hanging and dipping things, and this confirmed simple actions could be an end in themselves.

IC: The act of making removes the form from its source, and it's important for you that the form develops independently of the idea. You've previously referred to this as 'the destruction of an idea'.

PB: I've often spoken of the simile being a kind of curse; a desperate need to find a rationale for what we're looking at. To be abandoned with something that's only like itself, and refutes definition, is an extraordinary experience. Sculpture can really challenge one in that respect. When the idea is lost, something unknown starts to develop, and this relationship between maker and object is incredibly powerful – it's as if the work is fighting back. The object that doesn't yield is a

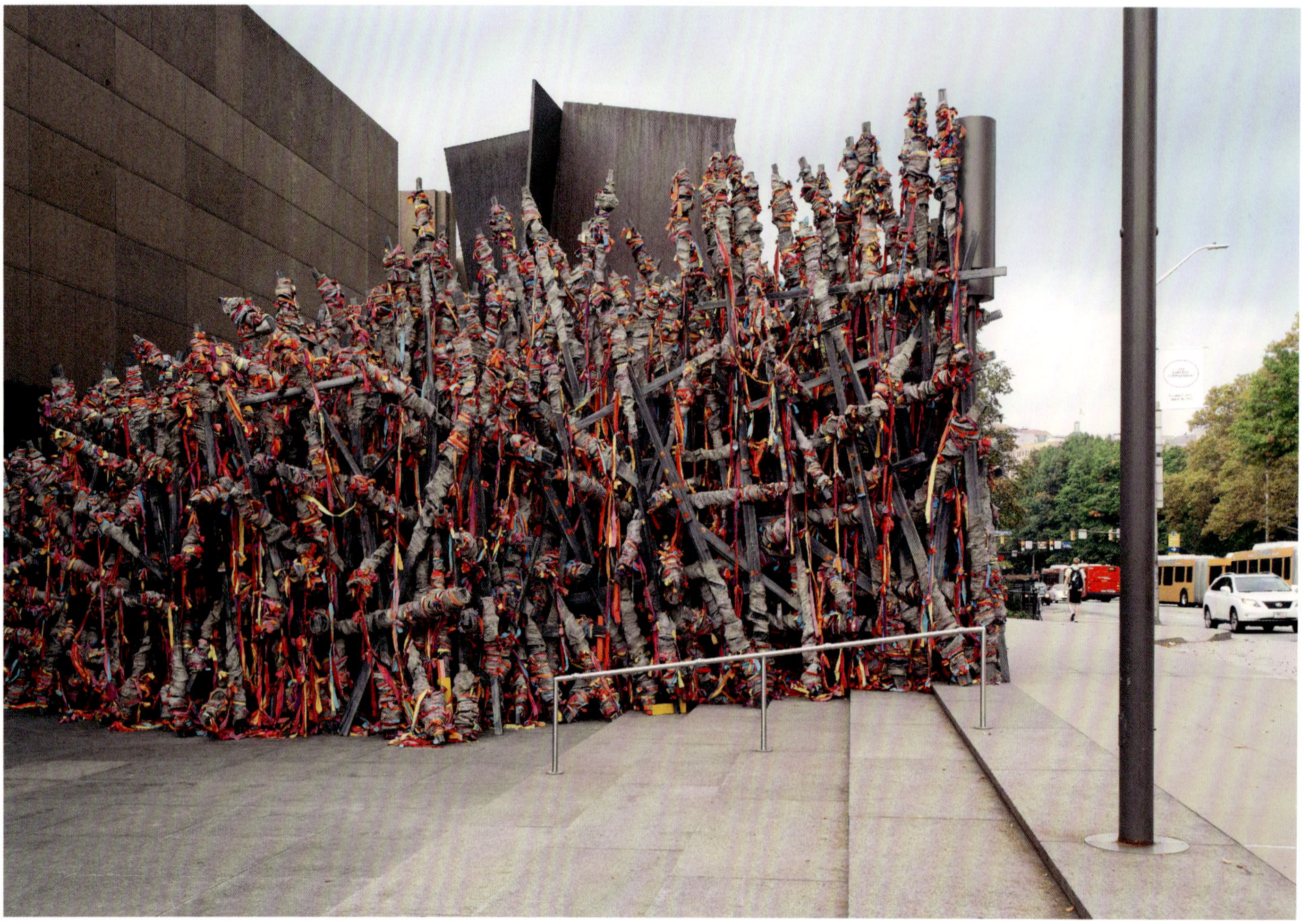

touchstone, giving another dimension to the toughness of life. So, ideas, or thoughts, happen during the process of production, rather than being concrete at the outset and resolved through the making.

IC: The way size informs your practice has been much commented upon, as seen in the exhibition 'tryst' (2015) at Nasher Sculpture Centre, Dallas, or in *TIP* (2013), for Carnegie Museum of Art in Pittsburgh, which utilized an array of coloured fabrics – yellows, pinks, greys – and appeared to be swarming from the building's interior out onto the street.

PB: I'm fascinated by the fact that each component of a work is 'handle-able', yet once assembled it becomes vast, out of reach. Colour has been present since the 1960s, when I decorated plaster with shapes. Sculpture doesn't need complete integrity; you can play with its surfaces as much as on canvas, and even how I tie fabrics onto armatures is similar to creating paint marks. *TIP* was made of cement, timber, steel mesh and lots of different fabrics. The curator said, 'You know we have to leave the Henry Moore and the fountains, as well as the rubbish bins.' And I replied, 'Look, if we're going onto the street we just embrace it all. It's not a problem.' At one point we had to dismantle a whole section, because it had spread and needed to be brought back. When returning from some of these installs, I can't shed them, as I've directed every single upright, diagonal and cross-piece needed, back and forth. One of the tragedies of these large projects is the pressure of what to do with them afterwards. I'd have liked *TIP* to disintegrate in its own time. After all, it survived the Pittsburgh winter and had snow all over it.

I always feel incredibly honoured that people want the work, since it's so troublesome. It's expensive to transport, difficult to install and requires a large team. Yet, for me, there's a wonderful sense of drama

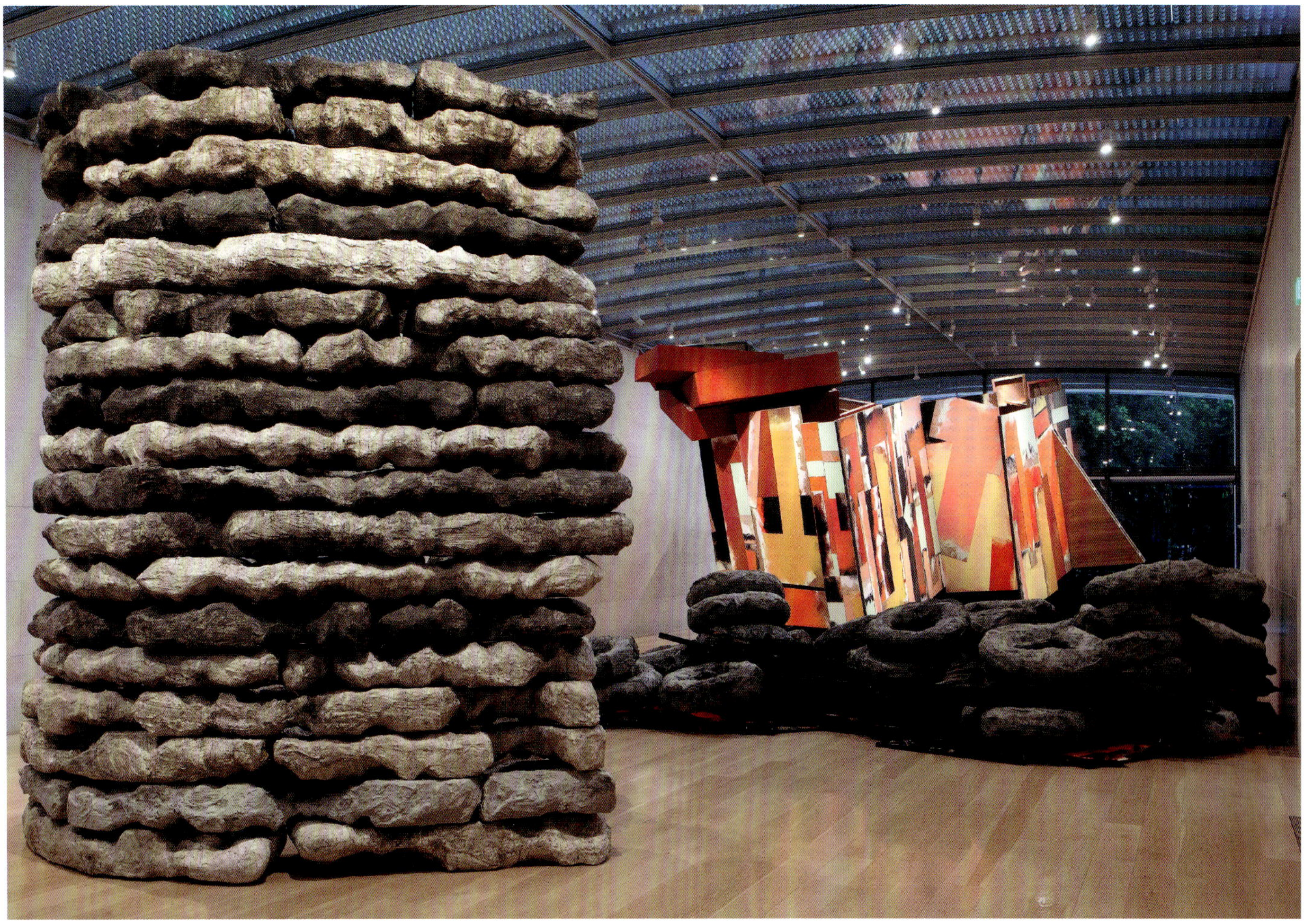

←
Phyllida Barlow
TIP, 2013

Timber, steel, spray paint, wire mesh, cotton, cement, fabric, varnish
701 × 914.4 × 2728 cm
(22 ft 12 in × 29 ft 12 in × 89 ft 6 in)
Installation view:
Carnegie Museum of Art, Pittsburgh, 2013–14

↑
Phyllida Barlow
tryst, 2015

Dimensions variable
Installation view:
Nasher Sculpture Center, Dallas, 2015

about that. The work has been laboured over in the studio, requiring several individuals to produce any one section. When arriving at a location I may have a sense of where pieces go, but it's never battened down. However, in the Nasher I could have left huge scars on the building's impeccable surfaces. There was much pre-planning, as I knew we couldn't simply trundle in and try things out.

IC: *dock* (2014), another vast installation, consisted of a group of separate, yet interrelated sculptures commissioned for Tate Britain in London. Here, you married the Duveen Galleries' interior with the Tate's riverside location by the Thames. The viewer didn't just look at *dock*, but into it, and by glancing through its mesh-like construction other fragments of the work could be seen, as well as the architecture. How did you achieve this?

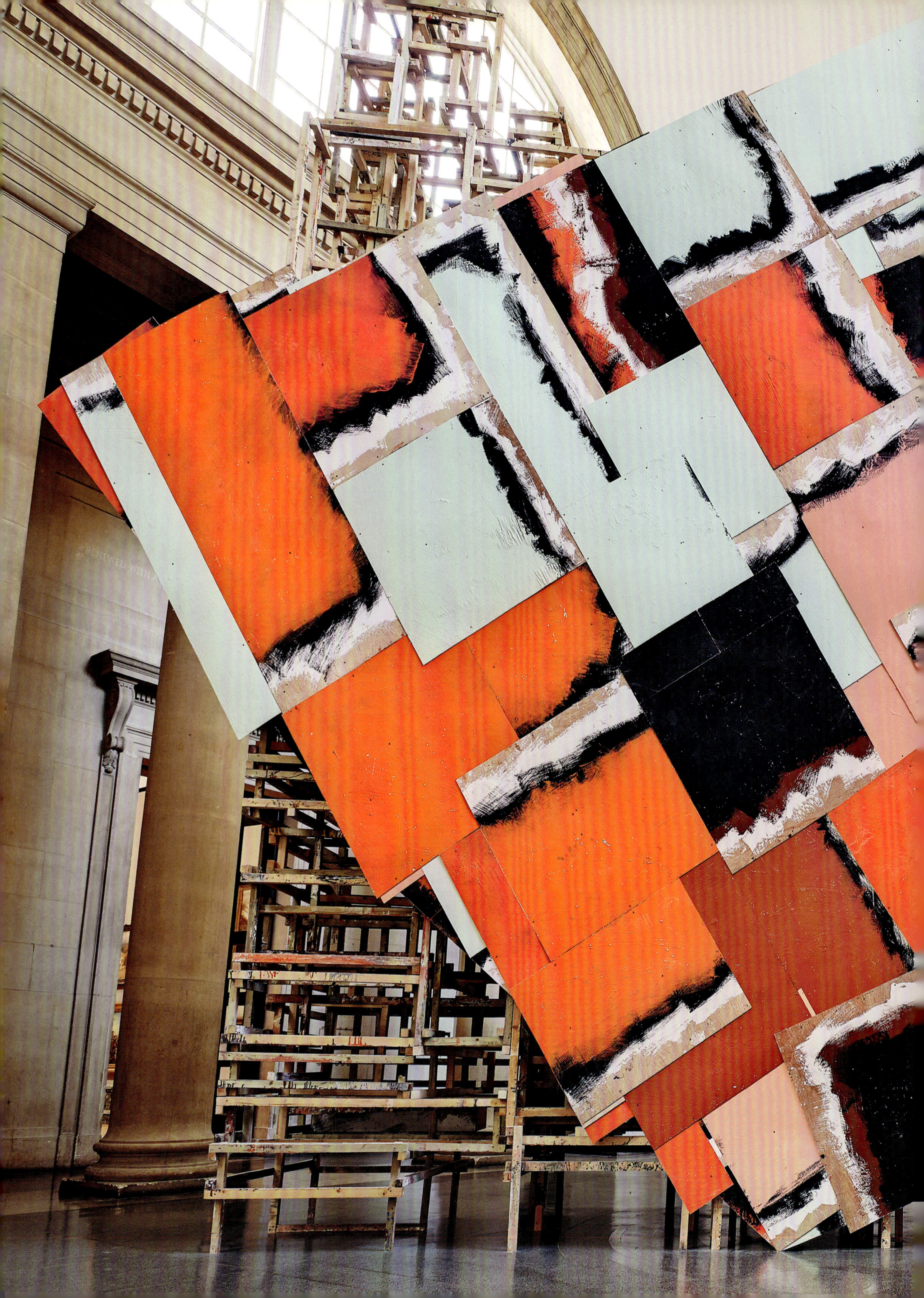

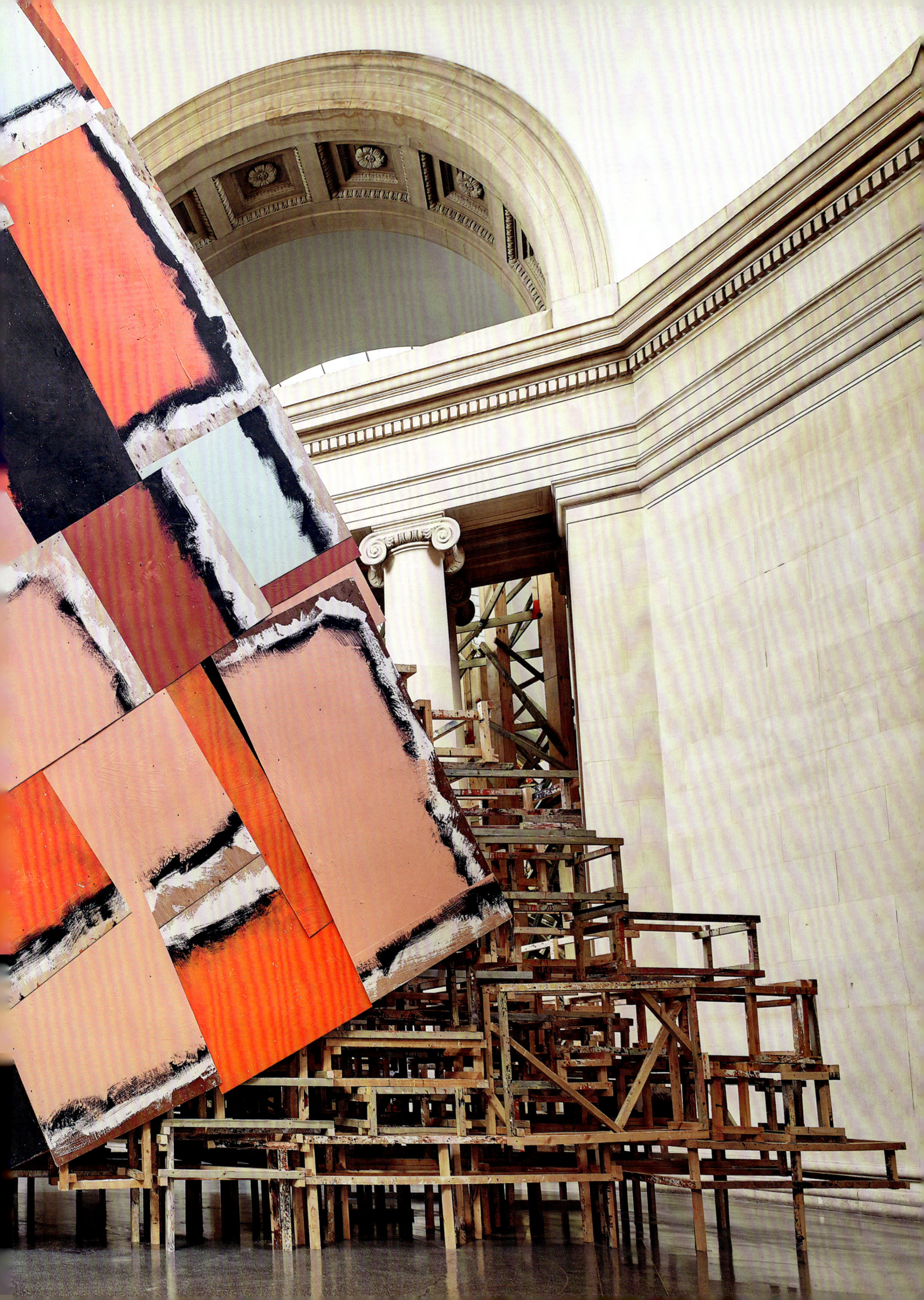

←←
Phyllida Barlow
untitled: dock: emptystaircasehoarding, 2014

Timber, paint, plywood
900 × 400 × 1000 cm
(29 ft 6⅜ in × 13 ft 1½ in × 32 ft 9¾ in)
Installation view:
Tate Britain, London, 2014

PB: Sitting on the Tate steps in a cold, late-November light, my attention had been drawn to river barges carrying containers, gliding ambivalently past, and their floating clinched what I wanted to do. *dock* wasn't about reinventing a riverside folly or environment, though. It was about appropriating that sensation of drift, of instability. I wanted to reach the arching space at the top of the Duveen, so freeing the floor was important, since that's owned by the audience. The plan was for nothing to touch the ground and for huge lintels to operate as supports. These wooden uprights had the banal architectural structure of scaffolding. They had to operate in contrast to the Duveen: fragment its elegance and act like a mesh playing over its beautiful surfaces, to offer different viewpoints and encourage people to walk through. However, the collapsed piece and the tower purposefully touched the floor; they were intended as two contrasting directions, or bodily experiences. One was fallen and the other upright and phallic – forms we're familiar with in terms of sculptural language. My take was playful, though, using debris and offcuts from the making process, as well as cardboard and tape, to bring an absurd informality into the space.

One of the conditions of the commission had been to reference Tate Britain's collection, which was my idea of heaven. It was fantastic to look at all the works that had made such an impact on me, especially in relationship to the phenomena of invented form among a certain trajectory of sculpture from the 1930s to 1950s, which stood in complete contrast to the readymade. I'd always been fascinated by that, intellectually, psychologically and physically.

IC: The transience of your installations, and the way pieces are stacked in disintegrating formations, gives your work the quality of a collapsed city, ravaged by political savagery or natural disaster. This is reinforced by the sheer scale of projects such as *TIP*, *dock* and 'tryst'. To what extent do world affairs impact on the development of your practice?

PB: The act of creativity is political by its very nature. It's a statement about an individual existence and, therefore, has to be political. It comments, however indirectly, on that individual's condition at a particular time, and I'm no different. Nothing is permanent. Nature constantly falls apart and rebuilds itself through tsunamis or volcanoes, or simply the change of seasons. Our mark on the planet is similar and, for me, sculpture is also about that, since I participate with materials which have their own way of being. I'm therefore interested in huge changes that happen to places and people, even the devastation of Palmyra in Syria, for instance. Although tragic and abysmal, it seemed to represent something within nature and humankind. Destruction and construction, or damage and repair, do somehow meet, however uncomfortably, and that's exactly what the sculptural process is about. So yes, there may be an oblique reciprocation with what I see in the world. I also caught the tail end of World War II. My father took us to bomb-damaged areas of London as children as a way of saying war is appalling and hatred is terrible.

→
Phyllida Barlow
folly, 2017

Dimensions variable
Installation view:
Venice Biennale, 2017

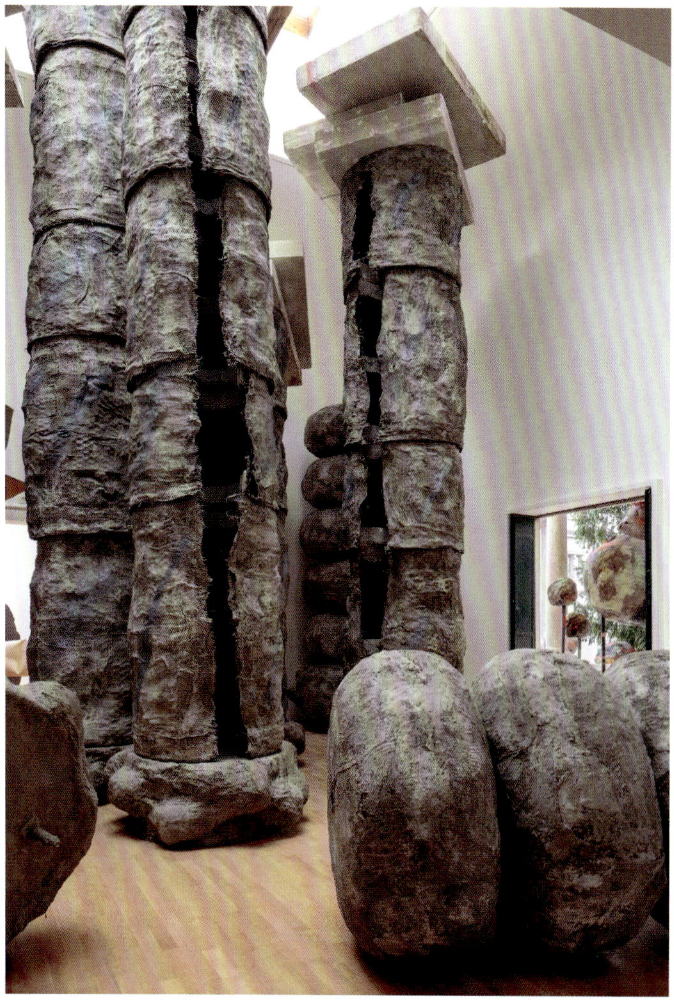

IC: You represented Britain at the 2017 Venice Biennale, where 'folly' generated a wonderful dialogue between your upright, fallen and suspended forms. You've said you're interested in the 'phantom state of objects as dreams or memories'. Did this apply to 'folly'?

PB: Yes, that was key, because I wanted the pretence of sculpture to be dominant. Why were there a stack of columns after moving through the absurd forest of baubles, for instance? Big political changes were happening, like Brexit. What did it mean to be in the British Pavilion at a time of such calamity? The political language had an almost *Ubu Roi* [a play by Alfred Jarry, 1896] ridiculousness, a pomposity to be explored. So, when making the columns I wanted to reach into that lofty, slightly out-of-proportion space on entering the Pavilion and create an oppressive overfilling. Of course, they weren't really columns at all, but phantoms of columns. Sculpture's ability to stand in for an original narrative, or become a phantom-like echo of a reality, intrigues me. Although it has this great claim on materiality, it's still not the thing it professes to be. Even a Brancusi, which has such a haunting presence of physicality, still escapes definition. You walk around to try and grasp it, yet it slips away and you're left with this extraordinary relationship to its materiality, and also to its ambiguity. As viewers, we occupy the space of sculpture in a fundamental way and are, therefore, forced into a union with it. That's equally phantom-like: our own reality versus something which claims an equal reality but refuses to totally give itself up to that.

IC: In contrast to 'folly', the exhibition 'tilt' (Hauser & Wirth, New York, 2018) was notable for the emphasis on smaller, autonomous pieces – *untitled: dancer*, *untitled: spree (green)* and *untitled: roadsidehoarding*, all created that year.

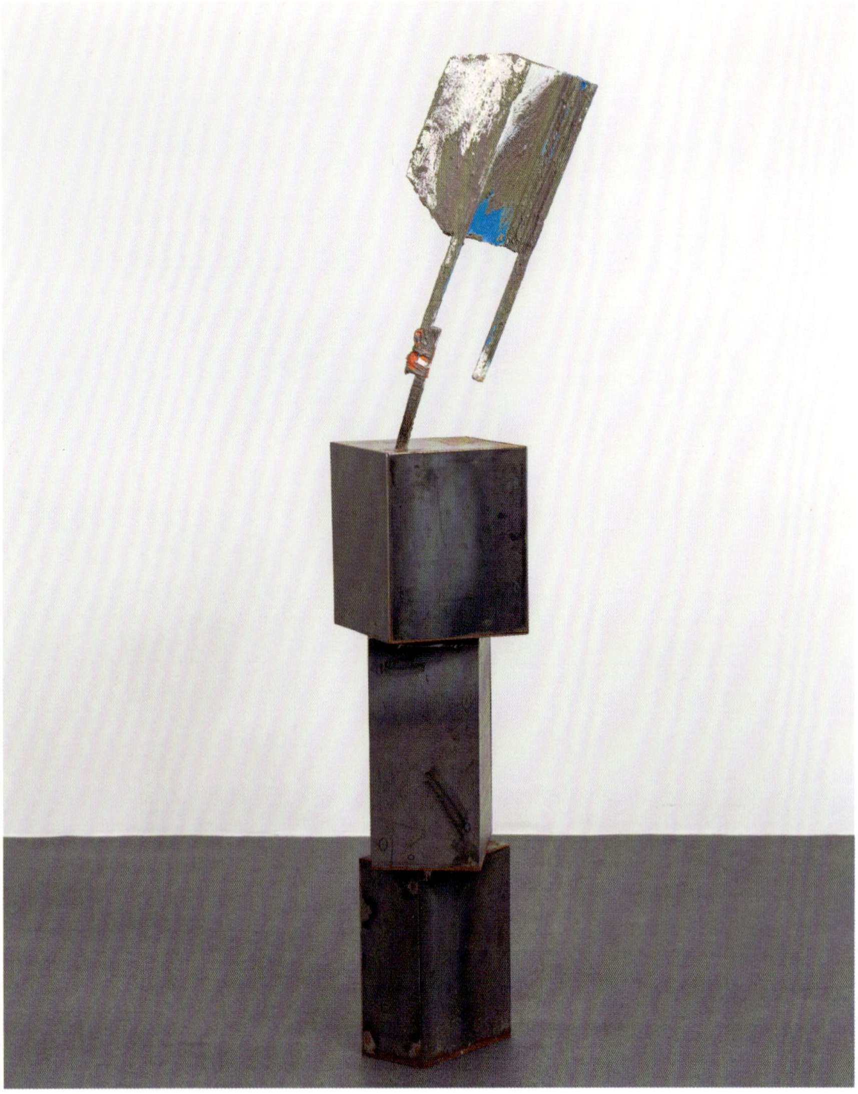

←
Phyllida Barlow
untitled: dancer; 2018, 2018

Bonding, cement, PVA, paint, plaster, plywood, poly cotton, sand, spray paint, steel
194.5 × 58.5 × 54.5 cm
(6 ft 4⅝ in × 23 in × 21½ in)
Hauser & Wirth, New York, 2018

→
Phyllida Barlow
untitled: spree (green); 2018, 2018

PVA, paint, plywood, sand, spray paint, steel
165.1 × 48.9 × 47.6 cm
(65 × 19¼ × 18¾ in)
Hauser & Wirth, New York, 2018

They reside on plinth-like bases, which adds to their sense of containment, yet they're off-balance, leaning, as if blown by the wind.

PB: After Venice, I became almost allergic to what I'd done there, and my work went through a process of eradication. Venice was so audience-orientated, with highly performative installations that often dealt with specific issues. Questioning the language of sculpture, and its relevance to now, suddenly became quite difficult. Hence 'tilt' was very cleaned out and reclaimed the idea of the single object. Smaller works are becoming more central to my practice, and don't need to be made at such ferocious speed. They're also versatile in how they find their place; they can fall, lie, or be turned around. 'tilt' was a new beginning, a stark contrast to Venice and a necessary evisceration.

It meant a lot, and I realized things don't have to be either/or. I can make standalone pieces and sculptures that have a connection to each other; I can use pretence and theatricality and the stark reality of what something is. I feel liberated, as if a glitch has passed. Between my shows in New York and at the Royal Academy of Arts in London, there was an opening up of my repertoire, and my work became honed into a much leaner language.

IC: You wrote an article on the teachings of George Fullard (*Tate Etc.*, 2016), in which you referenced Buster Keaton's unique physical relationship with inanimate objects. Does *untitled: lintelshadow* (2018), made for 'cul-de-sac' at the Royal Academy, propose a reference to that absurdist position?

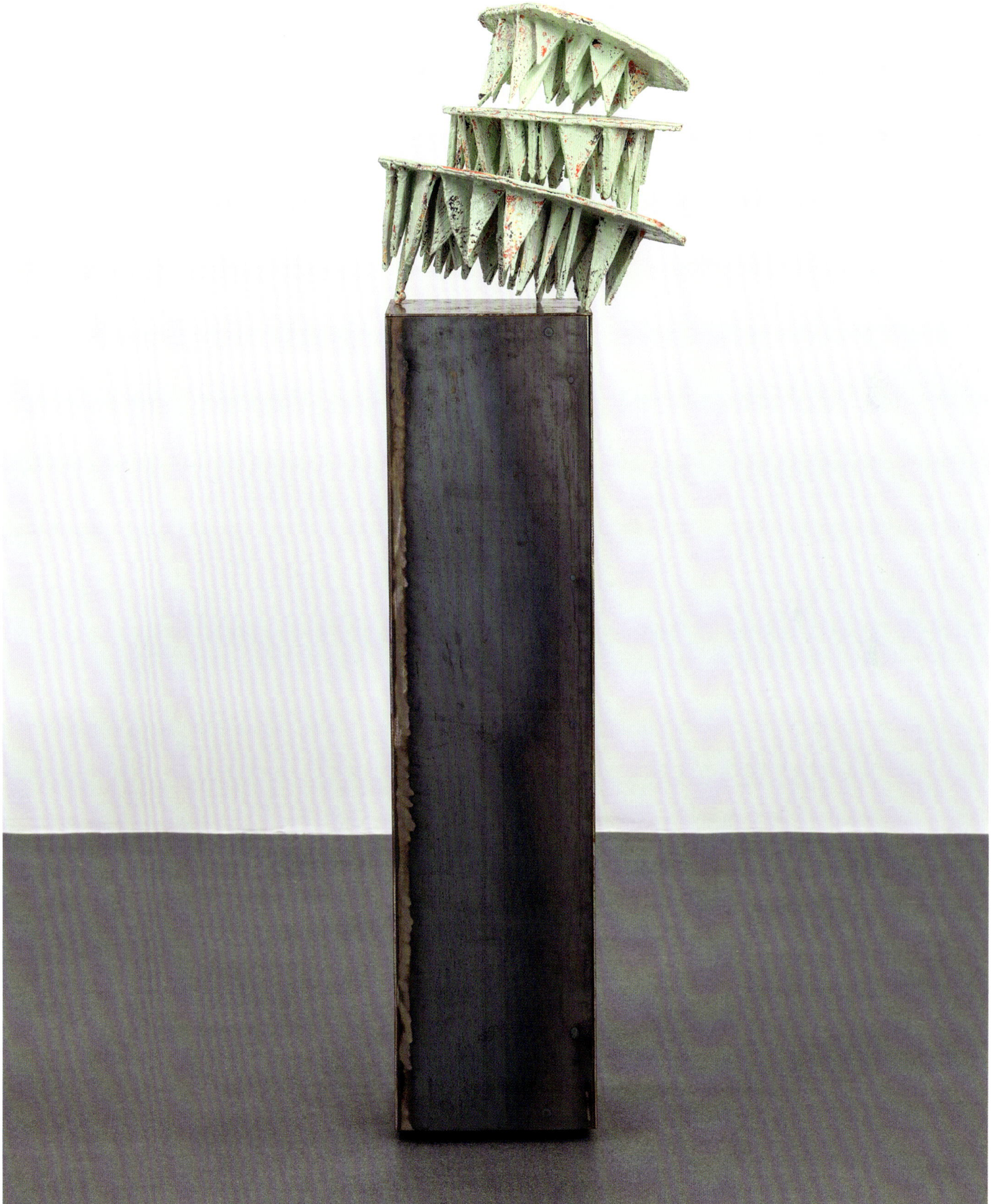

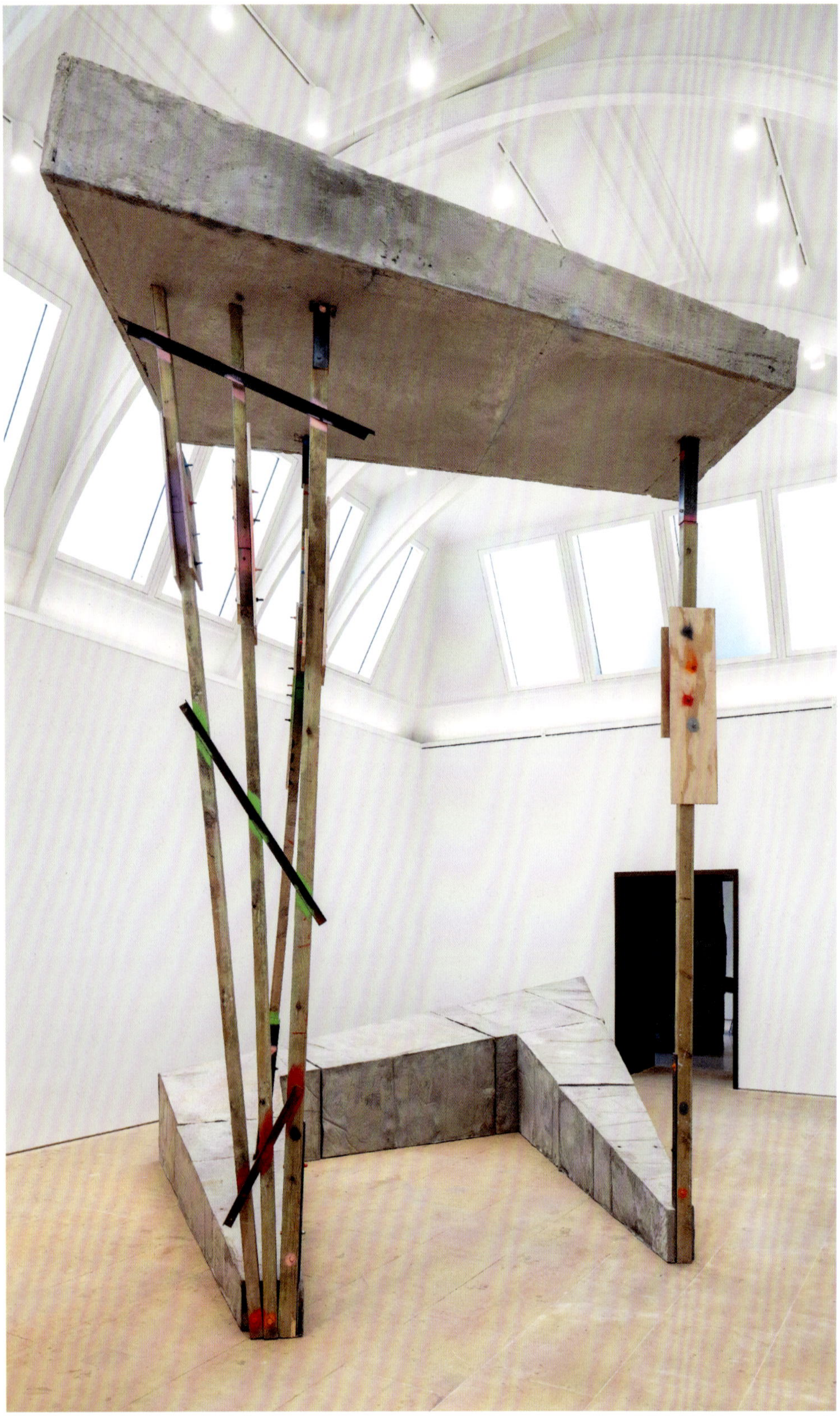

Phyllida Barlow
untitled: lintelshadow; 2018–2019,
2018–19

Cement, hessian scrim,
PVA, paint, pigment, plywood,
polyurethane board, polystyrene,
polyurethane foam, spray paint,
steel, timber
600 × 720 × 650 cm
(19 ft 8¼ in × 23 ft 7½ in × 21 ft 3⅞ in)
Installation view:
Royal Academy of Arts, London, 2019

PB: I'm intrigued by absurd and irrational objects that comment on the world through more obtuse references. Certainly, *lintelshadow* was an absurd architectural prop, attempting to contend with the architecture that was already there. The shadow's materiality is often in question, yet in *lintelshadow* it becomes more substantial than the thing it is shadowing. The lintel structure, as in the side columns, are very improvised, so the connection with Buster Keaton is quite apt. Certain elements had initially been put in for support, but I liked them and said, 'Just leave them there; they can become part of it.' I have a subconscious desire to make things that are inherently unreliable. They act as a mood or atmosphere, and a gesture in the space – stretching, reaching or appearing awkward in some way. Once something is locked into a space like the Royal Academy, it's imprisoned. Does the space or the sculptural intervention win out? Is the intervention a disruptive, or enhancing, influence? This constant questioning gnaws away at me.

Subject has become defined by politicized identity issues, so what is the role of sculpture that doesn't take those issues on? The irrational artwork is now at the outer limits, since the focus seems to favour what is clear about its subject and content. This leaves the field wide open for under-the-radar activity that stands in contention and explores beyond those particular dictates. The canon has been troublesome, especially for women, and the identity fever is good and necessary. It throws a huge challenge down for artists like me, who aren't fixed into a role that reveals a particular human condition. My practice isn't about a specific narrative, but much more slippery. And that's difficult because the qualities of form, material and physicality are still relevant to who and what we are. Sculpture is an experiential language and so much of it enters into this slightly amorphous territory.

IC: In the 1970s you felt your work was too idiosyncratic, yet it's precisely this quality that has brought you great acclaim. Has the journey been challenging?

PB: I never really expected to be at this point. Looking back, it seems curious it was such a struggle, particularly when trying to reconcile the technical demands with the gestural demands – the lightness of touch or single gesture that carries the work. Of course, it didn't, which is why a lot of work was destroyed. There were practical concerns about storage, and pieces were made in a way that didn't pay any regard to longevity. I'm now examining longevity and how to resolve these conflicting technical issues. Early on, when using fabrics, plaster, wood, plastics, ropes, strings and tape, things were only just held together. However, through the use of steel, as both a concealed and visible structural element, my making processes have greater flexibility. Materials can be changed spontaneously, yet held in place, and I can retain the gesture as the fixture is there from the off. I'm now able to show in venues in which I can take on challenges I never thought I'd have the opportunity to do. That's fantastic, at this stage of my life.

Interviewed in 2015 and 2020

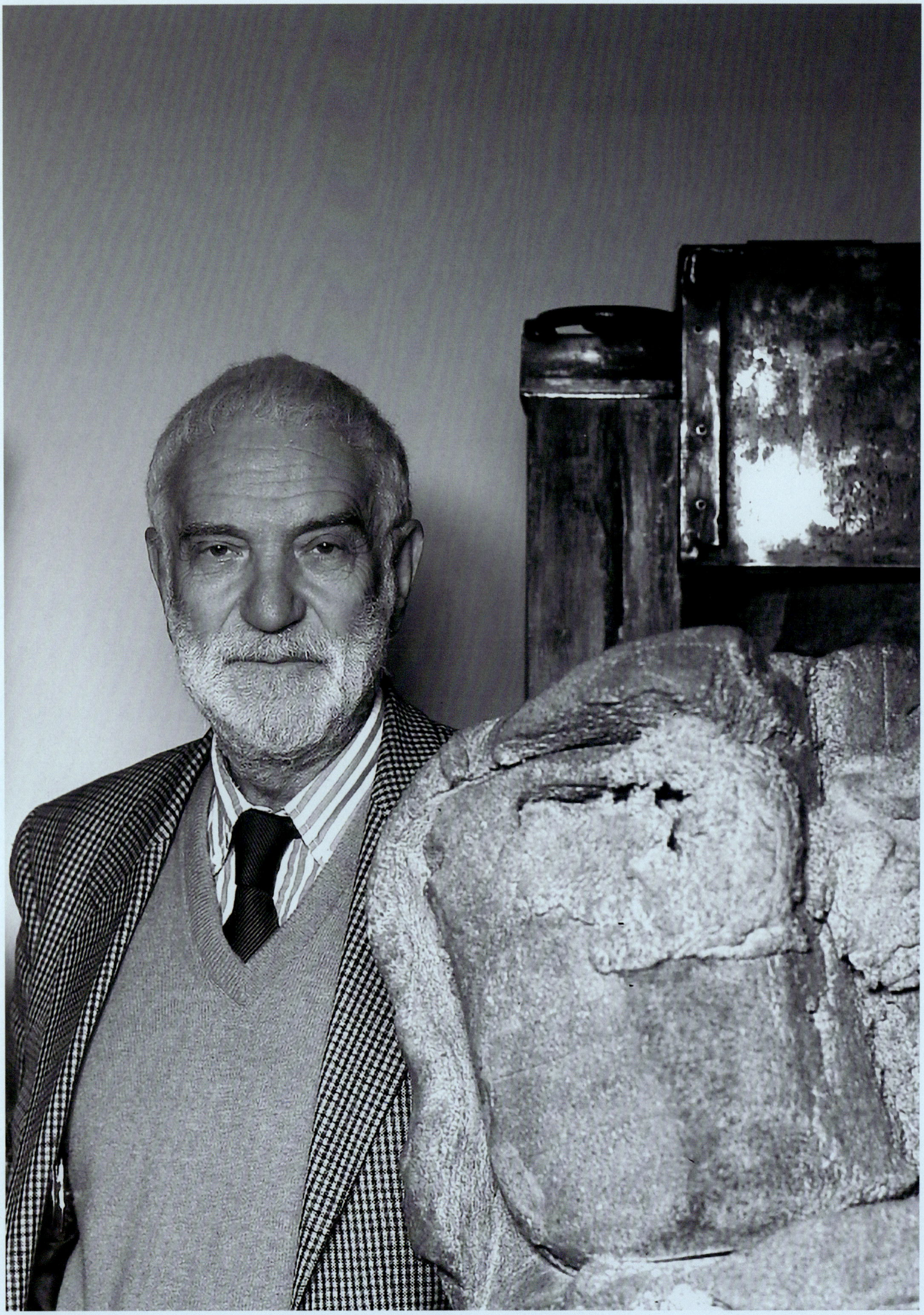

ANTHONY CARO

Born 1924, New Malden, Surrey; died 2013, London

Anthony Caro held a crucial position in the development of twentieth-century sculpture. His influential teaching methods at St Martin's School of Art (1953–81) gave rise to renewed confidence in sculptural practice worldwide. Caro became known for large-scale abstract constructions made from industrial metals and brightly painted, such as *Early One Morning* and *Sun Feast*. In these works, solid form has become replaced by a series of flat, interlocking planes, creating the illusion of lightness. His repertoire later evolved into powerful installations utilizing numerous components, as seen in *The Trojan War* and *The Last Judgement*. In 2000, he collaborated with the architect Norman Foster on Millennium Bridge, built to cross the River Thames. That same year he became the only British sculptor to be awarded the Order of Merit since Henry Moore, in 1963. In 2008, Caro's *Chapel of Light* was inaugurated at the Church of Saint-Jean-Baptiste in Bourbourg, northern France, generating a seamless union of art and architecture.

Ina Cole: You've always remained open to the possibilities of change in the making of your sculpture. How has your work evolved over the years?

Anthony Caro: I think I've brought the world in more. My early work had a strong focus on what sculpture can do, what it can be, how I can open it out and push it this way and that. More recently, I've let in machine parts and narrative, which would have been outside my limits in the old days. I've opened up, because I'm more confident about making things that previously would have looked crazy. I don't feel I have to be so guarded. When I was a student, sculpture was about the figure; it was quite rigid and always bronze, stone or wood. Then, when I worked for Henry Moore, there were things I couldn't do. I don't want to do what I know; I want to do what I don't know. That's why it's a great thrill to still be making art. It's very absorbing.

Anthony Caro
Sun Feast, 1969–70

Steel, painted yellow
181.5 × 416.5 × 218.5 cm
(5 ft 11½ in × 13 ft 8 in × 7 ft 2 in)

IC: When you look back on your life, at what point did you feel you had reached your pinnacle?

AC: I don't look back much, but the early 1960s were a bit of a breakthrough, when I made the first colour sculptures; then the late 1960s when I made *Prairie* (1967) and *Sun Feast* (1969–70), which were very abstract. I could have gone on with them, yet decided I'd got as far with that sort of abstraction as I wanted to. At my age, you might be making your best work, but you haven't got the same thrust of energy as in your thirties or forties. Suppose you asked that question to Monet: would he have answered *Rouen Cathedral*, *Haystacks* or *Water Lilies*? In the end we might like *Water Lilies* best, but I don't think they would have necessarily been a pinnacle for him.

IC: You developed an enduring transatlantic presence, especially in New York. Artistically, have you always had a closer affinity with Americans?

AC: Well, I haven't been to America for some years and that's extraordinary for me. I used to go up to five times a year, and a lot of my best friends were American artists. They had an appetite for abstraction, which the English don't have. We like a good story here. English

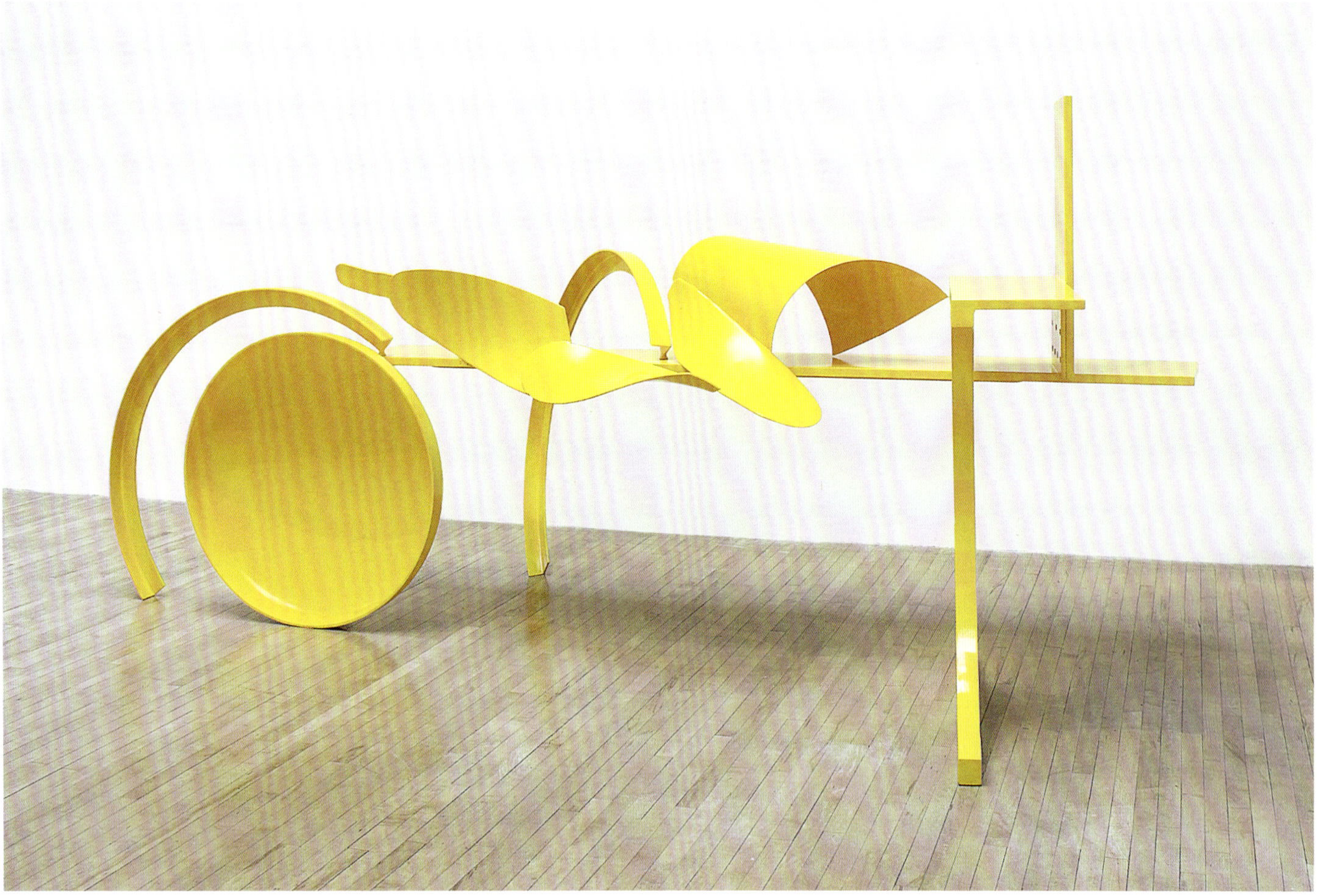

people tend to say, 'What does it mean?' and Americans say, 'I like it', 'I don't like it', or 'It's not quite right.' I don't think I'd have made the abstract sculpture had I not had that early contact with America. My American work was different from my English work. That was the funny thing. I learnt a lot from being there, then coming back to England; it was good from a practical and commercial point of view. It was tremendously stimulating, and my work was appreciated more there in the early days.

IC: A former piano factory has been your studio for several decades, and you've often acknowledged the importance of involving other people in the realization of projects. Do you actively seek a more collaborative approach, or does the nature and scale of your sculpture make this interaction necessary?

AC: The latter, but Pat [Patrick Cunningham] has been with me since 1969, so he knows what's going on in my head and can offer suggestions. The amount of work that goes into fabricating the bigger sculptures and engineering them so they can be taken to pieces and put into a gallery, is such a sweat. I don't want to spend time on it. In the old days, I had a one-car garage at home where I made sculptures like *Early One Morning* (1962), and I used to shout to my friends, 'Come and give me a hand.' That's not art time, though, its fabrication time, and those two things are different. I've now got a team as I'm making big things and, as a result, I've more time to make art. It's nothing compared to Rodin who had about 27 assistants. He could say, 'Make this, cast that', then do crazy things because he had the freedom.

IC: Can you describe a day in the studio?

AC: I get up between 5 a.m. and 7.30 a.m. and have my breakfast, then go back to bed and have at least another hour's sleep. I don't hurry. I'm in the studio by

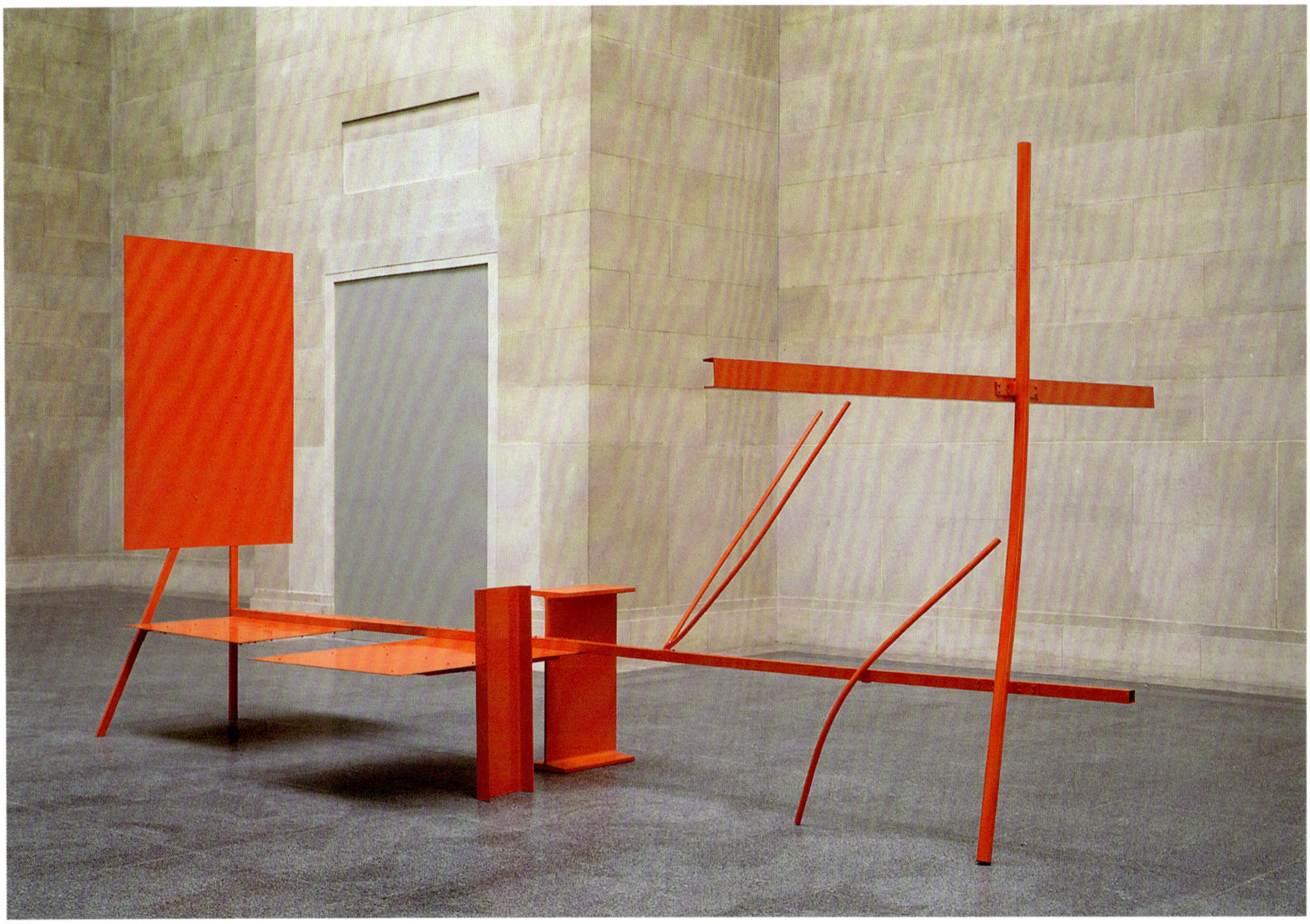

about 10.30 a.m., have a cup of tea and a look at what's going on. I'm not good in the mornings and don't really start to be creative until after lunch. As a student, the evenings and nights were the best times to work, but I now have to keep normal hours, as I'm dealing with a lot of people. So, I go on and make small changes, or big changes, or new work until about 5.30 or 6 p.m. I feel happy when I've worked like that but hate it if I have a day when I've been at a committee or talked about money. I try and get it over with as quickly as possible.

IC: How much room do you allow for spontaneity within your practice?

AC: Probably about 98 per cent. Well, not quite, but if I roughly know the direction I'm going, I can be as spontaneous as I like. For example, with Pat I say, 'I need a bit of that', and within ten minutes it's in the studio. Then I say, 'Well no, it's not right, I've made a mistake.' We can do a lot of playing around if I've got people who can move things easily. The ability to fabricate and feel at home with steel, or any material, is really important.

IC: The steel pieces, which secured your reputation in the 1960s, are truly innovative in the way they took sculpture from the hierarchy of the plinth onto the floor. Does the versatility of steel continue to provide new challenges?

AC: I love steel. I never thought I would, since it has some resistance, but I love it. Years ago, I saw some steel in Italy with the ends turned. It gets cast, then thrown away in America and Britain, yet in Italy they use it and cut it. I'd not seen that sort of thing before, so I used it too. I'm also using a lot of cast iron, which is a problem because you can't weld it to make it join; you have to bolt it, and this is much more arduous. I've used many other materials – paper, silver, clay, gold, bronze – and my method is to treat them all casually. Bronze has a preciousness about it, which I had to destroy by using cheap castings and pieces of bronze sheet, because there's no preciousness about them. The casting process takes such a long time, so people think bronze is special. In fact, it's just a material like any other. Silver is just a material, as is gold. They're all just stuff.

IC: Each material must provide you with different challenges, though.

AC: Absolutely. In fact, the material tells you which way it wants to go. Take clay; I can't mess about with that. If it doesn't work, I destroy it and start again. The time of spontaneous action with clay is completely different from steel. With steel you can come in the next day and change it, but you can't do that with clay. It's direct and quick. I always aim for directness, or a way of being spontaneous. I try and get that early-morning feeling whenever I'm making anything. When I first worked in paper, I had no idea you could make it stiff, or drape it, and that it was a soft material when wet. I always thought of it as sheets of paper. I also made some jewellery, and when working with gold it's so small I had to sit low with the table up high. These things are demanded of you.

Anthony Caro
Early One Morning, 1962

Steel and aluminium,
painted red
290 × 620 × 333 cm
(9 ft 6⅛ in × 20 ft 4⅛ in × 10 ft 11⅛ in)

IC: In a sense the material itself makes certain demands of you as the artist, as opposed to you having preconceived ideas about manipulating the material.

AC: Yes, and I think that's true of a lot of one's behaviour. You are your own person, but others can change your perception of how you see the work, or how you respond to it. The artist is like a radio receiver: rather than pumping out stuff all the time, they listen to the world's response to their work, or to the material. We are looking and listening instruments. Take Picasso: such a big person, such a big artist, yet we think of him as closed. When you start to read about him you learn he was responding to a lot of different people, and to the world. He knew when to pay attention and when not to. All these things do have an effect on you.

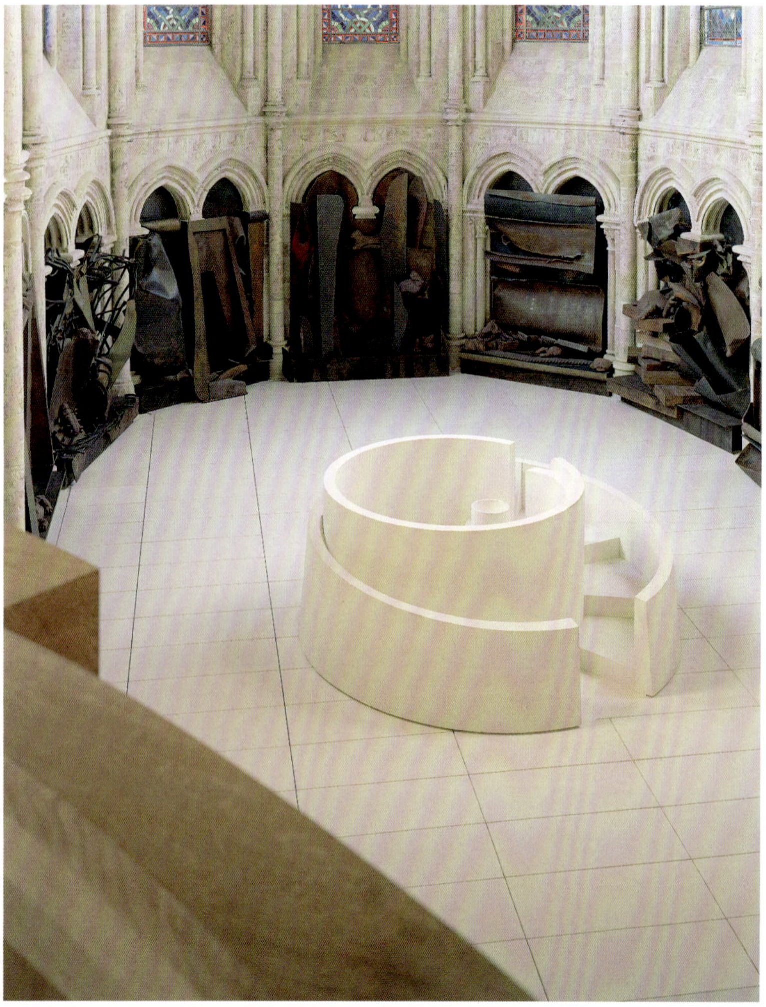

Anthony Caro
Chapel of Light,
2001–08

Steel, corten steel, French oak, concrete, stoneware, jarrah wood
Dimensions variable
Installation view: Church of Saint-Jean-Baptiste, Bourbourg, northern France, 2008

IC: Exhibitions of your sculpture have taken place around the world, and you were given a retrospective at Tate Britain, in London, in 2005. How do you prepare for the recognition this brings?

AC: As with all museum exhibitions there were a good many meetings and, sometimes, it was a bit gruesome. You talk a lot, minutes are taken and nothing happens. Then they change the dates. I think I invested too much and took it too seriously. It's easy for that to happen in your own country, as it's a big thing and you have to get it right. I used to be so nervous every time I had a show. Oh yes, I can remember, but that was quite a long time ago. It's a moment when you're on parade, visible; this is me, judge me. After the Tate show, I had a new lease of life. I took off, made a lot of new sculptures and sent them away for galvanizing, to paint and work on them afterwards. I'm a sculptor, so I should be making sculpture, not thinking about exhibitions.

IC: A commission, *Chapel of Light* (2008), for the church of Saint-Jean-Baptiste in Bourbourg is part of a restoration of the Gothic choir. When did the planning for this project start?

AC: In 2001, but Rodin took years to make *Burghers of Calais* (1884–9) because it was commissioned. I also remember complaining to Norman Foster about the amount of time we spent over Millennium Bridge. With Bourbourg, they just said, 'This is the place, do what you like with it.' But, of course, you have to cope with the bishop, who said it's got to be part of the church, and all the people from the city. Matisse had exactly the same problem with The Rosary Chapel in Vence. The archbishop was a real pain in the leg, yet as soon as it started to happen he wanted to take the credit.

IC: What was your reaction to the space when you first walked in?

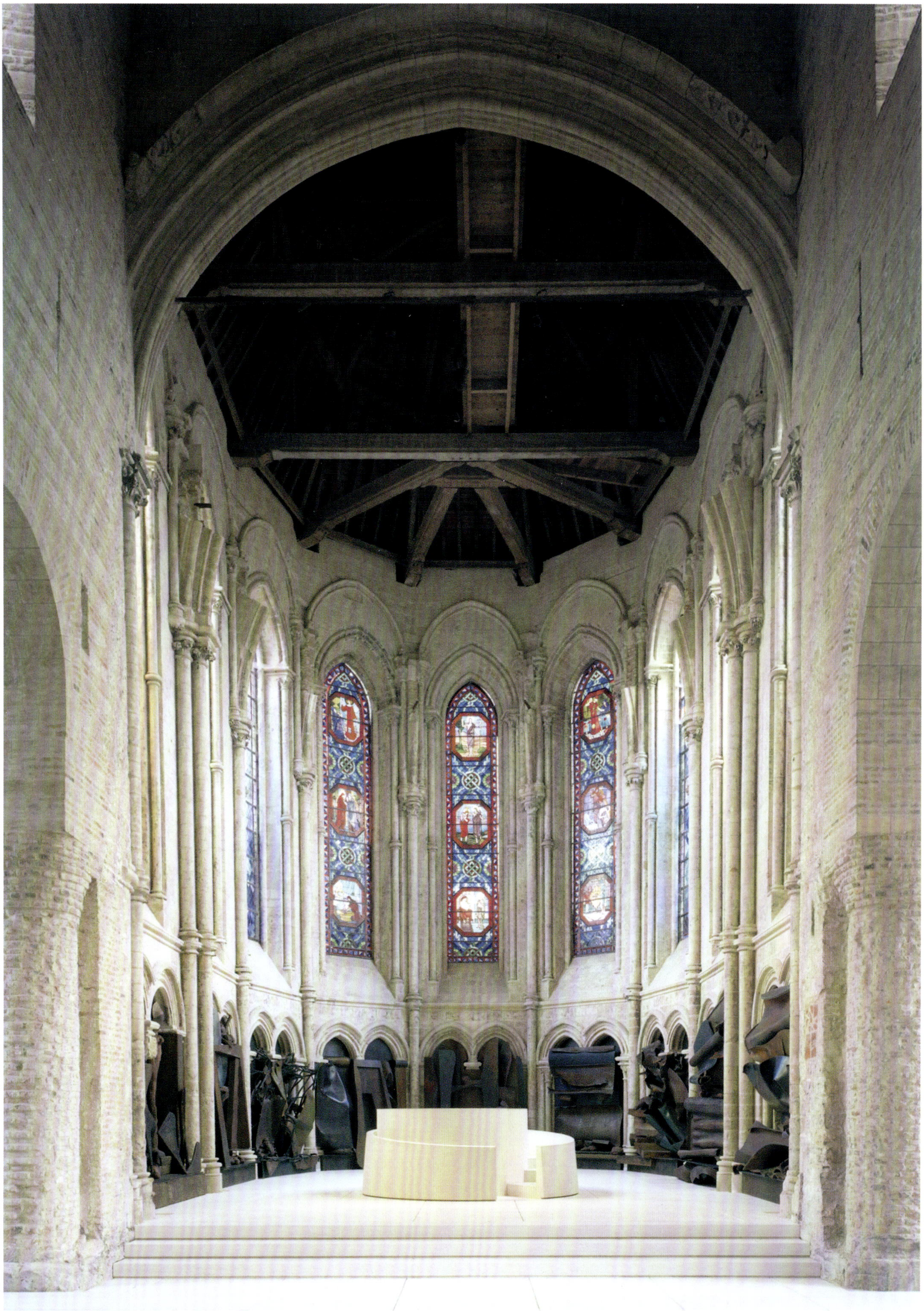

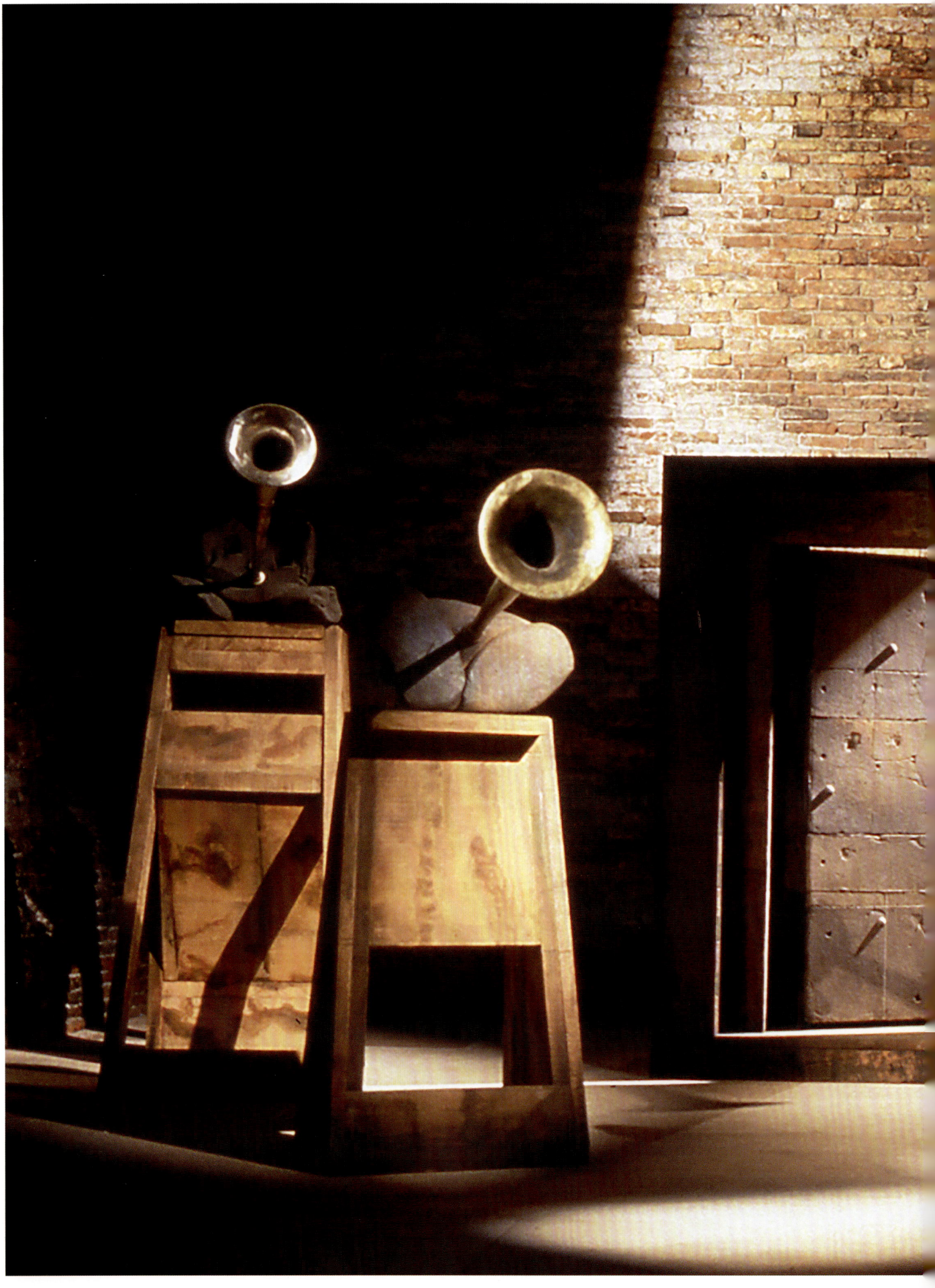

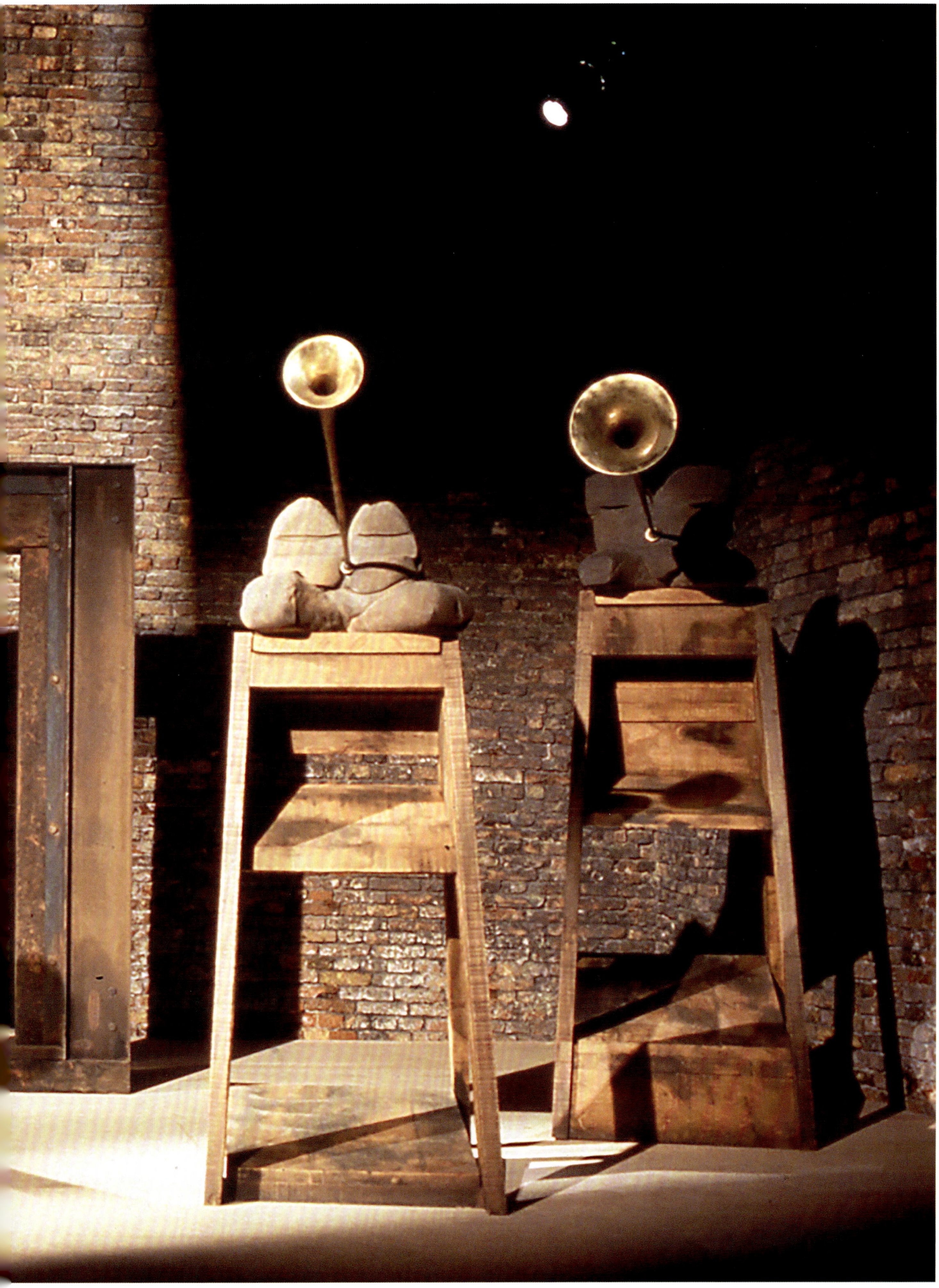

←←
Anthony Caro
The Last Judgement: Trumpeter 1, 2, 3, 4 and *Gate of Heaven*, 1996–9

Stoneware, steel, jarrah, oakwood, brass, bronze, concrete, plaster
Dimensions variable
Installation view: Venice Biennale, 1999

→
Anthony Caro
Child's Tower Room, 1983–4

Japanese oak, varnished
381 × 274.5 × 274.5 cm
(12 ft 6 in × 9 ft⅛ in × 9 ft⅛ in)

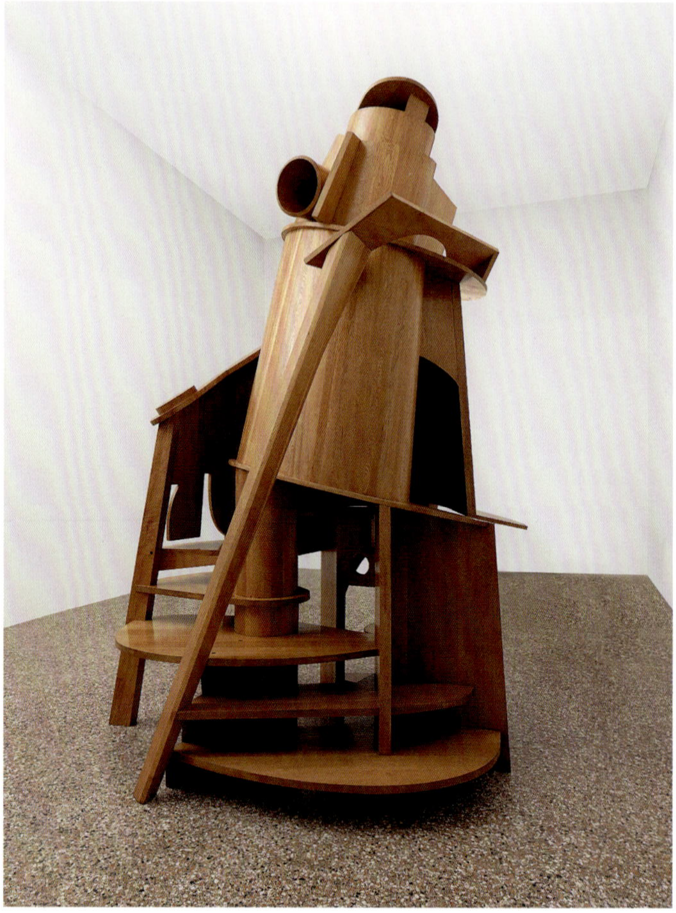

AC: It's an amazing space, incredible. When I walked in there were a lot of supports I thought I'd use. I played with the idea of having a single tower. Then I left it alone, the whole thing. I didn't want to talk or think about it anymore, so put all the parts away and forgot about it. When I took them out again it seemed clearer, and I made two towers that are much more integral. The height is amazing; I can imagine choirs singing and all sorts of nice things happening. The bishop wanted a baptistery with a baptismal pool, and a woman from the area arts council felt it could be like *The Last Judgement* (1996–9). Yet, in the end, it's about creation. However, I think I was chosen for the *Chapel of Light* because of the niches I'd made in *The Last Judgement.*

IC: The influence of architecture on your practice is well known. In which of your pieces do you feel this unification has been most successful?

AC: In *Millbank Steps* (2004), which you walk through. So much of sculpture is to do with where you see it and how you look at it. Do you look up; do you walk around to grasp it from the circumference; are you outside looking in; or do you look down? The idea of walking through is a different way of making it real. Sculpture gravitates between painting and architecture, and I was always attracted to painting in the old days. Now I'm more influenced by architecture. The Church of Saint-Jean-Baptiste in Bourbourg is a piece of architecture that I'm putting sculpture into, but the towers I made are certainly to do with walking up and into them. It's rather like the experience you have as a child, when crawling under a table to look at people's legs, or when you have a tree house. Those are very sculptural experiences when you begin to get a sense of how your body fits into the world.

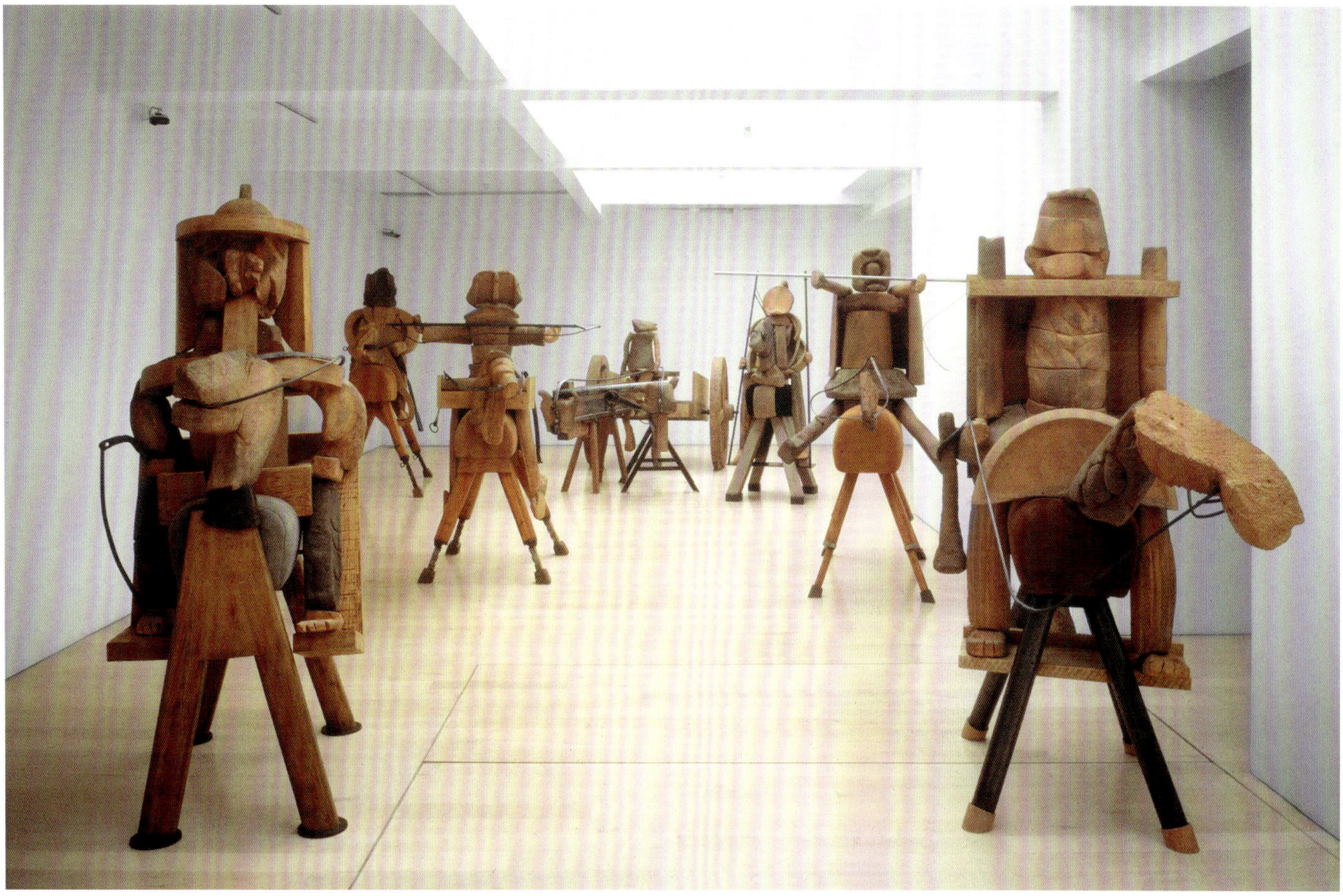

↑
Anthony Caro
The Barbarians,
1999–2002

Terracotta, wood, leather, steel
Dimensions variable
Installation view: Annely Juda Fine Art, London, 2003

IC: How do you explain the manner in which your sculptures move between the abstract and figurative, particularly in relation to the later installations?

AC: The last thing I ever wanted to do was make cold work. I wanted to make work that had a human feel to it, but found the figure was getting in the way, which was when I started to make the work abstract. In a different way, when I went to the South of France and began making clay pieces, I had no idea what I wanted to do. I just used the lumps of clay and stuck things in. Before I knew where I was, they were becoming figurative. So, I made *The Trojan War* (1993–4) and *The Last Judgement*. Then I saw some vaulting horses and thought, 'I must have those', and they became the set I call *The Barbarians* (1999–2002).

IC: *The Last Judgement* was made in response to the horrors of war and ethnic cleansing in Bosnia, Rwanda and elsewhere during the 1990s. The 25 pieces are each set in a box-like structure, closed from the light and reminiscent of the inside of a chapel, to create a path leading from *Door of Death* to *Gate of Heaven*. How did this idea develop?

AC: I got the idea from murals I saw in a tiny church in Crete. It was called *The Last Judgement* as a working title, then someone said, 'That's what you should really call it.' I made all the parts, which the ceramicist Hans Spinner fired and sent to the studio. Then I found a box, like an old wardrobe, all broken and bashed, and used it as a little house for the first one. I added to it, making more and more of them, and just putting the parts into boxes. As it evolved, I realized I needed a door, and so on. It was much more planned than *The Trojan War*, while *The Barbarians* was even more planned, too planned probably.

IC: With *The Last Judgement* was this the first time politics entered your work in such a prominent manner?

AC: I think it was just a reaction to the terrible massacres, genocide and bombs we see on television. Another example would be the series *Disasters of War* (1810–20) by Goya. We hoped it would all finish with World War II, but human beings aren't very nice. They just do this. It's something I feel strongly about, but, in a sense, it was the last thing I wanted to do, because I feel more involved with the abstraction of sculpture. You could say it's like someone who writes symphonies, then does an opera as well. *The Last Judgement* is like an opera; it reflects on what's happening in a human way. For the show's catalogue (Venice Biennale, 1999) I got a poet, a philosopher, a writer and a scientist to write about *The Last Judgement* from the point of view of their feelings. Therefore, the catalogue is not really a catalogue so much as it adds to the totality. It's not about people saying, 'I like this piece better than that one.'

IC: You prefer viewers to appreciate the unity of the installation?

AC: Well, you don't look at it in as pure a way as you do with abstract sculpture. I don't think one should tell people how to look, but I felt uncomfortable with *The Trojan War* when people said, 'That's my favourite.' It seemed to me that wasn't what it was about. I wanted them to get the entire picture of the war and feel like they were in the middle of a battlefield. And, in *The Last Judgement* I wanted them to get the totality of the chapel, as you call it, rather than making a choice in saying this one is better than that one.

IC: You've probably seen significant shifts in behaviour and society over time, and it seems the utopian ideals of the twentieth century have become extinguished. Where do you believe this will take us?

AC: I think I'm optimistic. It would be very hard to be an artist if you didn't believe in the possibility of good, although people seem to go through a lot of harm before they reach the good. I'm not a tragic person, or a miserable person. On the whole I'm a hopeful person, and whether it's because of the utopia of the mid 1960s or something else, I don't know. I've no idea what will come next, but I'm sure the lessons of today will be very useful. I do think that, in the end, we'll still be trying to get beyond the bad towards good, beyond violence towards peace; that peoples' lives will be more fulfilled, and that poverty will go. There's always a way through. This is nothing to do with sculpture, but it is to do with hope, and work does involve hope, belief and onwardness.

Interviewed in 2006

→
Anthony Caro
Achilles (The Trojan War), 1993–4

Stoneware and steel
168 × 94 × 53.5 cm
(66⅛ × 37 × 21⅛ in)

↘
Anthony Caro
Paper Sculpture No.5 – Blackbird, 1993

Paper, hand coloured
27 × 44 × 38.5 cm
(10⅝ × 17⅜ × 15⅛ in)

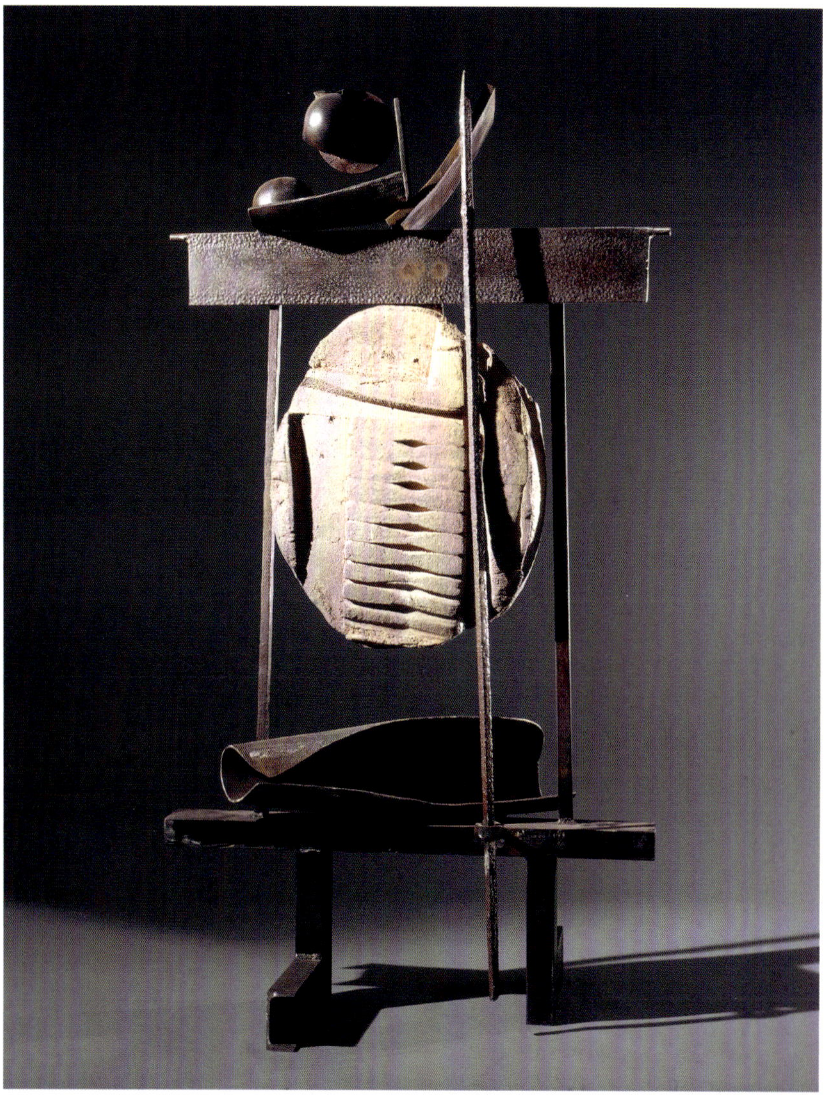

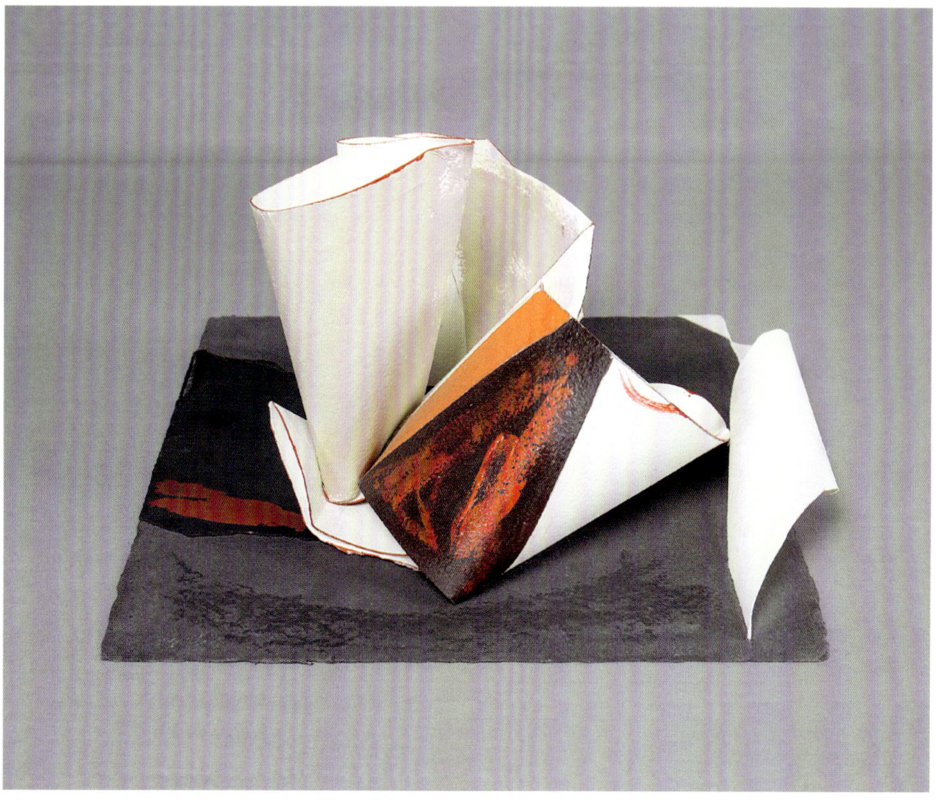

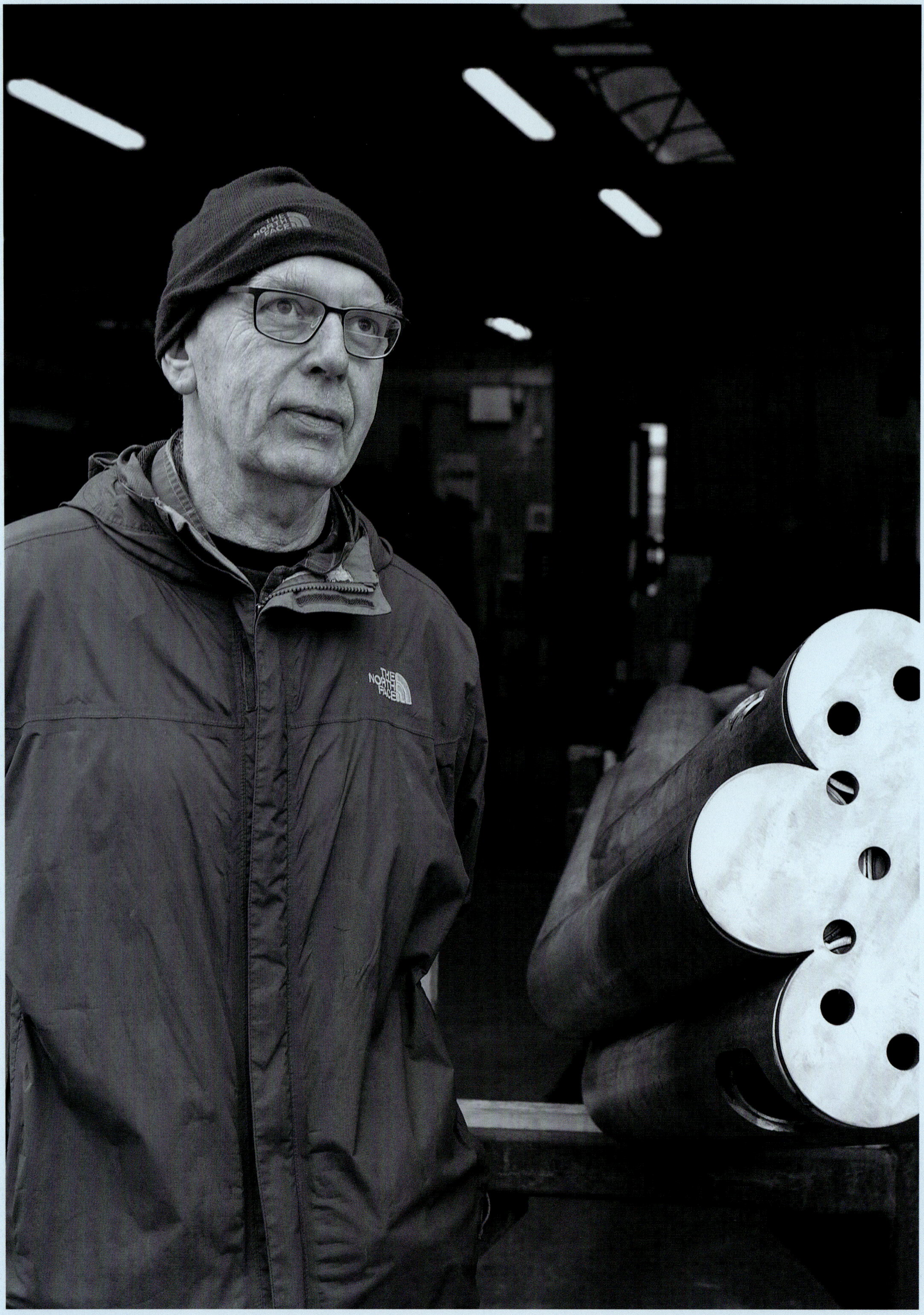
THE NORTH FACE

RICHARD DEACON

Born 1949, Bangor, Gwynned

Richard Deacon's practice frequently results in monumental forms that rely on a highly developed understanding of the fabrication process. Despite this, his work is fixed into allusive territory and it was a literary text, Rainer Maria Rilke's *Sonnets to Orpheus*, that contributed to his sculptural breakthrough in 1980. Words continue to exert a profound significance, as seen in his use of highly associative titles, which are descriptive, yet ambiguous. Deacon's works explore the connection between interior and exterior, mass and volume, surface and edge, to create a repertoire of forms that, although reliant on fabrication, align themselves to a more organic iconography. This is clearly apparent in *Laocoon, Out of Order* and *Under the Weather*, which appear to pulsate with unbounded energy, as if invisible forces were accelerating through their sinewy arcs. Deacon's sculptures are typically autonomous, only just making contact with the ground, and their particular relationship to the space imbues them with an undeniably commanding presence.

Ina Cole: Early on, you were inspired by Rilke's *Sonnets to Orpheus* (1923), which informed *For Those Who Have Ears #2* (1983) and *Tall Tree in the Ear* (1984). Both are open frameworks, their perspective continually shifting on circumnavigation. Did they constitute a significant development for you in the 1980s?

Richard Deacon: The breakthrough came in 1978–9 with a series of drawings related to *Sonnets to Orpheus*, called *It's Orpheus When There's Singing*, in which I transposed a way of making sculpture into more lyrical forms. In my work of the 1970s, a quantity of material was made into a shape and moved around, similar to cutting and folding. There was no need for prior thought because the process actually structured the material volumetrically. As an adjunct, the sonnets indicated areas where content might be involved. The drawings began from a geometric solid, with lines progressively moved around until I ended up with a final shape. They're like a rehearsal for a vocabulary that came into force later. As they involved curves, they were basically a manipulation of circular forms which quickly started to resemble other things. In the past, I'd found that association unacceptable, but there was a way in which the poems released ideas about content.

On the other hand, those 1980s pieces were an additional step forward, because there was a strong decision about scale and the relationship of the spectator to the sculpture. The work became a skin between an inside and an outside, and this seemed a positive process. So, there were two stages rather than one: the first was to have a vocabulary which allowed me to think of certain forms, then to translate that vocabulary into ways of manipulating material by bending, rolling or folding.

IC: Your sculptures are often given short descriptive titles, which can be unravelled like codes: *If the Shoe Fits* (1981), *The Eye Has It* (1984) and *Struck Dumb* (1988), for example. Even later pieces – *Shiver My Timbers* (2015–17) and *Under the Weather* (2016) – are enigmatic, allowing for multiple readings. How do you arrive at these titles?

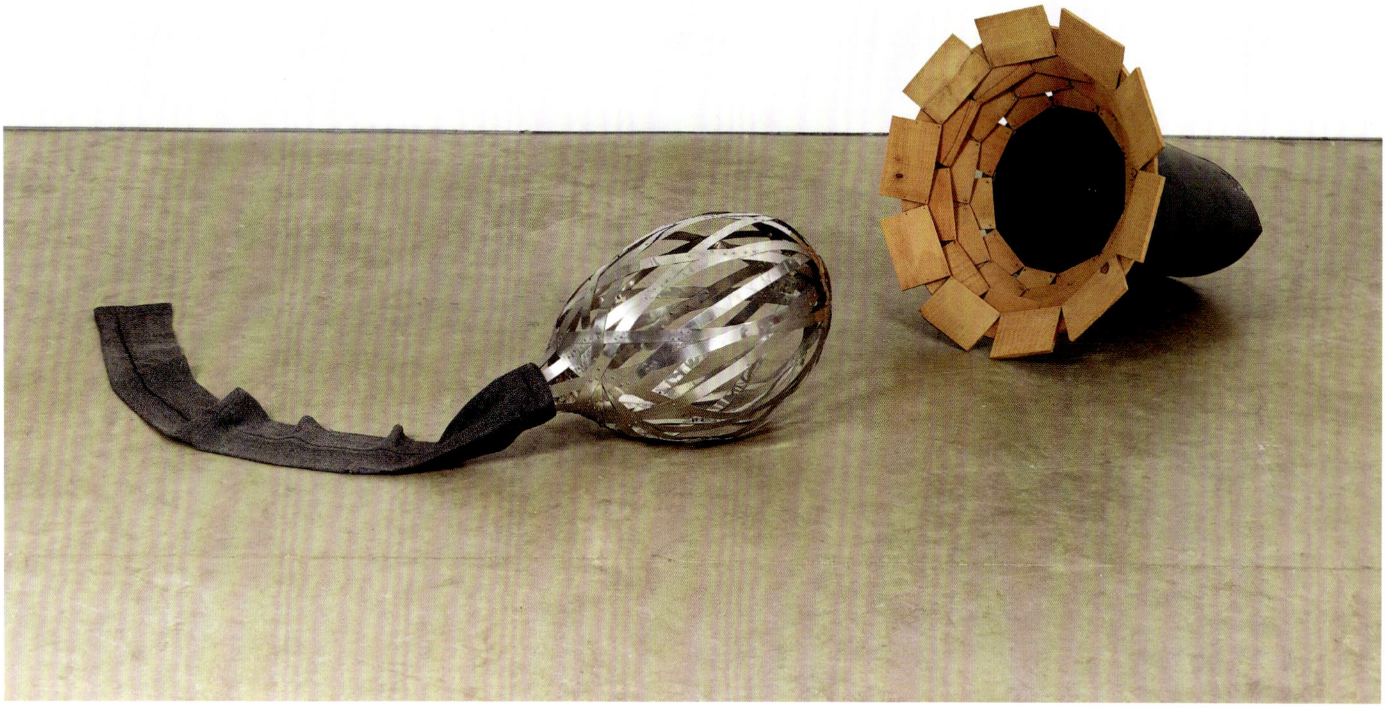

Richard Deacon
The Eye Has It, 1984

Wood, stainless steel, galvanized steel, brass, cloth
80 × 344 × 170 cm
(31½ in × 11 ft 3⅜ in × 66⅞ in)

RD: I've written fairly extensively in relation to my work. During my semi-performative practice in the early 1970s, I did a lot of describing in letters to my mother who was quite incapacitated. The idea was to build something in her head by describing it. Language became part of the working process, and using titles was an acceptance of the associative value of certain kinds of forms. It seemed natural, and the first really successful piece was *If the Shoe Fits*, which relates to the Cinderella fairy tale. Yet the sculpture's surface is studded with screws, so it wouldn't necessarily be a comfortable thing to wear.

Titles can help you to recall, guide you along, or lead you in the wrong direction. If you just use a number – a frequent convention of the 1960s to 1970s – that's quite hard to remember. Think of Caro's *Prairie* (1967), which is a very good title, or *Red Splash* (1966), for instance. Mine are generally after the fact, although there have been times when I've worked with slogans that became titles. I'm interested in the mechanisms of language, such as

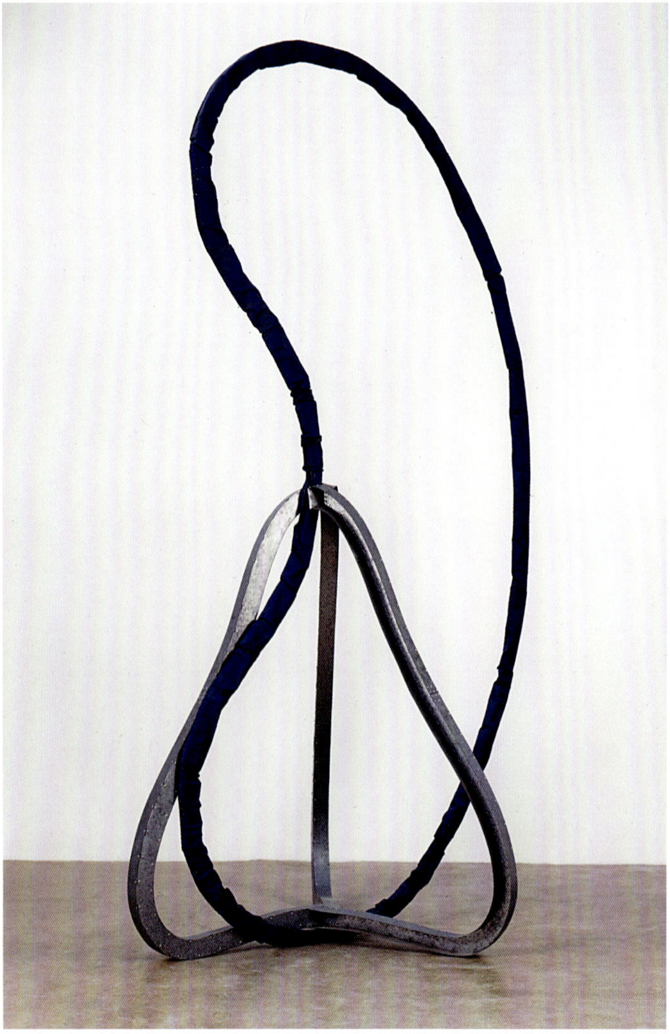

Richard Deacon
Tall Tree in the Ear, 1984

Galvanized steel, laminated wood, canvas
308 × 105 × 205 cm
(10 ft 1¼ in × 41⅜ in × 6 ft 8¾ in)

in a group of small sculptures titled as conjunctions, *If, And, But*. Or cliché, where the lexical meaning and actual meaning are different, is an interesting ambiguity to play with.

IC: You grew up in the 1950s and have vividly described playing on a half-finished housing estate in South West England, then moving to Sri Lanka and watching a snake charmer in the local market. You also revealed that you had your first sculptural experience at age seven, when seeing rock-carved Buddhas. Were these childhood experiences important?

RD: I think all childhoods are rich, whether they're impoverished or not, and they're important in how you construct the world afterwards. I was fortunate in having a broad spectrum of experiences; even a simple thing, like returning from Sri Lanka to find the arrival of television had changed everything. Yet it's hard to know if you turn out like you do because the path you've gone along led to that position. My father joined the Royal Air Force as an engineering apprentice and was extraordinarily capable with tools. I'm not really, even though I can make things, but a certain kind of clumsiness is useful. One of the reasons for adopting new ways of doing things is because you're clumsy at first, which brings a level of materiality into it. I was always intrigued by how tools work, and I'd abuse them, by cutting stone with a saw or rendering my shoes permanent with concrete. That fascination is inherent in me. It was a way of particularizing the world, so I could come to understand it, but whether that led to making art is another question.

At secondary school I didn't think my predilection for messing about had any place until I discovered the basement of the art room, where materials were available to be manipulated. My teacher, Derek Holland, was extraordinarily generous with his after-school time, and this was as important as what I was getting from my parents or contemporaries. An intellectual itch was being satisfied, but translating that into becoming an artist took another 20 years.

IC: In the 1970s, the sculptural object was becoming superseded by more insubstantial art forms such as performance. When did you realize you were on the track that would direct your future approach with regard to object making?

RD: On leaving St Martin's School of Art, in 1972, I was primarily involved with performance and documentary, but felt my ideas had missed the point. The reason I'd been involved in time-based practice was not to undermine object making; rather, to open up the space where objects could be made. There was a dreadful sense in which workshop practice meant you had to say what you wanted to do before you did it. Most of my activities involved devising things as I went along. I thought object making should be like drawing, less preconceived. There's a freedom to pencil and paper. In 1974, I attended the Environmental Media department at the Royal College of Art. I realized I'd never get into the sculpture department on the basis of the work I'd been doing, despite the fact I was interested in object making. However, all of that performance activity became a rehearsal for how to use a studio. Each of us in Environmental Media not only had to define what we did, but also to define the context within which that practice was located, and this was extraordinarily beneficial.

IC: Photography has also been important, and you wrote an insightful essay exploring the feelings you held towards your father's Leica camera.

RD: That essay is about liking apparatus. As I grew up with performance the relationship of film to performance is interesting, and photography was very much part of 1970s sculptural practice. Much later, I made a number of works by cutting holes in photographs, then placing drawings behind. It felt quite sculptural, as I had a physical cut in the paper, and the perspective of the camera pushed the drawing in front, out of the photograph. Then there came a point when I was completely discombobulated, as photography had become so ubiquitous. The changeover from film to digital was fast, and the link between time and image disappeared. Digital photography was printed linearly rather than holistically, and all of that disconcerted me. The photographic boundaries have expanded and its relationship to the truth has become blurred. So, the idea that the camera never lies is no longer true.

IC: You've produced a number of collaborative projects with fellow sculptors Bill Woodrow and Thomas Schütte, resulting in an intriguing fusion of sensibilities. How does this compatibility arise?

RD: I do have very longstanding relationships with other artists. In my last year at the Royal College I was actually setting up a studio and gallery for 30 artists at Acre Lane in Brixton, London. I strongly felt artists should determine their own futures and have a certain amount of control over the means of production – both in the making and the distributing. Despite there being no art market at the time, I was quite anti-market. Damien Hirst's activities on behalf of his fellow students at Goldsmiths, University of London, took a similar approach. There's also a bit of me that thinks, 'I don't necessarily feel my creativity is exclusive.' There are ways in which I can be open to other people. Well, as long as they do what I want them to – there is an element of that.

The collaborative object is interesting, as it's neither one thing nor the other. With Bill, it's as if we've created a third artist. He was a year ahead of me at St Martin's and we have a lot of shared interests. The collaboration with Thomas came about when he said, 'Why don't you come to the ceramic studio in Cologne, because it's not your studio or mine, but there are resources and materials we can use together?' Although we ended up producing two separate bodies of work, it did introduce me to clay again, and all my ceramic pieces since 1999 have been made in the Cologne studio. So, on one level the collaboration didn't succeed, but at another level it went fantastically well.

IC: The twists and turns in your sculpture are achieved by placing wood in a steamer, causing it to become more malleable. *Laocoon* (1996) derives from a Greek myth, in which a priest and his sons struggle with deadly serpents; *After* (1998) is equally snakelike in its writhing muscularity, while *Out of Order* (2003) and *Restless* (2005) are also suggestive of an extraordinary alien energy.

RD: I've collaborated with Matthew Perry since 1984, with whom I made a lot of the laminated pieces. When that came to an end in the 1990s, we began to explore new methods. We taught ourselves how to bend wood, starting ambitiously and learning quite quickly. Being able to manipulate wood with some plasticity surprised me and continues to surprise me. Once we learnt the parameters we were off, really. Those sculptures are quite muscular. They're also open-ended, which is quite unusual for me. Laocoon was a priest of the god Apollo and the statue, *Laocoön and His Sons* (c.2nd century BCE), was excavated in Rome in the sixteenth century, witnessed by Michelangelo. I'm interested in the way its discovery influenced the Baroque – it's an intriguing period. Although my sculpture *Laocoon* isn't a direct interpretation, I think my work is quite Baroque.

Richard Deacon
Laocoon, 1996

Steamed beechwood, wood, aluminium, steel bolts
430 × 364 × 357 cm
(14 ft 1¼ in × 11 ft 11¼ in × 11 ft 8½ in)

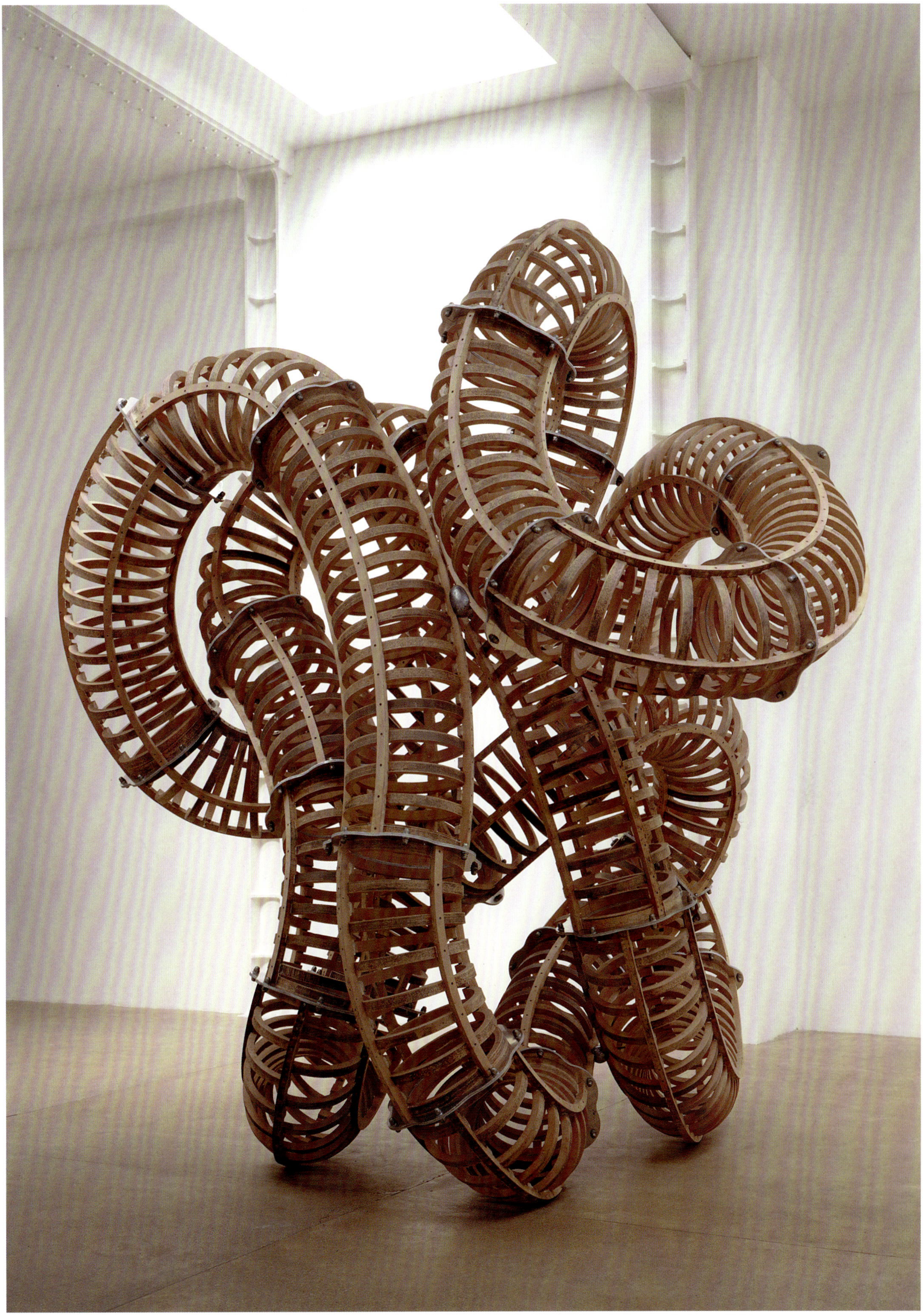

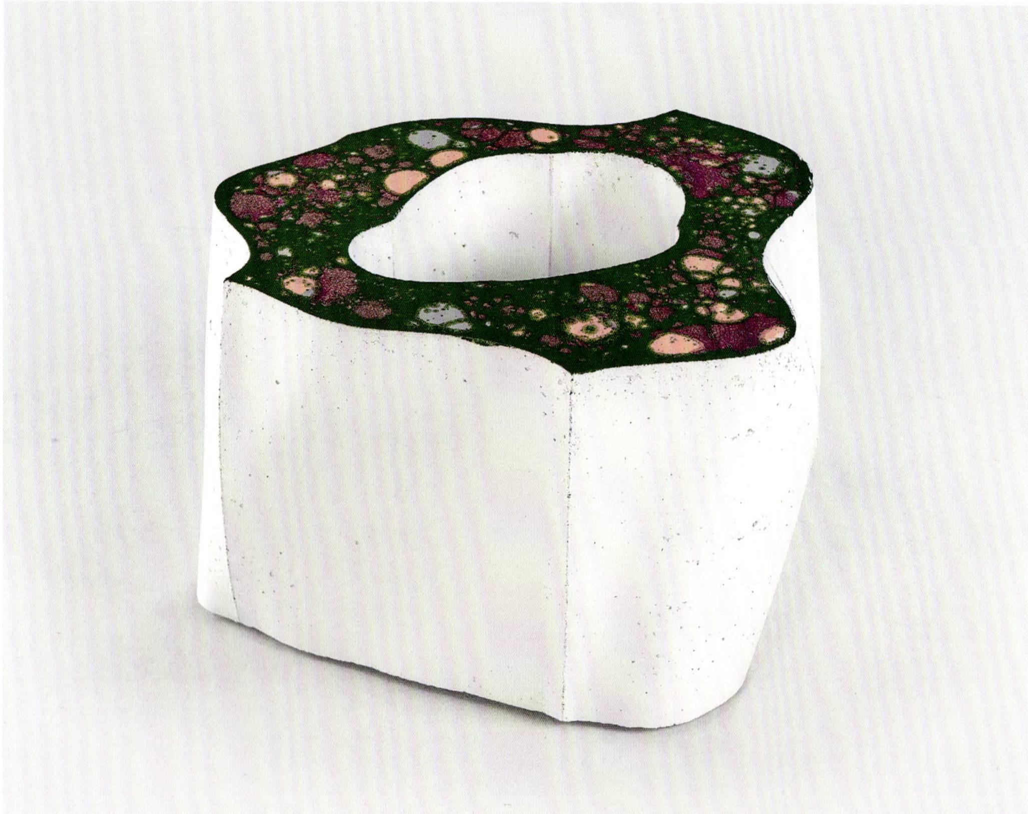

←
Richard Deacon
Flat 27, 2016

Glazed refractory concrete
34.5 × 52.3 × 44 cm
(13⅝ × 20⅝ × 17⅜ in)

→
Richard Deacon
Infinity #30, 2006

Stainless steel,
mild steel base
140 × 236 × 122 cm
(55 ⅛ in × 7 ft 8⅞ in × 48 in)

In *After*, the curve that produces the tubes is the result of an intense six-month period of repetitive making. At the time, we thought we could only bend in a single plane, so the tube is built up by repetitive elements. Then we said, 'We're not going to do that again', and began to think about bending in a spiral, as in *Restless*, or a twist, like *Out of Order*. It's less predictable and most of the subsequent works are based on those two ideas. Wood doesn't like being twisted from end to end, so it's better to twist a bundle than a whole. We also extracted bits of the bundle and *Under the Weather* is based on extracted elements.

The wooden pieces present technical problems that throw you into different territory. Technique is not always the solution, though. It's a question of experience, thickness of timber and knowing how long it has to stay in the steamer before coming out to be manipulated. Shipbuilders used to bend wood in the eighteenth century, but it was a slow process. We only have five minutes to bend it. It's a quick, one-way process, as the wood doesn't really go back again like steel, which is reversible. Sometimes, I think we've reached the limits of what we can do, but Matthew is very good at manipulating complex forms in wood.

IC: There's an evident physicality about those sculptures, yet smaller configurations, such as *Cuttings* (2018) and *Fold in the Fabric* (2018), are more reserved and reside on table tops. *Flat* (2016), a series of fragments that introduce colour, are similarly 'handle-able'. How do you decide on scale when starting new projects?

RD: I had a show at Galerie Thaddaeus Ropac in Paris (2017) called 'Thirty Pieces', where eight were on the wall and the rest on tables, made in a variety of techniques. It was a deliberate attempt to give myself a bit of space, and many of the subsequent gallery shows, in

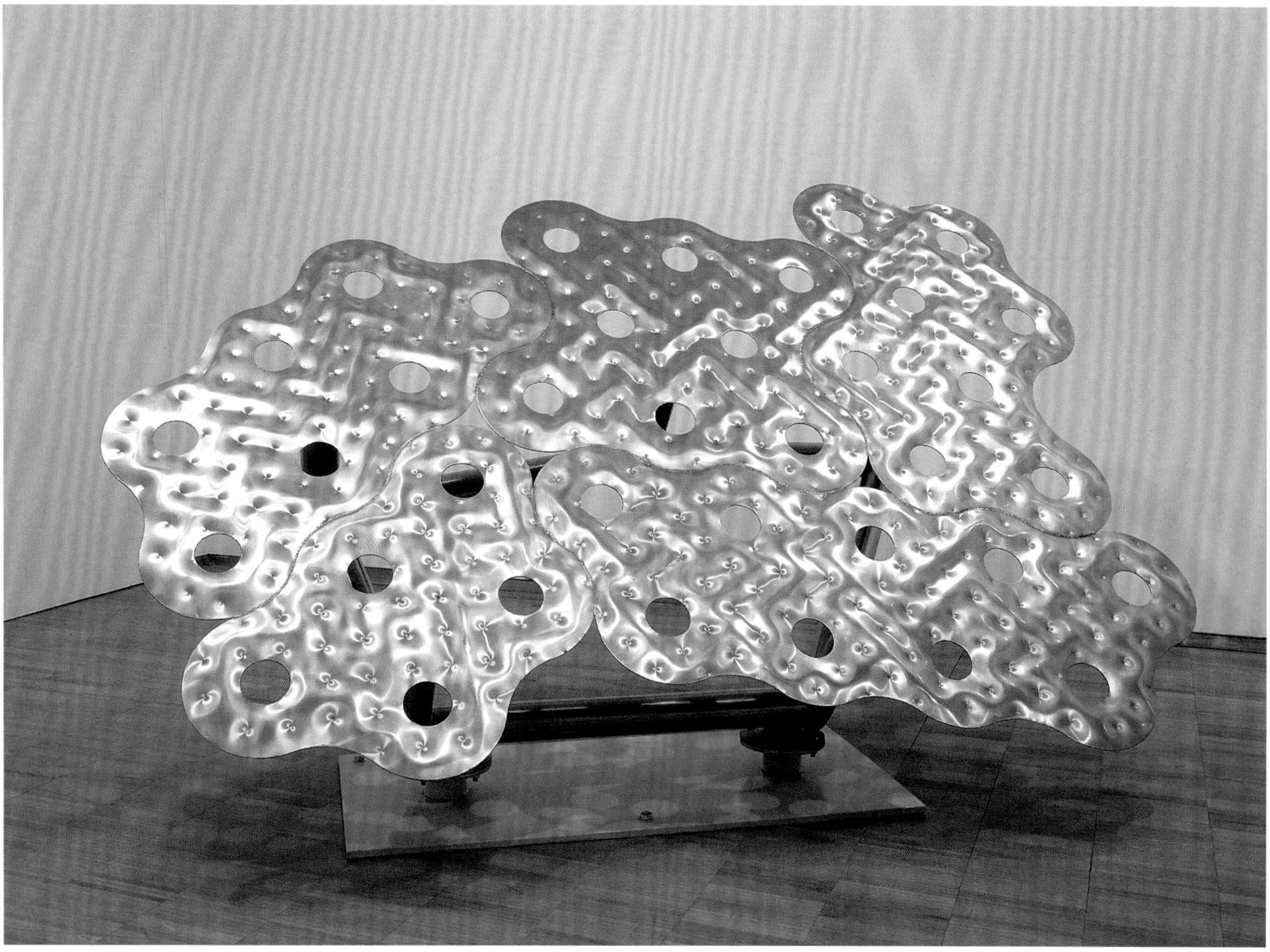

Los Angeles, New York and Berlin, continued this idea of small works. It was also to do with trying to open up unexplored avenues, and I'd begun using a saw and building the shapes from that. With *Flat*, I realized my ceramics were getting flatter and flatter, and I was becoming increasingly interested in the glaze. When you glaze a horizontal surface, rather than a vertical, it's a very different experience. I've always thought that the museum as the only home modern sculpture has, puts the cart before the horse, discounting the public and private space. The decision to make smaller work is to keep the space in which they're seen more open. It's not only to do with enabling a new approach: it enables me to utilize other spaces, or to approach a larger space with a different mindset.

IC: *Infinity* (1999–2008) is a series of modular shapes evoking molecular structures, fashioned from stainless steel. This systematic exploration of combinations generates an endless variety of forms and has preoccupied you for a number of years.

RD: *Infinity* was slightly born of failure. I'd wanted to make something on the floor that fitted together in any number of permutations, like a jigsaw puzzle. I had two-, three- and four-lobed puzzle bits, but hadn't accounted for the fact that they twisted when being made. They didn't really fit together very well, and I took the parts away and never showed them. Later, I realized those elements could be recombined to create a five- or six-lobe, and so on. They were welded together and wall-mounted at Lisson Gallery in London (1999), quite close to the floor. With the next group I had to resolve the twisting, and the solution was to put a hole in the middle of each module. Then I added stalks at the back for them to sit on the floor, rather than having to be wall-mounted. The stalked units were assembled into configurations, acting like cradles and resembling satellite dishes.

The 'infinity' idea was also to do with counting. When learning to count, I remember understanding that once you knew the rule you could go on and on enumerating. As a child, it was an incredibly powerful intellectual realization, and I became a bit like a speaking clock. Yet, within the material structure of the works, there's also the way they respond to light, which has qualities of the infinite as well.

IC: You have an equivalent interest in letter forms. What's the driving force behind *Alphabet* (2009–2018), a series that also explores infinite permutations?

RD: At the time, I'd been making ceramics based on an idea about carving. A lot of these ceramics involved manipulating a lump of clay and using it as a model for larger pieces. I hollowed out the lump, just leaving the edges, or punched holes into it. Then I visited Kailasa temple, at the Ellora Caves in India, which is basically a complete temple made by carving. The earliest Buddhist temples were caves, as were Christian churches. The cave as an architectural form doesn't have an outside, only an inside. The Kailasa is a huge lump that becomes a complete temple – it's amazing. It seemed to overlap with the hollowing out I was doing with the clay pieces, which I thought could become the basis for constructed sculpture. Then I wondered what would happen if I flattened them and began a number of drawings to do with the idea of flattening. By the time I'd run out of enthusiasm or inspiration, there happened to be 26 of them, and that's how they became the alphabet. I got to Z and finished. Those flat drawings were then made into reliefs, using many different configurations. They're very geometric, but geometry has become much more significant to me now.

IC: You've said it's important for your sculpture not to have points of interruption – that there needs to be a place for wholeness. Yet the larger ones have to come apart to be installed in an exhibition. How do you resolve this dichotomy?

Richard Deacon
New Alphabet ABC, 2018

Stainless steel and paint
264 × 206 × 47 cm
(8 ft 7⅞ in × 6 ft 9⅛ in × 18½ in)

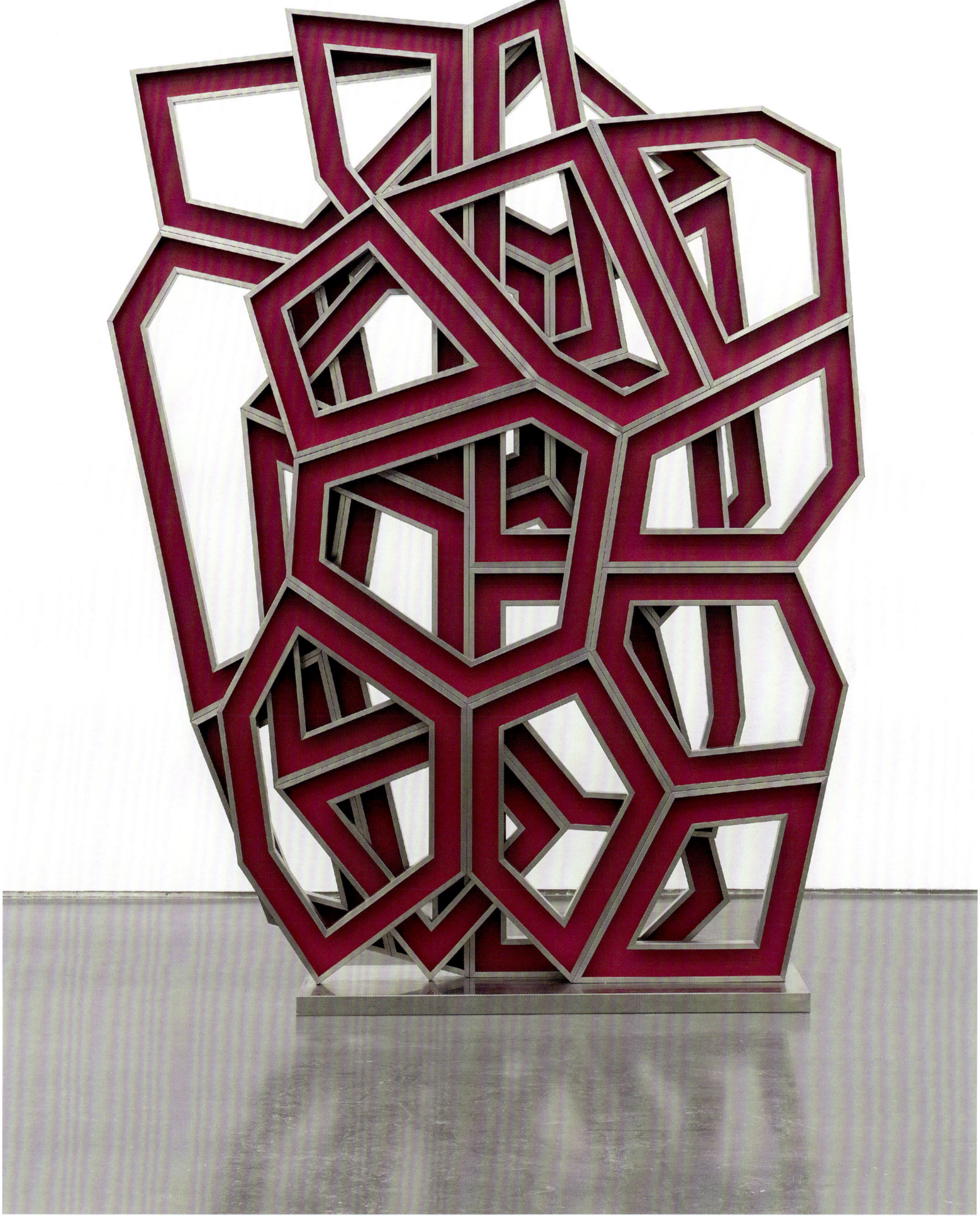

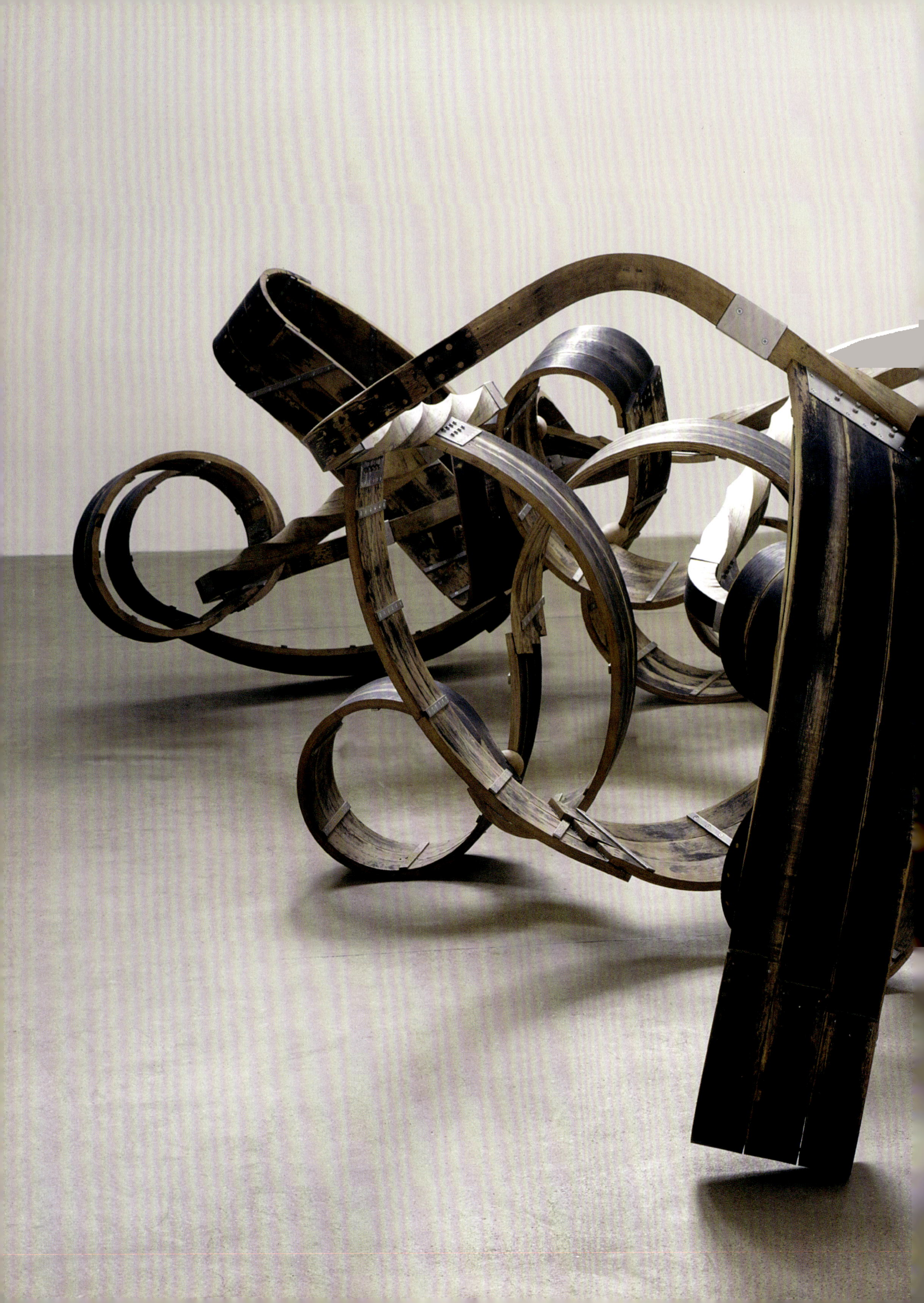

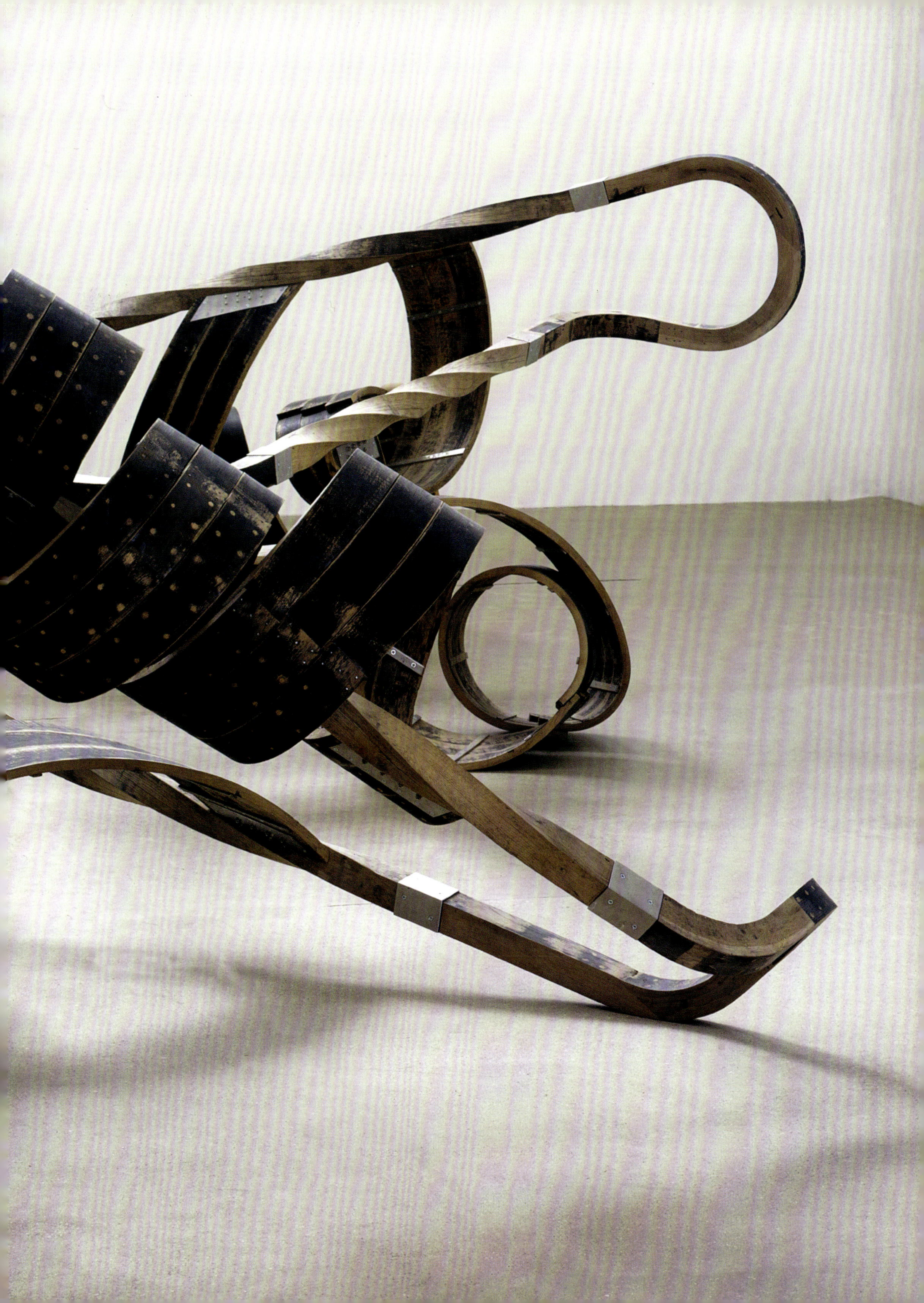

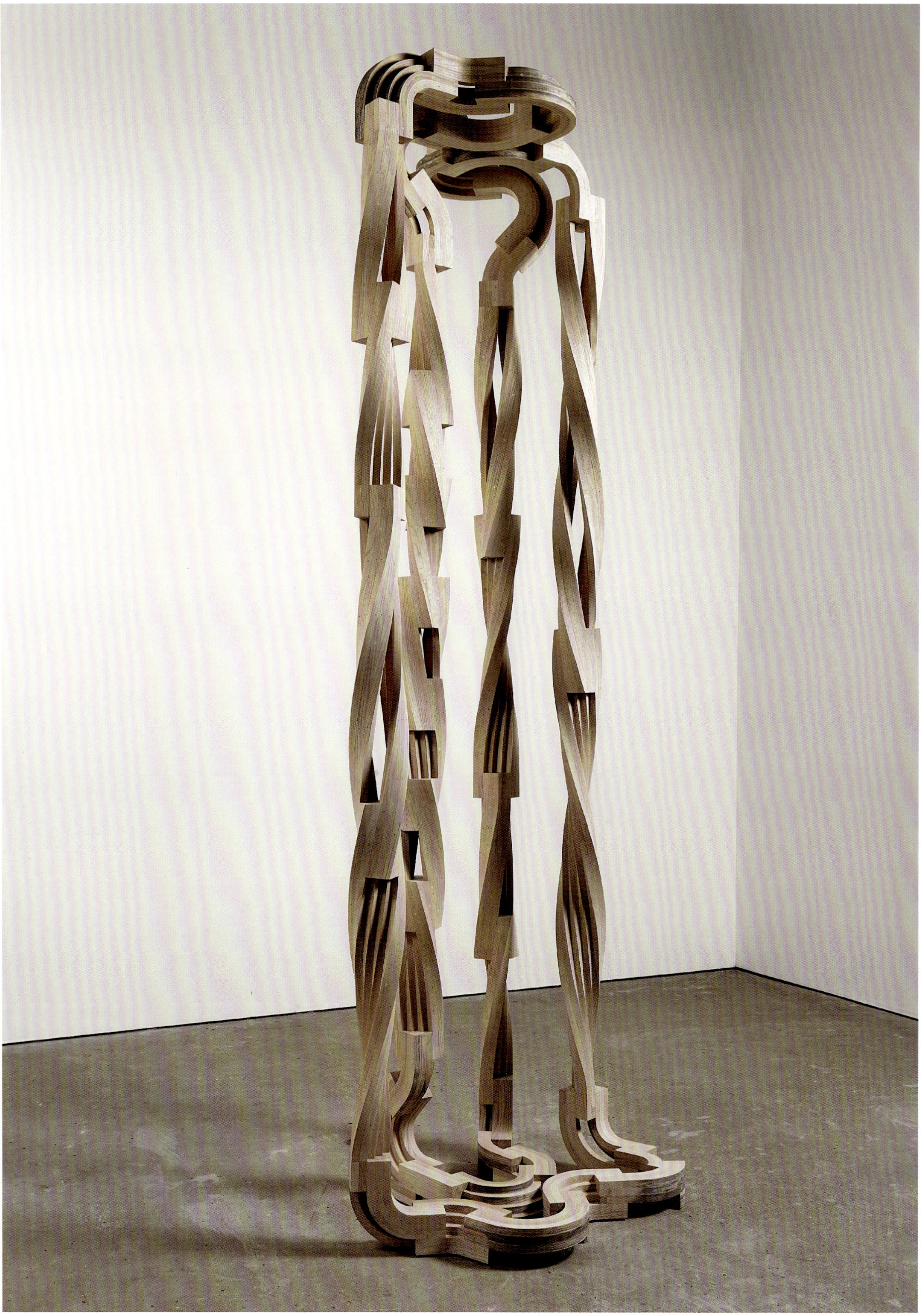

←←
Richard Deacon
Out of Order, 2003

Wood (steamed oak),
stainless steel
190 × 700 × 570 cm
(6 ft 2¾ in × 22 ft 11⅝ in × 18 ft 8⅜ in)

←
Richard Deacon
Under The Weather #2, 2016

Steamed wood
346 × 116 × 103 cm
(11 ft 4¼ in × 45⅝ in × 40½ in)

RD: Well, Gestalt theory was important in the 1970s. Although I've always talked about construction, I did think corners were difficult because they're stopping points in relationship to the whole thing. And there are practical problems, as you've pointed out, to do with making large sculptures which then come apart. One solution has been to use as many screws as possible, so you can't differentiate between the fixing screws and those that are part of the work. I multiplied the ways in which they were constructed, in order to hide the parts that came to pieces.

On the other hand, I thought wholeness gave the sculpture autonomy in the space, while also giving autonomy to the viewer. There was a fairly deep ideological reason for having autonomy. Although I've made reliefs on the wall, and incorporated the wall into the work, it's possible to criticize installation for being overly dependent on architecture, and works installed in charismatic spaces can become dependent on the space to carry their meaning. Making sculpture that's resistant to being appropriated by the space is a way of establishing its boundaries and your boundaries as a viewer. There's a dialogue in my practice between those two ideas. In the late 1970s and early 1980s I was very insistent upon autonomy. Then I realized that the larger pieces actually seem to reach out and embrace you, so there's an empathetic response as well.

Interviewed in 2019

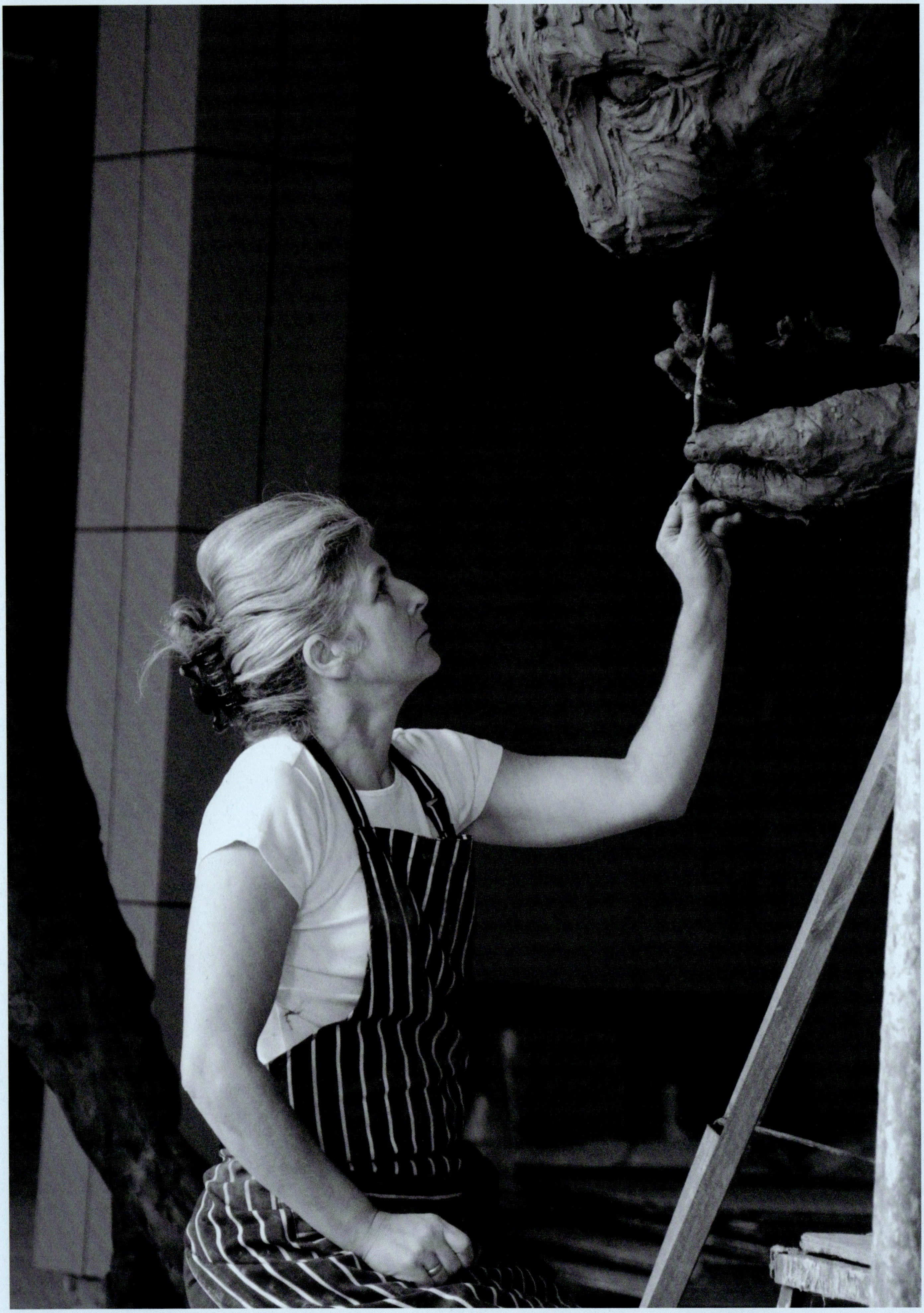

LAURA FORD

Born 1961, Cardiff, Glamorgan

In Laura Ford's sculptures, human and animal elements are often synthesized to create perplexing hybrids, as exemplified in *Headthinker VIII*, in which the weight of the ceramic donkey head contrasts with the apparent frailty of the human form on which it resides. Ford applies her acute observation of physical demeanour to a range of characters who exude humour and terror in equal measure. They plead empathy yet, on closer inspection, all is not as it seems. In *Rag and Bone*, a nomadic hedgehog wrapped in blankets occupies an interior; *Dancing Clog Girls* are impaired by roots that sprout from their feet; *Emissary Cats* pace nervously in expectation of impending doom; while *Three Bears* masquerade as politicians. Ford practices intuitively, through a ready supply of materials that are continually modified until the final result is achieved. Pertinent social and political issues are raised in a fantastical language that enthrals yet challenges the viewer.

Ina Cole: You grew up in a travelling fairground family. Children often have overactive imaginations, and this environment must have introduced you to a magical world. To what extent did this early experience direct your work?

Laura Ford: My mother left my father, who was a television announcer, just before I was born. So, we went to my grandparents. When not travelling, they lived in an old farmhouse that had previously been a zoo. My grandfather had a 'chipper': a three-storey lorry which opened out, where he made fish and chips and sold Coke at fairs. Performers came for their chips and, minutes later, they were covered in gold, sitting in a glass case full of rats. It was both extraordinary and mundane, yet that's just how people made money.

I also remember a tableau with a statue of Frankenstein in the centre, which was very sculptural. At a critical moment, the statue came alive, jumped up and chased me and my grandmother out of the booth. The sense something may, or may not, be alive has stayed with me. My uncles also had overactive imaginations, telling stories of escaped bears. One of them climbed a tree dressed in my grandmother's fur coat and, when his sisters were underneath, he dropped down, pretending to be a bear. There was much terror involved. At the time it seemed quite normal, but I can now see much of my work has come from fairground scenes.

Laura Ford
Giraffe, 2013

Cast bronze
800 cm (26 ft 3 in) high
Installation view:
Frauen und Hautklinik
Heidelberg, Germany, 2013

IC: Animals are a key feature of your practice, appearing in many different guises, and you capture the intrinsic essence of the animal you seek to portray. *Moose* (1998), an early sculpture, perfectly represents the expressive solemnity of this beast, while *Giraffe* (2013) is characteristically skew-whiff. Most children relate well to animals. Is this because animals function without language and, therefore, make no judgement on behaviour?

LF: Definitely. As a child I had an Alsatian. We were inseparable and went on many adventures together. When I got told off, I wept into her fur, and she responded with a little howl of understanding. So, I projected my emotions onto this dog. *Moose* is made

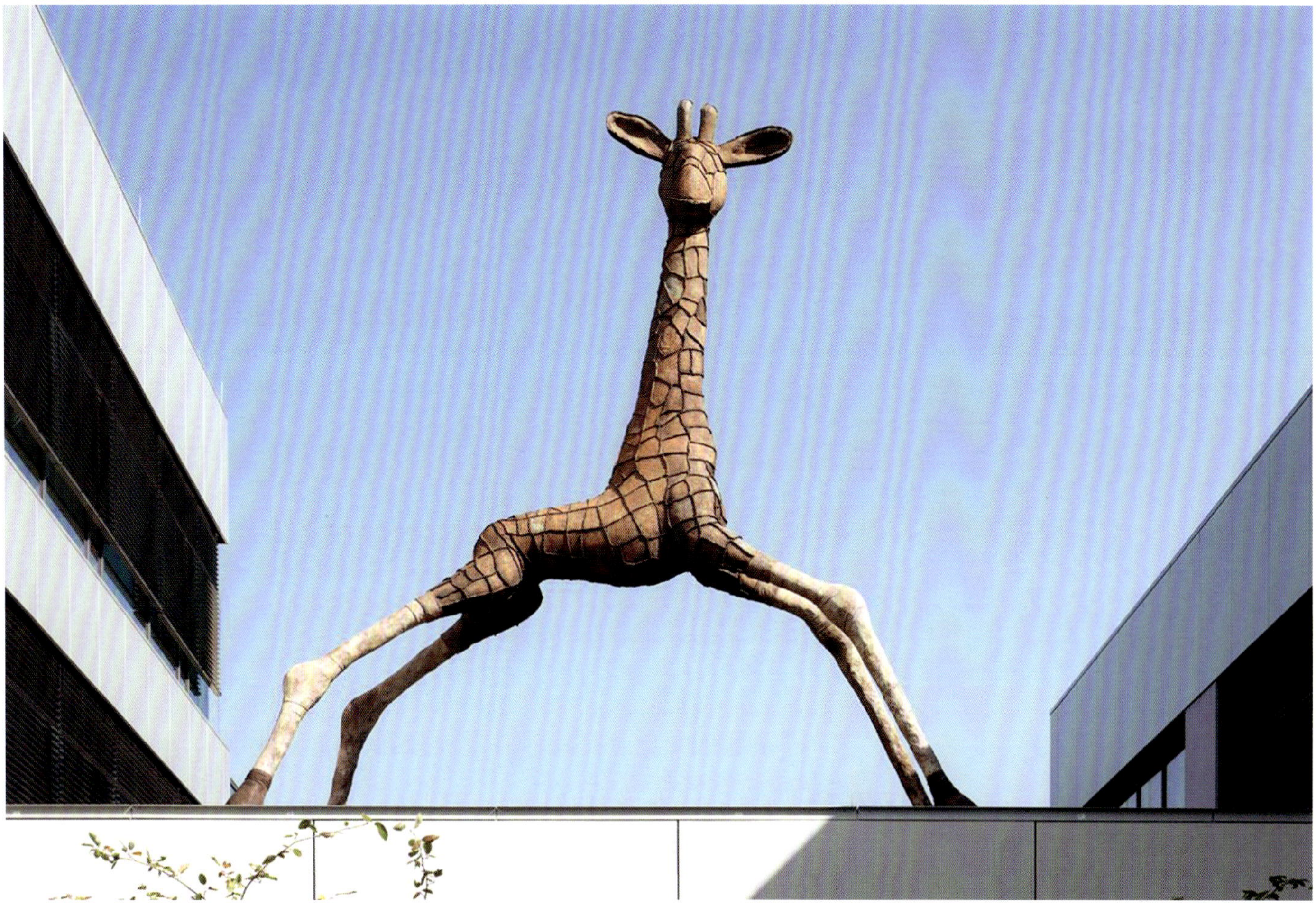

of felt and references my interest in Joseph Beuys. His materials – felt, wax, lard – are aesthetically gorgeous. And there's the whole mythology, the self-dramatization, which I enjoy. At the same time, sculptures like *Moose* also poke fun at that kind of macho showmanship. I made my first giraffe when my kids were very young, as I had a pass for London Zoo and visited once or twice a week. A lot of my time was spent looking at caged animals. This was probably because I felt like a caged animal myself, suddenly having to become domestic. It's an odd thing, being a parent and staying at home, as I'd never been at home that much before.

IC: Many of your sculptures employ metal armatures, which are dressed with fabrics, leather, canvas and wool. Each piece is handmade by you, in an era of mass production. Did this approach come about as an antithesis to the fabricated object?

LF: I can't really work in any other way; I get my ideas through the making and by the choices that come about that way. The sculptures would become too illustrative if I didn't do that; there would be no surprises or pleasure. There is some planning, of course, but the pieces are continually changing as I make them.

IC: You frequently use wit to impart hard-hitting messages, and your work is sometimes heavily politicized. *Bunny Boy* (2003), for instance, wears a suicide-bomber's belt, and *Armour Boys* (2006) is a poignant reflection on child soldiers.

LF: All my work comes from personal experience, and I had three children I was desperate to keep safe. News stories at the time made me think of my own position. As a mother, how do I keep my children safe, yet give them space to experience danger without dying? When watching my favourite cartoons, I noticed Bugs Bunny had explosives attached to him, and thought, 'This stuff is so violent.' *Bunny Boy* relates to how suicide bombers had strapped bombs to small children. Terrible things were happening to peoples' sons and daughters, which seemed horrific to me. *Bunny Boy* and *Armour Boys*, therefore, acted out the worst that could happen, in the hope it would never happen to me.

IC: Many of your pieces, such as *Bunny Boy*, fuse human and animal composites. Similarly, *Headthinkers* (2003–12) are a group of slight figures resting their oversized, world-weary donkey heads on plinths. What prompted this series?

LF: *Headthinkers* came about when I was putting up an exhibition in Salamanca, Spain. I felt exhausted, as my children were very young at the time, and I'd been creating work for quite a few exhibitions. But I had half an hour to sit in a café and think about my practice. Initially I wanted to make some work using the plinth as a place to lay my own head, and ceramics, as all the donkey heads are made of ceramic. The way they're chopped at the neck is quite violent and important. However, the idea of the donkey actually came from when I was schooled at a convent. My parents weren't religious, but they had a bit of money by this stage and thought a private school was the best place for me. There were a few other fairground girls there, as well. Some of the nuns hated me, and I had a real battle with one of them. I took an exam a year early and phoned to get the result. She said, 'D for donkey, you stupid girl!', and put the phone down. It turned out I'd got a C, but that stuck with me, so I've used it a lot in my work.

IC: In *Rag and Bone* (2007) you transpose Beatrix Potter's characters to the twenty-first century, where they've resorted to rough-sleeping, scavenging and substance abuse. As a nation, we're sometimes kinder to animals than to our fellow humans. Do we feel more empathy with this particular group because they're represented as animals?

LF: Yes, which I find extraordinary. I began making them one Christmas, for an exhibition at the Economist Plaza in London (2008). It's a time when we ensure the homeless get dinner, but what about autumn or summer dinners? Or what about trying to understand homelessness, rather than sentimentalize it at Christmas? Those sculptures were also provoked by a book, *Stuart: A Life Backwards* (2005), by Alexander Masters. We assume everyone wants the life we have, with a nice house and so on. Yet some people can't live like that because of their traumas, mental health issues or simply because they don't want to. Something has brought them to this point. It's a complicated situation which is too often simplified.

My ideas frequently come about through a series of events. At the time, I saw many homeless characters on the street that I really liked. There was an amazing woman, Mary, who sold books from a pushchair. She looked like a little hedgehog. And an old guy with a big white streak in his hair, like a badger, wore an apron and went through the bins of Camden. Another guy always

→
Laura Ford
Three Bears (Maquette), 2017

Bronze
Three elements:
32 × 30 × 11 cm;
24 × 22 × 8 cm;
17 × 12 × 8 cm
(12⅝ × 11¾ × 4⅜ in;
9½ × 8⅝ × 3⅛ in;
6¾ × 4¾ × 3⅛ in)

↘
Laura Ford
Rag and Bone with Blanket, 2007

Bronze
77 × 110 × 86 cm
(30¼ × 43¼ × 33⅞ in)

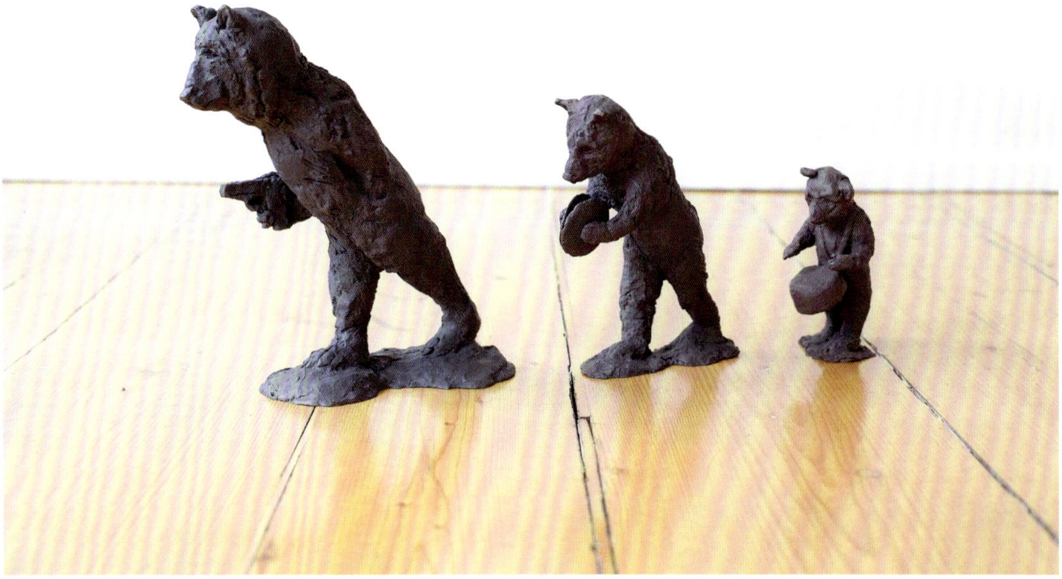

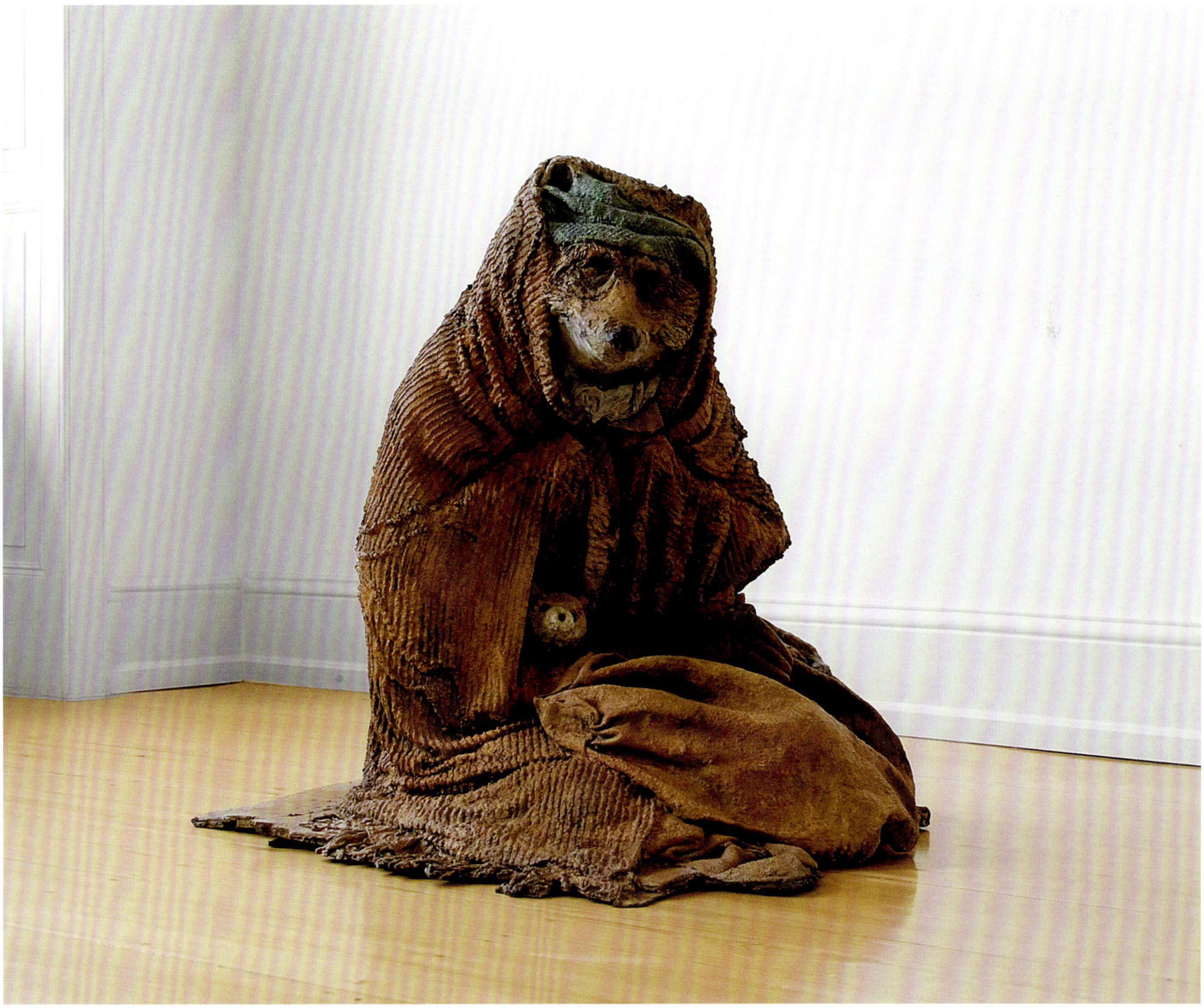

asked for change for the same parking meter, even though it didn't take change any more. He reminded me of the squirrels that came in and walked along the wooden beams of our house, when I was reading Beatrix Potter to the children.

So, the series came together like that. They're portraits, just as Potter created portraits of the animals she saw around her. When the hedgehog, Mrs Tiggy-Winkle, was shown at the Economist Plaza, a security guard saw it on camera and went to move it on before realizing it was a sculpture. I want people to react bodily and emotionally to the work, but in an unconscious way. If I'm trying to make you feel empathy, I give the sculpture a body language that causes it to look vulnerable or upset.

IC: Your works do often consider the extreme and irrational emotions of childhood, such as *Weeping Girls* (2009) and *Silent Howler* (2016). Why do these particular figures appear as such embodiments of despair and anxiety?

LF: They do, but it's as if they're making it up. They're wailing so much that they're in another place and really quite enjoying it. Emotion has tipped over to become a conscious act. Also, I've a particular fondness for Greek mourning figures; funerary sculptures of weeping women. I first made *Weeping Girls* for Jupiter Artland in Scotland, and they were sited next to Ian Hamilton Finlay's *Temple of Apollo* (2005). *Silent Howler* was created specifically for Blackwell House in the Lake District. There's a fabulous wall in the garden, and she's positioned there with her back to this incredible landscape, deep in her own misery, or not. Yet, there's a beautiful world behind her that she's not aware of. There is a terrible story about Blackwell, in that the owners' eldest son died in World War I, after which they stopped coming to the house because there was just too much sadness around. You could attach all this to the figures, which makes them sadder. However, you can also read them in many different ways.

→
Laura Ford
Dancing Clog Girls, 2013 (detail)

Bronze
Dimensions variable
Installation view:
Kunstsammlungen und Museen Augsburg, Germany, 2013

→→
Laura Ford
Weeping Girl 5, 2009

Bronze
127 × 60 × 45 cm
(50 × 23⅝ × 17¾ in)
Installation view:
Jupiter Artland, Edinburgh, 2009

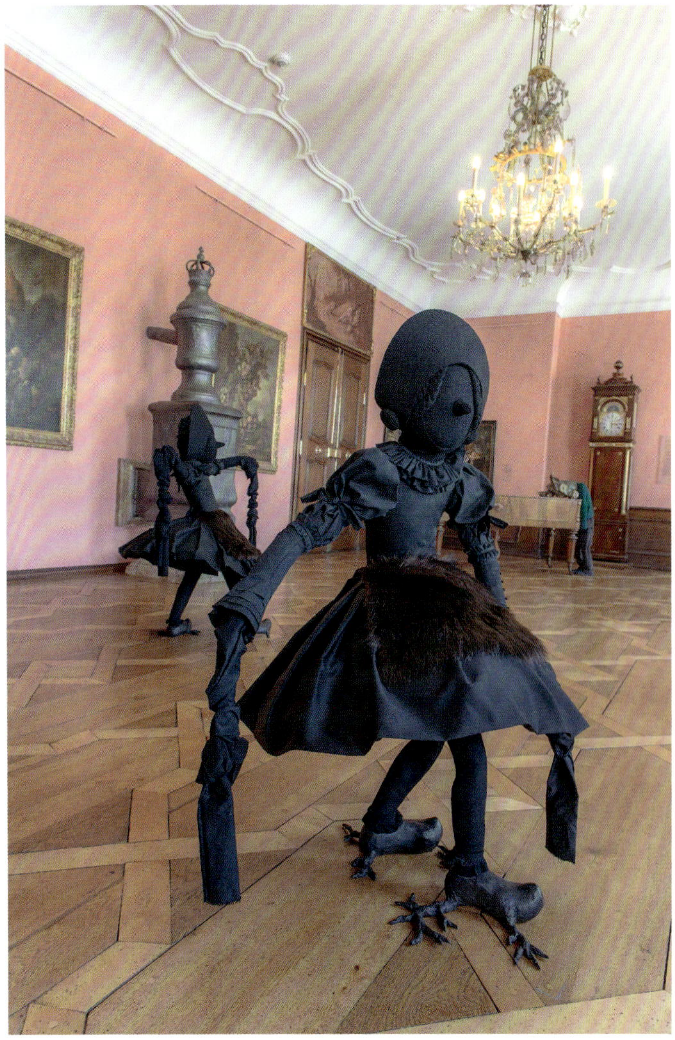

IC: Once a work is in the public realm it takes on a life of its own, and people bring their personal stories and emotions to it. Nonetheless, *Weeping Girls* and *Silent Howler* don't actively engage with the viewer. Their heads are tilted at an angle that obscures the face, and eyes don't feature, so they can't actually meet your gaze. It's as if they're acting out a very private ritual.

LF: The minute a face is added, peoples' ability to respond emotionally becomes limited, because the emotion is already there. If there's no face more effort has to be made in terms of reading the body language of the sculpture. When making those pieces, lots of materials were used – wax, plaster, fabrics, everything. They were then made stiff, after which moulds were taken from them. The patination gives them a washed-out appearance, and this makes them look like those Greek funerary sculptures. When I was at the convent, I sometimes stayed behind with the other girls to look at all the religious figures, which were painted white. We thought they would start to move when it got dark, as dusk does weird things to the eyes. And, because we sat there willing them to move, they did of course move. I remember writing my thesis on Jean Cocteau's film *The Blood of a Poet* (1932). I was deeply influenced by Cocteau and, in this film, all these Greek statues come alive, speak to the characters and take them to another world.

IC: The emotions of childhood become superseded by logic, but never wholly dissipate. They remain latent, often re-emerging in later life. There's a thread of uncanniness running through your work, which touches upon this notion of deep-rooted childhood sentiments remembered.

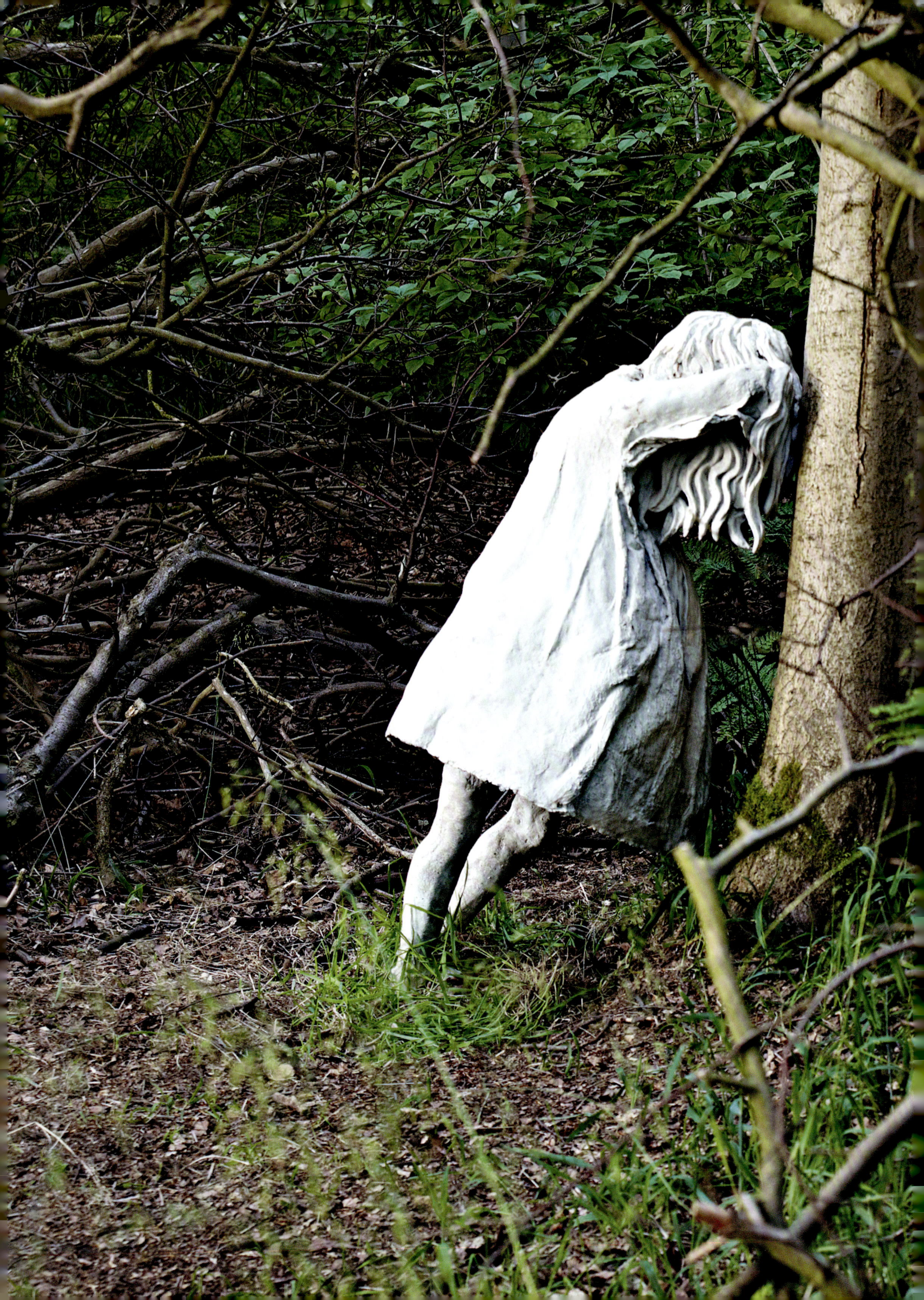

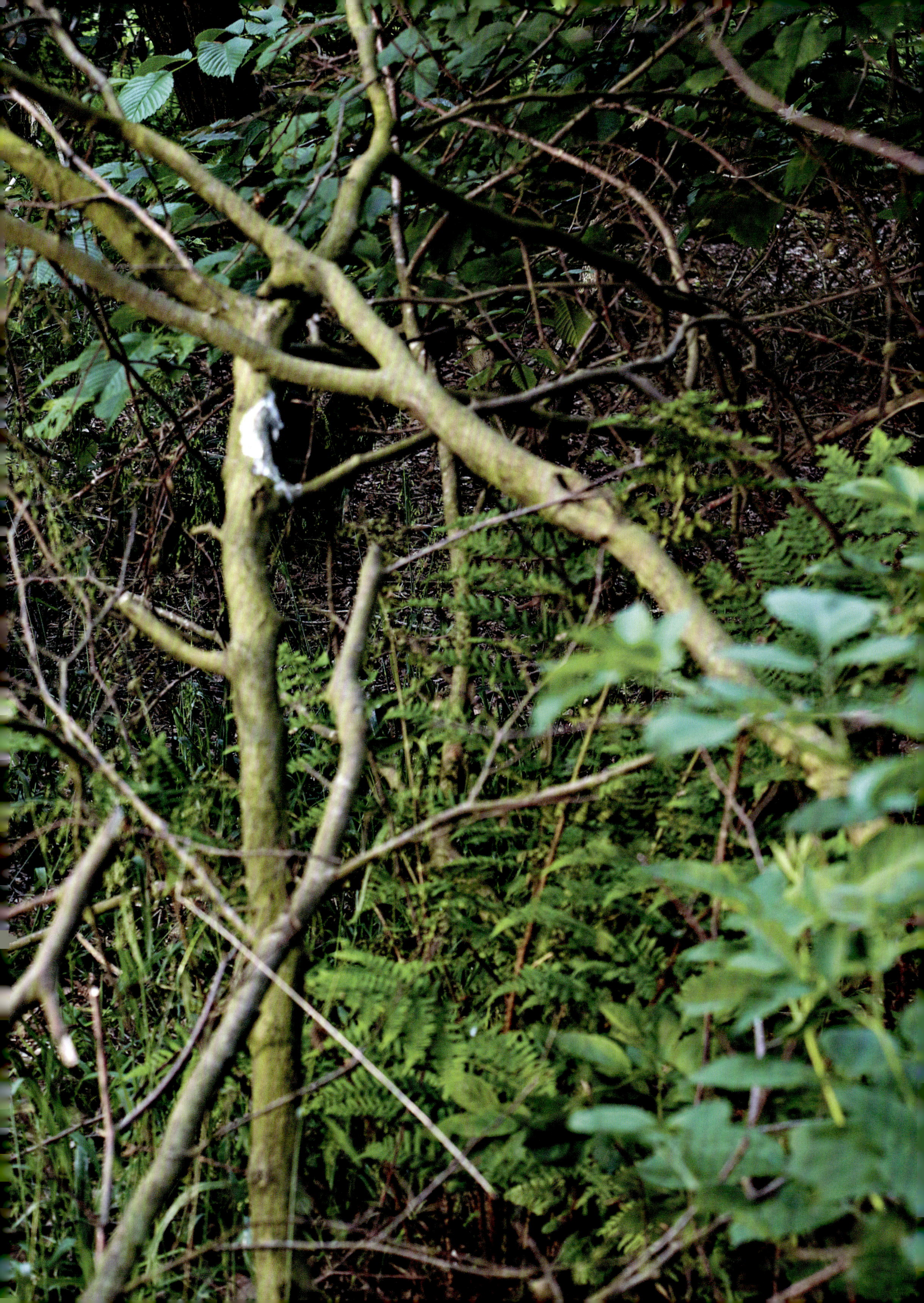

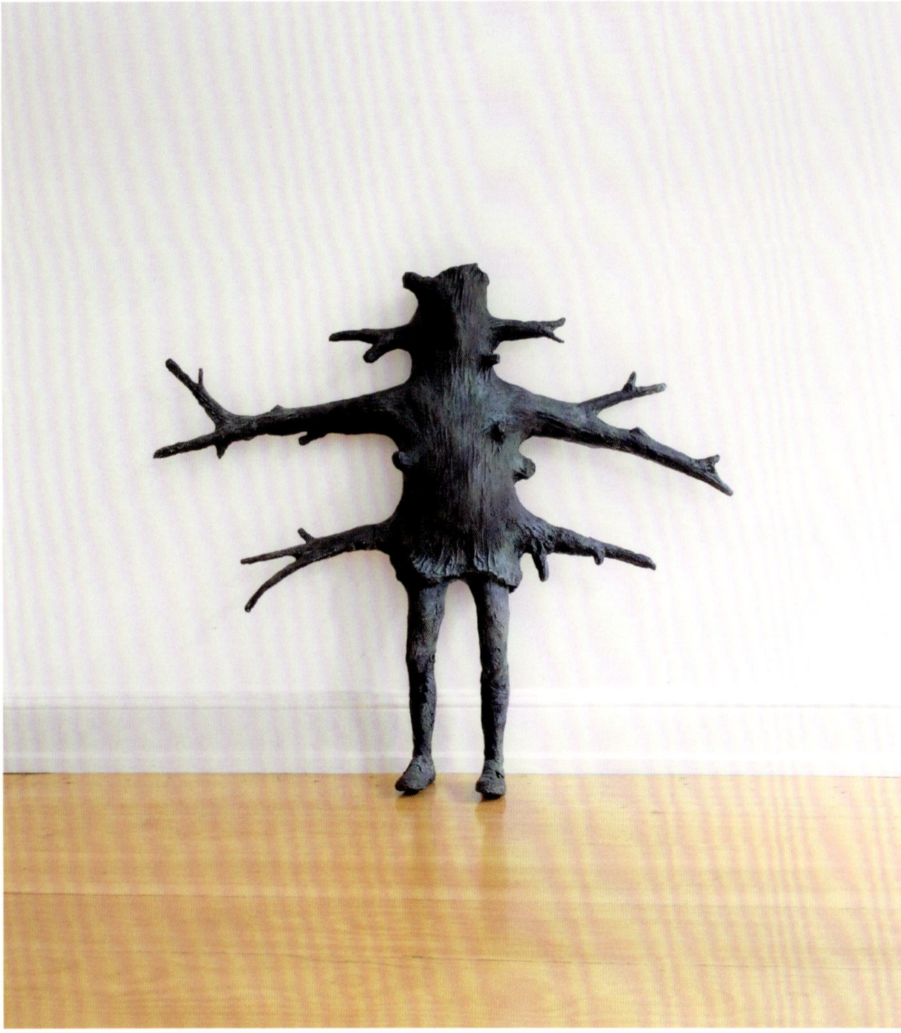

LF: It's sometimes said my practice is all about childhood. Actually, it's not; it's about the child within, which in terms of psychotherapy is really important. Unless the little people are given a voice, their responses can become very damaging. Freud was a favourite of mine at one point. Not that I think about him when I'm making sculpture, but his stories are fabulous to read and I was very influenced by him. In one of my earliest installations, *God Pot* (1992), the little figures gave the impression of wanting to be rescued from their dungeon environment. I aimed to create a dreamlike state, so they were dressed in sleep suits. Although you wanted to pick them up, they were incredibly creepy; a bit like the children in Henry James's novella *The Turn of the Screw* (1898) who are cute and need looking after, yet their minds may be evil. Also, we all have a totally different sense of personal history. In Tara Westover's memoir *Educated* (2018), the seven siblings perceive completely different histories, depending on what they thought they saw and what they had buried. The gap between people and their experiences is so interesting.

IC: Sometimes, your hybrids are part-human, part-flora, such as *Espaliered Girl* (2007) and *Espaliered Woman* (2007), of which you've made a number of versions. They're in a state of flux, undergoing a disconcerting transformation as they sprout roots and branches.

LF: My interest in females and nature is linked to the essentialist feminism I bucked against in the 1980s. The idea that women were pure and closer to nature seemed to play right into the patriarchy's hands. I wanted to poke fun at it, and also make it darker. There was a notion that anything natural was good, but of course it's not. As my kids were growing up, I thought about the effect you have on them as a parent.

←
Laura Ford
Espaliered Girl, 2007

Bronze
150 × 180 × 28 cm
(59 × 70⅞ × 11 in)

→
Laura Ford
Days of Judgment, 2012

Bronze
160 × 100 × 167 cm
(63 × 39⅜ × 65¾ in)

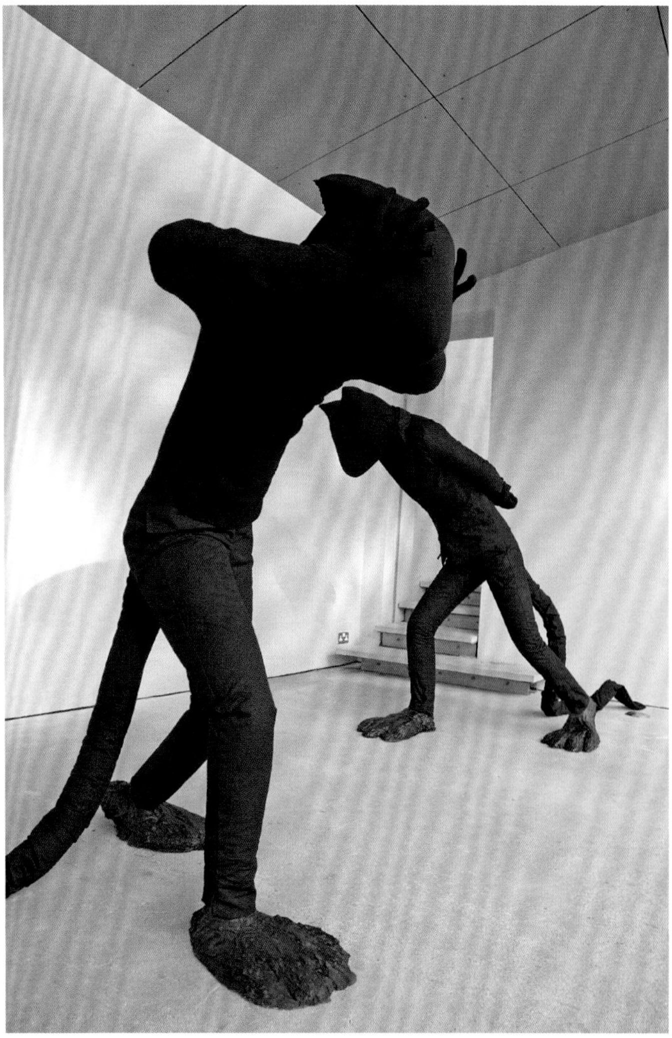

There are some espaliered trees in my garden, which look crazy as they're not very well trained, and I was inspired to draw a parallel with my parenting skills. The espaliered girls were Jesmonite [an acrylic-modified gypsum composite] originally, and then cast in bronze, whereas the espaliered women were always bronze. Their roots and branches are trying to grow and bust out, but in a contained way. It's as if the figures reflect a state of self-restraint.

IC: Your groupings often reference their historical location. For example, *Dancing Clog Girls* (2013), who also sprout roots, were exhibited at Schaezlerpalais in Augsburg, Germany. Similarly, *Emissary Cats* (2012) were shown in 'Days of Judgement' at Strawberry Hill House in Twickenham, London, in 2015, a residence built by Horace Walpole in the eighteenth century. Do you have an interest in our ancestral past?

LF: The Schaezlerpalais has an incredible ballroom, visited by Marie Antoinette who danced there. *Dancing Clog Girls* relates to that and to the story of Cinderella, who is the chosen one, lighter than air, not the one with a puppet-like face, peasant ankles and roots that grow down into the ground. The princess is blonde and flies away; she's not a grotty, earth-based creature. That's why the clog girls come to dance with the princess. They have aprons made of fur, so there's a sense of the animal and a reference to the grittiness of being a proper human. The clog girls are poking fun at royalty, and the way our class structure is based around silly rituals completely inappropriate for today's times.

Emissary Cats was created when the banks collapsed and governments grew desperate to lend support. That grouping is about a sense of catastrophe. If you catastrophize you don't actually have to deal with the problem, as it becomes too big to solve, and the banks too big to fail. So, we just go on as before. Like global warming, which tends to get ignored, as it's just too awful to deal with. My cats also reference Behemoth in Mikhail Bulgakov's *The Master and Margarita* (1967); the terrifying cat figure that does wickedly funny things. *Emissary Cats* looked good at Strawberry Hill because it's such a Gothic location. And at over 6 feet tall (180 centimetres), they came across as really thunderous. It's as if they became beatnik poets. I never stay on one single theme when making a work.

IC: Fairy tales habitually conjure malevolent aspects of humankind and the animal kingdom. Yet many of these stories hold an element of deep wisdom. In a perverse sense, do fairy tales offer the child a good grounding in what to expect of life?

LF: It might give them a good grounding, but it also weirdly makes girls want to become princesses, like Cinderella. There are other socially controlling aspects as well, of course. However, fairy tales can empower the child because they don't usually get gobbled up in the end. Children in these tales go through terrible times, but they get through it. Fairy tales are very powerful, and I often use them in my work – *Three Bears* (2017), for example. It's a tale we know well, yet I made it when Donald Trump was elected, and those crazy Brexiteers Nigel Farage and Boris Johnson brought on the circus. So, *Three Bears* was my interpretation of events at the time. Still, the connotations change depending on how the bears are positioned and where they're shown.

IC: The placement of your sculptures is key to their dramatic appeal. Is it important that your work ignites experiences personal to the viewer?

LF: I'm extremely interested in peoples' reactions. I was commissioned to install new work at Southmead Hospital in Bristol, in the west of England (2014): a group of animals with ailments, one of which was an elephant with a swollen trunk. The wife of a patient, whose husband had a tumour in his nose, was deeply upset by that piece. It was fascinating because the majority of people didn't have such a reaction; they felt reassured by the animals, but she wanted the elephant taken down. On the other hand, children dance and cartwheel around *Emissary Cats*. They search for the head, stroke it and try to understand the work physically by getting into a similar position. Children can understand anger and happiness just by the way a piece sits or stands, and they have an immediate reaction to it.

IC: Childhood is both magical and fearful, probably in equal measure. Even though enchantment and humour are clearly present throughout your work, it is nonetheless permeated by melancholy darkness.

LF: Yes, and I often ask myself why, as I had a really fun childhood. Perhaps darkness makes the sculpture feel true. I also seek out the darker side when watching movies, such as the films of David Lynch. However, humour is important. I've always been interested in how jokes are constructed. They're a really good way to talk about difficult subject matter and be provocative but, because there's identification and catharsis, it feels safe. That layering is key, and I think my work does have that quality.

Interviewed in 2019

Laura Ford
Headthinker VIII, 2012

Glazed stoneware, steel, fabric
136 × 37 × 70 cm
(53½ × 14⅝ × 27½ in)

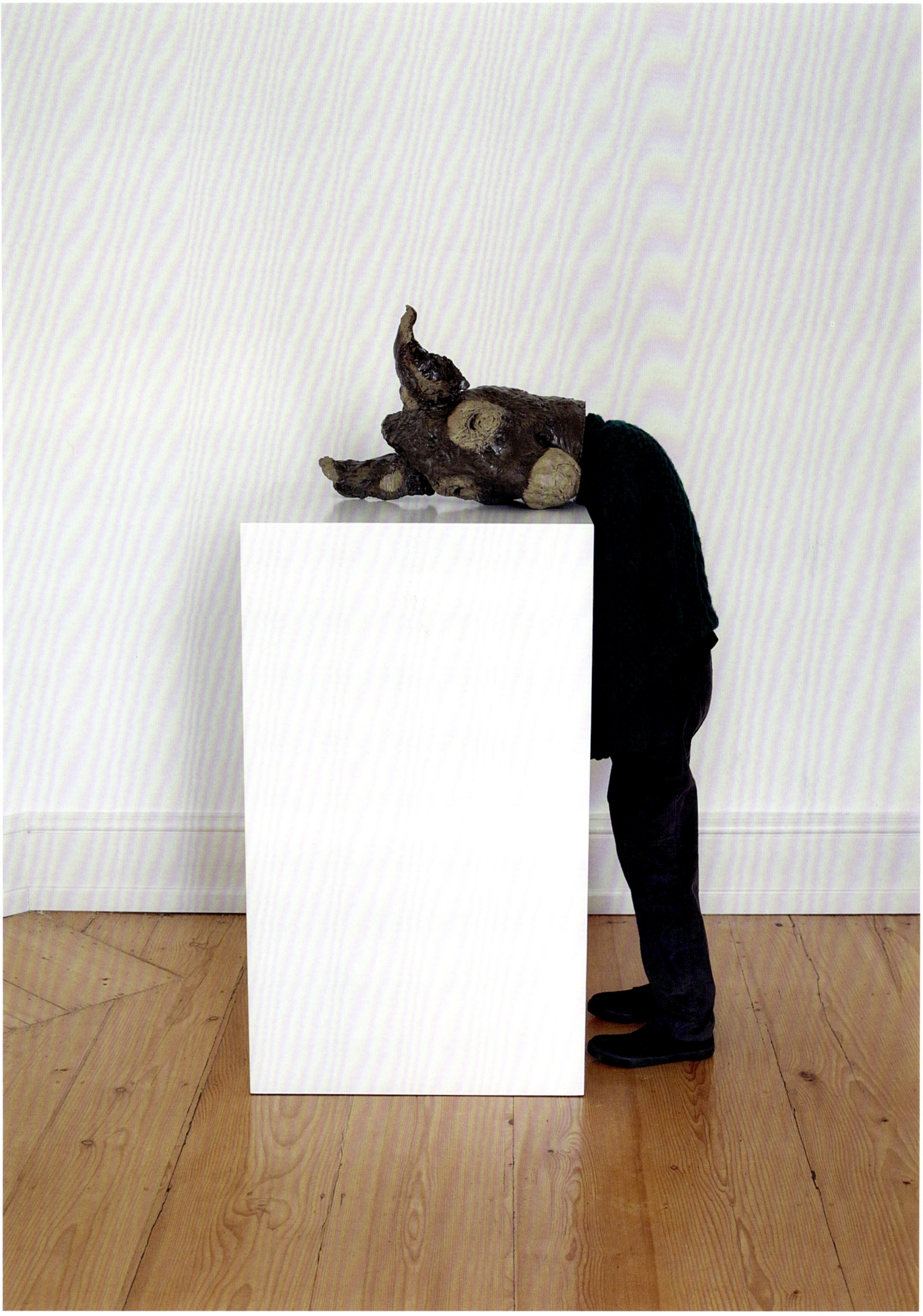

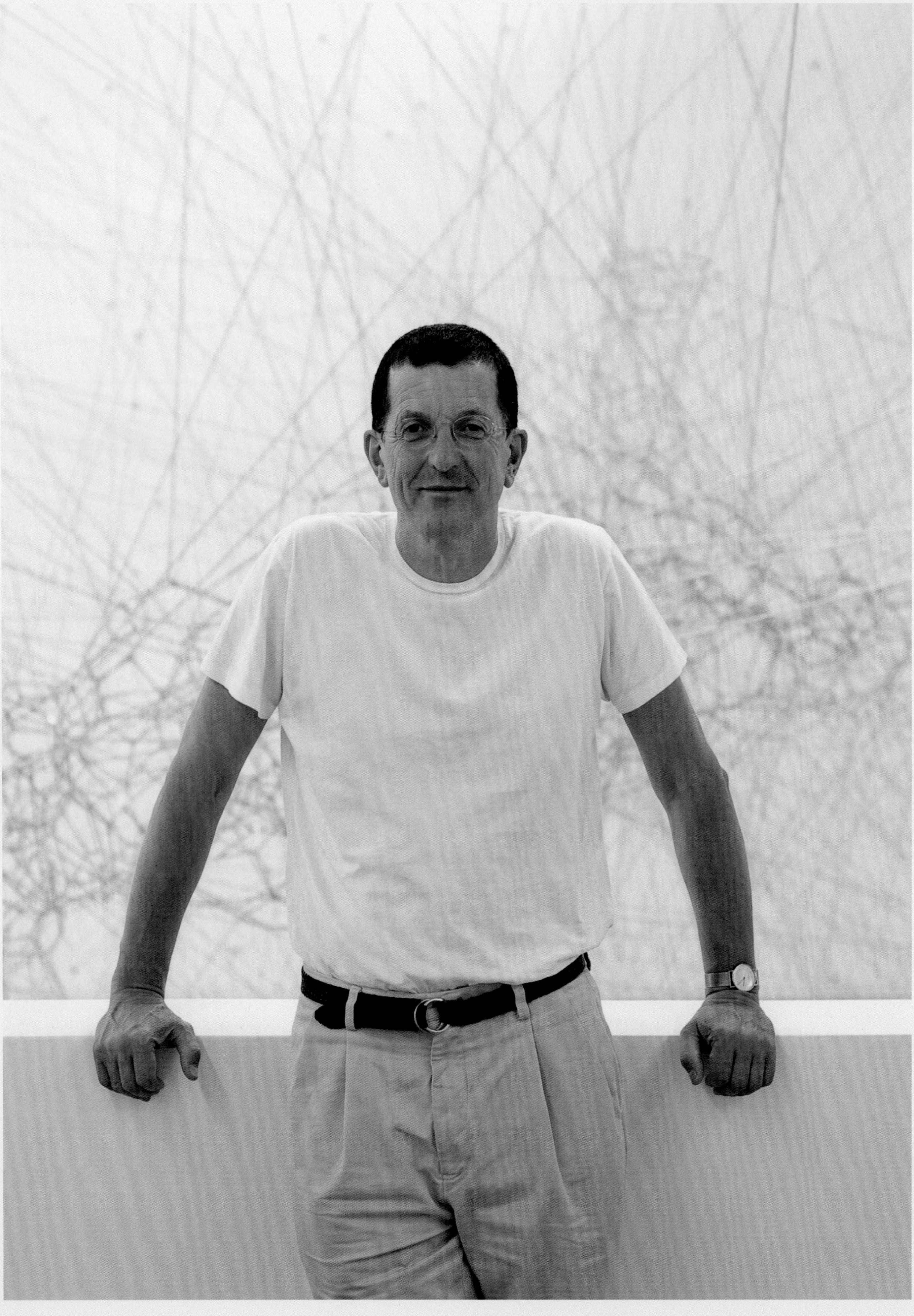

ANTONY GORMLEY

Born 1950, London

In the 1980s, Antony Gormley pioneered the concept of casting the body to evoke universal ideas relating to the human condition, a subject that has remained the predominant theme in his work. The 'mind and body problem' is fundamental to his practice in that the body is finite, while the mind is seemingly capable of limitless expansion. Gormley's sculptures range from the diminutive to the monumental. In *Field*, thousands of miniature terracotta figures confront the viewer, and these myriad watching eyes offer a haunting and emotional experience. Conversely, *Angel of the North* is located near the A1 road in Gateshead, North East England. Poised as if preparing for imminent flight, it stands 20 metres high (65 feet 7 inches), with a wing span of 54 metres (177 feet). Gormley's projects cross time and geographical boundaries, and are often spread over wide expanses of land, such as *Inside Australia*, created for an iridescent outback of around 10 square kilometres (almost 4 square miles), and *Sight*, installed on the sacred island of Delos in Greece.

Ina Cole: You're one of seven children, so were accustomed to a community from a young age. However, you have said that, as a child, you had an overriding anxiety as to whether you belonged in the world at all. This is interesting in relation to how you position figures in your installations, as they can appear quite alienated from each other. Do you view society as a collective force, or is the reverse more appropriate to your practice?

Antony Gormley: I'm intrigued by the twin facts of individuation: that we're all born with unique characteristics but evolve through time and experience. We have an encoded physical, genetic, intellectual and emotional imprint, yet the individual is really only defined in relationship with others. My interest lies in how these two models interact, as the shape the individual takes can't be disentangled from their place within a collective, however mobile and interchangeable it might be.

Being the last child in a large family made the possible spaces seem very limited. I was brought up in Hampstead Garden Suburb, London; a materialized ideal, a green nowhere, with perfect homes and gardens in a street with perfect privet hedges. People were civilized and wealthy, and my family was much the same. It was the 1950s and the birth of the 'nuclear family' – a well-organized organism. To an extent, I felt alienated by the way everything had been decided, and there wasn't a great deal of room for originality. This pushed me towards inventiveness, or fantasy, and an attempt to try and do something that lay outside the expectations of this determined world.

My work continues to battle with these issues around the social need for convention. I think we're at a point of crisis in terms of Western civilization, where it's clear that, in exercising the democratic ideal of individual liberty, we're involved in a loss of community. It isn't a crisis that art can necessarily heal, but art can certainly reflect this tension between personal freedom and collective restraint. My projects try to make an analogue for the collective body; ever since *Field* (1989–2003) this has seemed the most important task.

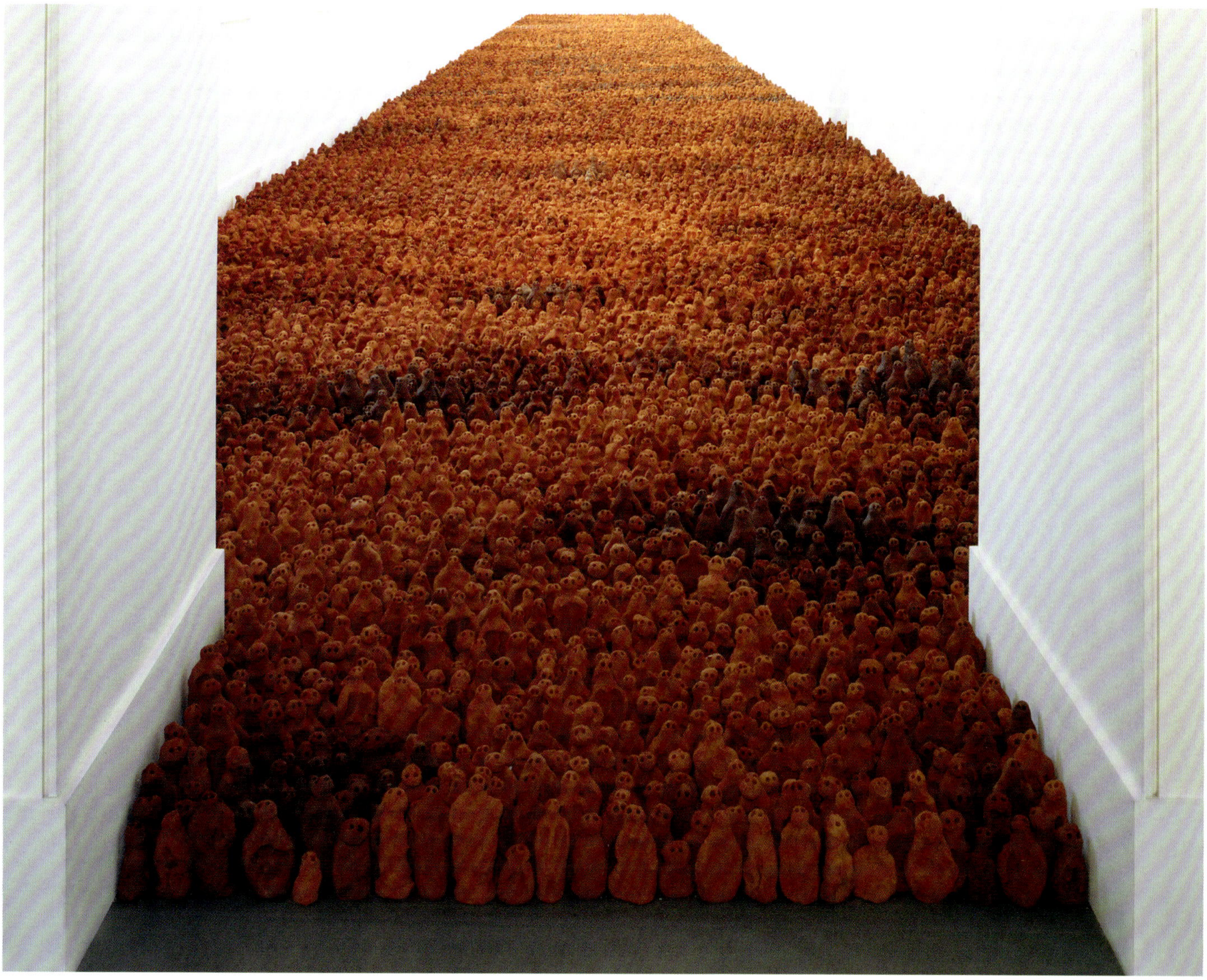

Antony Gormley
Field for the British Isles, 1993

Terracotta
Variable size: approx. 40,000 elements, each 8–26 cm (3–10 in) high
Installation view: Irish Museum of Modern Art, Dublin, 1994

IC: In the late 1980s and 1990s you produced a number of iconic sculptures that became imprinted on society's consciousness, particularly *Field* and *Angel of the North* (1998). How did these works impact on your future ideas?

AG: It's great to create works that have popular impact, although it's not the only criterion. All artists want to be loved, or certainly seen, but just because something is seen by many doesn't mean it's any better than something that's seen by very few. *Angel* is viewed by about 90,000 people a day, repeatedly passing at speed, yet one looks for the depth of contact over a period, and I hope it provides that too. It can't be a one-shot job; a slow bleed is important. *Field* also functions

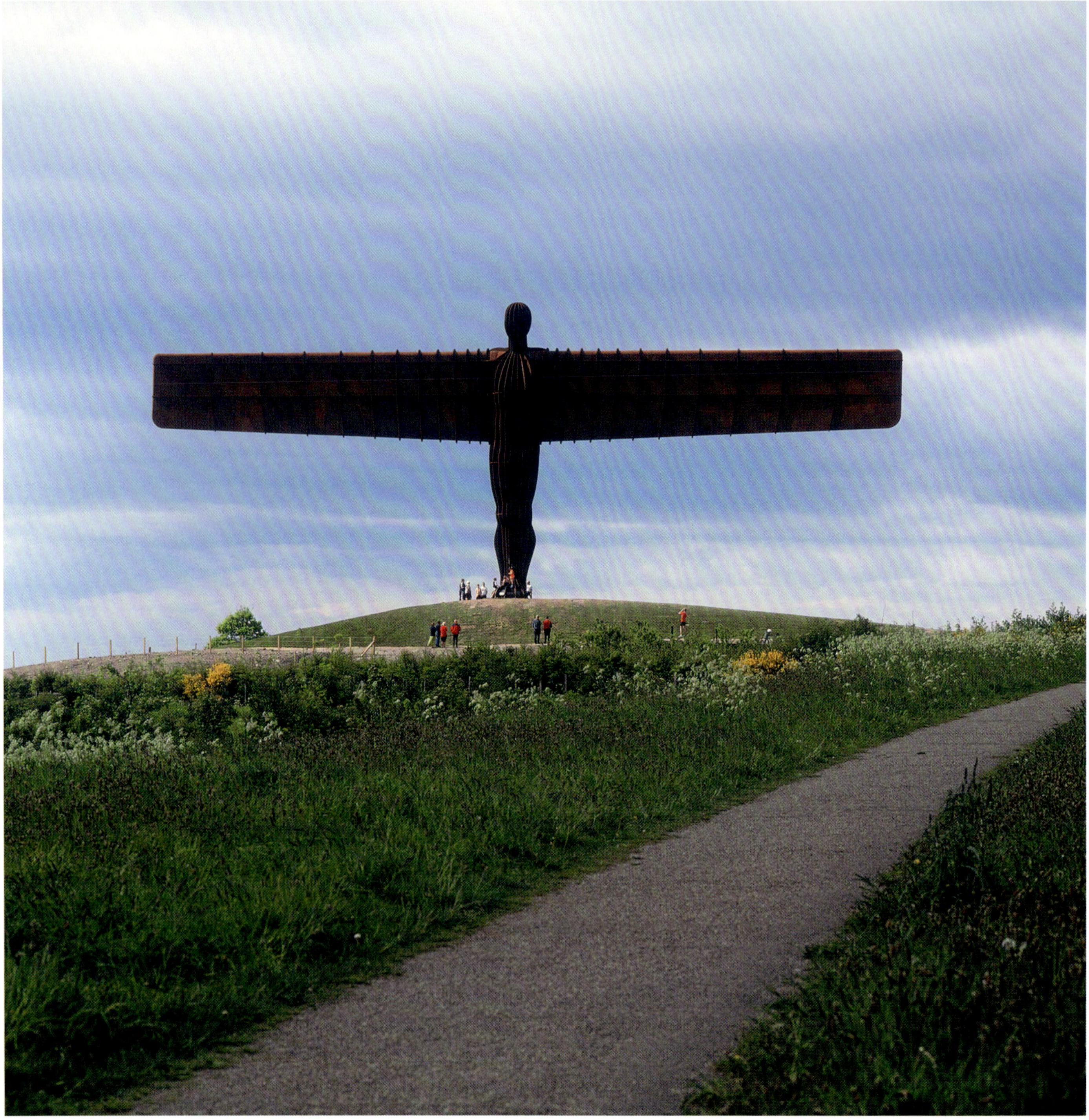

in a similar way: it has immediate visual impact, but your understanding of it changes over time. So, *Field* and *Angel* are benchmarks; two different ideas about extendibility in time.

IC: *Field* has travelled the globe and is created anew for each site, using volunteers from the immediate locality. Likewise, *Critical Mass* (1995), first made for the Remise Transport Museum in Vienna, has been shown extensively. Every location inevitably presents its own challenges, but how do you ensure each new installation offers a fresh interpretation?

AG: Every installation, whether of short or long duration, begins with a dousing or checking-out of the location. I think of exhibitions as opportunities to catalyze a space, not occupy it. In proposing the body itself as a site, the sculptures can absorb their site while interrogating it, making it strange and adding focus. I'd never claim they animate the site; the visitor does that. However, they can function as acupuncture: points of concentration and focus within a landscape or building. On each occasion *Field* or *Critical Mass* is shown, it evokes different emotions and demands different readings. I see the sculptures as diagnostic instruments, for viewers to connect with the sedimented emotional layers within themselves, and for the site and its history.

Antony Gormley
Angel of the North, 1995–8

Steel
20 × 54 × 2.20 m
(65 ft 7⅜ in × 177 ft 2 in × 7 ft 2⅝ in)
Installation view:
Gateshead, England, 1998

IC: Encasing yourself in plaster, as seen in *Critical Mass*, must give you a heightened awareness of your corporeal state, the organic nature of who you are. Is being incarcerated in plaster a kind of temporary death, from which you're constantly reborn – a quest for immortality perhaps?

AG: Every time I'm encased in plaster and moulded, it is a passage; a voluntary journey into the underworld and a rebirth, which has become ritualized and integrated into my way of living. It means more to me if the work starts from a lived moment, using my own physical existence as tool, subject and material. The process of casting is an hour taken out of the continuum of existence. I use my own body not because it's me particularly, but simply because it's an example of a common condition of embodiment. I'm interested in the mind and body problem, in that the body is finite, organic and only capable of being in one place at one time, while the mind is capable of seemingly infinite extension into realms of imagination, which aren't, strictly speaking, anything to do with the body. Yet the body is the place we live; it's the material we have to deal with.

From an early age, I used to sit in the car, or in trains, and look out onto a 1950s smog-filled London, or into lighted windows at dusk, and think, 'That could be my home; that could be my life.' I've transferred this to my work, as I realize my life and my body are one possible location for human identity. So, my sculptures are not representations of a particular person, but a potential place where life might rest. By inhabiting the space of sculpture, you can escape from your own condition into another's. We haven't evolved out of the need for transitional objects that function as objectifications of our deepest fears or most potent desires, and sculpture can act as a catalyst for those feelings.

IC: Although you've used yourself as a template since the 1980s, *Allotment* (1995) and *Domain Field* (2003) were made using volunteers from the community in which the installations were located.

AG: Here, I wanted to shift from bearing witness to individual identity, to an engagement with the idea of the collective. *Field* did it in terms of unformed, surrogate bodies that evoke 'species-ification' prior to the development of humankind. *Allotment* deals with the local, the village, and is a collection of modernist bunkers enclosing the exact dimensions of 300 living people, aged from two to 85, from the city of Malmö, in Sweden. These bunkers create a virtual city in 15 blocks of around 20 rooms each, with two avenues and four cross streets.

Domain Field was made out of the direct moulds of over 200 people from Gateshead, in the north of England, of a similar age range as *Allotment*. A domain is a random matrix of stainless-steel bars, welded together to describe the body's space and turning its mass into an energy field. It evokes the body through

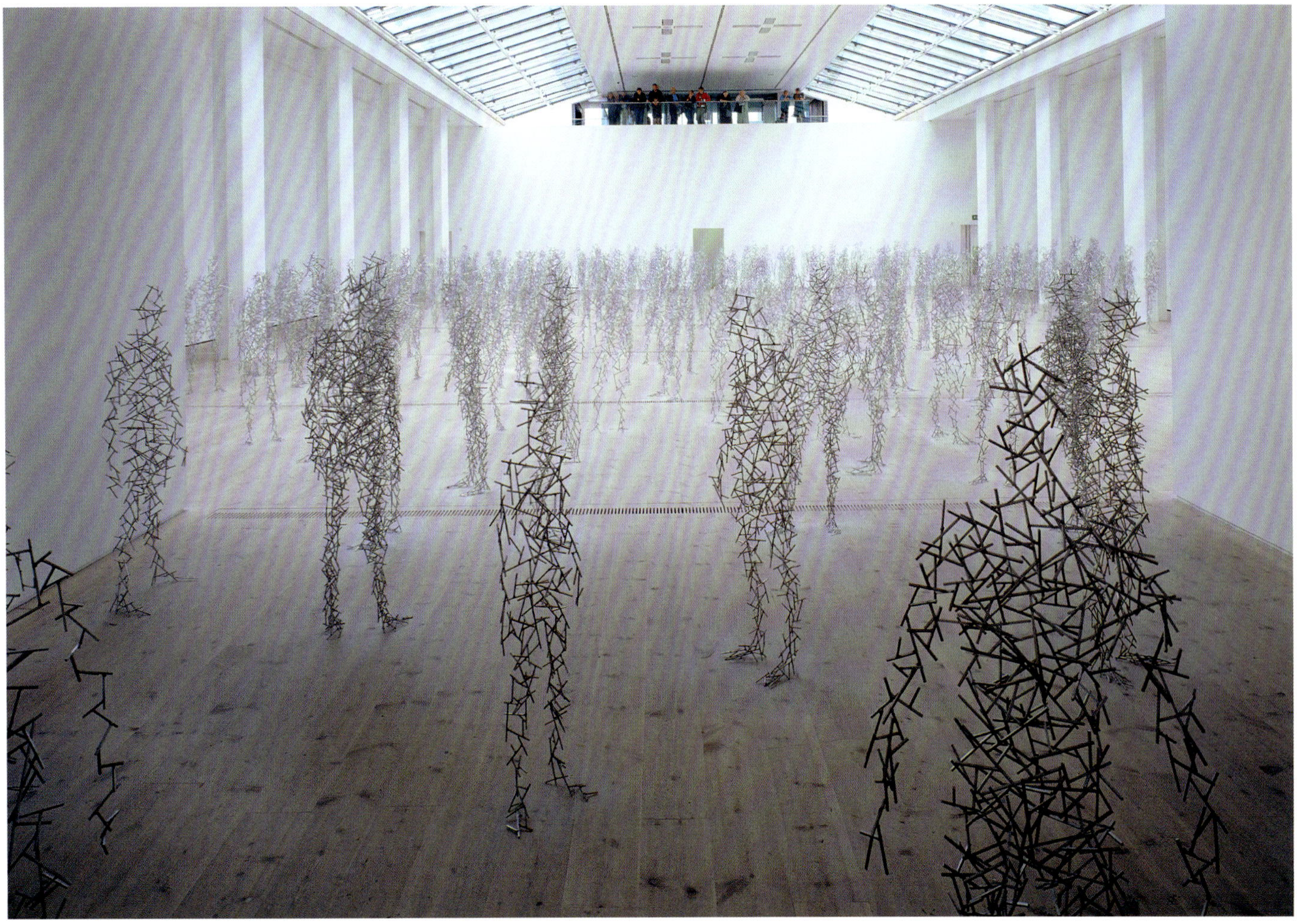

↑
Antony Gormley
Domain Field, 2003

4.76 mm (¼ in) square section stainless steel bar
Various sizes: 287 elements, derived from moulds of local inhabitants of Newcastle-Gateshead aged 2½–84 years
Installation view: BALTIC Centre for Contemporary Art, Gateshead, 2003

→→
Antony Gormley
Critical Mass II, 1995

Cast iron
60 life-size elements
Dimensions variable
Installation view: The Long Museum, West Bund, Shanghai, China, 2017

a structural principal that is neither architecture nor anatomy, but more like the random matrices found in stochastic systems. On entering, you're not aware of single forms, only that the whole room is filled with a mist of trajectories. Then, once you walk around, you begin to recognize the individuality of each work: the yearning energy and vulnerability of a child, or the composed compression of an older person. In all these projects, what I'm trying to do is make you see the everyday in a new way.

IC: *Expansion Field* (2014–15) explores how the body enters unbounded territory when we close our eyes and succumb to darkness; in *Room* (2014) the body is embedded in a host building, whereas *Drift* (2009) is one of your most dematerialized installations. In continually pushing the realm of possibility, what is your ultimate goal in relation to the mind and body problem?

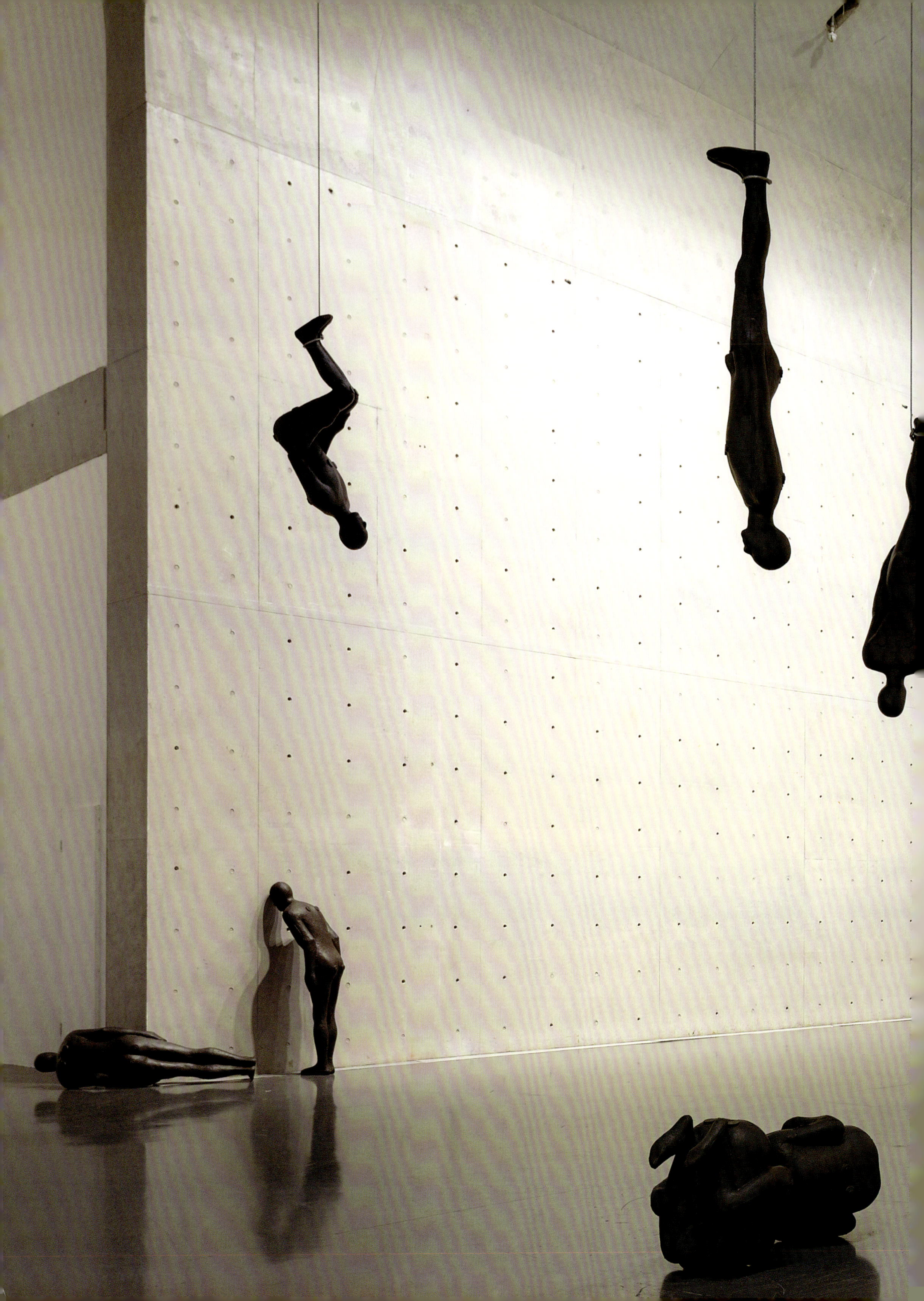

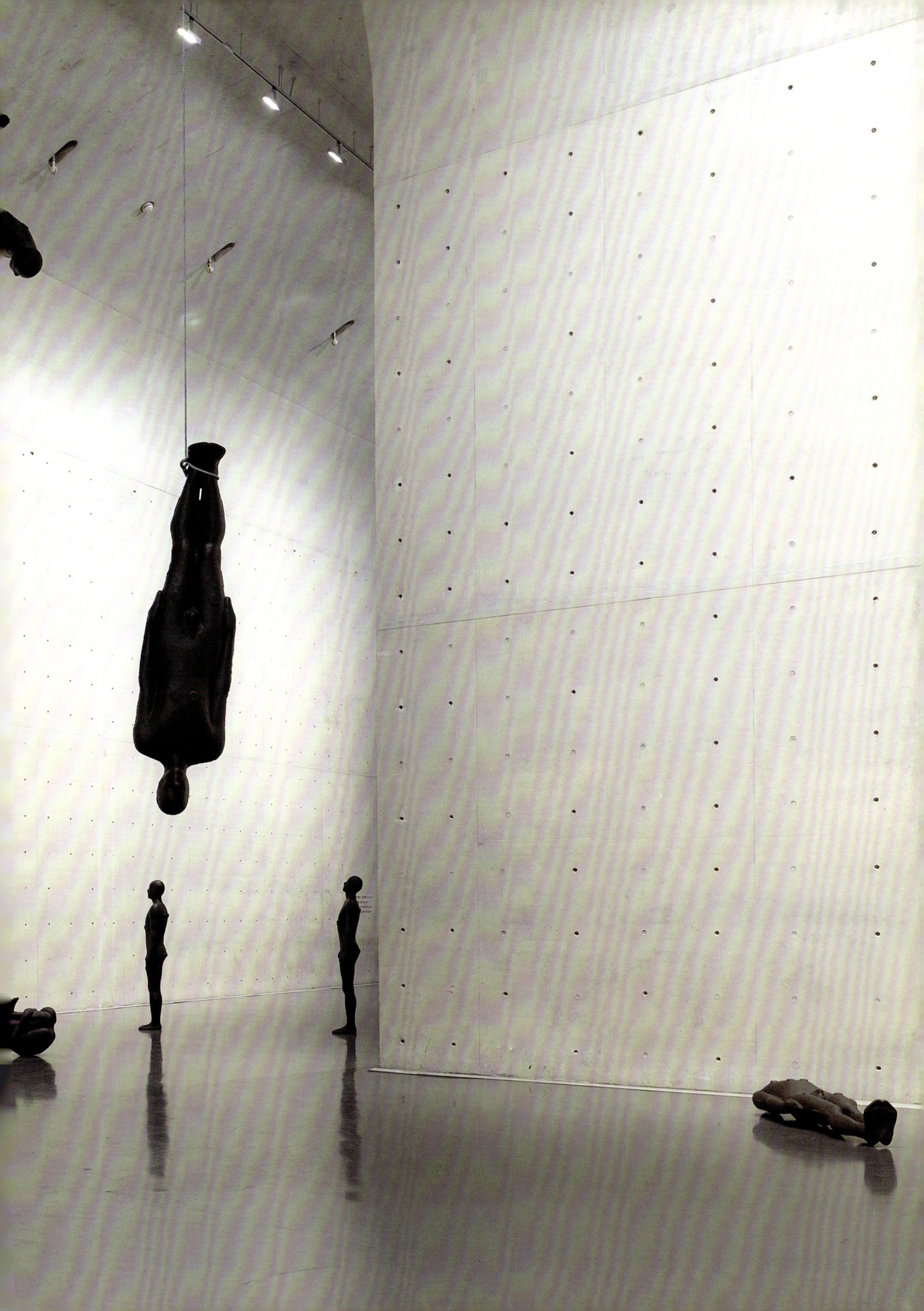

AG: Sculpture uses material means to make material propositions and, for me, getting to grips with post-particle physics is a natural need for someone that uses material means. However, all of these intellectual pursuits are of very little use when it comes to how sculpture functions. I want to encourage first-hand physical experience; it's not simply a matter of making something, but of creating an arena in which transformation of physical space becomes the transformation of emotional and intellectual space. To explore the potential of sculpture, I use all the tools and tropes of our era's materials and technologies. Sculpture is by its nature silent and still, yet it can produce extraordinary internal transformation. The only solution to the mind and body problem is to collapse its oppositional dialectic. We have to take the body seriously as the vehicle through which our contribution to the world must come. I'm not interested in using it for narrative or idealization, but as the universal basis of human experience.

IC: There's an archaic thread running through many of your projects. Ideas to do with time and geology, for instance, are central to *Planets* (2002), a commission for the British Library in London.

AG: *Planets* evokes the relationship between thought and matter. That might be what sculpture is about; an attempt to leave on the face of an indifferent universe a sign of thought and feeling. A standing stone is an early example of a natural object placed to become a marker against which human life can be registered. I've taken that idea and made it more polemical. I used eight ancient rocks – one is Cambrian and the rest are probably Devonian – on the surface of which I carved the trace of eight people, one to each rock. Each work is a testimony to a lived moment, in which a body and an individual rock were brought together. Stone is an important material because we sense it comes from a time before mind. Now we know the universe was created about 13 billion years ago, these rocks become messengers from a time before life.

In *Planets* the bodies conform to the shape of the rock, rather than the other way around, as in

Antony Gormley
Expansion Field, 2014

4 mm (1/8 in) Corten steel
60 elements
Dimensions variable
Installation view:
Zentrum Paul Klee, Bern,
Switzerland, 2014–15

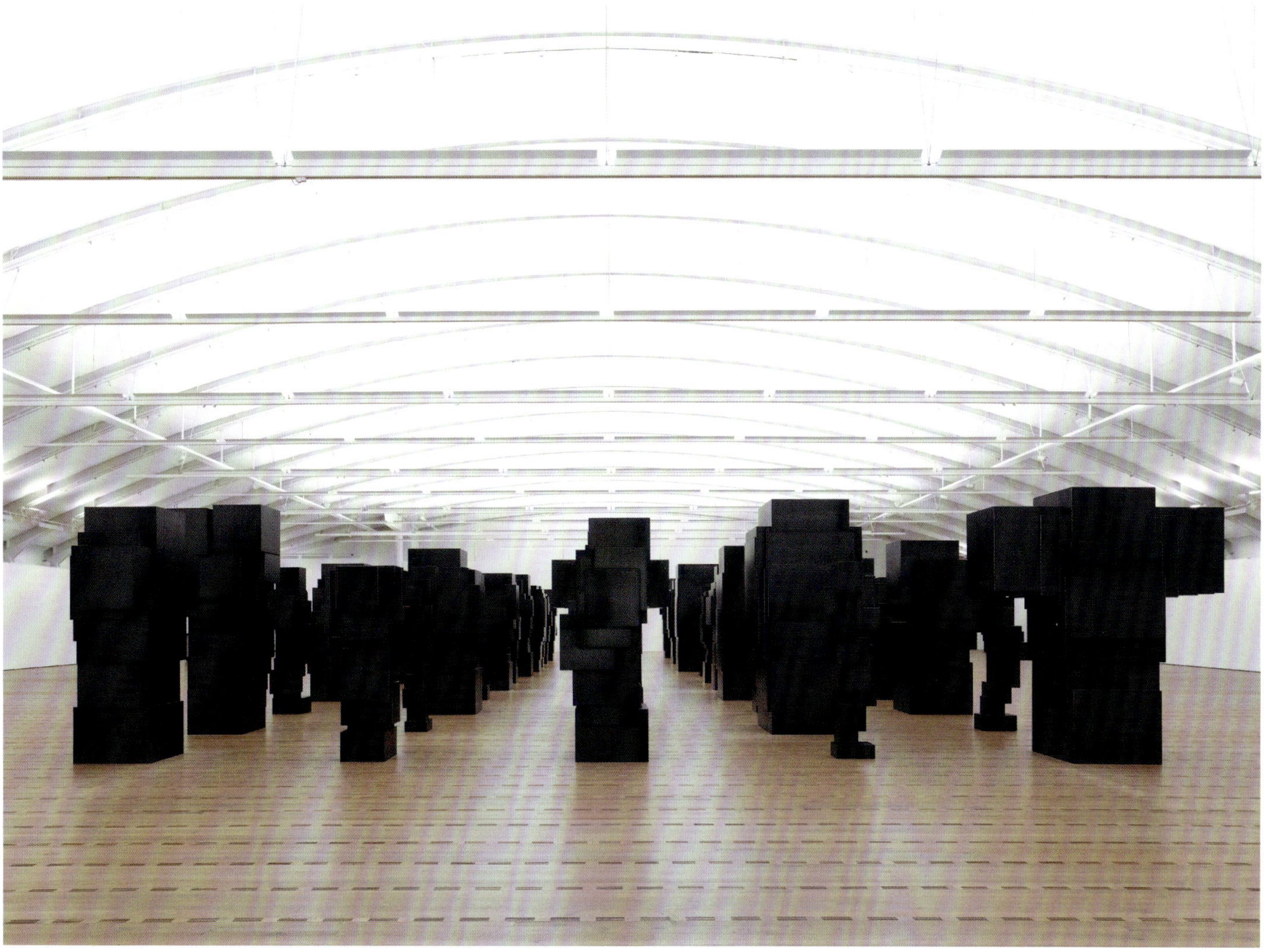

Michelangelo's *Slaves* (1513–16), and that's important. These are traces of people hanging on for dear life. It's an indication of the mind's dependency on the body and the body's dependency on the planet, which has particular poignancy at the British Library – a depository of the fruits of human mental activity over millennia. Sculpture can communicate over vast periods, and I think art has always been an attempt to create a bridge with what lies beyond the horizon of perception.

IC: *Inside Australia* (2003) comprises gaunt, blackened figures that infiltrate their location like an alien incursion. The drama of this installation derives from the figures' emaciated appearance and the fact that they reside within such a remarkably enigmatic landscape setting.

AG: Western Australia has some of the oldest rocks on the face of the planet. Around three billion years old, these Archean rocks contain an enormous wealth of mineral deposits (uranium, iron, copper) and stranger, more recently arrived elements on the elemental table (iridium, vanadium, molybdenum and titanium). For *Inside Australia*, I made an alloy based on high-grade stainless steel 316, which includes many of these new elements. It's a kind of concentration of the elemental memory in these very old rocks.

Inside Australia is located in the sodium landscape of an outback area, a salt lake, Lake Ballard, where I placed around 50 sculptures called *Insiders*. An insider is a residue, a concentration of the body, where around 60 per cent of its mass is lost, and a third of its volume retained, but only in one axis. So, these figures are the same height as the original person, yet vastly reduced laterally. They're placed about 700 metres (almost 3,000 feet) apart on this extreme white, optically acute, chemical landscape. At the west end there's a raised mound about 40 metres (131 feet) high, from the top of

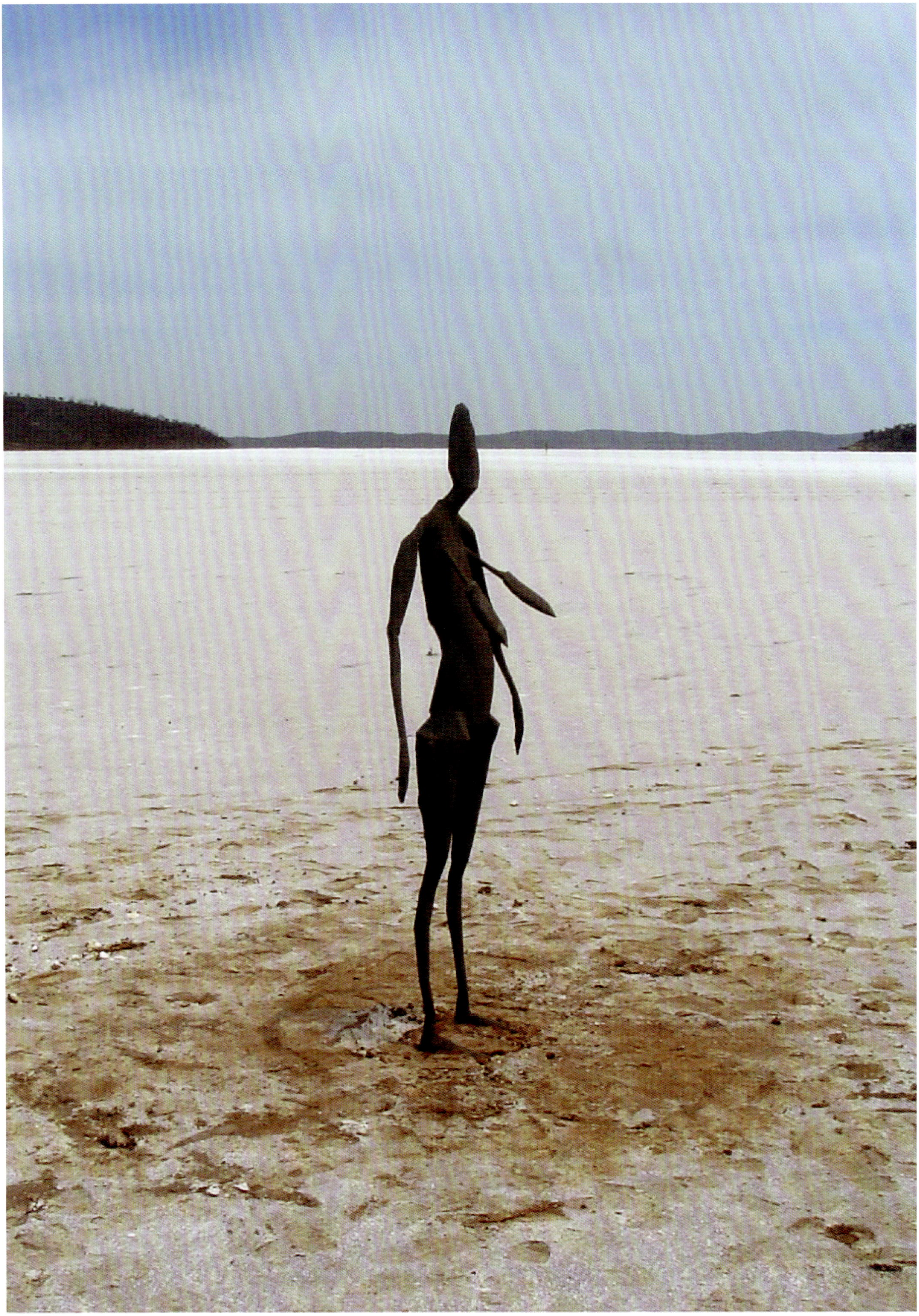

which most of the installation can be seen, covering an area of around 10 square kilometres (almost 4 square miles). The works are carbonized, so they're black stick figures that evoke, as in *Field*, the spirit of the ancestors, and also something futuristic.

IC: In 'Sight' (2019), installed on the island of Delos in Greece, sculptures were empathetically integrated into a particularly potent location. This requires not only an in-depth knowledge of the place, but a respect for the memory of our forebears. What considerations does such a project involve?

AG: Delos became a vibrant sacred and economic centre of the ancient eastern Mediterranean and home to thousands of figurative sculptures, now almost entirely removed from the site. I was keen for my sculptures to acknowledge its surprising position in relation to neighbouring islands – Amorgos, Paros and Naxos – and start with the geology of the island itself, essentially a granite rock with some metamorphic and marble intrusions. I placed six bodyforms in standing positions on the island's periphery, all looking to the horizon, thereby acknowledging both the geology and the extraordinary relationship of island states to each other in the time of classical Greece.

Moving inland, I had an increasing desire to enter into a dialogue with the deconstructed architecture found everywhere on the site. Delos has been deconstructed and reconstructed through 150 years of archaeology. It's become like a gameboard with the plans of buildings outlined by foundation stones and stylobates, the higher stones numbered and set in serried ranks in construction order. I arrived before any major reconstruction had happened. The dialogue between the remembered and the deconstructed was therefore still alive and could be translated into the forms of my *Blockworks* (2003–7), *Slabworks* (2014–19) and *Rooters* (2017–19). These bodyforms all use orthogonal language to animate the part–whole dialectic, creating a bridge between bits and bytes, and slabs and blocks, as constructive principles.

I was looking for resonant relationships with context, and five extra works were made for Delos: *Signal II* for the steps by Mount Kynthos; *Water* looking down

Antony Gormley
Inside Australia, 2003

Cast alloy of iron, molybdenum, iridium, vanadium and titanium
51 elements based on 51 inhabitants of Menzies, Western Australia
Installation view:
Lake Ballard,
Western Australia, 2003

at the Minoan fountain; *Rule* sitting on the antique capital outside the museum; *Chute II* for the Grotto of Hercules; and *Prop* in the theatre district. The challenge, and joy, was to make the entropy of this ancient site into an active ground for thinking about our future in the digital age. All the works were made out of iron, which brought the materials of the Industrial Revolution to a site that had only seen marble and bronze as a sculptural medium. The iron's red oxidization, seen against the white marble buildings and blue Aegean sky, had a particular resonance that was both disturbing and animating. It was important to respect the island. All I could do was send whispered questions amongst its picked-over remains, in a hope of using the site as a ground for contemporary contemplation, rather than simply as a background or historical frame.

IC: When considering indigenous cultures, do you think that, apart from our physical state, there are other stages of being, or are we purely organic matter, existing for a limited period after which there is only oblivion?

AG: Rather like the horizon, what lies outside this stratosphere is something we can only dream about. I feel the same sense of potential about what lies on the other side of life as what lies inside the body. Darkness is often seen as a denial. It isn't; it's a zone of potential. People see death as the end of everything, but it could well be a beginning. It's an acknowledgement of the necessary relations between night and day. Most vibrant cultures of our time have managed to accommodate the notion of death within their living, yet we live in a culture where death is the big trauma. The cult of youth and bodily beauty, in some desperate way, tries to ignore the inevitability of death, whereas in the great cultures of Mesoamerica, Chan and Tibetan Buddhism, or in the Egyptian *Book of the Dead*, there's no sense in which it wasn't acknowledged and celebrated in life. All of them, in different ways, have imaginative projections about the continuity, or the relationship, between the living and the dead.

IC: We're witnessing an era of phenomenal scientific and technological acceleration, yet the divide between world excess and deprivation is an ever-widening chasm. Despite unquestionable progress, people seem increasingly confused and dissatisfied. How hopeful are you for society's future?

AG: We've been living in the Kali Yuga, the era of Kali, goddess of night, sex and death according to the Hindus, and I think that just about fits. There is huge confusion and fear, but also an acknowledgement that, in some way, change is necessary. We don't know what the next stage of human consciousness and physical existence will be. It could be wipe-out or total transformation. I like how we've globalized the world with mind; the Internet is the manifestation of that. This is the noosphere: the encirclement of the globe by intelligence carried by the human organism. What this does in terms of the biosphere isn't clear. It's evident we need to transform our needs to achieve sustainability, as we have a finite world with finite resources, and the 'there's more where that came from' mentality won't persist without us becoming the agents of our own destruction. I believe art is a zone in which we can imagine the necessary transformation.

Interviewed in 2002 and 2020

→
Antony Gormley
Stream, 2018

Cast iron Rooter
131.6 × 192.7 × 65 cm
(51¾ × 75⅞ × 25⅝ in)
Installation view:
Busan Museum of Art,
Korea, 2019

↓
Antony Gormley
Shore, 2012

Cast iron
88 × 47 × 57 cm
(34⅝ × 18½ × 22½ in)
Installation view:
Delos, Greece, 2019

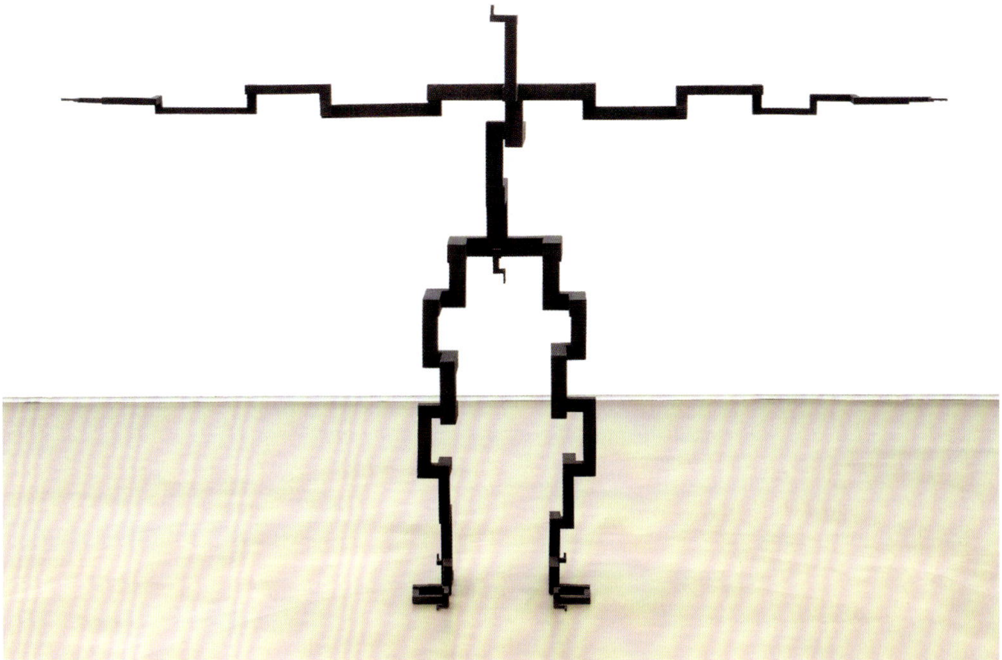

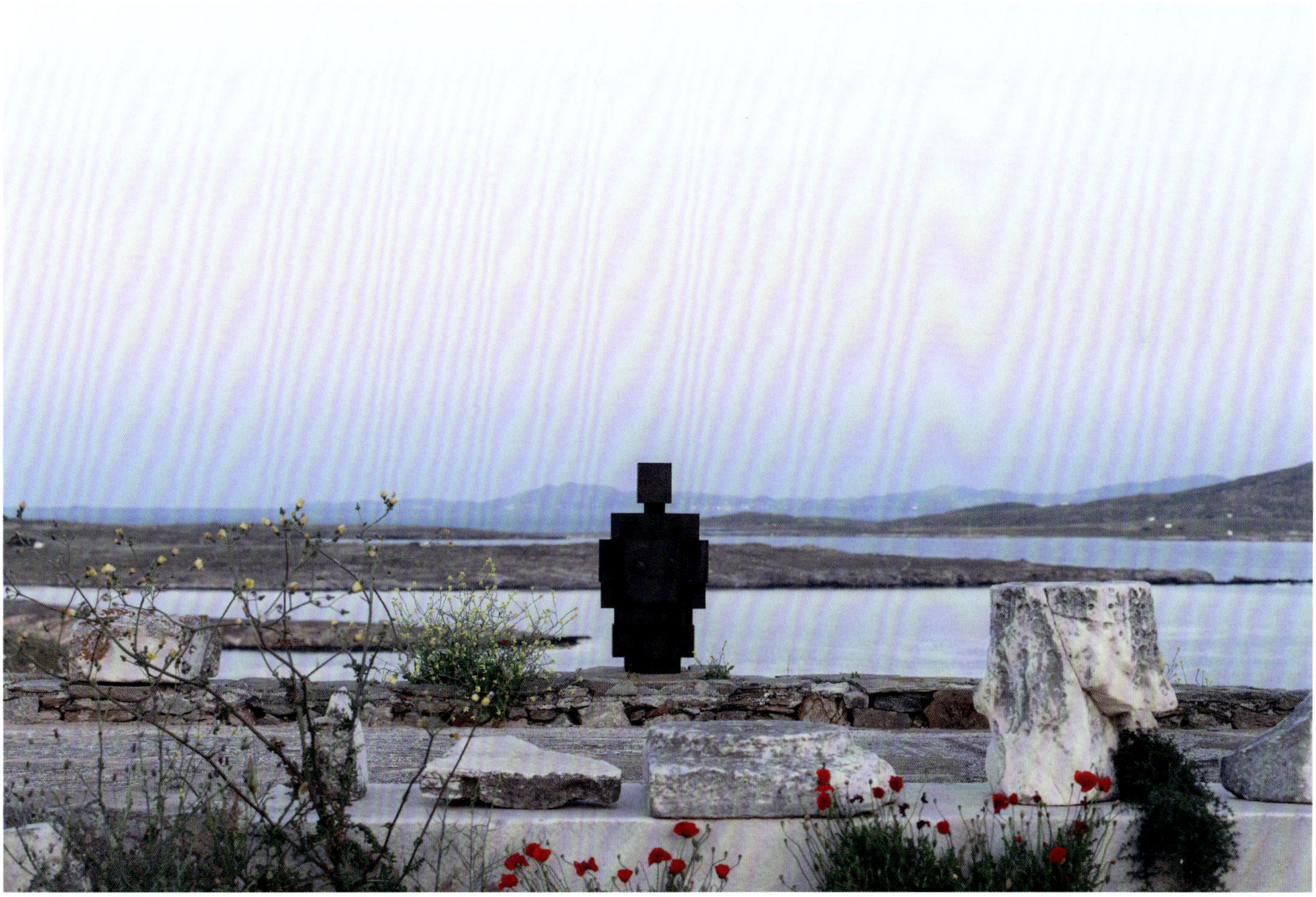

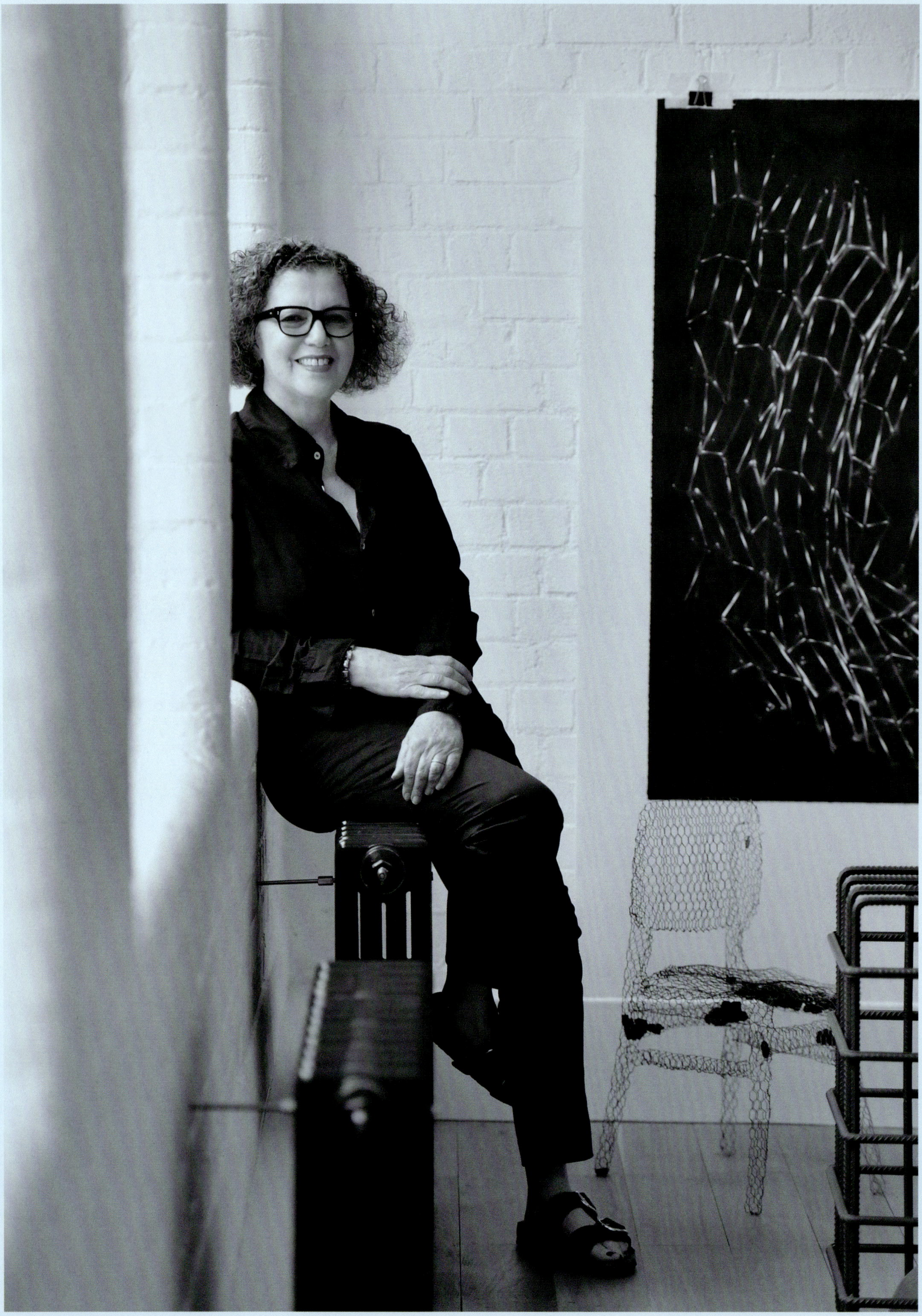

MONA HATOUM

Born 1952, Beirut, Lebanon

The power of Mona Hatoum's work resides in her ability to universalize pertinent themes, through a sculptural language that is implied rather than didactic. Although her practice explores issues of conflict, its message can apply to the personal, political or geographical. Hatoum's early work encompassed performance and video, as seen in the poignant *Measures of Distance*, after which she returned to an exploration of the phenomenology of materials, where ideas correlate in a more oblique manner. In her arrangements, electric current and lighting are frequently choreographed to astonishing and hypnotic effect. *Current Disturbance* utilizes crackling acoustics and synchronized lights to draw the viewer towards the enclosure's periphery; while *Homebound* assimilates domestic furniture and appliances via a network of electric cables, to create a sense of foreboding in a hazardous environment. Later projects become more overtly political, as epitomized by the devastatingly scarred structures of *Bunker* and the incinerated fragility of *Remains of the Day*.

Ina Cole: You were visiting London in 1975 just as civil war broke out in Lebanon, which meant you couldn't return there. An early video work, *Measures of Distance* (1988), considers that separation. It's complex and intimate, but why was it important for you to make?

Mona Hatoum: *Measures of Distance* differed from anything I'd previously made and, in many ways, was the conclusion of all my narrative work. It's layered with meaning and was the first time I used the autobiographical. I've always tried to keep my statements open so that, when reflecting on war or displacement, any number of conflicts could be conveyed. Despite this, it was often thought that my practice is linked to my personal history, which is why I eventually decided to tell my story in this one piece. *Measures of Distance* is structured around letters my mother had sent me from Beirut, a conversation recorded with her in 1981 and 12 slides of her in the shower. These three different elements became the video.

It was then the early part of the war and I was constantly in fear of losing my parents. So, the subject is the mother–daughter relationship, but in the background there's an articulation of war and separation, and a sense of tremendous loss. In the video, my mother speaks on how this situation affected her life. This was lacking in the media, in that reports on the Middle East presented Arabs as herds of faceless people. By foregrounding the voice of an individual, the stereotype of the Arab female as passive was contradicted.

The images of my mother taking a shower are intimate, revealing a closeness between us. They're overlaid with the letters, which creates a grid reminiscent of barbed wire, and this acts as a veil denying total access to the images. The voice-over is also layered: it's a conversation in which I ask her questions in Arabic, overlaid with my voice reading a translation of her letters. There's a sense that the narrative is fragmented, since the competition between the Arabic and English is quite confusing.

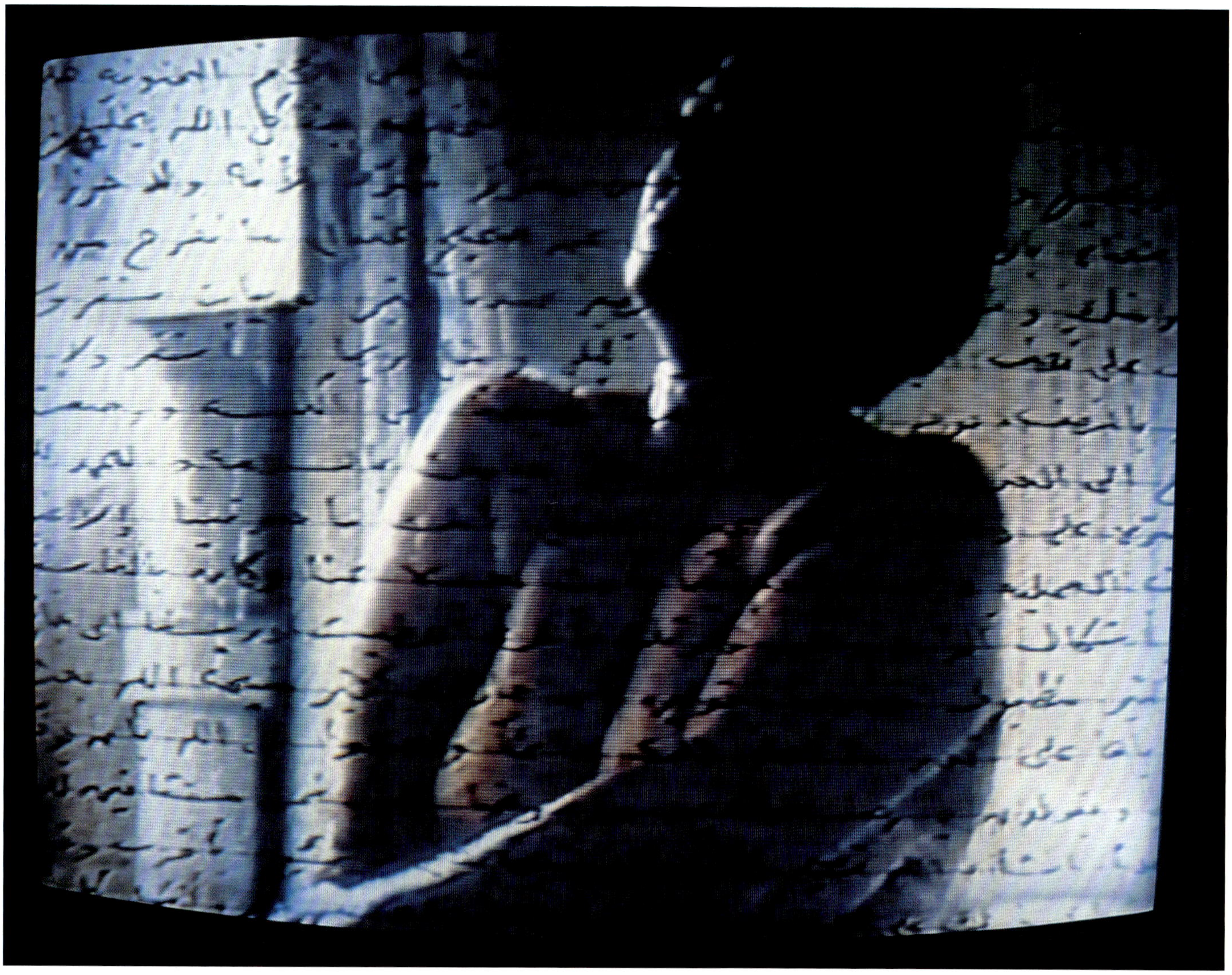

Mona Hatoum
Measures of Distance,
1988

Colour video with sound
15 min 35 seconds
A Western Front
Video Production,
Vancouver, 1988

IC: Despite the complexity of the layering, the theme remains universal, in that the relationship between a mother and daughter can be seen as the most enduring union of all. It's primal, and a subject everyone can relate to.

MH: That's true; *Measures of Distance* had a huge impact on people, especially younger women. I was prompted to make it because of my involvement with the discourse around psychoanalysis and feminism, which led me to explore the relationship with my mother. In Freudian theory, the Oedipus complex referred to the relationship of the child to a parent of the opposite sex, and, in many ways, feminism privileged the relationship between mother and daughter for the first time. My mother was of a certain age and revealing her naked body seemed daring, taboo or exploitative, from a feminist point of view. I was terrified of what might come of this, yet rationalized it by thinking, 'I'm not just showing her as a sexual object, but in the full complexity of a mother caring for her children, affected by war and loss.' She was portrayed in her completeness, and I therefore decided to make it and bear the consequences later.

Measures of Distance is a tribute to my mother. She was an incredibly intelligent, intuitive and admirable person, very strong in so many ways. Before video and performance, I'd made sculptures and installations and, in a sense, this video work gave me permission to return to exploring the phenomenology of materials, where ideas can resonate more indirectly.

IC: As a student at Slade School of Fine Art you created installations, conducting volts of electricity through household objects. Were these untitled works prototypes for the later pieces?

MH: At the Slade, I had ideas about experimenting with invisible forces – electricity and magnetism – but both were considered dangerous and many restrictions were placed upon me. The bureaucracy was difficult, and the only way around it was to carry out a controlled demonstration, or experiment, to a small invited audience. It took ten years before I revisited the idea of using electricity as a threatening force, with *The Light at the End* (1989), a site-specific installation for The Showroom in London. From a distance it looked like bars of light, but, on getting closer, intense heat was experienced from the electric heating elements, which formed the bars of a gated structure blocking the end of the gallery. Balance between material and meaning was created by the fact *The Light at the End* looked like an abstract structure yet became much more sinister when drawing closer.

Hot Spot III (2009) also relates to this idea in that it uses delicate red neon to outline the contours of the continents. The globe is a cage-like stainless-steel structure and, although the heat is metaphorical, the work buzzes with a seemingly dangerous energy. As early as 1978, while at the Byam Shaw School of Art, I made a piece with magnets and iron filings – materials utilized many years later for *Socle du Monde* (*Foundation of the World*) (1992–3). This is a large cube in which the magnets and iron filings covering its surface appear ambiguously soft and furry, with a pattern reminiscent of the lobes of the brain or intestines. So, these early ideas have often reoccurred within my practice.

Mona Hatoum
Hot Spot III, 2009

Stainless steel and neon tube
234 × 223 × 223 cm
(7 ft 8⅛ in × 7 ft 3¾ in × 7 ft 3¾ in)
Installation view:
Fondazione Querini Stampalia Onlus, Venice, 2009

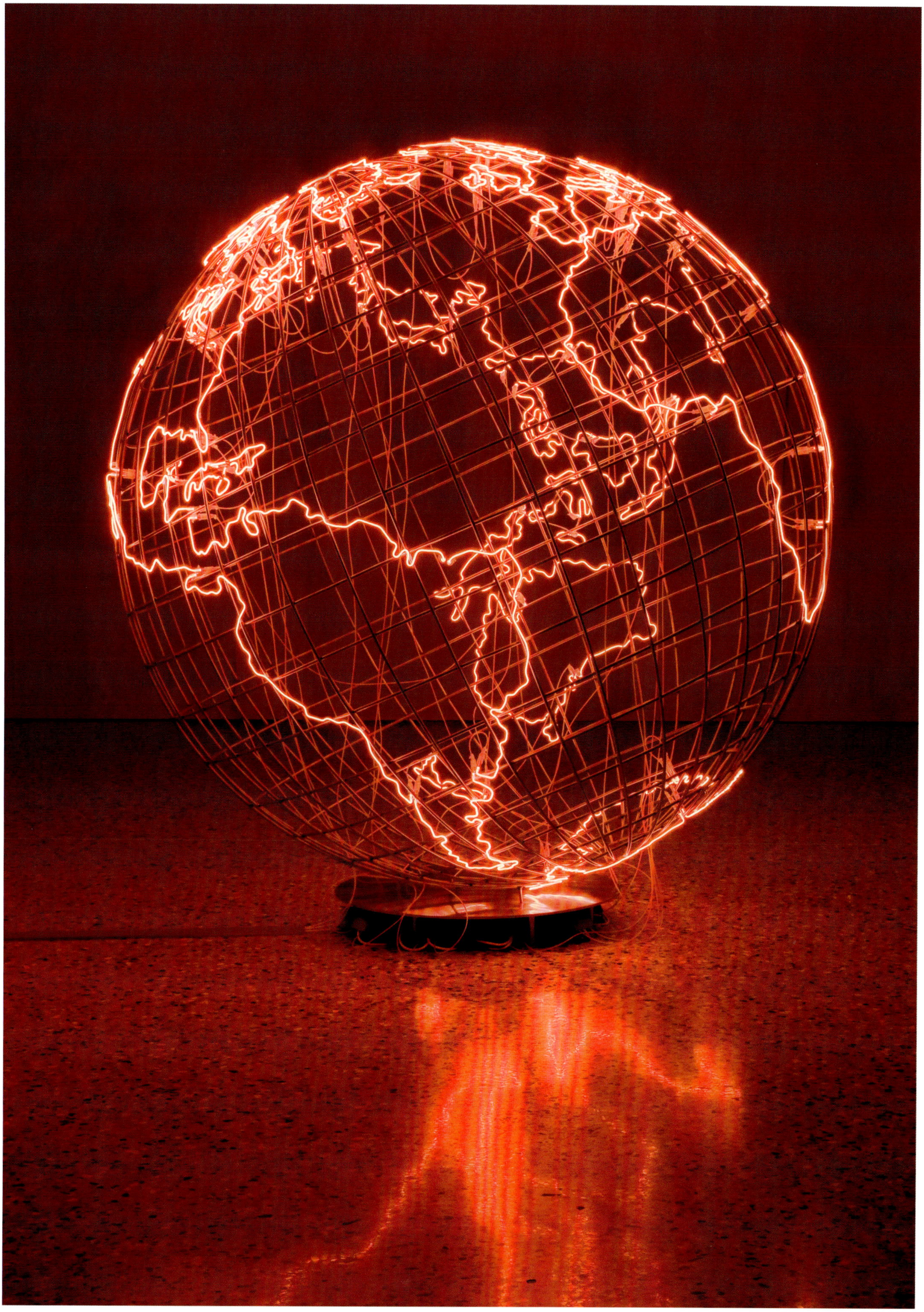

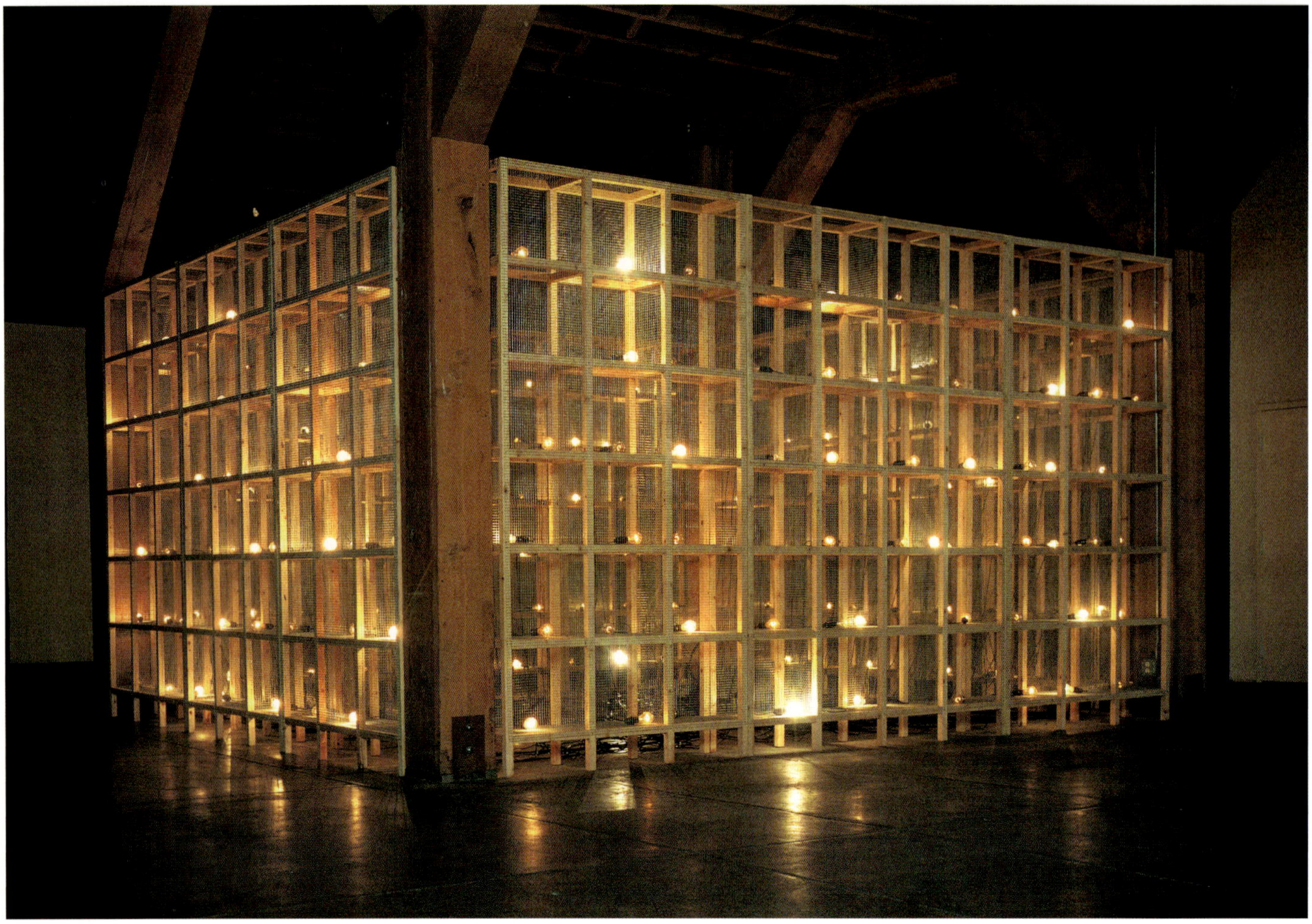

IC: *Light Sentence* (1992) and *Current Disturbance* (1996) retain the legacy of Minimalism through the use of grids; their emotional charge is generated by synchronized lights, destabilizing shadows and acoustics that hum and crackle. They belong to a larger group of constructions reminiscent of prison cells holding noncompliant occupants. Throughout history, the shadow, whether actual or psychological, is usually perceived as clandestine, but what is its relationship to these two installations?

MH: The aesthetics of Minimalism – pared-down form, devices like the grid, seriality and repetition – as well as the intellectual rigour of conceptual art all influenced my own practice. I like to articulate concept through the phenomenology of materials, and the shadow adds a performative element. *Light Sentence* merges concept and form in the way *The Light at the End* had done. It has a rigid structure made of wire-mesh lockers – higher than human height, so they aspire to architecture – and resembles a government project that houses people in basic, prison-like environments. A naked light-bulb, operated by a motor, moves up and down in the centre of the structure, which creates huge moving shadows. *Light Sentence* was an early installation in which I still thought in performance terms. The body of the spectator interacts with the work as, when they enter the space, they're immersed in the shadows and it seems like the ground is shifting under their feet. Although *Light Sentence* communicates instability, or displacement, it's also very beautiful and poetic because the shadows are fluid and contradict the rigidity of the metal lockers. I always like to emphasize the contradictions; it's not all doom and gloom. The title, *Light Sentence*, also refers to a sentence that's not too heavy; a prison searchlight penetrating the lockers, or little inhabitation units indicating surveillance and control.

←
Mona Hatoum
Current Disturbance, 1996
Wood, wire mesh, light bulbs, dimmer unit, amplifier and four speakers
279 × 550.5 × 504 cm
(9 ft 1⅞ in × 18 ft ¾ in × 16 ft 6⅜ in)
Installation view: Capp Street Project, San Francisco, 1996

→
Mona Hatoum
Homebound, 2000 (detail)
Furniture, kitchen utensils, electric wire, light bulbs, dimmer device, amplifier and two speakers
Dimensions variable
Installation view: The Menil Collection, Houston, 2017–18

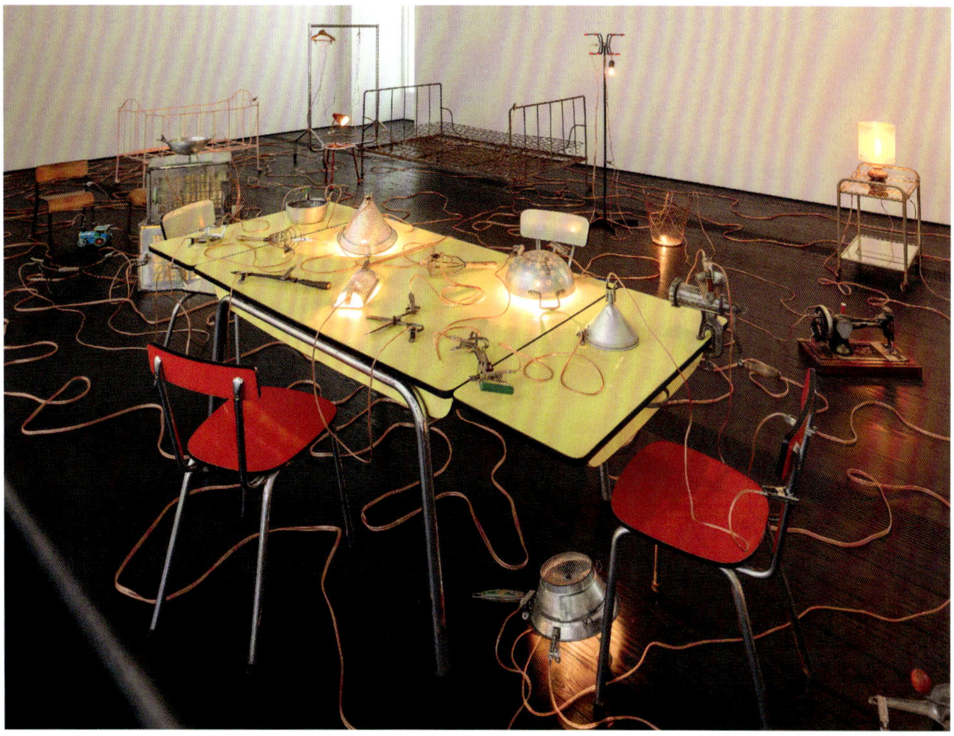

Current Disturbance was made specifically for a space in San Francisco (Capp Street Project, 1996). I built an enclosure and constructed 240 cages out of wood and wire mesh with a light-bulb in each. It was the first time I amplified the sound of the electric hum, so you were simultaneously aware of the lights and the sound of electricity. As usual, context can dictate specific connotations: the space was close to Alcatraz, so *Current Disturbance* was read as prison quarters with rioting inmates. However, when the same work was shown at Whitechapel Gallery in London (2011), it was seen to resonate with the council flats surrounding the gallery. So, it's also a crowded housing project, where people freak out in their little compartmentalized lives. I'm not interested in prescribing a specific reading. Meaning is fluid and changes depending on the situation, which is essential in many ways. The spectator completes the work by bringing their own interpretation, thereby playing an active role in creating meaning. It might be quite different from what I'd intended, but my intention becomes irrelevant once a work's out there. The title might offer a hint, yet sometimes even that's a contradiction. Anyway, the language of art is very ambiguous, especially when using abstraction or formalism rather than articulating a didactic message.

IC: *Jardin public* (1993) echoes René Magritte's *The Rape* (1934), and *Why Not Squeeze* (1995) references Marcel Duchamp's *Why Not Sneeze Rose Sélavy?* (1921). How important have the tenets of Surrealism and the readymade been to your own practice?

MH: Surrealism, the readymade and Duchamp are all significant. I became interested in Surrealism when growing up in Lebanon. My eldest sister studied psychology at university and I dipped into her books, even though I could hardly read English and had to use a dictionary. I was fascinated by Freud and the interpretation of dreams, and when I came across Magritte and the Surrealists it felt like they were visualizing the subconscious, or our unconscious desires and fears. *Jardin public* is both surreal and humorous but makes a serious statement. I exhibited *Jardin public* at the Menil Collection in Houston, Texas (2017–18), where it was placed next to Magritte's *The Rape*, a painting that turns the face of a woman into her sexual parts, as seen through the projection of male desire.

In *Jardin public* a triangle of pubic hair was inserted into the holes of the seat of a curved French garden chair, thereby subverting the objectification of the female form. I called it *Jardin public* because female sexual parts are always on public display, yet it's also nonsensical, and was my earliest humorous work. Similarly, *Why Not Squeeze*, a little cage with two hairballs, is also sexual. I often use cages, and this is one of an ongoing series. I felt that Surrealism created work from the interior reality of the person, rather than from what emerges through the logic of the mind. In a way, reality doesn't exist; there is only interpretation. Personal experience colours your interpretation, which is what Surrealism presented to me in the early days, before I started making art.

IC: A seminal essay written by Sigmund Freud in 1919 posits the idea that the uncanny resides in the familiar which has changed shape, rather than in the unfamiliar *per se*. To what extent has this concept informed your domestically inspired sculptures?

MH: I was specifically interested in Freud's concept of the uncanny. It's when aspects of everyday life suddenly become sources of dread, because some kind of trauma has been associated with them. This can happen on many different levels, from the mundane to the experience of war, displacement or loss. I'm fascinated by how the psyche processes trauma. Trauma can take you in a weird direction that's totally illogical. One way of making the familiar unfamiliar was to enlarge kitchen utensils until they became architectural or menacing. *Grater Divide* (2002), for instance, is based on a Victorian three-panelled grater bought from Camden Market in London, enlarged nine times to become an aggressive object cutting through space. As a child, I was drawn to a painting by Magritte (*Personal Values*, 1952) in which an innocuous bedroom becomes threatening because objects, such as a comb and shaving brush, had become so enlarged. Another way of making things appear unfamiliar, or dreadful, is to introduce a disturbance, like an electric current surging through everyday objects.

IC: As humans we crave comfort and familiar territory, yet your practice suggests this is provisional and that our homes and borders can, conversely, become our prisons. *Homebound* (2000), a ground-breaking work, utilizes electric current to evoke a jarring terror, epitomizing a traumatic inversion of the home.

MH: There's nothing homey about *Homebound*. It has a very cold atmosphere because most of the objects are made of metal and lack soft padding. Fluctuating electrical current courses through the furniture and utensils, which are connected by electric cables attached to light-bulbs, while the noise of the 240-volt current is amplified, creating a cacophony of crackling and buzzing sounds. The installation is fenced off by taut wires that create a cage-like environment and protect the viewer from being electrocuted. It's a lethal, unwholesome setting, fraught with danger on a physical, emotional and metaphorical level. The title *Homebound* is ambiguous; it could relate to heading home, or being bound by the home, as in the confinement of domesticity or domestic entrapment. Home is supposed to be a caring and nurturing environment, a role that remains the responsibility of women, but that can be a prison in itself. The title could also refer to house arrest, the notion of a barricaded home, or a denied homeland. In *Homebound*, I introduced a disturbing element, to turn your expectations of the home upside down.

IC: Later work, in particular *Remains of the Day* (2017), also renders the home uninhabitable through a catastrophic event, evidenced by the abandoned fragments of a life once lived. Yet, here, the overriding emotion is one of great sadness.

MH: It is sad. *Remains of the Day* was inspired by a trip to Hiroshima when I was awarded the Hiroshima Art Prize (2017). It's one of a series consisting of domestic furniture, burnt and charred to look like precarious ghostly remains, barely held together by a covering of wire mesh. *Remains of the Day* resembles a family environment hit by sudden destruction, which, in the context of Hiroshima, reminds us of the near total annihilation of the city after the dropping of the nuclear bomb. At the same time, it feels like quite a universal occurrence, representing the aftermath of war, violence or even ecological disaster anywhere in the world today. We're very vulnerable to all this, and *Remains of the Day* evokes the precariousness of human life, our insecurity, as well as malaise about the state of the world.

I think politicians conspire to create an atmosphere of fear and anxiety about the future to keep everyone restrained. It seems that the economic situation, political and religious fanaticism and the depletion of natural resources are all coming to a head. It may be simplistic, but if we were all more tolerant and kinder to each other, and to the planet, everything would be more sustainable. As long as profit and greed are favoured, at the expense of peoples' health and wellbeing, the whole system is bound to collapse.

IC: There's a distinct feeling of absence in some of your installations in that you create environments in which occupants are rendered invisible, as if the collapse you refer to has already occurred. In *Suspended* (2011), all the seats are empty, yet they sway as if animated by ghosts. Likewise, *Bunker* (2011) presents an urban sprawl, but the cut-steel tubing is riddled with puncture holes suggestive of devastation and mass exodus. When encountering installations like these, it's as if one is witness to an event, and this engenders a lingering feeling of disquiet.

MH: *Suspended* is 35 swings hanging by heavy chains from the ceiling, with a city map carved into the surface of each seat. They start to move when people walk past and take a long while to settle down, so it feels like something eerie is activating ghosts in the space. *Bunker* is like a cityscape of generic modernist

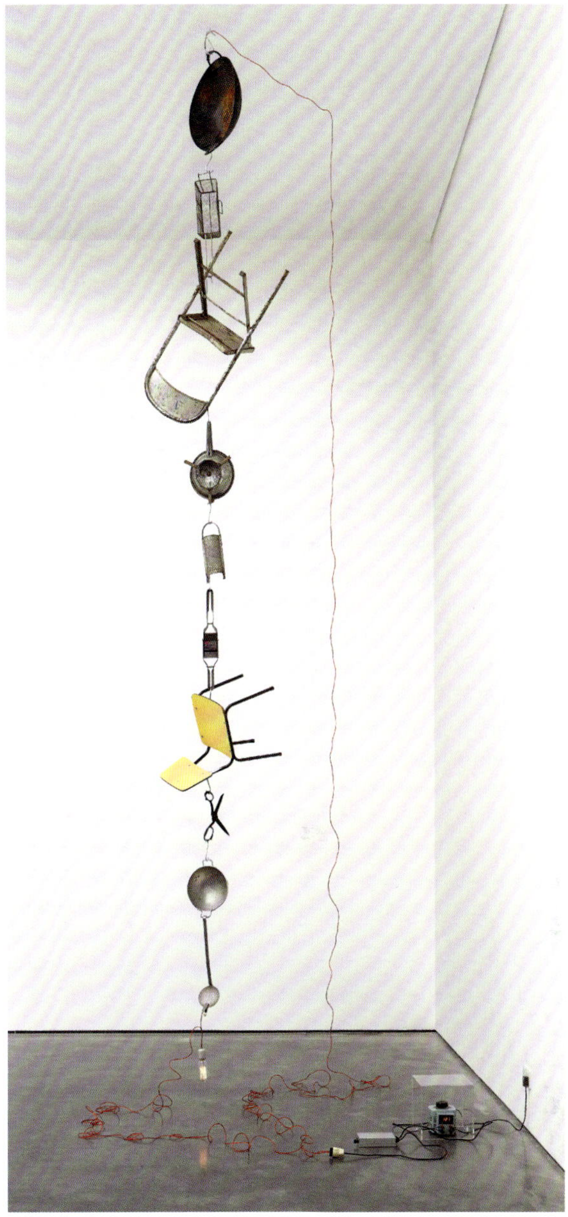

↑
Mona Hatoum
Electrified (variable II), 2014
Kitchen utensils, furniture, electric wire, light bulb and variable transformer
Dimensions variable

→→
Mona Hatoum
Remains of the Day, 2017
Wire mesh and wood
Dimensions variable
Installation view: Hiroshima City Museum of Contemporary Art, 2017

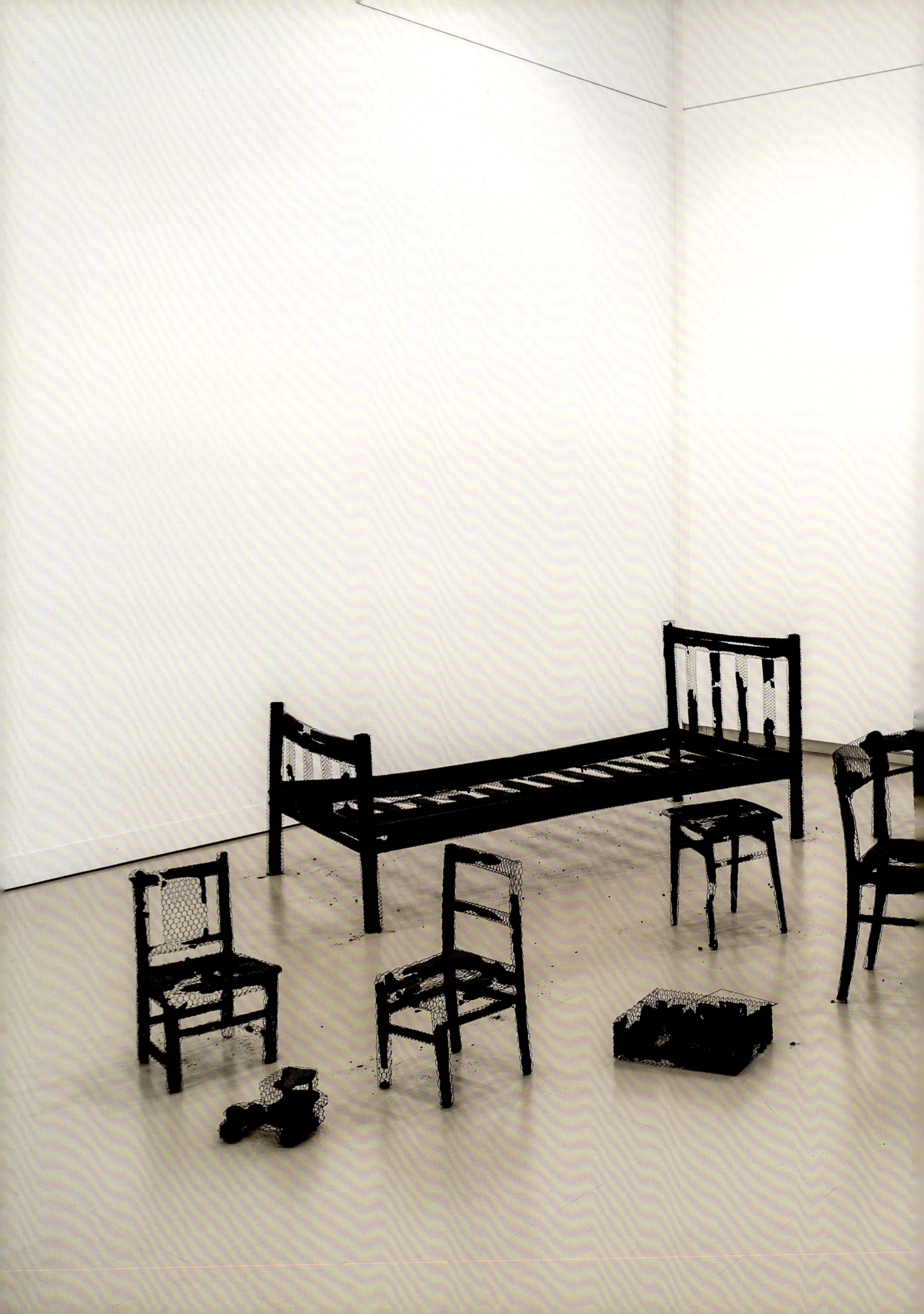

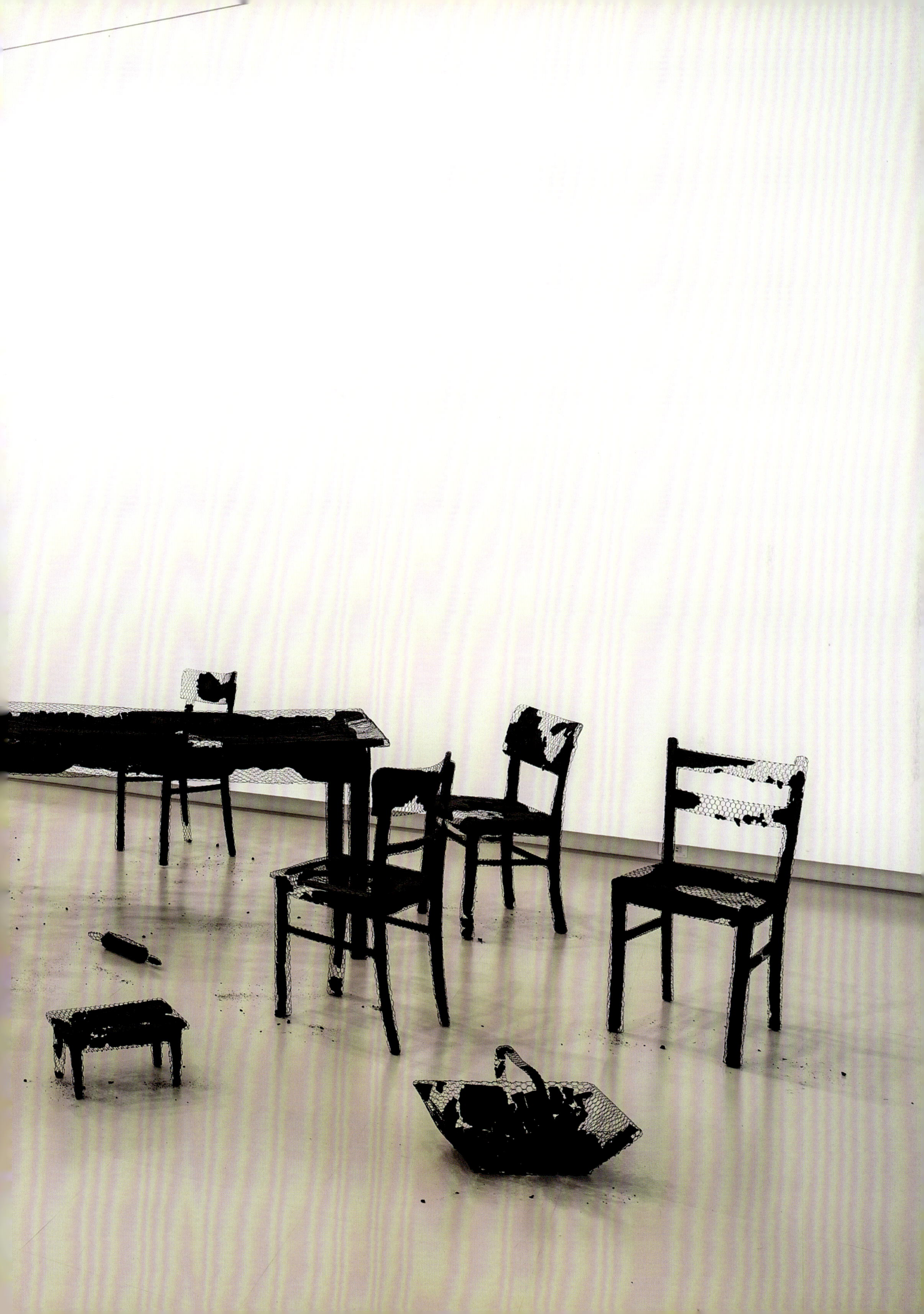

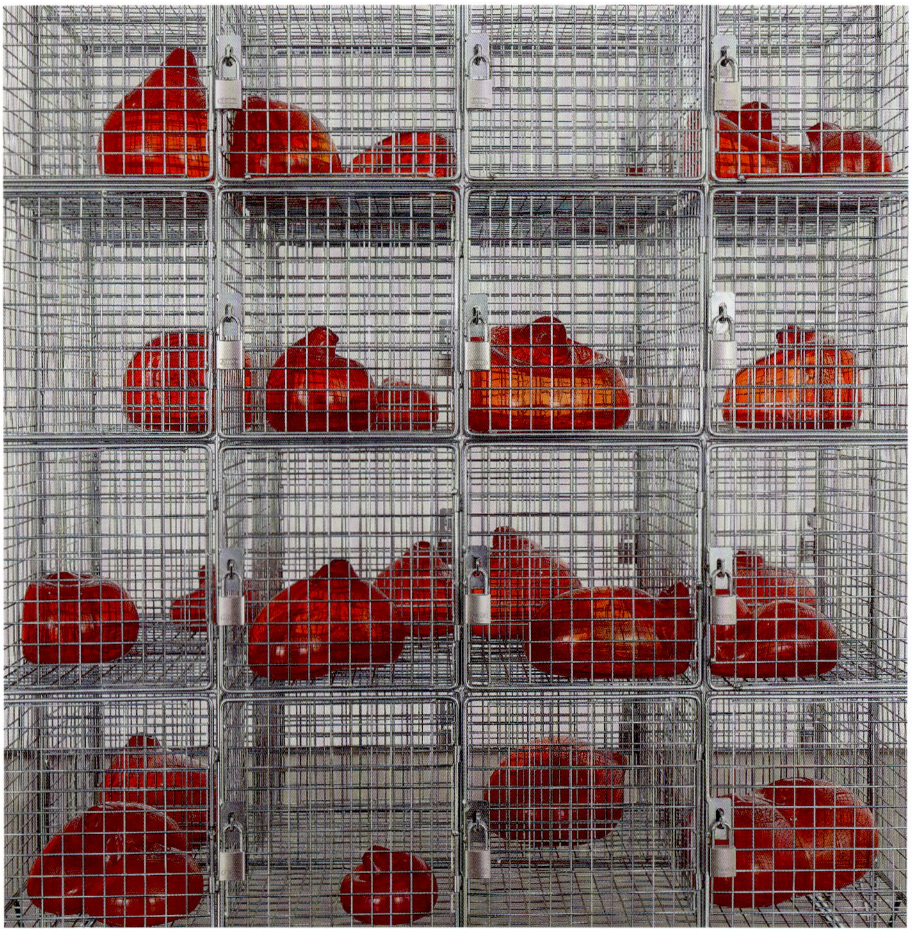

←
Mona Hatoum
Cells, 2014 (detail)
Zinc plated steel and hand-blown glass
136 × 121 × 65.5 cm
(53½ × 47⅝ × 25¾ in)

→
Mona Hatoum
Bunker, 2011
22 mild steel tubing structures
Dimensions variable
Installation view:
White Cube, London, 2011

buildings and, again, uses seriality, repetition and altered grids – minimal devices to create models of around 20 derelict and desolate architectural structures. Each structure is made up of rectangular steel-tube sections that had been subjected to cutting and burning, giving them the appearance of buildings scarred by conflict. Half of the structures specifically refer to buildings in Beirut; others were invented to fill the gaps. It's ironic because they're like maquettes, resembling plans for a future construction project, yet the signs of destruction are already present, as if accounted for in their design. These two installations feel empty, but they're also environments that can be populated by viewers.

IC: Your practice demonstrates great technical prowess. Although there have been significant advances in imaging technology and sound recording, a seminal piece such as *Corps étranger* (1994) retains the impact it had when first made. Is this kind of resilience important to the ongoing life of a work?

MH: It's incredibly important. My practice transcends the specific to reflect the essence of threat, conflict or destruction, which I hope makes it survive over time. *Corps étranger* was, again, an idea I had as a student at the Slade, but technology was then rudimentary and the medical centre, which was part of my university, refused to film me with an endoscopic camera. This idea was actually shelved until I was commissioned by the Pompidou Centre to create a video installation in 1994. By then the filming process could be seen on a monitor, and I was filmed by a French doctor.

Corps étranger, which is French for 'foreign body', comes from an interest in surveillance that struck me when first arriving in London. I felt observed and controlled by 'Big Brother', as opposed to protected, and this work pushes the idea of surveillance to an

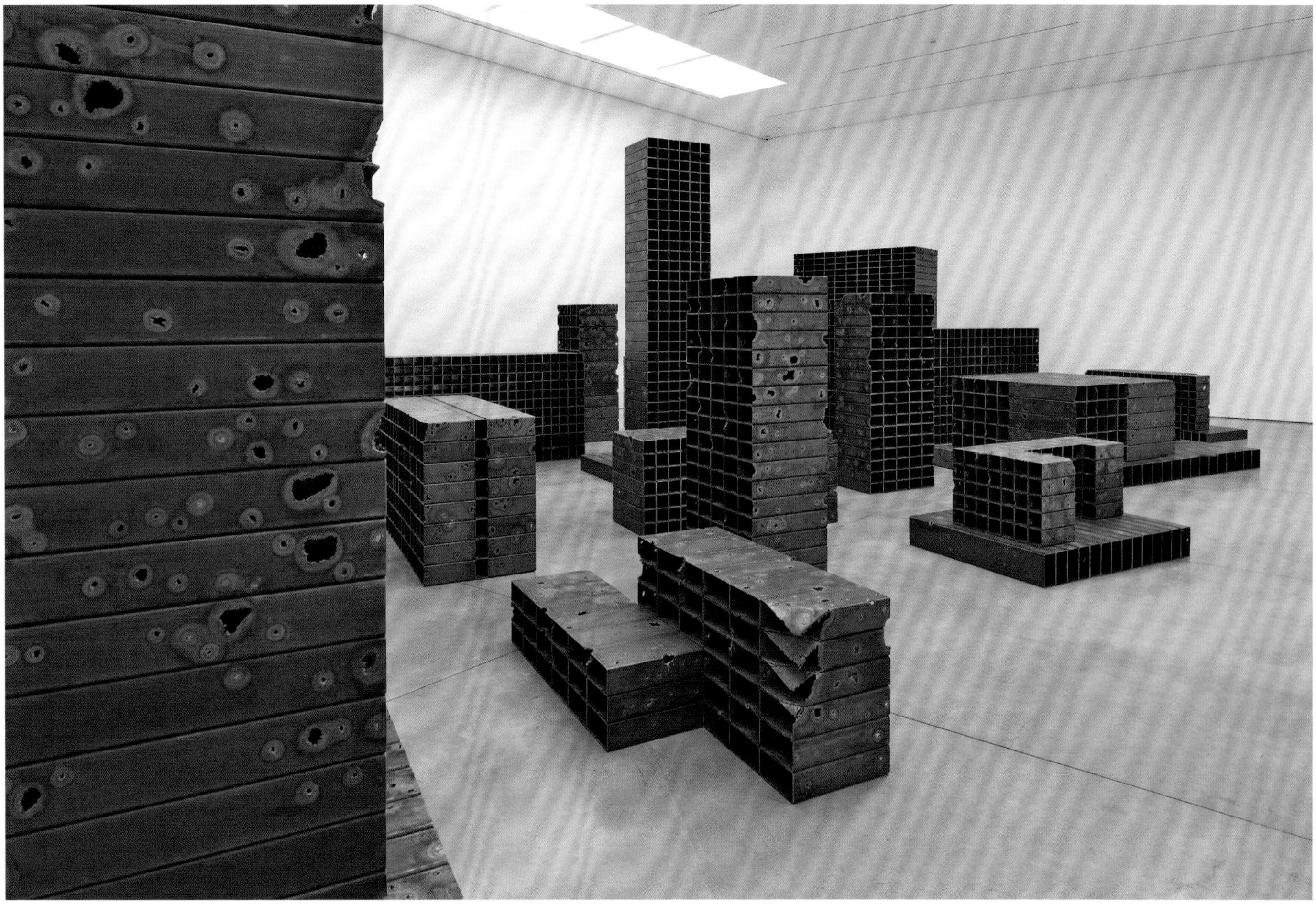

extreme, as if it could even penetrate your inner core, deconstruct and objectify you. *Corps étranger* is a video projection on the floor of a circular room you can enter. A camera travels through the oesophagus, stomach and intestine – an abyss full of goo, fascinating but disgusting – while the body is pulsating and whooshing. I think women are more comfortable with it; men are mostly horrified and don't even want to walk in. The body of the female is debased, as it's on the floor and could be walked over, yet it's also presented as dangerous territory and a source of anxiety, as in the Freudian concept of the devouring womb.

When you refer to the idea of resilience, *Corps étranger* is resilient because it transcends time. In the same way, I'm amazed how much interest there still is in *Measures of Distance*, which was made in 1988. Although it's focused on my parents' experience of living through the Lebanese Civil War, and our closeness and separation, it communicates the universal themes of exile, displacement and disorientation. A work like *Measures of Distance* will continue to resonate because it deals with a reality that many people experience.

Interviewed in 2019

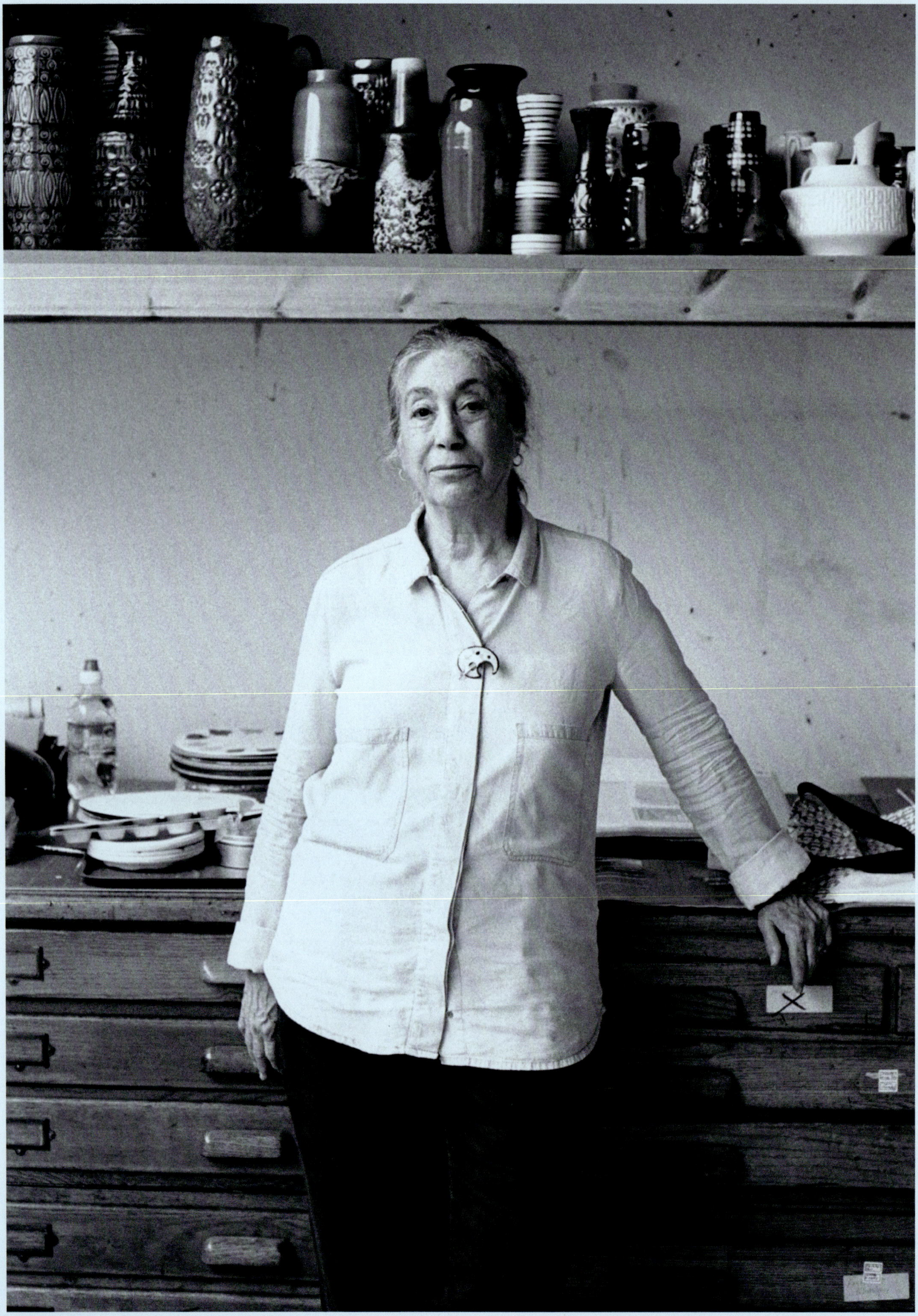

SUSAN HILLER

Born 1940, Florida, United States; died 2019, London

A pioneer of multimedia installation art in the 1980s onwards, Susan Hiller created a complex body of work that subverts our understanding of reality, offering an intellectual investigation into the darkest recesses of the human imagination. Her practice revolves around a fusion of conceptual art with subject matter that is usually dismissed, or overlooked, for being peripheral or paranormal, as demonstrated in *Belshazzar's Feast*, *Witness* and a series of *Homages* to well-known artists and writers. Accepted arguments are swept aside as Hiller constructs an enquiry into alternative modes of representation and explanation, where science and the irrational challenge each other through sculptural ensembles. She presents innovative ways of making the private experience public, in installations in which the spectator often becomes a participant. Hiller's multifaceted use of materials and technology immerses the viewer in a world of imagery and sound, to provoke an altered state of consciousness that questions the very nature of existence.

Ina Cole: You've lived in the UK since the 1960s, but what memories do you have of growing up in Florida, particularly in relation to your early fascination with anthropology and art?

Susan Hiller: I was born in Tallahassee but grew up in Cleveland, Ohio, until my parents moved back to Florida, to Coral Gables. As a child I was always interested in art. My father, an amateur painter, was very supportive, and I had a corner of my bedroom set up as a workspace with art supplies. The anthropology came about in high school, when I found a fascinating booklet by Margaret Mead called *Anthropology as a Career for Women*. Mead, who was responsible for the first generation of women anthropologists, offered the field in a gendered way which seemed terrific. At that point, I'd thought being an artist was impractical, but while at university in the US I took art courses to keep up with it. So, my career as an artist was partially formed by a vaccination of anthropology, but it doesn't mean my work is anthropological. It's simply my definition of art is anthropological, which leads me to be interested in certain things.

IC: Part of your early practice involved recycling paintings into three-dimensional forms, such as *Painting Block* (1974–83), or burning them and displaying their ashes in glass cylinders, as seen in *Hand Grenades* (1969–72).

SH: There's an idea that sculpture's existence as an object is the most important way to define it. My work isn't committed to objecthood in quite the way of traditional sculpture. With the recycled works, I want to see how far you can go before something doesn't exist materially anymore – it's an investigation.

Some years ago, I was invited to participate in a conference on Henry Moore at the Sainsbury Centre for Visual Arts in Norwich because of a shared interest in ethnographic art, and I explained that my decision to leave anthropology had taken place during a lecture on African art. The writer D.H. Lawrence had criticized the 'photographic' idea of sculpture, as opposed to the African commitment to 'all-roundness' that characterizes Moore's work. My own commitment to the idea of sculpture being all in the round, rather than flat against the wall, has emerged in my installations in a fundamental, but less obvious, sense. Some installations document particularly well, as you see them from one angle like a theatre set; mine less so, because they're in the round and use sound, which goes back to the very beginnings of my interest in African sculpture.

IC: *Monument* (1980–1) is a signature work, a moving exploration of how people continue to live through the thoughts and voices of others. How did it represent a breakthrough for you?

SH: It was the first work I'd made like that. The photographs are inset into a wall and presented with a park bench and sound. The soundtrack is in analogue format, so you can rewind the tape machine and my voice unwinds in your ear in a physical way, which doesn't happen with digital. Viewers approach the work from a distance, move closer, stop and read the panels, then notice there's a place for them to sit, listen and become part of the ensemble. The memorials are from a London park, which is wonderful now but was overgrown and melancholy, and I photographed them because I found the texts poignant. People sat on benches with their backs to these plaques, and I then realized the fate of memorials or monuments of any kind. They're ignored; no one pays attention to them. The idea of this invisibility became important in the work.

IC: *Monument* also reflects on our difficult relationship with temporal existence.

SH: It was made up of one panel for each year of my life. The element of time, so important in sculpture, is fundamental in this piece, since the subjects of the texts exist longer as representations than as living creatures. If I die and someone keeps a photograph of me, I'll be around as a representation for other people, not as myself, which is curious. Our society is obsessed with conserving histories because we can't conserve ourselves, and this is explicitly addressed in the soundtrack.

Monument is built up around the idea of memory and commemoration, but it doesn't provide answers;

Susan Hiller
Hand Grenades, 1972
(from paintings made in 1969)
Ashes of paintings in 12 glass jars, rubber stoppers, labels, Pyrex bowl
11 × 18 × 18 cm
($4\frac{3}{8} \times 7\frac{1}{8} \times 7\frac{1}{8}$ in)

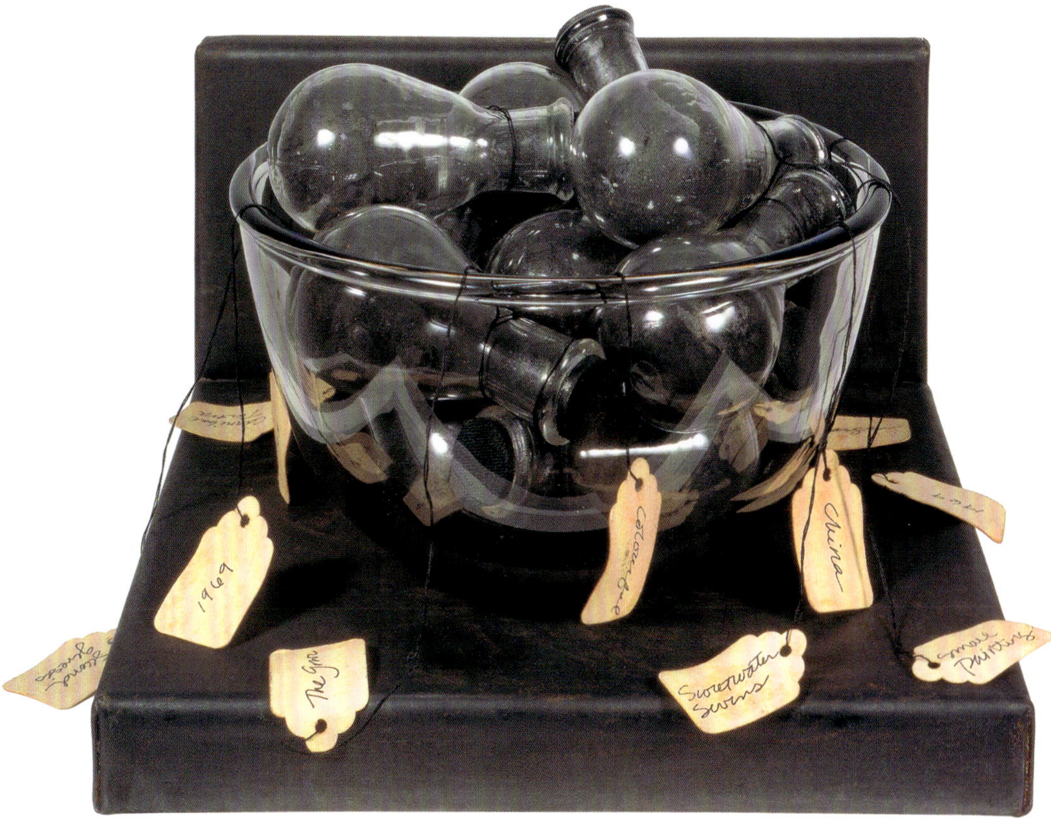

it just raises more questions. Empirical explanations don't satisfy our yearnings for continuity. There's a kind of Hollywood mishmash of cult fantasies and beliefs, a desperate groping for something that religion used to take care of. A lot of work needs to be done to address these issues, as the fantastic explanations posited by physics about the nature of reality don't match the boring, common-sense, empirical view pounded into society. When people wonder about other possibilities, others usually laugh at them. It's a big problem, and our society is in crisis. Do you feel that?

IC: Yes, I think we've reached a crisis point in terms of human consciousness. People still pursue answers, but their experiences tend to be individual and quite insular rather than of collective significance.

SH: *From Here to Eternity* (2008) explores the medieval idea of creating an altered state of consciousness, by metaphorically undertaking the great pilgrimage to Jerusalem. This work is based on the idea that time and space can be experienced from a diagram. There are three slow, silent video projections of three different labyrinths, with little dots moving round a pathway, similar to an early computer-game graphic, or a Frank Stella painting. There's something very interesting about the concept of a labyrinth, as opposed to a maze. A maze is a place to get lost; a labyrinth has only one right way to go, but it's complicated, and you often seem to go backwards, or in the wrong direction. You think, 'This can't be right', but it is, and that's why it's such a great statement about life. If you follow the dots, you can feel your attention moving from one side of your brain to the other in a very physical way. My work is increasingly designed to create situations in which people begin to understand something about themselves, and *From Here to Eternity* does it without text or sound.

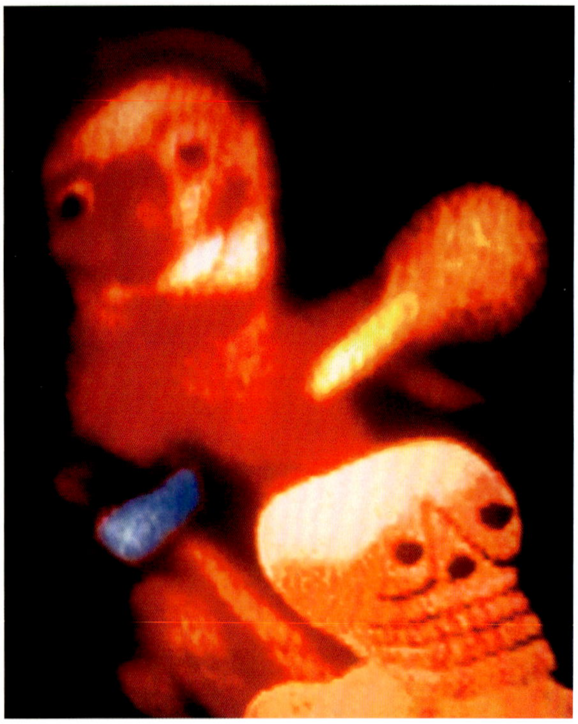

IC: In *Belshazzar's Feast, The Writing on Your Wall* (1983–4), the central element is a television screen set within the configuration of a living room. In films, the screen frequently serves as a paranormal device through which victims become obsessed with occult transmissions. Here, it creates tension through its dual nature as an accepted everyday object that nonetheless has the power to subsume us all. Can you discuss the ideas behind this work and explain why the screen shows footage of flames?

SH: Communication at a distance, starting with the radio and telephone, opened up new possibilities of spookiness in the history of Western culture. *Belshazzar's Feast* is based on newspaper articles about apparitions appearing on screens after a broadcast had ended. The Canadian philosopher Marshall McLuhan had a very rational explanation about the lure of television when he said it had replaced the living-room hearth. Deconstructing television isn't my primary interest; I'm interested in the phenomenon of reverie that can happen regardless of what programme is on, which is similar to what happens if you stare into a fire, because of the little blips of light. If you're good at imagining, you'll see pictures and make up a story. It's probably the origin of image-making.

The biblical story of Belshazzar's feast describes a collective hallucination, during which everyone sees a hand writing a message of doom. The relationship of this story to my piece is that numerous people rang the BBC after close of broadcast saying they could still see images, which they found very spooky. My work is about projection, and this can be a source of great pleasure if you enjoy imagination – otherwise, it's scary.

IC: *An Entertainment* (1990) offers a moment of high drama, presenting itself as a visual and acoustic shock to the senses. Here, the spectator becomes victim, boxed within a four-screen installation. Is it important for you that viewers feel complicit in the interpretation of a work, so, by experiencing it, they become something like collaborators?

SH: In *An Entertainment*, I wanted to put the adult in the place of a child. The only way to revive the hypersensitivity of a child was to make things big and make us feel small. All the repetitions in the piece are from Punch and Judy shows, and since the puppets perform from a box, I thought, 'Let's put us in a box.' So, I invented a projection system that surrounds the viewer with images coming from all sides. I went to many puppet-shows when my son was growing up and I'd hear the littlest children crying and wanting to leave, and their parents saying, 'Oh, look at Mr Punch, isn't he funny?', or 'Don't be so silly, there's nothing frightening here.' I realized denial is a ritual in our society; we're trained to deny our own experiences and laugh at our fears.

An Entertainment has the attractiveness of a certain kind of fear because it triggers childhood memories in which you're terrified of something that turns out not to be real. In childhood, you don't anticipate and, with *An Entertainment*, the sound and image suddenly come from behind, forcing you to turn around. This uncertainty

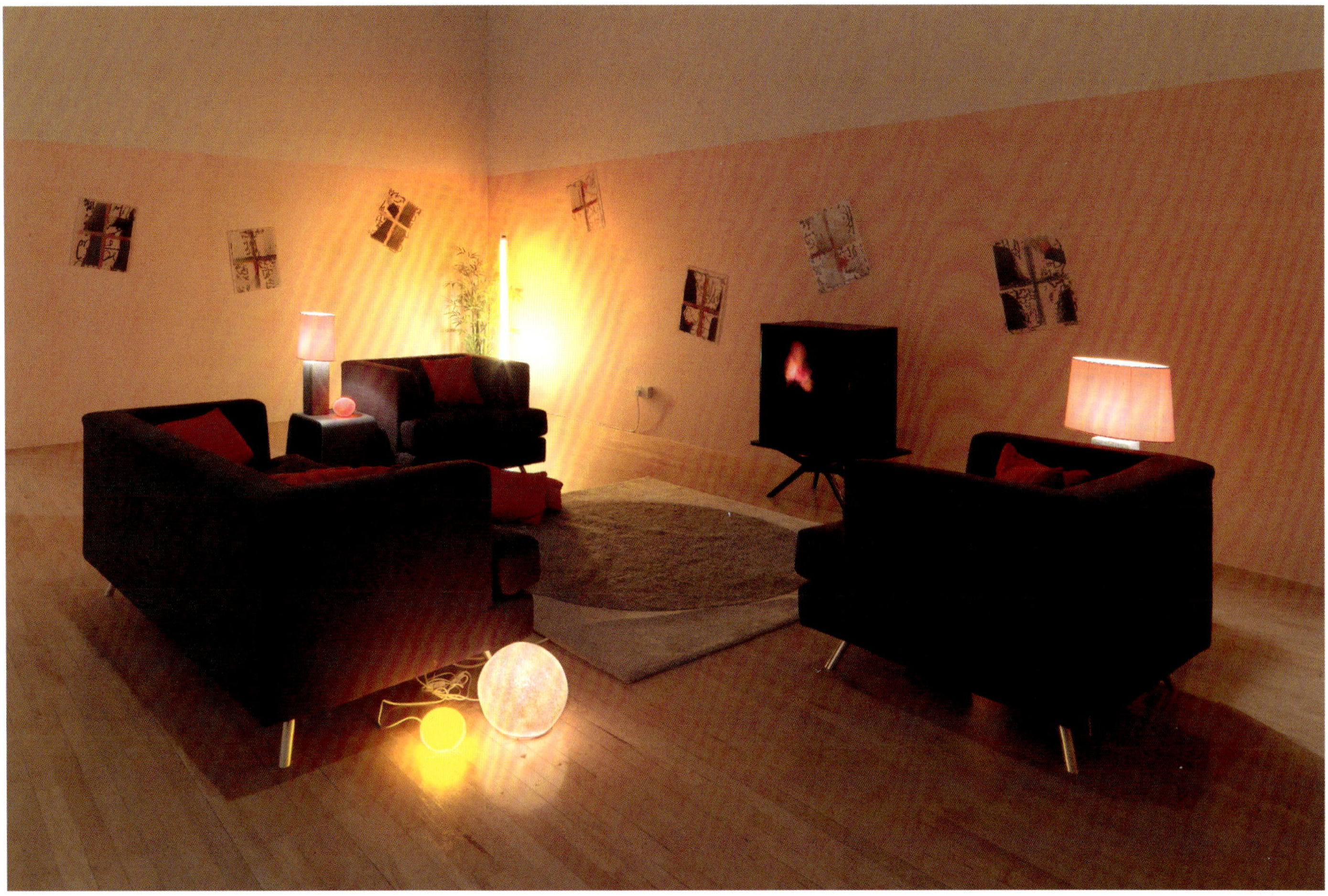

is a deliberate part of the piece. With my installations, the degree of involvement and three-dimensionality increases through time, starting with *Monument* which you can just walk past, to *An Entertainment* and *Witness* (2000) where they become greater.

IC: In *Witness*, hundreds of suspended microphones emit a cacophony of voices recalling stories of alien encounters from across the world. In the past, people looked to religious icons, while contemporary witnesses often see spectral or extraterrestrial phenomena. Does this represent a yearning for something greater than ourselves – something to make our earthly existence more tolerable?

SH: In the past, there was a context for heightened psychological experiences, which could be translated into known iconic figures and, therefore, made acceptable. We're now out on a limb with this because society is more

←
Susan Hiller
An Entertainment, 1990
Four synchronized video projections, quadraphonic sound
Dimensions variable
Programme duration 26 minutes

↑
Susan Hiller
Belshazzar's Feast / The Writing on Your Wall, 1983–4
Video installation and photographs
Dimensions variable
Installation view: Tate Britain, London, 2011

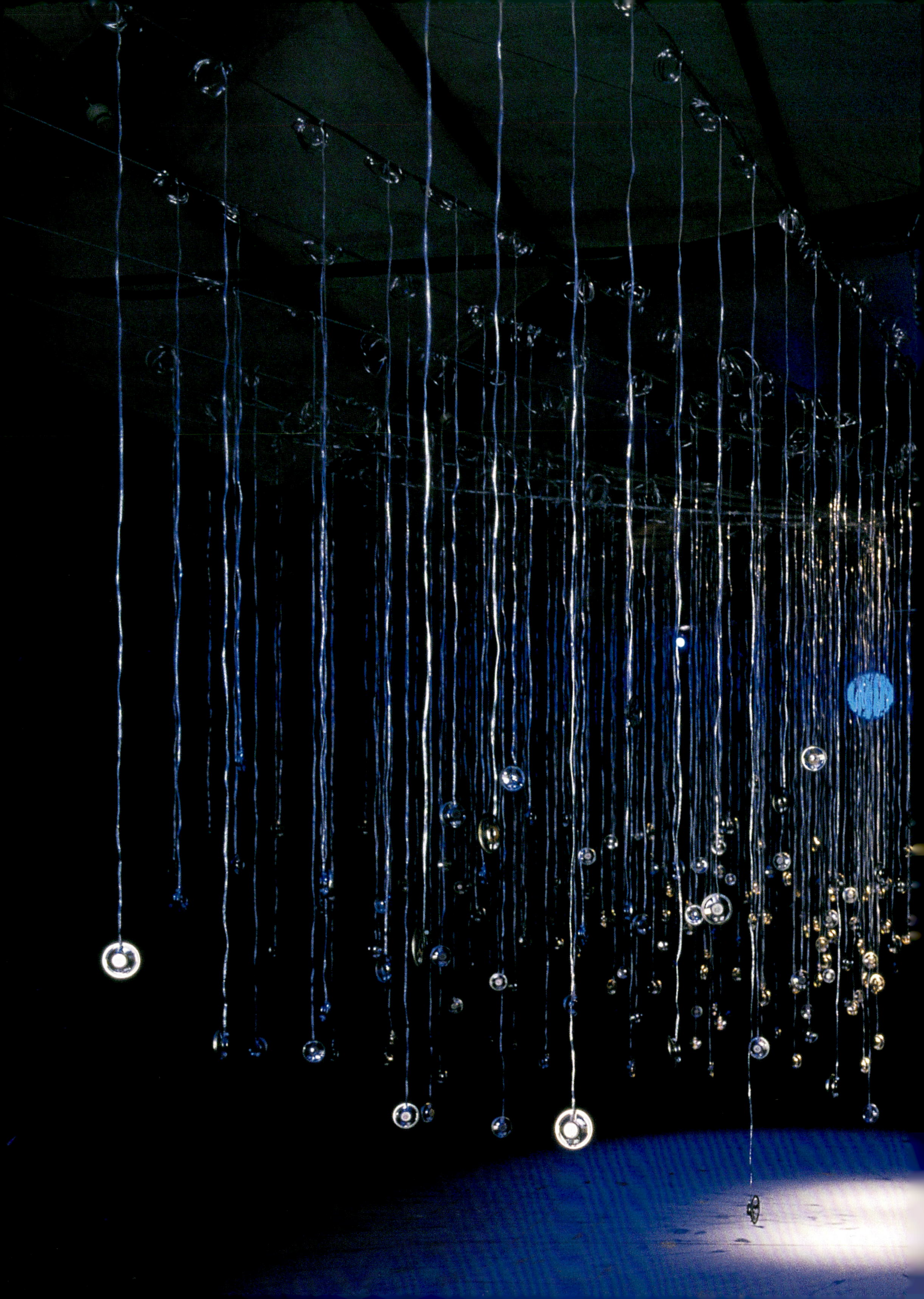

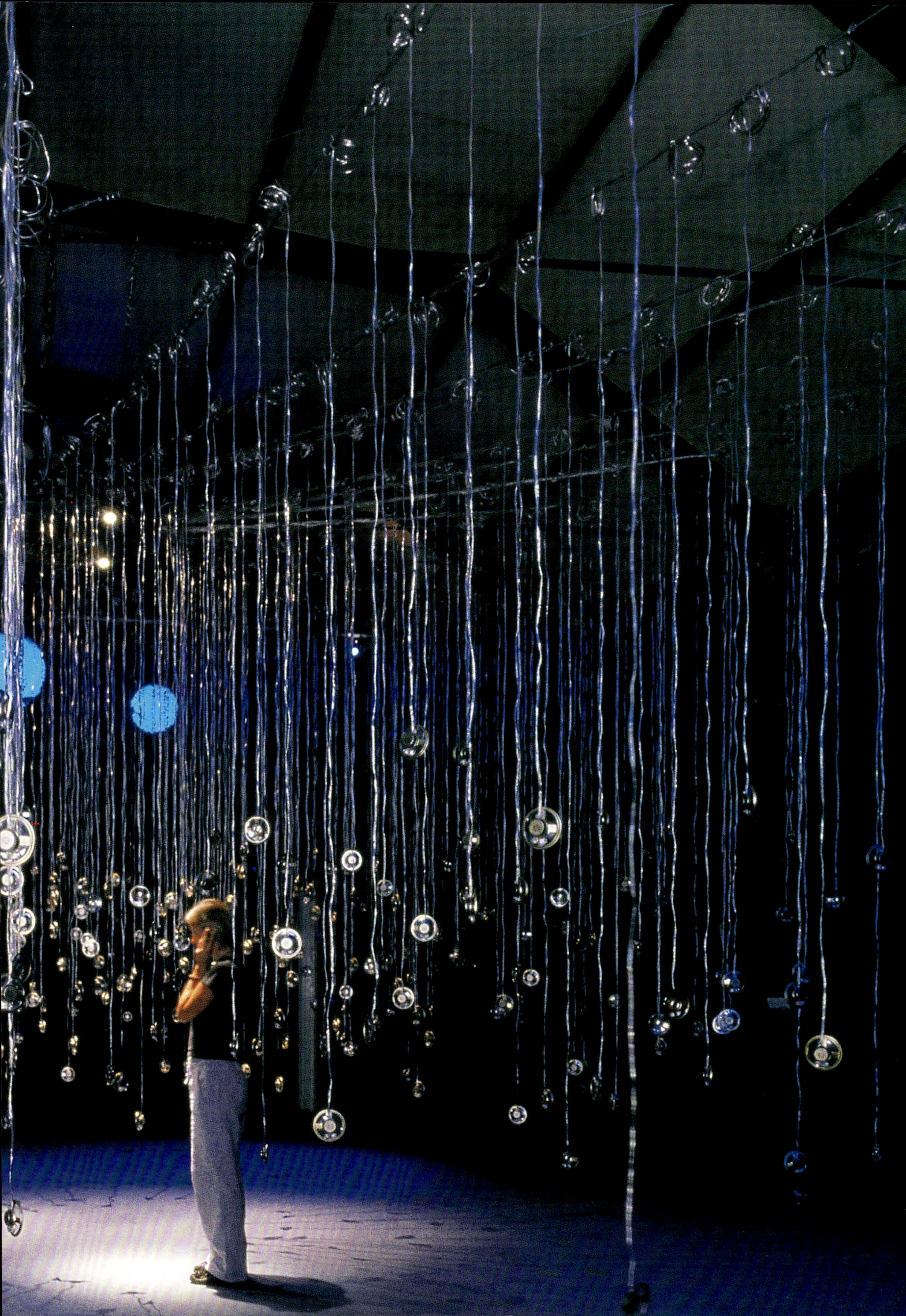

←←
Susan Hiller
Witness, 2000

Audio-sculpture: 350 speakers suspended from ceiling, 10 audio tracks, switching equipment, steel structure, amplifiers, wiring, lights
Size approx. 1800 × 900 cm (59 × 30 ft)
Installation view: Artangel at The Chapel, London, 2000

→
Susan Hiller
Die Gedanken sind frei (Thoughts are Free), 2012

Interactive audio installation: 100 songs on customized walnut jukebox, vinyl wall texts, 'Songbook' artist's books, benches
Configuration and dimensions variable
Jukebox dimensions 152 × 81.4 × 64 cm (59⅞ × 32 × 25¼ in)
Installation view: Documenta 13, Kassel, Germany, 2012

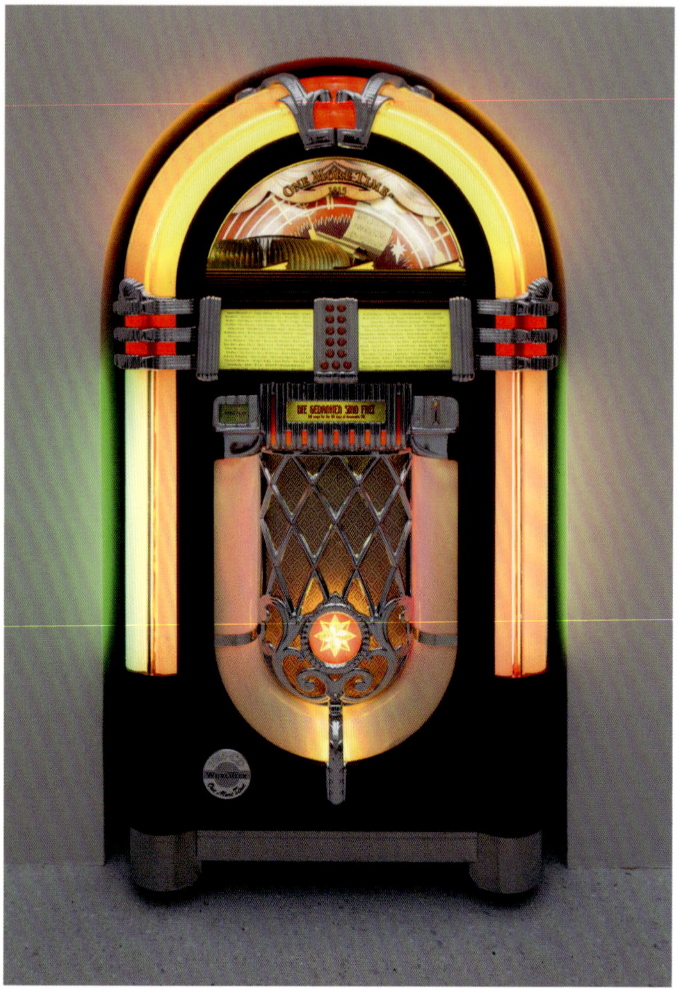

and more on the surface; we don't have metaphysical ponderings and depth. Freud said that the lost pleasures of life on this earth are compensated for by a belief in occult theories. He saw there was a need and was sympathetic, even though he didn't believe. That's the place to be – tolerant but sceptical – and I think more work needs to be done on these issues by psychologists and scientists.

In *Witness*, the UFO experiences usually begin when someone's driving through empty countryside at night, as the monotony triggers receptivity. It's hard to talk about these experiences, so people create straightforward narratives. Was it an angel, a flying saucer or just a bright light? It depends on the person, and these stories have a very long history. William Blake saw angels. Are we supposed to mock Blake? No, I don't think so. So, what do we do with these stories?

IC: Perhaps science ignores the workings of the subconscious mind at its peril?

SH: Yes, and since we don't allow people to have regular paths to unconsciousness, certain issues become big social problems. Everyone yearns for peace, but we have more war than ever because, unconsciously, something's happening that we can't get at. It would require a fundamental shift of focus to change things, and I can't see how we're going to achieve that. In *Witness*, these experiences are eruptions in consciousness when the person's in a state of receptivity. We have a capacity to see the most beautiful things, which may, or may not, be there. Scientists tell us there are nine dimensions and everything is happening simultaneously, but how are we supposed to put that together with the stupidity with which we're brought up? We're the prisoners of our senses; we have bodies, and that's why we invented the idea of the soul. I don't think we're ever going to resolve it, but it's interesting to provide experiences which allow people to think about it.

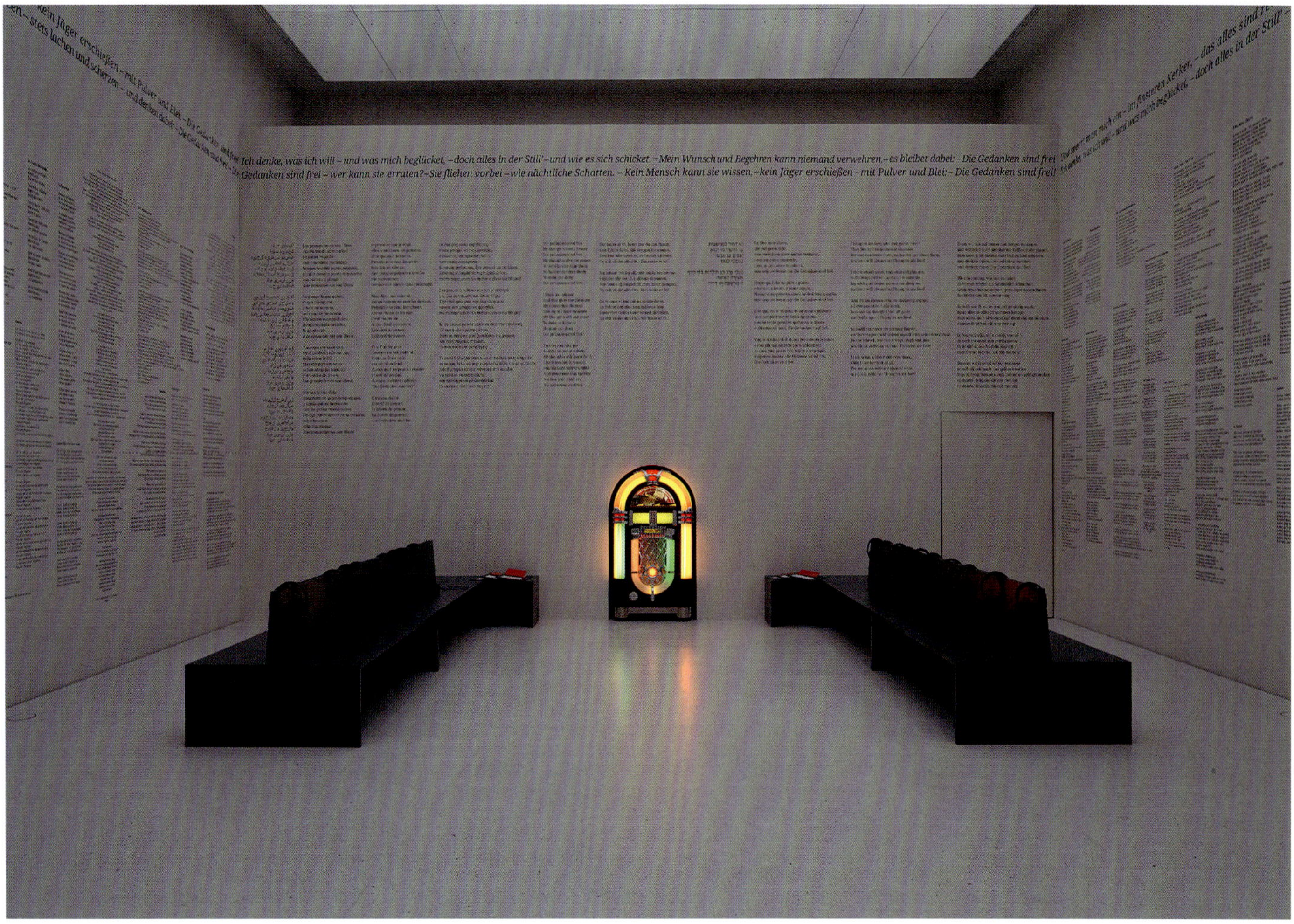

IC: *The Last Silent Movie* (2007–8) amasses a collection of extinct and endangered languages, while *Die Gedanken sind frei (Thoughts Are Free)* (2012) is a collection of songs on a jukebox. Is civilization becoming more homogenized, with individual traits conveniently erased?

SH: You could say I'm erasing the individualism of languages by collecting them, but I'm not; I'm pointing out their existence and uniqueness. In *The Last Silent Movie*, the decision not to have pictures is important, as it takes away one of our senses. We listen to voices, and every voice is unique, like a fingerprint. We have a closeness when hearing the recorded voice of someone who's dead, because the voice is still living; although that wasn't my first intention, which was to look at the phenomenon of disappearing languages.

The fact that languages are collected and shut away in academic archives is very peculiar. So much effort is made by anthropologists and linguists to record languages as the last speakers become old and fade away. We should be asking, 'Why are these languages dying? What's going on?' But we never ask these questions because we're stuck on the implications of our own way of life, which is eating up the rest of the world. *The Last Silent Movie* makes this disappearance visible.

In the same way, *Die Gedanken sind frei* is a collection of songs that were popular in certain political and resistance movements, yet still have a charge when you listen to them now. They act as memory triggers for events long forgotten. Sound is very important in that way, more than vision, and I'm fascinated by its potential.

IC: *From the Freud Museum* (1991–6) responds to Freud's lifelong passion for collecting. The installation, which you've referred to as 'an archive of misunderstandings', includes 50 archaeological storage boxes filled with mementos, relics and talismans you acquired. Can you elaborate?

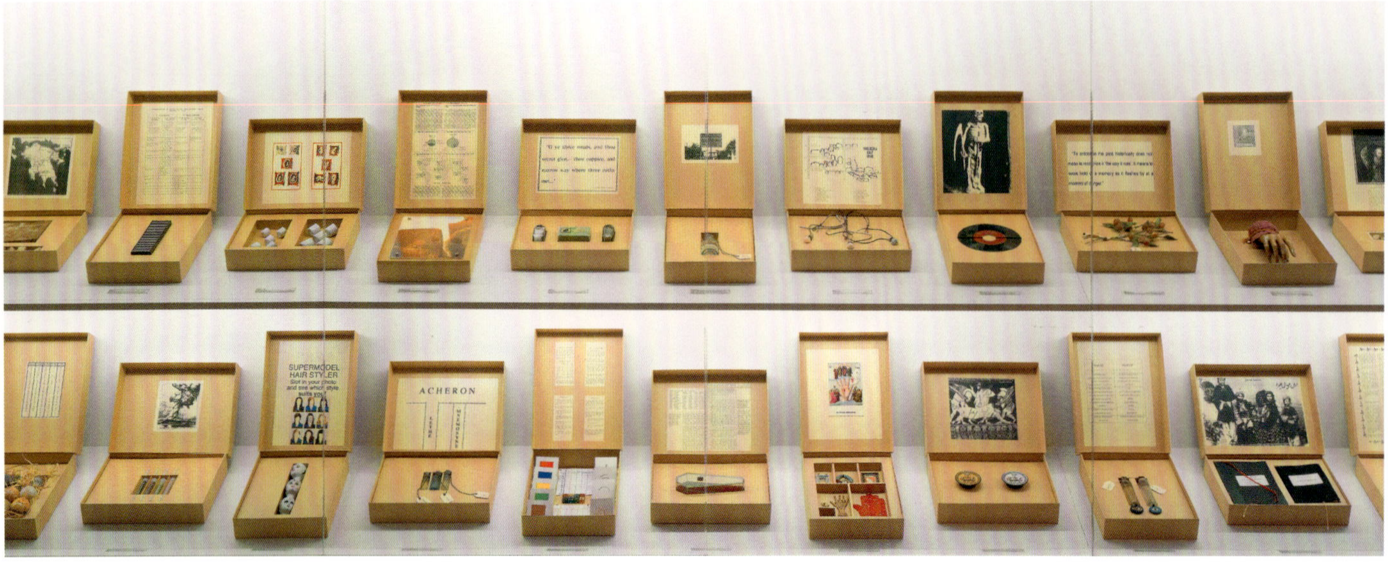

SH: Freud collected everything, and his collection was of the kind any cultivated European of his period with sufficient income would have acquired. I'm not saying it wasn't personal, but it's typical of a middle-class man of his time, whereas the things I collected have no value other than they're perplexing or curious. The misunderstandings are of various kinds. Each box has its own title referring to a particular discourse – art history, anthropology, psychoanalysis. They're juxtaposed randomly so the different perspectives problematize each other, with each individual box deciphering other kinds of misunderstandings.

One box holds coloured salt from a mine near Auschwitz. The mine contains beautiful carvings made by the miners and has a ballroom with semi-transparent walls that glow when lamps are placed behind them. It was used as a TB sanatorium because of the pure air, and as a facility for advanced technologies, since there was no dust. One of these advanced technologies was the basis for a Nazi armament factory using slave labour. Hundreds of people died, but the tour and tourist map of the mine don't mention the slave-labour camp. I found a book about this mine, with a chapter on the camp. So, I placed a photocopy of the tourist map in a box, along with these lovely orange, green and grey samples of salt, drawing the location of the slave labour camp in red. That kind of juxtaposition is what the boxes are about.

Another box contains a praying mantis in a painstakingly made glass coffin, with a big red glass jewel set in the top. I juxtaposed this with an excerpt from a 1970s House of Lords debate on UFOs, because the words 'mantis' and 'mantic' both, through their Greek origin, relate to prophecy and supernatural knowledge. I thought of someone placing a praying mantis in a coffin, thinking it was a creature from outer space, and ceremonially treating it as if it were holy. The fact that the House of Lords had an official debate on

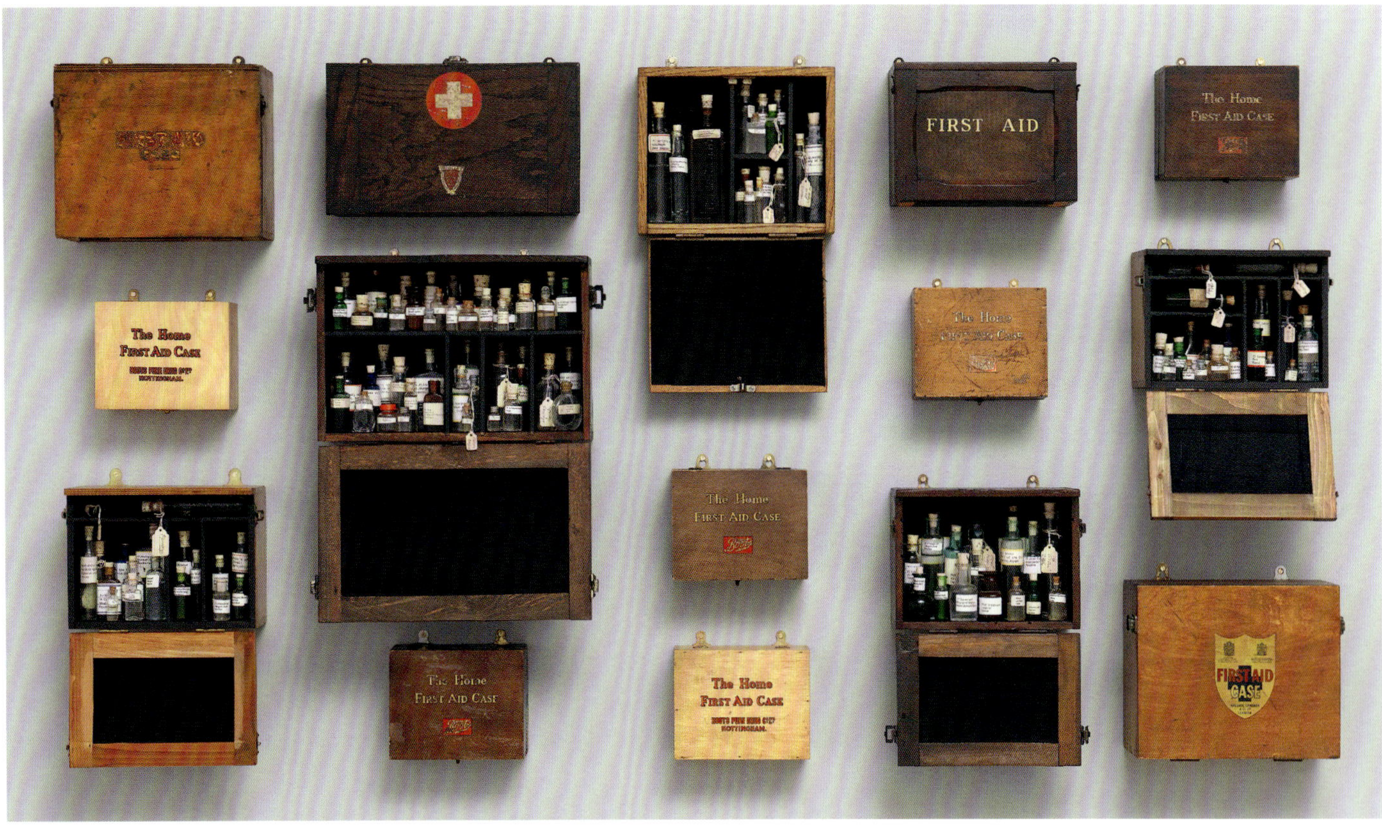

↖
Susan Hiller
From the Freud Museum, 1991–6 (detail)

Vitrine containing artefacts and notes in 50 custom-made cardboard boxes
Vitrine 220 × 1000 × 60 cm
(7 ft 2⅝ in × 32 ft 9¾ in × 23⅝ in)
Boxes each 25 × 32.5 cm
(9⅞ × 12¾ in)
Video duration 15 mins

↑
Susan Hiller
Home Nursing: Homage to Joseph Beuys, 1969–2011

15 wooden felt-lined first aid cabinets, 116 bottles of holy water, vintage first aid supplies
110 × 191.3 cm
(43¼ × 75¼ in)

UFOs was irresistible to me. A touch of humour had to enter into this work from time to time, which relates to Freud's idea of the joke, the misreading and the omission. The individual boxes work by association, and viewers' associations probably override my own.

IC: You've created a series of *Homages* to twentieth-century artists and writers, including Marcel Duchamp, Gertrude Stein and Joseph Beuys. All were radical thinkers, but why did you select them in particular?

SH: I'm interested in what's hidden, left out, or which continues to haunt us. The history of modernist art includes elements from occult traditions that are underplayed or ignored, yet it was through these artists, and others of their generation, that occult concepts were transmitted down to the present. Duchamp quested for a vehicle for many years after giving up retinal painting. It isn't generally acknowledged that he went through various occult movements before finally ending up with alchemy. In *Portrait of Dr Dumouchel* (1910) – a portrait of his friend, a radiographer – Duchamp deliberately conflated the idea of the occult aura with the light of radiography. I wanted to explore what that means in a digital age and showed images, sourced online, of people who presented themselves as disembodied through light.

As a student of psychology, Gertrude Stein conducted experiments on automatic writing, but spent the rest of her life denying she had. I found a wonderful piece of Art Deco furniture that reflects her roundness – after the sculpture of her behind New York Public Library, which exaggerates her fatness – and I stacked it with books on automatic writing and on other forms of advanced thinking of the time. So, *Homage to Gertrude Stein* emphasizes an aspect of her work that tends to be suppressed or ignored.

Beuys haunts contemporary art, and his controversial pose as a shaman mediating between two worlds is both seductive and repellent. I was interested in representing how he tried to stay on the edge of that by using bottles of holy water. The UK has a superabundance of holy springs, and I started collecting such waters years ago. *Homage to Joseph Beuys* situates these bottles in a felt-lined vitrine, connecting Beuys to a current in popular belief that is both credulous and sceptical. Even though people return from sites like Lourdes with water, I don't believe they think it's actually magic. Beuys tried to create a bridge between some of the things we've talked about, but his shamanistic pose and biography as a celebrity raises a problem. It's an encouragement for credulity rather than for thinking.

Interviewed in 2011

Susan Hiller
Lucidity and Intuition: Homage to Gertrude Stein, 2011

Art Deco writing desk containing books on automatism and related subjects, dossier by the artist, plinth
72 × 47.5 cm
(28⅜ × 18¾ in)

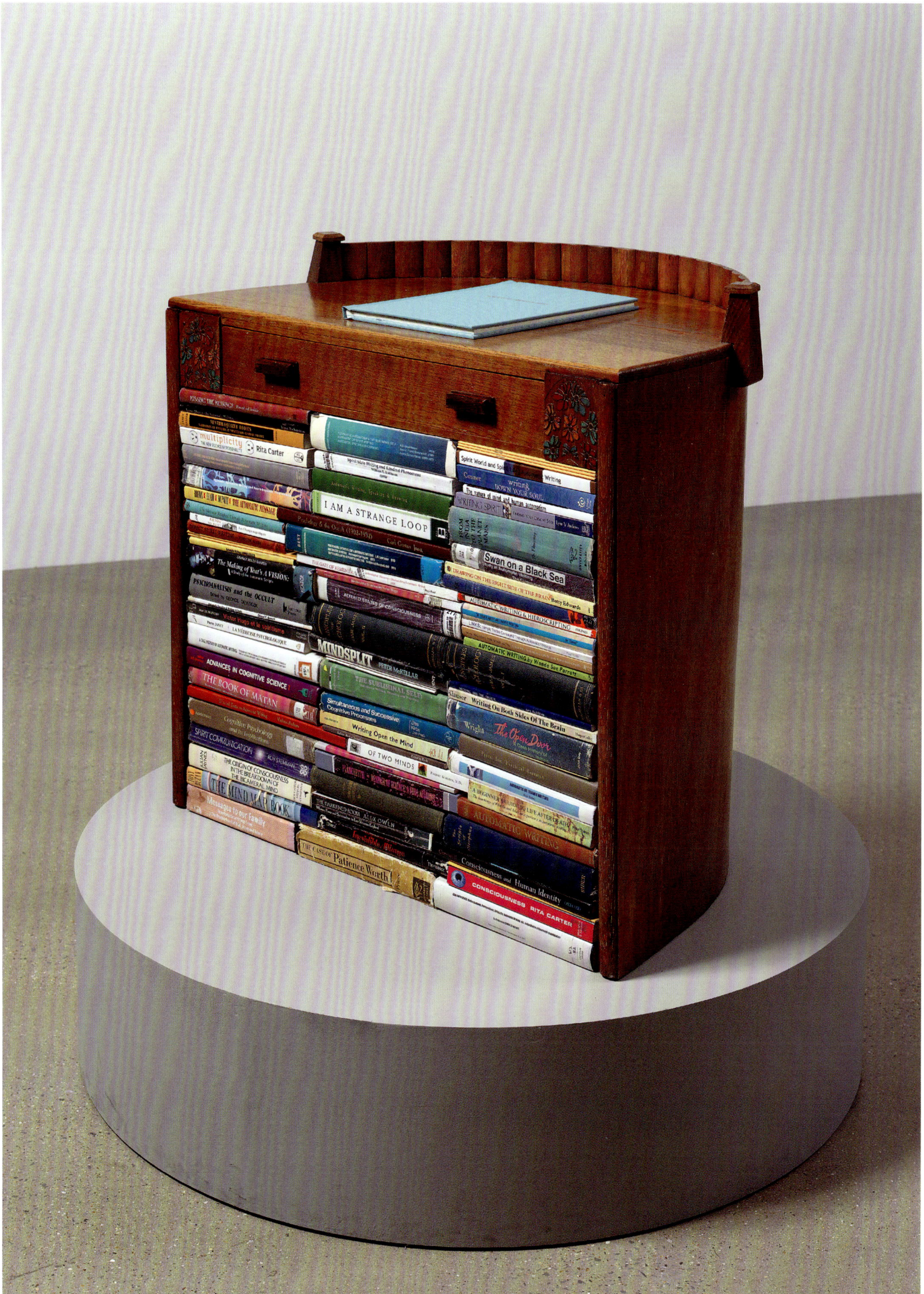
multiplicity
Rita Carter
I AM A STRANGE LOOP
Swan on a Black Sea
DRAWING ON THE RIGHT SIDE OF THE BRAIN
PSYCHOANALYSIS and the OCCULT
MINDSPLIT
ADVANCES IN COGNITIVE SCIENCE
THE BOOK OF MATAN
THE SUBLIMINAL SELF
Simultaneous and Successive Cognitive Processes
Writing On Both Sides Of The Brain
The Open Door
SPIRIT COMMUNICATION
Writing Open the Mind
OF TWO MINDS
THE ORIGIN OF CONSCIOUSNESS IN THE BREAKDOWN OF THE BICAMERAL MIND
THE MIND MAP BOOK
AUTOMATIC WRITING
THE CASE OF Patience Worth
Consciousness and Human Identity
CONSCIOUSNESS RITA CARTER

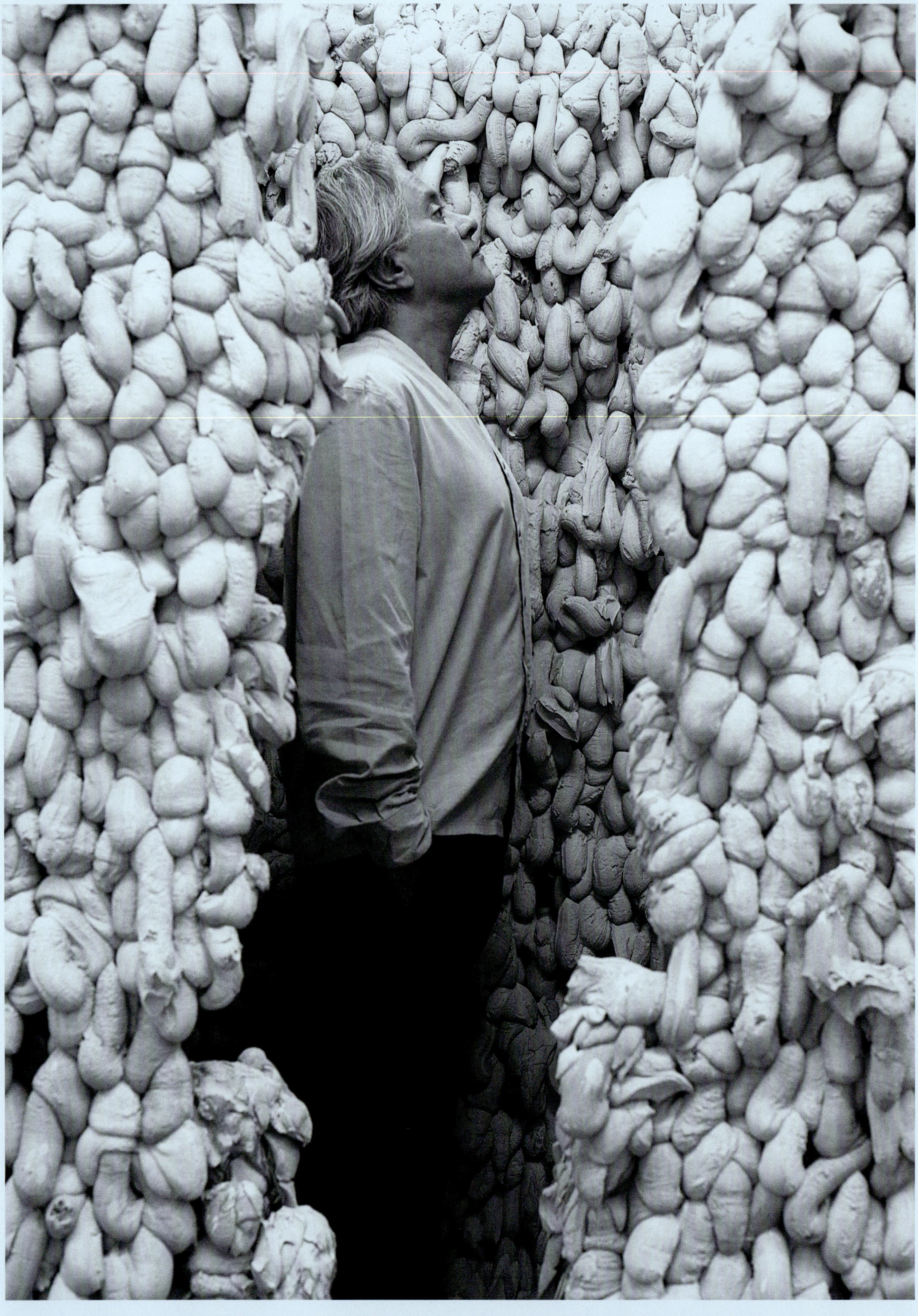

ANISH KAPOOR

Born 1954, Mumbai, India

The sculptures that brought Anish Kapoor to public attention in the 1980s were geometric and biomorphic configurations, covered with luminously coloured powdered pigment. They were aligned to the modernist tradition through form and colour, yet these beginnings led to the development of a sculptural language reaching far beyond the object, into deeper realms of physical and psychological experience. Kapoor's sculptures hover between the material and the non-material. Although their presence commands attention, they possess an illusory quality that plays havoc with the senses and our application of logic. These transformative properties are applied to *Sky Mirror* and *Cloud Gate*, which appear to exist by their own volition. Highly reflective, they are simultaneously present, yet tantalizingly out of reach. Space and scale are a fundamental preoccupation within Kapoor's practice: *Orbit* soars to a height of 115 metres (377 feet); *Leviathan* is a colossal, all-engulfing inflatable; while *Shooting into the Corner* commandeers its space by blasting wax shells from a cannon, to leave an oozing red trail in its wake.

Ina Cole: In the early 1970s you emigrated from India to Israel, after which you hitch-hiked to Europe, before arriving in London. How has the convergence of all these different influences defined your practice over the years?

Anish Kapoor: I grew up in India, I have Jewish origins and, of course, these things mix with each other. Much of what I grew up with in the Indian context, mythologically and psychically, keeps returning to me. One can't help it, it's there, which is rather wonderful because it gives access to deeper human questions about being, death, mythological origin and consciousness. They're key bits of matter that emerge in spite of oneself; a connection with old culture. But what is old culture in relation to new culture? Is new culture independent of old culture? Is old culture to be used as a political tool to establish nationalism? These are the great dangers, but there is this inevitable back and forth that says the two are deeply related.

In my mirrored sculptures, the viewer is part of what is looked at. They include your reflection, so it's as if they follow you around the room. I can't help but think of late-medieval painting in which the pursuit was to have the eyes of Christ follow you around. What do you have to do, technically, to have the eyes follow you? Where does that come from? It obviously comes from the notion of an all-seeing god, ever present, sitting on your shoulder. They're beautiful ideas, but can we make them contemporary?

IC: It's well documented that your sculpture is inspired by opposites. Where have these polarities been most successfully combined?

AK: I'm not interested in opposites *per se*, yet what I've observed in the process of making my work is that opposite entities are one of its abiding languages. It's not a pursuit, but something that has been there from the beginning. Since it's there, it is my duty to recognize that and work with it. At one level, the role of art is to give a voice to conflict, and all I've done is acknowledge the conflict is there. One could say that the history of sculpture is the history of material. I've always been drawn to the idea that for every material there's an equivalent non-material, and my particular history of sculpture includes the non-material. We can speak of that as opposites.

The process of being an artist is to recognize that the unknown is a workable reality. I've often proposed I've nothing to say as an artist – and allowing there to be nothing to say is a really important condition. So, I'm shifting the project into a psycho-physical space in which I try to bear witness to the inner life of material. That's where the real work happens.

IC: *Sky Mirror* (2006) was commissioned for the Rockefeller Plaza in New York, a most vibrant location. The mirror's ability to transmute was remarkable. In low light it seemingly dissolved into its surroundings; in bright light it had a dominant presence, reflecting an inverted impression of the Rockefeller skyscraper on its concave side and Fifth Avenue on its convex side. By placing an optical illusion at this site, did you want to create a hiatus in the city, particularly in relation to what you've said about the non-material?

AK: My first non-objects were pigment objects made of illusory matter, which were both physical and, at some level, uncertain about their physicality. About ten years later, the void objects were an emptying-out of form and the making of a container, normally dark and painted blue, black or deep red. Although they seemed to have a non-physical presence, I was still using colour as a quasi-physical entity. Then, in the early 1990s, I made some concave mirror objects to see if a mirrored surface could have the same non-object status. The void objects worked with the traditional sublime: the idea of a surface leading to deep space. The mirrored objects seemed to work with a different kind of sublime, or 'modern sublime': the mirror inclusive of the viewer, yet of a different kind of space. If the space of the void is beyond the picture plane, then the space of the concave mirror is in front, and I suggest this is a new kind of space.

Sky Mirror engaged the Manhattan skyline by turning 30 Rockefeller Plaza, an iconic New York building,

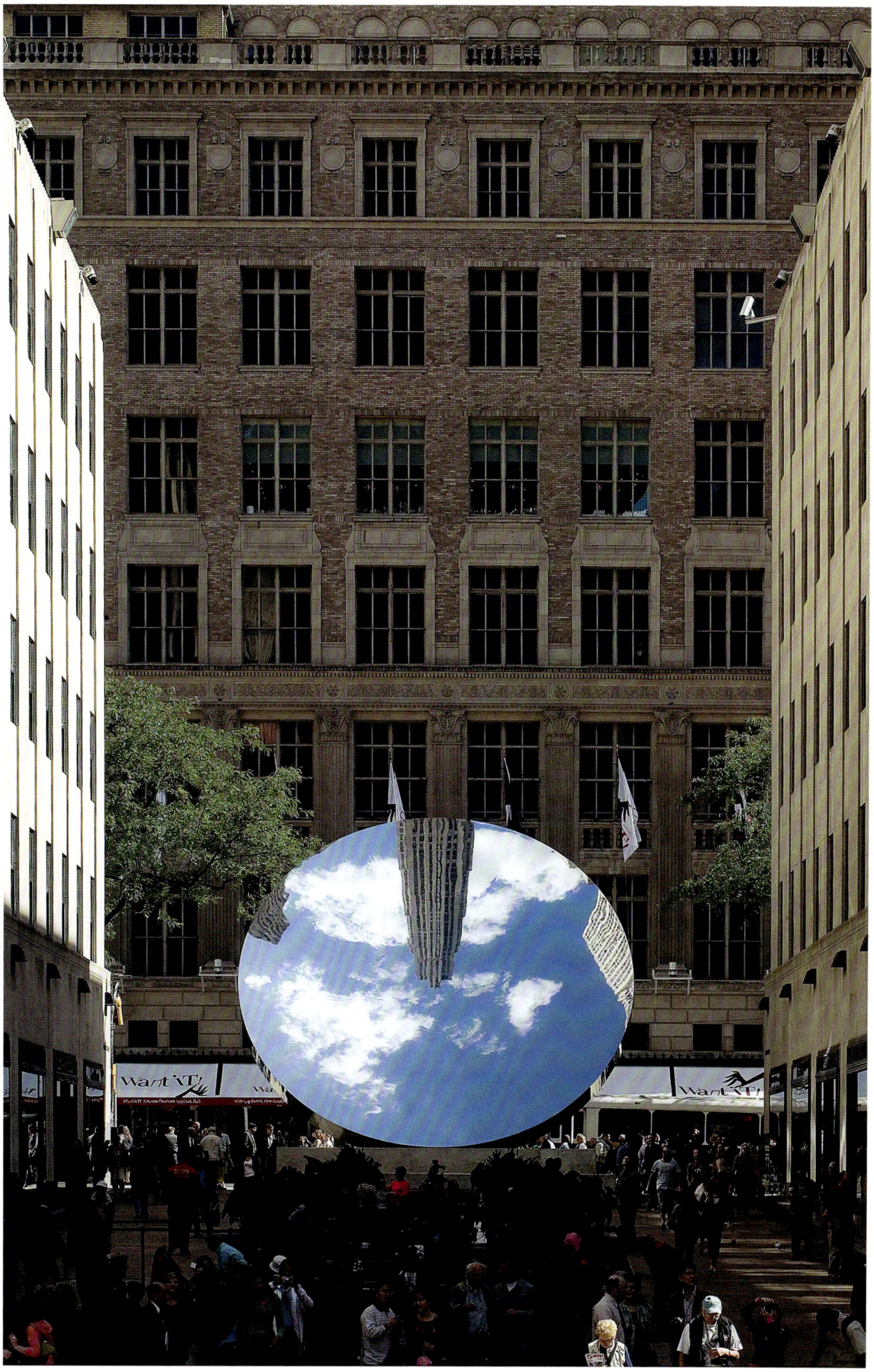

Anish Kapoor
Sky Mirror, 2006
Stainless steel
Diameter 10 m
(32 ft 9¾ in)
Installation view:
Fifth Avenue,
New York, 2006

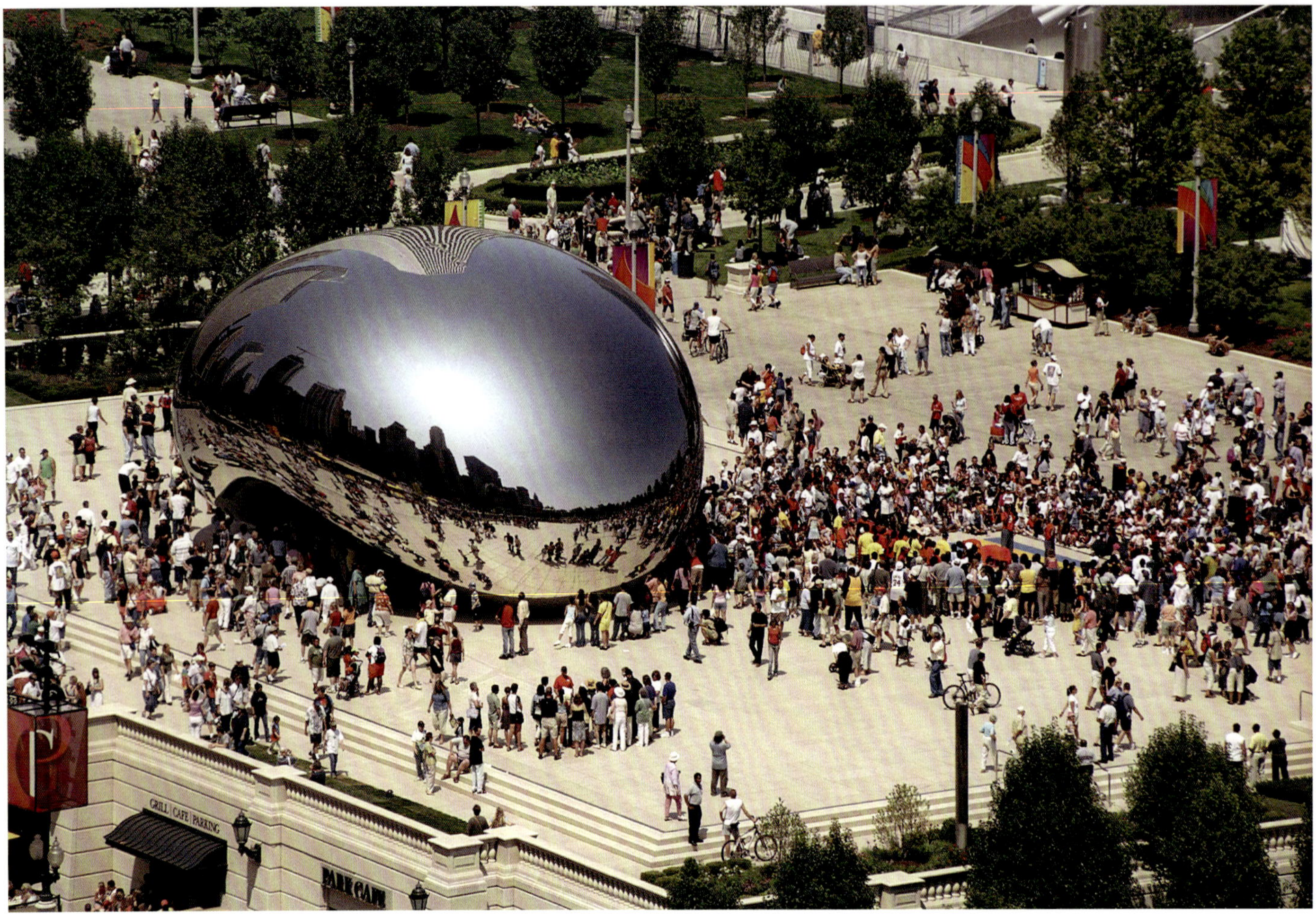

upside down. Spatially, *Sky Mirror* is rather confusing, in that it is concave and it's therefore hard to read where the surface lies. Then, of course, it's bringing the sky down to the ground. The sky is an ever-changing picture. Sometimes it's blue, or has clouds floating through it; at other times it's grey and rainy, much like an eighteenth-century landscape painting. So, the illusory intent of *Sky Mirror* is part of its non-material purpose.

IC: *Cloud Gate* (2004), like *Sky Mirror*, has a highly reflective surface and, because of this, appears as a living, breathing entity, capable of engulfing both viewer and surroundings. How would you describe the sculpture's relationship to its location in Chicago's Millennium Park?

AK: Firstly, *Cloud Gate* is beautifully made, staggeringly so. There's a kind of unreality in how it sits in the world. Because of its seamless wholeness, it's hard to understand its scale. When you're close it looks enormous, then as you step away the scale shifts, and this makes one's physical relationship to it uncertain. *Cloud Gate* is a quasi-architectural object you enter into. You go underneath and look up into the belly of it, which is an involuted closed form. Its enigma has to do with the way it sits on the ground and invites participation and yet, because of its indeterminate scale, eludes capture. It has a mysterious quality that holds the sky and the body in some strange relationship.

Similarly, *Marsyas* (2002), for Tate Modern's Turbine Hall, in London, was a big sculpture in a big space, but there was nowhere you could truly look at it. You were always in it, part of it, though not able to view it as an image. This resistance of view is an important feature of the illusive scale I look for. With *Marsyas*, I wanted to make the object bigger than the space of the Turbine Hall. I've always believed the philosophical context

←
Anish Kapoor
Cloud Gate, 2004
Stainless steel
10 × 20.1 × 12.8 m
(32 ft 9¾ in × 65 ft 11⅜ in × 41 ft 11⅞ in)
Millennium Park, Chicago

→
Anish Kapoor
White Sand, Red Millet, Many Flowers, 1982
Mixed media and pigment
Dimensions variable

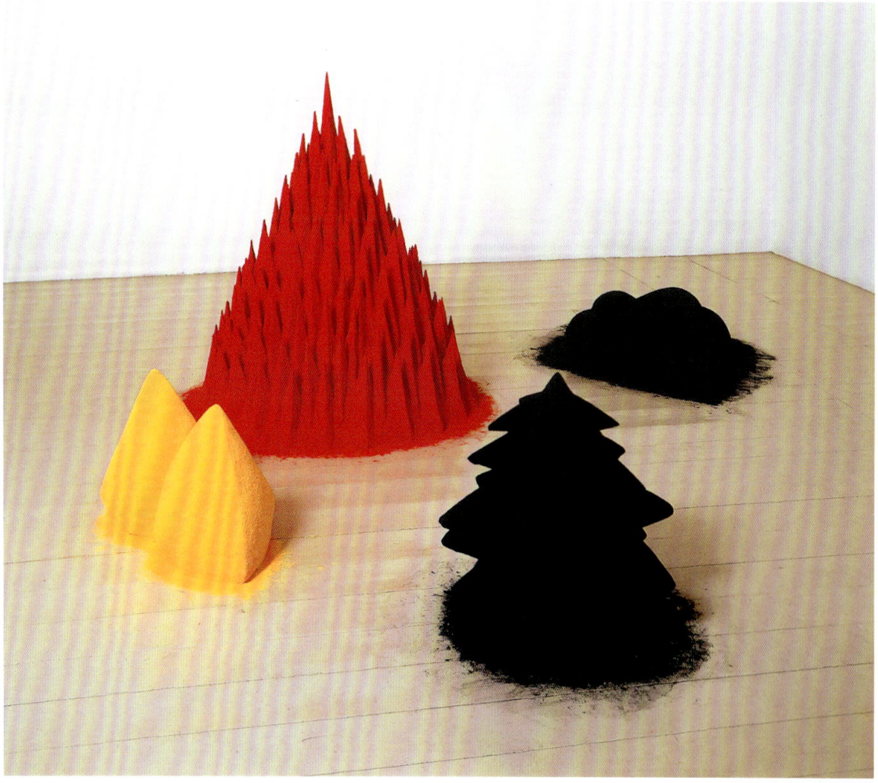

of a work is twofold: firstly, how it lives in the space and, secondly, how it addresses itself to the viewer. The manipulation of a place of viewing is as old as art itself, and I believe in it. It's not a casual encounter, it's particular and formal.

IC: Although the interaction between *Cloud Gate* and *Sky Mirror* with their respective locations was key, both gave the impression of having arrived at the scene of their own accord. There's a term you've used in relation to your practice – 'self-manifest'.

AK: Well, the proto-object – the first sculpture or original moment – was a preoccupation of early modernism and is part of my inheritance. *Past, Present, Future* (2006), for instance, is a big wall that slowly moves from left to right, then right to left, describing an object as it moves, and it's as if the object were being made by the process. The fiction of its forming is an idea about an original moment, a proto-moment – a fiction of the self-made object. Many of my works point to the beginning. One might say it's what ties Brancusi to Barnett Newman: Brancusi's sculptures of birds, eggs, the newborn and infant heads, and Newman's zip paintings, are all seen as proto-moments. This concept of the beginning is fundamental to abstract art.

IC: Your work elicits a sense of awe which is, in part, due to its sheer size. Yet awe can, conversely, also be felt when viewing a tiny object. It's not necessarily scale-dependent.

AK: Absolutely. The art world is very strange about scale, perhaps less so now than it was. The general view is that bigger isn't better. I understand; that's probably right. As Barnett Newman said many times, scale is a matter of content, not of size, which is key. However, scale is also one of the tools of sculpture, and we must not be

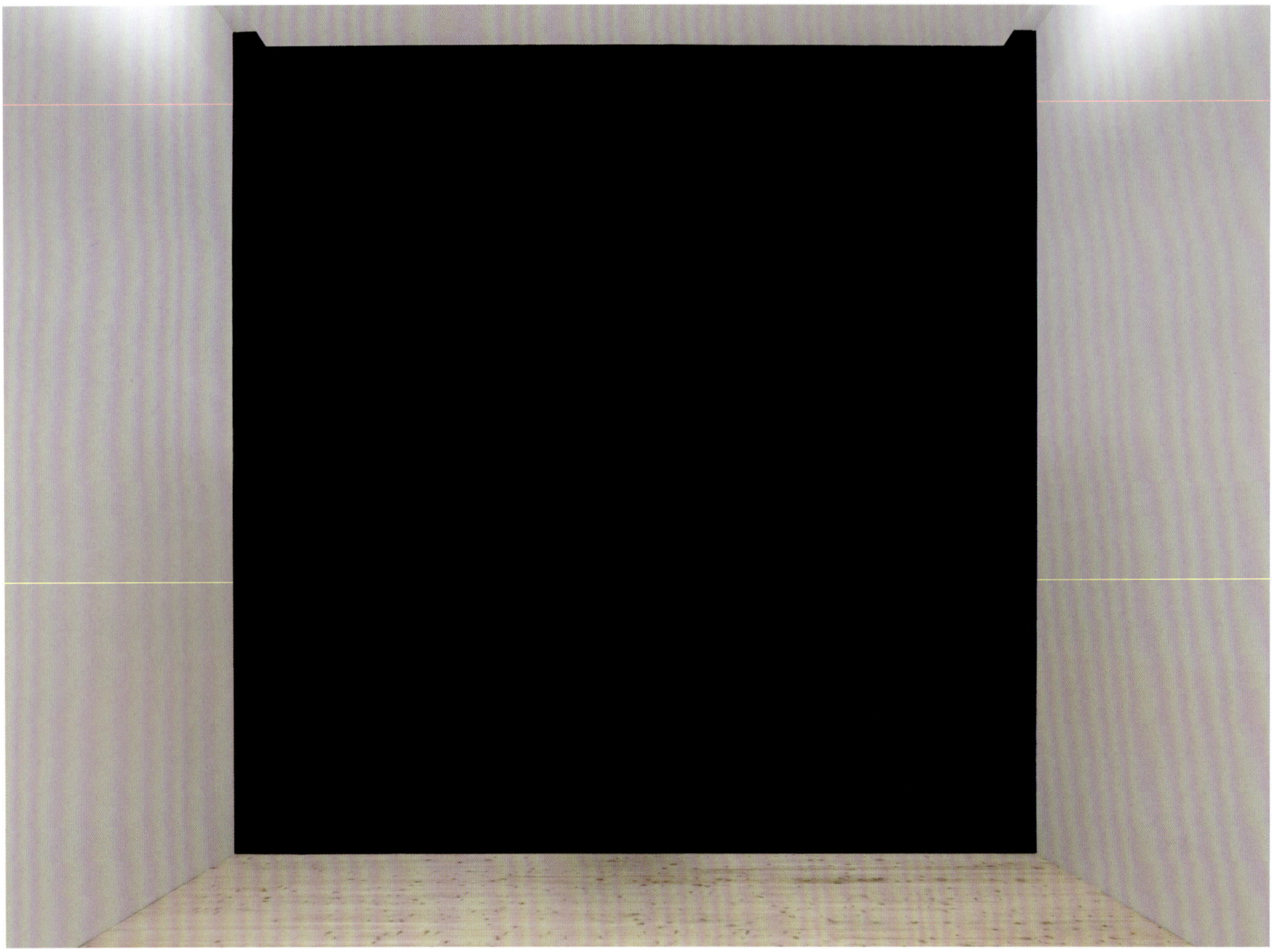

shy of it. I'm interested in making things that force the viewer into a situation where they enter the space, are confronted by something and their jaw drops. Scale, if it's right, can do this. When scale, meaning, size and place come together, scale is a truly poetic magical quantity.

IC: Earlier projects such as *Descent into Limbo* (1992) and *Building for a Void* (1992), as well as later work such as *Void Pavilion VI* (2018), also place the body in an inexplicable relationship to its location, but this time through your particular use of black. Yet there's an element of terror associated with a space full of darkness, or void.

AK: In the last few years I've been working with this super-black material, taking on a project with a certain finality. I've always used very dark blue, simply because blue is much harder to focus on, from a purely biological perspective. Black, generally speaking, is much more material; you can actually see black. But this material is the blackest material in the universe, absorbing 99.8 per cent of light. Our eyes are astonishingly efficient and even 0.2 per cent can be seen in certain conditions.

In Renaissance painting, the purpose was to give appearance to objects. What this material does is make things disappear; it's the opposite of painting, and towards the non-object. There were two great ideas in the Renaissance, perspective – which places the human being at the centre with all lines converging away into the distance – and the depiction of the fold, a fantastic late medieval invention. The fold in a piece of fabric is a sign of being, the body present. So, if the fold is 'being' then this super-black is beyond being, like Malevich's suprematist object made real.

Yves Klein jumping off the building with his hands outstretched [*Leap into the Void*, 1960] speaks of an aesthetic leap into the unknown. The truth is, however,

←
Anish Kapoor
Void Pavilion VI, 2018

Wood, concrete and pigment
600 × 600 × 1200 cm
(19 ft 8¼ in × 19 ft 8¼ in × 39 ft 4½ in)

→
Anish Kapoor
ArcelorMittal Orbit, 2012

Steel
Height: 115 m (377 ft 3½ in)
Queen Elizabeth Park,
Stratford, London

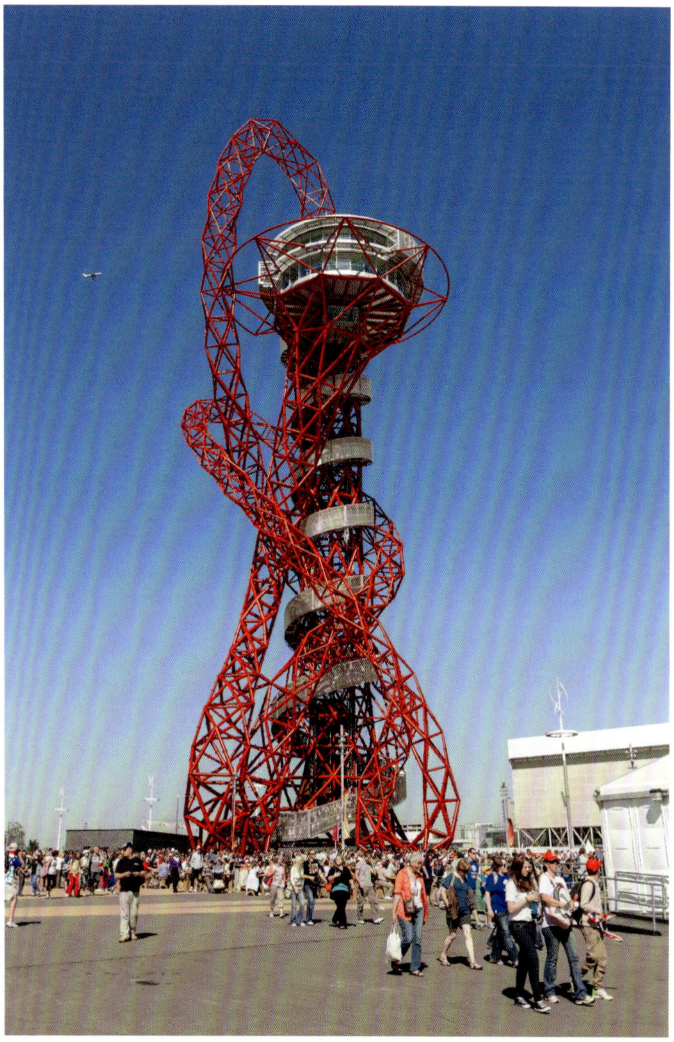

that the sublime, as we know from Kant, is full of fear. It is the end, the abyss. *Descent into Limbo* proposes a leap into the void. I hope it's beautiful and terrifying. Fear has to be part of the equation. I'm deeply interested in how black can bring terror, wonder and even awe.

IC: Many of your monumental projects intersect with architecture, which can present a challenge, in that they serve a functional purpose, but are essentially sculptures. *Orbit* (2012) for instance, a 115-metre high (377-foot) tower for Queen Elizabeth Park in London, has a sinewy awkwardness, as if it's attempting to resist its function.

AK: *Orbit* is an object with all its elbows sticking out. Awkwardness was very much part of the agenda. I worked with Cecil Balmond, the engineer, and we looked to find a structure that didn't have a classical A-frame or tripod configuration. There's a sense that the structure struggles to support itself, because of all its rounded snake-like forms. I hope its unwillingness to fit in will give it life. One can't tell. *Orbit* was made as an artwork and has now been turned into a so-called public attraction. I have to let the sculpture fight its own space.

IC: *Shooting into the Corner* (2009) addresses the complexity of the corner within architecture, but this time through truly performative means.

AK: *Shooting into the Corner* started its life at MAK (Museum of Applied Arts), Vienna. I'm a great fan of all those Viennese action artists and playfully wondered to myself, 'What these guys haven't done is something as crazy as putting a canon in the middle of a room and shooting at the corner.' The corner is an old obsession of sculpture and architecture. One might argue it's a deeply cultural proposition where three planes meet – where the space beyond is indicated but not

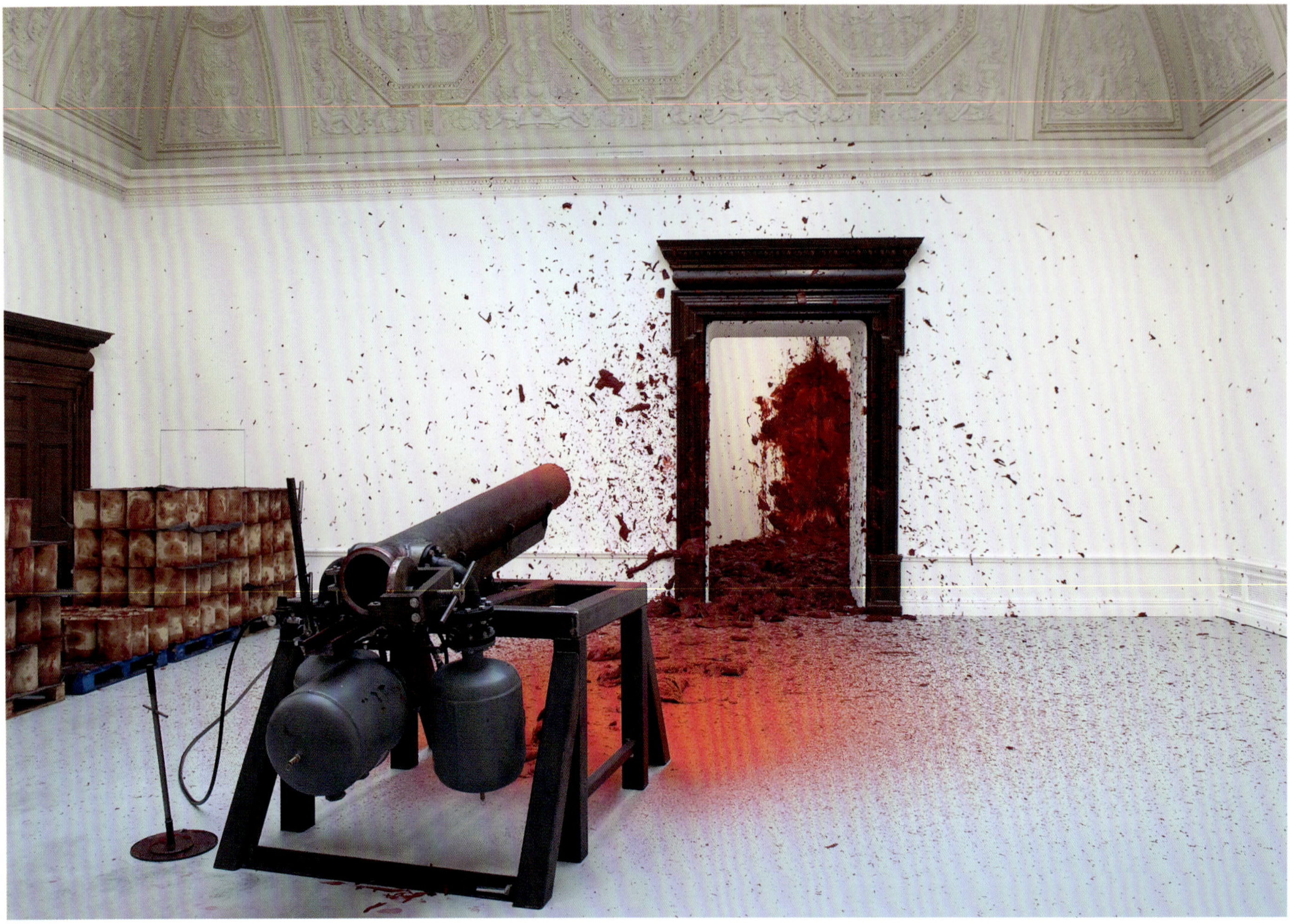

there. It's imaginary and has all kinds of metaphorical implications. And it's deeply human in the sense that the body just about fits into a corner. It's also a place of punishment, from school. Many other late modernist artists – Robert Morris, Joseph Beuys – worked with the corner.

I put a cannon into the room to shoot into the corner without really knowing what was going on. This is what we do as artists. I wanted it to be a performative action, so every 20 minutes the cannon fires wax pellets into the corner at about 50 miles an hour. Then I realized, 'This is action painting: Jackson Pollock; it's Goya and the massacre of the innocents; it's Duchamp and the male and female.' There's the accumulation of wax as the room fills up, the noise and the way the wax separates and becomes liquid then solid. All sorts of things are going on simultaneously, which gives it significance. I'm interested in that melodrama, of course. It's an operatic psychodrama.

IC: *Blood Relations* (2006), made three years earlier, utilizes red wax and bronze. It involved a collaboration with the author Salman Rushdie, who wrote a text specifically for the project. How did this partnership develop?

AK: Salman and I have been friends for many years, and often spoke of collaborating. He came to the studio at the time I was making a series of 'blood' paintings, rather rough and drippy. On seeing them he decided to write a text about blood and wrote about *One Thousand and One Nights*. The text had an overwhelming narrative, which presented a problem. At a formal level, what could I do with a text? Where would it go – on the wall, on the work or in the work? I decided to include it in the work and made boxes around which the words could wind themselves. The boxes are waist high, rather like Donald Judd boxes, and provide the forum for a kind of shrine, while reading the text forces

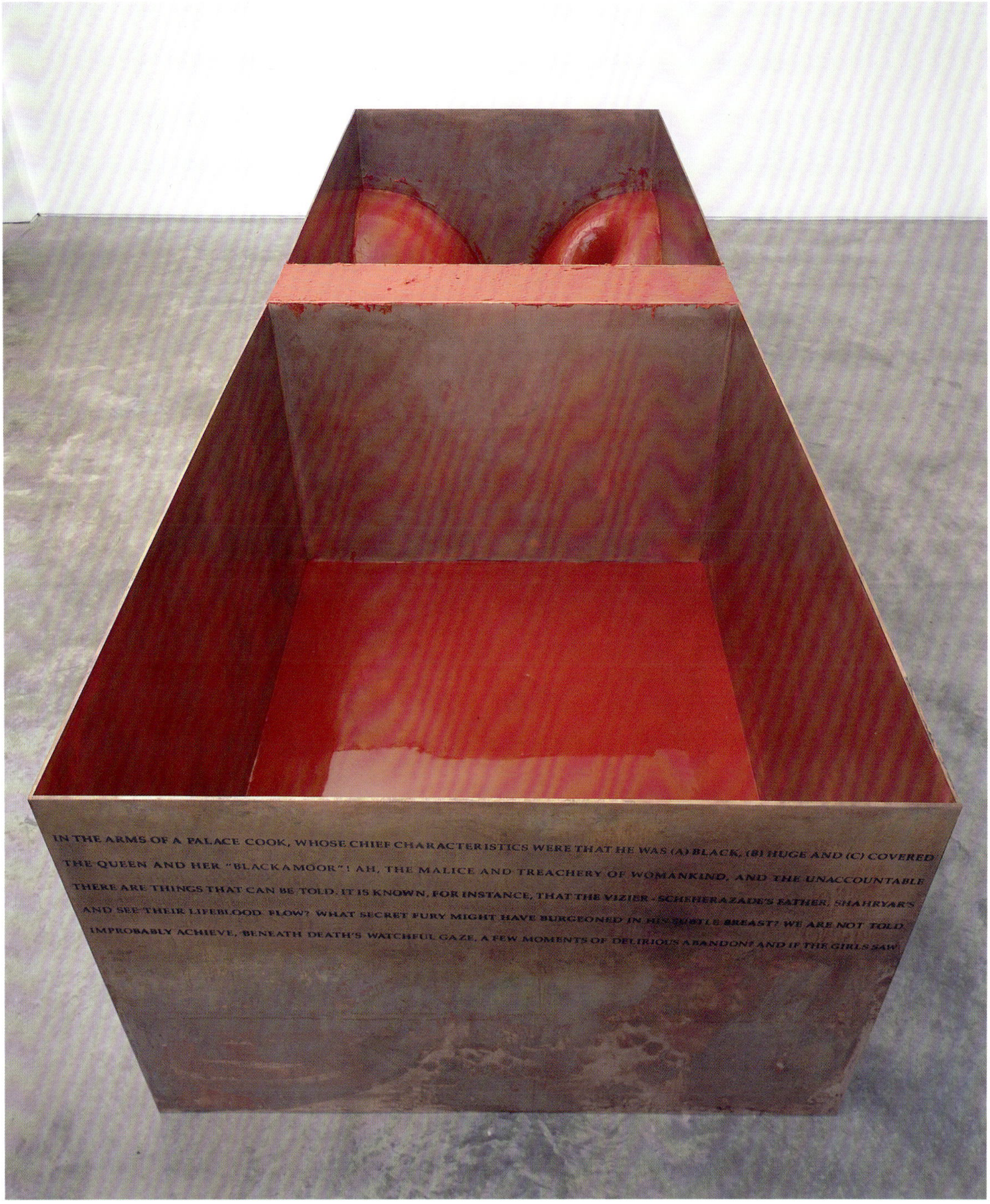

↖
Anish Kapoor
Shooting into the Corner, 2008–09

Mixed media
Dimensions variable
Installation view:
Royal Academy of Arts, London, 2009

↑
Anish Kapoor
Blood Relations, 2006

Bronze and wax
100 × 432 × 151 cm
(39⅜ in × 14 ft 2⅛ in × 59½ in)

→→
Anish Kapoor
Leviathan, 2011
(exterior and interior view)

PVC
33.6 × 99.89 × 72.23 m
(110 ft 2⅞ in × 327 ft 8⅝ in × 236 ft 11¾ in)
Installation view:
Grand Palais, Paris, 2011

one to walk around them. This circumambulation fitted well.

Although Salman and I are very different, we have one important passion in common: the idea that form can be condensed into a context, or a formal reality, which gives it mythic possibility. I've always been interested in the Greenbergian idea that there can be form without resorting to contamination from content; that somehow there is such a thing as abstract art. I'm not sure there is. It seems most configurations lead to meaning, and my notion of sculpture is that those meanings are manipulable, even if the form is carefully condensed.

IC: *Leviathan* (2011) was created for the Grand Palais in Paris (Monumenta, 2011), and dedicated to Ai Weiwei, who had been under house arrest in China. Its title alludes both to the mythological sea serpent, and to a book written by Thomas Hobbes in 1651, which discusses the structure of society and legitimate government. Yet the most notable feature of *Leviathan* is its colour – an all-consuming primordial red.

AK: *Leviathan* relates to Hobbes's book on the State and its place, and the whale-like gigantic beast engulfing all. The Grand Palais is a strong, strange building and I wanted to interfere with it rather than display an object. What I did was to inflate a PVC membrane, with three spherical forms joining up to a central nave. The public entered the object first through its interior, then out through a side door into the space between the object and the Grand Palais. It's an inside-out, outside-in question: the idea that the space we hold within us is not the space we describe ourselves by. What I have within me is bigger than my physical body. So, there's a sense that the object is bigger inside. It relates fundamentally to darkness, to interiority.

Black and blue aside, red is the central colour. It is interior, dark and messy, bloody and of the earth; it is emotive in ways neither blue nor black can be. We live on the ground, die on the ground and go back to the ground. Red returns us to that primal, horizontal space. It's full of power, and that's what I'm after. This is essential matter and, as artists, we can speculate about the great themes of the universe. Science claims to do it better, but science can't do consciousness. As artists we can speculate about consciousness. I'm a Barnett Newman fan, and it's not surprising his works are called *In the Beginning* or *Day One*. The beginning: consciousness?

IC: The metaphysical connotations in your work often suggest a considered approach to some 'other' world, yet the message remains essentially elusive.

AK: If you're asking me if I have something to say, the answer is no. If you're asking whether the work proposes a kind of utopia, I don't believe it does. However, if you're asking whether it proposes an infinite luminescence, darkness, mystery and other such Romantic notions, then the answer would be yes. These propositions are not there just for Romantic purposes. The tradition of the sublime is a tradition I understand to be among the highest ideals of art, and they're to be fought for. This poetic 'nonsense' is a nonsense that's worth the struggle. People often refer to my work as spiritual, and if spiritual means the recognition of a state of being, then I'd say yes, it is spiritual. The reason the void sculptures succeed is because darkness is a condition we recognize as an interior condition. It's not just what happens when the lights go out.

IC: You once said the idea of art born out of pain is a myth, that the best art is born out of joy. Do you still believe this?

AK: At one level I do believe that the human condition is that we're here for a few moments and then we die, and those around us die, and our attachment to them can only be expressed in terrible pain. So, ours is a condition of pain. But it also has to be true that one's creative forces must flow better when they're freed from that pain. While there is some really great art made out of pain, I think there's some even greater art made out of a celebration of being.

Interviewed in 2006 and 2020

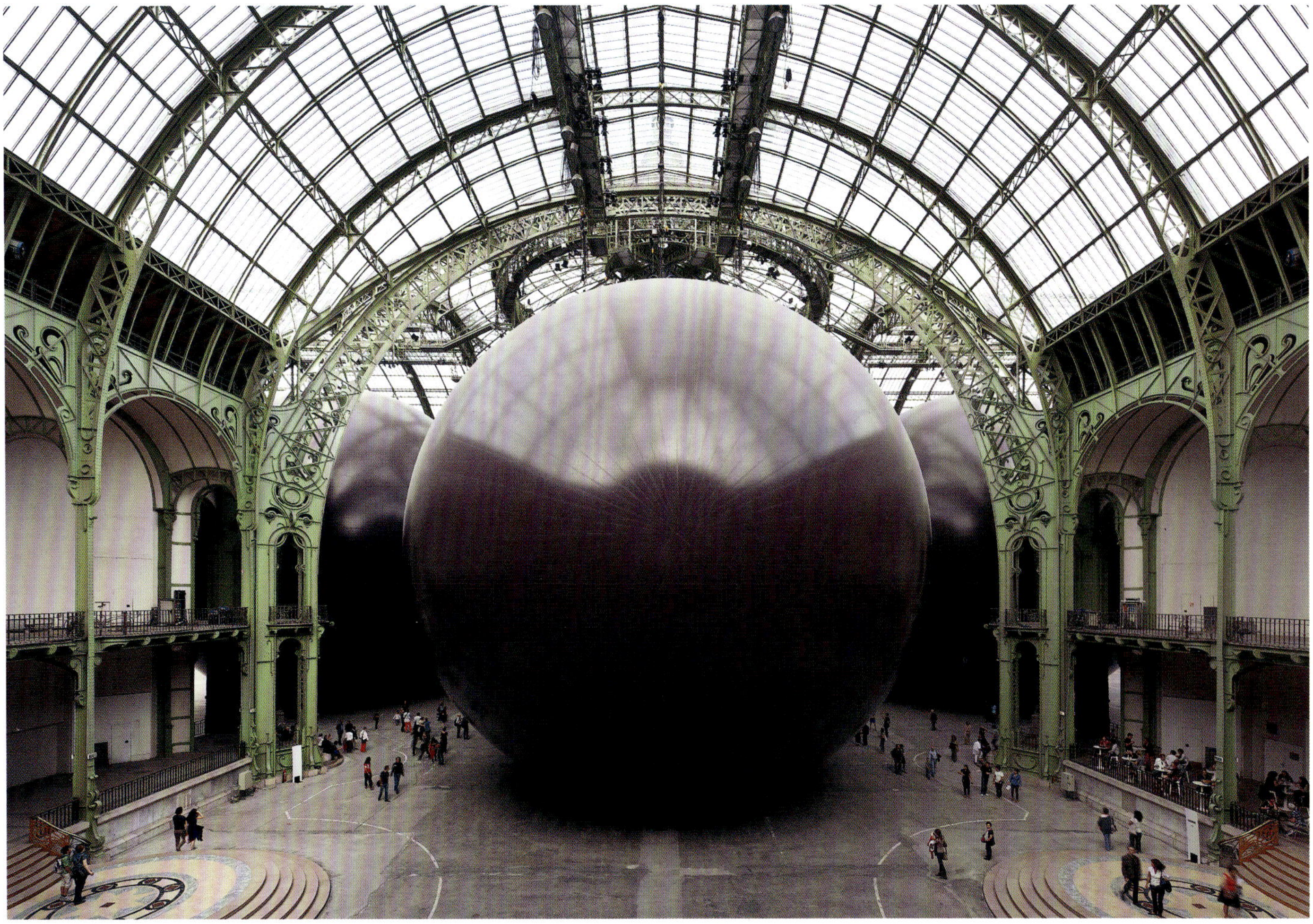

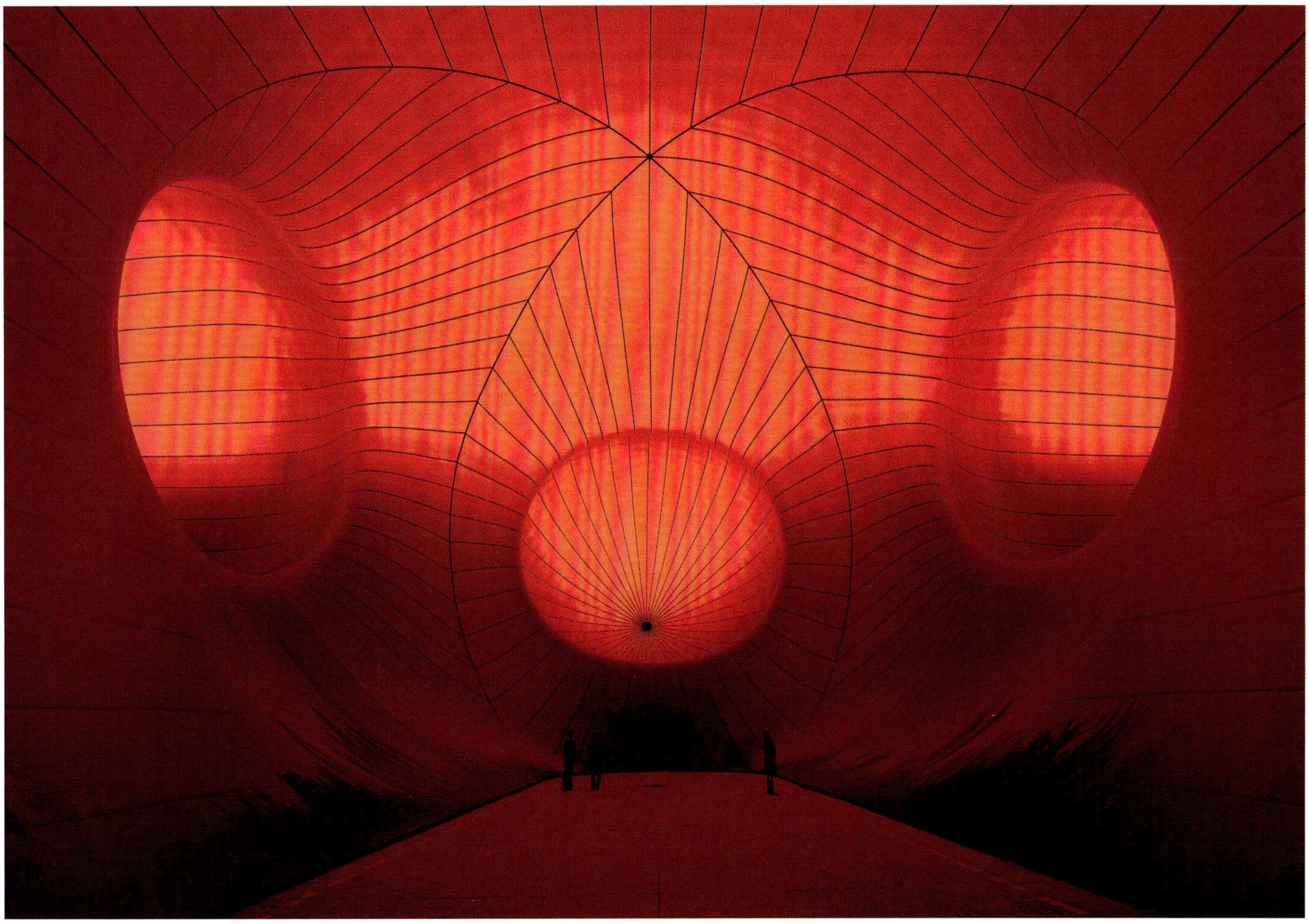

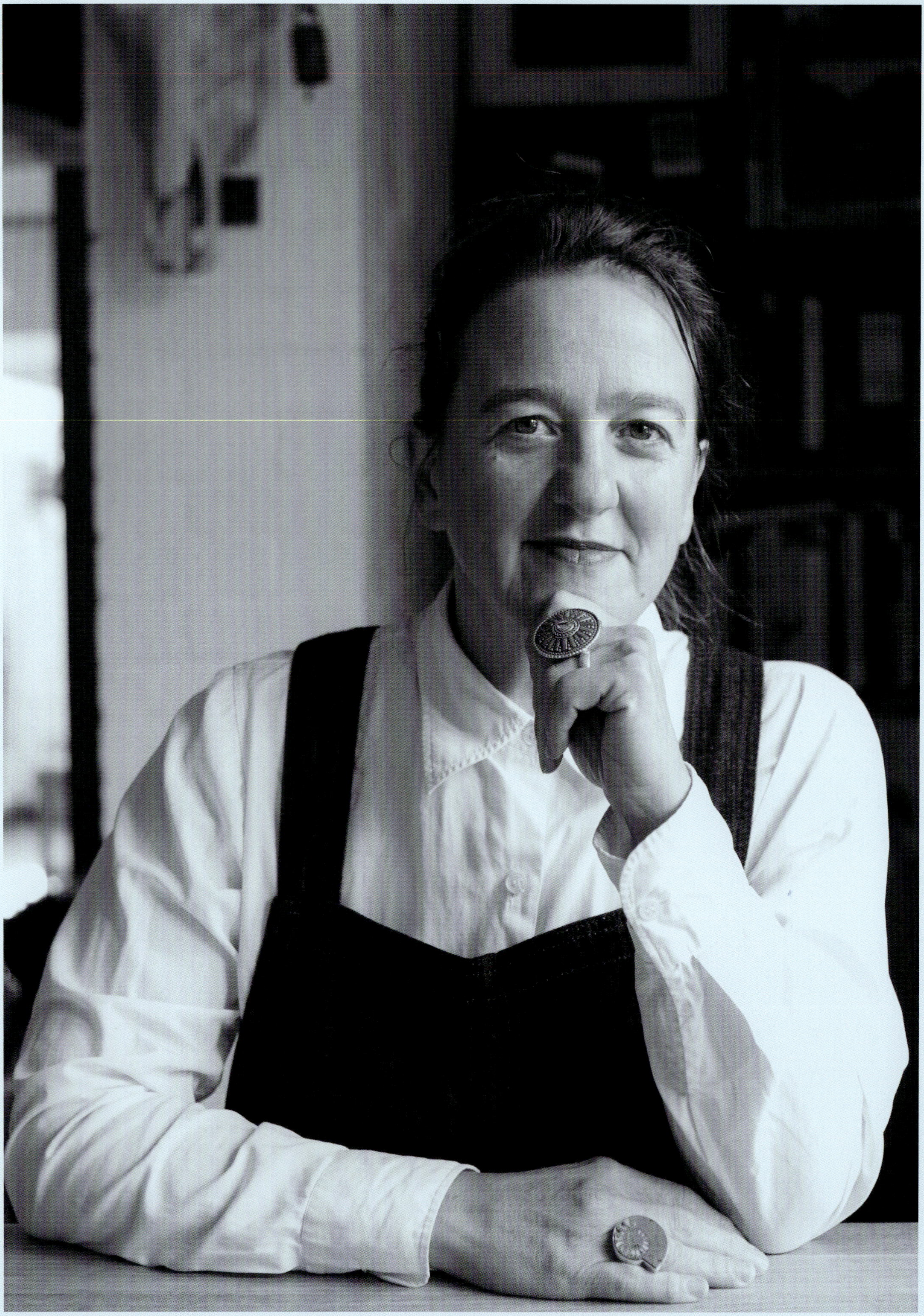

TANIA KOVATS

Born 1966, Brighton, Sussex

Tania Kovats' practice offers an investigation into the layered experience of landscape: that which lies beneath and beyond what is perceived with the naked eye. These unknown spaces – shifting tides, weathered rock faces, wood grain and the uncharted territories of the ocean – are mysteries to be unravelled. Projects such as *Meadow*, a travelling artwork; *Tree*, made for the ceiling of the Natural History Museum in London; and *Dirty Water*, resulting from an artist's residency on the River Thames, epitomize her concerns. Interconnectivity is key to Kovats' practice; every action, however minuscule, sends a ripple that expands beyond its core to connect to all that surrounds it. Our relationship to the planet forms the basis for much of her work: as a fragile yet resilient entity in constant flux, it provides infinite scope as a subject. This allows Kovats to bear witness, reflect and communicate her findings through permanent and transitory installations, which point towards a profound physical and psychological union with the land.

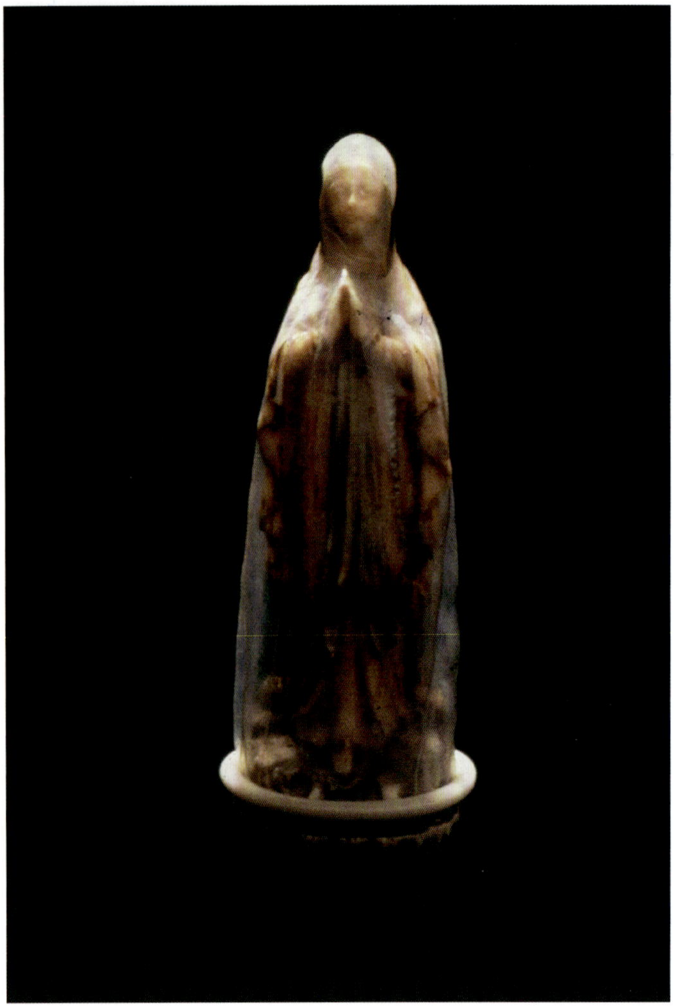

Tania Kovats
Virgin in a Condom, 1992
Resin and latex condom, Virgin Mary statue
10.5 × 4 × 3 cm
(4⅛ × 1⅝ × 1⅛ in)

Ina Cole: An early piece, *Virgin in a Condom* (1992), garnered public attention at a time the so-called YBAs (Young British Artists) entered British consciousness. Their work often generated a sense of outrage, as was also attested to here, but your ideas quickly progressed into intensively researched and more reflective projects, drawing inspiration from the landscape.

Tania Kovats: For me, *Virgin in a Condom* was reflective. At a formative point in my career it made me realize the sort of artist I did, and didn't, want to be. The YBA phenomenon had incredible momentum, providing a steady supply of copy for the press, but I didn't enjoy the attention the piece generated. I had my own reasons for making it, but it got caught up in a tornado of controversy I had very little to do with. *Virgin* was part of 'Pictura Britannica' (1997–8), a British Council touring show, and it created a storm when exhibited in New Zealand. The curator received death threats and the work was stolen and had to be replaced. Mass hysteria broke out with prayer meetings in the gallery and protests outside. In retrospect, I can understand why this happened. In New Zealand Maori culture is hugely respected, and Maori artefacts are revered as highly prized museum objects. The somewhat disenfranchised Catholic community couldn't understand why one of their icons, the Virgin Mary, wasn't given the same respect in the same museum. So, *Virgin* became a catalyst for these concerns and absorbed some of that tension.

I was then quite young and my response was to withdraw and say little publicly. *Virgin* really came from the fact that I was conditioned by Catholicism when growing up and held strong feelings of resentment towards patriarchal structures that influenced how a woman felt about her sexuality and fertility. The condom was seen as protection which, as a Catholic, you were denied. *Virgin* was also a sculptural coincidence; a simple case of 'that fits over this'. Yet, when I first put a condom over the little statue I wasn't sure if I'd protected or suffocated her, which was an interesting dilemma in itself.

IC: Following *Virgin,* you created a number of landscape-inspired sculptures resembling extracted sections of the earth reinterpreted as craggy, standalone pieces.

TK: My first landscape work was *Grotto* (1995). In classical mythology, grottos are gateways to another world, and Virgin Mary grottos are located in places closest to heaven. So, I worked with the place rather than with her. She wasn't present, only her smell was, as I used rose oil to generate a perfumed cloud around *Grotto*. At this point, I made my first trips into remote and challenging terrain. Visiting the Grand Canyon and Israel to see exposed vistas, with deep layers of time written into them, was incredibly powerful. The beaches of the Salton Sea in California and Dead Sea in Israel are just above being a crust of salt. I've also been to a number of salt flats in Bolivia and Argentina. Seas come and go, and it's fascinating to recognize how land changes over millennia, whether through vast canyons, coastal erosion or glacial processes.

For me, landscape isn't actually a place, but a process, and how it evolves became a central sculptural question to play out in the studio. I shared my thinking with geologists in order to better understand geological systems and mapping. In geology, you're mapping time as well as location and that was an interesting visual language to explore.

IC: Your father was born in Transylvania, a place you've described as a pre-industrialized agricultural landscape. It has a complex history and was part of the Austro-Hungarian Empire prior to being claimed by Romania. Your mother spent her childhood in rural Somerset, South West England. You were born in Brighton, but did your parents' early experience, and their relationship to the land, foster your deep understanding of the natural environment?

TK: Both my parents had a rural idyll they felt had been taken from them during childhood. My dad left Hungary at age 19, at the outbreak of World War II when his family decided that he should be sent away rather than be conscripted. My mum's childhood was nomadic because the family didn't stay anywhere for long. So, when my parents met, it was as if they'd come home. I once visited Transylvania while on an artist's residency in Hungary and can only describe it as a psychic shock. I kept seeing things that felt completely familiar, and was very confused by these experiences. I called my dad and said, 'I really love Transylvania,' and he replied, 'You do know I was born there? It's where I spent my early years.' He'd never told me this before, which, in part, explained why I'd had such a visceral relationship to it. I woke at dawn to see people cutting meadows by hand with scythes, then loading up donkeys and carts. It was as if I'd time-travelled and ended up in a Van Gogh painting. It's essentially peasant living, yet people didn't seem unhappy. I don't want to romanticize poverty, but how you live on the planet and within communities is incredibly important.

Tania Kovats
Meadow, 2006
Meadow grown on trays, butty boat
12 m (39 ft 4½ in) long

IC: Does your affinity with the nomadic way of life, and the notion of flux, feed through into works such as *Meadow* (2006) – a seminal piece inspired by Transylvania, which broke the boundaries between liquid and solid, and travelled via England's canal network?

TK: Definitely. *Meadow* was a breakthrough moment and came directly from my experience of Transylvania. In my mind, it belongs to my father. I've always been interested in peeling back the top layer of a landscape, to reveal its geology, but *Meadow* was grown in trays so it could be moved, and I worked with the top layer. It was a travelling artwork that moved via the inland-waterway system from the South West of England to London. The cuts canals make are exquisite and sculptural and, when managing the flow through a lock system, you're effectively sculpting the water. *Meadow*'s central question was, 'When you move through a landscape does it move through you?' I see myself as nomadic: I'm not from anywhere necessarily and it's important for me to feel mobile.

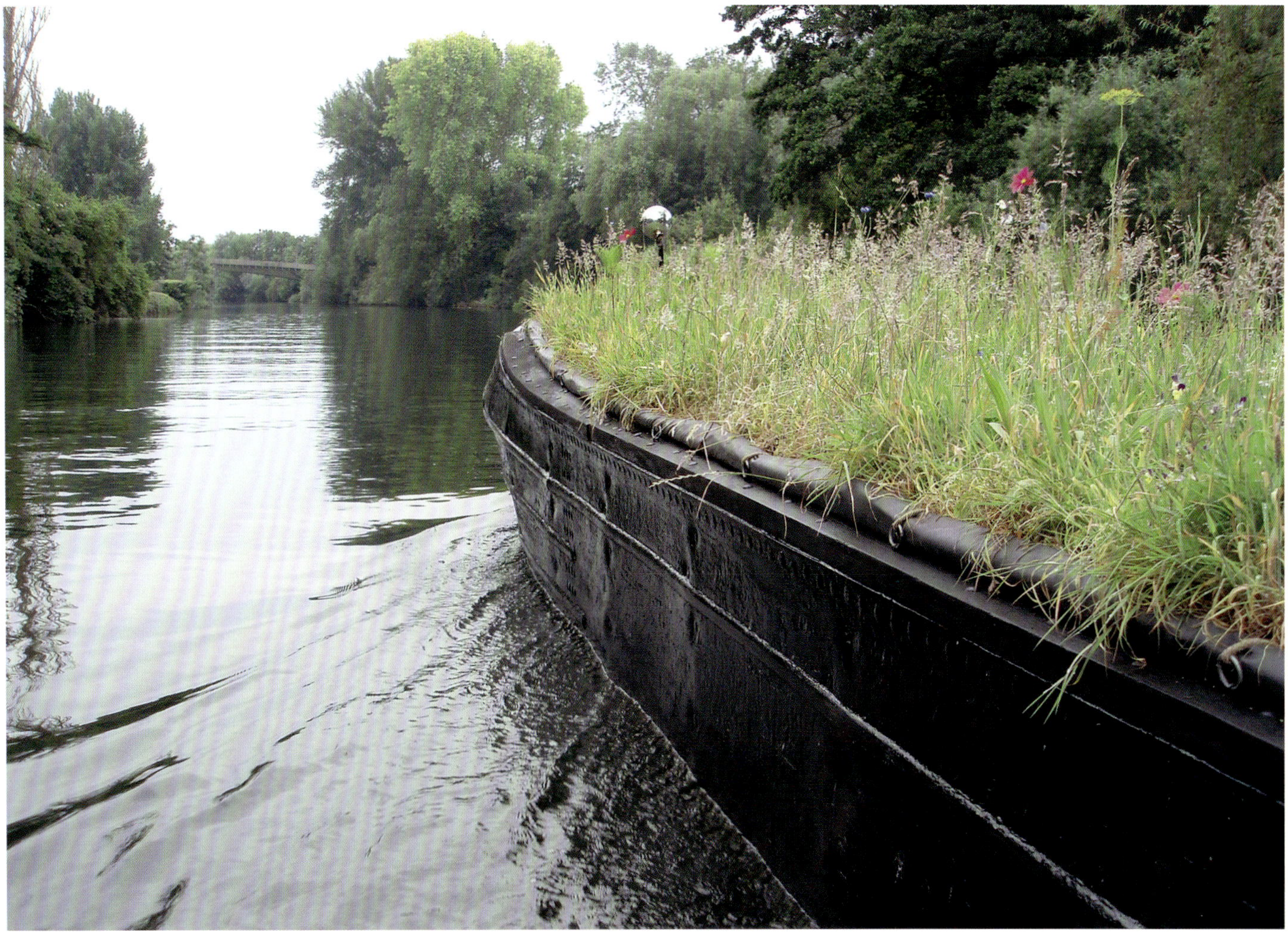

Meadow travelled on a 12 metre/40 foot-long butty boat, towed by a tugboat. It was an epic journey, even at four miles an hour. As I journeyed with it, that polite triangle between artwork, artist and audience collapsed. I encountered a towpath audience and this dissolved the sanctity of the white cube. The butty was beautifully contained by the canals but looked very small when we reached the Thames. When I came off at Brent I felt gutted, as I just wanted to continue out to sea. In some ways, *Tide* (2015) and *Dirty Water* (2017) completed the yearning *Meadow* left me with.

IC: *Tide* was created on the 2015 autumn equinox, when you cast a 12-kilogram/26½ pound bell on Porthcurno Beach in Cornwall for a Trust New Art commission, 'One and All'. What did the process involve and why did you choose this location?

TK: For 'One and All' I worked with an itinerant foundry on a beach close to Land's End, using an ancient tradition of casting. I had a wax bell and two furnaces: one melting an ingot of bronze and the other bringing the mould for the bell up to temperature. When the correct temperature was reached, the fires were turned off and the molten liquid was poured into the mould. It was bright orange, liquid light, like a bit of sun had fallen down. I've never stared into such light. The cast bell took a long while to cool, so it was taken out of the mould the next morning and baptized in the sea, which is traditional.

Tide was commissioned by the National Trust to celebrate 50 years of Project Neptune – their custodianship of the coast. My approach was driven by the unique tidal edge we have in the UK. A bulge of water comes in off the Atlantic twice a day, splits at Land's End, wraps itself around the UK, then joins the River Thames at the point it discharges into the sea.

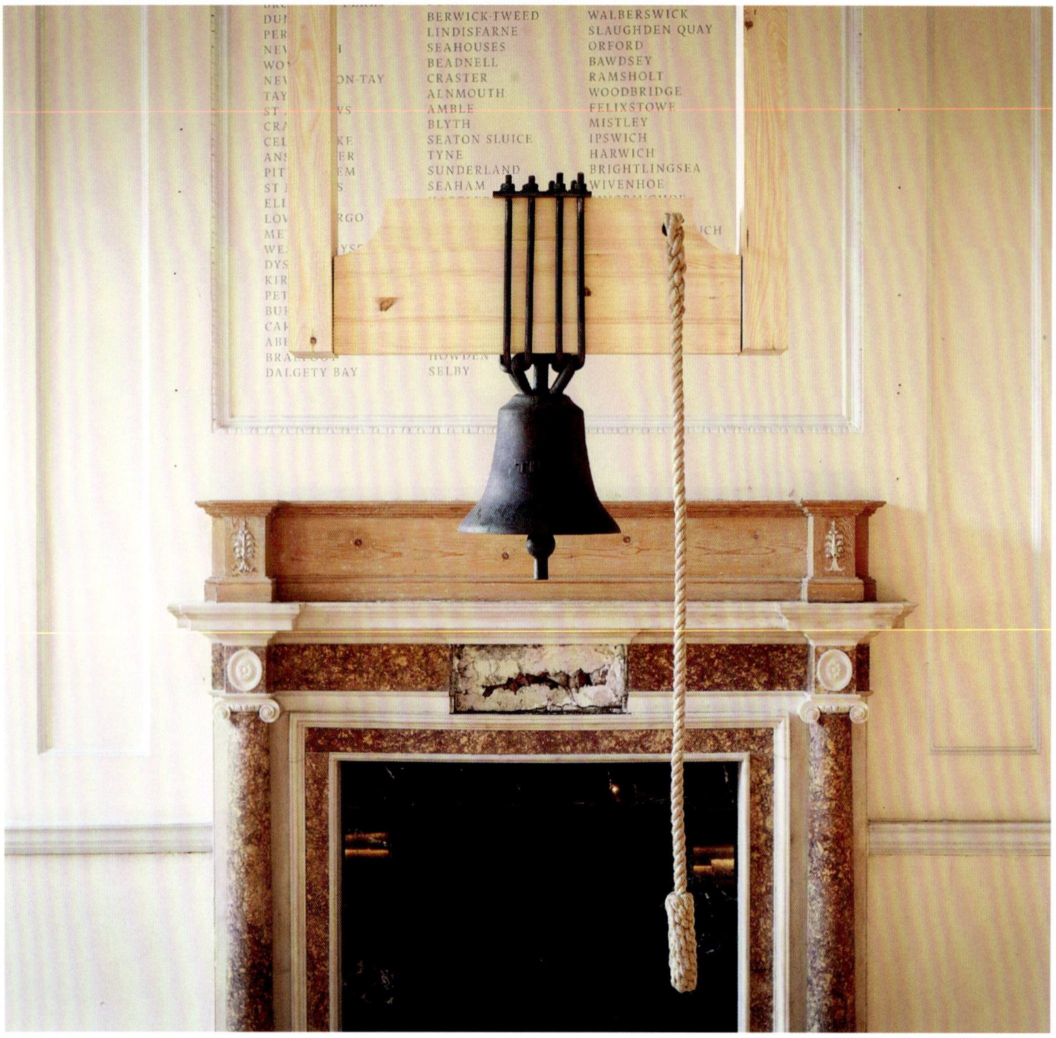

Tania Kovats
Tide, 2015
Bronze, wood, rope
Dimensions variable
Installation view:
One and All,
Somerset House,
London, 2015

That's why I wanted to cast the bell close to Land's End. It was shown in 'One and All' at Somerset House in London (2015) and, at the moment of high tide on the Thames, a member of the public rang the bell. We have all these alarms, notifications and signals, but I wanted to mark time as tide time and point to a slower rhythm.

IC: You then became artist-in-residence on the River Thames (2016–17) in a project sponsored by Tideway, a company responsible for London's super sewer. This resulted in the limited-edition artwork *Dirty Water*, which incorporates drawings and text with the Thames acting as a wise and aged story-teller. Why was it important for the river to become a conscious entity in this way?

TK: If we were less ego-driven, the natural world could have more of a voice. By giving the Thames a voice, it changes our relationship with it. So, I appointed the river as editor of *Dirty Water*, in which she remembers high- and low-tide moments. Some memories are celebratory, others tragic; sometimes she's deeply ashamed of the river's dirtiness. I don't make a distinction between the urban and non-urban, as I think of the city as a living organism, full of interruptions and connections, much like the density of a hedgerow. It's just that I'm looking at its guts and flush, which isn't very glamorous but crucial for its health. The city excretes a lot, and what we do with our waste is an environmental and ecological question across all our activities. Also, the Thames is part of the dynamic nature of the city. It's where money originally came from. The financial industry is built on shipping and insurance, and this is tied up with the river, docks and trade.

While participating in the 'Drawing Ecologies' project in New Zealand (2019), I came across a river extremely important to Maori rights. Activists have campaigned for many years, using the slogan, 'I am the river and the river is me.' The river has now been attributed the same rights as a human because, in their eyes, it's an ancestor, and how can you own, extract or pollute an ancestor? I'm not naïve, as some of their practices are just as extractive and polluting as anyone else's. But there is this particular rhetoric, or belief system, which is sensitized to an embodied relationship to the land, and I'm keen to find ways of communicating that through my own practice.

IC: When you created *Bleached* (2017) for Hull City of Culture, a devastating coral-bleaching event had occurred, affecting over 90 per cent of the Great Barrier Reef. How did the event impact on the development of this work?

TK: *Bleached* was made with scientists and researchers from The Deep aquarium in Hull. The constructed habitats, presented within vitrines in the aquarium, interested me sculpturally. So, plaster casts were created from coral salvaged from The Deep, which made *Bleached* look like whitened memorials resembling those horrific ghost reefs. This exploited the corals' sculptural worth, as they're enticing but, on pressing your nose against the glass, you suddenly realize, 'Where's the colour?' When sea temperature rises, corals expel the zooxanthellea algae that give them colour. As environments, the reefs are under huge stress, and some of the causes of bleaching aren't going way. It's an environmental crisis in that a whole ecosystem is failing. It's also a human crisis, because the reefs provide shelter from storm surges, as well as protecting the land and providing protein for people who are fishing. Land will now become less habitable due to the ingress of sea water and lack of food sources. Art has to keep this in the conversation in a way that's different from data and statistics.

IC: An earlier sculpture, *Tree* (2009), also underwent a process during which it became a spectre of its former self. It's a lengthwise cross-section of a 200-year-old oak, inserted into the ceiling of the Natural History Museum in London to celebrate the 200th anniversary of Darwin's birth.

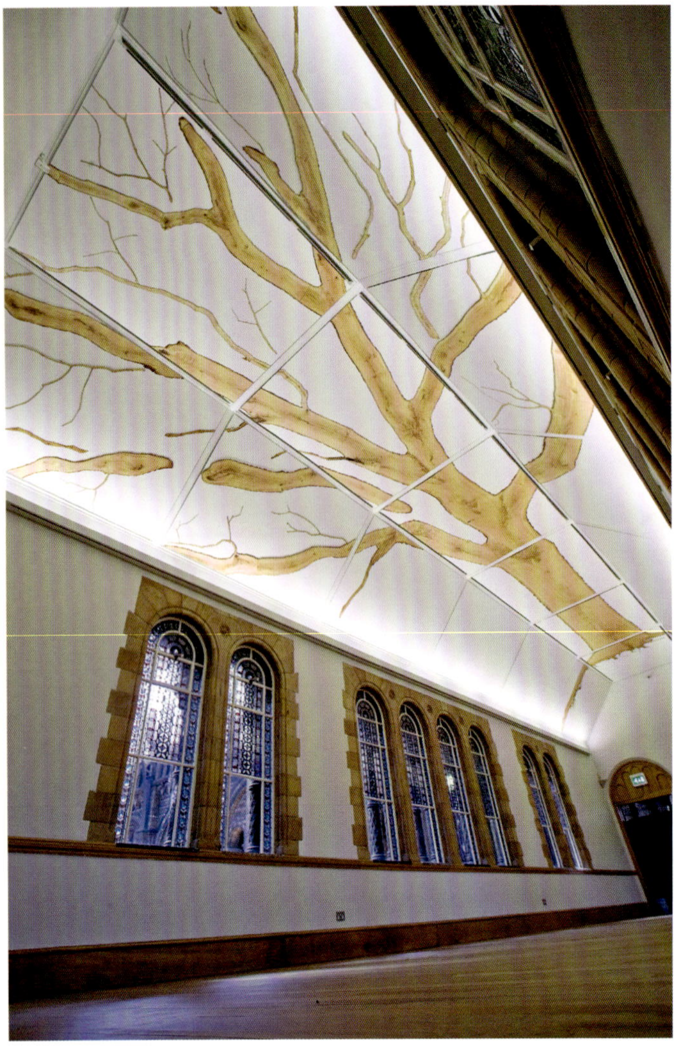

←
Tania Kovats
Tree, 2009
Wood
17 m (55 ft 9¼ in) long
Installation view:
Natural History Museum,
London, 2009

→
Tania Kovats
Colony, 2012
Mixed media
160 × 190 × 180 cm
(63 × 74¾ × 70⅞ in)

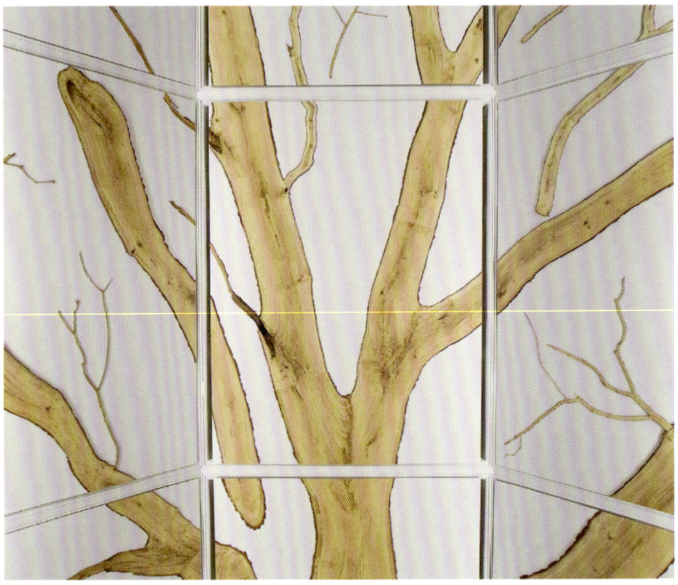

TK: *Tree* was complex, given I only wanted a slice of 4 millimetres (about ⅛ inch) through its roots, trunk and branches, but I worked with a great team of woodsmen. Forestry people think in long timelines, as do geologists; tree knowledge is, therefore, old knowledge that gets passed down. The oak was cut up and the timber numbered and tracked in a drawing. It was then 50 millimetres (2 inches) thick, and wood takes an age to dry and season, so the drying process had to be accelerated. The wood was then put onto panels and skimmed to the required thinness with a big-bed router. *Tree* was a heavily documented puzzle and yet we could always follow the line of the wood grain from the root, through the trunk and out through a branch. Our thoughts are arboreal, in that we identify with trees and think of families as trees. So, we were meticulous in sourcing the tree from sustainably managed woodland, and 200 saplings were planted as a response to taking this one oak.

Tree also references Darwin's notebook, in which he first visualized his theory of evolution. At the top of the page he'd written, 'I think', but, instead of continuing in words, he drew a branching form, based on a tree. Drawing is the most direct way of visual communication, and this is a beautiful spindly drawing mapping out one of his biggest ideas.

IC: Shortly after *Tree*, you undertook the Gulbenkian Foundation's Galapagos Artists' Residency Programme (2010) to collaborate with the local scientific community. This was a fruitful period in terms of generating new work, such as *Colony* (2012), a clustered piece inspired by barnacle formations.

TK: *Colony* came about through my interest in Darwin, who had collected and studied barnacles for 12 years. He procrastinated before publishing *On the Origin of Species* because he knew it would pose a threat to

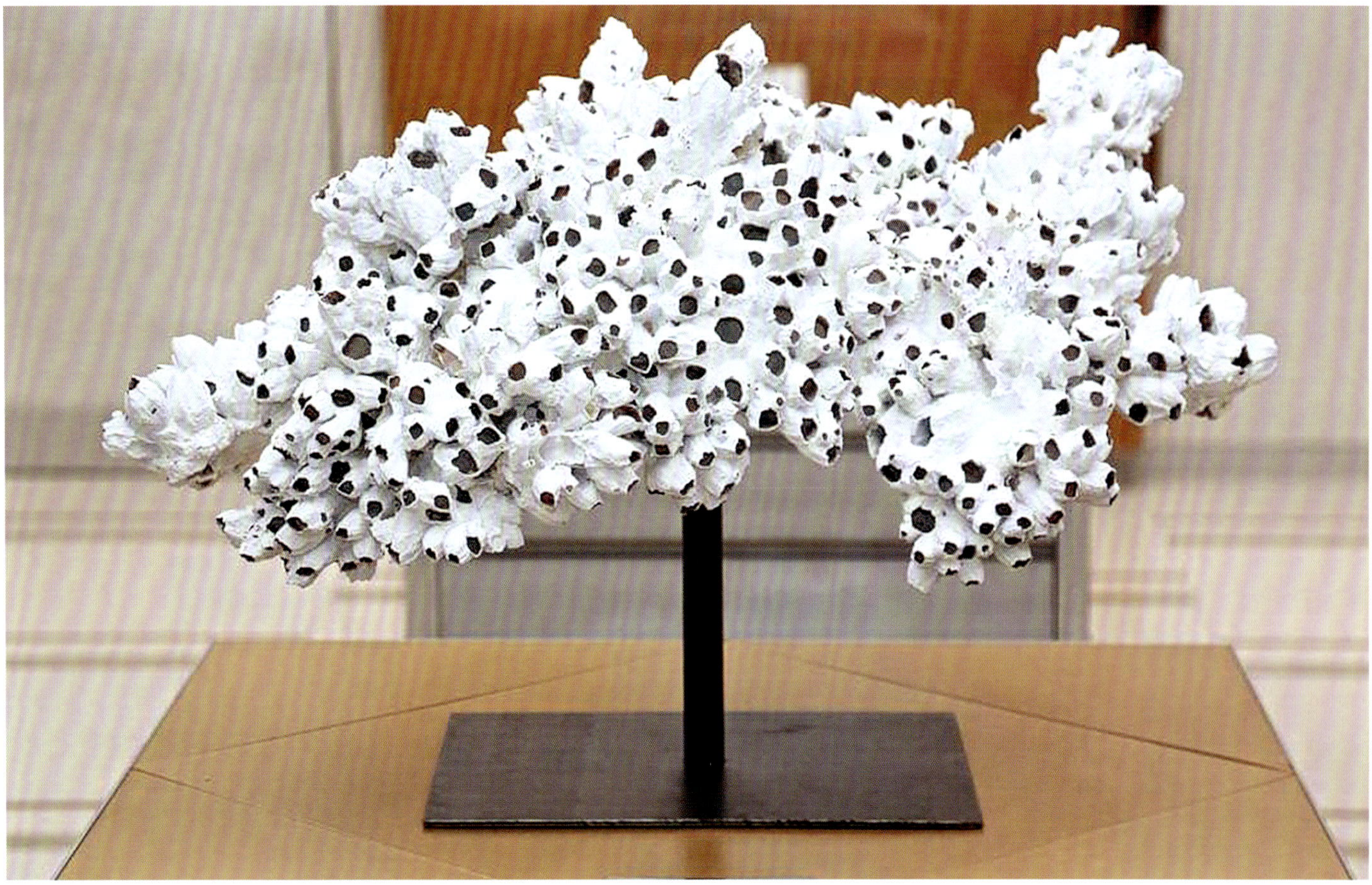

the orthodox view, and therefore wanted to prove his reputation as a scientist before introducing his theory of evolution. Poor health meant he couldn't leave home to study barnacles – people just sent them to him from all over the globe. Barnacles grow in clusters and are hermaphrodites. They belong to the liminal shoreline: part-animal and part-geological.

Seeing the effects of an exploding population on the main port of the Galapagos had a big effect on me. People from mainland Ecuador had come from the coast, jungle, mountains and city to relocate for a better standard of life, but resources were limited. There was a massive imperative from the scientific community to conserve, but the prohibitions had created a lot of tension amongst island residents. Observing this colony was fascinating; it was as if the world's problems were being acted out in miniature.

IC: In *All the Seas* (2012–14), you collected seawater from across the planet, assisted by a network of contributors, which was then decanted into glass vessels and installed on shelving. Water has history; it travels, bringing with it echoes of the past and intimating the future. It's a fusion of all time, metaphorically speaking. Is this work a portrait of the ocean – a way of capturing an unwieldy entity in order to fully understand it?

TK: *All the Seas* came from an impulse to gather the world's seas into one place. In *Rivers* (2012) – a little-sister work to *All the Seas* – I'd previously collected water from 100 different rivers in the UK on a similar impulse. The experience of watching flowing water, for me, is an image of time. We've talked about deep geological time and tree time, and watching water pass is very much of the now. I do think of water metaphorically as well: that our histories are dissolved in it. Water performs a role as the ultimate solvent, physically and psychologically, yet it also brings you to the now.

In *All the Seas*, I had 365 bottles representing 260 separate bodies of water. I hadn't made a participatory installation before and put a social-media callout with The Fruitmarket Gallery in Edinburgh (2014), so *All the Seas* completely relied on other peoples' generosity. What began as a reflection on my relationship with the sea, became a collection of stories associated with the water that people sent. I was a custodian of these gifts and wanted to gift them back as an artwork. So, I decanted the water, choosing glass bottles that could have appeared in a painting by Morandi, Picasso or Cézanne. The bottles had to have simplicity and not look too scientific, or like food or perfume vessels. As a sculptor, I'm interested in material, as well as de-material, and it was important that *All the Seas* wasn't only about the idea of water: it *was* the water. There were a few seas I didn't get in the first round, which were represented as empty bottles, but if people have access to those waters they're invited to contribute on each occasion the work's shown.

IC: Landscape is continually in flux and, therefore, offers infinite scope for investigation, as does the unfathomable ocean. It's remarkable to think that 70 per cent of the earth's surface is covered in water, yet only around 5 per cent of the ocean floor has undergone detailed mapping. What might we find should our knowledge begin to increase?

TK: I'd have to draw a parallel with what we know about human consciousness. Our understanding of the brain is also limited, so maybe this knowledge will progress together. Water isn't even our element: we can't survive in it for long. However, it is life and we depend on it. Although I say my subject is landscape, that's misleading. It's more a way of exploring the self without being there. The self is as big as any of the landscapes we've talked about. In particular, working with water represents our liquid selves, our unknowable selves. Art is a container we can pour ourselves into, and exchanges are possible when that art reaches someone else. That exchange is my motivation.

Interviewed in 2016 and 2019

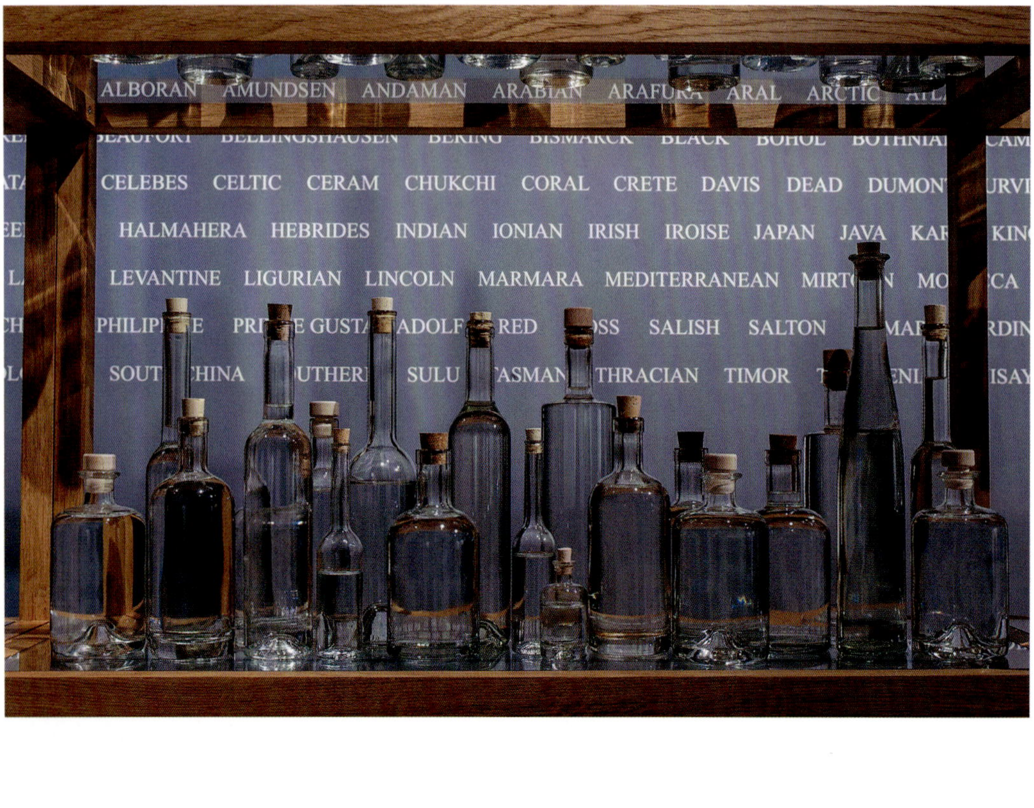

←
Tania Kovats
All the Seas, 2012–14
Seawater, glass, cork, oak
(365 bottles)
600 × 278.5 × 40 cm
(19 ft 8¾ in × 9 ft 1⅝ in × 15¾ in)
Installation view:
Museum of Science & Industry, Manchester, 2015–16

→
Tania Kovats
Rivers, 2012
River water, glass, rubber, boathouse
Dimensions variable
Installation view:
Jupiter Artland, Edinburgh, 2012

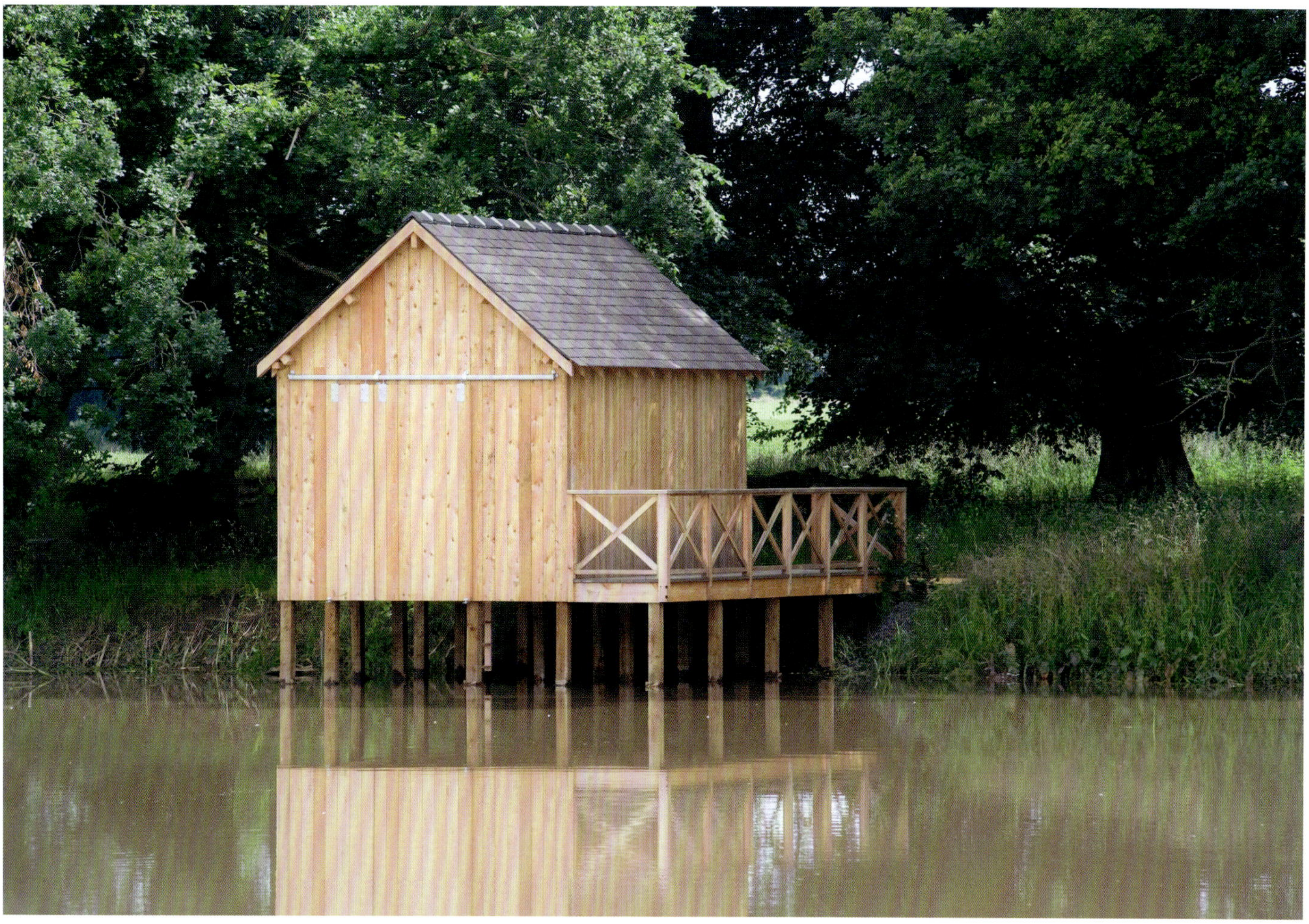

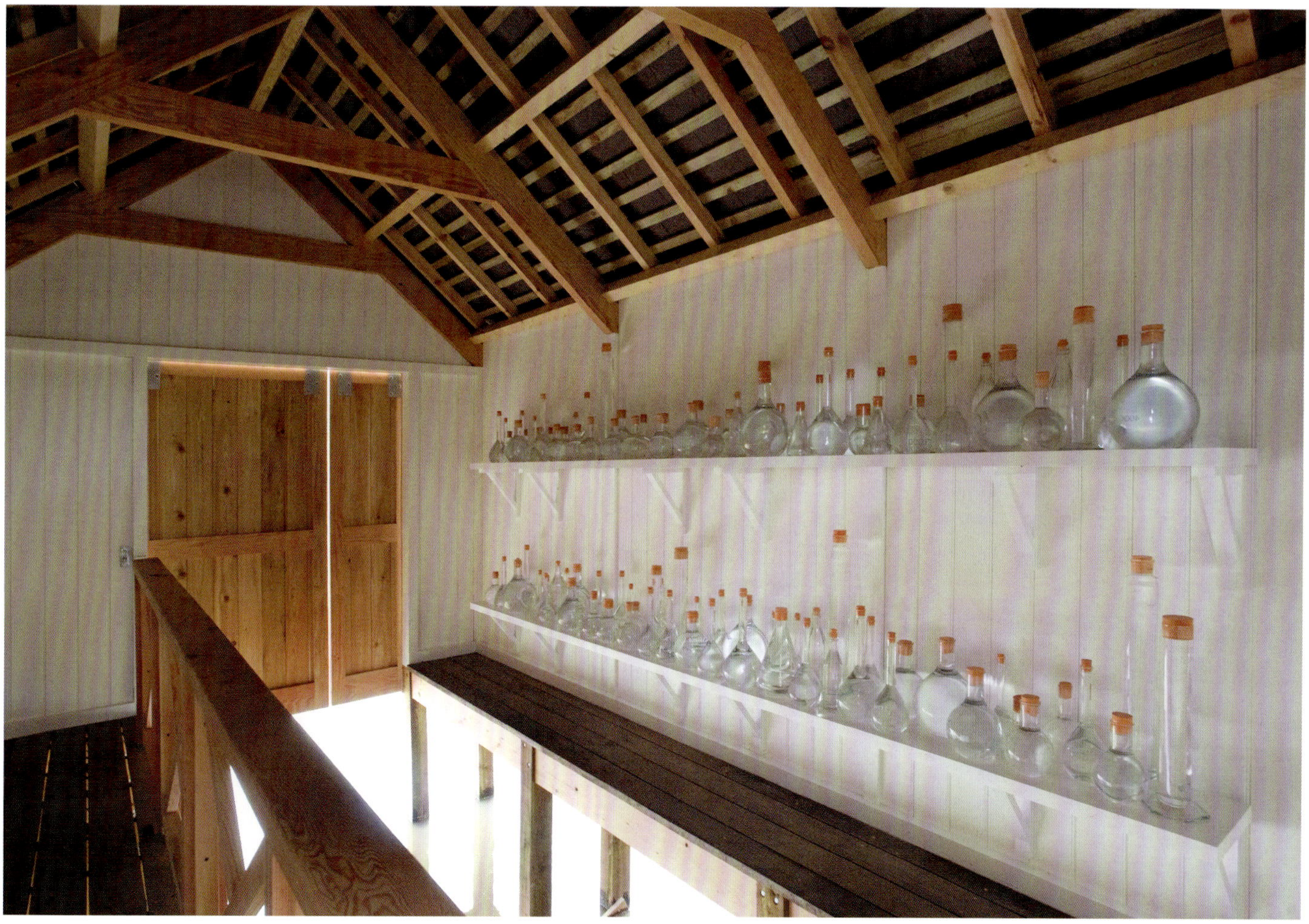

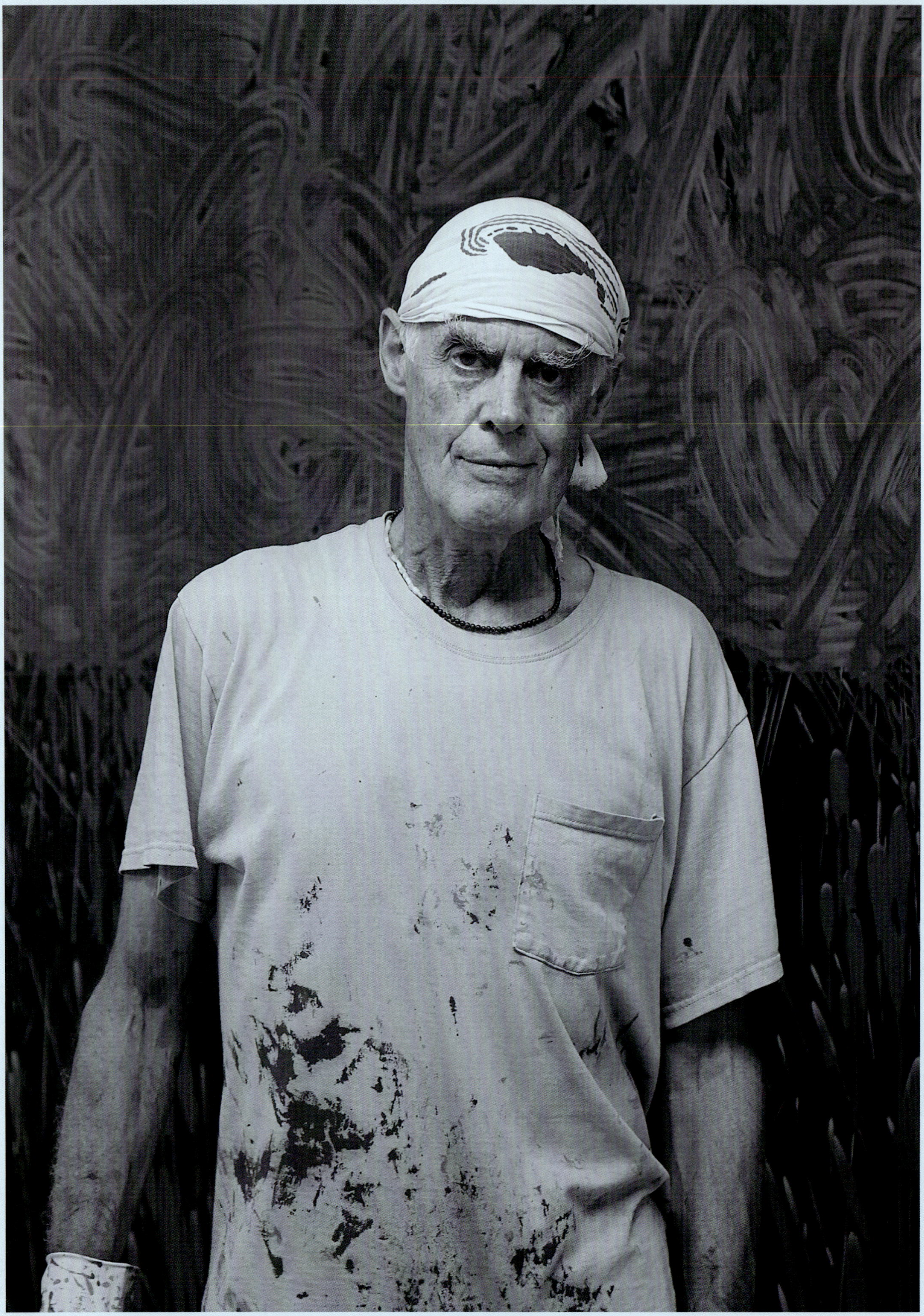

RICHARD LONG

Born 1945, Bristol

Richard Long's practice involves walking in the wilderness, then pausing to leave a mark or arrangement with sticks, stones and driftwood, referencing natural and cosmic phenomena discovered *en route*. Sculpture can, therefore, be sited anywhere and at any time – on top of Mount Kilimanjaro, in the middle of the Sahara or by a glacier below the icefall on Everest – releasing him from the constraints that many other artists encounter. Long's chosen terrain exerts its own laws of regulation over the end result, and his arrangements are often reabsorbed, their transience acting as a metaphor for the mutability of nature and, ultimately, humanity itself. Mud and clay, which possess an inherent drama when used in the right mix, form the basis of his enormous wall works situated within museums and galleries. Long acts as witness to the world's uninhabited vastness and his practice relies on a swiftness of gesture, combined with an inherent sense of order and harmony.

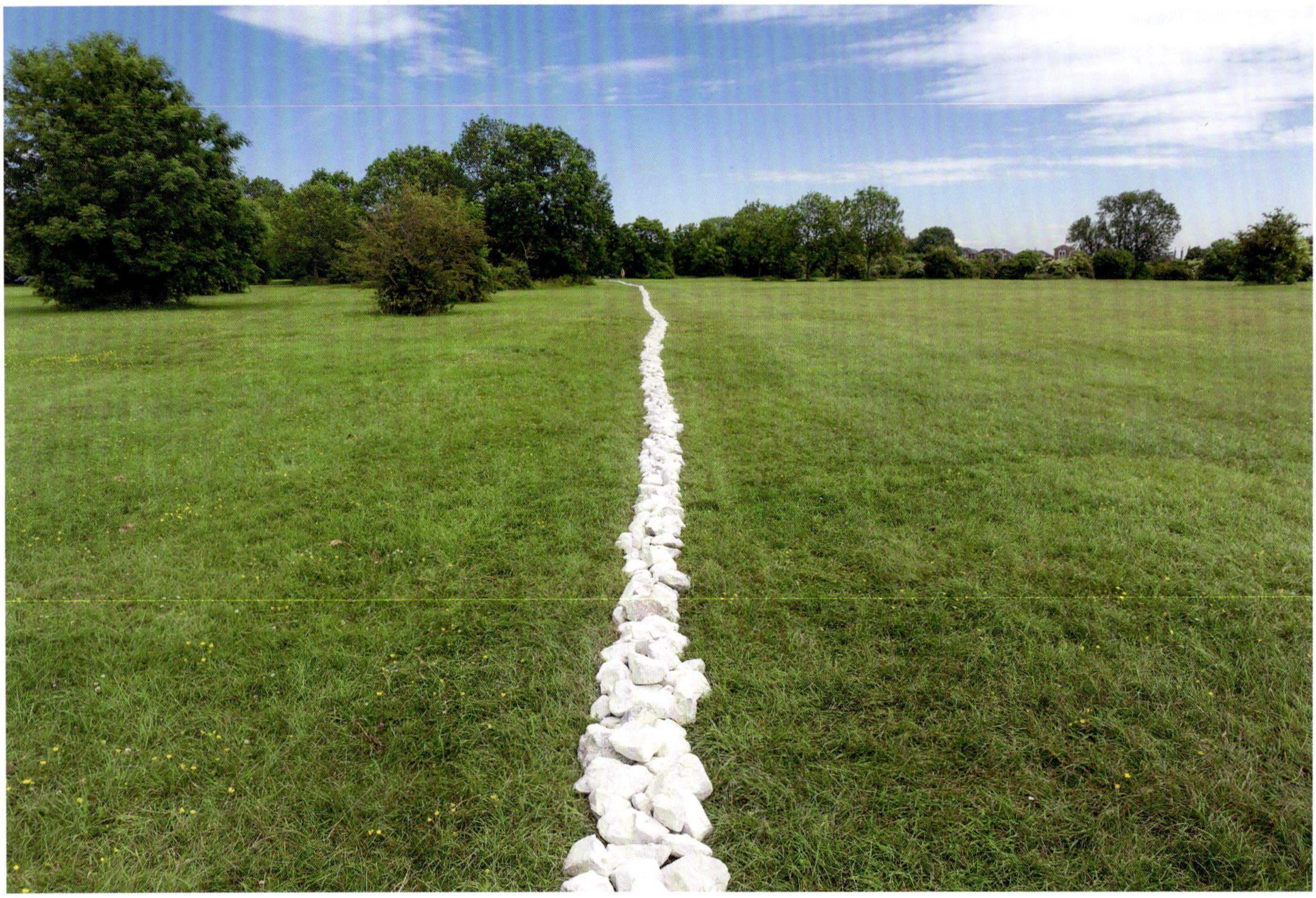

Ina Cole: You were born in Bristol, a place that exerts its influence on works such as *Boyhood Line* (2015). It seems you found your artistic language at a young age and that this early experience still sustains your approach.

Richard Long: Yes, Bristol has been important in that sense. *Boyhood Line* was, literally, a sculpture on a footpath, as stones were placed along an existing path and the shape took its form from how people had walked across the grass over the years. I chose the location to have good sight lines, then realized it was only 50 yards from where I'd made *A Snowball Track* (1964), my first sculpture using the materials of a place, and 100 yards from *England 1968*. So that whole territory – the plateau on the Avon Gorge, the gullies, screes and caves – was my early testing ground.

Although I was a city boy, family holidays were in the West Country: visiting my grandparents on the edge of Dartmoor or youth hostelling with my father. In a way, I've just followed my childhood pleasures into my professional life, making things I did as a kid part of my work – bouncing stones across rivers, building cairns, playing on the beach with pebbles. When growing up along the towpath in Bristol, the river was sometimes so full and at other times completely empty. I was fascinated by that great physical phenomenon and, simultaneously, I was always drawing and painting. While at the West of England College of Art, I tried many different things, as all young artists do. There came a point towards the end of college when I realized that weather and landscapes offered me far more potential to engage with the world than plaster casts and drawing classes.

IC: In 1968, you were taken on by Galerie Konrad Fischer, and many of your early exhibitions were abroad rather than in the UK. Did you have more empathy with artists such as Carl Andre and Joseph Beuys than with the British avant-garde?

RL: In my last month at St Martin's School of Art, I got a letter from Konrad Fischer, asking me to take part in an exhibition at his Düsseldorf gallery. So, I sent a bundle of sticks over, with instructions on how to make a sculpture, for this group show. Konrad was an artist himself and, just on the evidence of seeing that, he offered me an exhibition a year later. That was Konrad for you: he had a fantastic nose for art. After the opening, he said, 'There's this manifestation down in Amalfi in Italy, a new art movement called Arte Povera. Why don't you get on a train and check it out?' Which I did. That opened up a new world of Italian artists to me, who all became interested in my work.

I was recognized abroad at least two years before becoming known in Britain. In some ways, the British art scene was then independent and insular but, in Düsseldorf, I found a world of experimental practice, including Joseph Beuys, who I first met in 1968, and Carl Andre, who took news of my work back to New York. All the support in my early days was from other artists who found the walking and lines in fields interesting. I had photographs of *A Line Made by Walking* (1967) and *England 1968*, so the medium of the photograph was important in spreading the word.

Richard Long
Boyhood Line, 2015
White limestone
170 m (557 ft 8⅞ in)
Installation view:
The Downs in Clifton, Bristol, 2015

IC: You then went on to travel across every continent on earth, seeking unoccupied terrain – mountains, deserts, shorelines, grasslands – breathtakingly spectacular topography.

RL: Wild, empty landscapes, that's my love. Many people live in cities, whereas I'm a witness to the still relative emptiness of the world. So, every sculpture is an emotional response to me being there at that moment. It doesn't mean I'm unique, but maybe I was one of the first artists to somehow use the world as one place. Theoretically, I felt I could go anywhere to make art. Also, I'm of a generation who could do that with hardly any money. For example, I bought a ticket to fly to Kenya in 1969 for almost nothing, partly to make a sculpture on the top of Kilimanjaro, and I hitch-hiked

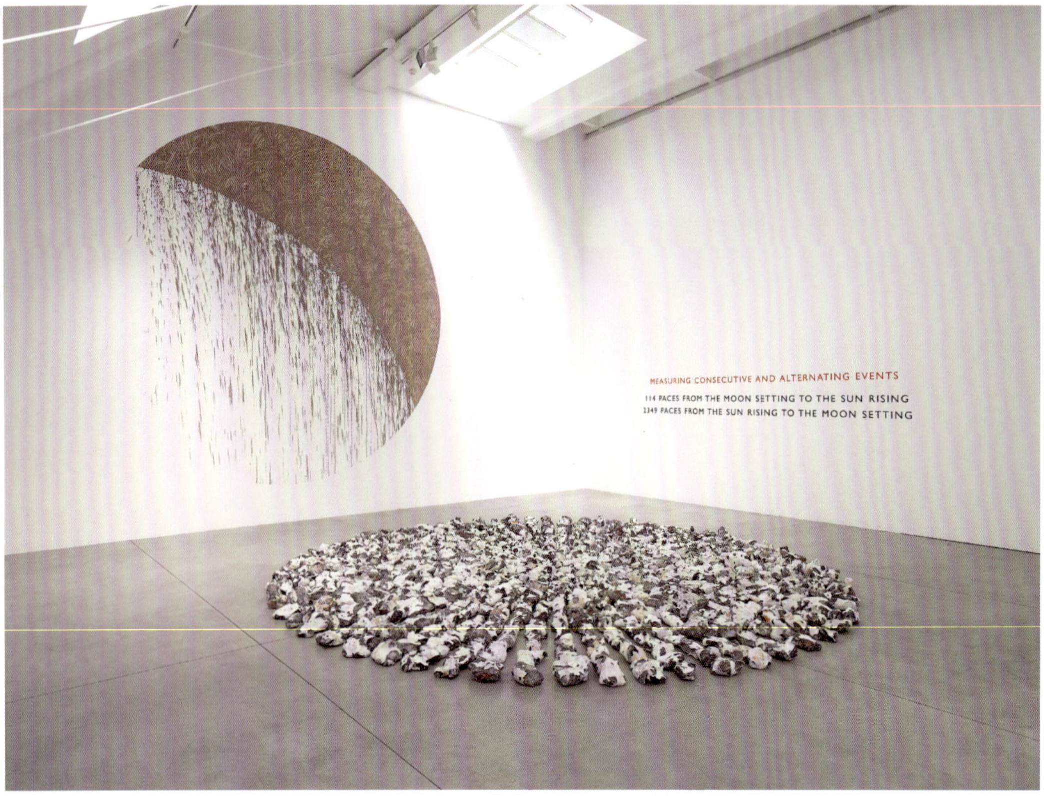

←
Richard Long
Circle to Circle, 2018
Installation view:
Lisson Gallery,
London, 2018

→
Richard Long
Circle for Sally, 2016
Granite and marble stones
520 cm (17 ft) diameter
Installation view:
Centro de Arte
Contemporáneo de Málaga,
Spain, 2016

across Route 66, in the US, in 1970. Being out in the world makes me optimistic. It's a vast, empty place and nature is very strong.

IC: Yet humanity is now far removed from the basic principles governing life on this planet. Do you subscribe to the view that different landscapes are charged with their own potent energies, retaining echoes of past uses and the footprints of our ancestors?

RL: Absolutely. Mongolia is still occupied with the culture of the nomads; the Australian outback is redolent with aboriginal culture; while New Mexico is suffused with the history of Native Americans. However, I can relate that to the English landscape as well. Yes, we have become somewhat removed. You might say climate change – floods, warming, melting ice caps, sea-level rises – are nature's new rhythms. Nature always adapts, as it did after the 1883 Krakatoa eruption, or when the meteor hit Arizona, which probably ended the dinosaur era. So now it has to adapt to our man-made disasters, and the future won't be the same as the past. It never is. *In extremis*, our industrial societies will invent the capacity to eliminate greenhouse gases. That's my hope.

Intellectually, I'm aware of the politics, but I'm not a political person. When in the middle of a sandstorm, the pouring rain, or freezing cold, I'm faced with a different reality. I bring the geometry of an avant-garde, minimal artist from the Western world to the middle of Mongolia, for example. Yet when I'm there, I use the materials of the place, and every work in the landscape is a union of who I am and the characteristics of the place. Every location is different and, even though I might be repeating circles, every circle is also different. The archetype of the circle actually emphasizes the cosmic variety of everything, and this gives it its power, beauty, understandability and resonance.

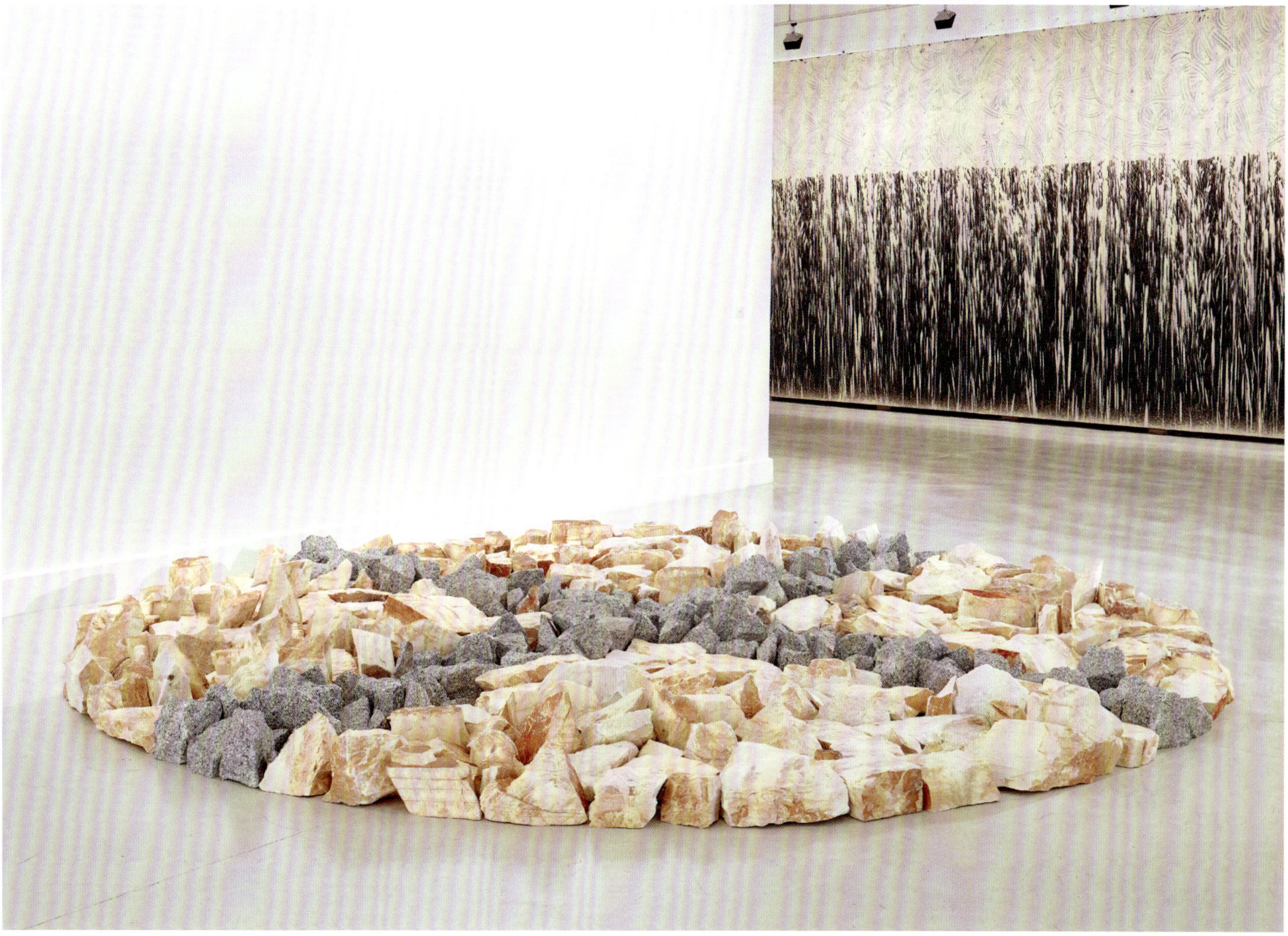

IC: *Circle for Sally* (2016) combines two archetypal forms, a cross sitting tightly within a circle. It's made from the materials of a particular locality that evoke the memory of your grandmother. Is a narrative piece like this unusual in your practice?

RL: It's good to have something unusual. The granite is from Madrid and the light-coloured stones from Sierra Nevada, near Málaga. My grandfather was a travelling man who had many different jobs in his life. One was as the representative for Hispano-Suiza cars in Spain, so he relocated the family to Madrid. When my grandmother, Sally, got tuberculosis they moved to the coast in Málaga, where she later died. Then, with the Spanish Civil War, there was a gun battle close to where they lived, and the remaining family were picked up by the British Royal Navy from the beach at night. That was the end of their life in Spain. I once climbed over the wall of the English cemetery there to visit my grandmother's grave, after one of my walks in the Sierra Nevada. You don't need to know my backstory, but, once you do, it adds to a richer experience of the work.

IC: Your textworks summarize the stimuli pervading your senses when travelling and, occasionally, offer glimpses of a backstory. There's a play on typographic layout, as seen in *Those Blue Remembered Hills of Somerset* (2019); while 'Circle to Circle' brought together a textwork with other elements, to create a lyrical three-part astronomical installation, referencing a continuous walk from moonrise to sunrise (Lisson Gallery, London, 2018). You always choose and position words very carefully.

RL: Of course, just as I choose my stones and places carefully. Those three pieces combined a textwork, sculpture and a mud work, which each have some 'cosmic' connection. The textworks are another strategy:

they describe a walk or the story of a sculpture. If I'm carrying a stone in my pocket and placing it on the road, when walking from day to day, it's more practical to tell its story with words than to photograph it. The early textworks were deliberately simple and direct, descriptive but non-literary. Words and language are flexible, so I sometimes choose to use them more creatively now: scrambling the chronology, playing with time or making a work that reads both across and down. *Those Blue Remembered Hills of Somerset* is, in some ways, nostalgic, full of my history. I still live in North Somerset and have frequently crossed the county over the past 50 years. It's familiar ground.

IC: Some of your walks take weeks to complete, yet the act of producing an artwork, or marking the terrain, can take only 30 minutes. It's clear you get immense pleasure from your practice – the physicality and sheer freedom of being outside, the touch of natural materials – but can you describe how it actually feels?

RL: That's such a big question. To explain it is the wrong way to look at it. If I'm in the wilderness, I believe in being open to instinct, to chance. I could do a long walk and not find a place to make anything at all, yet another in the Sahara yielded many sculptures. It's emotionally satisfying to be on a walk, with all the hardships, the camping and the campfires, and it's similarly pleasurable to make sculptures along the way. In Antarctica, it was like being on the moon, except it was white. It was one of the most unique places I've been to; absolutely lifeless with not a single minute insect.

IC: When you're camping do wild animals ever become inquisitive?

RL: I once woke up in Lapland and found the footprints of a bear around my tent. It had been a snowy night and he had checked me out. That doesn't bother me. It's just what happens, sometimes. Well, there was one terrible moment in East Africa when lions suddenly ran towards us from out of the grass. I really thought that was it. There were two of us, and a guide with a gun – but there's no way he could have got the gun off his shoulder in time. The lions weren't charging; we'd just surprised them, and they ran through us. Luckily, there were no males among that particular group, they were all lionesses. Even so, it was a heart-stopping moment and, in retrospect, stupid to go walking in the bush.

What you see in my work is what I've chosen to edit from my experiences, but I've been travelling for decades and have many amazing anecdotes. If I was a writer, I'd be writing stories, but as an artist I'm doing something that hasn't been done before – discovering new ideas about movement, time and space. The textworks, for example, are often a ritualized simplification of these rich experiences, an abstraction. However, as you can tell from the photographs, I do encounter interesting things *en route*. I may stay in amazing little taverns or get given tapas when stopping for a drink on a road walk in Spain. Many incidental human occurrences happen that don't enter the work.

IC: A photograph of *A Walking and Running Circle* (2003), in the Warli tribal land of India, shows a group of children looping around. This is unusual because the incidental human occurrence, as you put it, remains in the photograph. How did this interaction come about?

RL: It was the end of the harvest in Maharashtra and they'd cut the paddy and burnt all the chaff, which left fields of black ash. Being an opportunist, I walked around and around to make a white circle in the black ash. Out of the corner of my eye I saw village kids watching me, fascinated, but they were too shy to come close. Then, when I'd finished, I stood back to take photographs and they all came up to the circle and spontaneously started running around it. I'd made the walking circle and they the running circle, hence the title.

Quite often, I think a work is finished, but then something happens, and it becomes much more interesting. In Mexico, I once made a water line along a footpath and, just before taking a photograph of it, there was a snow storm. All the visual characteristics of the place changed, and the photograph reveals what it

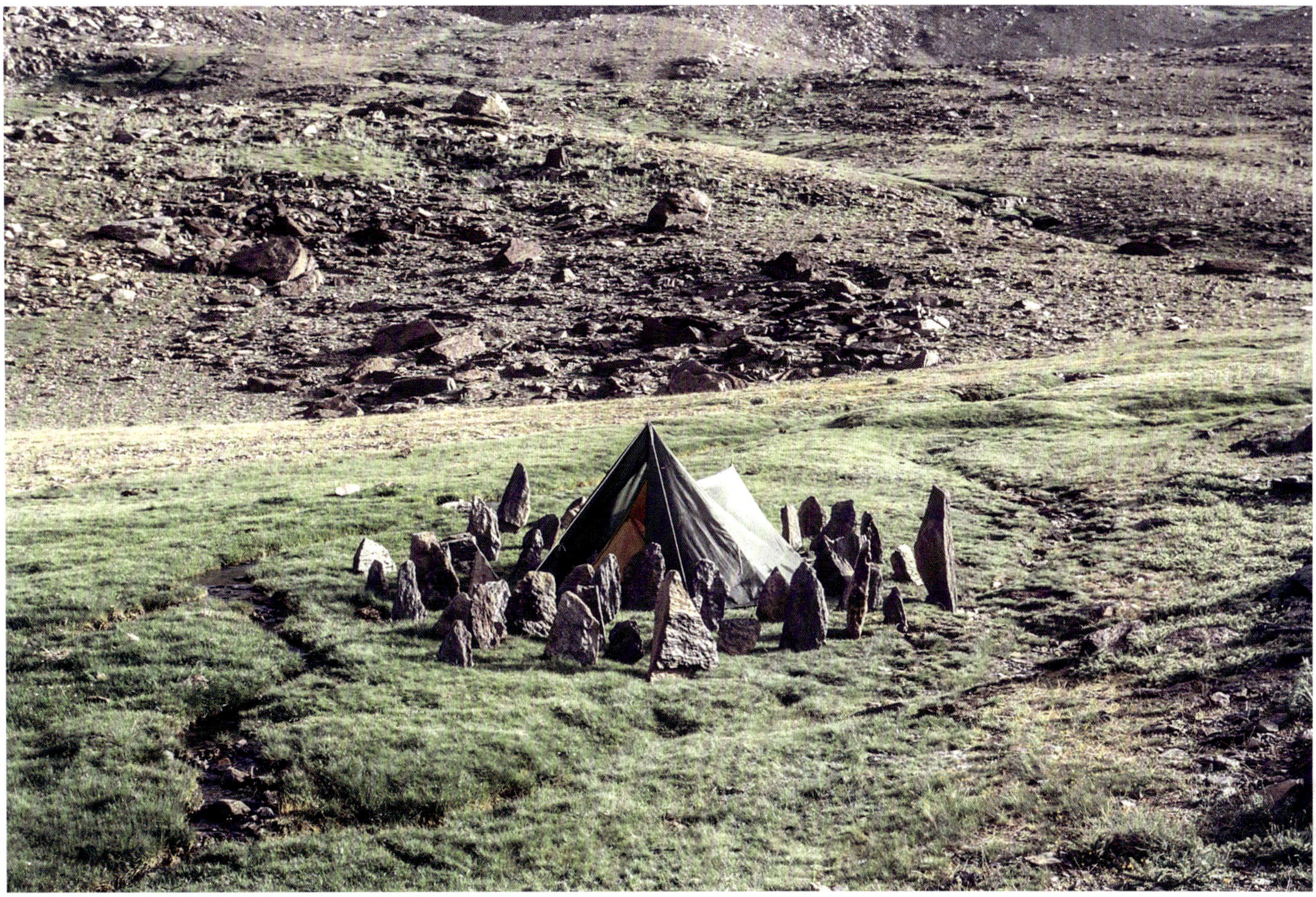

Richard Long
Camp-Site Stones, 1985
Stones
Dimensions unrecorded
Sierra Nevada, Spain

looked like after the snowstorm. That's an example of how the landscape works are open to the vagaries of change and chance.

IC: Your works are habitually sited in inaccessible locations and often don't have an audience. It may be that only you see them, and, even then, only for a short while before they dissolve with time and the effects of weather. You do, however, consider longevity, as attested to in your photographs, textworks and artist's books.

RL: Ideas can last forever. Even stones in a landscape can last forever; it's only that one might not recognize them as a work of art. I've the freedom and capacity to make something anywhere I happen to be. As you say, it can be in an isolated and inaccessible place, and might disappear after a short time, but I hope that's why it's interesting. Ephemerality is just a by-product. The idea

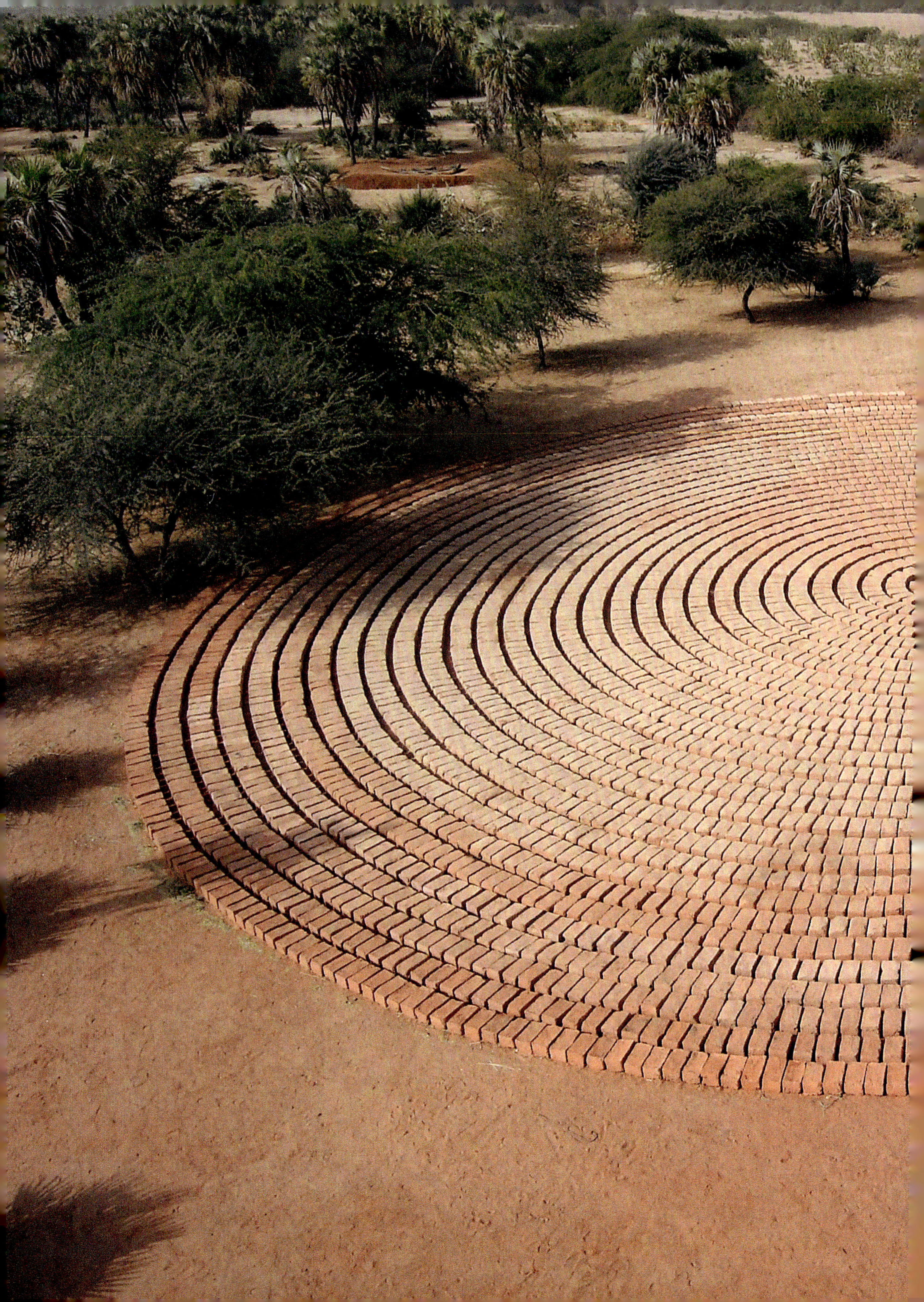

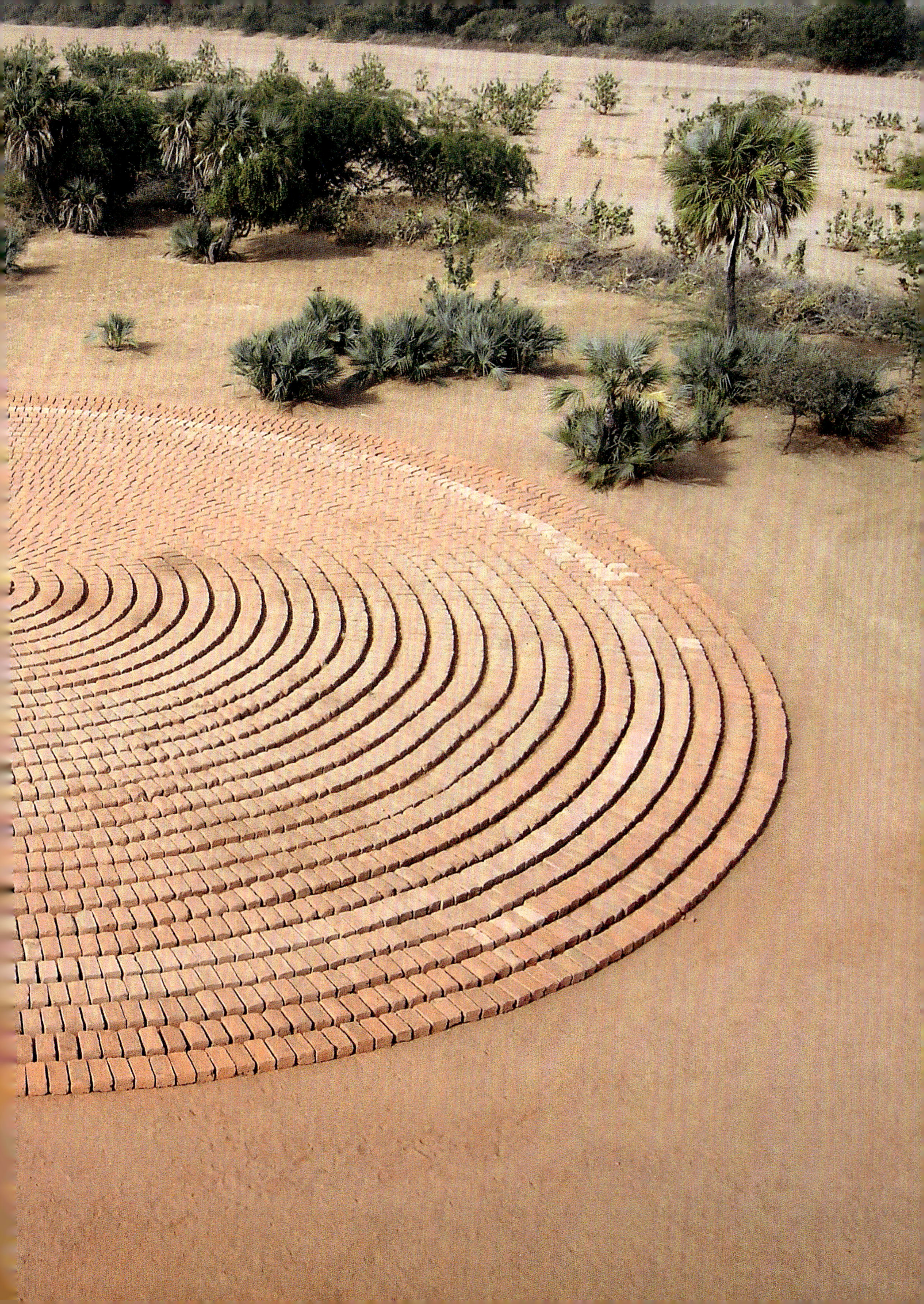

for *A Line in the Himalayas* (1975) was to make a line on a glacier below the icefall on Everest and to take a photograph to record it. The fact that it subsequently broke up and disappeared was logical and natural, but not part of the idea.

Likewise, *England 1968* was a man-made mark in a place that already had a pattern of daisies. I superimposed my cross onto the natural pattern by removing the daisies' heads. The fact that they grew back afterwards was neither here nor there, because the work had been finished and photographed, and the image was in the world as I wanted it to be. I also show in galleries and museums in the middle of cities, so it's not either/or. If somebody gives me a grand space, I can make a grand work, and I use the beauty of great architecture, like the Guggenheim in Bilbao, or the Hearst Tower in New York.

IC: I watched you create *Porthmeor Arc* (2002) for the curved, sea-facing wall at Tate St Ives, using River Avon mud. You were up on scaffolding, and I was struck by the intense physicality of the act, and how you blocked all peripheral distraction to focus solely on the task in hand. It's as if body and mind were fused into a highly disciplined instrument. Is that level of concentration learned or inherent?

RL: I have to be focused and can't make any mistakes because there are no second chances. It's no different from a musician playing a piece of music. That's not to say what I do is a performance, but it requires a similar level of concentration. I'm equally wrapped up in the moment, yet no different from any other artist. It's simply a bit more dramatic when you're watching me up on scaffolding. What's important is that I make all my own work, whether it's walking a thousand miles or placing a fingerprint. I'm not an industry; I don't have a studio; I don't have assistants. That's not a value judgment, it's just how I am. It's all based on my strength, or even my lack of it. In a way, it's a portrait of me without being figurative.

IC: *Sunset Circles* (2006), in Agadez, Niger, was conceived in response to a tower built by the Swiss

←←
Richard Long
Sunset Circles, 2006
Adobe bricks
Dimensions unrecorded
Installation view:
Agadez, Niger, 2006

→
Richard Long
Popocatépetl Line, 2020
Black volcanic stone from Ecatzingo, Estado de México
310 stones
31 × 2 × 0.4 m
(101ft 8½ in × 6 ft 6¾ in × 15¾ in)
Installation view:
Cuadra San Cristobal,
Mexico City, Mexico, 2020

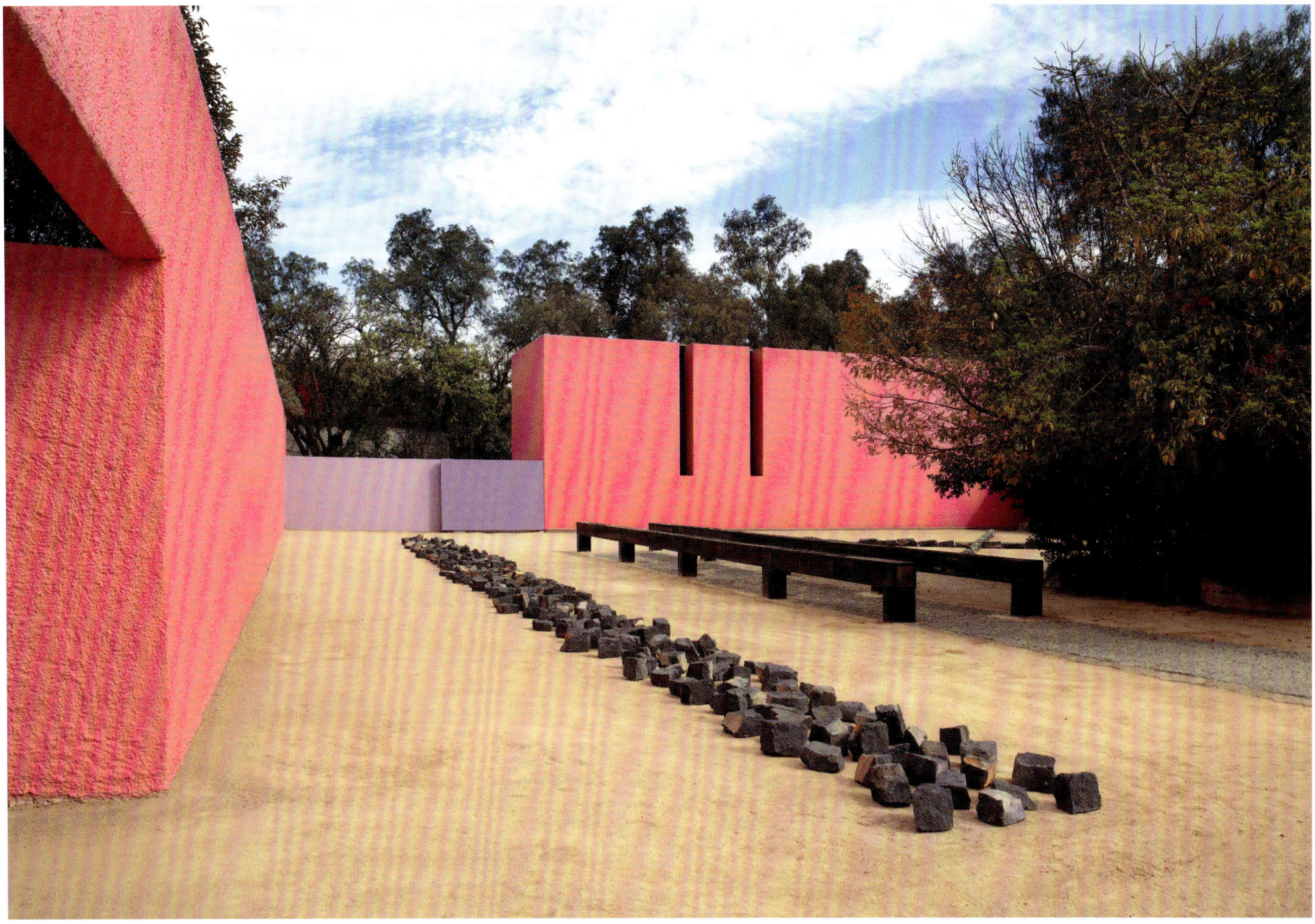

artist Not Vital in 2005, and *Popocatépetl Line* (2020) was created for Cuadra San Cristóbal in Mexico City, Luis Barragán's 1968 modernist landmark. This must require a particular sensitivity to a site's characteristics and history?

RL: Not Vital's work is a cross between sculpture and architecture, and he made a beautiful tower in Niger from which to watch the sunset. *Sunset Circles* is a complementary homage, which you can look down upon from his tower. I'd never heard of Luis Barragán or his work before doing the Mexico project. So, I first went on a reconnaissance visit to see the location, which was very impressive – with amazing colours. I also went on some great road trips looking for stones. One memorable day, we cooked lunch over a fire with the men who were hewing stones from the ground by hand, in the forest on the slopes of Popocatépetl. As usual, the shapes 'chose themselves'. *Popocatépetl Line* turned out to be quite similar to my 'scattered but straight' lines in the wilderness.

IC: You utilize a defined sequence of abstract variables – lines, circles, crosses and spirals – forms that take us back to the beginning of time. Are you trying to retain a sense of Paleolithic engagement lost through human evolution?

RL: Yes, I do have an affinity to primitive man. Using mud, with my hands on a wall, isn't so far removed from cave painting. I'm leaving a mark and being human, yet also being human by way of adding something new to the story of art. It's more like rock 'n' roll. I feel a primitive energy when making a huge mud work or a circle of stones. It's primal, physical, emotional – a celebration.

IC: It's also a tangible means of confirming one's existence in the present. Do you feel able to reach a higher state of being through this process of making?

RL: I feel in a state of grace when I'm on a wilderness walk on my own, with just my rucksack on my back and my camping food. I'm mentally free from the stuff of modern life. It's a poetic idea, but it is powerful. It's good to be able to touch that psychological place once in a while. So, when making my work, I am fulfilled and happy.

Interviewed in 2015, 2017 and 2020

↗
Richard Long
Heaven (Portrait of Carl Andre), 2011
Thassos marble
10.2 × 305 × 307.3 cm
(4 in × 10 ft × 10 ft 1 in) overall

→
Richard Long
Stones/Years, 2015
157 basalt stones
Height: 40 cm (15¾ in)
Radius: 352–364 cm (11–12 ft)
Installation view:
Konrad Fischer Galerie, Düsseldorf, 2015

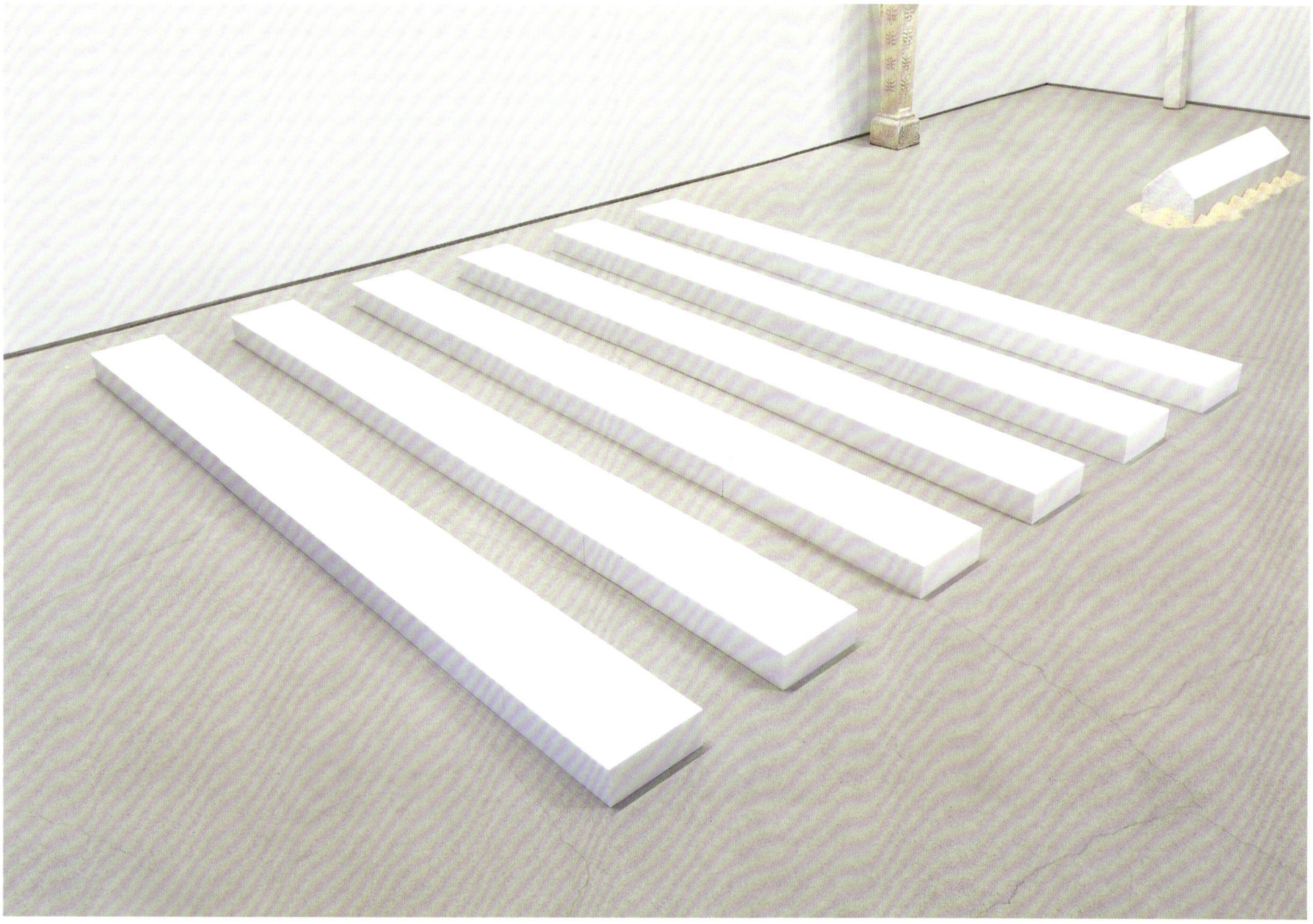

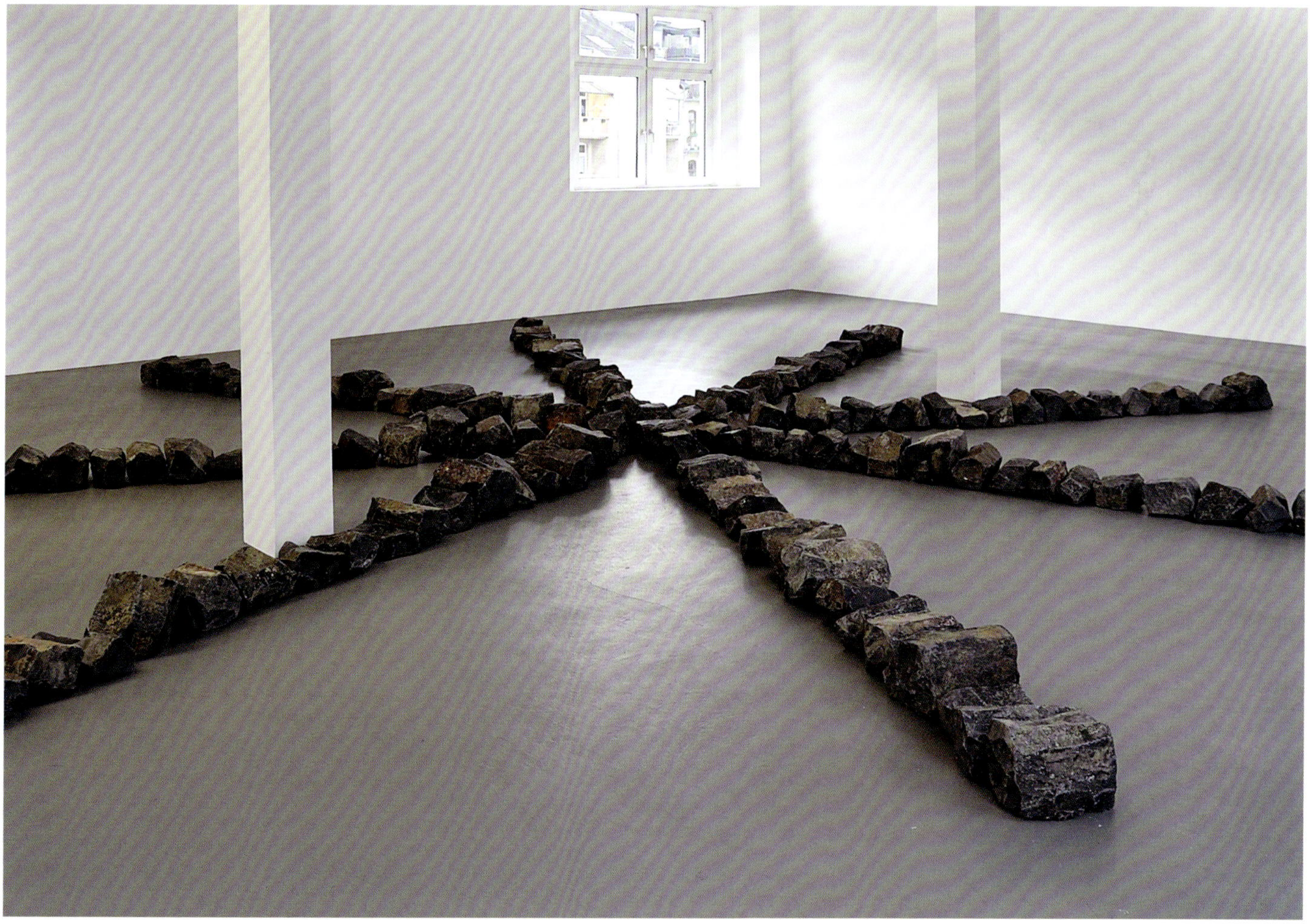

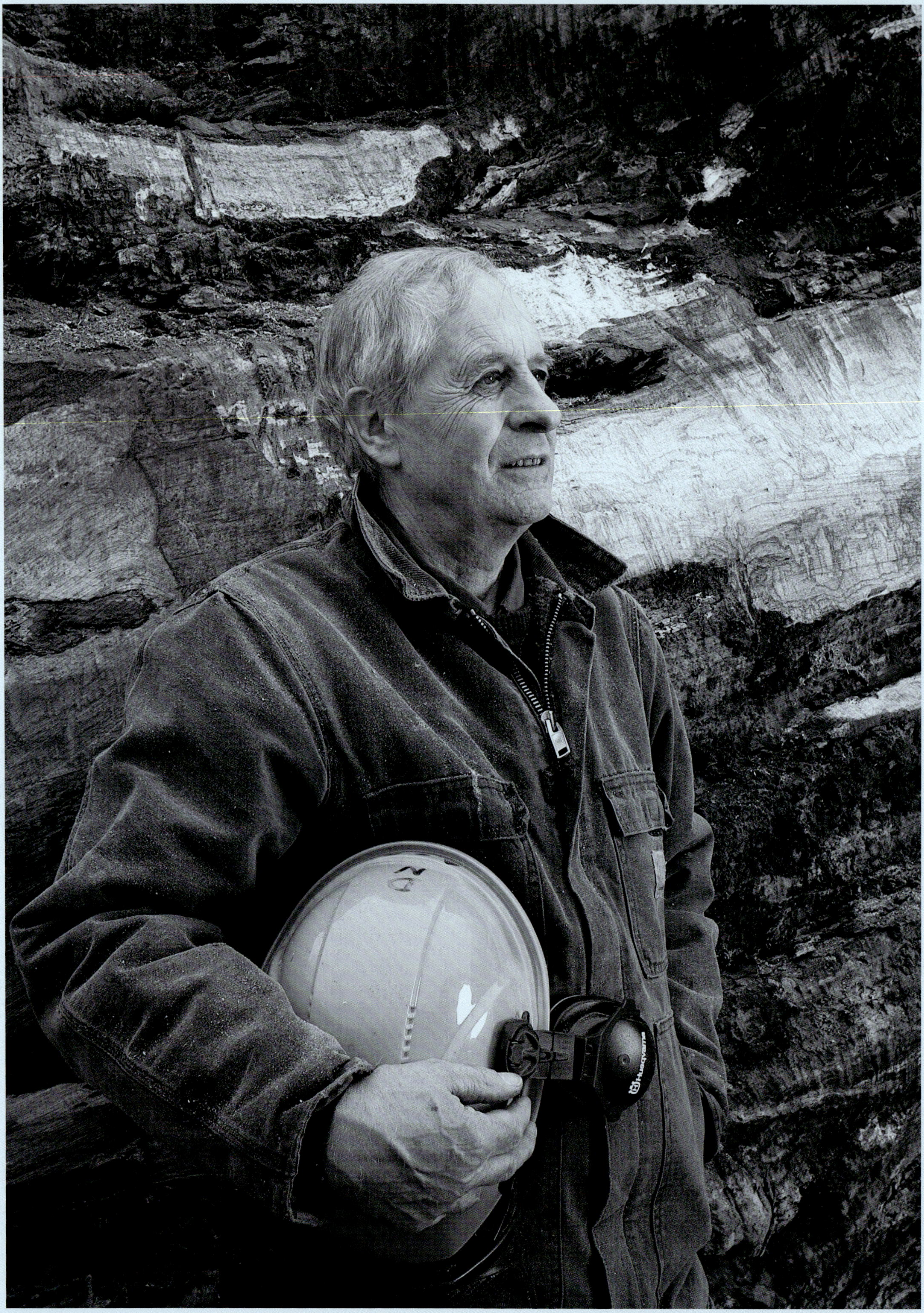
Husqvarna

DAVID NASH

Born 1945, Esher, Surrey

The sculptures of David Nash are rooted in a tree's life cycle, borrowing their material from its sequence of growth and decay. During the process of making, Nash engages with the elements of earth, air, fire and water, and also the dimensions of time and space into which the works are launched. Trees are fundamental to human existence, imbued with deep wisdom derived from their longevity. Despite frequently drawing upon allegorical nuances, Nash's sculptures are essentially configured to embody the physical characteristics of a species. The idiosyncratic traits of a particular genus, therefore, have an important bearing on the artist's approach. Towering shapes and squat forms convene in animated fashion, while wraith-like carbonized works shimmer enigmatically. There is an almost primal need to get close to their rich and textured surfaces – the cracks, crags and undulations that offer such a poignant reminder of the inescapable passing of time.

Ina Cole: You purchased Capel Rhiw in 1968, and it has evolved from a working studio into a space housing a changing display of sculptures. It lies in Blaenau Ffestiniog, North Wales, an area you've known since childhood. Is this sense of attachment important?

David Nash
Wooden Boulder, 1978
(image from 2014)
Oak
1 × 1 × 1 m
(39⅜ × 39⅜ × 39⅜ in)

David Nash: My grandfather had a house in North Wales, with acres of amazing woodland, and in 1948 my father bought a cottage nearby – an evacuation house, being convinced we'd soon be at war with the Soviet Union. We went there every holiday and, as a young child, I experienced the four seasons in Ffestiniog valley, which were much more vivid than in Weybridge, Surrey. So yes, the attachment is very deep. Then, in my second year at Kingston School of Art, I bought two cottages in North Wales for £300. Three years later, Capel Rhiw came up for sale for £200, so I sold the cottages for £1,500, which gave me enough money to install water and electricity in the chapel, buy tools and have the year making sculpture. Everything was done for practical reasons. Also, I stammered badly and wanted to bury myself somewhere I liked, and where I could scrape a living but be free.

Capel Rhiw and Blaenau are base camp, but I've worked wherever circumstances lead me. Some of the sculptures made on these journeys stay where they're made, but many come to Capel Rhiw to be further developed, or recycled. Capel Rhiw is really an ongoing installation: it's where the work congregates and, when new pieces arrive, they wake everything up. Several have remained as members of the congregation, while others move to new homes via galleries that represent my work. At Capel Rhiw, thought and reflection have a more natural pace compared to the frenetic pace of projects. I travel far less now, making sculpture here in Blaenau and working through unresolved pieces that still have potential.

→→
David Nash
Capel Rhiw (interior), 2018
Blaenau Ffestiniog, North Wales

IC: Blaenau Ffestiniog is where you created *Wooden Boulder* (1978), a seminal early work made from part of the limb of a giant oak brought down by a storm. You then released the boulder into the valley and documented its comings and goings for decades, but it hasn't been seen for a while.

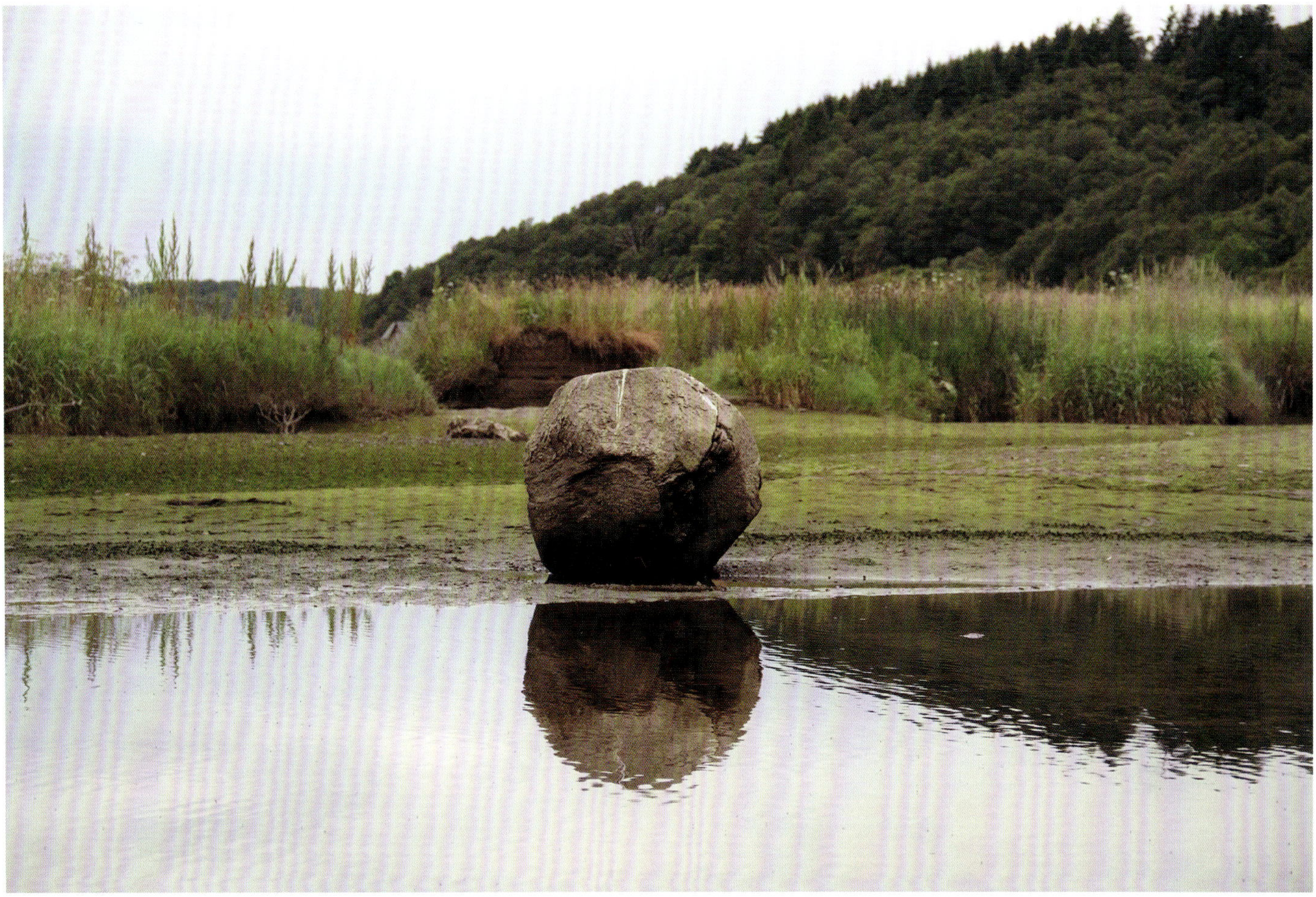

DN: *Wooden Boulder* is somewhere, just out of sight. Although I'm its guardian and watch and tell its story, it is its own being. I thought it had gone to sea in 2003, but it hadn't, as it suddenly reappeared in the Dwyryd estuary. 2013–15 was a special period, in that it was static but there was always the possibility it could move on. I would love to see it – like a dear friend not seen for many years, the attachment is still there to be revived in a moment if we met again.

IC: Showing sculpture at Capel Rhiw, or in a gallery, must present different challenges than when creating pieces that live within the landscape, such as *Wooden Boulder.*

DN: I don't consciously work with the landscape. It is as it is – outside, inside. When I make something inside and take it out, it diminishes by a third, whereas if I make it outside and bring it in, it grows by a third. Ninety per cent of what I do is actually for the indoors: made outside, then brought inside. Wood is a material you can borrow from – through its cycle of growth and decay – by bringing it inside. Then, if you put it back it will return to the cycle of reintegration. I'm very theatrical, and galleries are like little temples to me, where I can create an experience I can't do outside. When I had my exhibition at Yorkshire Sculpture Park (2010), I was able to establish a journey of multiple layers, in which the sculptures looked like theatrical characters, gesturing. Much earlier, in 1973, through a beautiful set of circumstances I showed at York festival, followed by the Arnolfini in Bristol, and the Serpentine and Hayward galleries in London a few years later. I've had some amazing moments of luck, but my fallback position was always to live in Blaenau.

IC: Your knowledge of the different characteristics of trees is fundamental to your practice, and there's a

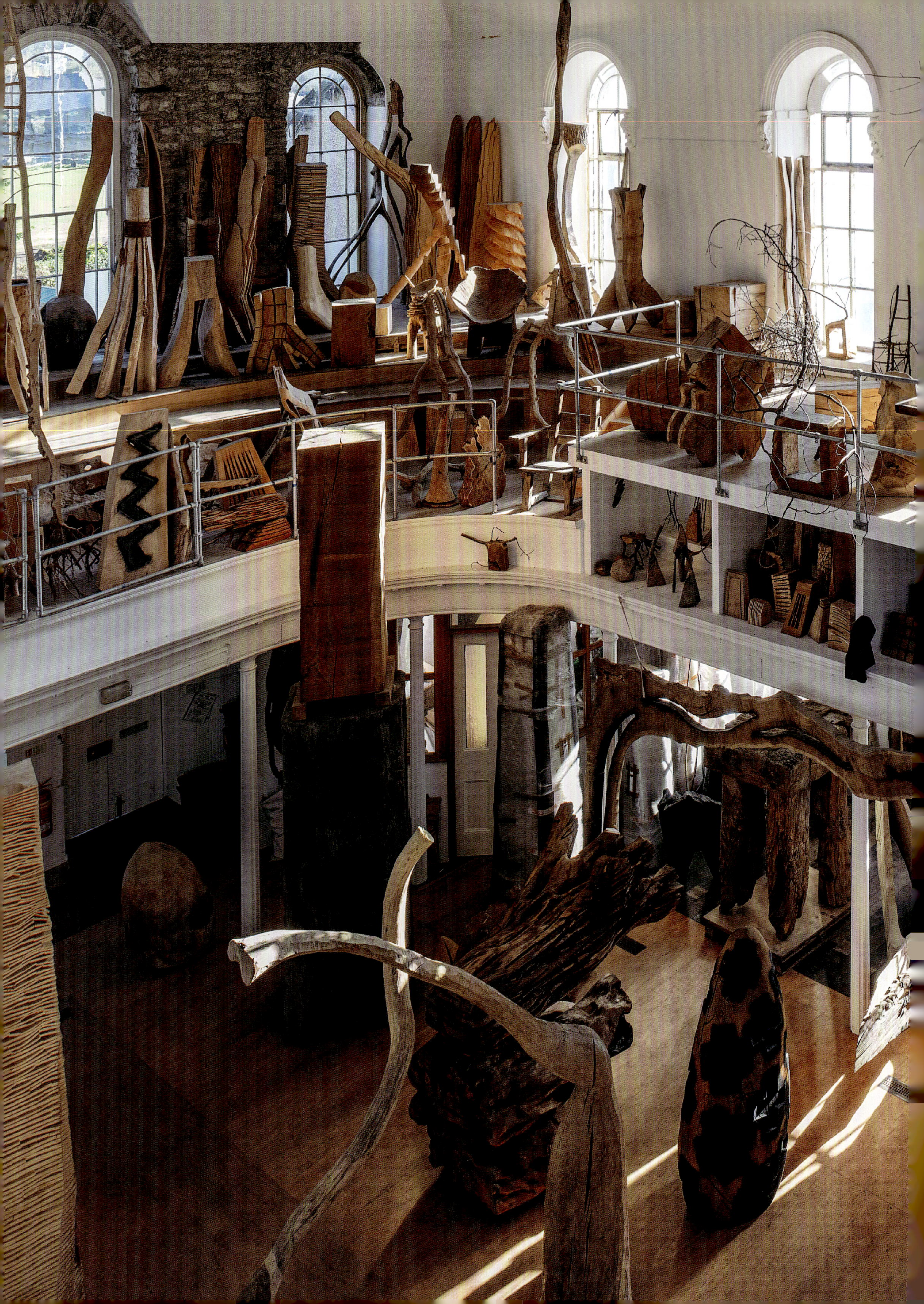

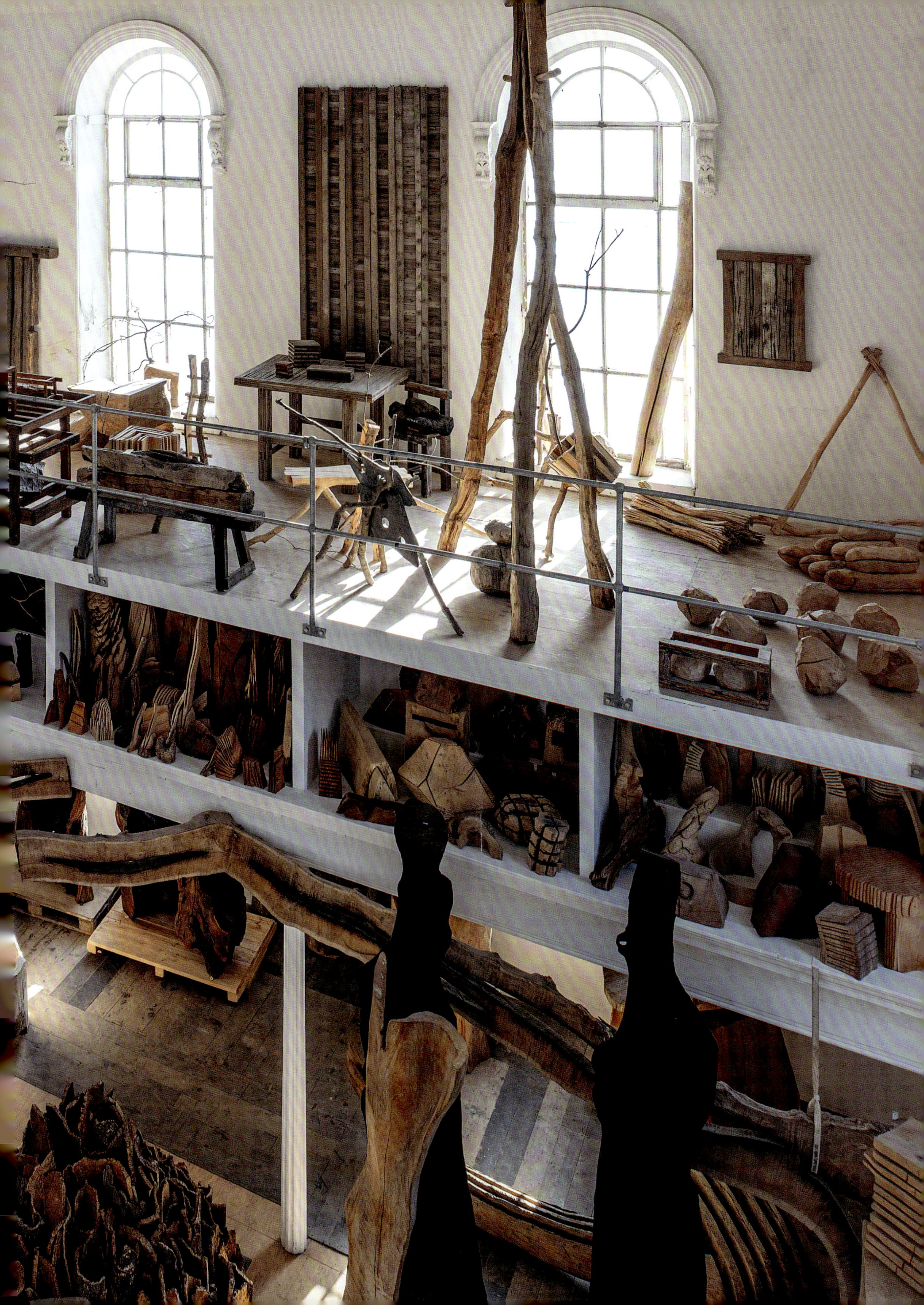

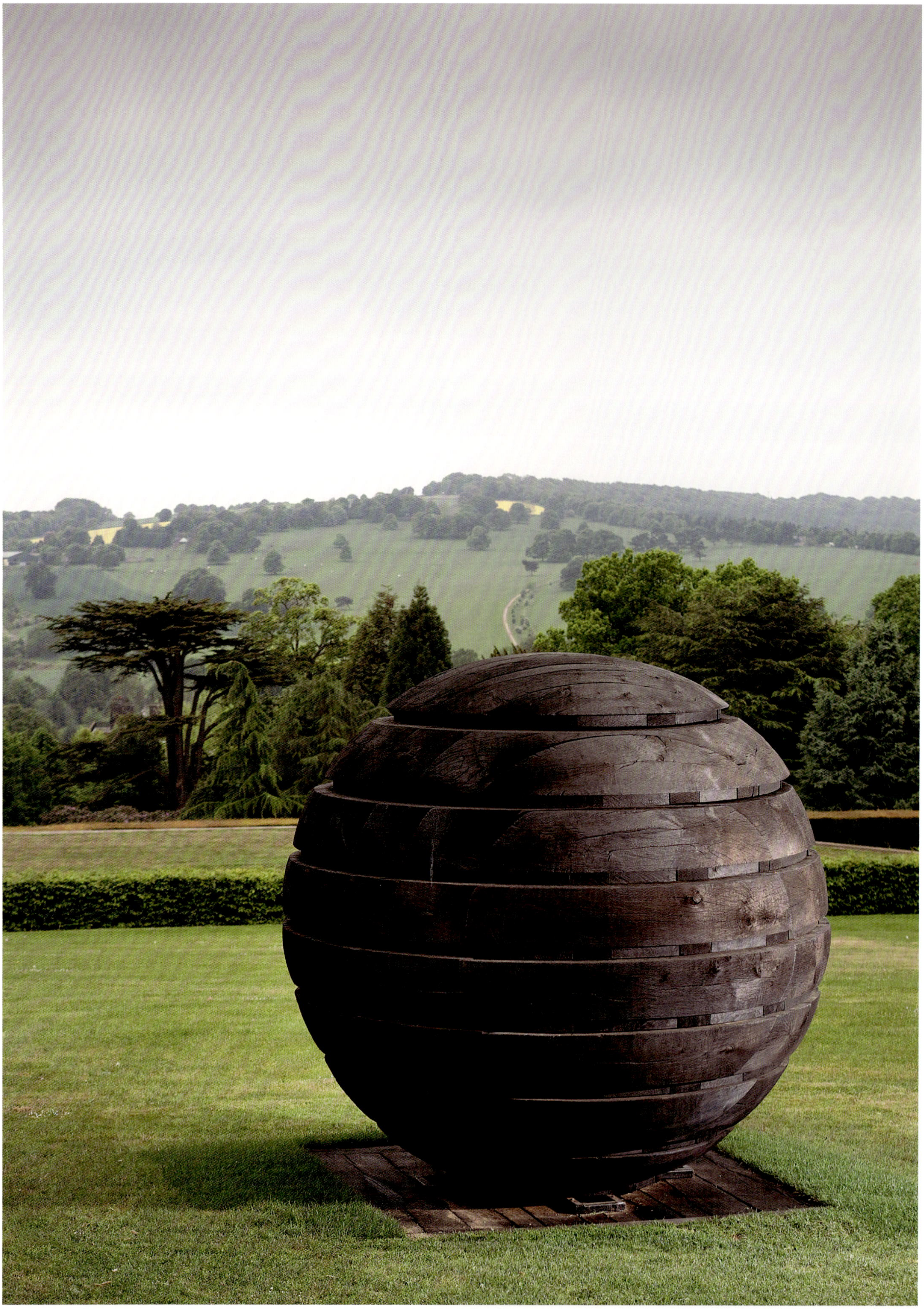

David Nash
Black Sphere, 2010
Charred oak
250 × 250 × 250 cm
(8 ft 2⅜ in × 8 ft 2⅜ in × 8 ft 2⅜ in)
Installation view:
Yorkshire Sculpture Park, 2010–11

distinct progression from the rawness of the first cut shapes to the poise of later sculptures. How has your work evolved since you began using wood in the 1970s?

DN: It has evolved, but I'm not that conscious of it, because the knowledge is deep within and I just deal with it. If the wood's red, I make the most of its redness; if it's a yew, I do something which doesn't split; if it's a certain size, I work with that size. Although my material is wood, my tools are steel, with edges that are for hitting, cutting like an axe or spinning like a chainsaw, which has lots of sharp little chisels going round. I cut as little as possible to get the form, leaving the mark of the tool on the wood, so a sense of the original shape remains. Sometimes I'm criticized for not doing much. Quite right – these are spontaneous sleights of hand.

I also work with cast iron, as it has a similar quality to wood. It has behaviour, it changes, and I like its rawness. I've experimented by pouring molten bronze to mesh around charred wood. Bronze is a mineral when cold, an earth element. By applying heat, it becomes molten, and changes into a 'water' element when fluid. When I pour it into a space, the air element, it cools and goes back to being an earth element. I've also reproduced the black sculptures in bronze, because, when burned, they're no longer a wood experience but a mineral, carbon experience, which translates well into bronze. I'm interested in how all these elemental forces can be amalgamated and worked on by human hand.

IC: Through this process of charring by controlled burning, as seen in *Husk* (2009); *Black Sphere* (2010) and *Two Sliced Cedars* (2010), doesn't the carbonized sculpture become a ghost of its former self?

DN: Yes, that's what carbon does. The experience of carbon is of deep time. Wood is closer to our mortality, but, once blackened, it enters another time zone altogether. I trial the works in a fire to get big texture, thick carbon, and scrape it off because the texture distracts the eye from the form. Then I burn it again with propane to get that ethereal quality. I remember once looking across a green field with black cows, and the cows appeared like holes in the landscape, in the

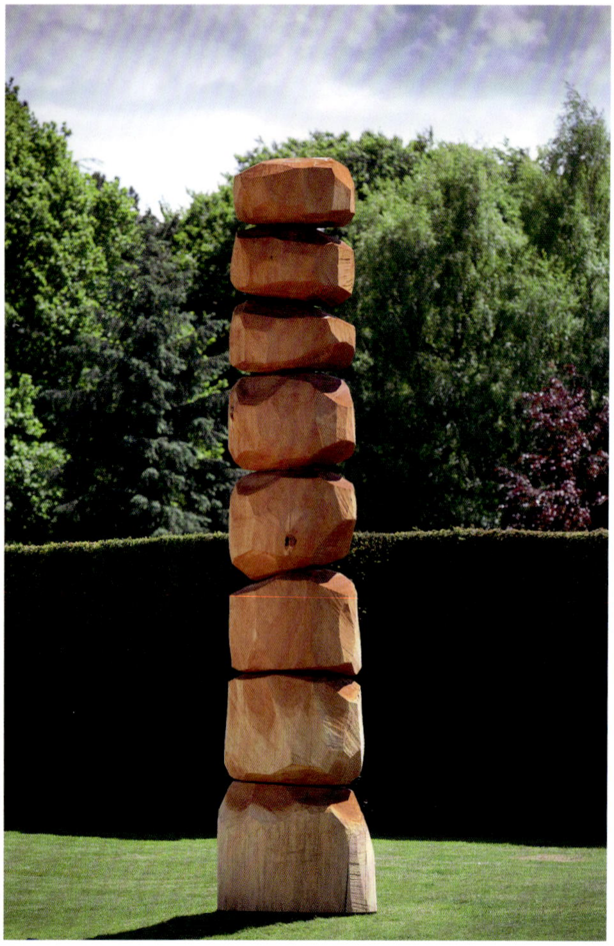

←
David Nash
Red Column, 2010
Redwood
135 × 135 × 600 cm
(53⅛ in × 53⅛ in × 19 ft 8¾ in)
Installation view:
Yorkshire Sculpture Park,
2010–11

→
David Nash
Ash Dome, 1977
(image from 2009, matured)
Dimensions variable
Cae'n-y-Coed, North Wales

same way blackberries appear like holes in a bush. When a piece is black you see the form before the material, so, in a sense, those sculptures aren't really there because they've become like holes.

IC: You give trees human characteristics and have described ash as vigorous and impatient, beech as vain and the redwoods as benign and calm. *Red Column* (2010) has an affinity with Brancusi's *Endless Column* (1926). However, you've accentuated its organic vertical growth, whereas Brancusi was more interested in the rising undulation of New York skyscrapers.

DN: Brancusi's column breathes; it pushes out into space, then comes in, and pushes out again. It's very different from *Red Column*, which is a big pile of lumps. Trees are columns; a tree has its root and its leaf, and it's building a column throughout its life. That's its capital, and the leaf is its revenue, with the root pulling up the resources it needs. If a piece is going to be successful, the way it begins is really important. So, *Red Column* doesn't stay red; it starts to go grey after nine months. I put forms into time for them to behave in time, and surprising things can happen.

Humans need wood; it's fundamental to survival. The commonality of this experience makes my sculpture accessible, which is partly why I choose wood as a material. I get on with it and can work quickly. So, my materials are the four elements, through which I launch pieces into time and space. This loosens me from a sense of ownership and sentiment, in the same way that I had to relinquish ownership of *Wooden Boulder*.

IC: *Ash Dome* (1977) is an example of a work that's been launched into time and space. You planted this ring of trees in North Wales as an act of optimism during a period of economic gloom. However, it

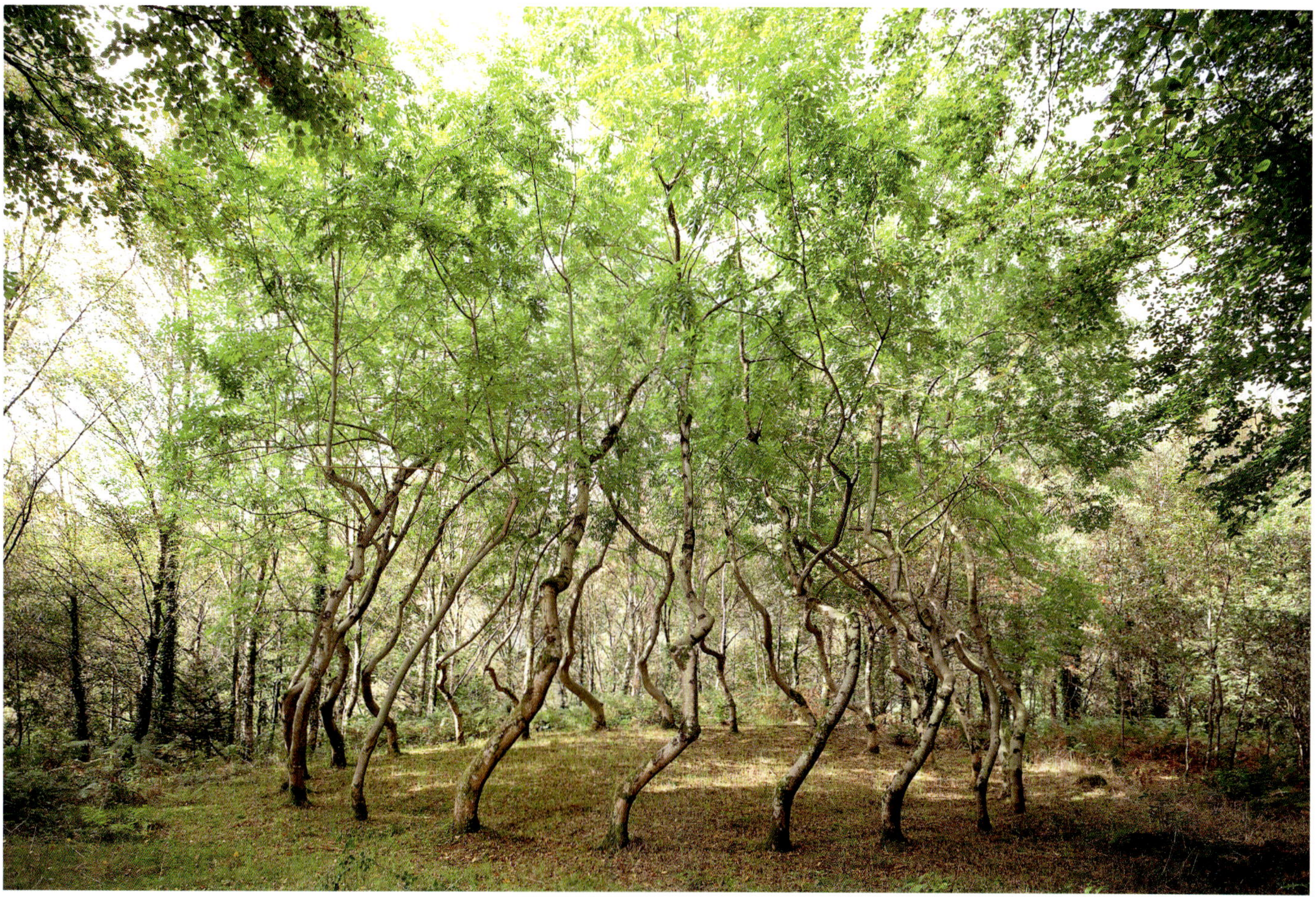

succumbed to the natural cycle of life and death. To counteract its decline, you planted a circle of 22 oaks around its circumference, so, as the ash fade, the oaks will thrive. Is this the ultimate act of regeneration?

DN: Maybe it's the regeneration of an idea. *Oak Dome* (2019) is a way of keeping the spirit of the idea, the initial concept, alive and present. To have *Ash Dome* dying, at Cae'n-y-Coed, is such a dispiriting prospect. *Ash Dome* meant a lot to so many people, and *Oak Dome* is as much for them as for Cae'n-y-Coed and me. Apparently, in the Napoleonic Wars, the Navy planted forests of oak, from which a fleet could be built hundreds of years later. It's fantastic long-term thinking, and, as I use trees for my sculpture, I thought I should also plant them.

Ash Dome was always an artist-attached work, and I needed to be near it and take responsibility. Its concept was longevity, as governments were changing and policies were short-term. At the time, people thought we wouldn't see the end of the century, so, with *Ash Dome*, I threw a grappling iron into the twenty-first century. It had no interest in the millennium, but that was its graduation. It is continuously spontaneous and genuinely of its place, not made somewhere else and brought in. That was the first piece that needed more interference than I'm comfortable with, but I've learnt a lot from it.

IC: This concept was further explored with *Sabre Larch Hill* (2013), an installation of 60 saplings planted at a 45-degree angle at Frederik Meijer Gardens and Sculpture Park in Michigan. How will the saplings' visual appearance alter as they reach maturity?

DN: The native American larch is much slower growing than the European larch, so the form is slow to emerge. Its curving growth is known as 'sabre growth', which is common in natural larch. The young saplings are pulled down by collapsing bracken and brambles, or by snow. They curve up towards the light and are then pulled down again until they're sturdy enough to resist, but, in the meantime, they've developed sabre growth. In *Sabre Larch Hill*, the saplings are spaced and planted at an angle, so each one has a discernible direction. They criss-cross on either side of an avenue up the hill. The planting pattern is quite loose, and each larch will find its own individual form, but all with that characteristic curve.

IC: *Two Ubus* (1988), made of oak and ash, is a significant sculpture from the 1980s. It was inspired by Rothko's *Seagram Murals* (1958), which were shown at the opening of Tate Liverpool. How do your two vaulted forms relate to Rothko's paintings?

DN: I first saw Rothko's paintings at the Tate in London when I was 21 and had been encouraged to sit with them, not just browse and walk through the gallery. Over a few minutes, they became luminous with profound human warmth. This revelation was very important to me at the time. Then, 21 years later when I was 42, I saw them again at Tate Liverpool, and it was a completely different experience. They were less atmospheric and more structural or architectural, like rudimentary temple buildings. The paintings hadn't changed, though; I suddenly got a recognition that I'd changed.

One of Rothko's long horizontal paintings seemed to have a column at each end that narrowed to a neck, then grew a branch across the top to meet and form an arch. I imagined a sculpture made from a trunk with a horizontal branch and resolved to look for that form in my next project, near Mâcon in France. I had two trees, an ash and an oak, and the oak had the right length of trunk and a good-sized lower branch, not horizontal but near enough to try. So, I stripped off the bark and axe-carved the diameter of the branch to meet the diameter of the trunk. One of the French students helping said it resembled Père Ubu, from Alfred Jarry's play *Ubu Roi* (1896), and, in an onomatopoeic way, the name felt correct for that elephant-like form. So, I made another from the ash. They were like Mr and Mrs Ubu from the play.

IC: You have a longstanding interest in the pyramid, sphere and cube generated by Cézanne's belief that nature could be simplified into geometric shapes. What is it about this configuration that continues to inform your practice?

DN: Cézanne's paintings allude to geometric shapes, but he wasn't ideologically dogmatic about it. And Odilon Redon's apprenticeship was with an architect who made him draw cubes endlessly. When Richard Long was asked why he creates lines and circles, he responded that it's because they don't belong to anyone, which is brilliant. These forms are universal. Our whole experience is geometric, and yet emotional, and everybody identifies with these forms, even children. The footprint of the pyramid is a triangle, the sphere a circle and the cube a square. In *Pyramid, Sphere, Cube* (1997–8), I've put them together in a way that people find satisfying. The physical world is a threshold to the spirit world, and people relate to these forms because they speak a truth they recognize, a fundamental truth – the vertical is awake, the horizontal passive and the diagonal hugely dynamic.

IC: *Oculus Block* (2010) is a vast semi-geometric cube fashioned from four naturally fused eucalyptus trees, the most incendiary of materials. Literally translated, *oculus* is Latin for eye, or, in architectural terms, a circular opening inviting the elements, such as in the Pantheon in Rome. Is this definition pertinent to the piece?

↗
David Nash
Two Ubus, 1988
Oak and ash
Oak: 345 × 180 × 74 cm
(11 ft 3⅞ × 70⅞ in × 29⅛ in)
Ash: 340 × 240 × 72 cm
(11 ft 1⅞ in × 7 ft 10½ in × 28⅜ in)
Installation view:
Towner Art Gallery,
Eastbourne, 2019–20

→
David Nash
Oculus Block, 2010
Eucalyptus
285 × 195 × 222 cm
(9 ft 4¼ in × 6 ft 4¾ in × 7 ft 3⅜ in)
Installation view:
Yorkshire Sculpture Park,
2010–11

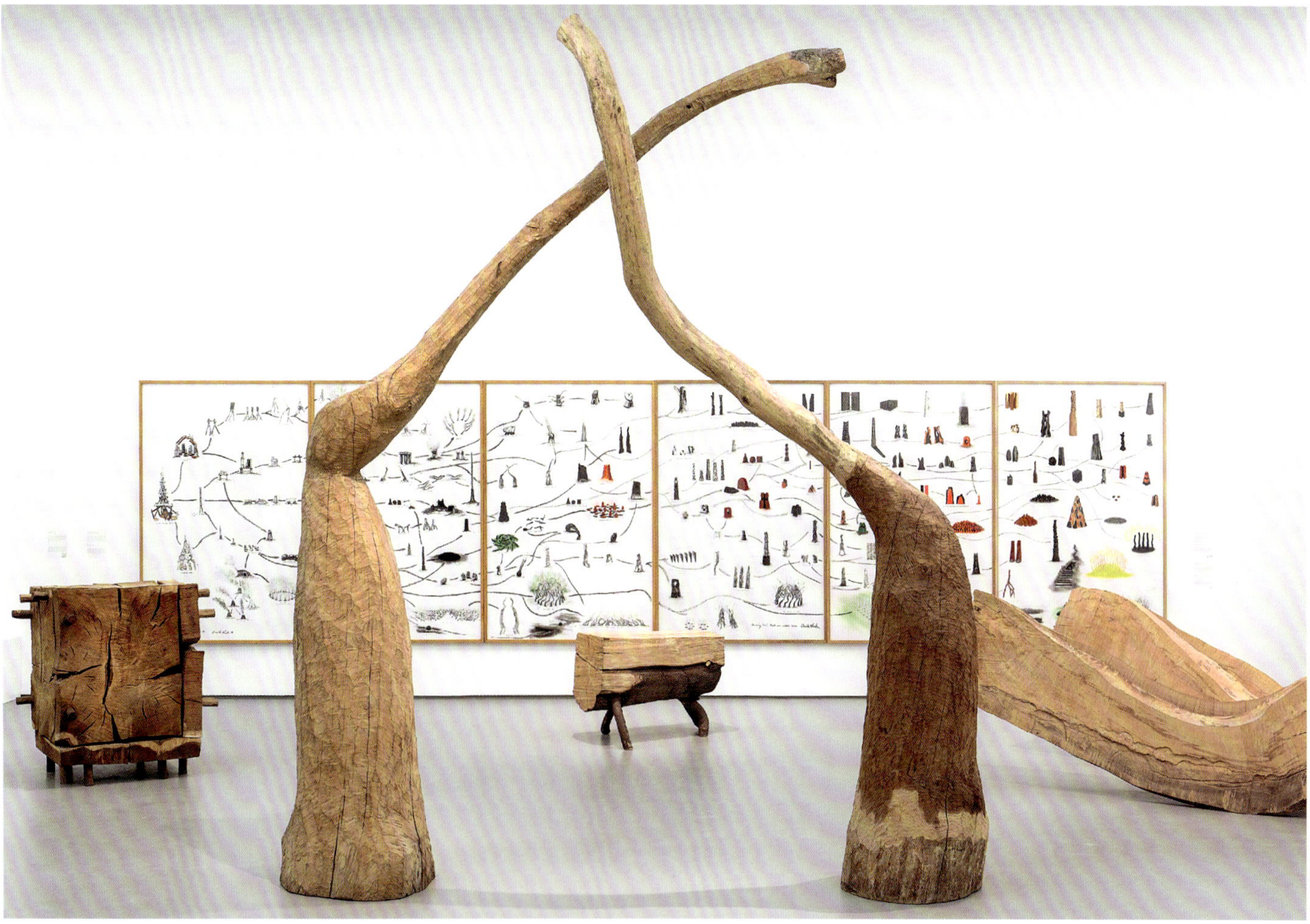

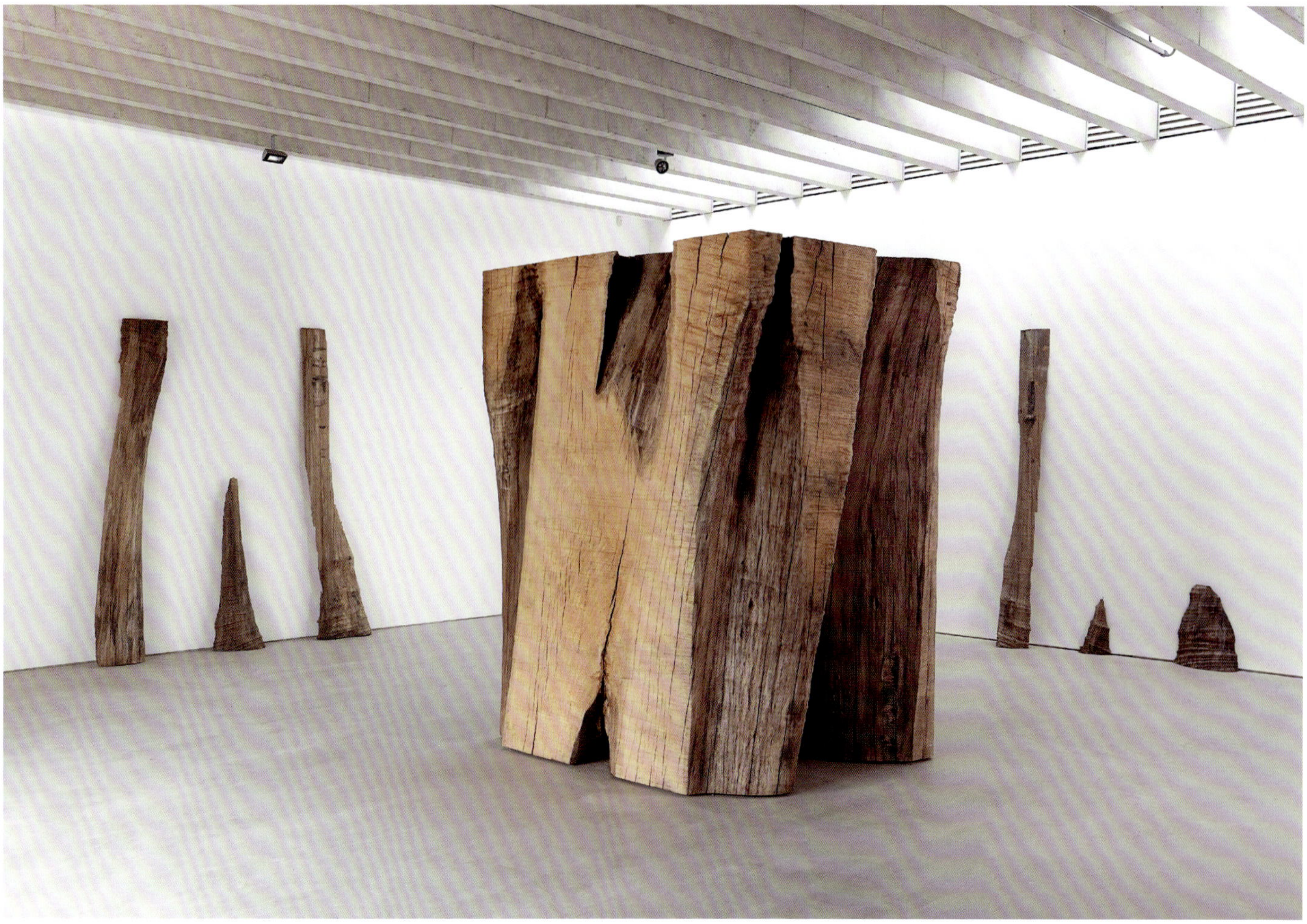

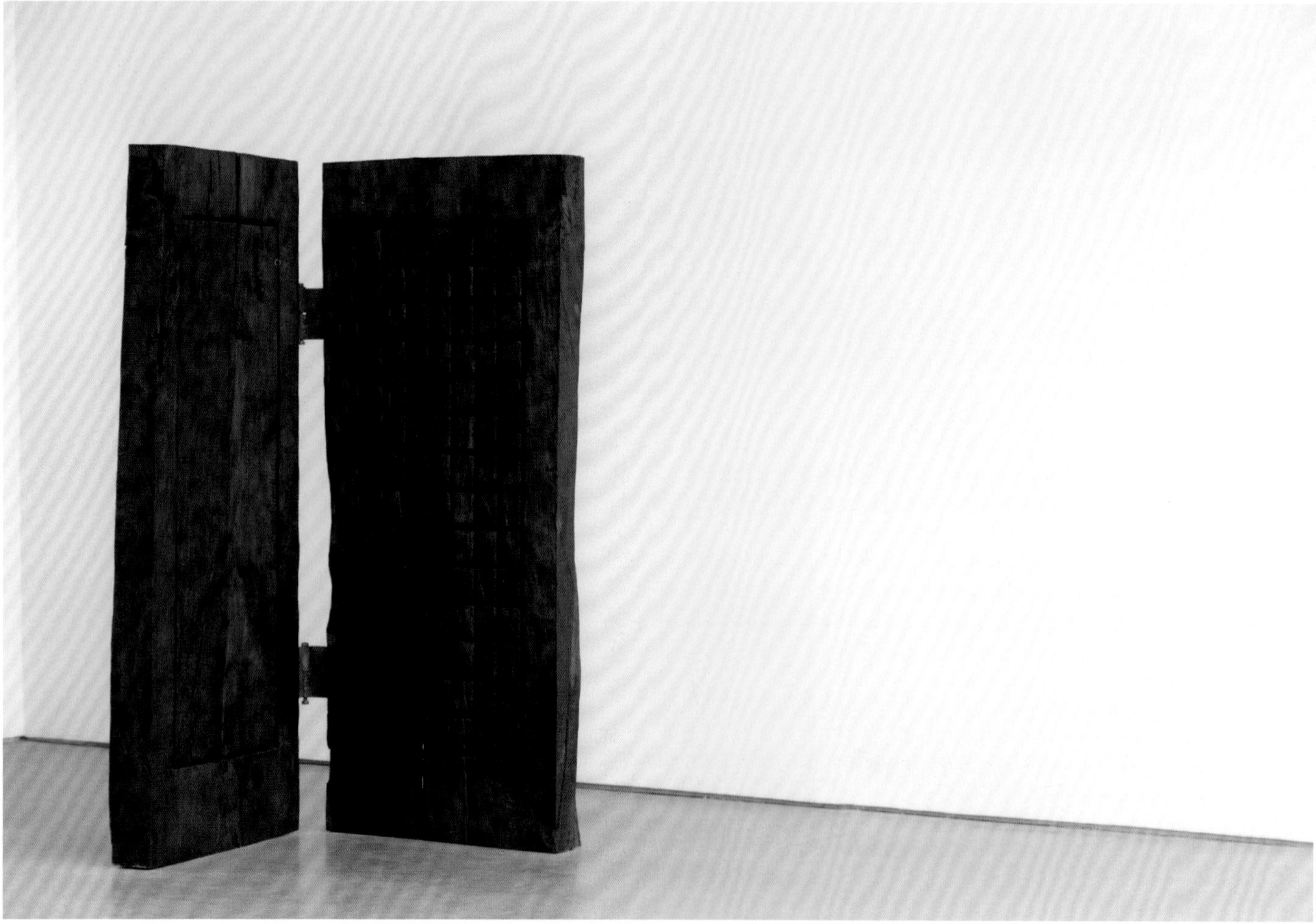

DN: *Oculus Block* has a natural hole at the top, the eye, which you can't see unless you're inside it. You have to turn sideways, go in and look up – that's the oculus. The work is only just square; it's not carved into a square with flat sides. The squaring is just breathed across, in the same way that the best Inuit sculptures retain the size of the original stone, with the image only just visible. Evan Shively, who has a wood yard in San Francisco, called the work *Oculus*, because of the eye. He's a Harvard man and loves words. Eucalyptus is an Australian tree that was grown in California for locomotive fuel, as there wasn't any coal. Steam had to be made and eucalyptus is 80 per cent as efficient as coal, because it contains a lot of oil. It's one of the densest woods and grows quickly, so it started swamping out the indigenous trees and had to be cut down. I have another studio in the South of England where Alan Smith, who I've worked with for many years, lives. He sources the wood and knows a good tree. Many of the bigger pieces are roughed out there, where he has a yard, and then hauled back to Wales.

IC: With exploitation and utility so prevalent in forestry, does your practice open our eyes to a more sentient experience of the forest?

DN: My work reflects an attitude towards the environment and to others. A basic tenet has always been an economy of means, only working with what comes available by natural process. I have strayed from this with the bronzes, but, in essence, that tenet remains my starting point. I hope people can see this interface between the living, elemental world – the environment we're all dependent and interdependent on – and the human mind, which is in its infancy, in terms of consciousness. Tree species are far older than us, and there's a level of wisdom in ancient things because of the longevity of their truth. I like to think my work touches on these truths.

←
David Nash
Millennium Book, 2000

Charred beech
and rusted steel
Each piece 231 × 101 × 18 cm
(7 ft 7 in × 39¾ in × 7⅛ in)

→
David Nash
Crack and Warp Column,
1989

Birch
218 × 53 × 53 cm
(7 ft 1⅞ in × 20⅞ in × 20⅞ in)

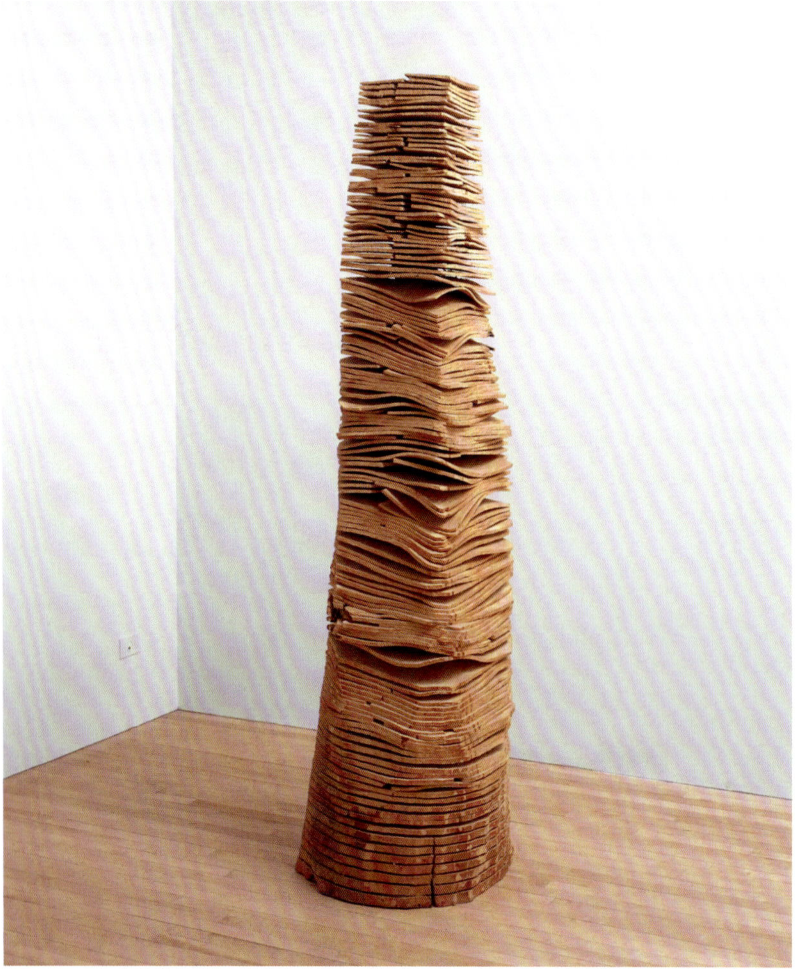

IC: *Millennium Book* (2000) and *An Awful Falling* (2001), made within a year of each other, emit a powerful message. *An Awful Falling* is reminiscent of 9/11, and *Millennium Book* echoes Rodin's *Gates of Hell* (1917), Rodin taking his inspiration from Dante's *Inferno* (c.1308). Although you've reflected on the unprincipled nature of human beings, your work remains essentially optimistic.

DN: The atrocities people perpetrate, along with capitalism and greed, is appalling. Of course, they always have, but it just goes on and on; nothing is ever learned. We do too much, expect too much and demand too much of nature's resources. Flying a family on holiday is the norm. This has all been evolving for the last thousand years and is accelerating. So, *Millennium Book* just pitches something to the viewer, but I'm not controlling where their thoughts go. I'm just offering a theatrical gesture. The two panels were originally going to be on a wall, but they were joined to become freestanding. It was then I got the book idea, hence the rusty hinges.

An Awful Falling wasn't intentionally associated with 9/11. I'd actually flown to Switzerland two days after 9/11 for an exhibition of my *Crack and Warp Columns*. At the time, it felt like the Western world was in such turmoil. On returning home, I found an offcut with spires sticking out of it. It stood up on its own and looked like the twin towers, and that's how it started. Then I made more but kept them in a room separated from my other work. Whenever I entered that room, my hair stood on end. It felt like war and peace, because most of my sculpture is about life. It is optimistic. I want people to feel joyous and uplifted by my work, but that needs to be balanced by the darker side of our human nature.

Interviewed in 2010 and 2019

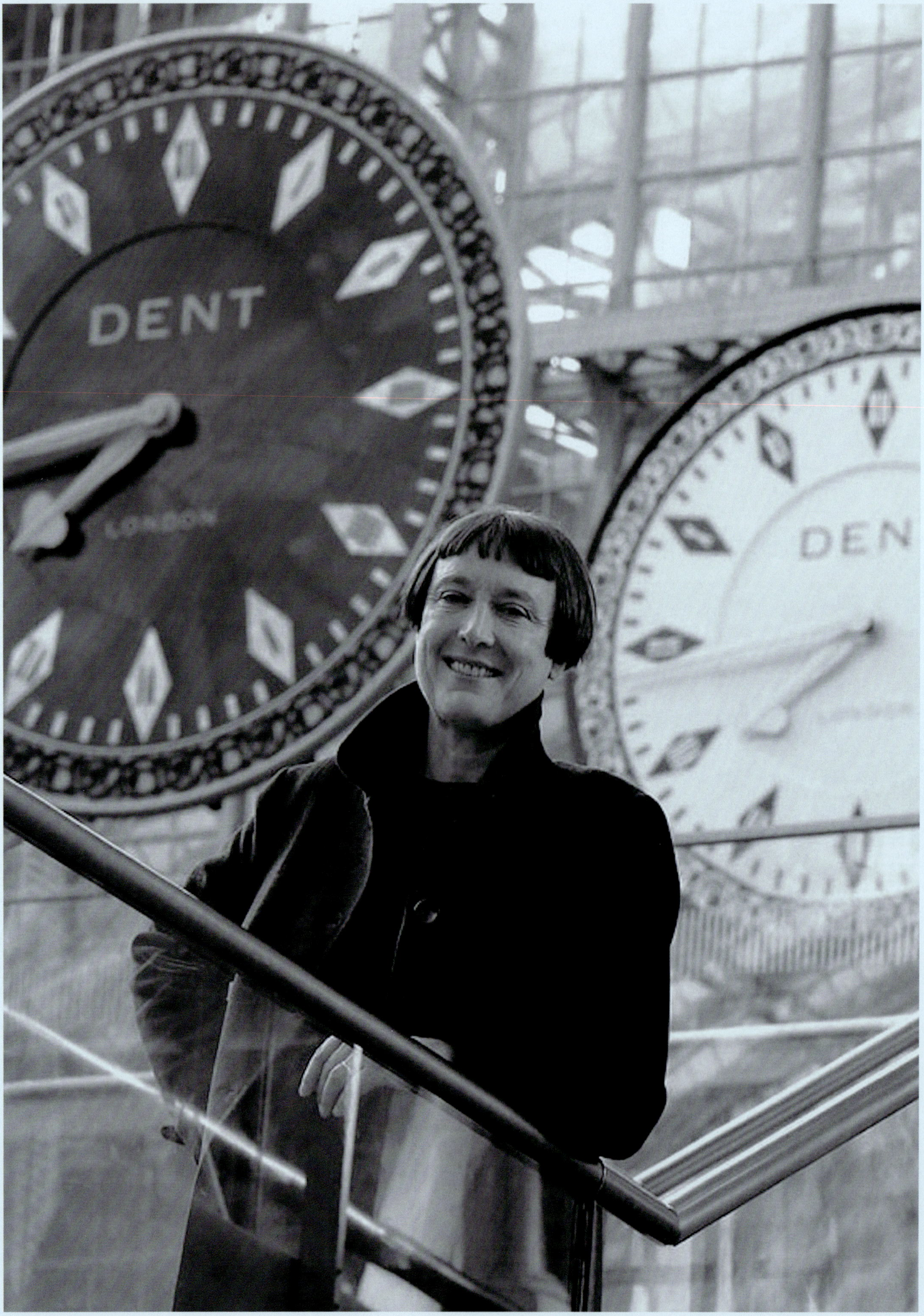
DENT
LONDON
DEN

CORNELIA PARKER

Born 1956, Cheshire

Cornelia Parker's approach is inherently experimental, in that recycled materials are often subjected to extreme processes, then suspended from the ceiling by near-invisible wires. For her seminal work, *Cold Dark Matter: An Exploded View*, she commandeered British Army personnel to blow up a garden shed, then salvaged the scorched remains to create an explosion held in mid-air. Through the opposing forces of destruction and reconstruction, the most surprising configurations reveal themselves. *Subconscious of a Monument*, a key work inspired by the Leaning Tower of Pisa, is loaded with history and memory, while *Transitional Object (Psychobarn)* is psychologically and politically multi-layered. Parker grapples with societal issues in unexpected ways, as seen in *Magna Carta (An Embroidery)*, shortly after which she became Britain's official Election Artist in 2017. Her practice is channelled by a dark undercurrent that questions humanity's increasingly perilous relationship with the planet and its fragile resources.

Cornelia Parker
Thirty Pieces of Silver, 1988–9

Steamrollered silver plate, metal wire
Dimensions variable
Installation view:
Museum of Contemporary Art Australia, Sydney, 2019

Ina Cole: The materials you use go through a dramatic process of transformation, often becoming crushed, exploded, burned or extracted. You have said your work harnesses all the friction that exists in the world.

Cornelia Parker: Friction has been going on in sculpture for centuries, ever since someone first knocked two stones together. My activity is about that friction, which happens naturally or can be premeditated. Materials are subjected to many different processes, and I particularly like using materials that have symbolic meaning in society – like a silver spoon – stretching them to see how far they can go. Metals can stretch; they have adaptability, precious metals particularly.

I've had the longest relationship with silver, and one of my first projects, *Thirty Pieces of Silver* (1988–9), was silver-plated objects crushed with a steamroller. Some years later, I made *Breathless* (2001), a flattened brass band for the Victoria and Albert Museum in London. This caused huge furore because it was thought I'd robbed the nation of all these musical instruments. However, I only used instruments that had already lost their puff and were at the end of their natural life. I've always used recycled materials, not through any environmental motivation, but because I find things which had a previous life more interesting. So, I'm not deliberately making provocative work. I just take objects that already have their own place in the world and recontextualize them to give a different meaning.

IC: Your practice often takes the form of a series, or themes, yet your projects are not consciously planned. To what extent do you rely on intuition?

CP: Intuition is a subjective act that artists often use, and I have to trust it. When I was teaching at Goldsmiths, University of London, my students were sometimes overwhelmed by critical theory. I told them to do what they felt intuitively driven to make, after which we could explore the possible meanings. That was my teaching gambit, to try and help students who were blocked. Several strands of my work have emerged and expanded intuitively over the years: it's not consciously plotted out, but added to. It's almost like groping around in the dark, and only through the making do I realize what I'm trying to do. However, titles can pull the artwork back to becoming a conscious object. Words, for me, are another material, and can have a friction all of their own. For example, in *Cold Dark Matter: An Exploded View* (1991), 'cold dark matter' is an unquantifiable piece of the universe, a scientific term, while 'exploded view' is a functional diagram. They're oppositional.

As an artist you have to surrender to your subconscious. Picasso's sculpture, for instance, is quite coherent but intuitive, which allowed him to make radical choices. The sheer variety is stupendous, as is the way he switches scale. He's obviously the consummate artist, just like Matisse who, on his deathbed, made the cut-outs. Look at *Snail* (1953). It's incredible how abstract it is, so ahead of its time. How modern and full of verve they both were.

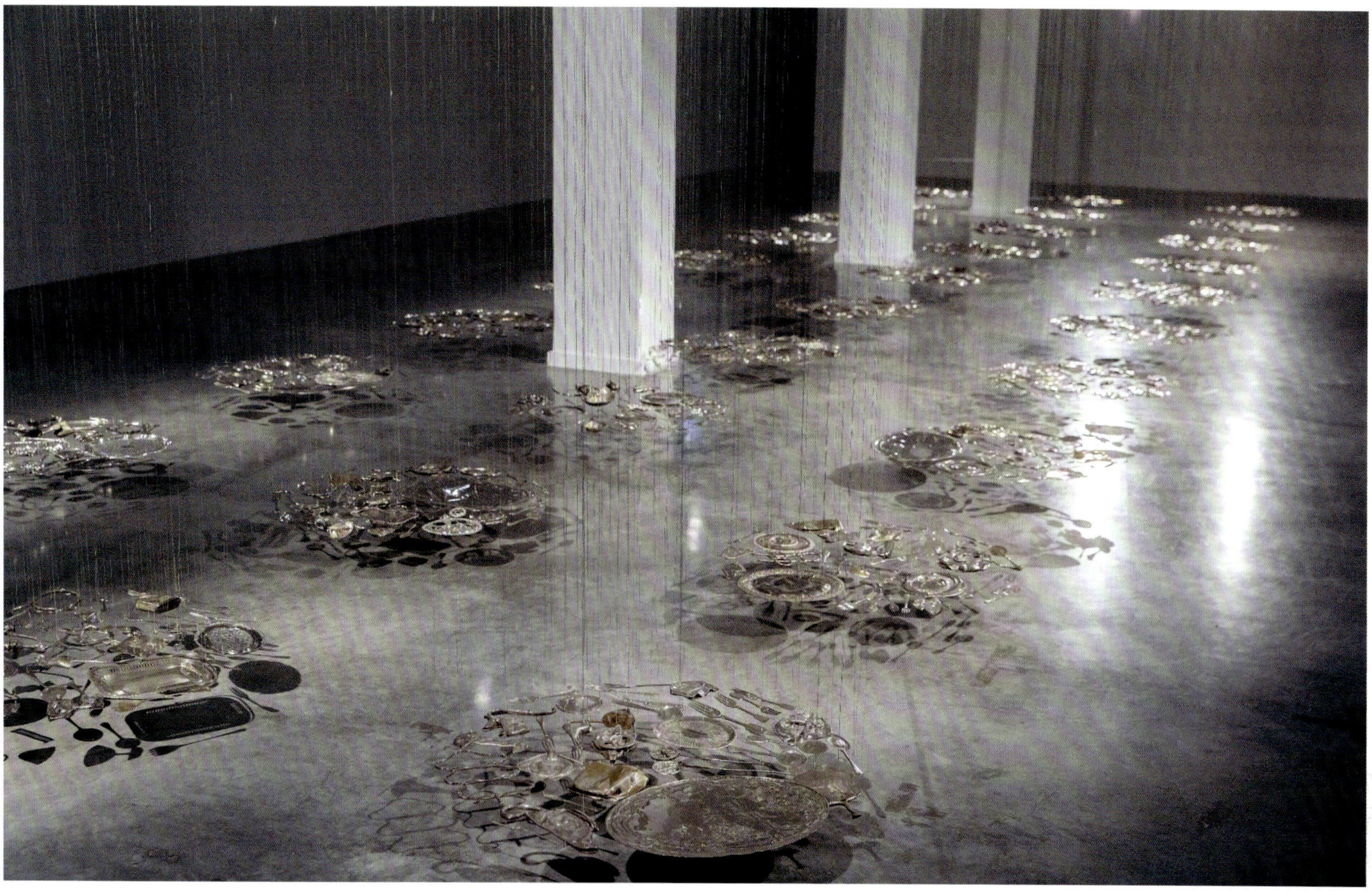

IC: *Cold Dark Matter: An Exploded View* is one of your most celebrated installations. Walking into the room to become engulfed by shadows cast from a central light-bulb is a mesmerizing experience. It featured in Ian McEwan's novel, *Saturday* (2005), but what was the context for this?

CP: He visited Tate Modern in London where he saw *Cold Dark Matter,* really enjoyed it and put it in his novel. I've read Ian McEwan's books and was happy he enjoyed my work too. We all make allusions to other art forms, and, once created, artworks go on to have their own lives. However, when first installing it, I didn't realize the shadows would be so effective. It was just like recreating the explosion. Viewers walked between the shadows and the light and became part of this particular moment. For me, art is about moments of revelation which I cannot plan. In the Easter Sunday Mass at St Paul's Cathedral, London, in 2003, the minister giving the sermon used *Cold Dark Matter* as a metaphor for the Iraq war. He then took the whole congregation, hundreds of people, over the bridge into Tate Modern to see it, which I thought was incredible. *Cold Dark Matter* isn't about Iraq, but about every explosion that has ever happened. I just felt the explosion had become ubiquitous in terms of expression and our own anger. As a subject, it was another friction, another mini apocalypse.

IC: Many of your installations, such as *Cold Dark Matter,* defy gravity and appear to be levitating. How did your interest in suspending objects begin?

CP: The idea of suspension, literal or metaphorical, has always been there, even as a student. There's a history of sculpture being about stability and grounded to the earth, yet with Arte Povera and the dematerialization of the art object, things changed. My work is constantly in flux: leaning against a wall, hovering, or so fragile it

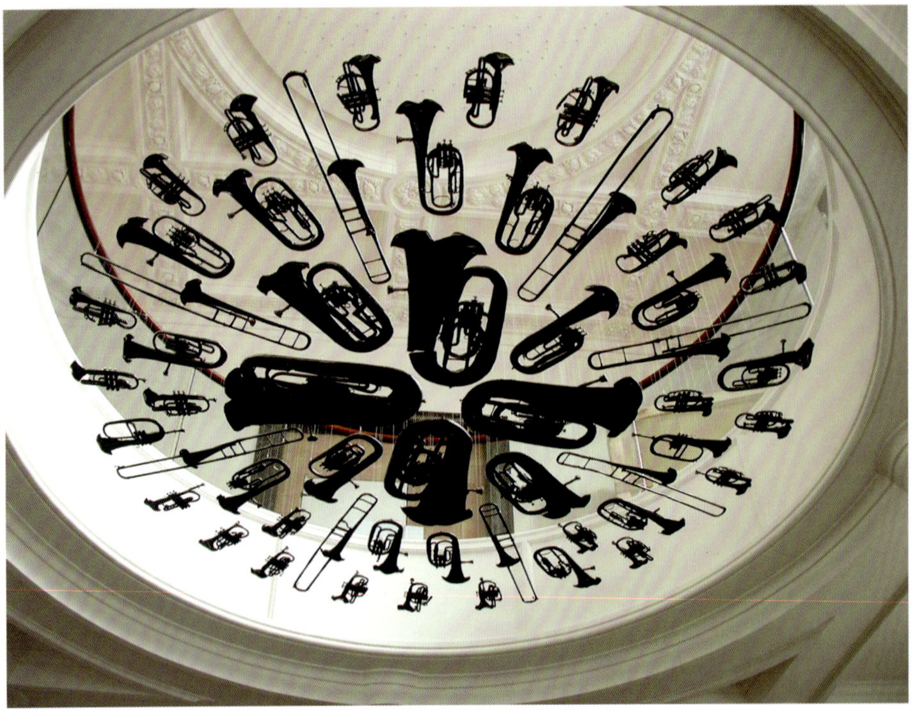

←
Cornelia Parker
Breathless, 2001

Brass musical instruments flattened, wire
Dimensions variable
Installation view:
V&A Museum,
London, 2001

→
Cornelia Parker
Cold Dark Matter: An Exploded View, 1991

Blown-up garden shed and contents, wire, light bulb
Dimensions variable
Installation view:
Chisenhale Gallery,
London, 1991

might collapse. Perhaps that's what I feel about my own relationship to the world. Vulnerability is a universal condition. We don't have solid, fixed lives; we're constantly in transit.

IC: In *Subconscious of a Monument* (2003) you used extracted earth from beneath the Leaning Tower of Pisa. By resurrecting and suspending this discarded material, you not only give it renewed life, but also reveal another dimension – a hidden, enigmatic aspect.

CP: Much of my work deals with gravity, and occasionally famous monuments or famous people. The Leaning Tower of Pisa is one of the world's most iconic buildings, associated with Galileo's gravity experiments. It was finally saved from falling when engineers slightly rectified its lean by extracting some of the earth from underneath it. The thought of humble earth supporting a beautiful Romanesque tower and that, by extracting some of it, the tower could be saved, interested me. However, it took long negotiations with the Italian bureaucracy before I was allowed to have some of this earth. It came out as waterlogged mud, and I first showed it as a pile in a solo exhibition at GAM in Turin (2001). When it was later shipped to me in bags, it had dried out into smaller lumps, which meant I could suspend it. I liked the idea of the subconscious of this monument – the Leaning Tower of Pisa – defying gravity and giving it a chance to expand and fill its own space. In New York, there's a permanently sited earth room by Walter de Maria (since 1977), and mine is a suspended version, a small homage.

IC: *The Maybe* (1995), which featured actress Tilda Swinton sleeping in a glass case, attracted over 20,000 visitors in a single week when shown at Serpentine Galleries in London. It was quite a brave act on her part, but why did *The Maybe* create such intense curiosity?

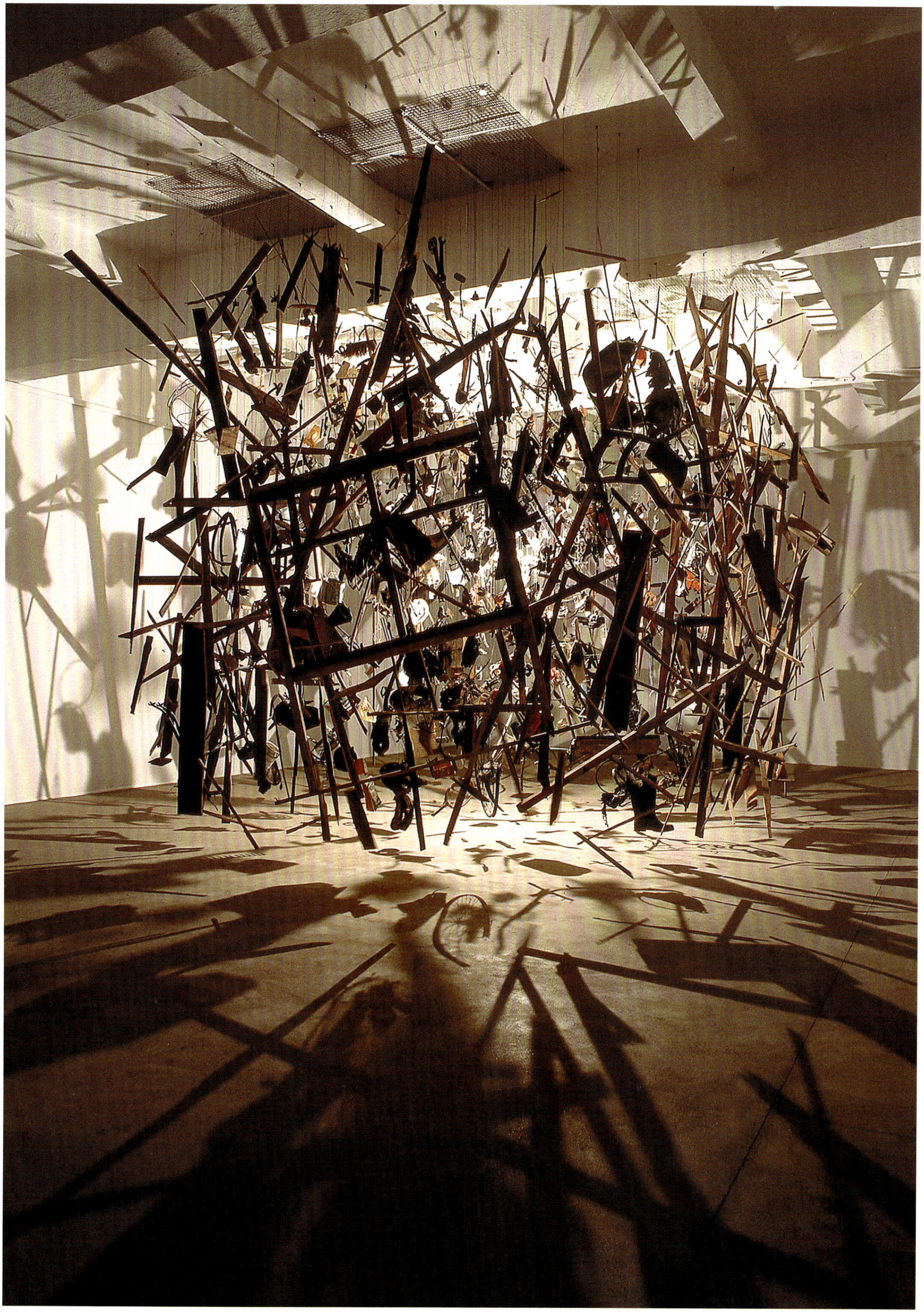

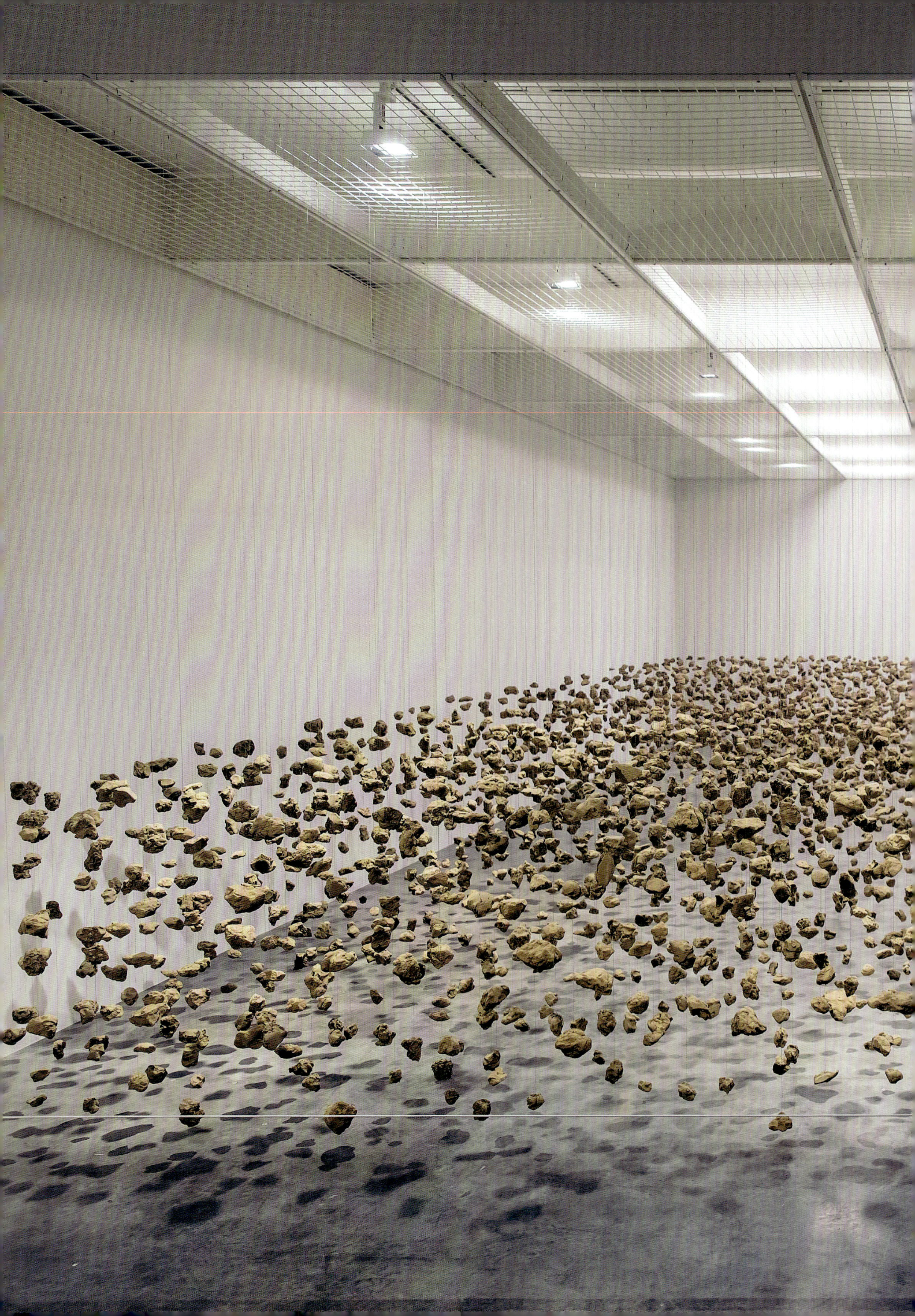

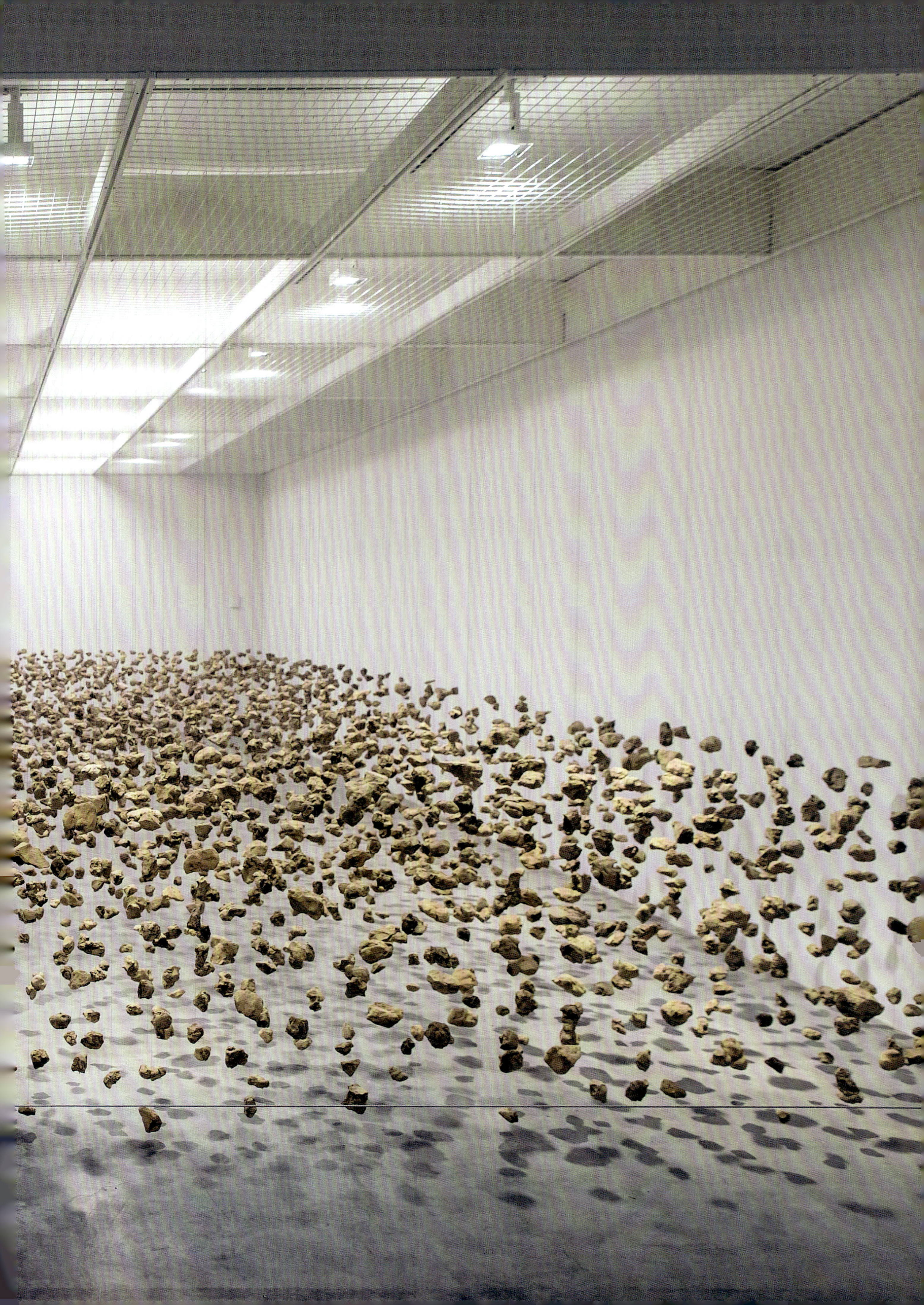

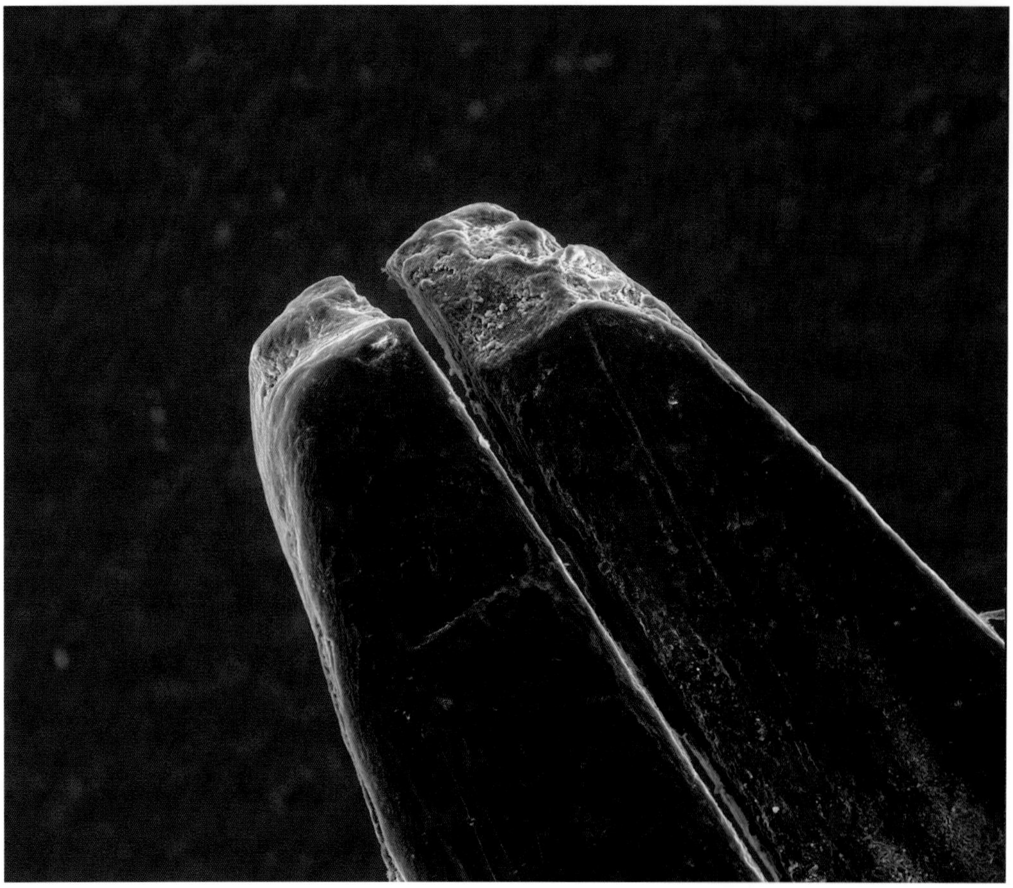

←←
Cornelia Parker
Subconscious of a Monument, 2003
Soil excavated from beneath the Leaning Tower of Pisa, wire
Dimensions variable
Installation view:
Museum of Contemporary Art Australia, Sydney, 2019

←
Cornelia Parker
Brontëan Abstract (Emily Brontë's quill pen nib), 2006
Silver gelatin print of an SEM Image
44.5 × 49.5 cm
(17½ × 19½ in)

CP: It was hugely brave, and she had a strong desire to do it. *The Maybe* was quite maverick, as it was funded by a new collaboration grant for practitioners from different art forms to make work together: my obsession with materials and histories, and her performance skills, and the fact she could lie still, seemingly asleep, for eight hours a day. At the time, Tilda was an art-house movie star rather than a household name, and I think *The Maybe* created a lot of curiosity because she had this enigmatic quality people were attracted to.

Tilda wanted to create a performance piece sleeping in a glass coffin as Snow White. It's funny, but when I first went to talk to her about the project, enthusiastic male friends of mine said, 'Oh, bring me back one of her stockings.' This gave me the idea of creating a reliquary, exhibiting objects belonging to famous historical figures, long dead, such as Churchill's cigar, Charles Dickens's quill pen, and Charles Babbage's brain. In this context, Tilda was unfinished business. It wasn't about fame; it was about mortality and immortality, and the relic standing in for someone else. She was dressed simply as herself, framed in a nondescript glass case, like the other objects. Although part of this reliquary, she just happened to be a living, breathing Snow White, not dead, but in limbo, which we all are. However, the installation needed viewers in the gallery to activate it as art, otherwise it was merely a collection of objects. People connected them, and the energy flowing through the spaces was electrifying. It made everybody draw on their own sense of mortality. It was more about them as individuals than about Tilda, or the other exhibits, which were extraordinary only because of their history. There was an almost Frankenstein feel to it all.

IC: *Brontëan Abstracts* (2006) also draws upon inconsequential 'relics' once owned by famous

→
Cornelia Parker
Transitional Object (PsychoBarn), 2016

Life-size
Installation view:
The Metropolitan Museum of Art,
New York, 2016

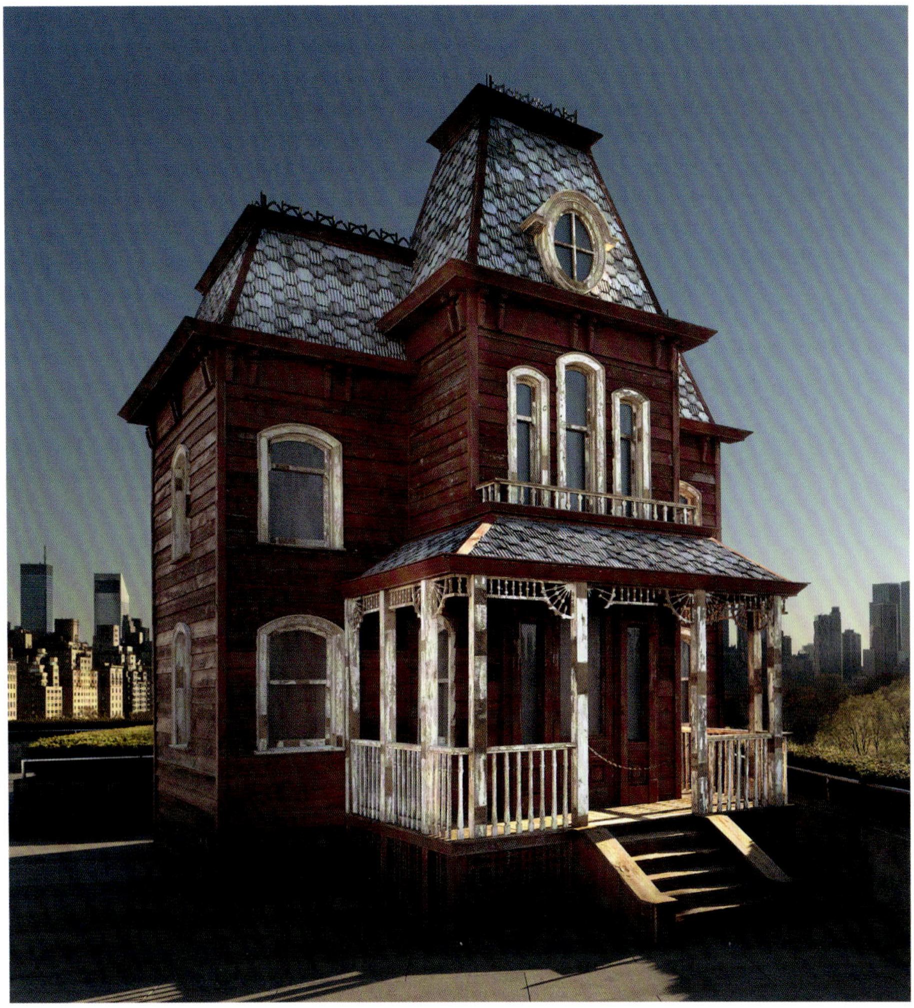

historical figures, this time Charlotte and Emily Brontë. This project was developed during a residency at the Brontë Parsonage Museum and reveals a fascination with the minutiae of human existence, the poignant details so often forgotten. How did your forensic interest in the life of the Brontës develop?

CP: The Brontës are such iconic figures, and every particle of their lives has already been picked apart. I therefore found abrasions they had unconsciously created, which couldn't be seen with the naked eye, and I enlarged them using an electron microscope. Emily's feather quill pen was worn down through friction, perhaps through scribbling away at *Wuthering Heights* (1847), and it resembles the beak of a bird when increased in size. Charlotte's pin cushion was covered in blue paper that she had pierced many times with her pin, and I enlarged one of the holes, so it appears like a gaping black void.

As children, the Brontës wrote these tiny cryptic books, and I also used the microscope to blow up small details, so you can see the narrative. I found the original *Jane Eyre* (1847) manuscript in the British Library, and when Charlotte neatly copied her last draft she had crossed out a few words that didn't make it into the book. I decided to save those discarded words and give them another showing. All these little frictions, which nobody was concerned about, became the subject of *Brontëan Abstracts*. They were abstracts made by them, rather than me. I simply captured them. When I'd finished the project, I felt very close to the Brontës. Those little abrasions they had created told me much about their characters.

IC: *Transitional Object (Psychobarn)* (2016) was commissioned for the roof of the Metropolitan Museum in New York. It takes its inspiration from Hitchcock's film *Psycho* (1960). How did you decide on the subject matter and the positioning of this work within its assigned space?

CP: It was built using wood from an old red barn and takes the shape of the Bates house from Hitchcock's *Psycho.* In the film, the house only consisted of two facades, propped up from behind, and I replicated it using photographs of the old set. *Transitional Object (Psychobarn)* was commissioned for the Metropolitan's fourth annual roof project, so was created with the roof in mind. It was set against the backdrop of New York, because you can see propped billboards on many roofs all over the city.

My first thought had been to raise a typical American barn onto the roof, but I then realized it would be too large, so revised the proposal. New York used to be New Amsterdam, an area made up of fields, with farmers who most probably had barns. In fact, I later discovered that the Metropolitan was built on the site of a big red barn. Also, during the Great Depression of the 1930s, Central Park was covered with a shanty of makeshift wooden houses nicknamed Hooverville. I learnt that Hitchcock had used Edward Hopper's painting *House by the Railroad* (1925) as inspiration for *Psycho*, in addition to which Hopper painted a lot of red barns. American politicians often stand in front of them, as they're symbolic, a metaphor for wholesomeness. I wanted to create the opposite of that. The Bates house is about evil, a murderer becoming his mother. That's why I called it *Transitional Object*, a term used when a child is weaned off the mother by the use of a blanket, or teddy bear. Hitchcock was from Britain and I used to live in Leytonstone in London, where he was born. I was playing with polarities and this work is a mutation of all these ideas.

IC: You often use the gun and bullets in the development of projects. This has taken the form of an ongoing series called *Bullet Drawings*, and guns that have been dismantled, as in *Sawn Up Sawn Off Shotgun* (2015), as well as *Landscape with Gun and Tree* (2010) at Jupiter Artland, in Edinburgh.

Cornelia Parker
Sawn Up Sawn Off Shotgun, 2015

Shotgun sawn off
by criminals,
sawn up by police
Dimensions variable

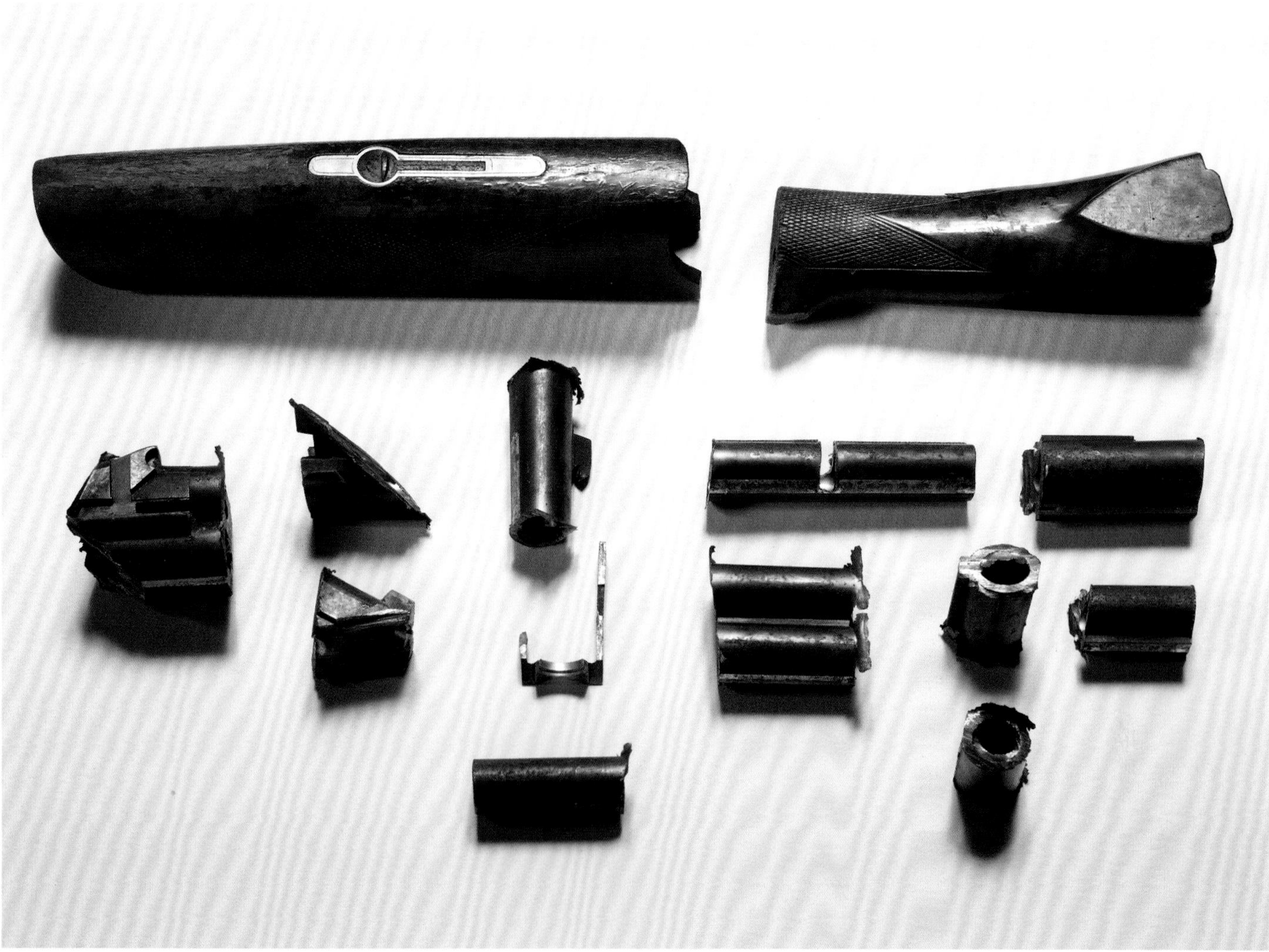

CP: Guns are prevalent in society, especially in America. Yet the gun and bullets are also clichés, like *Transitional Object*. Clichés are interesting because they're very reinforced, a much-visited spot. When first starting out, I used familiar objects to describe something unfamiliar, and that's still true of my work. Bullets are pliable, and in *Bullet Drawings* they're melted down and drawn into wire. A bullet's worth of lead wire is then trapped between two sheets of glass and framed to resemble a pencil drawing. This process of making wire from melted-down objects is called 'drawing'. There's always a hail of bullets in the world, so *Bullet Drawings* are ongoing.

Sawn Up Sawn Off Shotgun is a gun confiscated by the police. They had to decommission it before giving it to me, by chopping it into bits. Sawn up is done by the police, and sawn off by criminals – two sets of sawing. *Landscape with Gun and Tree* was commissioned by Robert and Nicky Wilson for Jupiter Artland, where gun cartridges can often be found in the long grass. I wanted it to be alarming and borrowed Robert's gun, which was enlarged to 9 metres (29½ feet) tall, so it could lean against a tree, albeit reinforced. I was inspired by Gainsborough's painting *Mr and Mrs Andrews* (1750), in which Mr Andrews stands with a gun over his arm while his wife sits demurely. Initially, I considered calling it *Mr and Mrs Wilson*, as the landscape of Jupiter Artland reminded me of that painting. However, in the end, I decided on *Landscape with Gun and Tree*, a much broader title.

IC: More recently, politics and the law have entered your practice. *Magna Carta (An Embroidery)* (2015) was created in collaboration with over 200 individual contributors. It was initiated by Ruskin School of Art in Oxford, for the 800th anniversary of the Magna Carta, in collaboration with the British Library. How did *Magna Carta* develop?

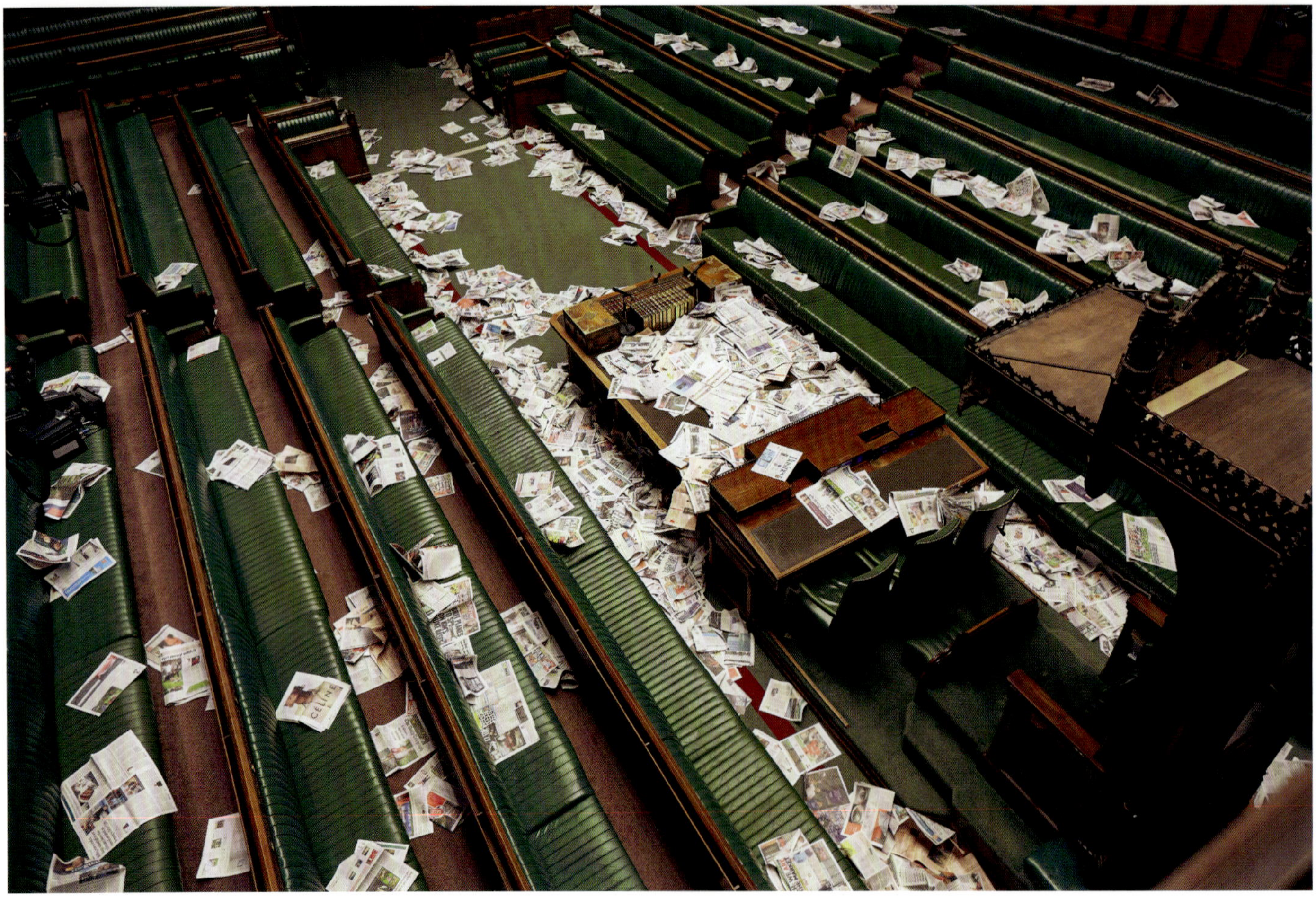

CP: *Magna Carta* is a 14 metre/46 foot-long hand embroidery that took a year to complete. It's based on the Wikipedia page of the Magna Carta, as of 15 June 2014. The text was first printed onto canvas, then cut into strips and sent to male prisoners in jails around the UK – prisoners who had been trained in embroidery by a charity called Fine Cell Work. Then I made a list of other contributors I wanted, most of whom touched on an aspect of the law: a human rights lawyer embroidered his words in Guantanamo Bay, while attempting to free a prisoner; Paddy Hill, one of the Birmingham Six, embroidered 'free man'; and Doreen Lawrence, whose son Stephen was murdered, stitched 'denial delay justice'. Whistle-blower Edward Snowden contributed the word 'freedom' from Russia; and I met Julian Assange, of WikiLeaks, in the embassy of Ecuador in London, from where he also took part. There were many others; all available information is here, in this embroidery. The online encyclopedia, Wikipedia, is made up of entries that are crowd-sourced; hundreds of stitched-together testimonies that change every day. It's a fantastic concept, and Jimmy Wales, inventor of Wikipedia, who embroidered 'user's manual', set up a website to link the embroidery to the main Magna Carta page.

IC: Following *Magna Carta*, you became Britain's official Election Artist in 2017, at a time when the whole world order seemed to be changing. Your work generally doesn't force its message – it allows for multiple readings – so was this quite a challenging prospect?

CP: Yes, very, but it was also quite liberating, in that I couldn't divulge my political position. I was asked to use a diaristic approach and took to Instagram with gusto. *Election Abstract* is a three-minute film from those Instagram diaries, using 1500 images. However, the main film, *Left Right & Centre*, was set in the House of

Commons at night, where I placed three months' worth of newspapers on tables in separate piles – left wing, right wing and centre. It was pitch black and a drone with a light was filmed by a camera in slow motion. The drone moved along the seats while light played over the newspapers, teasing you along. Next morning, the drone returned, went over to the tables and dive-bombed all the newspapers, which flew up into the air revealing their headlines. This continued for a few minutes until everything was completely covered in newspapers. Finally, the drone moved out of the House, into blackness.

IC: There's an undercurrent of volatility in many of your projects, irrespective of the materials you've used. You have said that you grew up thinking the apocalypse was just around the corner.

Cornelia Parker
Left Right & Centre, 2017
Video

CP: I had a frugal upbringing in the countryside, programmed by my parents never to waste anything. You can get much pleasure from minimal acts; you don't need excess for enjoyment. I now feel we're on a downward slope, consuming far more resources than are available. The population has reached a certain point and infrastructures are collapsing. There's not enough energy to power the world's demand, not enough nutrient in the soil and not enough water to satiate everyone's thirst. This capitalist, consumerist society is failing and we can't continue like this without a massive depopulation. The planet can probably go on for a long time; it's the human race that's at stake. People aren't paying attention. Before global warming and the possibility of nuclear annihilation, there was always the thought that a meteor could hit the earth. I don't know which is going to happen first; they're all distinct possibilities. Perhaps I do have an over-developed sense of the apocalypse, but I think we have to be alert and not sleepwalk into oblivion. In my life and work, I always try to engender the idea of not being wasteful and of respecting what we have.

Interviewed in 2008 and 2020

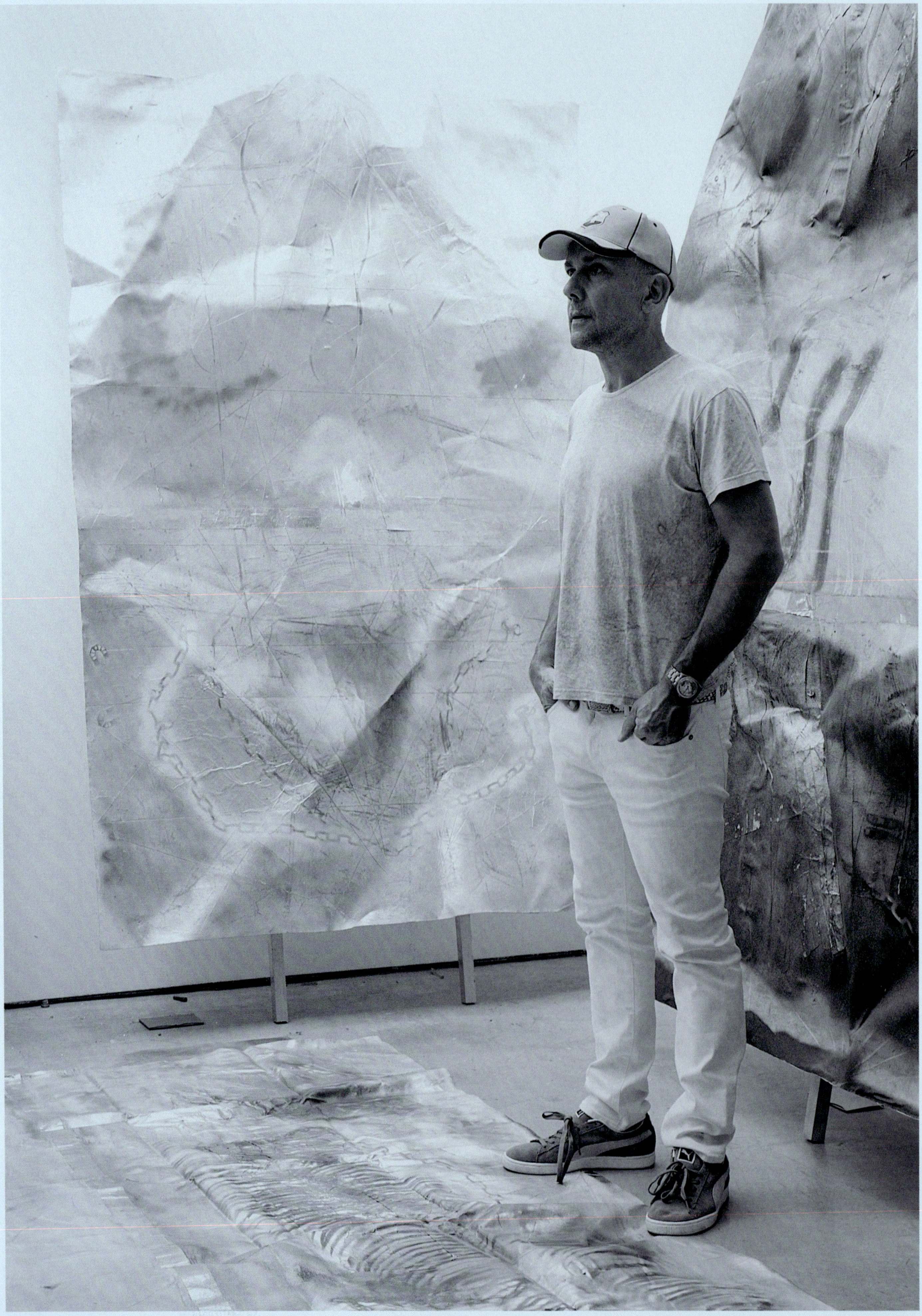

MARC QUINN

Born 1964, London

Through a fusion of scientific knowledge and artistic means, Marc Quinn creates an investigation into the body, identity, genetics and humanity's complex relationship with nature. His early work utilized organic and degradable materials, such as *Self*, a cast of the artist's head made from 10 pints of his own blood and immersed in frozen silicone. The transformative, and elusive, properties of material are an important feature of his practice, yet later projects also assimilate the permanence of marble, bronze and concrete. Quinn's work often alludes to art history, particularly the classical forms of antiquity, which resulted in *100 Heads*, a contemporary interpretation of Greco-Roman portraiture that raises awareness of the mass crossing of refugees in the Mediterranean. This series challenges the perception of refugees as homogeneous masses and celebrates their individual identities instead. Quinn's repertoire can be seen to echo life's manifold paradoxes, thereby also serving as an outlet for social interaction and debate.

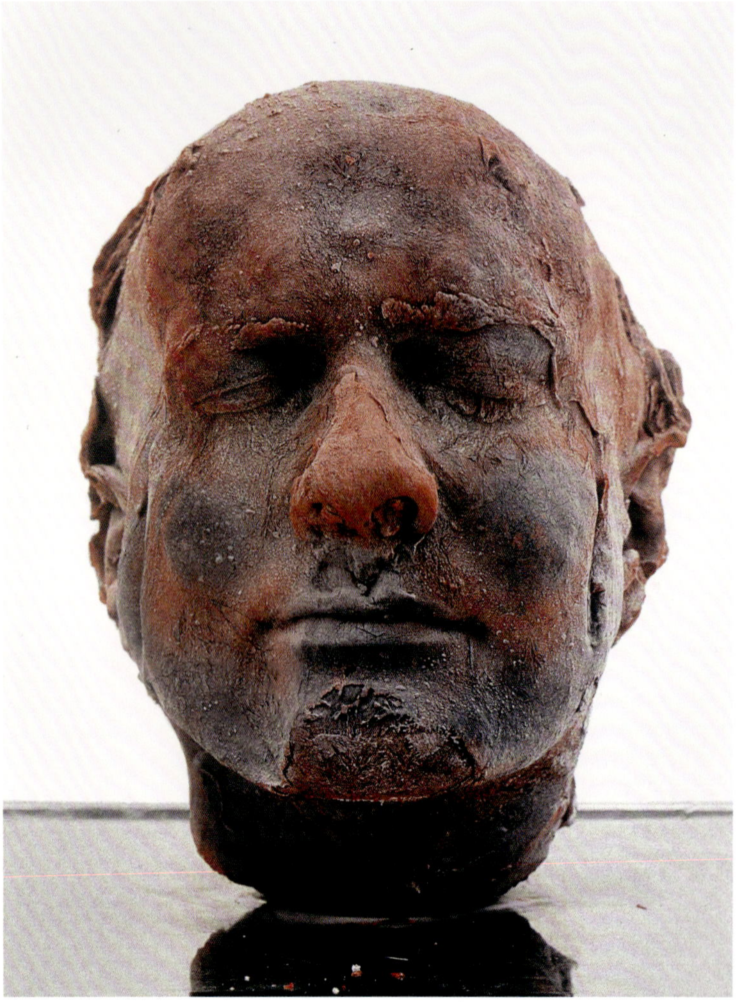

←
Marc Quinn
Self, 1991

Blood (the artist's), stainless steel, Perspex and refrigeration equipment
208 × 63 × 63 cm
(6 ft 9⅞ in × 24¾ in × 24¾ in)

→
Marc Quinn
100 Heads (Adiam Yemane), 2020

Concrete and stainless steel
181 × 33 × 25.5 cm
(71¼ × 13 × 10 in)

Ina Cole: *100 Heads* (2020) are concrete portrait busts of a cross-section of the global refugee population. Concrete is particularly versatile, as it can be modelled, carved or cast. What compelled you to create this work?

Marc Quinn: When watching the refugee crisis on the news it struck me as being, firstly, a really human story, and secondly a defining one of our time, in that it speaks of where the world is headed. This crisis has become part of history, and I'm interested in bringing contemporary history into art. As a contemporary artist, it's important to make work that reflects the time you live in, and this is a critical story to tell. I used concrete because it's like an urban twenty-first century marble. We usually only see it in the built environment, but it's a nuanced material that can be modelled and shaped with an incredible level of detail. It has the feel of being classical and contemporary all at once.

100 Heads is part of a wider outreach project in which I take art into the 'real' world. It's important to put challenging content into the public realm. People rise to the occasion when presented with public art, and a proper discourse can then occur. Historically, sculpture has always been used for this purpose, and it suits me to be part of that dialogue. So, the whole ethos behind *100 Heads* is a collaboration with refugees who joined the project as part of a global recruitment process. I had to form a charity and join up with other non-profit organizations and the International Rescue Committee. All this might not traditionally be seen as sculpture, but I believe it is. I was a big follower of Joseph Beuys when younger, and made artwork out of debate and social connections, not just physical materials.

IC: You've had a long interest in the portrait, and previously used 10 pints of your own blood for *Self*.

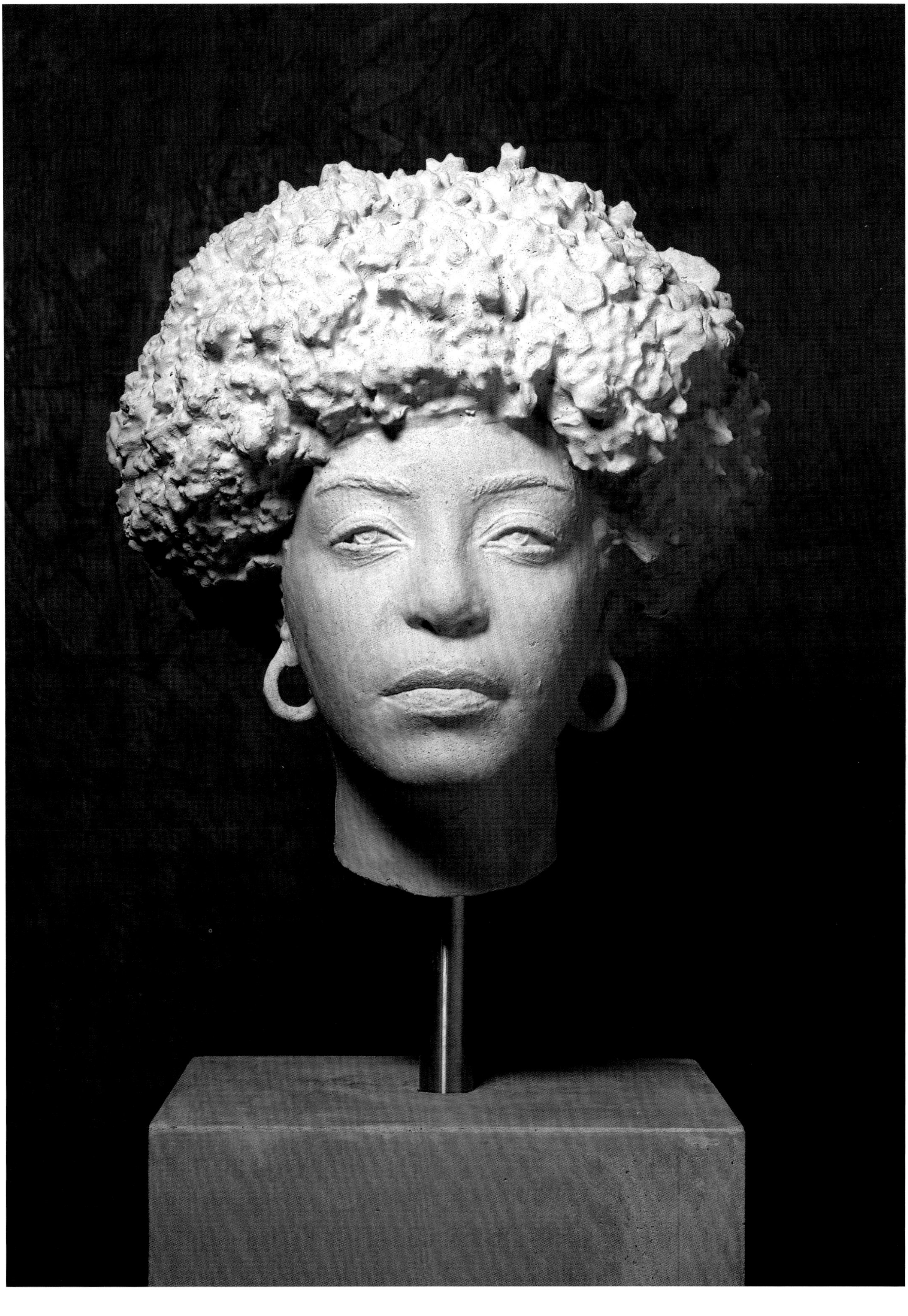

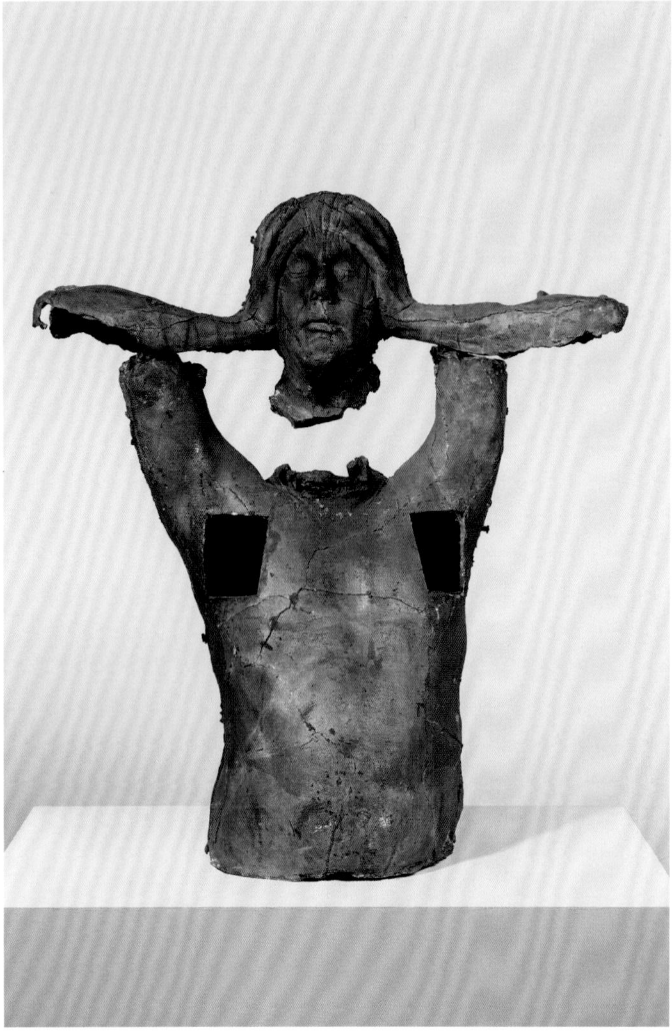

Marc Quinn
Emotional Detox, The Seven Deadly Sins IV, 1995

Cast lead and wax
90 × 80 × 30 cm
(35⅜ × 31½ × 11¾ in)
(approximate)

The first of these self-portraits was conceived in 1991, and a new one on the theme is made at regular intervals. Am I right in thinking there's an instruction for the last cast in the series to be taken from your deceased body?

MQ: I haven't decided yet, but it would be a shame to waste the material. Even better, if I'm brain dead my children could keep my body alive on a ventilator and continue making post-posthumous copies of *Self*. This would take the idea of the posthumous cast to another level. The body can be kept alive and it can keep producing blood, therefore I could potentially continue with those artworks after my death, which is an interesting idea.

With *Self*, I wanted to bring real life into art. I thought, 'How do I make a self-portrait that's real – that looks like the sitter and is also made of the sitter?' And, 'What part of the body could I use which wouldn't disfigure or kill me to take?' Blood seemed like the right material: it symbolizes life, the body remakes it, and yet it's classed as an organ. It has sculptural qualities because it's a liquid, but when the atmospheric conditions change it becomes a solid, so there's a sense of being able to transform it in a sculptural way. *Self* uses electricity to maintain its frozen state, and, to me, that reflects our dependence on society and infrastructure – how we rely on others and external mechanisms to keep ourselves alive.

IC: This fascination with the self has a powerful historical descent: Franz Xaver Messerschmidt created around 60 'character heads' in 13 years, beginning in 1770, using his own head as a template. Did you consider this descent when making *Self*?

MQ: Absolutely. I love Messerschmidt. I think he felt inhabited by the 'spirit of proportion', which he exorcized by making a head of every possible facial expression. His heads are cast in lead, so the fumes of lead casting could easily have sent him a bit mad. The titles were then added after his death. In a way, he's a shamanistic artist. I did a whole series much more directly inspired by Messerschmidt: *Emotional Detox* (1995), seven lead sculptures cast from parts of my own body, made when I gave up drinking in 1993. They're contorted, not only facially, but bodily. So, I'm a great fan of Messerschmidt.

IC: At the point of creating *Self* and *Emotional Detox*, the British art scene was presided over by the so-called YBAs (Young British Artists). What you all had in common was an openness towards materials and process, and a predilection for the theme of mortality. Looking back, do you consider the YBAs as a coherent group, or somewhat disparate?

MQ: It's quite a disparate group, but what is coherent is the fact that everyone made and showed art at the same time. The common denominator was how we used real-life subjects and concerns. It was a reaction against art becoming essentially formalist and post-Minimalist. Art about art just seemed slightly irrelevant. We had a post-punk attitude and didn't wait around to be chosen, or for value to be placed on our work. Creativity was the driver, rather than an inferred value placed upon us by an establishment that didn't understand what we were doing. We did it all ourselves, from the bottom up.

IC: Your father was a physicist, and much research goes into your projects, often involving a close alliance with scientists. *DNA Portrait of Sir John Sulston* (2001) was commissioned by the National Portrait Gallery in London. You were with John at the BBC in September 2001, just as planes hit the Twin Towers in New York. The disparity between this terrorist act and the heroism of his research in sequencing the human genome is immense. Although we share 99.9 per cent of our genome with the rest of humanity, does it not seem we're essentially much divided?

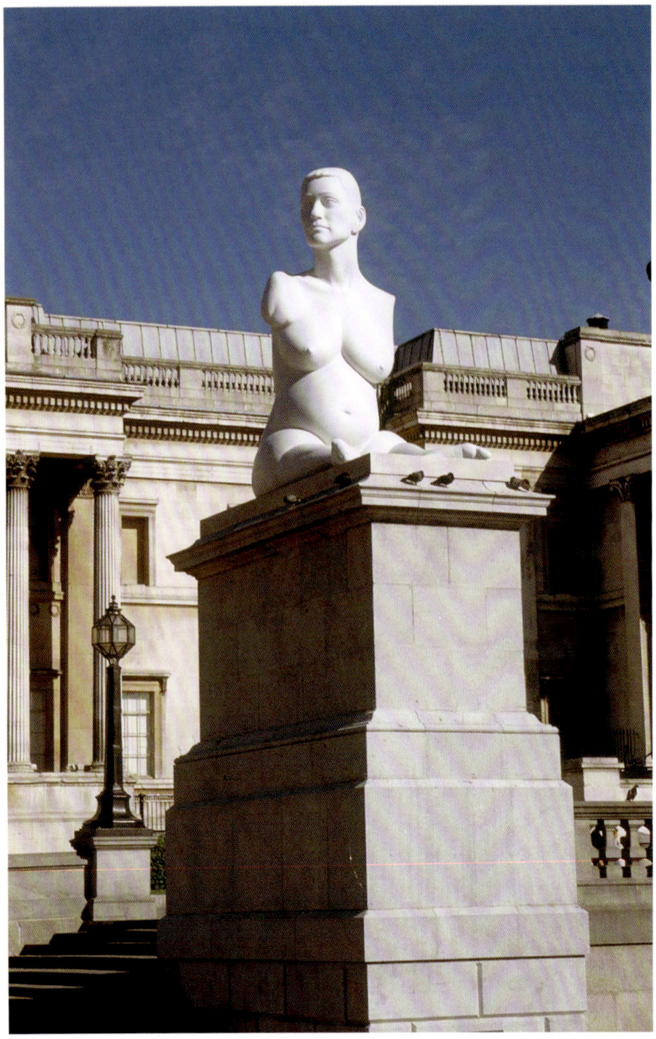

←
Marc Quinn
Alison Lapper Pregnant, 2005

Marble
355 × 180.5 × 260 cm
(11 ft 7¾ in × 71 in × 8 ft 6⅜ in)
Installation view:
Fourth Plinth,
Trafalgar Square,
London, 2005

→→
Marc Quinn
Garden, 2000

Cold room, stainless steel, heated glass, refrigeration equipment, mirrors, turf, plants, flowers, acrylic tank, low viscosity silicon oil held at -20°C
320 × 1270 × 543 cm
(10 ft 6 in × 41 ft 8 in × 17 ft 9¾ in)
Installation view:
Fondazione Prada,
Milan, 2000

MQ: As we walked into the BBC, televisions were showing planes hitting the Twin Towers. It was weird; very surreal. John's research is all about how we're connected, and I believe the similarities between us are much greater than our differences. A terrorist act is essentially about differentiation; it's a way of saying, 'We hate you because you're not like us.' However, you have to fight difference, don't you? For instance, the whole migration issue pushes people to take extreme positions, but, by hearing an individual's story, those prejudices can dissipate.

DNA Portrait of Sir John Sulston explores the border between abstraction and figuration. It's a plate of agar jelly-covered bacteria colonies, containing John's genome. Although it seems the most abstract thing in the world, it actually contains the instructions to remake the sitter. It presents the idea of figuration as informational, rather than something that resembles someone. At the time, it was the most realistic portrait in the National Portrait Gallery, even though it was the only abstract one. I worked with John for a while, as we made a few different DNA pieces together. He was a great guy.

IC: *The Complete Marbles* series (1999–2005) also deals with issues of differentiation. They're of a group of people missing limbs through birth, accident or illness, created using the whitest marble from Macedonia, and partly inspired by the Elgin Marbles at the British Museum. One of these, *Alison Lapper Pregnant*, was installed on the Fourth Plinth in Trafalgar Square, London (2005), and then became a centrepiece at the 2012 London Paralympic Games. Did this particular work change our perception of the body?

MQ: I've heard that many involved in the disability sector felt it had changed things. *Alison Lapper Pregnant*, like *100 Heads*, uses content in the public realm for people to feel, think and change their views in a direct way, because it bypasses intellect and hits you emotionally. What was interesting about *Alison Lapper Pregnant* is that the rest of Trafalgar Square is full of dead guys who conquered the world, and her sculpture is about a woman who's alive. In fact, it's about the future, because she's pregnant. It's also about making the most of your life despite being given various difficulties to overcome.

The Complete Marbles were originally a reaction to looking at fragmented classical statues in the British Museum and seeing the admiration audiences had for them. Someone whose real body is 'incomplete' – like those fragmented statues – would be met with a different reaction. So, my sculptures are photorealist, idealized versions of a body that isn't traditionally seen as ideal. It's like they're of the future, from a more enlightened society where difference, diversity and inclusivity are celebrated rather than marginalized. When looking at the history of art, I felt it was time to reset the clock. But things have changed a lot since making *The Complete Marbles*.

IC: Your interest also lies in the manipulation of nature. *Garden* (2000) is a hallucinogenic botanical paradise, which brings all the flowers on the planet into one location. It seems to epitomize the notion of desire, yet it's only an illusion, as the flowers are housed in a refrigeration unit and would crumble at the slightest touch.

MQ: Yes, they're dead essentially, frozen in silicone. There's a kind of purity in taking a living thing and making a sculpture of it using the same atoms that existed in the living version. Taking the life out of it, and changing the condition from ambient to frozen, is the moment of creating the sculpture. It's as if an invisible transformation between object and image were taking place. The real flower is the object, and when it freezes it becomes an image of itself, made from the same atoms that were in the original flower. It's the magic trick of art, in a way. The flowers represent desire, as most of these plants only exist in great numbers because humans buy them in such quantities from shops, or flower markets. In nature, these flowers wouldn't all exist at the same time. Now, because of human desire and globalization, they're flown from all over the world to arrive in one place.

IC: Yet the flowers in *Garden* have to sacrifice their own quite limited lifespan to become everlasting.

MQ: Exactly. You have to die young in order to stay beautiful forever. *Faust* (1988), my first sculpture of a head cast in lead, was about the same idea. I started with wax, which was then enveloped in plaster and put into an oven, where the wax was melted down. The metal then went in to make a permanent version. However, in order to get that version, I had to sacrifice the wax, which is mutable and could have become anything at all. So, its potential was sacrificed in order for the object to become permanent.

IC: Much of your work is only kept intact through artificial means. It would disintegrate without a support system, and this belies its permanence. Is there a deliberate dichotomy taking place?

MQ: Yes, absolutely. While some of it is temporary, that temporariness can be permanent as well. Certain pieces, like *Garden* and *Self*, need someone, or an external mechanism, to look after them. They're artworks on life support. Then again, my sculptures are also made of marble, bronze, cement or even plastic bags which can last for a thousand years. I practise on many different levels. Part of my interest in material is its half-life. How long it lasts is part of its meaning.

Other work, such as *1 + 1 = 3* (2002), is more performative, in that light and water emerge together as the properties of a rainbow, then evaporate, or dissipate, and I have to start again. In a way, *1 + 1 = 3* is about how the creative process happens, and the beauty and purity of art. Similarly, by absorbing culture we can come up with something new. It's like a flame on a candle: although it can be explained scientifically and rationally, there's still a sense of magic. These fleeting experiences, and images, are why life is worth living. Like the frozen flowers – they're fleeting but

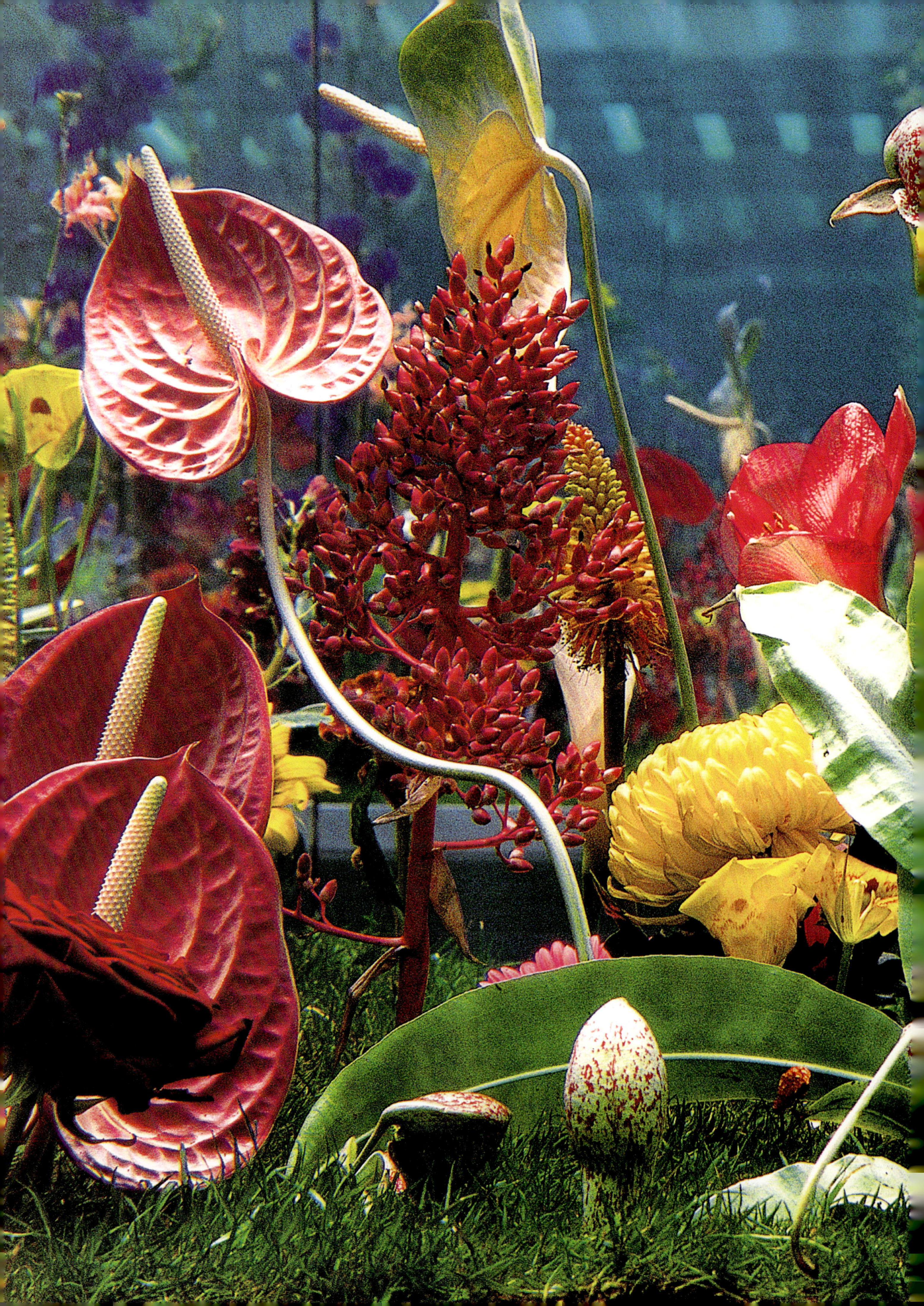

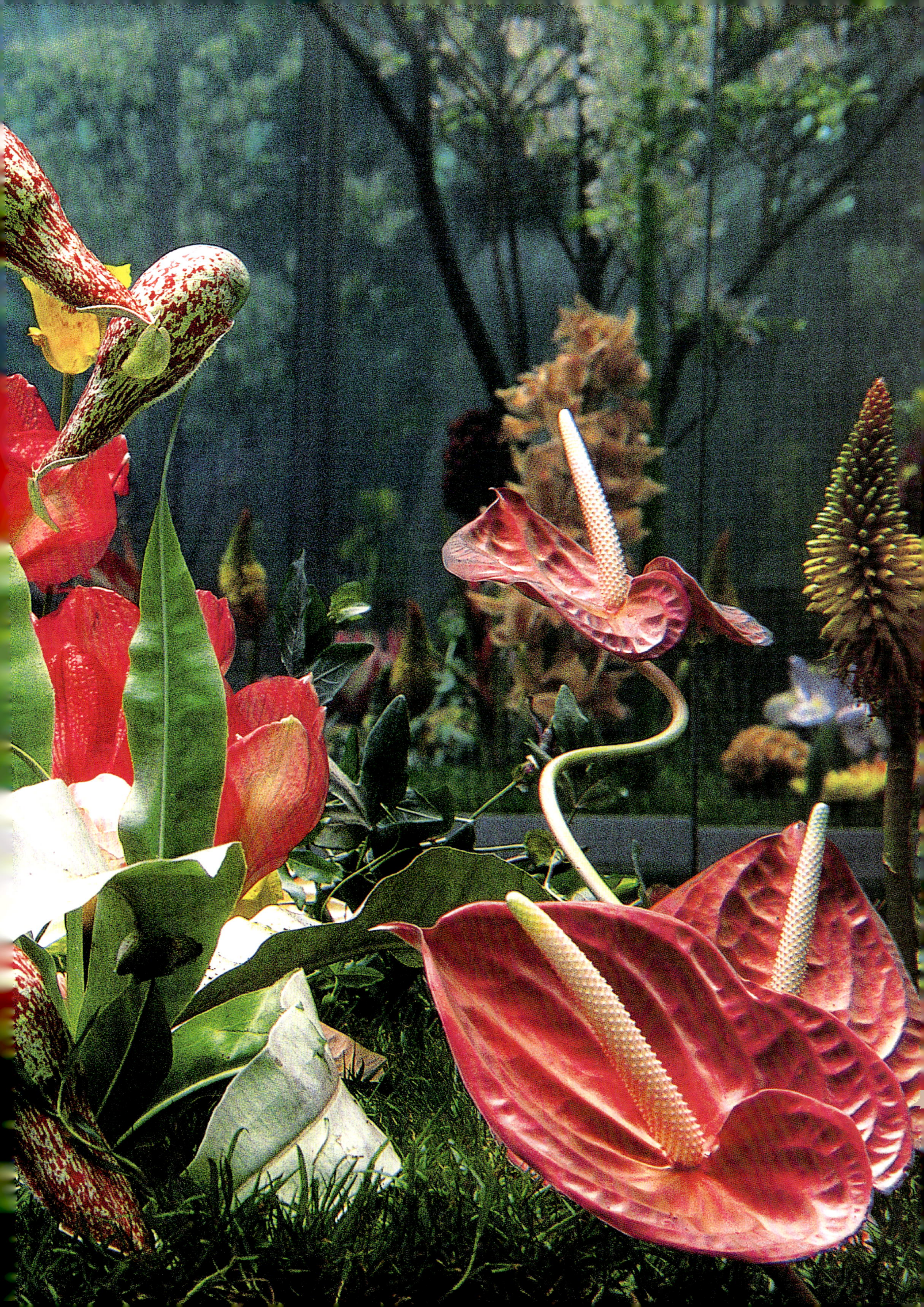

were made to remain in one place by extending their relationship with nature. This could all be considered as a commodification of nature, and I suppose a human desire to control comes through too. It can be read in many ways.

IC: *Evolution* (2005) is a group of nine marble sculptures, while *Planet* (2008) is a monumental 10 metre/32 foot-long baby hovering above ground level, using painted bronze and steel. These two pieces seem intrinsically linked. Were they intended as a celebration of life?

MQ: *Evolution* is the genesis of a baby; it's an abstraction, an idealization. I was also inspired by Michelangelo's *Slaves*, for the tomb of Pope Julius II (1513–16), in which the figures look as if they're struggling out of the marble. In *Evolution*, the figures of the foetus appearing from the marble look like life emerging from the material world. *Planet* was made when I had a child. Although those two works are connected to my biography, they're also about the creation of a person in the womb more generally. It's the most primordial form of sculpture; the most magical thing. There's a chemical reaction that creates something that grows to become a fully formed human being. It's almost impossible to believe, and yet we've all come from there. That is really the most extraordinary form of sculpture.

IC: Conversely, from 2006–11 you made a number of works using skeletons, such as *Waiting for Godot* (2006), a praying skeleton awaiting guidance. Is its inherent irony premeditated?

MQ: Definitely; you could wait forever. The skeleton is interesting because it's an abstraction of the human body. Even though it has no particularity or singularity, everyone can identify with it. Obviously you would only usually see one if someone's dead. Well, on one hand it's not alive, but on the other hand it is, as it's the architecture of the body, the geology. The skeleton is amazing sculpturally because it results from a process of mineralization: the body takes minerals from your diet and turns them into bone, which is a form of sculpture in itself. The body creates bones and teeth made of calcium carbonate, which are essentially stone. It's extraordinary to think you have stone inside you.

IC: Death is a recurrent theme in your practice. In some ways it's an inconceivable prospect, partly because we're contained by the body, while the mind is capable of infinite flights of imagination. In a sense, we're all living this strange, paradoxical existence. Do you fear the concept of death?

MQ: No, I don't think so. Once you're dead, you're dead. Maybe I fear dying, but that depends on how it will happen. I don't worry about not having lived during all the millennia before I was born, therefore why should I worry about it afterwards? Yet, obviously, being alive is great and I don't want it to end. Also, having limited time adds impetus, otherwise you'd just sit around doing nothing.

IC: *All About Love* (2016) is a group of 12 life-casts, which echo the fragmented forms found throughout art history. They're incredibly intimate, so much so that, on viewing them, it feels one has inadvertently intruded upon a prohibited and very personal space.

MQ: I like the series a lot. They are very personal. I wanted to take the idea of the fragmented artwork and animate it so it becomes present and personal. They're about life, and life is about relationships and love.

Marc Quinn
Evolution VIII, 2005

Pink marble
253.5 × 116 × 85.5 cm
(8 ft 3¾ in × 45⅝ in × 33⅝ in)

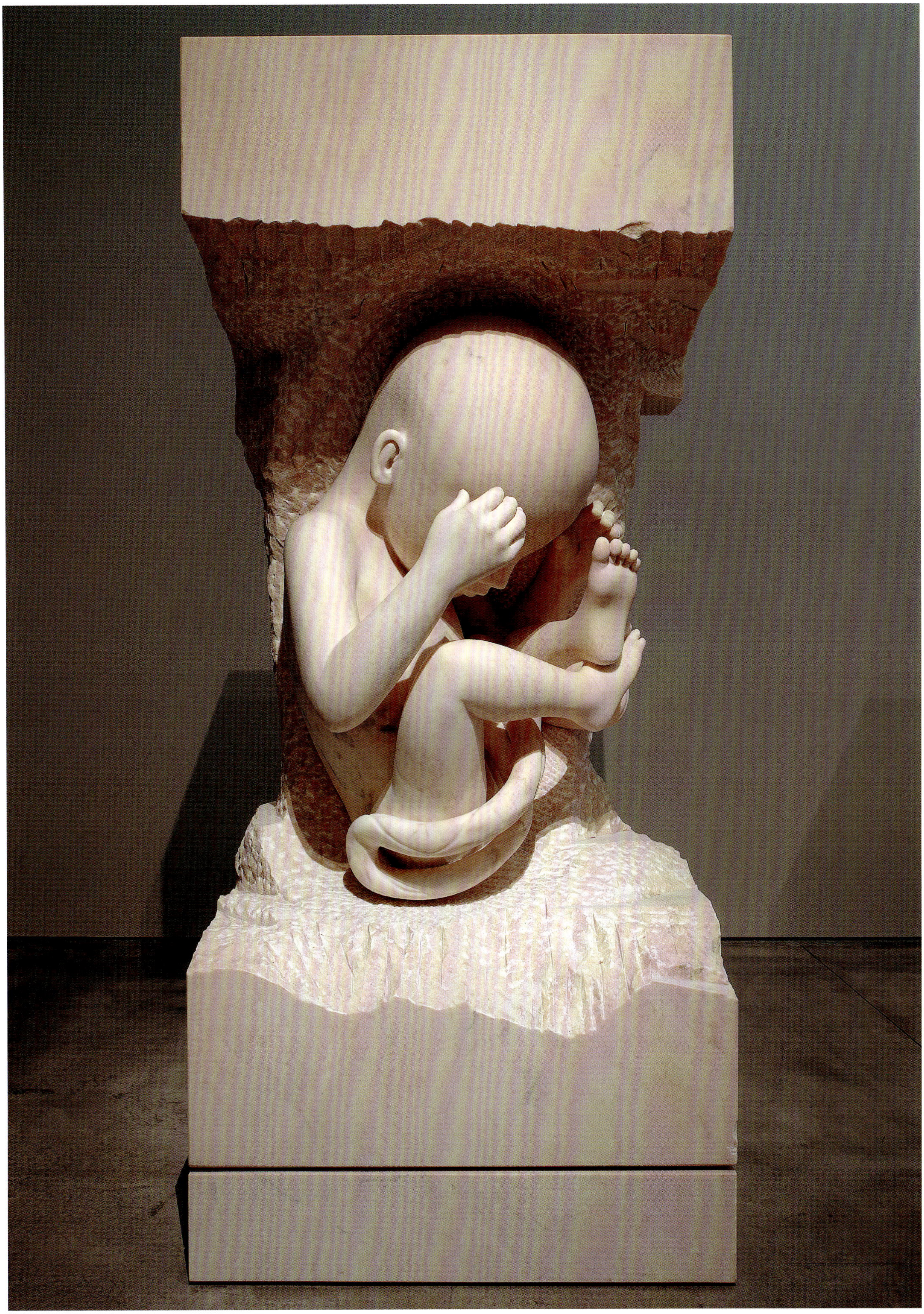

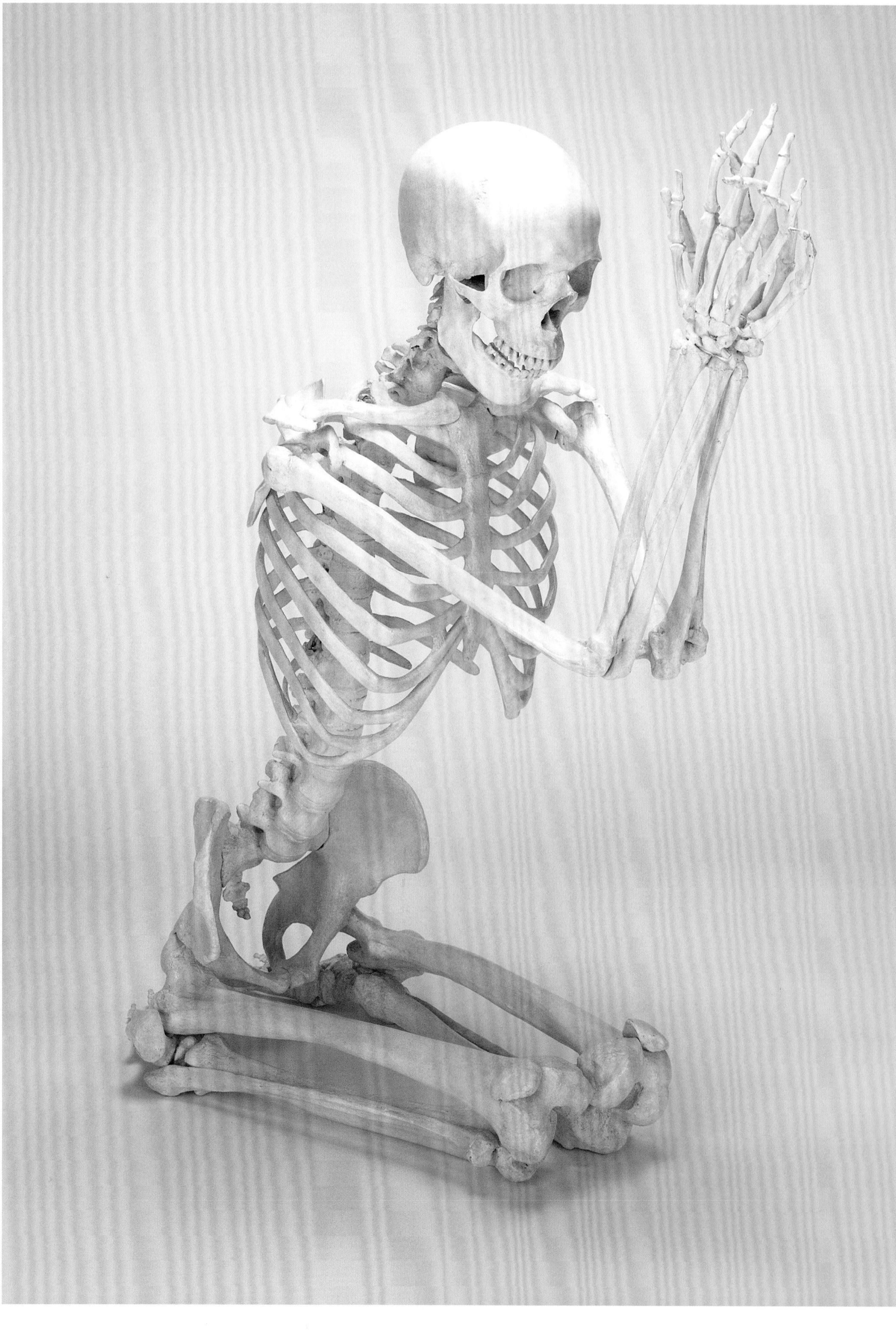

←
Marc Quinn
Waiting for Godot, 2006

Patinated bronze
77 × 37 × 76.5 cm
(30¼ × 14⅝ × 30⅛ in)

→
Marc Quinn
All About Love (Breathe), 2016

Glass-reinforced polyester and biresin polyurethane, stainless steel plate and rod, split shaft collars, softwood and far eastern ply
214 × 64 × 63 cm
(7 ft ¼ in × 25¼ in × 24¾ in)

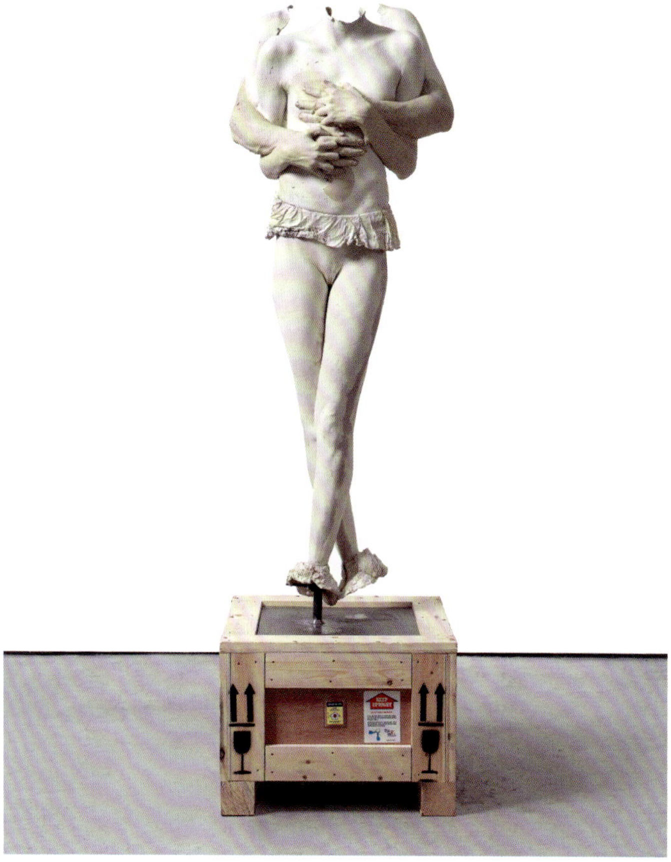

However, they were made through a language which seems paradoxically inappropriate, that of ancient sculpture. I brought the figures back to life by using this incredibly detailed dental rubber. This picks up each little pore in the skin and every hair. Even though they're made of fibreglass, an industrial material, they appear like real bodies. By not having heads they become universal, as they're not portraits of anyone. Well, they are, but without faces. Once you add a face, the sculpture loses universality. They're all about the language of gesture and how bodies connect to each other, rather than the language of the face.

IC: The human ability to love is a noble attribute, yet we're living in an increasingly simulated era. Are we at risk of losing the ability to project feeling onto anything that lies beyond our defined personal territory?

MQ: The more virtual our existence, the more necessary reality will start to become. One of the great qualities of art, and particularly sculpture, is that it's not downloadable. You have a physical interaction with it, and it unfolds in time as you walk around it. Art has become universal because it's reproduced so frequently, but the experience of being with a unique artwork is now really essential in a world where everything is replicated. Virtual reality makes you forget about your body in some way, but I think people do yoga and go to the gym because they're trying to get back into their bodies. I believe our incarnation, our sense of being in the body, will become more and more important.

Interviewed in 2019

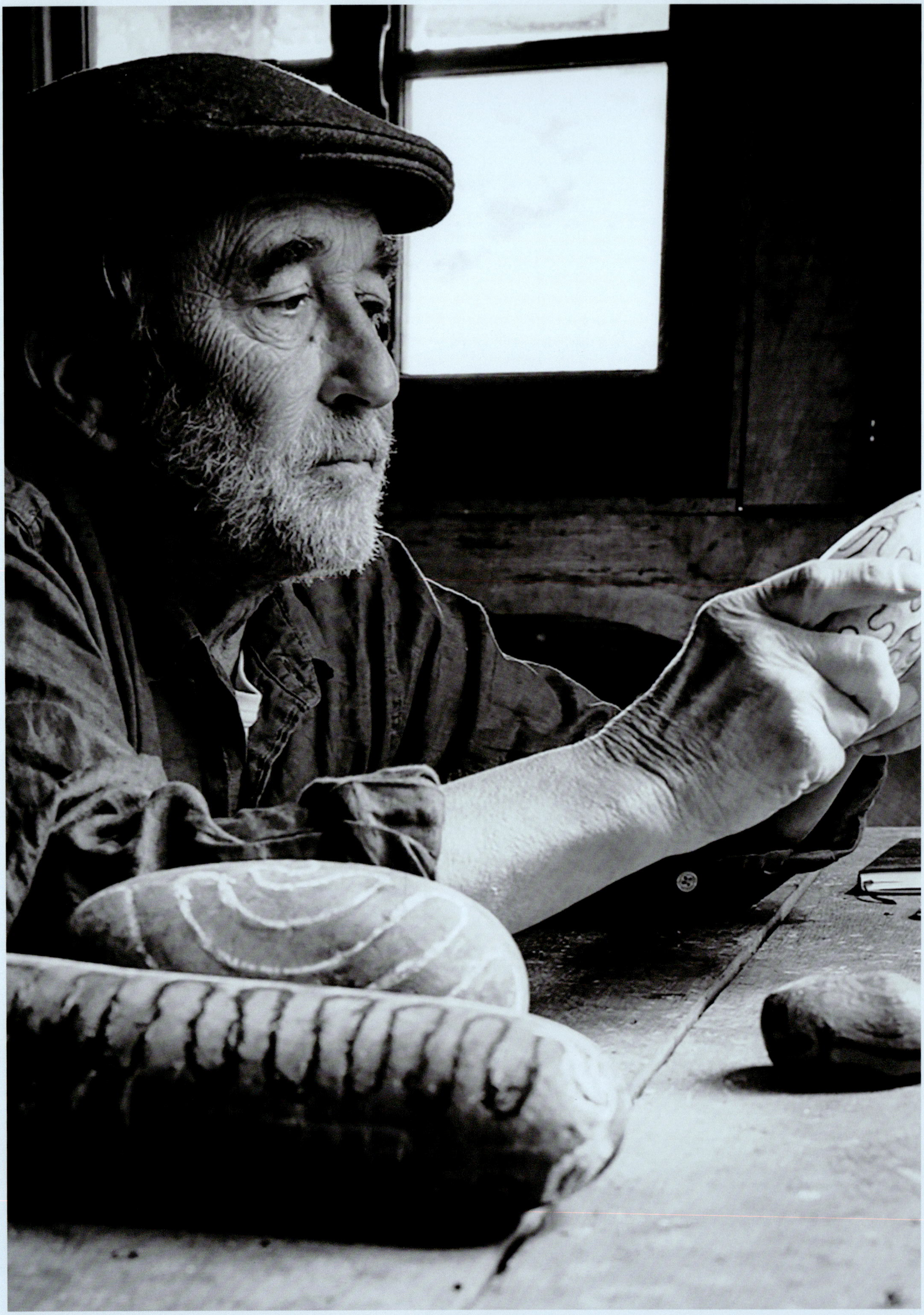

PETER RANDALL-PAGE

Born 1954, Rochford, Essex

Peter Randall-Page's practice relies on technical precision and a deep understanding of the natural world. Nature, which provides a multifarious range of forms, is held in suspended animation between the polarities of stasis and transformation, and his sculptures link these forms to explore analogies between seemingly unrelated phenomena. His practice can be seen as an investigation into symmetry, camouflage, tessellation and deep time, in which formal and intellectual concerns become fully assimilated. The series *Shapes in the Clouds* is a sculptural interpretation of the five Platonic solids, the only totally regular polygon, while *The One and The Many*, commissioned for Fitzroy Place in London, is a 24-tonne (26.5-ton) obelisk incorporating the world's writing systems. Randall-Page's sculptures dance to their own beat – a mellow, archaic rhythm. Although solid and weighty, they are never still; instead, they appear on the cusp of mutation, seemingly humming with compressed energy, as exemplified in *After Bessie Smith*, *Rocks in my Bed* and *In Mind of Monk*.

Ina Cole: You had an early fascination with the underlying principles of growth, and this interest was reinforced when you worked on the restoration of Wells Cathedral in Somerset, South West England. How did these experiences impact on your practice, particularly in relation to the 'New Milestones' project in Dorset, initiated by Common Ground in the 1980s?

Peter Randall-Page: As a child, I was dyslexic and couldn't access information through reading. Instead, I spent time in my father's studio – a garden shed where he made dioramas. I understood the world through direct observation, drawing and experimenting. Early on, I was given a microscope, magnifying glass, a little telescope and binoculars. I kept collections of shells, pebbles and plants, and noticed the similarities in different phenomena, even though they're produced by diametrically opposite processes. It's as if there's an underlying pattern-book of forms everything can be rationalized into.

After art school, I wanted a job in which I could still be involved with sculpture, but make some money, and it was a great privilege to work so high up on Wells Cathedral. To me, it seemed revelatory that the pre-empirical age had such a different sense of the world. The cathedral has wonderful stiff-leaf carving for the capitals and finials, which are a rationalization of plant growth. On the cathedral, figures are set within niches – a device for incorporating art into architecture. For the 'New Milestones' project, I therefore created niches in sections of wall to shelter the *Wayside Carvings* (1986). The Dorset landscape is spectacular: chalk cliffs with huge views of the sea and sky, which I couldn't compete with in scale, so the niches provided intimacy. I used Purbeck marble for the carvings; it's a material found in lots of churches and cathedrals, made of the fossilized remains of innumerable gastropod shells.

IC: The fact that growth systems in nature mirror bodily organs, in their structure and regularity, confirms that we're an intrinsic component of the natural world – a small cog in a greater whole. Although this is reassuring, do you think it also emphasizes our insignificance?

Peter Randall-Page
Wayside Carving III, 1986

Purbeck marble in
Purbeck stone walling
48 × 36 × 38 cm
(18⅞ × 14⅛ × 15 in)

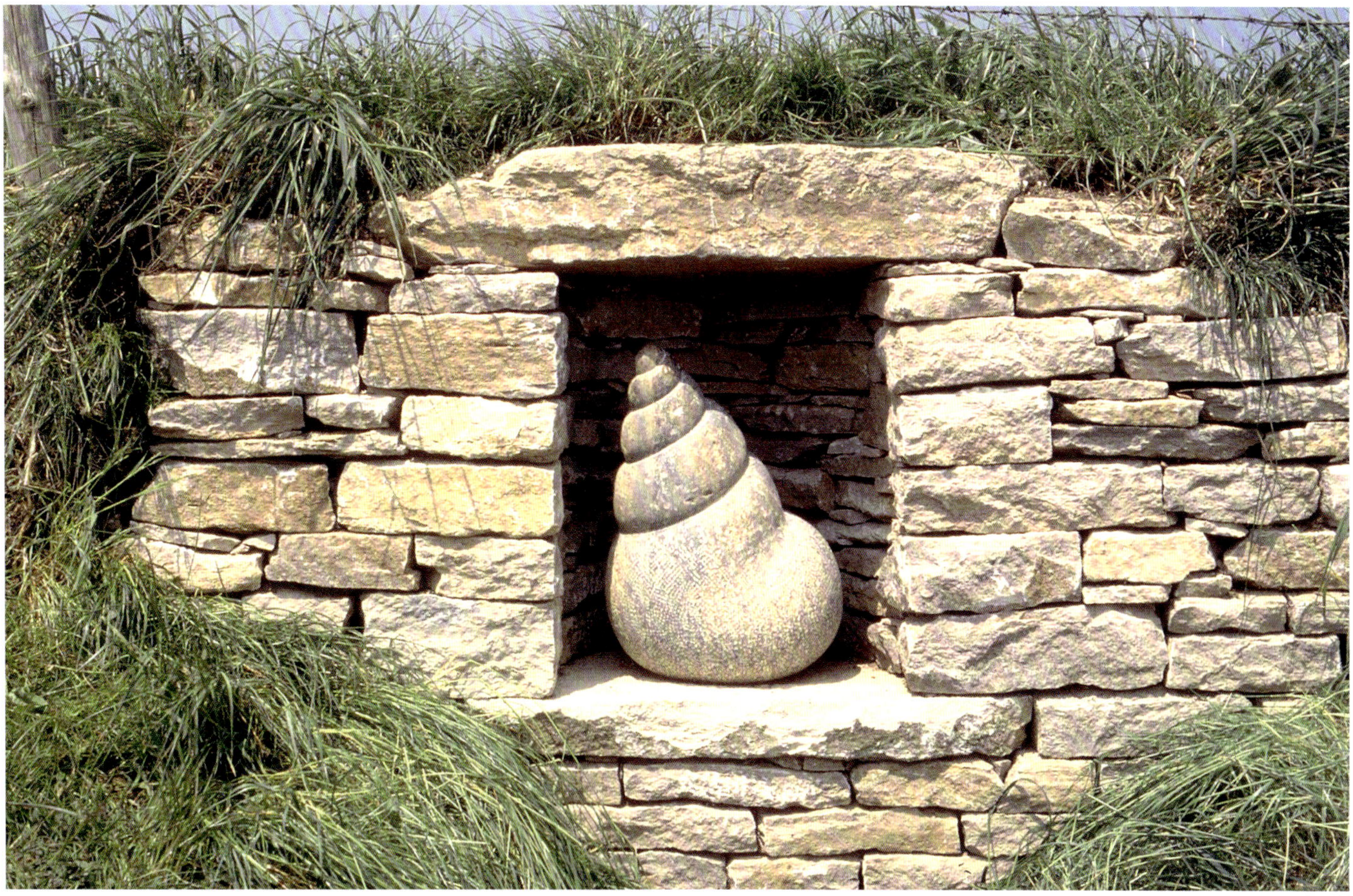

PRP: Similar branching patterns are found in river systems, cardiovascular systems, neural connections and plants, all resulting from different physical processes. I've always drawn a lot, and my branching drawings – *Blood Tree* (2013), *Sap River* (2013) and *Ink Flow* (2014) – are made by pouring ink onto paper, which is then inverted so that the drawings appear like espaliered trees. I was influenced by an exhibition of the methods Antonio Gaudí used when designing La Sagrada Família in Barcelona. He wanted the spires to appear to be reaching up to the heavens, so he poured plaster onto hanging strings, then turned the hardened forms upside down, effectively inverting gravity. It was extraordinary.

Looking closer through magnification, further away through telescopes or into the body, makes everything equally significant. Humans are keen to find pattern and meaning. When asked about their life, everyone has a narrative, otherwise they would just feel at the mercy of events. Intrinsically, I don't think the world has any human meaning whatsoever, other than we're a part of it, but it's wonderful that we're able to imbue it with meaning. I've always been interested in understanding the very fundamentals about being human. I'm not interested in stone, clay, charcoal or ink *per se* – only insofar as they're vehicles to explore the human condition.

IC: Our first, primal understanding of physical form comes from ourselves and those closest to us. *The Bridge* (2011), at Dartington Hall in Devon, can be navigated, and *In Praise of Trees* (2012) acts as a seat. Both pieces were created with the human body in mind, in that they're functional and can therefore act as conduits to many other experiences.

PRP: The relationship of the body to sculpture is vital. For me, the most successful works are those you can turn in your palm, or get your arms around. Outdoor sculpture has to relate to the scale of the landscape or the architecture as well and, when putting a work into a particular place, the net result, on an emotional level, can be more than the sum of the parts. Sculpture could be seen as a blunt instrument for communicating, given the many ways of conveying information we now have, but there are still areas of human experience in which making and showing an object is the most efficient way of communicating. Although technology can bring us closer in a virtual sense, it distances us from the multi-sensual physicality of the world. Sculpture comes into its own when words fail.

Of course, if I wanted to talk about sociopolitical issues, choosing to make an object would seem clumsy, but sculpture articulates the experience of inhabiting a physical body in a physical world. Imagine a Martian who's never seen a tree. Even if you described it every way you could, they still wouldn't know what it was like to sit under a tree. That's where sculpture is most potent: through direct experience. It's a matter of using the appropriate expressive language. In a way, it's the least abstract of the arts. Music is temporary; it's there, then gone. Painting and photography act as windows into an imaginary space, so are abstract in that sense. Sculpture, on the other hand, you can definitely stub your toe on.

IC: Your practice requires intense time and effort – a perfect choreography of hand, eye, tool and material. I'm thinking of *Ridge and Furrow* (2011), commissioned for the University of Iowa – a 17.2-tonne (19-ton) granite boulder that took five months to carve. Did you develop an empathy with the material's characteristics during this time?

PRP: The boulder was chosen for *Ridge and Furrow* because of its shape and character. I first drew, then carved one continuous line covering the stone's entire surface. An axis of symmetry was introduced into the pattern, and the line had to cross the axis twice during this process. The stone developed a kind of 'beingness' for me. Plotting its surface provided an understanding of its unique distribution of mass and form. The process became a meditation on randomness and structure,

Peter Randall-Page
Clay Bodies, 2009

Clay
Each piece: 18 × 13 × 9 cm
(7⅛ × 5⅛ × 3½ in)

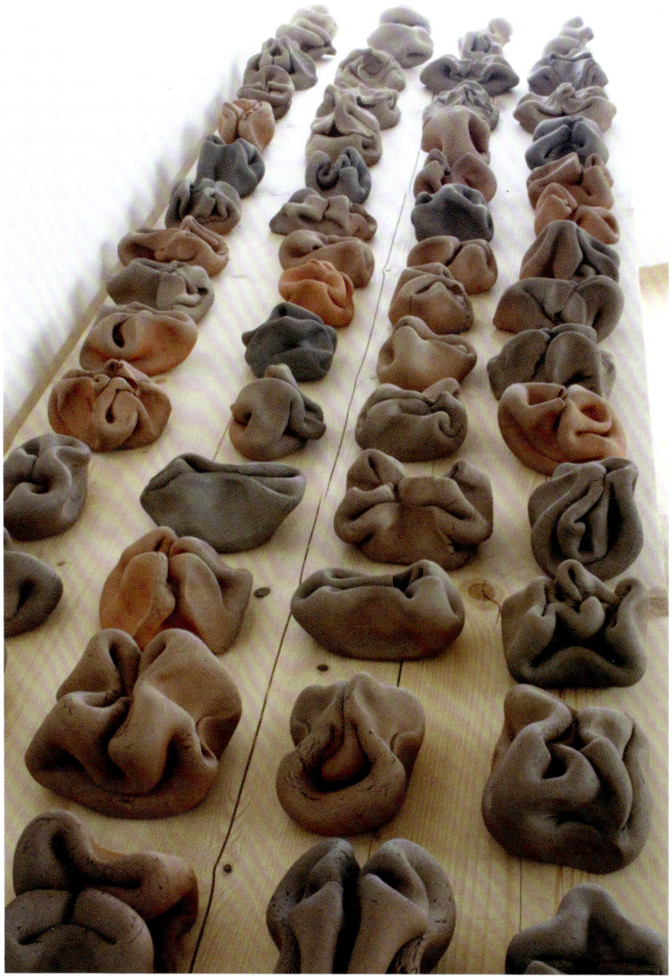

with plenty of space to play in between those polarities. There are, of course, an infinite number of ways to circumnavigate a form with a line. It's surprisingly difficult to set up a situation in which you can improvise unselfconsciously, yet that's how you find out more about the nether reaches of your mind.

Ridge and Furrow is nicknamed the 'brain stone' because of its hemispheres and convoluted pattern. It's become legendary, as students queue up and hug it before exams to guarantee good results. They all reckon it works and believe it's a benevolent object. It's amazing how you can put something into the world, and it takes on its own meaning.

IC: Even though you set up situations for improvisation, there must also be planning, as different materials present their individual idiosyncrasies and, therefore, require specific tools and methods.

PRP: Yes, but the same fundamental principles apply with any material. When making *Clay Bodies* (2009), for example, one of my assistants threw the clay cylinders onto a potter's wheel, and, when they reached the right consistency, I systematically collapsed them, rather like folding a flower back into a bud. So, the cylinders were the ordering principle imposed on the chaotic nature of the clay, while my collapsing of them was improvisation.

For *Inside Out* (2014), naturally eroded boulders were cast in foundry sand mixed with sodium silicate and carbon dioxide. Once the mould had hardened, the stone was removed, and I got into the moulds to carve from the inside so that my concave indentations became a swollen convex shape in the final cast. It was more like something grown than carved. Improvisation and variation bring expression to the theme, and the theme gives structure to improvisation. In Bach's music, for example, he strays so far from the theme that you don't know if he's ever going to get back. It's the same

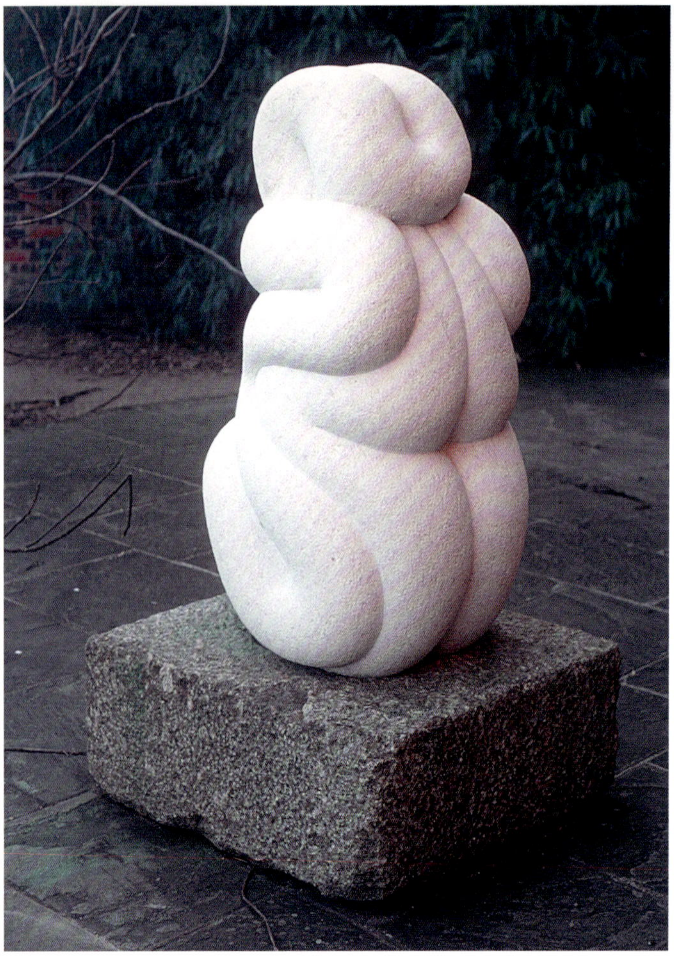

←
Peter Randall-Page
After Bessie Smith, 1995

White marble and blackenstone granite
Sculpture: 123 × 76.2 × 58.5 cm
(48⅜ × 30 × 23 in)
Base: 34 × 88.5 × 80.6 cm
(13⅜ × 34⅞ × 31¾ in)

→
Peter Randall-Page
Fructus and *Corpus*, 2009

Kilkenny Limestone
Fructus: 265 × 180 × 180 cm
(8 ft 8⅜ in × 70⅞ in × 70⅞ in)
Corpus: 254 × 178 × 178 cm
(8 ft 4 in × 70⅛ in × 70⅛ in)
Installation view:
Yorkshire Sculpture Park, 2009–10

→→
Peter Randall-Page
Rocks in my Bed, 2005

Canvas and boulders
400 × 200 × 200 cm
(13 ft 1½ in × 6 ft 6¾ in × 6 ft 6¾ in)
each

with improvised jazz, like Charlie Parker's. Coming back to the theme, or coming home, is immensely satisfying at a very basic level.

IC: *After Bessie Smith* (1995) is a personification of the remarkable blues singer, *Rocks in my Bed* (2005) is named after a song written by Duke Ellington, while *In Mind of Monk* (2008) references the jazz musician Thelonious Monk. Do you liken the sounds of jazz to the rhythm of hewing a sculpture, in that you can lose yourself and succumb to a more subliminal state of being?

PRP: Absolutely; music has always been incredibly important. It is, for me, the most powerful of the arts, going straight to the emotional solar plexus. I aspire to being in a state in which thought and action become fused in the working process. The act of carving is rhythmic by its very nature, so I'm chipping and making decisions unselfconsciously. *Bessie* is one continuous coil that wraps around, like a knot. At the time, I listened to a lot of her songs and was besotted, yet it was only on completion I realized I'd carved a portrait of her voice. The stone had belonged to Barbara Hepworth; it was unworked and given to me by Alan Bowness, the trustee of her estate.

Rocks in my Bed came from observing high-magnification images of chemicals that don't mix, but which form fascinating patterns with their own rules. Throughout evolution, organic life has harnessed these chemical phenomena to create the stripes and spots on tigers, zebras and on the back of mackerel. In *Rocks in my Bed*, this pattern continues from one canvas to another, then comes down along the floor and across the stones – random boulders painted in the same system. It's made of rocks and cloth, hence *Rocks in my Bed*. With *In Mind of Monk*, the three spheres are covered with a variation on that same chemical pattern

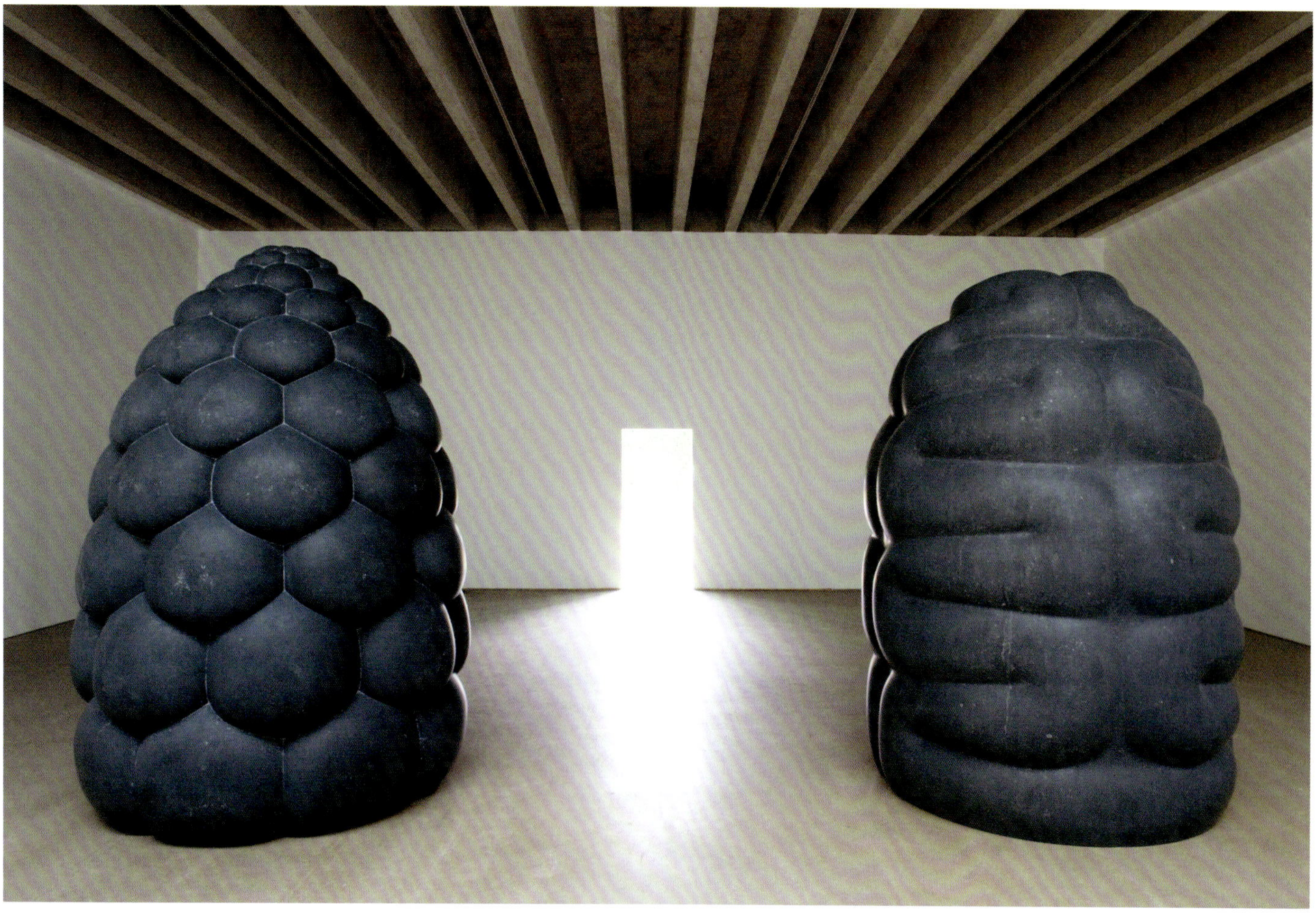

phenomenon – but more zigzag, or staccato – and, because of the curved surfaces, there's a sense that the triangles are appearing and disappearing, as one moves around the work. Monk's music is wonderfully awkward, yet perfect and emotional; it's like someone singing a beautiful melody, then digging you in the ribs. His sense of rightness is just slightly out of sync and unexpected. I wanted to bring that angular awkwardness into the perfection of these marble spheres.

IC: You gravitate towards certain materials, such as Kilkenny limestone, a distinctive dark-blue stone with white fossil formations which you used in key works including *Corpus* (2009), *Fructus* (2009) and *Phyllotaxus* (2013). Although linked, they appear as self-contained entities, and don't necessarily rely on their environment or interaction with each other. Would you agree?

PRP: I would, with a couple of caveats. There's a way in which a series of related pieces can build up an expressive vocabulary, because I'm establishing a thematic link. On the other hand, I like making self-contained objects and nearly always work all the way around and underneath, because the sculpture has to have integrity, like a pebble or shell. These three sculptures are archetypal examples of different formal preoccupations I've had for a long time. *Fructus* is about botanical fecundity: how fruit grows and swells, and the tension created between the skin and pressure from within. *Corpus*, as the name suggests, is bodily; it's more disturbing than *Fructus*, which is straightforwardly sensual. As a coil, *Corpus* alludes to the convoluted quality of the brain or gut, or even snakes and worms.

Kilkenny limestone is perfect for implying that sense of tension from within, even though we know it's just dumb matter. If *Corpus* was actually soft and squidgy it would be quite off-putting, but, when translated into

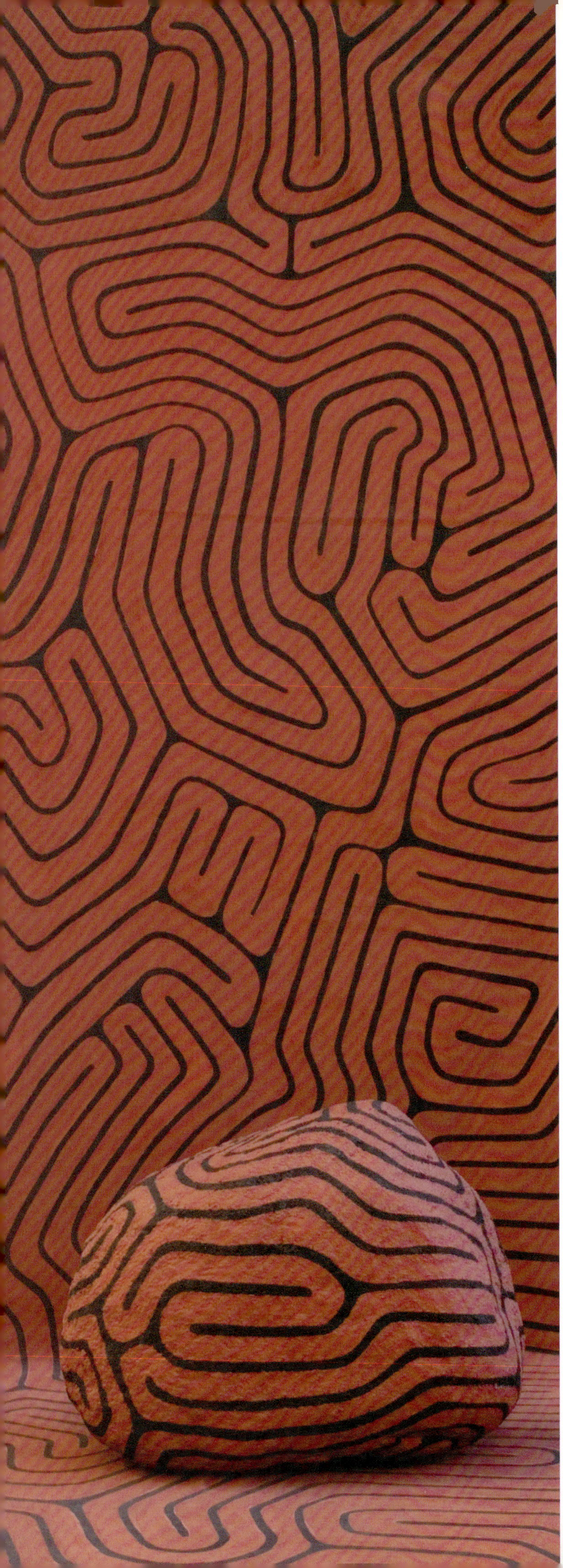
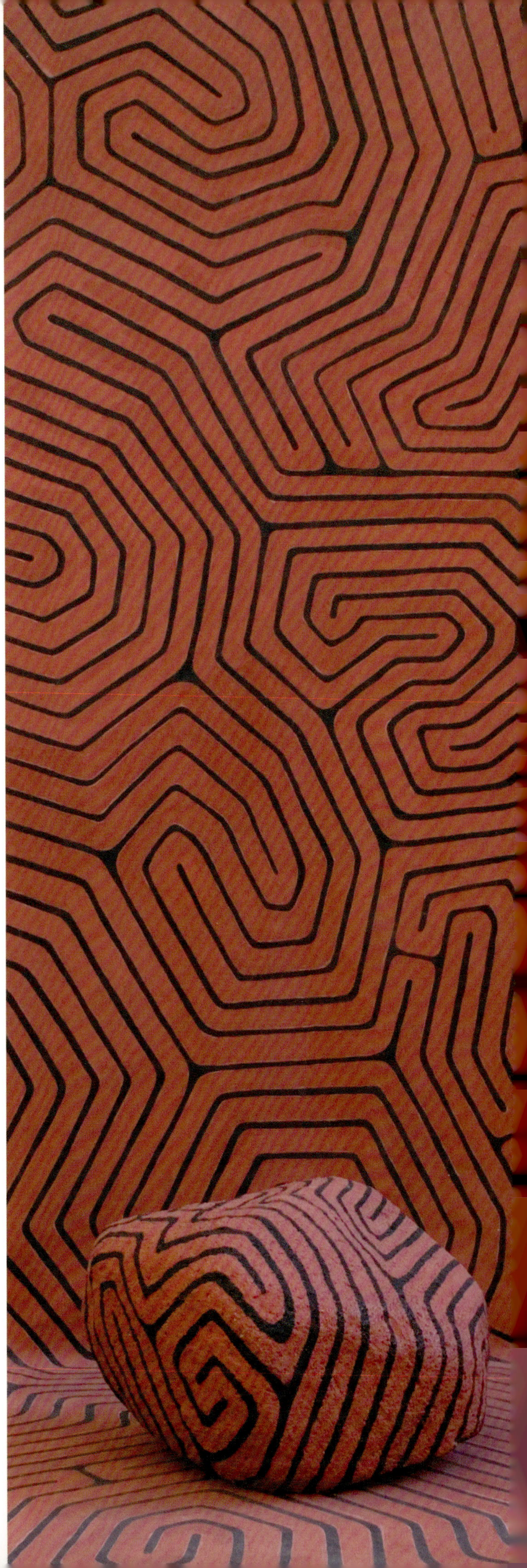

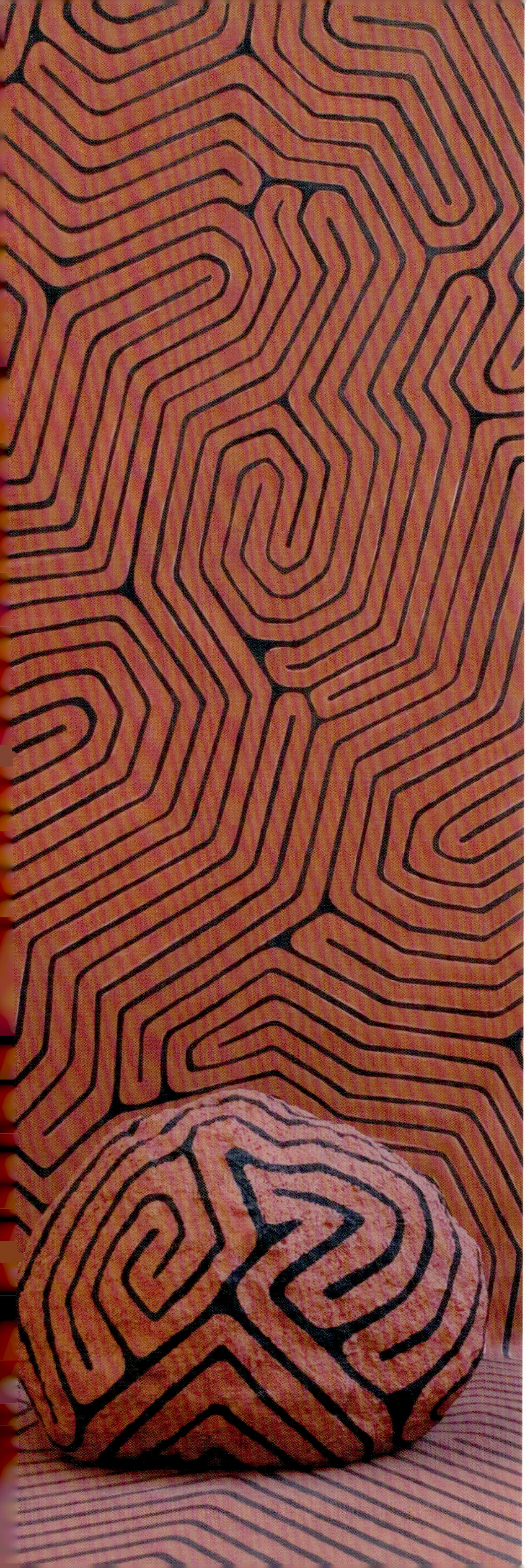
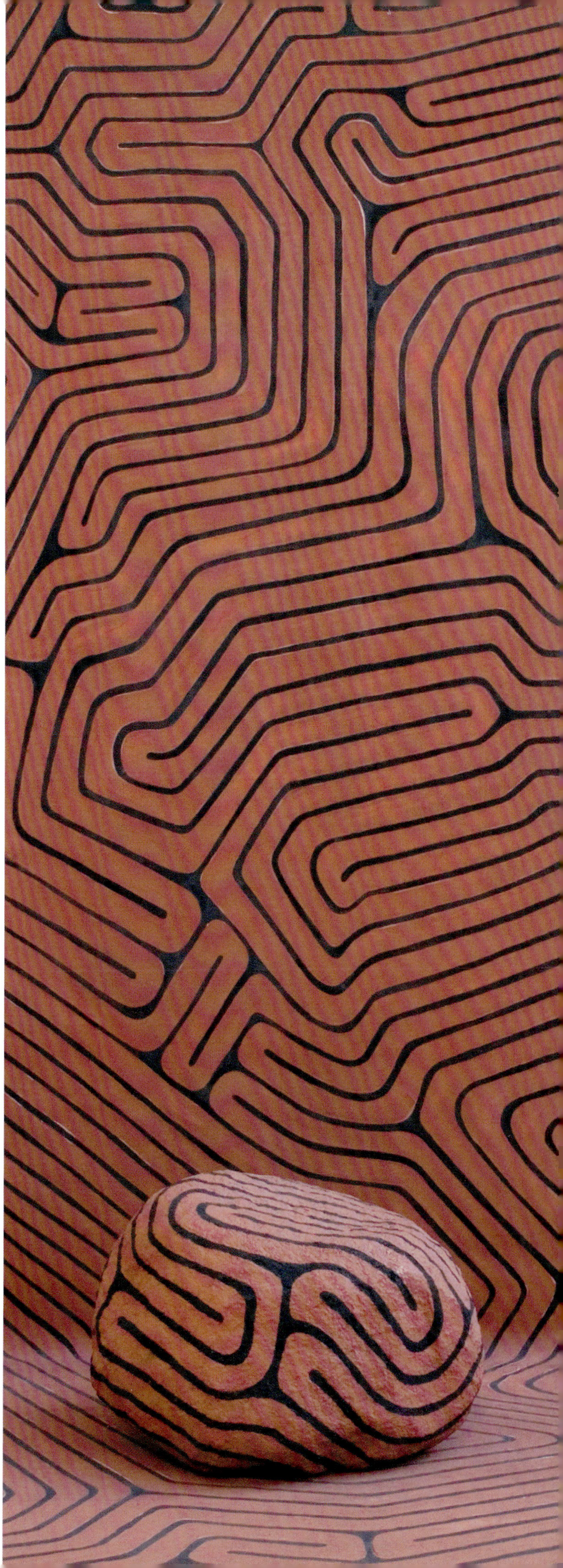

stone, you become aware of its structural beauty, rather than being distracted by inbuilt human revulsions. The third, *Phyllotaxus*, was made later and completes the group. It's based on plant patterns, but is more geometric and less bulbous, somewhat like *Seed* (2007), which was commissioned for the Eden Project in Cornwall.

IC: *Shapes in the Clouds* (2014) is a group of sculptures based on the five Platonic solids. Each piece has a seemingly buoyant quality that belies its weight, while the marble's configuration gives the impression of infinity. Plato associated four of the solids with the elements of earth, air, water and fire, and the dodecahedron with the ether. What provided the impetus to interpret them in sculptural form?

PRP: These sculptures are very ordered, derived from stacking spheres to create rounded versions of the five Platonic solids. However, Rosso Luana marble introduces a wild element, as it has a highly figured, distracting, chaotic pattern. By bringing together this random element with a structuring principle, I can concentrate on reconciling these two opposing forces. There's a strange contradiction in that each piece weighs around 5 or 6 tonnes, but the figuring evokes planetary systems, cloud forms or falling water, with the title obviously reinforcing this idea.

The Platonic solids are fundamental to how our universe fits together: they're found in atomic, molecular and crystalline structures. In the natural world, there's tension between spontaneous pattern formation and random variation, and the evolutionary process relies on that tension. If we only had pattern formation there would be stasis, and I couldn't even imagine what it would be like to have only random variation. So, I use that duality to invent and play in the space between order and chaos.

Plato's concept of ideals was that all we perceive are imperfect versions of some perfect forms out in the ether. We don't think in those terms now, but the essence of his idea is profound and relevant. Pebbles aspire to the minimum surface-area-to-volume ratio, but you never find a spherical pebble. Planets aren't

Peter Randall-Page
Seed, 2007

De Lank Granite
417.6 × 315 × 315 cm
(13 ft 8⅜ in × 10 ft 4 in × 10 ft 4 in)

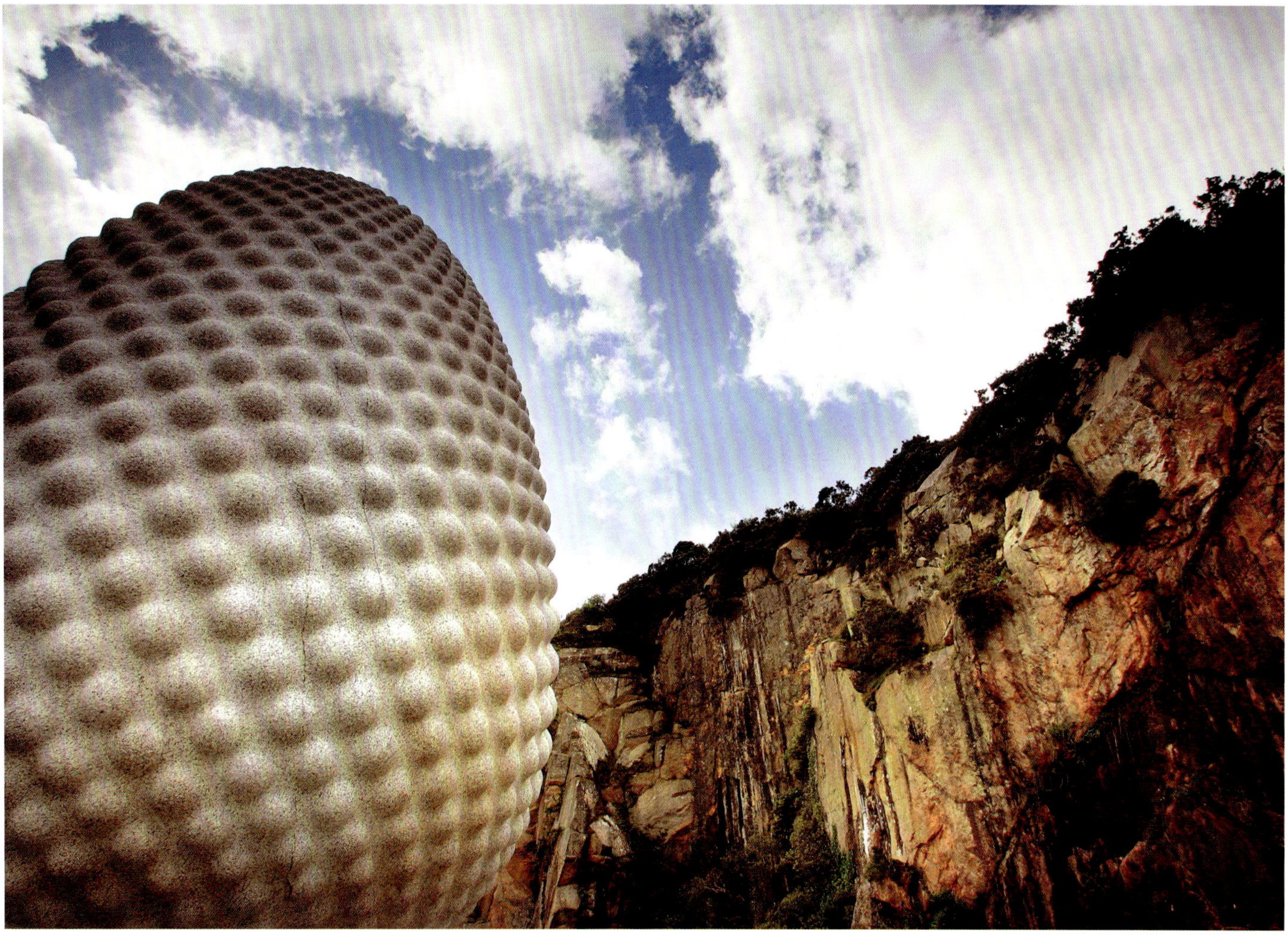

perfect spheres either, yet we can imagine what the perfect sphere would be. That's geometry, but it's completely theoretical, predicated on the idea of an infinitely thin line and an infinitely small dot, which don't exist, as a seemingly precise pencil line seen through a magnifying glass is actually quite chaotic. So, my fascination with the Platonic solids grew from the fact they don't exist in their pure form, yet we can extrapolate to imagine what the ideal form might be.

IC: *Playing God I & II* (2018) references creation stories from around the world. Similarly, *The One and The Many* (2014) incorporates writing systems through time, in an attempt to understand the very beginnings of creation.

PRP: *Playing God I & II* references stories in which the gods create figures from clay and imbue them with vitality by blowing, or breathing, life into them. These clay pieces had their origin in 1977, in my last year at Bath Academy of Art, when I simply put a stick into the ground and squidged mud, straw and cow dung onto this simple armature. It's basic modelling in one hit – just making imprints with my hands. Years later, the two elements of *Playing God I & II* were made from clay, then cast into iron. Although reminiscent of a leaf or fern, they're also spinal, and one approaches them as personages because they're figure-size.

For *The One and The Many*, I researched creation stories from around the world. It's an eroded granite boulder, obelisk in shape, weighing 21.7 tonnes (24 tons) and standing 3.5 metres high (almost 11 feet 6 inches). It incorporates the earliest cuneiform from ancient Mesopotamia to contemporary writing systems: creation stories from different cultures that try to imagine the unimaginable – how did it all start? Every culture has asked this same question. The first writing systems were all about accountancy – I owe you three camels, and

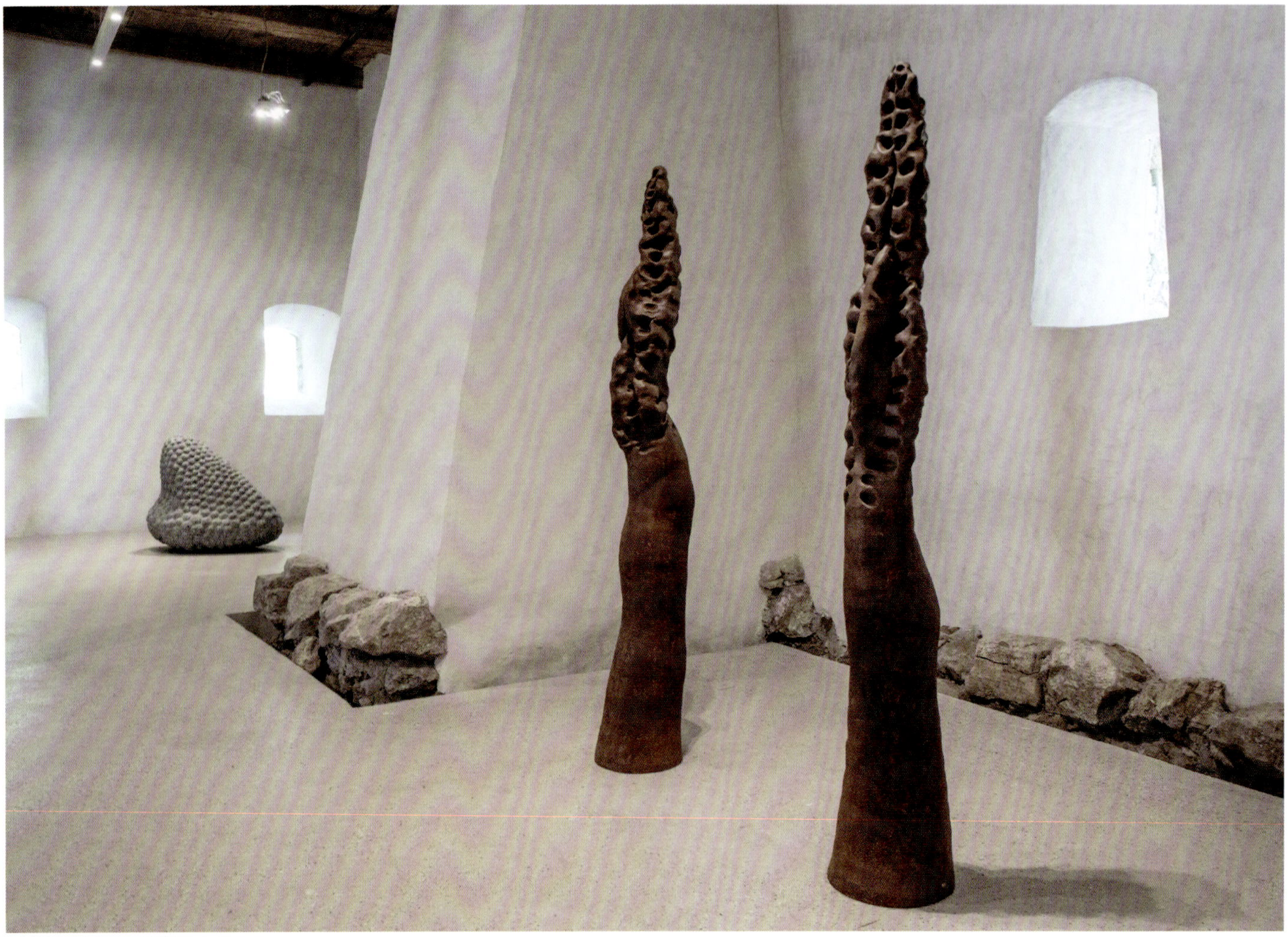

so on – but, in a short time, people started to use these writing systems more profoundly to imagine how the world, or universe, began. The stories span 5,000 years, from the *Epic of Gilgamesh* (c.1800 BCE) to astrophysics. I've also included a quote in braille from *The God's Script* by Jorge Luis Borges (1949), and a quote in Morse code from Samuel Beckett's *Endgame* (1957). The writing systems are like patterns incised into the stone's surface – some vertical, others horizontal – arranged in columns and bands according to the golden section. They're humble marks scratched into a boulder, but resonant of so much meaning and imagination.

IC: All your work appears linked by the imagination's astonishing capacity to forge connections between seeming disparate elements.

PRP: I'm interested in metaphor, particularly in relation to a pre-Descartes understanding of the world. Art

↑
Peter Randall-Page
Playing God I and II, 2018

Cast Iron
Playing God I:
180 × 31 × 27 cm
(70⅞ × 12¼ × 10⅝ in)
Playing God II:
182 × 30 × 29 cm
(71⅝ × 11¾ × 11⅜ in)
Installation view:
Kloster Schoenthal,
Switzerland, 2019

↗
Peter Randall-Page
Shapes in the Clouds IV, 2014

Rosso Luana marble
150 × 150 × 150 cm
(59 × 59 × 59 in)

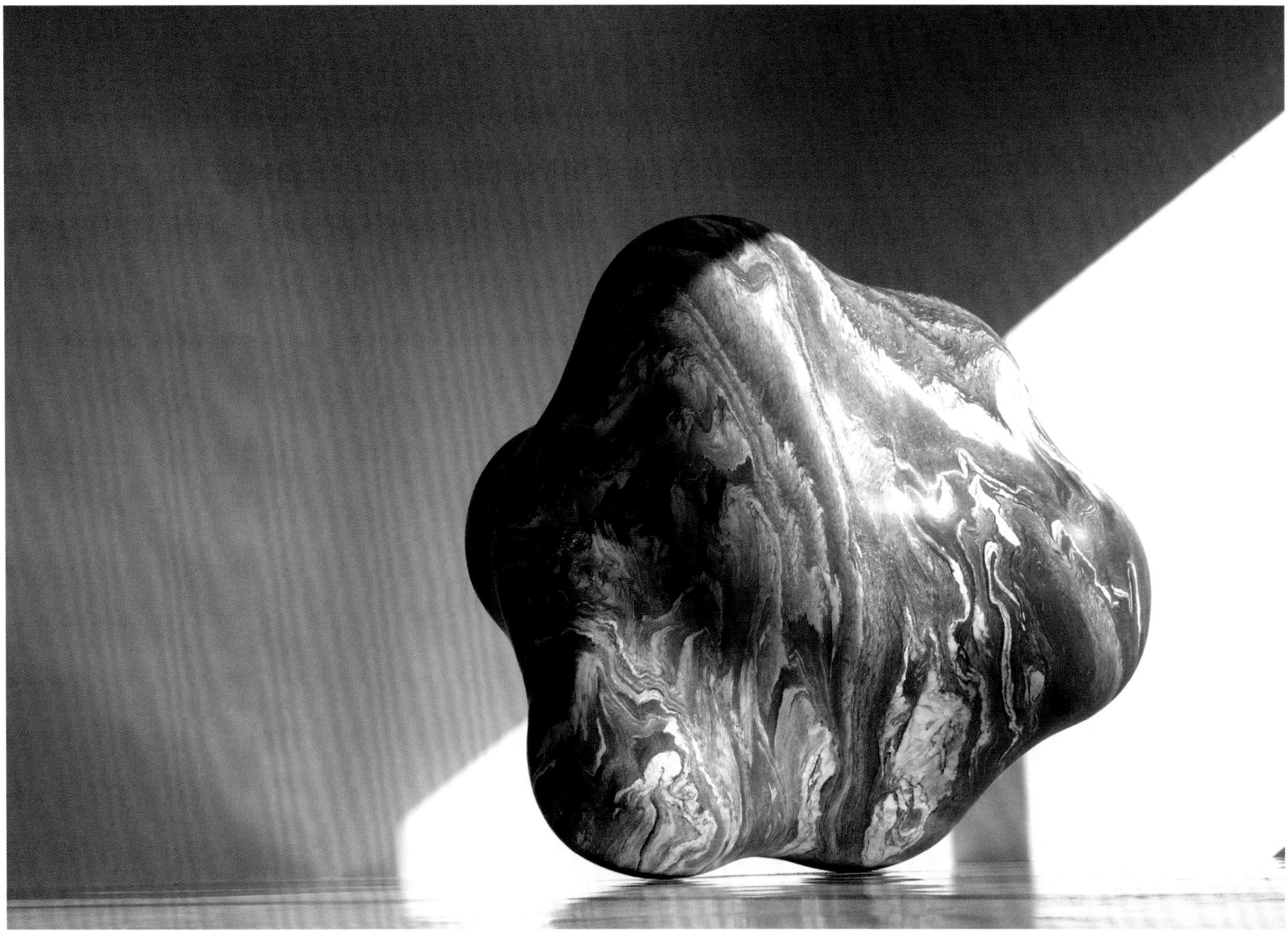

is a pretence, but it contains psychological truths about how we make sense of the world. These days, we're obsessed with literal proof, and a lot of artwork relies on knowing what it's made from for its meaning. For me, art is absolutely to do with metaphor, and I feel this has become lost over recent decades. When coming across something unknown, you relate to it by creating a metaphorical connection to something known; like Kandinsky, who linked painting and music in a kind of synesthesia. D'Arcy Wentworth Thompson's seminal work *On Growth and Form* (1917) has been an important influence. He pointed out that organic life isn't exempt from the laws of physics and is not, therefore, just determined by natural selection. This is how great leaps in imagination happen. I can link metaphor to just about everything I do.

A meaningless world becomes meaningful through metaphor, not science. The evolutionary process has produced a kind of mirror – our human consciousness. This means we're able to reflect, which, for me, is the magic. I don't need any more meaning than that.

Interviewed in 2014 and 2019

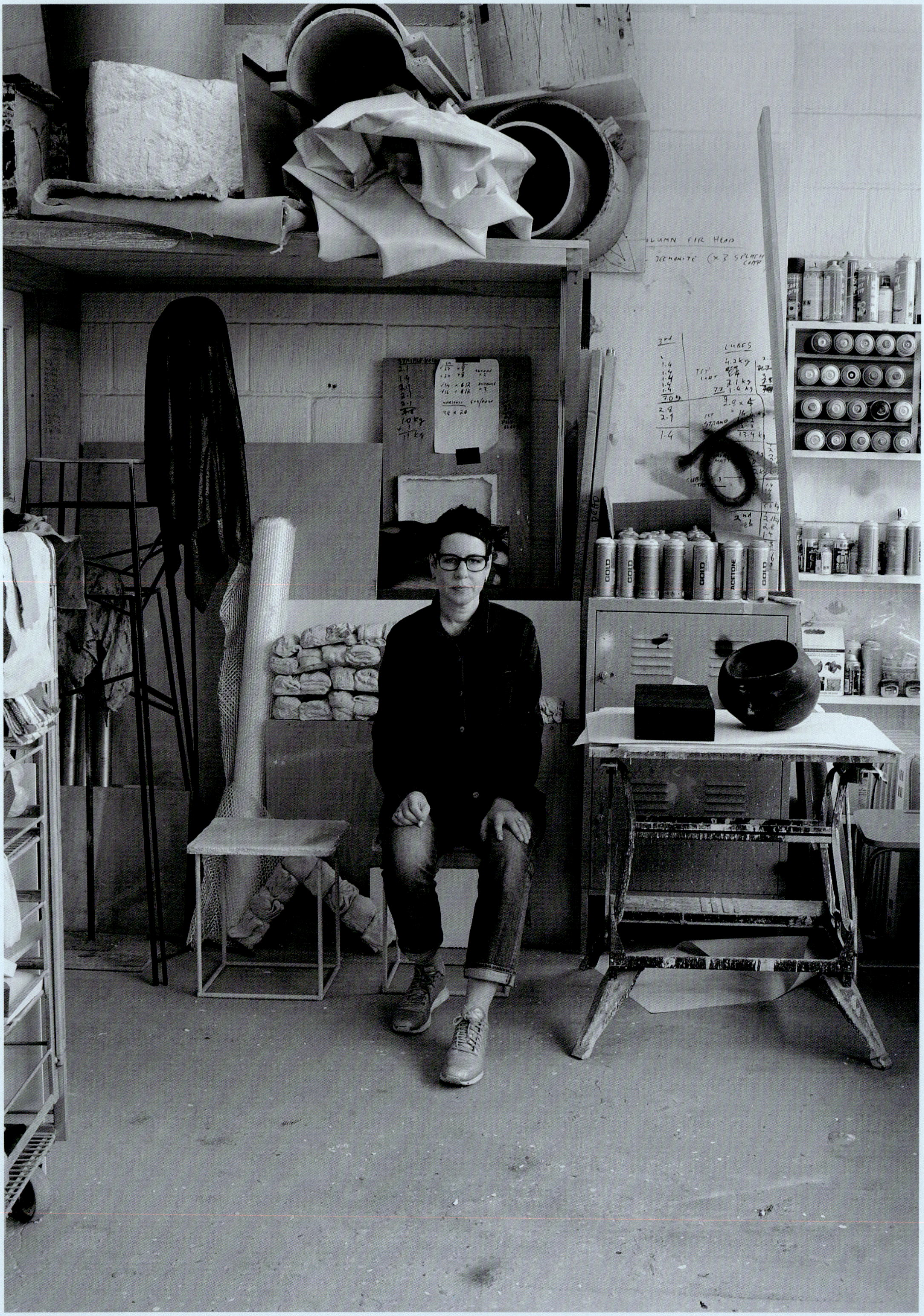
GOLD
ACETONE

EVA ROTHSCHILD

Born 1971, Dublin, Ireland

Eva Rothschild's practice expands on the modernist tradition, with a lexicon that is immediately recognizable: fragile geometric forms seemingly waver in mid-air, teeter on spindly plinths, or twist and turn through space. Her sculpture is characterized by an ordered clarity, and a network of closed and open arrangements made from materials including wood, Perspex, steel, aluminium, polystyrene, fabric, leather, beads and Jesmonite. As a materials-based sculptor, Rothschild creates surfaces that are immaculate, indicative of studio-based handcrafting. Works are often constructed from repeated units, allowing the notion of transformation to continue into the finished piece. Spheres, columns, arches and triangulated frames appear to rely on neighbouring structures for support; their ultimate success is contingent on a coexistence with other elements. Key to her practice are the aesthetics of protest and spirituality, through which she examines how objects acquire significance peripheral to their static reality, through inferred societal beliefs and ideologies.

Ina Cole: You grew up in Dublin and studied at the University of Ulster in Belfast from 1990–93, after which you spent time in San Francisco. Does *Burning Tyre* (2004) reflect on that early period?

Eva Rothschild: At art school in Belfast my course was multidisciplinary, and I didn't really think of myself as a sculptor until Phyllida Barlow offered me a job teaching sculpture at the Slade School of Fine Art much later. Belfast was a tricky place. There was a clear presence of the Troubles, but this offered a bizarre kind of security to a young person not involved in the conflict. Due to police and paramilitary presence, there was little petty crime. It was a heavily controlled environment, while San Francisco, which *Burning Tyre* refers to, was completely uncontrolled. I'm interested in the checks and balances around the extreme, and was there on a student visa, living within a volatile situation.

I felt under threat in San Francisco, so, on returning to Ireland, I noticed a shift in my sense of security. I'd gone to the US because of my curiosity about the cultural changes that had taken place there in the 1960s, but I didn't realize how that kind of individualization can lead to a lack of care. There was such a disconnect between the progressive ideas of the countercultural movement and the hippy lifestyle I encountered. *Burning Tyre* brings together the urgency demanded by protest and struggle yet undermines it through the use of incense sticks – empty signifiers of a spiritual search typified by a lazy appropriation of Eastern religions. It's one of the few pieces using ready-made elements, and an important work for me.

IC: *Actualisation* (1998) features two seemingly perfect glass spheres, one black, the other white. It was shown in 'Strange Powers' (2006), a Creative Time exhibition in New York exploring art and the occult, and then in 'The Dark Monarch: Magic and Modernity in British Art' at Tate St Ives (2009–10). You've previously spoken of how we project meaning onto objects that remain unaware of our intention, and the crystal ball is certainly indicative of this intent.

Eva Rothschild
Actualisation, 1998

Glass
Two orbs
Diameter 10 cm (4 in) each

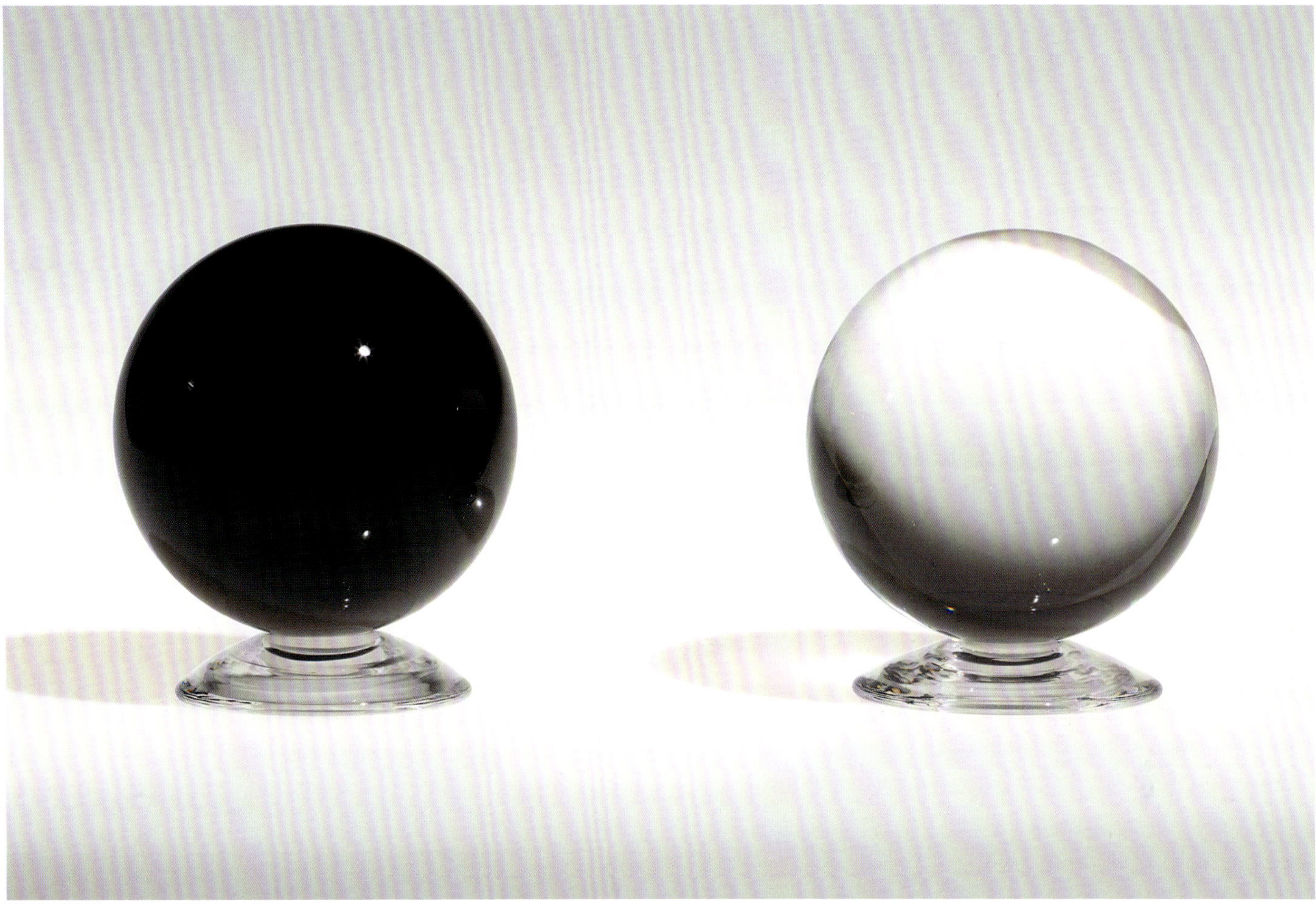

ER: People can allow themselves a level of communicative desire around an image, or object, in a way that doesn't happen elsewhere. When looking in religious ways, we're searching for something we perceive to be greater than ourselves. A different mode of looking occurs in a secular context, which is less goal-orientated and offers more equality. There's a divide between people who desire something greater and those who are more empirical. Art is an interesting place to work with those ideas.

In *Actualisation*, the two spheres are essentially imperfect, because they're formed by hand and not machined. They refer to the pursuit of fortune telling, which I find scary. Although I'm interested in religion and belief, it can open the door to anything, potentially – even the impossible. The crystal ball is the perfect form for this. It marries the idea of the minimalist object, yet can never be that object, because it's so loaded. *Actualisation* was my first sculpture and embodies all of my concerns: corrupted perfection, esoteric modernism and minimalism shrouded in mystery. In a sense, this is what we do when we make art – an actualization.

IC: *The Inside of Your Head* (2007) and *Horn of Plenty* (2011) are ovoid pieces pocked with large holes. Both reference the pierced form that played such a central role in the history of modern sculpture, particularly in the work of Henry Moore and Barbara Hepworth. Although your repertoire echoes the modernist tradition, the resulting configurations are unmistakably your own. Is this a difficult balancing act to achieve?

ER: Nothing is lost by looking at how someone else has practised; it's part of the process of discovery. Their sculpture was carved, so it's subtractive. They started with a whole and ended with a hole. That method isn't available to me. Carving, or subtracting, and adding are very different processes. With *The Inside of Your Head* and *Horn of Plenty*, I wanted to make something from an additive point of view, but mimic the subtractive process. They're like a kind of skin, a three-dimensional net, in that nothing was ever there. The first, *The Inside of Your Head*, was heavy, made from a strange mixture of materials and painted in many layers. Both are shown on stands, so they're about head height, and the relation of your head to the sculpture is important. I also applied spray paint, which just leaves a mark where it lands. There was a conscious disconnect between the object and the trajectory of the spray, as you can't control it like a brush. Approaching those pieces in that way allows them to appear freer.

Eva Rothschild
The Inside of Your Head, 2007
Jesmonite, plaster, gesso, papier-mâché, armature, painted steel
197 × 76 × 76 cm
(6 ft 5½ in × 29⅞ in × 29⅞ in)

IC: A site-specific project, such as *Cold Corners* (2009), was also extremely pared-down in its construction, yet this leanness contributed to the way it zigzagged through Tate Britain's Duveen Galleries in London, generating ever-shifting perspectives as the viewer followed its jagged path.

ER: I was once asked if I view my practice as sculpture or installation. I always think of my works as sculpture because they're made up of singular objects, but by occupying space in the way they do, they can be considered installation. *Cold Corners* was an episodic piece that could, potentially, have continued forever. It wasn't elaborate or detailed, though; it was economical. I wanted it to appear complete yet be everywhere at once. It also had to have a sense of motion. In photographs, it looks very coherent, but when you were in the gallery you had to dodge and duck. *Cold Corners* had scale, so the individual was dwarfed by it at certain points, but it was completely accessible to them at other points. You could touch it, lean on it, and it would have been strong enough to sit on; it wasn't precious on contact. It was created to respond to the Duveen's neo-classical environment, yet operate on different terms, like an alien within the architecture.

I'd previously made a series of photographs with people holding snakes, which relates to *Cold Corners* in that we may have a relationship to it, but it doesn't

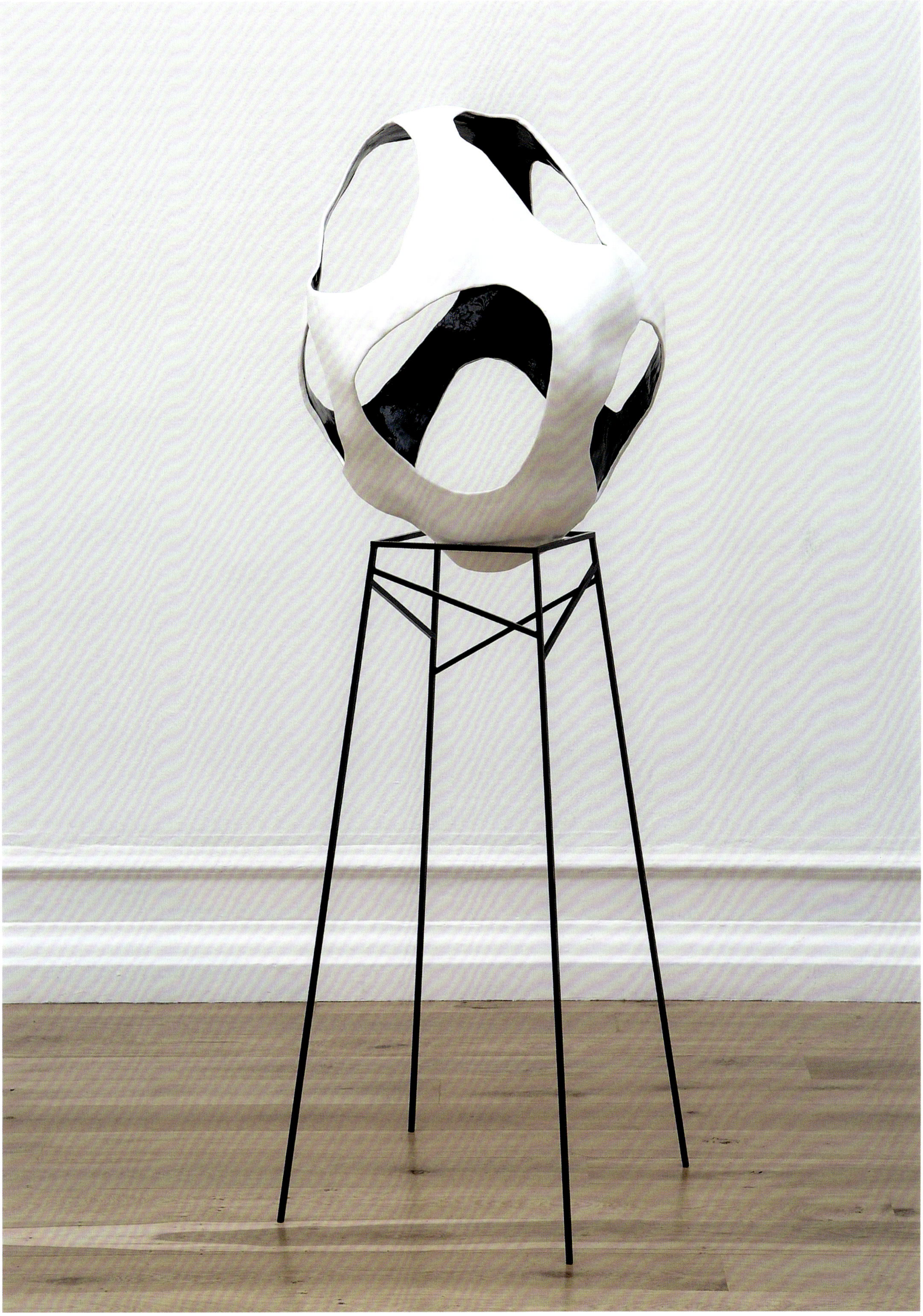

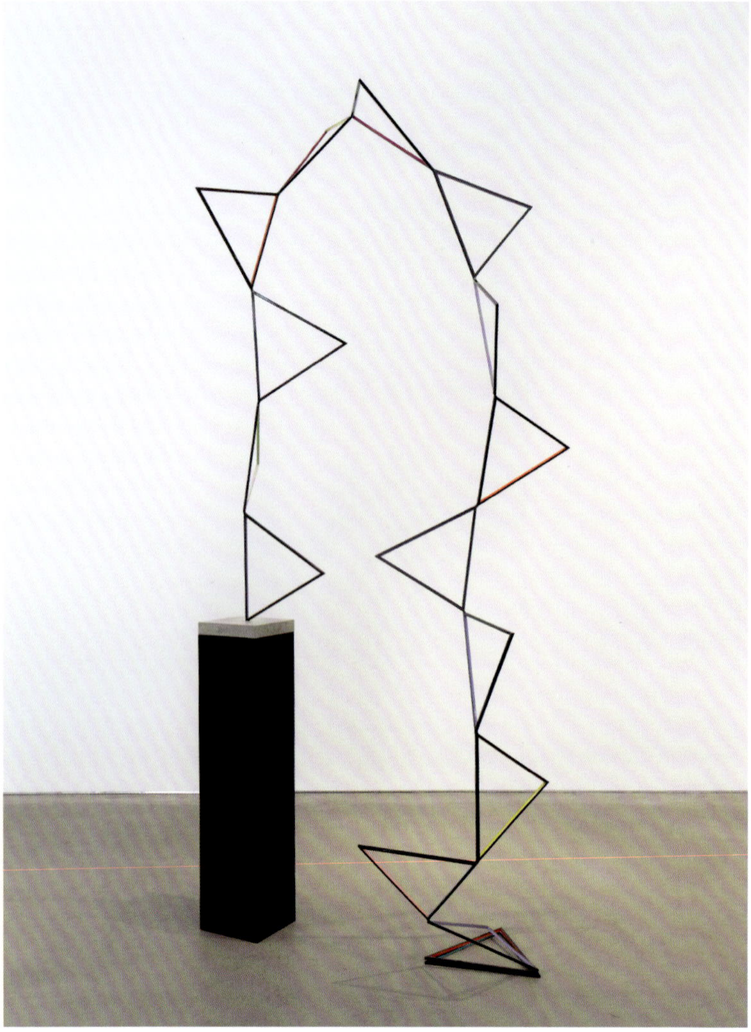

←
Eva Rothschild
The Leanover, 2018
Aluminium, paint, oak, concrete
333 × 148 × 89 cm
(10 ft 11⅛ in × 58⅝ in × 35 in)

→
Eva Rothschild
An Array, 2016
Jesmonite, plaster, fabric, rebar, steel, aluminium, perspex
310 × 305 × 200 cm
(10 ft 2 in × 10 ft ⅛ in × 6 ft 6¾ in)

care about us. Snakes aren't emotional creatures and don't develop attachments. The human holding them is no different from a rock or tree. Similarly, I wanted *Cold Corners* to have an aggressive appearance and to colonize the space.

IC: Although you frequently use familiar geometric shapes, they're altered in the most unexpected ways. This was clearly apparent in *Cold Corners*, but a sculpture such as *Fall, Fall, Falling* (2014) is equally surprising, as it shifts from being a horizontal arrangement of five open cubes to a scramble of lines when viewed side-on. Similarly, *The Leanover* (2017) sweeps upwards from its plinth, then cascades to the floor; it seems quite implausible, appearing to defy gravity. You've said you prefer not to demystify process, that a level of confusion when looking at art is a liberating experience.

ER: I don't like giving everything away, as it can devalue the final work. Because of their purity and completeness, geometric shapes have always been party to occultism. My practice is about making a known form more unstable, or less easy to absorb, often due to a strategic application of paint. The eye is troubled, as the form isn't doing quite what was expected, which leads to a more engaged way of looking and seeing. *Fall, Fall, Falling* was very intuitively created. The tumbling geometric form is a touchstone of my practice, but, instead of being on a plinth, this sculpture is ground-based. The application of paint takes that element of visual confusion through the different planes, creating an explicit sense of joy. Pleasure shouldn't be overlooked as a valid reason for making art.

Likewise, *The Leanover* is pure pleasure, like watching a waterfall. Here, I first made a model from stiff card, glued it, then faithfully translated it into

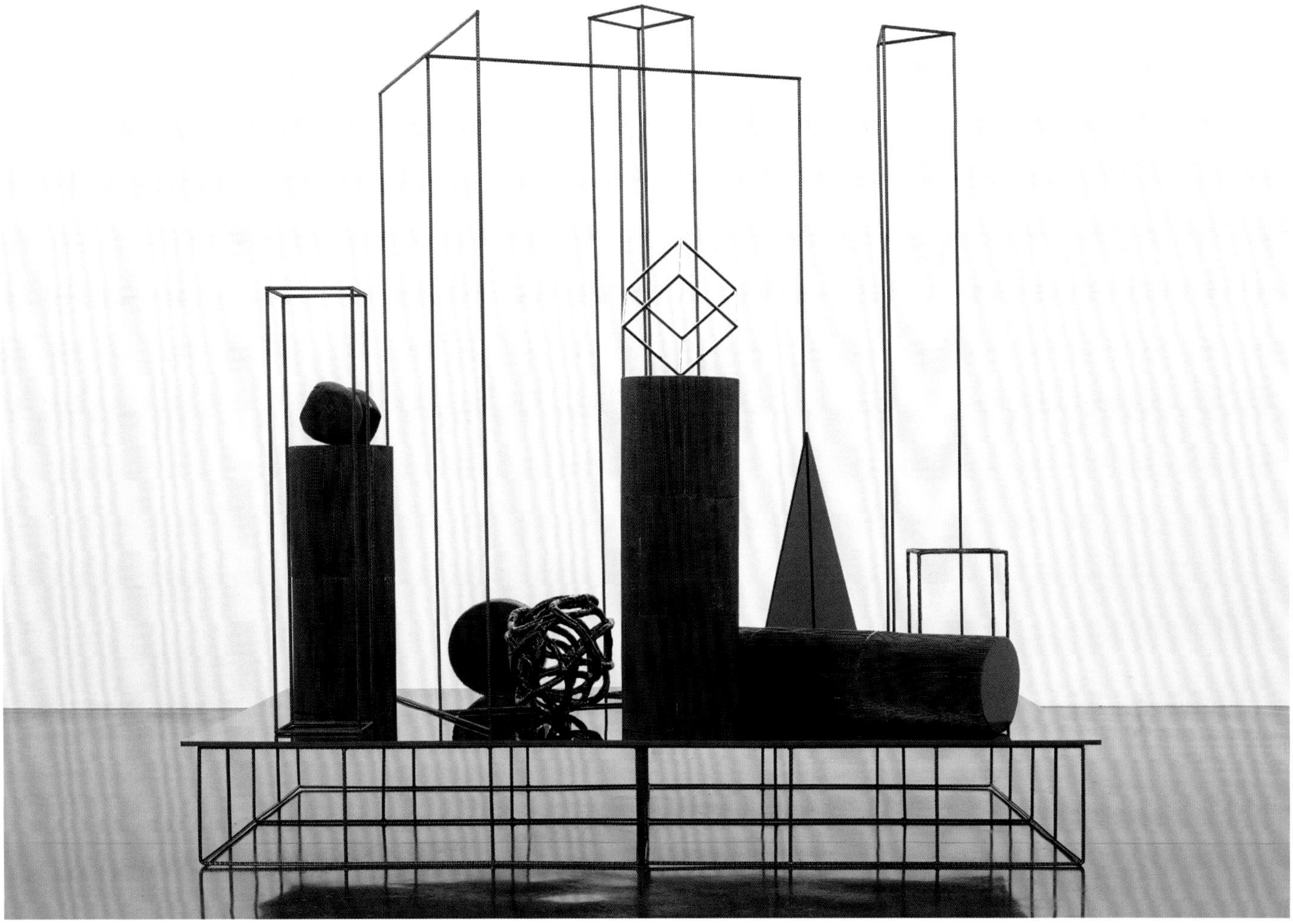

steel. The sculpture's balance, support and joins were discussed with a fabricator, since it could have just concertinaed. There's a white one and a black one, as I find that transference of colour fascinating. The two operate very differently, and I also change the plinths in relation to the colours. I think you can respond to the permutations of geometry and colour as you do to nature. Keeping a degree of confusion, or anxiety, between the pieces is important, so in an exhibition I may place this pirouetting form next to something that's gritty and almost abject in its realization.

IC: *An Array* (2016) and *Hangouts* (2018) both feature a collection of forms housed within an architectonic frame. Here, geometric elements exist alongside darkly mysterious, less well-defined components, to establish an enquiry into organizational space and the hierarchy of objects.

ER: When thinking about organizational space I always refer to Théodore Géricault's *The Raft of the Medusa* (1818–19). It's a lexicon of shape and movement, emotionally and compositionally, and became very important for those two sculptures. Initially, I wanted *An Array* to act as a museological display, but it then became something very different. *Hangouts* has a metal structure, and contains a column, so what's in service to what? Both hold a group of objects on a Perspex base. This base occupies a hierarchical position because it does the most with the materials it's been given. It can reflect, and has a perfection which the other objects, being handmade, can't achieve. Hence, it heightens their presence by providing a hierarchical platform, metaphorically and physically, for them to occupy. This platform also acts as a unifier in that the objects, despite their differences in materiality and making, are bound together, in the same way that the captain and galley boy are joined in *The Raft of the*

Medusa. There's a sense of equalizing in which each component is elevated by the other.

My practice is generally additive, and *An Array* and *Hangouts* expands on this to show how objects operating in unity have a greater prevalence. I've long been interested in the idiosyncratic display of Brancusi's work at MoMA New York, and in his notion of episodic form. He built up the different elements until he reached the right height. How did he get *Endless Column* so high at that time? It's really hard to build a high sculpture.

IC: Many of your works, however, are totemic columns – *Us Women* (2011), *Technical Support* (2018) and *Spektor* (2019). Can they be lengthened or shortened depending on their location, and is this transformation essential to our reading of them?

ER: The thought that these columns could continue, or that a decision was made that they're at the right height, is important. *Technical Support* has been installed desk to ceiling, and floor to ceiling, for instance. It can go anywhere, at any height; it is an endless column in a way because you can add and subtract. *Spektor* is cast from polystyrene moulds, and hovers between traditional form and the disposable object. Polystyrene is used all the time as a hidden base for things. It comprises smaller elements, and this refers back to the totemic quality of *Spektor*, which is also constructed of smaller individual pieces. The fact that polystyrene takes a mark really well allows for an expressive quality of making without getting into carving marble or stone. Instead, this swiftness of mark-making can be rendered permanent through casting.

Us Women is a series that came, indirectly, from seeing footage of protesting crowds around the world. They were my first beaded pieces: circular head-shaped forms held on top of each other, made quite intuitively. The title refers to women as spectators in protests, rather than participants, usually due to fear or safety concerns. Yet there's often a sense of stoicism. *Us Women* are watchers, and totemic sculptures often perform that function, acting as onlookers, or as a sight for activity that bears witness. I was brought up

Eva Rothschild
Technical Support, 2018
Jesmonite, steel bar
16 × 16 × 550 cm
(6¼ in × 6¼ in × 18 ft ½ in)
Installation view:
Australian Centre for
Contemporary Art,
Melbourne, 2018

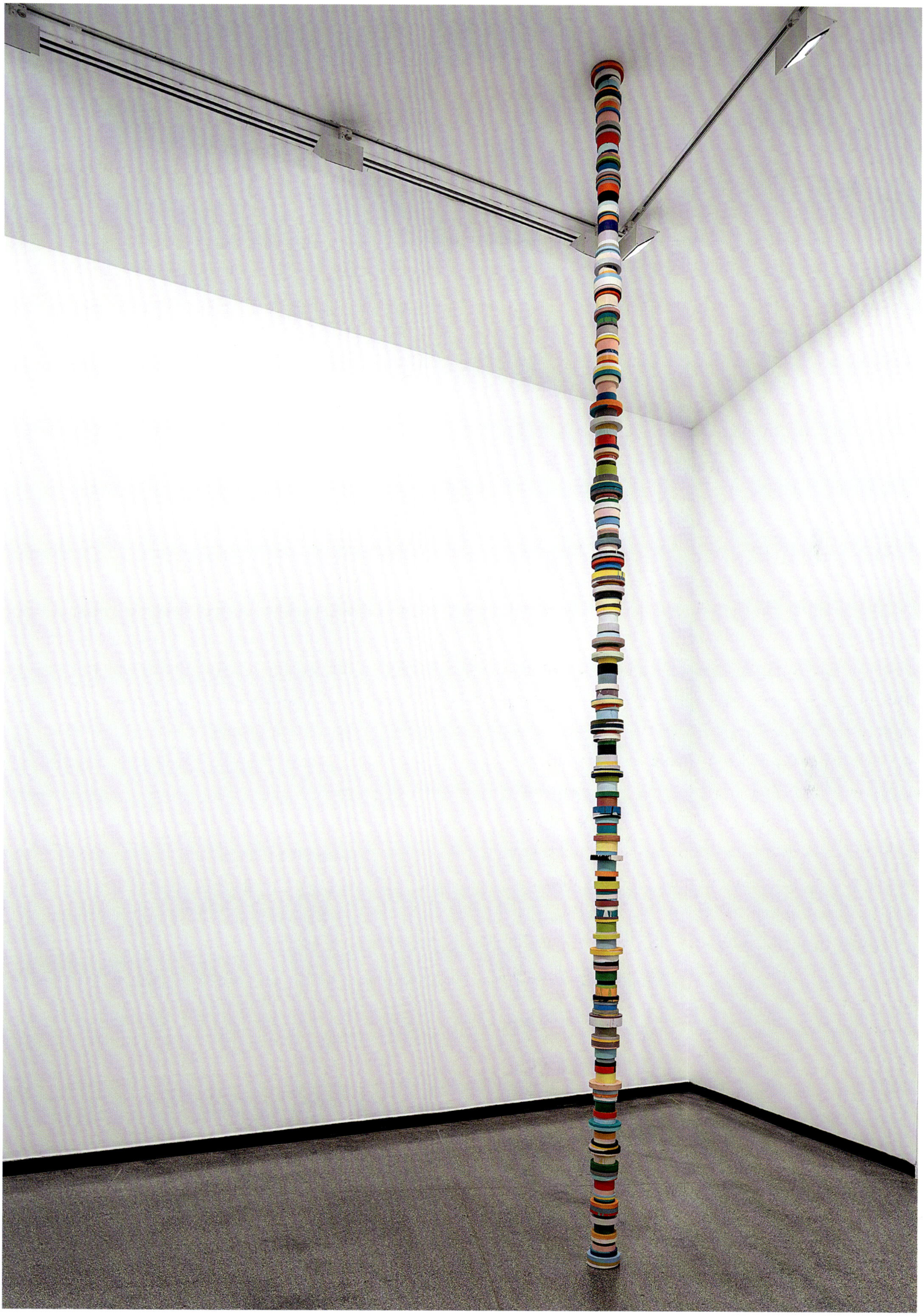

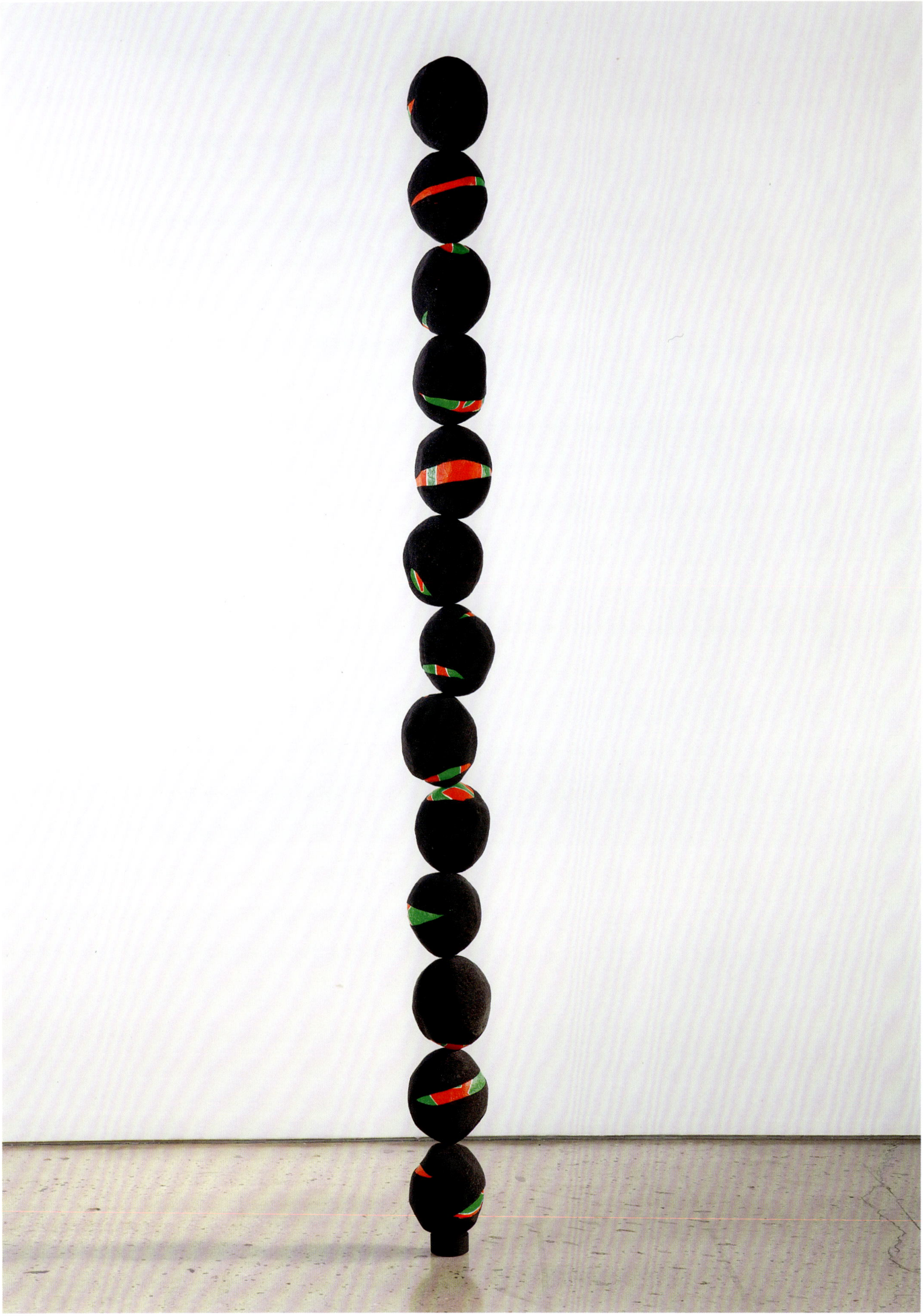

a Catholic, and, in the Bible, the cities of Sodom and Gomorrah were dens of wickedness, with Lot the only just man, as judged by God. On the destruction of the two cities, Lot and his family were spared, on one condition – they couldn't look back. Of course, Lot's wife did, and was turned into a pillar of salt. So that's where the idea of the static witness comes from.

IC: *Cosmos*, *Border* and *Iceberg Hits* were shown together at Modern Art in London (2018). They're extremely self-contained and poised. You like your work to be seen within a designated space one has to enter. Is this because it causes the viewer to fix their attention, reinforcing the notion of transference?

ER: Sculpture is very experiential. That's why, for me, it's vital as an art form. Titles are also fundamental. When looking at art, we're often casting about for the crutch of language, so it's important to have a poetic, expansive or even baffling sense around the titles. *Cosmos*, *Border* and *Iceberg Hits* sound quite geographical, for instance. There's a rhythm between them. In a prosaic way, I've also introduced seating into my exhibitions. Giving consideration to a location and the experience of crossing a threshold is key. What I dread is when people just glance from the door without entering. The seats, therefore, serve a practical purpose by inviting the viewer to stay, as well as allowing contact with the materiality of the work. This is significant, as I use a lot of transformed or changed materiality. Porosity is also important. *Cosmos*, for example, is very physically present, yet has a sense of dematerialization. Although it took up space, it didn't deny access to *Border* or *Iceberg Hits*.

In the same way, *My World and Your World* (2020), installed at King's Cross in London, epitomizes the idea of a huge structure able to coexist with everything else around it. My practice has become more socially engaged and less hermetic, in that the world has crept in. It's become increasingly hard to hold it at bay. All the structural issues we've swept under the carpet have come home to roost: inequality, the harassment of women and colonialism. My work isn't polemical; it doesn't have an axe to grind, but it does acknowledge

←
Eva Rothschild
Us Women (New York), 2011
Polystyrene, modroc, glass beads, paint and steel
355.6 × 22.9 × 22.9 cm
(11 ft ⅛ in × 9 in × 9 in)

→→
Eva Rothschild
Amphi, 2019
Resin, spray paint, wood
Dimensions variable
Installation view:
Venice Biennale, 2019

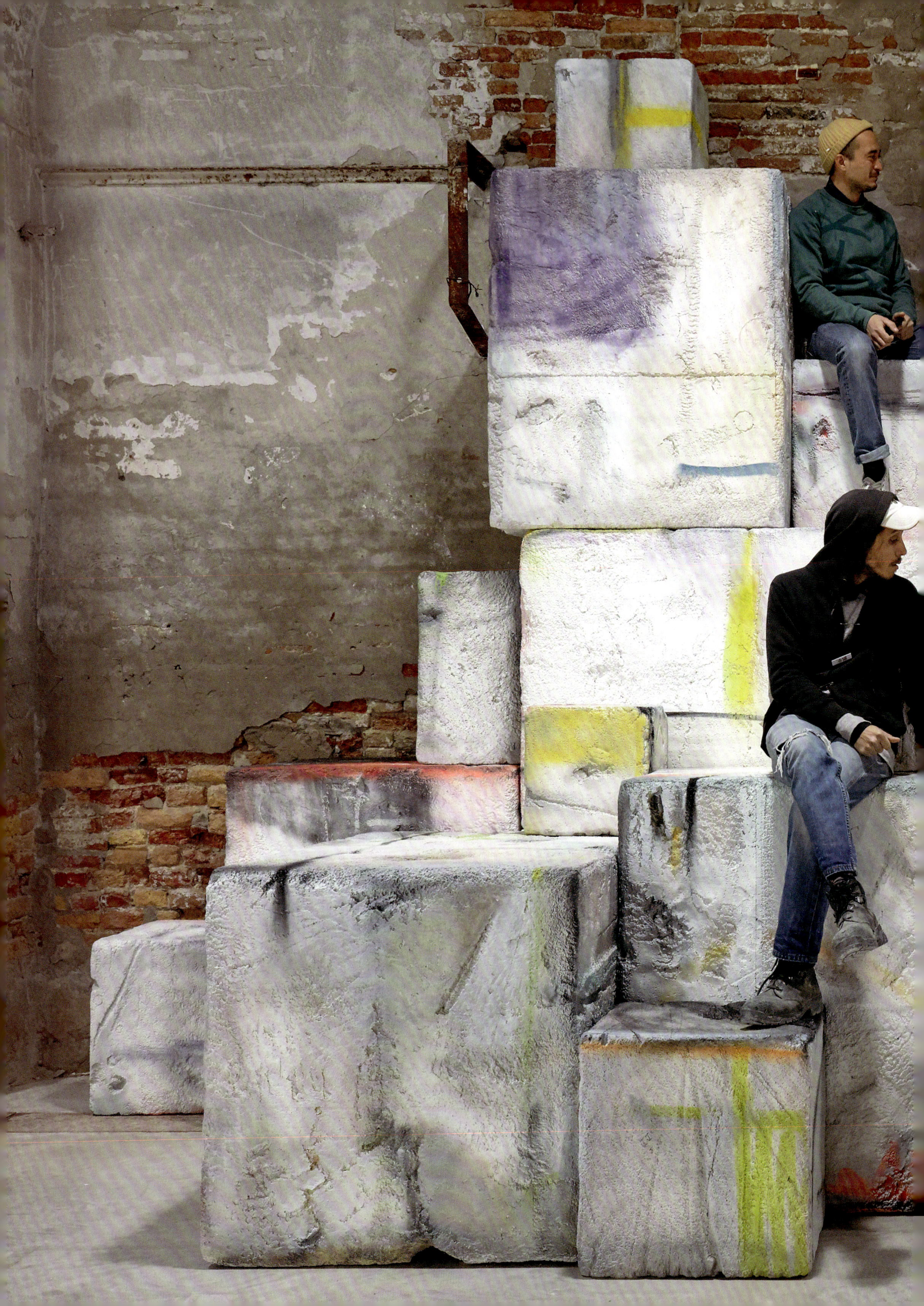

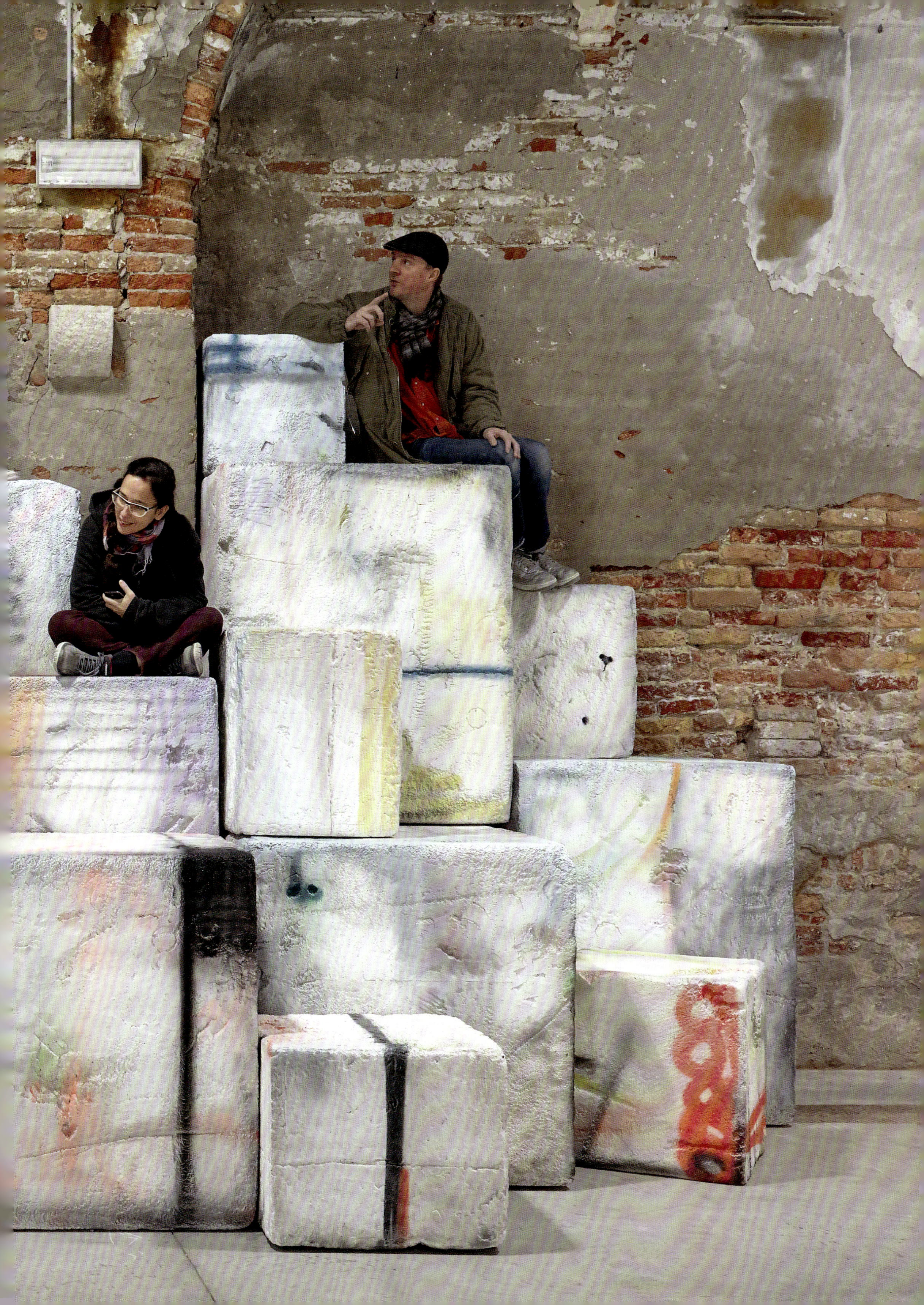

the time in which it's been made. I'm particularly conscious of borders and walls: I left school in 1988, and the Berlin Wall came down in 1989; I also witnessed the Good Friday Agreement in 1998 in Belfast. So, *Border* functions as a full stop or halt, whereas the other pieces are much more of a meander.

IC: You represented Ireland in the 2019 Venice Biennale with 'The Shrinking Universe', an immersive environment in which spectators could climb and occupy cast polystyrene blocks. This installation could be seen to embody your aim of producing work that's less hermetic. How significant was this social interaction, and why was the exhibition titled 'The Shrinking Universe'?

ER: The pace of the individual entering, and their experience in the pavilion, was important. So, the room had to be as light as possible for the sculptures to acknowledge both the space and the physical presence of spectators. Making furniture from similar materials to the work creates a scenario in which it's clear that the viewer is supposed to be there, and it also absolves the sculpture itself from having to be welcoming. 'The Shrinking Universe' went one step further with *Amphi*. This was a construction of blocks referencing historical forms and hazard architecture, the semi-permanent structures of coercion found within our cities. Climbing to seek out a viewpoint was therefore crucial; there was a chosen engagement rather than just a walk-through. Venice is such a spectacular event, and, when climbing onto the blocks, you immediately became a participant and part of the spectacle.

In terms of physics, the orthodox view is that the universe is expanding. But there's a contrary view that it's shrinking. Empirically, that's not the case, but experientially it is, as we travel and communicate in unprecedented ways. We inhabit the universe and experience it subjectively, and the gap between the subjective and objective is something I feel very keenly. The universe has its own metric; it has no use for our feelings. Even though we influence our world in the planetary sense, the universe is much greater. Like with *Cold Corners*, we often develop a subjective response to something that doesn't care. This disconnect put a parenthesis around the whole exhibition. 'The Shrinking Universe' also referenced the map of structural and historic power between countries, in terms of how the geography within the Biennale is organized. Post-colonial countries like Ireland, Ghana and Chile rent alongside still-emerging countries such as the Republic of North Macedonia, while the historically powerful flex in the permanent pavilions of the Giardini. That sense of the quantum and the minutiae interests me. It's as if the world is being squashed, even though our subjective view is at odds with the physical reality.

IC: Despite projects such as 'The Shrinking Universe', *My World and Your World*, and *Cold Corners*, studio-based practice has remained key for you. When first visiting Barbara Hepworth's Palais de Danse in St Ives, you were struck by its purpose, as opposed to the theatricality of Brancusi's studio in Paris. How would you describe your relationship to your own studio?

ER: It's very intense. One of my big anxieties is the idea of my home being under threat, and I feel the same about my studio. I really need it; it's vital to my practice. People often say you can work anywhere as an artist, but I can't. Where would I make the work on a daily basis? What would I do without tools and materials? That relationship is under threat, because of the precarious nature of even having a studio now. If you're experimental, but don't have a space to try things out, you may not have the latitude to arrive at a different conclusion. A studio is essential to everything. It's a room of one's own, in the largest sense.

Interviewed in 2018 and 2020

Eva Rothschild
My World and Your World, 2020
Painted steel, zinc and polyester
1193 × 1180 × 1597 cm
(39 ft 1⅝ in × 38 ft 8⅝ in × 52 ft 4¾ in)
Installation view:
Lewis Cubitt Park,
King's Cross, London, 2020

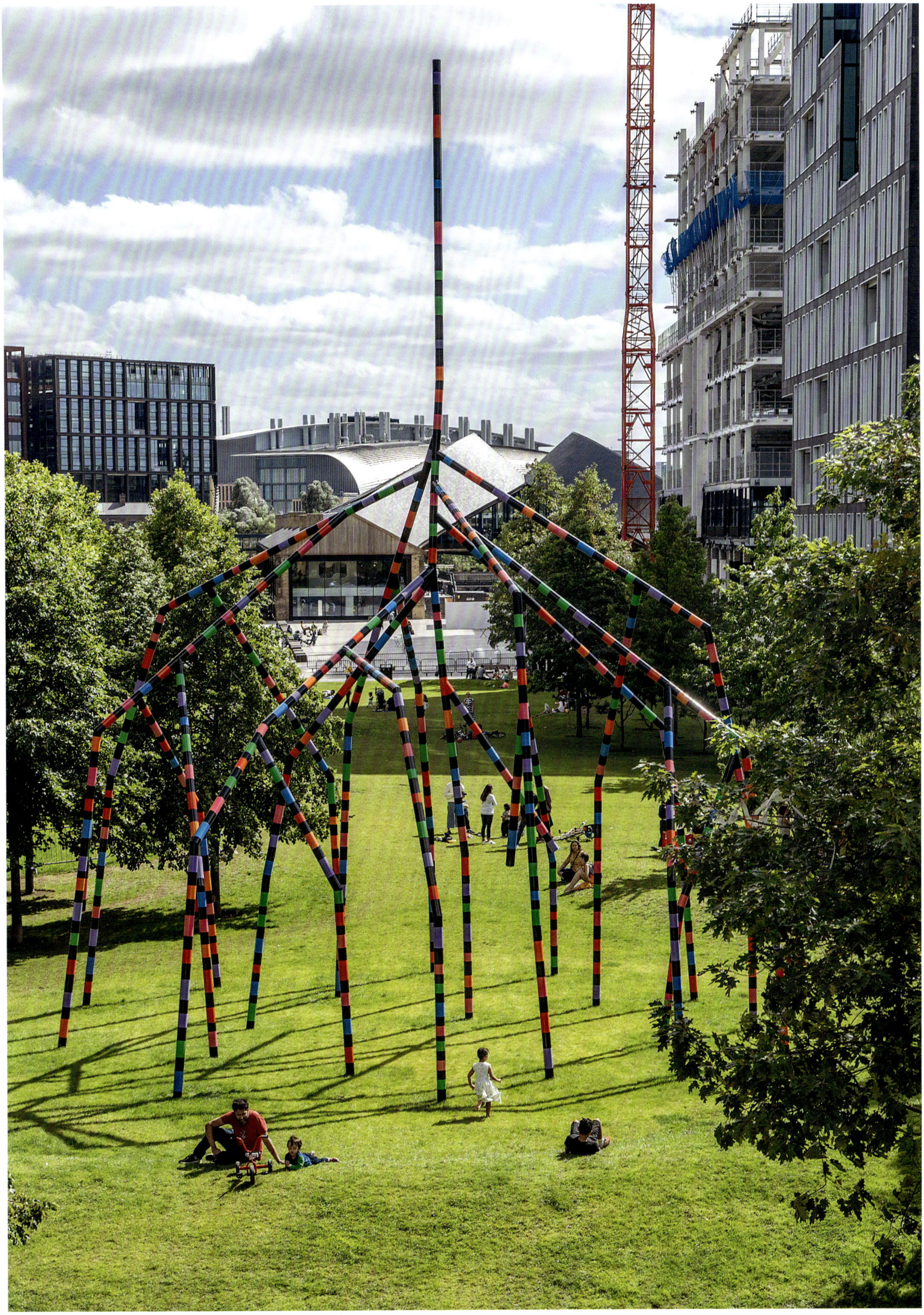

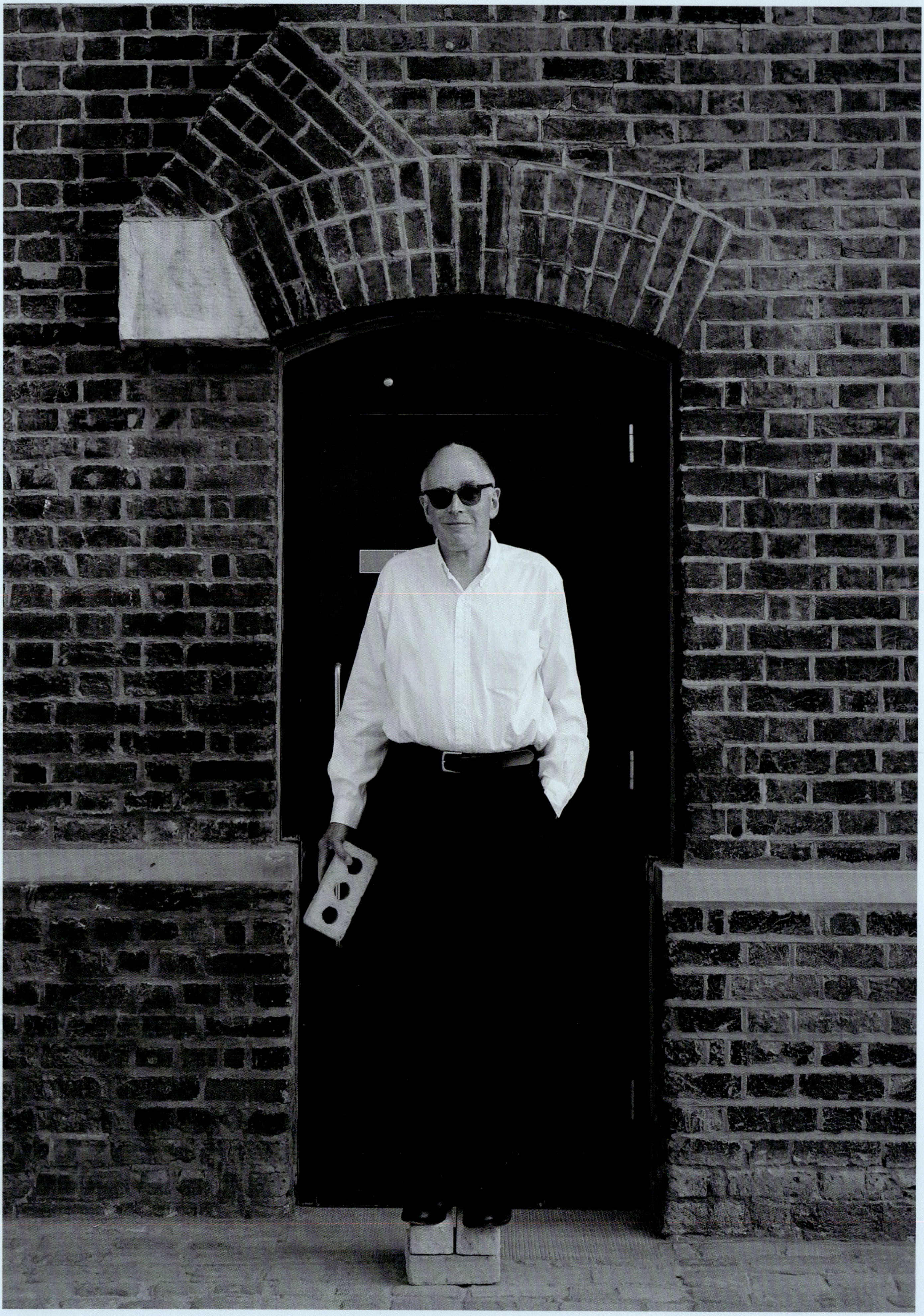

RICHARD WENTWORTH

Born 1947, Samoa

Richard Wentworth's way of seeing recognizes the world as a system of interlocking signs. He habitually walks the streets of London detecting minutiae often missed by the untrained eye, and these observations provide the nucleus for new ideas. This has resulted in projects that transform the established definition of sculpture, as well as photographs capturing the idiosyncrasies of the urban landscape, as seen in the series *Making Do and Getting By*. In his work, inanimate objects are energized by their placement alongside other objects that just happen to reside in the same environment. It is a game of chance which conjures seemingly implausible juxtapositions, resulting in a perplexing riddle for the viewer to unpick. Wentworth's projects range from all-encompassing installations – such as *Black Maria, A Room Full of Lovers* and *False Ceiling* – to smaller sculptures transforming utilitarian entities into aberrant arrangements.

Ina Cole: Your early practice often featured ready-mades, melded into pairings that render them unserviceable – *Stile* (1991), *Twain* (1992) and *Mode - Module - Modular* (2004). Even in later work, such as *A Room Full of Lovers* (2013), this idea is sustained. You operate without recourse to established techniques or principles, an approach offering certain freedoms with regard to perception and manipulation, both within the studio and outside on the street.

Richard Wentworth: Pairing is a kind of comedy for humans – bilateral symmetry, our parents, sex, and so on. I'm very aware of the autocratic extemporizing in our culture, and much of my motivation lies in that friction. We have a deep sense of what things 'are good for', and most of the time they're doomed to become images, which is why I find genre painting and Spanish vanitas so interesting. The concept of 'use value' is also interesting to me and the way we recognize it when things are passive – an empty watering-can, closed book or inactive torch. There's probably a deep sense of retrieval in my actions – a feeling that everything has a meaning yet, in combination, they could have more than twice their energy.

I'm particularly aware of the real dimension of objects, and, when I was a child, looking after things was a ritual – saving string, bottle caps and little handbooks on how to mend and repair. Tinkering, when it meant something. There are 'studio artists' and 'studio producers' who have a much greater sense of quasi-industrial activity. Then there are others who are in-between. Although I can work well in the studio, I'm not romantic about it, while, on the street, I'm always astonished by the multiple concatenation and corruption of objects. In some ways, my conduct is like the fox Francis Alÿs released into the National Portrait Gallery (*The Nightwatch*, 2004).

IC: You spend much time wandering the city, observing the way inconsequential items migrate to the most unlikely locations. As a subject, London provides a never-ending supply of opportunities, but you must have witnessed great changes over the years?

Richard Wentworth
Mode - Module - Modular, 2004
Wood and steel coat hook
47.5 × 50 × 35 cm
(18¾ × 19¾ × 13¾ in)

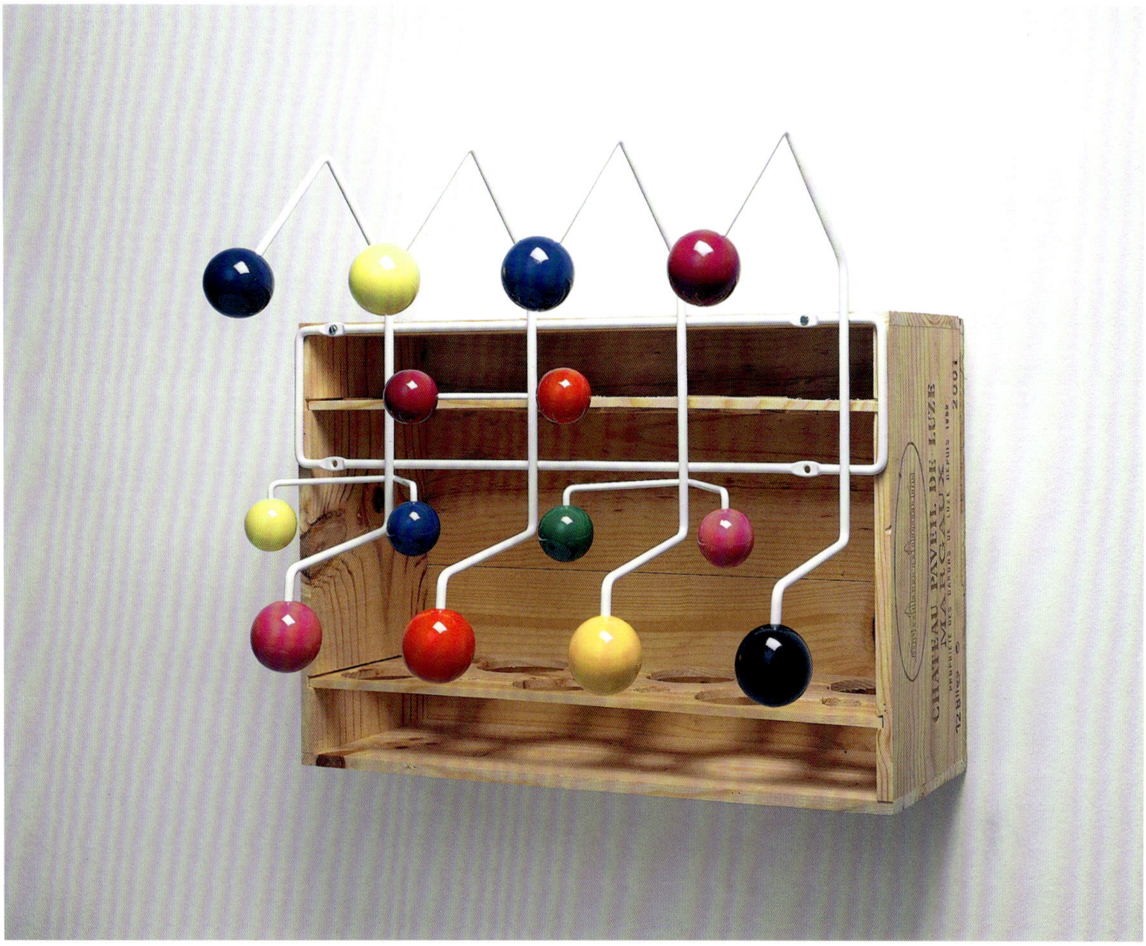

RW: London wasn't very fluid when I studied at the Royal College of Art in the 1960s, with few similarities to the London of now. Its populations had lived there for a long while, if they hadn't been bombed during World War II or moved out through slum clearance. When I studied sculpture, the atmosphere was gently European; Giacometti's ghost was prominent, as he'd had a Tate show in 1965 and died in 1966. London was a dirty, modest and quite conventional city, with a kind of parsimony right across the classes and powerful codes as to how things should be done. What characterized that period for me was how much disposable time and little disposable income everyone had. Yet, the delusions we now live by were then being invented: the idea one could have everything or be in touch instantly. Also, it was a period when many of the world's mysteries were revealed. I saw the city being made and unmade, so felt close to the fabric of it all. If you want to get behind the surface now you have to be much more inquisitive. However, I'm at a point where a lot of what I watched being built is being demolished.

IC: You taught at Goldsmiths, University of London until 1987 where you exerted a powerful force over the so-called YBAs (Young British Artists), who were then your students. This was an extraordinary period in British art. Looking back, what do you think lay at the core of its success?

RW: The entire story is extremely circumstantial, and one should pay attention to the circumstances. The YBAs were students in an isolated building rented by Goldsmiths in the middle of Camberwell, South London, who often saw each other and ate together. Some of these things are so simple. We were a group who felt we could do what we liked, in an unregulated city offering plenty of space. It was a time of energy. The atmosphere generated by the collector Charles Saatchi was that of the illiterate intellectual: smart and observant, yet not highly educated. Technology now allows the world to be regulated, which isn't sinister, but it's a big shift that could become sinister. So, if you're asking, 'How did those Goldsmiths artists obtain such confidence?', I'd say, 'Partly because they saw they could react.' The city is around you, stuff happens, and you give it due accord.

I once met Henry Kissinger, the US statesman, in Berlin, who said, 'Nobody had the luck of the English.' Historically, that luck relates to the actions of those we'd now call brigands – people who took enormous risks. The impetus to behave like that – which is partly informed by other empires – runs deeply in our culture and is practised in all sorts of ways. People seize an opportunity and create energy. With the YBAs, much of that energy was about the outer ring coming in and getting excited about the bright lights. There was a sense that the streets were paved with gold, but any serious city is an attractant and what happens because of the form of its attractiveness is quite mysterious.

IC: The notion of a brigand performing a reconnaissance suits your own practice, which involves a complex process of lateral thinking. How does photography as a mode of documentation aid this approach?

RW: My photographs act as a private place of recognition, like a little child's jewel box. It's important to make the most of reverie – the condition of wonder. But I'm not going out to observe; I'm just going about my business. I operate at quite a fluid level in the city and encounter the leftovers of other peoples' actions or conversations. It's like eavesdropping or overhearing, which, depending on your point of view, could be seen as alert or sinister. I'm particularly interested in peripheral vision: the moment we sense something, fall in love, recognize danger or invasion. It's like a magnetic field.

IC: The novelist Franz Kafka walked the streets of Prague, observing the populous in quite a similar manner. Yet he felt that the photograph falsifies, rather than represents, the reality; that it focuses one's attention on the superficial and doesn't offer the capacity for deeper contemplation.

RW: But I think I'm proving him wrong. Photography is such a complicated subject. What are images; why do we see them; how do we nominate something to become an image or not? Just think how many images I've seen today, and the way my brain has edited them. People often say they're bombarded by images, but images are passive. How we see and what we remember is mysterious. It's extremely luxurious to be able to use one's time like this; it's quite selfish, as the act of taking photographs is a form of possession. I have very high levels of coincidence. In the city, objects seem to lie in wait for me, like an ambush, and that kind of epiphany is to do with the way things are energized. It's odd to be affected by intentions, which are often anonymous. I can walk around a corner and see a building declaring, 'Give me some attention', yet have no idea of the architect's name. What exactly is that transaction for the passer-by?

Humans are so eager for meaning, and they exist inside a social code which moves around forever. As I get older, I realize I might even be responsible for generating a code that's being interpreted by those who wouldn't necessarily know why it ever came about. I'm a profferer of experiences, but there's no accounting for what the consequences of those experiences might be. People are image-sensitive; they're alerted to something and maybe that is art. How else do a few words thrown together, with the word Kafka underneath, become so full of meaning?

Richard Wentworth
Ifs and Buts, 2005
Galvanized steel with mirror
(two parts)
Dimensions variable

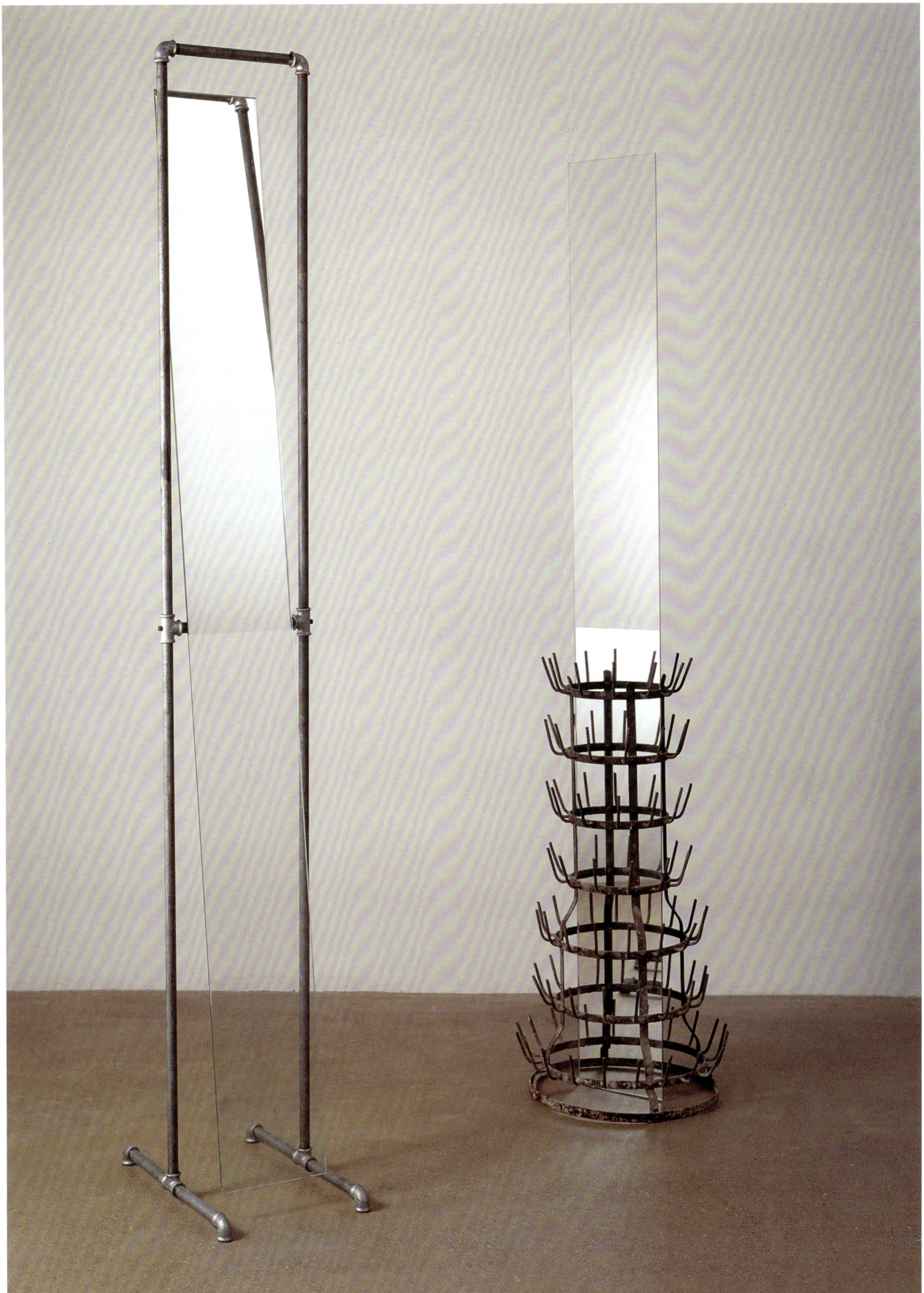

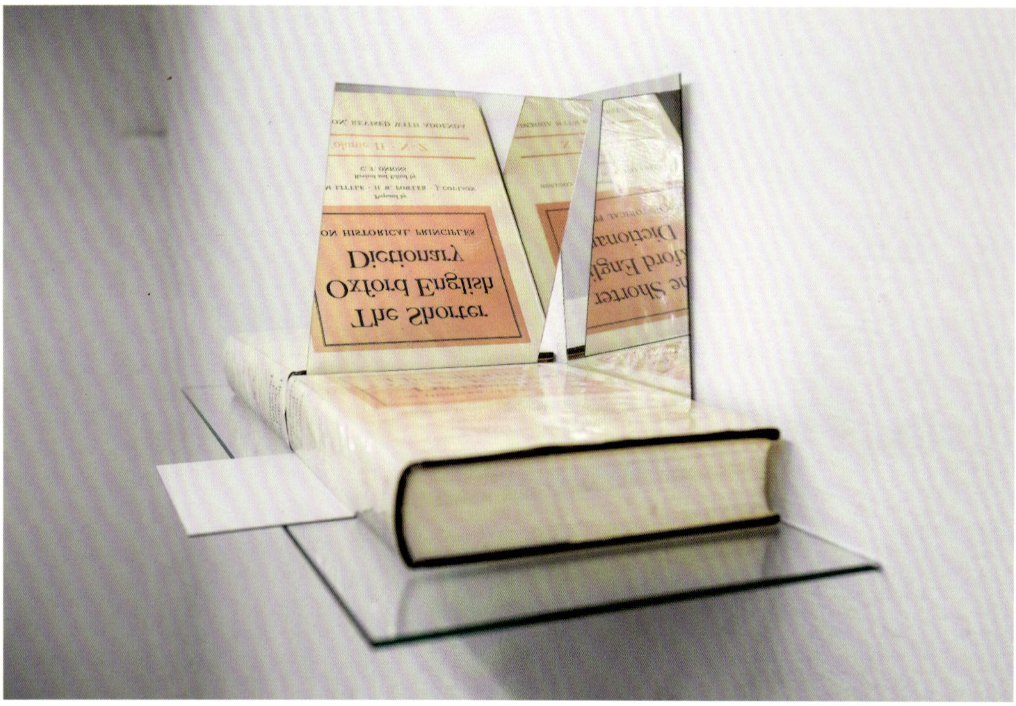

←
Richard Wentworth
Marginalia, 2019

Glass, mirrors and books
24.5 × 70 × 30 cm
(9⅝ × 27½ × 11¾ in)

→
Richard Wentworth
False Ceiling, 1995

Books and steel cable
Dimensions variable
Installation view:
Lisson Gallery,
London, 1995

IC: In much the same way, mirrors – which often feature in your installations – can be read as carriers of the truth yet, conversely, of deception. They're loaded with symbolism and feature in *Mirror, Mirror* (2013), *Ifs and Buts* (2005) and, most notably, *14 Rooms Upended* (2005), created for Felbrigg Hall in Norfolk.

RW: Mirrors seem miraculous to me, and the mirrors at Felbrigg paid a small homage to the country house. They were assorted ellipses and ovals that looked like quasi-domestic insertions into the interiors, which made you aware of the complexity of the different spaces. Sometimes, they appeared quite erotic, in that you could see round corners or into spaces, which felt illicit. There was, in fact, a very funny upset where a mirror that enabled you to see underneath another shapely shiny object, a piano, was removed for fear people might see up other visitors' skirts. This led to quite a vigorous discussion about the role of the spectator. Art is like a moving target: I had created something completely honourably, yet someone else had interpreted my intentions very differently. So, *14 Rooms Upended* constantly deals with points of view, and I'm always aware that my point of view is an accident. If I was sitting where you're sitting now, I'd see the world differently. Without all these considerations, and the underlying pleasure of a 'point of view', I don't think I could work.

IC: Books have also remained a constant in your practice – *Foglio/Foglia* (1997), *Time and Place* (2004) and *Marginalia* (2019). Throughout history, the open book is indicative of learning and wisdom, yet yours are usually closed. Why do they feature so prominently as objects in your work?

RW: The history of my work with books has an unusual relationship to the coming of the Internet. I am, by

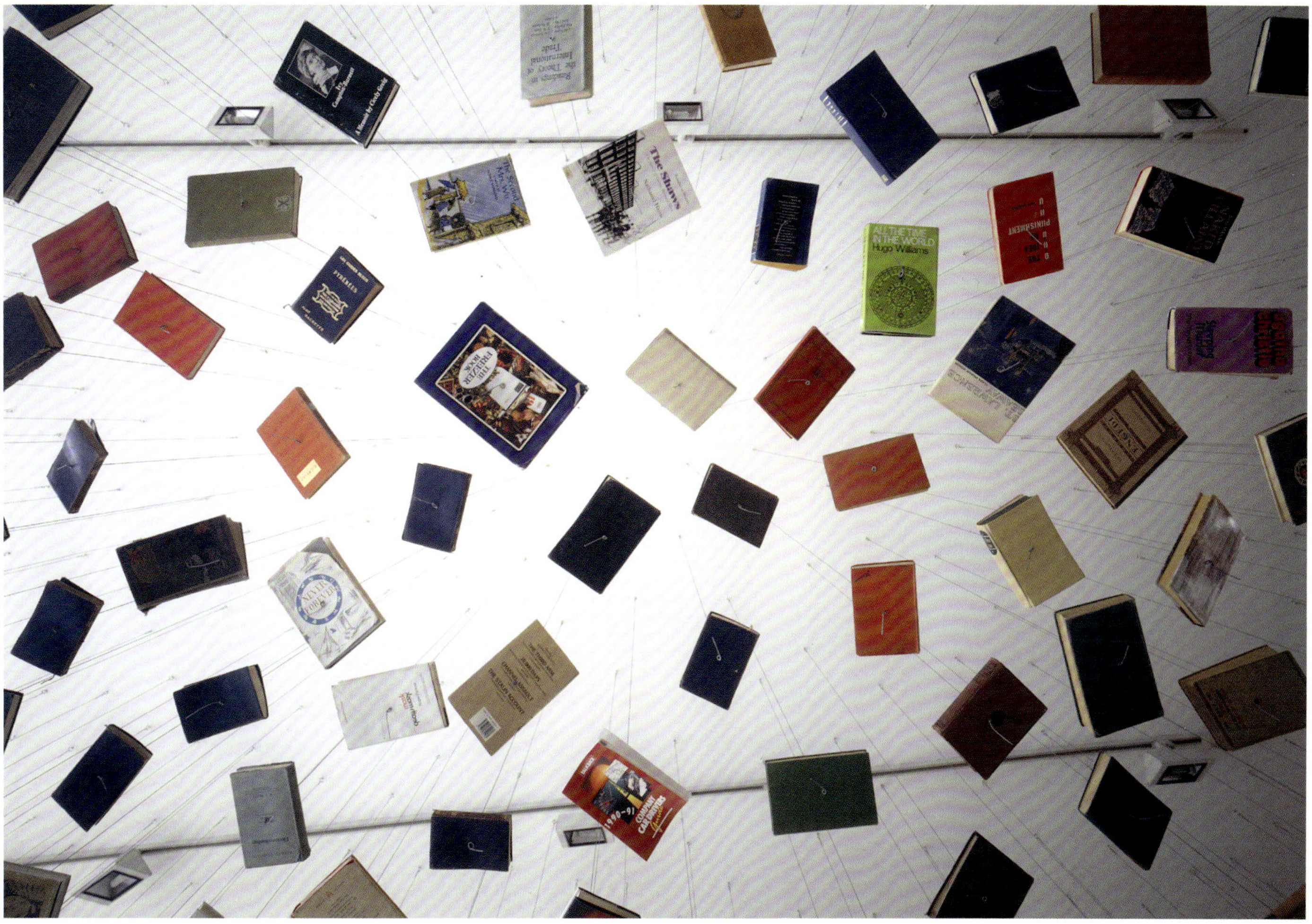

nature, somebody who finds rather than seeks. I was once at a village fête in the Cotswolds, when an announcement was made that 'all the books are now free'. I raced over to seize a two-part Oxford dictionary, now commonly abandoned because of the Internet. I noticed how well cared-for they had been and enjoyed the simple dedication at the front. I then laid them on the floor – on top of each other, side by side, inverted – and just watched their different geometries.

On returning to London, this feeling of the unmatched pair continued to impress me, and I took them to the studio. The exceptional 'architecture' of a book – a hinged sandwich of ideas and thoughts arranged between covers – is a parallel world to how I work as an artist. The pages mirror each other, but, then again, not. Think, perhaps, of all the ways we scan and assemble our thoughts and feelings – from the most dominant to the most peripheral – and share them. In one sense, a book, even a fresh one, is always in the past. It is us, as lookers and readers, who perpetually bring it into the present. Even when unopened, it is a set of proposals, a feeling of expectation, which might be indicated by its typography, colour or binding. Certainly, we have a good sense of the age of a book and its period. We do that when we meet humans too – how they dress and deport themselves as much as the experience worn in their faces.

IC: You initially created *False Ceiling* for Lisson Gallery in London (1995), then for Indianapolis Museum of Art (2015–16), where a call was put out inviting the museum's visitors to donate their unwanted volumes. It's a vast installation, with all the books suspended from the ceiling. How did this piece come about?

RW: Art still gets measured by its size, the time it takes to make, its weight or the cost of materials. I hope

Duchamp didn't pay too much for his urinal (*Fountain*, 1917) and just got on with it. When I lived in Berlin, in the early 1990s, I witnessed the consequences of mass distribution, which was a mass throwing-out. Enormous numbers of books were being sold by weight, most of which I couldn't penetrate, as I don't read Russian, Polish or German. That experience turned into *False Ceiling*, made for the eccentric architecture of the older of the Lisson Galleries. I wanted *False Ceiling* to vigorously assert itself against the architecture but honour it at the same time. If you suspend, the impulse to recognize an image and to read run parallel. It's not normal to do that above your head, and you become very physically aware. It's an odd place for the body to be, yet it's enjoyable and quite voyeuristic to watch people. They don't have a choice, it's what humans do; they look up, create sequences, then realize they're defeated. Deeply contradictory things happen because the subject matter of one book is completely different from the next.

The Indianapolis Museum of Art has an interesting architectural typology, and I used the foyer – an enormous area housing escalators. It's the main circulation point and quite hard to read as a space. It has architectural vanity, and *False Ceiling* had to cut through that, but surreptitiously, like whispering. It's not as if I wanted to confront this atrium space, though; just give it a good talking to and make something that was courageous yet gorgeous.

IC: *False Ceiling* also seems to suggest the unattainability of knowledge, as the books hover above peoples' heads, teasing and alluring, as if all we can do is strive but not quite grasp.

RW: But I don't think it's patronizing. We hear words like 'learning', 'processing information' and 'acquisition of knowledge': a lot of grand terms, but, on examination, they're rather technocratic. Think how capable humans are, whether educated or not. We have profound responses and amazing sentiments, even if we don't always know where the sentiments have come from. There is something about the weight of the books, and their sheer physical condition, but there isn't a wagging finger in there.

Richard Wentworth
A Room Full of Lovers, 2013

Steel welded chain
Dimensions variable
Installation view: Lisson Gallery, London, 2013

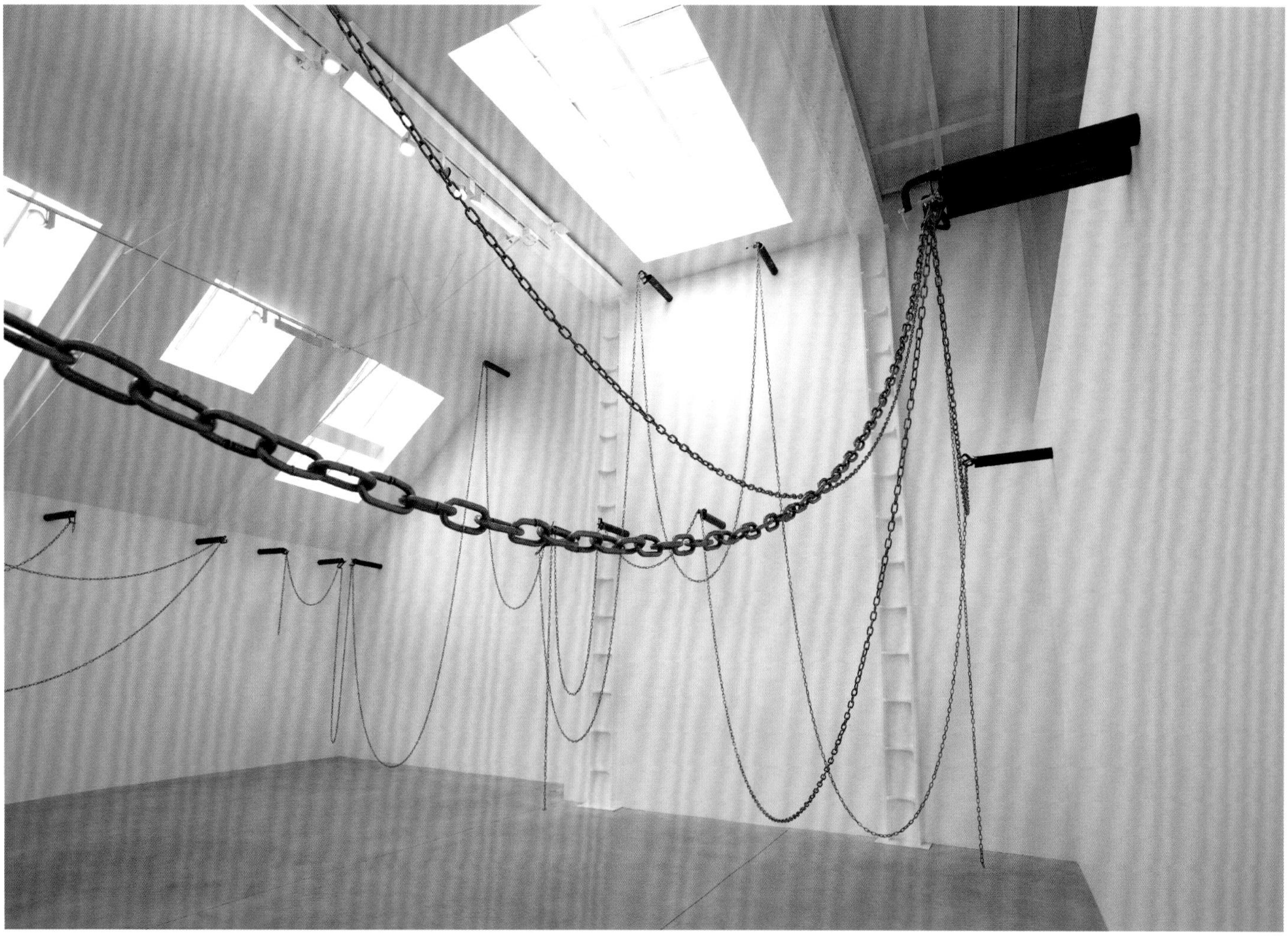

IC: It's more a sense of yearning, which is also present in *A Room Full of Lovers* (2013), particularly in the way the chains cascading into the space are anchored up high, remaining essentially elusive.

RW: *A Room Full of Lovers* and *14 Rooms Upended* share certain formal qualities, as I'm partial to gravitational curves. I see them everywhere. The chains in *A Room Full of Lovers* are so strange in that, when holding two links, you realize they're always in contact, and the point at which they're in contact is almost invisible. I'm very interested in certain kinds of pairing, and it's important to understand how elaborately the world is woven. Also, it's not unusual for me to play with ideas of impotence. Perhaps it's because one hasn't got much time to be effective, and a large part of our lives is worrying about being ineffectual. That's why we don't feel great when waking up in the morning, and constantly have to reinvent ourselves. Everyone carries a burden. We haven't got very long; we're not going to touch all the cultures of the world. I'm not going to meet a senior aboriginal or have a conversation about the Kalahari Desert anymore. We all have a story, but a short time to exercise our imaginative energy, so we do what we can.

IC: *Black Maria* (2013) was a major installation devised for The Crossing at King's Cross in London, in collaboration with the Swiss architects, Gruppe. You named the work after Thomas Edison's film studio, and it took the form of a timber atrium designed as a place of interaction and debate for London's communities. *Concertina* (2017), in collaboration with Apparata, then continued this aim. Do you think of your practice as altruistic?

RW: The discipline of architecture is so procedural, rigorous and litigious it really can't connect to my

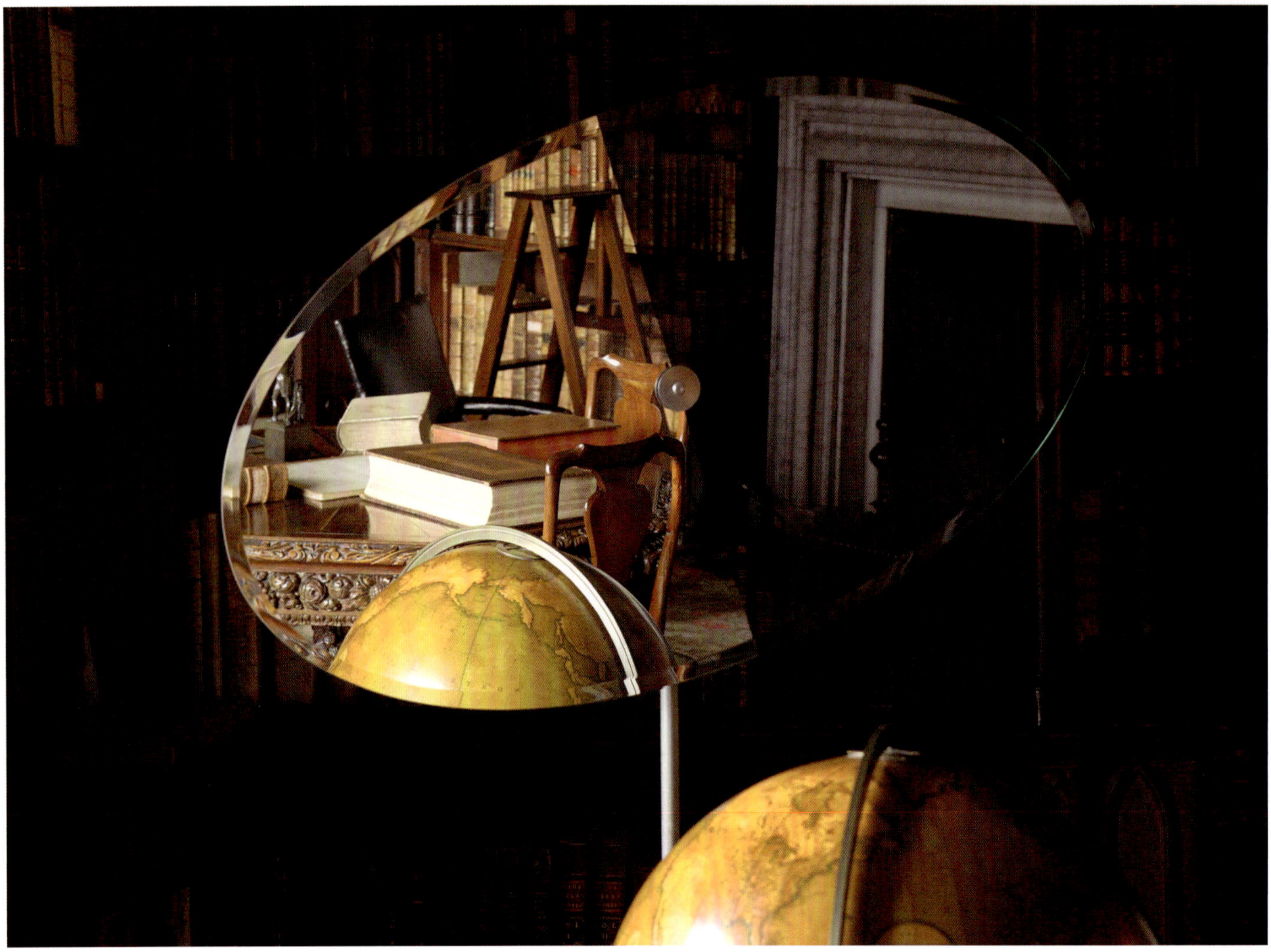

playroom approach, while the constraints on architects are steadily driving out their playfulness and formal curiosity. Only once have I felt that dynamic to be reversed, when Gruppe responded so vigorously to my thoughts. *Black Maria* was a brilliant triumph for them and well remembered by those who experienced it, while *Concertina* was a brave attempt to keep the yo-yo spinning.

I like the strangeness of relationships and meeting new energies that match mine; I see it as two-way traffic. Collaborating with Gruppe meant working with people I admired and trusted but didn't know very well. I didn't really own *Black Maria*, and anonymity can be a great companion. It was a noble piece of work made in difficult circumstances, but altruistic? It's a word that sits with 'sermonize', 'missionary' or 'evangelical', but what else are artists doing when they make something and let it out into the public space? It's loaded or charmed, and maybe that's the test of whether it's good or bad. I don't like the conventionalized language used for these projects. Words like 'participatory' or 'relational aesthetics' are alarming. It's as if someone's dropped a damp blanket. I don't quite know what *Black Maria* was, so the language used – like 'intervention', or the dreaded 'respond to the space' – was weak.

The organizational requirements for art-making can drive out much of the essential happenstance and fun. We're a bit low on critical energy, as visual-arts activity has become so industrialized that everything has been tidied into boxes. Yet some artists travel confidently. They're handed their coat and they wear it, whereas I've politely taken mine off. I'm not quite sure exactly what it is I do, but I have the confidence to believe it has content and meaning, and somehow penetrates the world.

Interviewed in 2015 and 2019

←
Richard Wentworth
14 Rooms Upended, 2005

20kg (44lb) weights, glass, mirrors and galvanized steel
Dimensions variable
Installation view:
Felbrigg Hall, Norfolk, 2005

→
Richard Wentworth
Stile, 1991

Steel and linoleum with brooms
155 × 141 × 77 cm
(61 × 55½ × 30¼ in)

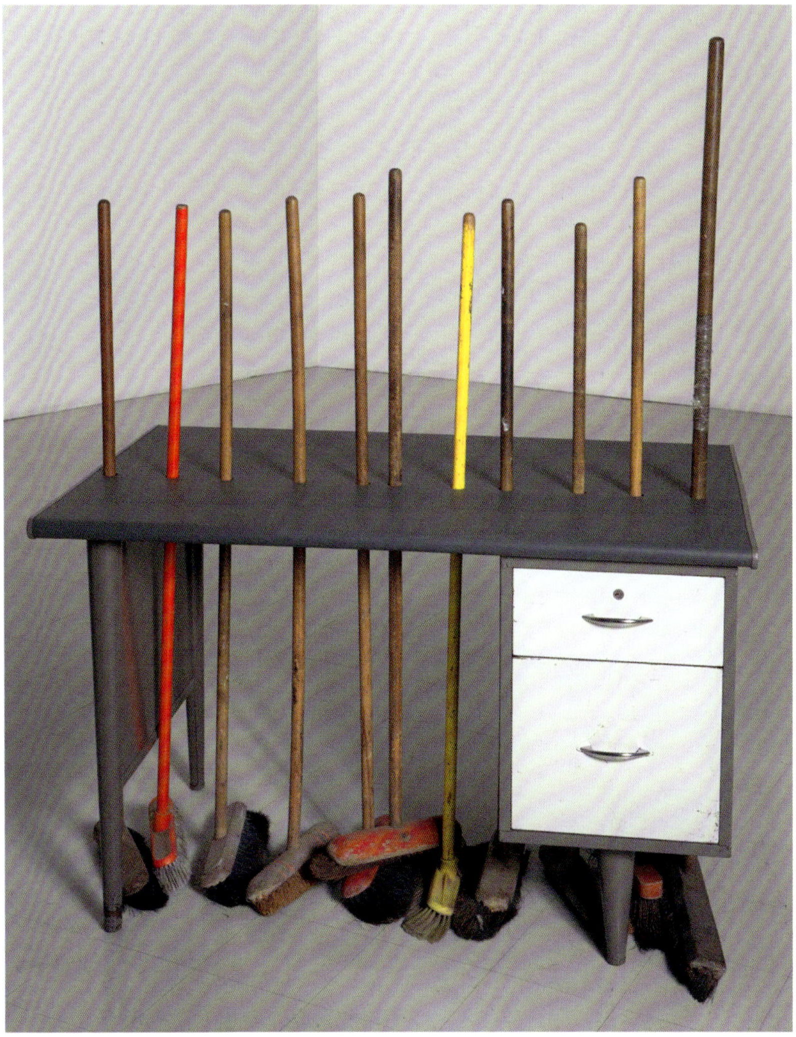

↘
Richard Wentworth
Foglio/Foglia, 1997

Mixed media
20 × 65 × 25 cm
(7⅞ × 25⅝ × 9⅞ in)

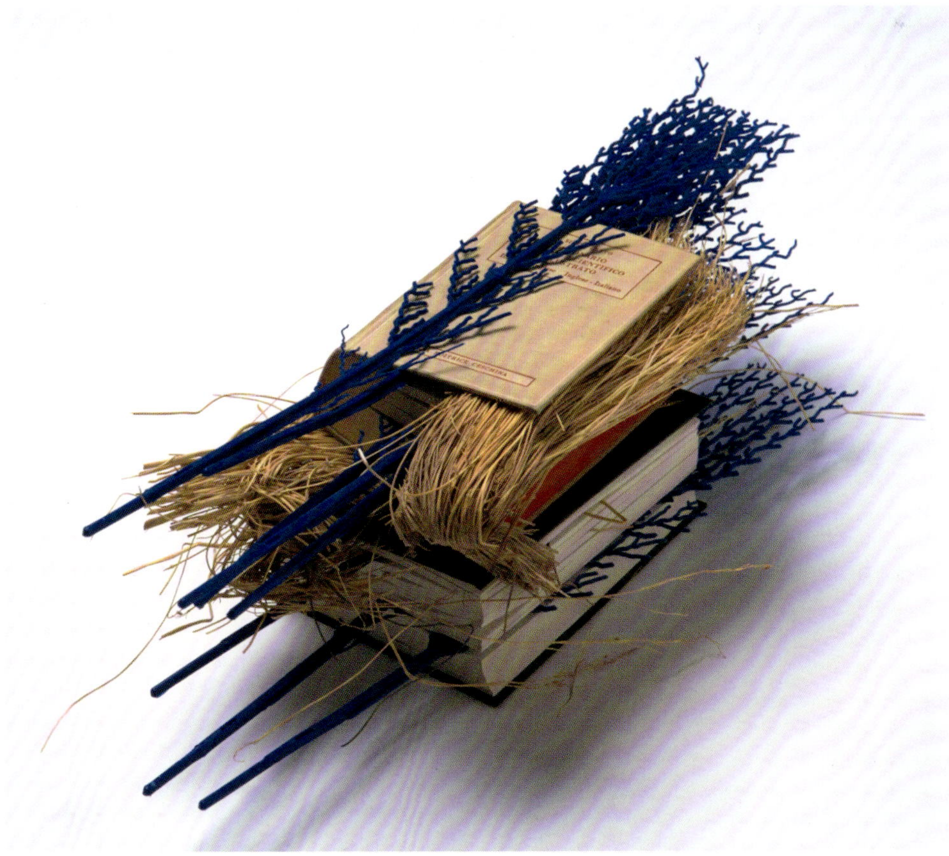

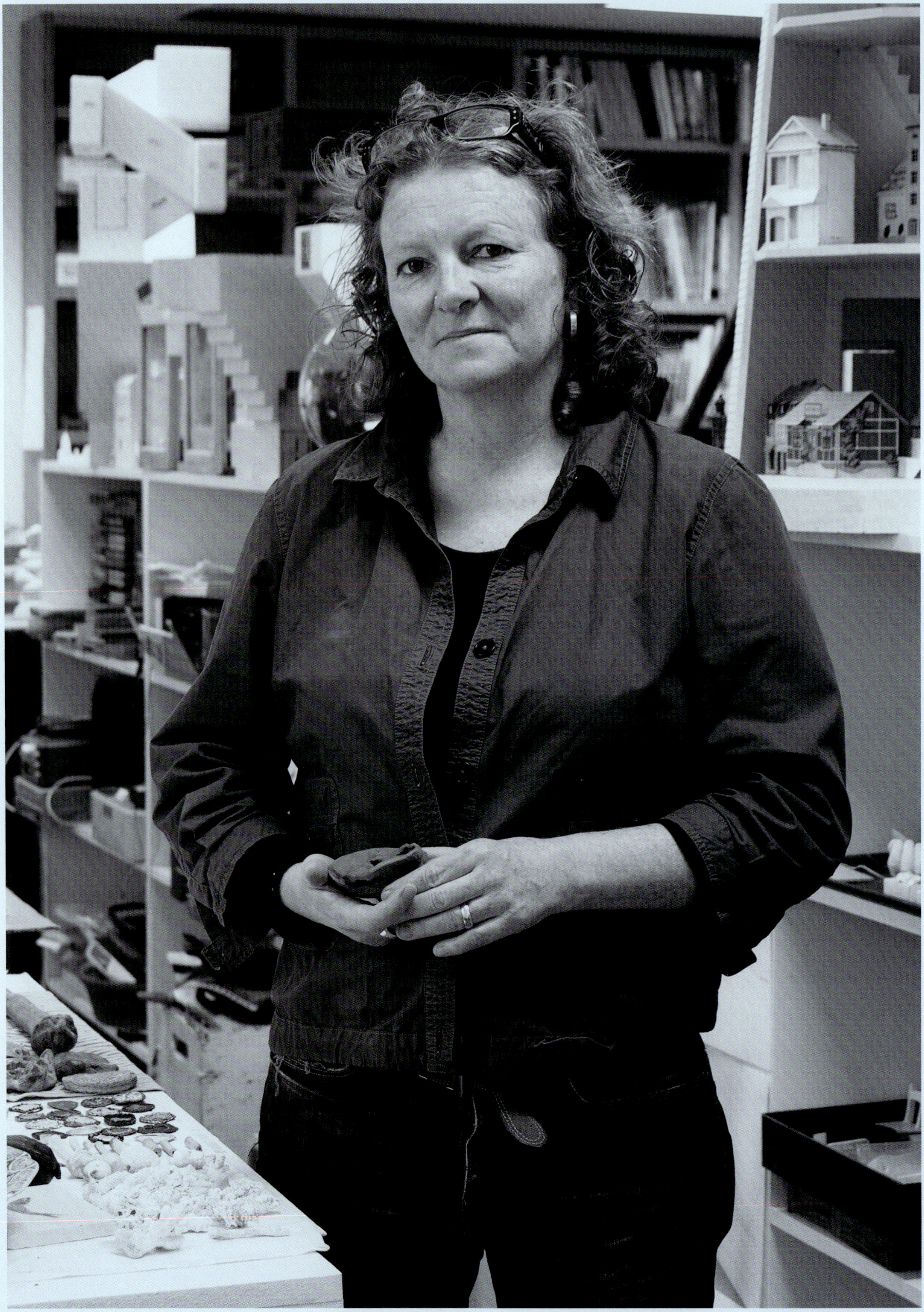

RACHEL WHITEREAD

Born 1963, London

Rachel Whiteread's practice involves casting the space within and around objects, using materials such as resin, plaster, concrete and rubber to generate negative impressions. Her sculptures resonate with the traces of human existence, history and memory. She created her first architecturally scaled work with *Ghost*, after which she made *House*, a cast of the inside of a terraced house in East London. Her commissions have come under much public scrutiny, none more so than *Holocaust Memorial* for the Judenplatz in Vienna, created to mark the genocide of Austrian Jews in World War II. These early, ground-breaking works led to projects across the world, including *Cabin* – sited on the top of Governors Island, overlooking New York Harbour – which purposefully juxtaposes a modest cabin with the grandiosity of Lower Manhattan. Whiteread's work includes casts of architectural features – stairs, doors, windows – and domestic objects such as water bottles, all of which act as a counterpoint to the large public commissions. They are infused with an inimitably dignified presence, offering a quieter, more intimate experience of form.

Ina Cole: You have memories of hiding in a wardrobe as a child, and one of your first pieces, *Closet* (1988), was a cast from the inside of a wardrobe. By making a void solid you are effectively shutting viewers out, as you're sealing off the space they would normally access. Is there also a psychological intention at play?

Rachel Whiteread: My first exhibition consisted of casts from a wardrobe, dressing table, hot-water bottle and a bed, in a gallery that doesn't exist anymore (Carlisle Gallery, London, 1988). These four elements sat in this gallery as though it were a bedsit. I'm not from a wealthy background, and it was simply a memory of my childhood: my grandparents and my parents. So some of the early sculptures were autobiographical, and very much to do with my childhood and my father dying. I took an introspective look at my life and that's where the pieces came from.

Over the years, the work has still come from there, but from all sorts of other places, too. I think *Untitled (Stairs)* (2001) is as psychologically loaded as *Closet*, or the bed, *Shallow Breath* (1988). I prefer using the word 'physiologically' because, although it's psychological, it's also to do with the body: how you use space, how space is connected and how you sit on a chair and put your legs under a table. This is something I use all the time and will continue to use, whether a sculpture is about absence or presence.

IC: Nineteenth-century sculptors referred to the stages of casting in bronze as life, death and resurrection: the object is destroyed through casting, only to live again in bronze. Your objects remain at the stage where they've shed life yet retain the potential for transformation. Do you always maintain control, or are there interruptions in the process that sometimes surprise you?

RW: Yes, definitely. If I'm in the studio and an accident happens, I'm happy to embrace it and make decisions based on that. However, if accidents happen in the foundry, the work has to be destroyed and remade. The stages of going from the plaster, to the mould, to a wax, to a metal, already involve enough changes. I have to be clear about the end result, so I can instruct people. It's really satisfying when I've made something in the studio, sent it off and it comes back exactly as I wanted.

If I have an idea I think will succeed, it's almost like an addiction and I have to make it happen. I felt like that when I was at Brighton Polytechnic, but it wasn't until reaching the Slade School of Fine Art that I thought the work was getting close to what I wanted. When making some of the early rubber sculptures, I wasn't sure how they were going to turn out. They were cast flat, and I literally wrestled around with them in the studio. Then they slumped against a wall and that was perfect; they found their own home.

Those things become part of your vocabulary, but, in order to work with a full deck of cards, I had to spend 15 years developing the language. It's a linear yet organic process, as I'm always thinking in a straight line, but these little accidents can happen along the way. The casting process has to be structured, because I can't create a 7-tonne sculpture and think, 'Well that hasn't worked', but the language will always change and develop.

Rachel Whiteread
Untitled (Fire Escape), 2002
Mixed media
736 × 547 × 600.5 cm
(24 ft 1¾ in × 17 ft 11⅜ in × 19 ft 8⅜ in)
Installation view:
Luhring Augustine,
New York, 2003

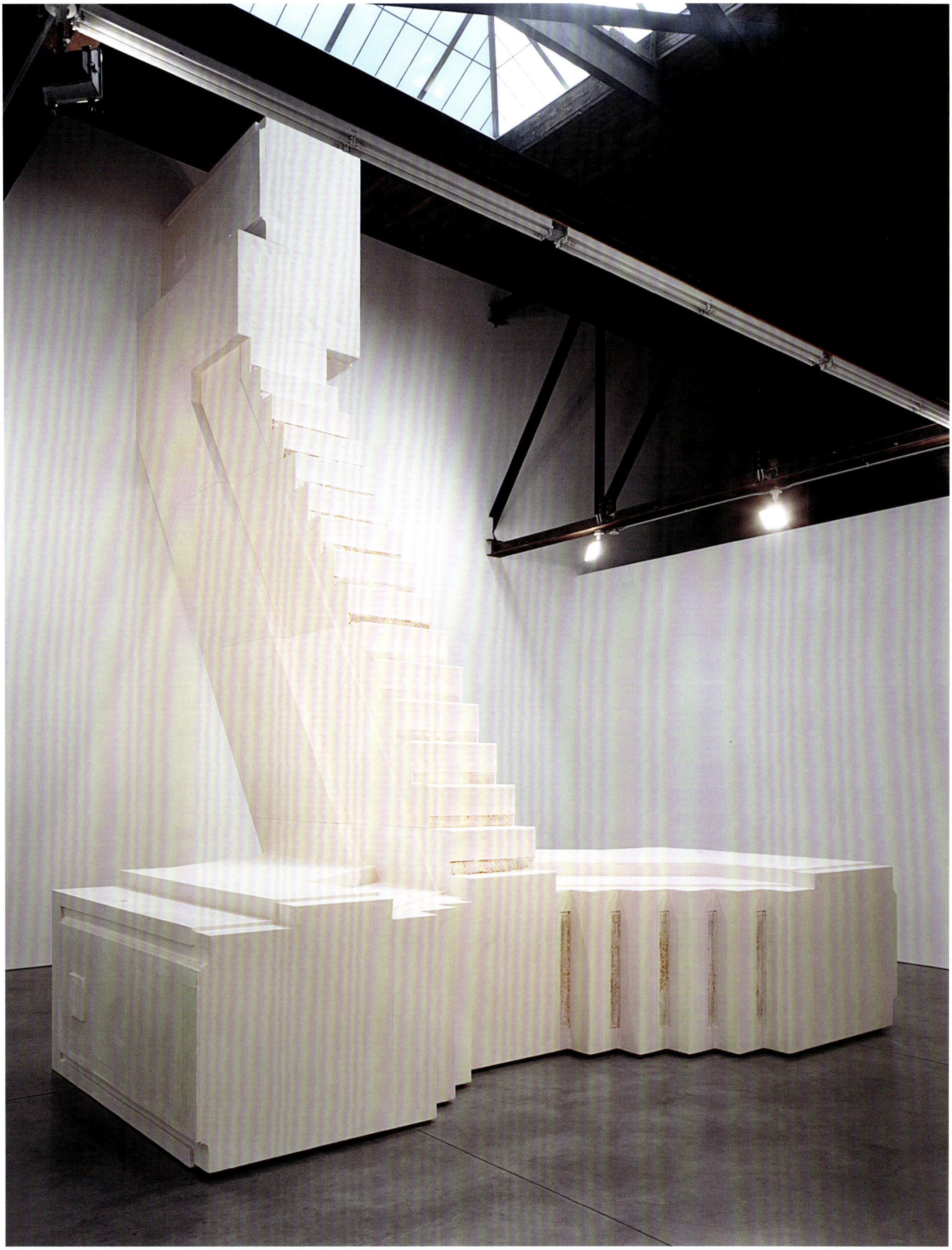

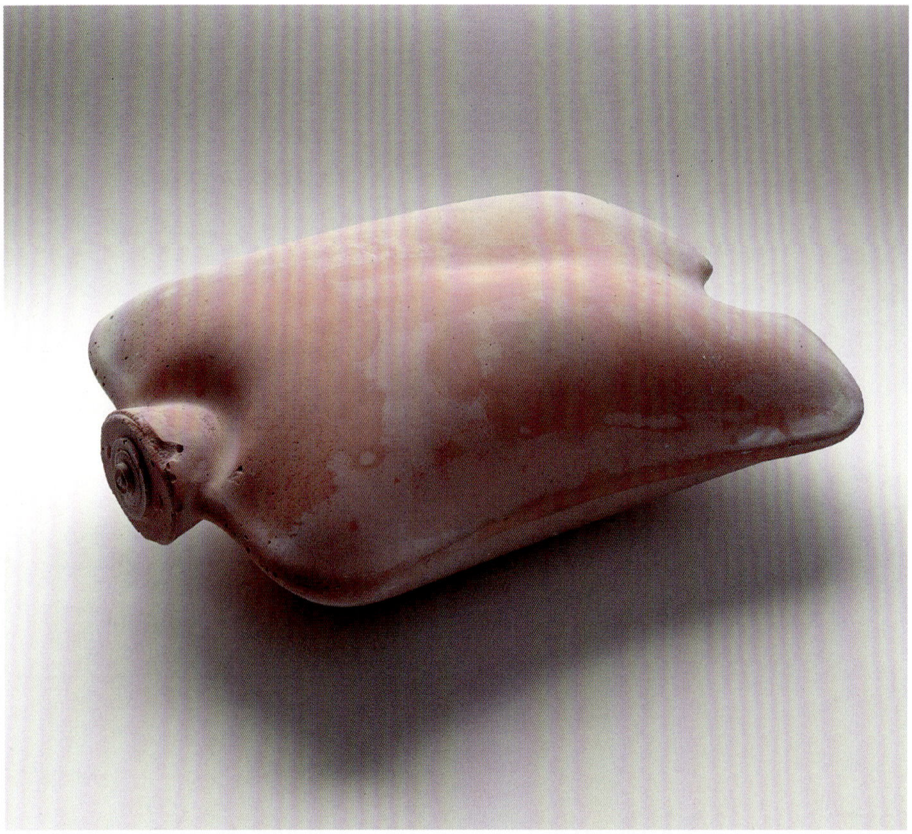

←
Rachel Whiteread
Untitled (Pink Torso), 1991

Pink dental plaster
9.5 × 17 × 23.5 cm
(3¾ × 6¾ × 9¼ in)

IC: Your sculptures have been compared to the work of Donald Judd, Bruce Nauman, Carl Andre and Gordon Matta-Clark. However, you pushed the boundaries in making the invisible visible, particularly in monumental projects such as *House* (1993) and *Holocaust Memorial* (2000). The demolition of *House* caused a public outcry. Were you saddened by its destruction, or did you feel ephemerality was important to its meaning?

RW: I didn't want to see *House* as a permanent piece, because it wasn't made with that in mind. I'd have liked it to stay up for a year, but it was only there for about four months. When *House* was demolished, the main reason I felt sad was because I never really had a chance to see it properly. Creating work in the street is very different from being in the studio. It was all just crazy; I was actually quite ill when I'd finished. I used to go to the site virtually in disguise, sit in the car around a corner, and each time *House* would be mobbed by people who screamed, shouted and painted it with graffiti.

It was an unfortunate set of circumstances. One particular council member wanted it demolished, as he thought the middle classes were lobbying for it, and it wasn't a middle-class neighbourhood. In order that *House* could stay up for an extra month or so, I ended up renting the ground it was on from the council. I also suggested a park with swings for children, but the council said no, as they didn't want any memory of the piece. However, people continue to tell me their memories of seeing it. I'm very proud to have made *House*, yet I am sad. I don't think it completely lost its dignity, but its dignity was rather hijacked.

IC: *Holocaust Memorial* in Vienna is an inverted concrete library, featuring rows of books with their closed pages facing outwards. This was another difficult and emotive commission, involving

→
Rachel Whiteread
Untitled (House), 1993

Concrete, wood, steel
Life-size
193 Grove Road, London E3
Destroyed on 11 January 1994

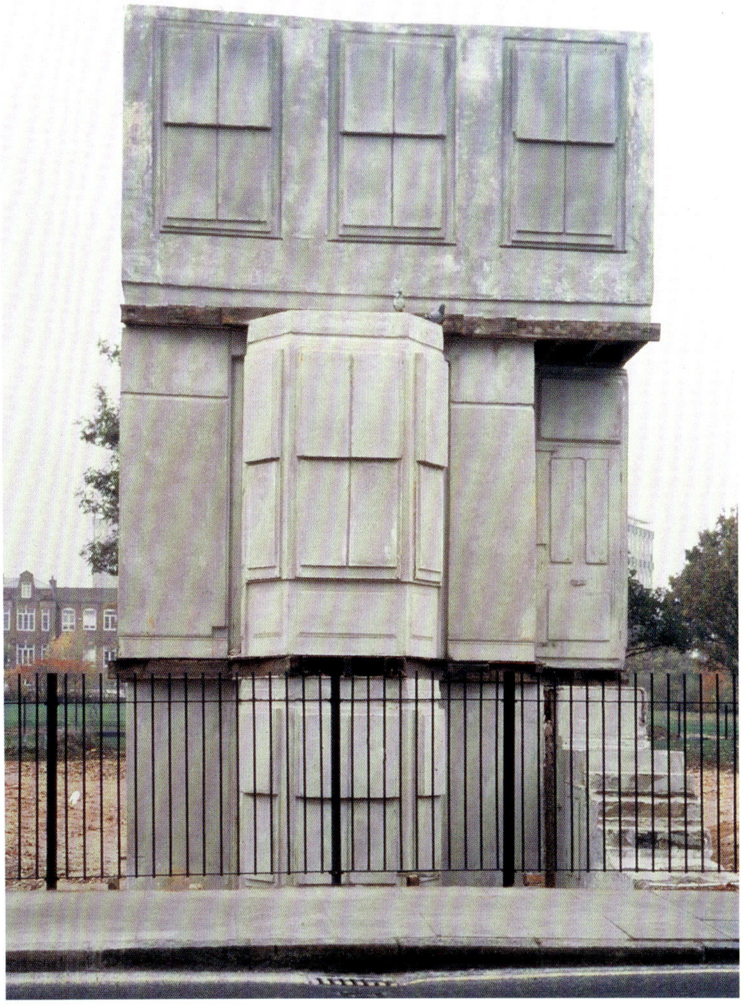

↓
Rachel Whiteread
Cabin, 2015

Concrete
Life-size
Installation view:
Governors Island,
New York, 2016

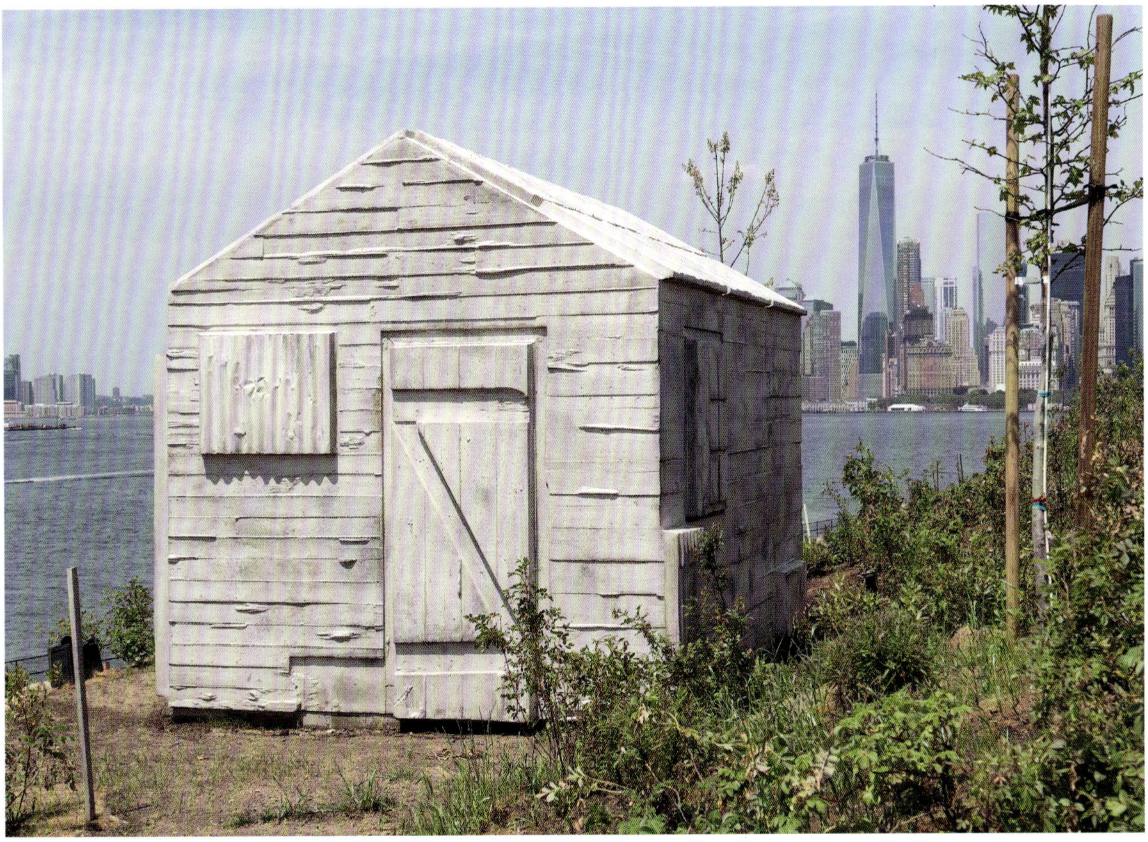

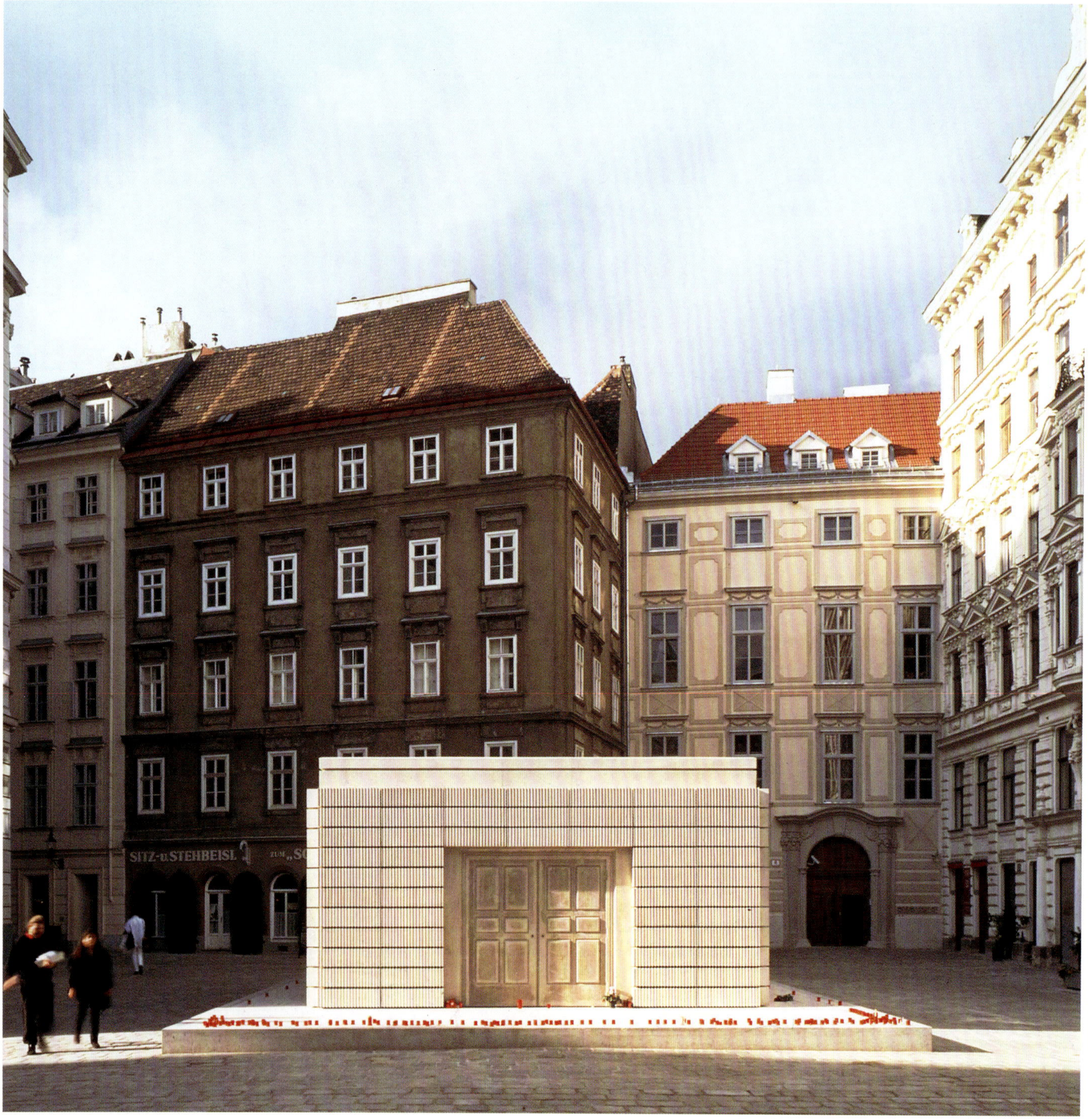

Rachel Whiteread
Holocaust Memorial,
1995–2000

Mixed media
3.8 × 7 × 10 m
(12 ft 5⅝ in × 22 ft 11⅝ in × 32 ft 9¾ in)
Installation view:
Judenplatz, Vienna, 2000

politicians, local residents and factions within the Jewish community, and there has been much speculation about the challenges you faced. Why did *Holocaust Memorial* become so contentious?

RW: At that time, Austria was a strange and complex place politically, and because of the political struggles in Vienna, ministers involved in the project were always changing. Some were desperate for *Holocaust Memorial* to happen, while others didn't care. It just went on and on, and it's hard to work with all of that. I got absolutely frustrated in the end when I was just being used as a political pawn, and I refused to go over there. Without the guidance and support of the architects, Jabornegg & Palffy, and Andrea Schlieker as liaison, I wouldn't have managed to complete the project. However, I'm happy to have made it, and I'm proud it's there. *Holocaust Memorial* hasn't been graffitied, extraordinarily, and I think it's well received in the city. I don't really go back there, though. There has to be a very good reason for me to return.

IC: How important is the historical casting of space to the development of your practice? I'm referring to feats such as Egyptian sarcophagi, the making of death masks in the fifteenth century, and the excavation of Pompeii, where entombed organic remains had left voids, which archaeologists could use as moulds to create plaster casts. Are these issues you consider?

RW: In the past, yes. Casting has become the language I make work in, but when searching for that language I definitely looked at sarcophagi. I didn't go to Pompeii, quite intentionally, as the image I had of it in my mind was probably stronger. Places can become so gargantuan in your mind, and I didn't want to be disappointed. I had a period when I looked at volcanoes and, for me, this was as interesting as going to look at a pyramid, in that they're elemental and unpredictable, rather than man-made. I also remember seeing a travelling show by Dr Gunther von Hagens called 'Body Worlds', which I thought was extraordinary at the time. When I was in Vienna, working on *Holocaust Memorial*,

Rachel Whiteread
Ghost, 1990

Plaster on steel frame
269 × 355.5 × 317.5 cm
(8 ft 9⅞ in × 11 ft 8 in × 10 ft 5 in)
Installation view:
National Gallery of Art,
Washington, 2004

the exhibition was there. The exhibits – plastinated human body parts – were dreadful, but there was something fascinating about them as well, with casts of blood vessels and a whole artery system in the body, which looked like fantastic sea plants. It was the casting of the body's interior that really interested me, rather than the fact that the exhibition was a macabre twenty-first-century circus.

IC: Your casting of staircases has resulted in a number of important works such as *Untitled (Stairs)* (2001), *Untitled (Domestic)* (2002) and *Untitled (Fire Escape)* (2002). Here, the use of inverted space taps into the realm of dreams and reverie, in that the stairs lead to nowhere. *Untitled (Stairs)* was taken from your former home and studio in East London. The stairs are poised at an incomprehensible angle, as you're looking at the space where they were, not the stairs themselves. How did your fascination with staircases come about?

RW: It really started a long time ago when I made *House*. I work in a linear way and, when making *Ghost* (1990), I thought it would be interesting to explore the possibility of casting an entire house. So, *House* came from *Ghost*. Then, when *House* was completed there was something missing. I was slightly irritated by the fact that I'd left the walls in, and that the staircase hadn't actually been taken out. It was as if the mould hadn't been completely taken apart. I tried to work through that and, about eight years later, finally resolved it. I'd previously tried to cast stairs, but never really had the right materials or the expertise. I also didn't have the staircases. Although certain demolished buildings had offered the possibility, it just didn't feel right.

When we purchased the building in East London, a former synagogue, it was in a dishevelled state, as it had also been used as a textile warehouse. We weren't sure what to do with it, but knew we wanted to try to live and work in the same place. There were three staircases in it, which was fantastic, and I just worked with those. I cast the first one and was so excited by it that I ended up casting all of them. It's very difficult to turn a space into an object in your mind, so I made models and played around with them, trying to decide which way up they should go, and how they might sit. When the actual object was cast and put in the studio it did something, psychologically and physiologically, that I hadn't felt for a long time with a sculpture. The simple act of making and then rotating an object to find the right way up really excited me. I enjoyed mapping the building, and also made casts of the floors and the two apartments, which felt like a way of getting to know the building and understanding it.

IC: You've always had an inherently experimental approach to making, and the 'Snow Show' in Finland (2004) was devised as an artistic collaboration between artists and architects. Although your sculpture was based on a familiar form, that of a stairwell space turned by 90 degrees, this project also provided an opportunity to utilize previously untested materials.

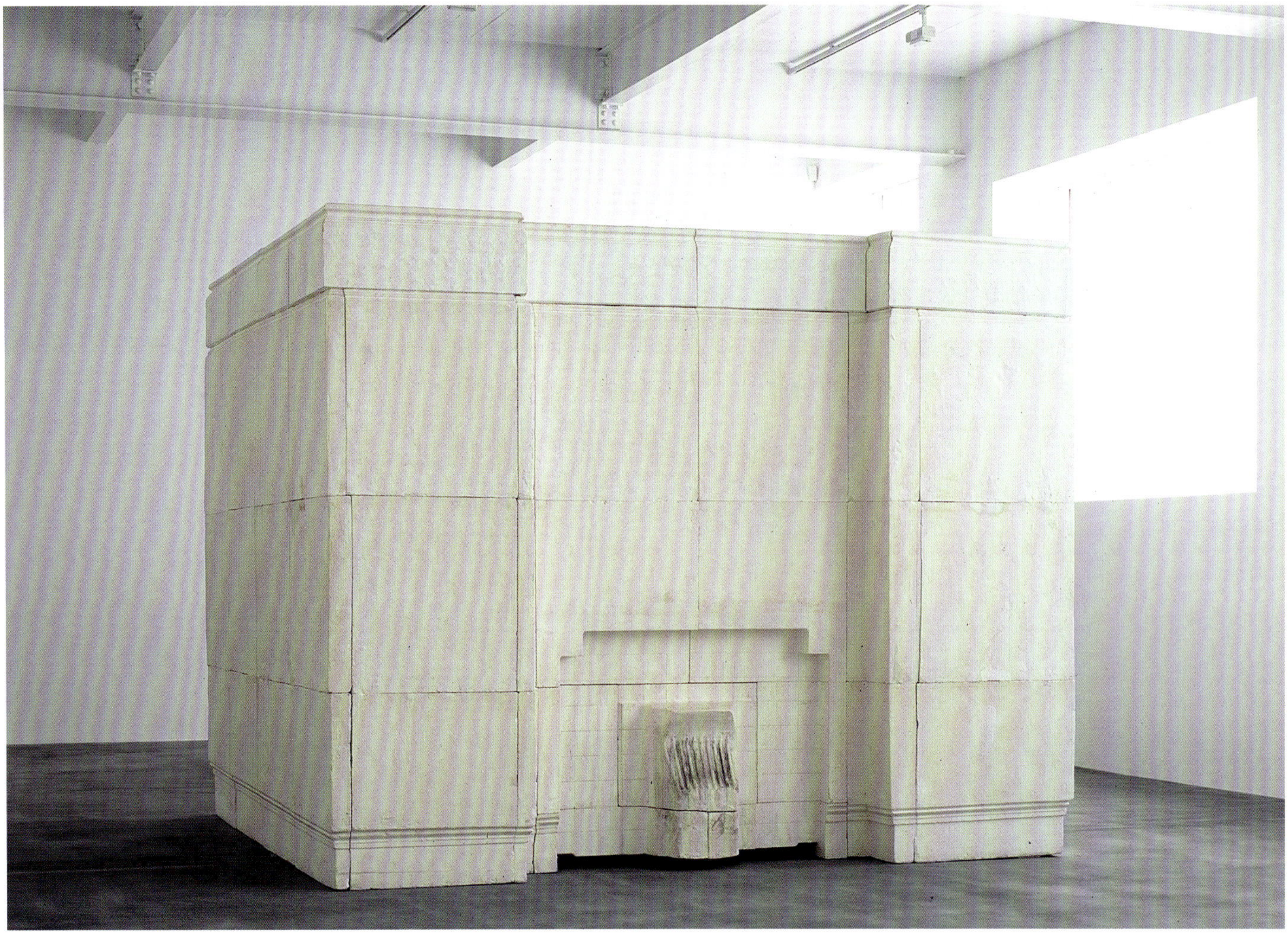

RW: I've done a lot of research in the past, and will continue to do so, because I'm curious about materials. I don't think of a piece and then try to find the material. It's equally balanced. Creating new work for 'The Snow Show' was experimental, as it was the first time I'd used snow and ice. Artists and architects were paired to make installations dotted over two areas, Kemi and Rovaniemi. With the architect, Juhani Pallasmaa, I worked on ideas for an inside-out, upside-down architectonic staircase structure, using models and drawings. Because of the weather, the show was only up for a couple of months before it became too dangerous for people to visit. It was an interesting move forward, in that it was a collaboration, which made me think about new ways of making.

IC: The spaces you cast often feel quite private, offering a moment of reflection within the cacophony of urban life. This is particularly evident in the smaller sculptures of architectural features and domestic objects, but even a major work such as *Monument* (2001), made for the Fourth Plinth in Trafalgar Square, London – which echoed the vacant plinth upon which it sat – seemed to provide an opportunity for contemplation.

RW: I'm essentially quite a private person and need time to stare at a white wall. I don't mean literally, but meditatively. As you become more successful, it's much harder to find that time and to plan ahead. I can remember living in the depths of the East End and cycling to the studio. The freshness of that period was easier, but, as you get older, you change, and your life changes. However, I get as much from the hubbub as from anywhere else. I also lived in Berlin, a much quieter city, and made more work in 18 months than ever before, as I was on my own and really able to concentrate. I definitely need time to go to the country and take a deep breath, but I also need the hubbub of city life around me. I use it as my sketch book.

When making *Monument*, I wanted to create a pause in the city, and place something that felt very quiet in Trafalgar Square. I've done a lot of travelling, during which time I take photographs, walk around markets and back streets, and drive out into deserts. That's research, as I know it's going to feed back into my work. I just go and look at these places, absorb, and think about sculpture. I then like returning to that intimate process in the studio, which gets taken over when making the large pieces, as I end up producing, rather than physically creating, them. So, I simply need time to take stock of things and reflect on how other projects will happen. By taking a pause, I can start to play again.

IC: Do you feel you're standing on the outside looking in, in order to observe aspects of life that can often otherwise go unnoticed?

RW: Yes, but I think a lot of artists do; it's part of being an artist. You seek things that are hidden and draw them out of their environment. I do that, but also scratch around with the residue of cities. When I was in East London, the building was designed so that we lived on the roof and overlooked the ever-changing East End environment. The area was made up of a varied community, with lots of artists and smaller independent galleries, which is what I particularly liked about it. We were on the edge of Brick Lane market, and sometimes couldn't even get out of the door for people selling their wares. However, London has changed enormously, with all the construction that's gone on. Many of the second-hand shops and other places where I got things all moved further out. Priorities change, and you just have to work with the day-to-day.

IC: You've called what you do 'mapping, a process of making traces solid'. You are, in a sense, immortalizing the spaces that you, and all those before you, have entered. Do you actually consider your casts as tombs, containing the ghosts of previous inhabitants, as well as traces of yourself?

RW: Maybe; that's a very rounded way of looking at it. With *Room 101* (2003), for example, all six sides are cast – the floor, ceiling and the walls. It was the first time I'd made a room that wasn't solid. There's an interior to it, yet it's completely sealed, and that does feel tomblike. *Ghost*, for instance, didn't feel tomblike because it doesn't have a ceiling. I never try to make something look like a tomb; I just make it as I want the object to be, and then it will have these other associations and connotations.

Room 101 came about when the BBC asked me to cast a room at Broadcasting House in London, which George Orwell had apparently used as his office – Room 101 from his novel *Nineteen Eighty-Four* (1949). It was an opportunity I couldn't say no to, as the room was about to be demolished and this was a way of making an imprint of it. I made an enormous sculpture, which was then shown at the Victoria and Albert Museum, in the Cast Courts (2003–4). When I first saw Room 101 it was a plant room full of all the gubbins that kept this big building breathing – all metalwork and pipes. Everything was ripped out, and I was left with a blown-up, pock-marked room. This was at the beginning of the Iraq War, so it seemed like a response to that. It actually felt like a room that had been bombarded with shrapnel. When you look around London and inspect the outsides of buildings, they often still have pockmarks all over them from both World Wars. *Room 101* looks very much like that, which felt quite Orwellian.

Interviewed in 2003 and 2020

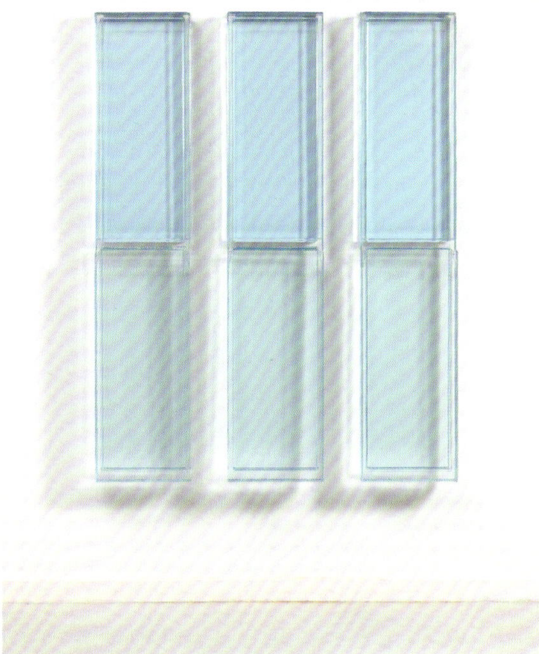

←
Rachel Whiteread
Look, Look, Look, 2012

Resin (three panels)
189.5 × 39.5 × 15 cm
(74⅝ × 15½ × 5⅞ in)

↓
Rachel Whiteread
Monument, 2001

Resin and granite
900 × 510 × 240 cm
(29 ft 6⅜ in × 16 ft 8¾ in × 7 ft 10½ in)
Installation view:
Fourth Plinth, Trafalgar Square, London, 2001

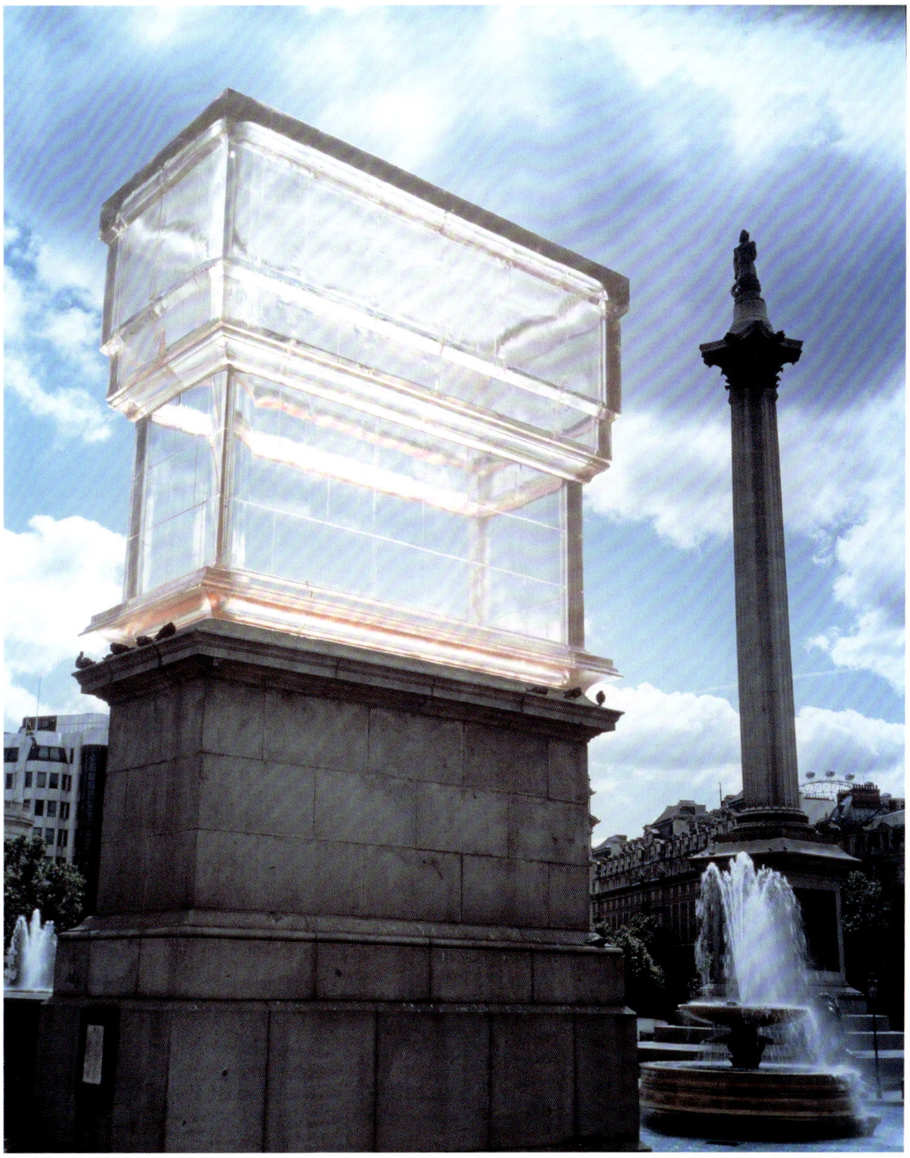

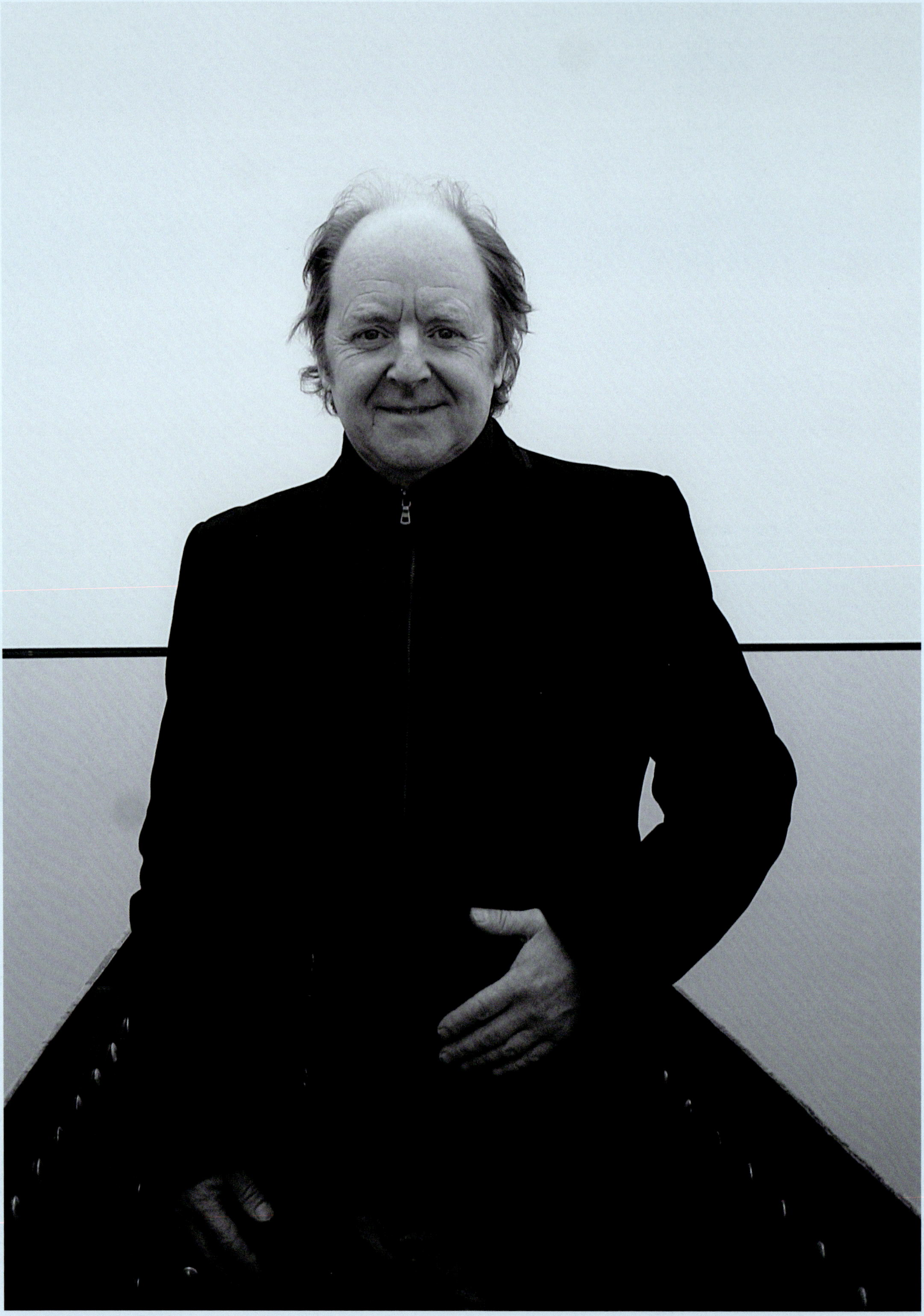

RICHARD WILSON

Born 1953, London

Richard Wilson's practice challenges the way our environment is perceived and navigated. He often employs industrial materials through which the locations inhabited by his installations become dramatically altered. In a seminal work, *20:50*, sump oil was utilized to create a puzzling, highly reflective space that questioned the relationship between viewer and artwork. Wilson's interventions in architecture rely on an understanding of engineering and construction practices, as seen in *Turning the Place Over*, in which an ovoid section of a building's façade oscillated on a pivot, and *Hang on a Minute Lads, I've got a Great Idea*, a hydraulically functioning coach balanced on the roof of De La Warr Pavilion in Bexhill-on-Sea, East Sussex. In his work, objects are often manipulated to the point at which form and function cease to relate. This can be seen in smaller pieces, like *Blocka Flats* which was made from reconfigured furniture, and in large projects such as *Huangpu Hold*, constructed from parts of a discarded ship and given new life on Huangpu riverfront, in Shanghai.

Ina Cole: Many of your projects challenge architectural space in fundamental ways. By doing so, any preconceived notions a viewer may have of their environment becomes subverted. When did you realize that creating work driven by the location would direct your approach?

Richard Wilson: I started conventionally but wasn't comfortable making objects, because I felt I didn't have the vocabulary to conjure form into anthropomorphic shape. I was at Hornsey College of Art from 1971 to 1974, instructed by Hubert Dalwood, Ken Draper, Martin Naylor and Paul Neagu, and the training had been formal. But I was always more interested in making work that was dictated by the space it was located in. It was a slow process, but my breakthrough came with an exhibition at Chisenhale Works in London (1984), when I made a wooden mould, filled it with sand, then angled it up towards the ceiling. Over several days, I poured melted aluminium into the shallow in the sand, building a solid ring of all these poured moments. When chilled, the sand was excavated, and the wooden structure removed, leaving the ring fastened to the site, as it was cast around one of the building's columns. This begged the question, 'To remove the work do I cut the ring, or take the column down?' They were integral to each other – the ring inspired by the column and the column acting as fulcrum to the ring.

When the exhibition 'The Sculpture Show' was held at the Hayward Gallery in 1983, this process of casting on site was denied for health-and-safety reasons, but in 1985 I had a solo exhibition at Matt's Gallery, then on Martello Street in East London, where I made *Sheer Fluke*. Again, I created a mould, melted aluminium to its liquid temperature, poured it, let it freeze in the mould, and, once excavated, I had a solid.

IC: At that time, Matt's Gallery was a pre-eminent space for breakthrough work. It was where you first made *20:50*, in 1987, which was then displayed at Saatchi Gallery on a permanent basis until 2015. It's still cited as your seminal installation, shown across the world and reconfigured for each new location.

Richard Wilson
20:50, 1991

Used sump oil, steel, wood, gate valve
Dimensions variable
Installation view: Saatchi Gallery, London, 1991

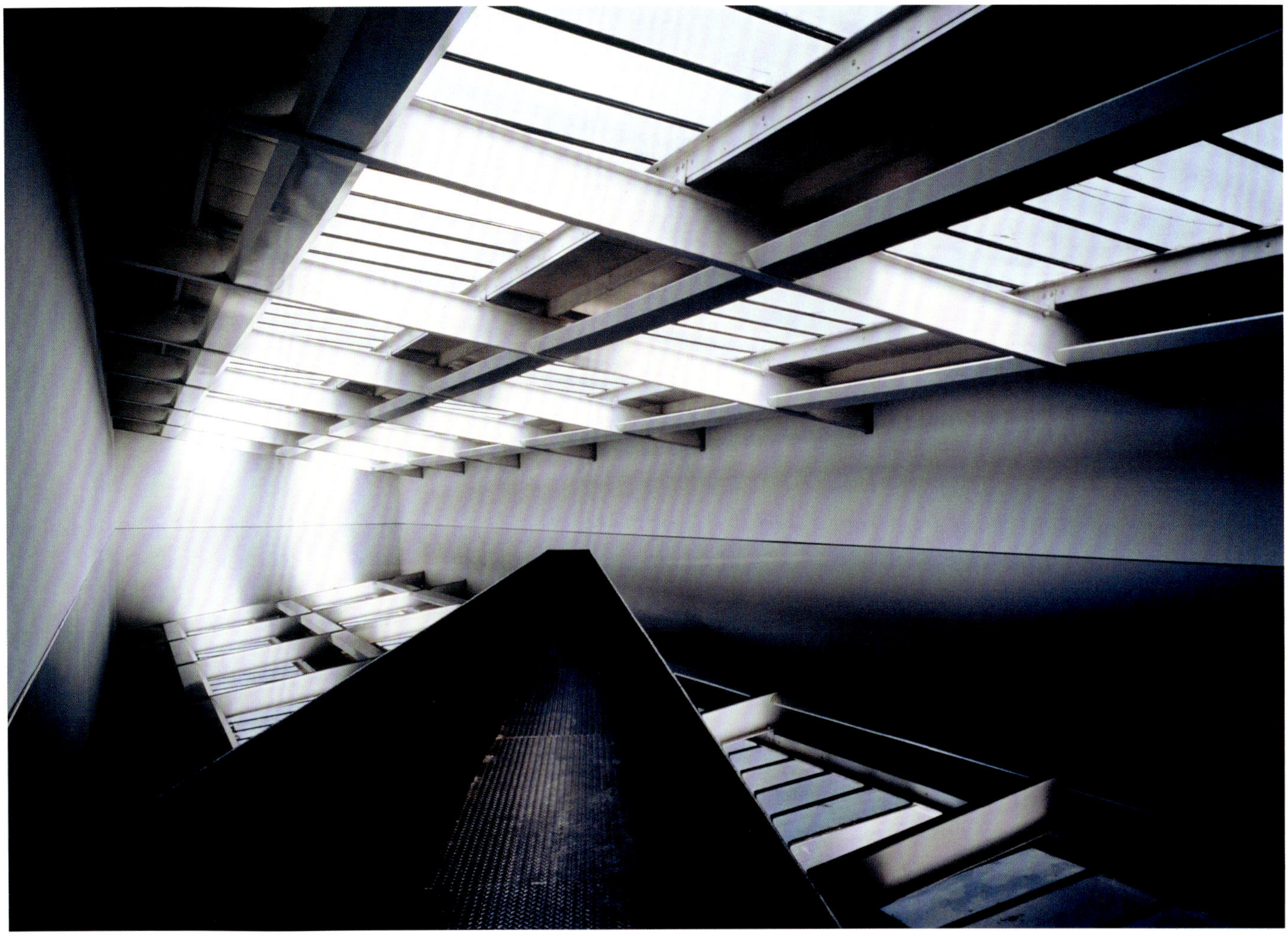

RW: *20:50* was a forward reading from *Sheer Fluke*, in which I could further the processes I'd previously employed. The words 'site-specific' and 'installation' were emerging, but there weren't many artists working like that. It was still very object-based, which I wanted to challenge. What was a site-dependable but not site-specific anti-object? With *20:50*, I transformed the gallery, to make a Tardis space, as in the BBC series *Dr Who* – a spatial conundrum. In my old Chisenhale studio I'd been annealing metal in a tank of oil, which produced an extraordinary reflection. After pouring some oil into a maquette, I decided to flood Matt's Gallery with oil, to create an illusory and psychological experience during which the viewer becomes the object. I made a tank and acquired the oil locally. It was really done on a pound, and we had to break a few rules. By filling the tank and building a walkway to enter the centre of the gallery, an extraordinary other world was experienced, like *Alice Through the Looking Glass*, or Narcissus. On looking down and across the oil, my refracted vision perceived things that weren't normally visible. It was a knockout.

When we opened, the gossip went national in a day, with a queue around the block at Martello Street. One evening, the collector Charles Saatchi walked in, after which he decided to acquire it. Although I own the copyright, he bought the intellectual rights, and this means I can remake but not sell it. It's not site-specific because it isn't fixed to the building, so can go anywhere in the world. The ingredients remain the same, only the focus changes.

IC: Many of your installations involve making changes to a building's structure. Following the success of *20:50*, how difficult was it to persuade other galleries to agree to a project?

RW: Certain works require tampering with the architectural structure in which they're located,

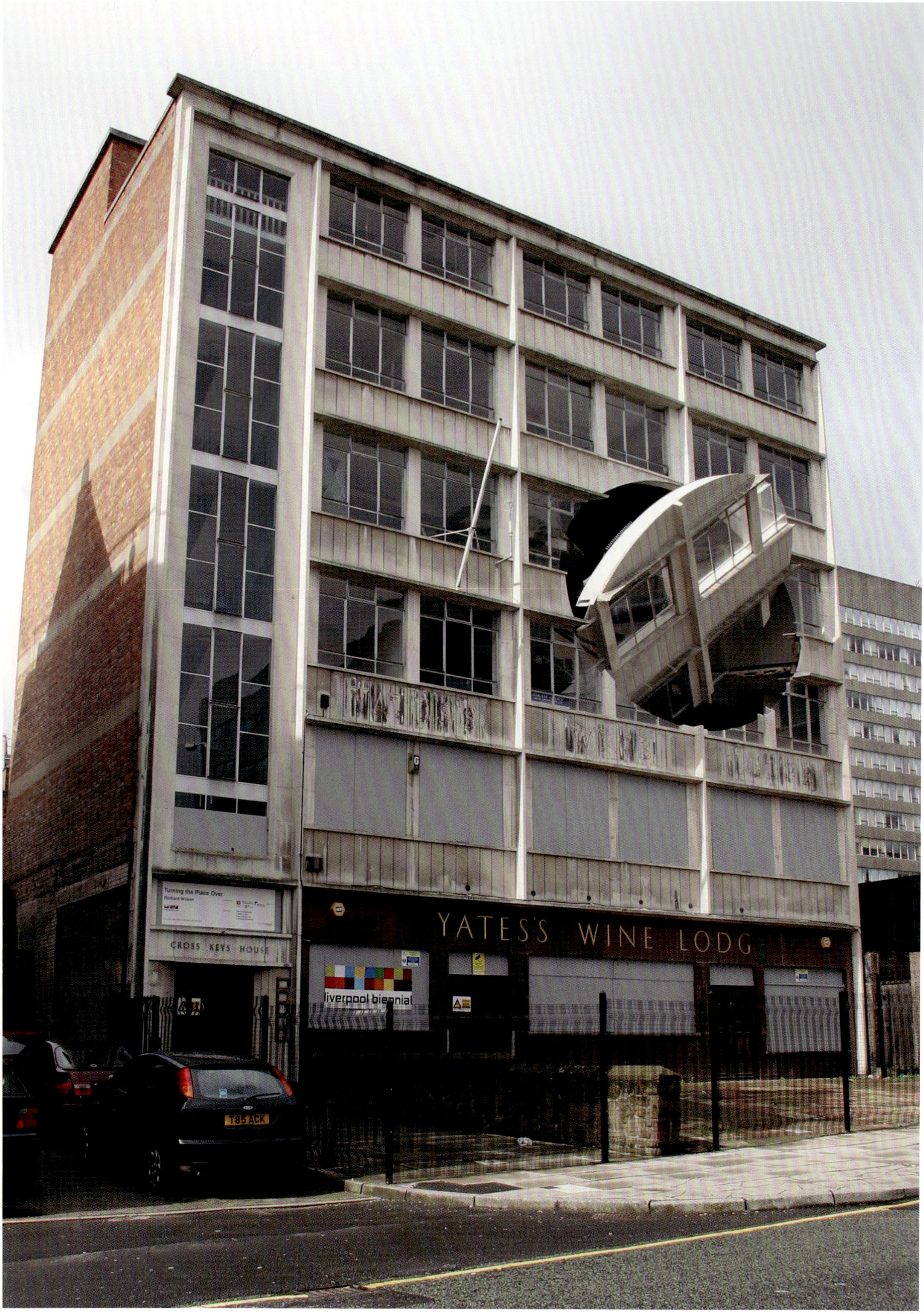
Turning the Place Over
Richard Wilson
CROSS KEYS HOUSE
YATES'S WINE LODG
liverpool biennial
T85 ACK

but with *Turning the Place Over* (2008) I could do what I wanted because the building was derelict and due for demolition. Likewise, *Jamming Gears* (1996), at the Serpentine Gallery in London, happened before it was closed for renovation. I wouldn't go into a museum and say, 'I want your tongue and groove maple floor lifted.' I can see that being a problem, and I'm sensitive about choreographing spaces. Even though some curators think I violate architecture, nothing could be further from the truth. Think of Gordon Matta-Clark. His choreographed pieces were incredibly sensitive, and most took place in disused buildings due for demolition. With a work like *Turning the Place Over*, people from all over the world come to look at the forlorn, lost and forgotten, because the artist's hand can transform an eye-sore in the city to become something splendid.

IC: In *Turning the Place Over* an 8-metre (26-foot) ovoid section of the building's façade oscillated on a pivot. It was installed during Liverpool's year as European Capital of Culture in 2008, but it had taken almost a decade before the right opportunity presented itself, which is a lengthy incubation period.

Richard Wilson
Turning the Place Over, 2008

Steel, electrics
8 m (26 ft 3 in) diameter
Installation view:
Cross Keys Building, Liverpool, 2008–12

RW: It started with *Over Easy* (1998) for Stockton-on-Tees – an 8 metre/26 foot-diameter bearing placed into the façade of the Arts Centre. The building surrounded the bearing's circumference but was inside it as well. As the ovoid oscillated backwards and forwards at 300 degrees, the windows rotated down and round, and the brickwork rotated up. It turned slowly, like the minute hand on a clock. Then, one evening, I'd left the studio having glued a spindle vertically onto a circular disc of balsa wood. The glue hadn't quite stuck and the spindle slid from vertical, stopping at 50 degrees. Next morning, when I picked it up and turned it, I had *Turning the Place Over* in my fingers, and thought, 'That's such a genius idea'.

However, it took very special circumstances to be realized; a derelict building, lots of money, and mechanical and structural engineers. The alignment of those conditions didn't happen until 2006, when I had a meeting with Lewis Biggs, artistic director of Liverpool Biennial. He immediately invited me to Liverpool and took me to six buildings. We chose Cross Quays House, which was ideal, as it's north of the city centre, near the station and *en route* to Tate Liverpool. Lewis wanted to put the word Liverpool on everyone's lips, and *Turning the Place Over* just blasted people away. It was so successful we didn't turn it off until 2012.

IC: Working in the public domain does mean these projects are subject to the whims of others. It also suggests that they're temporary and can be switched off, or dismantled, at any point. Is this problematic?

RW: I work on the premise that all that surrounds us, including architecture, is a fast- or slow-moving event. Everything is in a state of flux and, therefore, I automatically have to take on a sense of impermanence. *Turning the Place Over* is kinetic – designed to run for a period of time. I was on a fabrication not an engineering budget, and there's a difference. Everything is still there, but if it was switched back on it would need a maintenance schedule. How long is permanent? 'Permanence' is really just an expression for a period of time. Impermanence is the only permanence.

Today's emphasis is on object making and permanence, because of a buoyant market. Property prices rise and fall; money in the bank accumulates little interest, but artworks can make millions. So, the art world looks to buy the object, which means you have to be in that secondary market to have value. I've probably missed the boat; I don't have a secondary market. Had I gone down that route would I be any better or worse off? I just happened to be in a situation when the secondary market didn't exist, and I made pieces that, for whatever reason, didn't last. I can always make another *Turning the Place Over, 20:50* or *Slipstream* (2014). I'm flexible, having had a career that always looked at the demands of the location, budget, bureaucracy and the technical agility of what's possible. It's the sleight of hand and structural daring that gets people to say 'Wow!', and everything is backed by engineers who guarantee nothing will fall.

Richard Wilson
Slipstream, 2014

Steel, plywood, aluminium, rivets
74 × 8 × 8 m
(242 ft 9⅜ in × 26 ft 3 in × 26 ft 3 in)
Installation view:
Heathrow Airport,
London, 2014

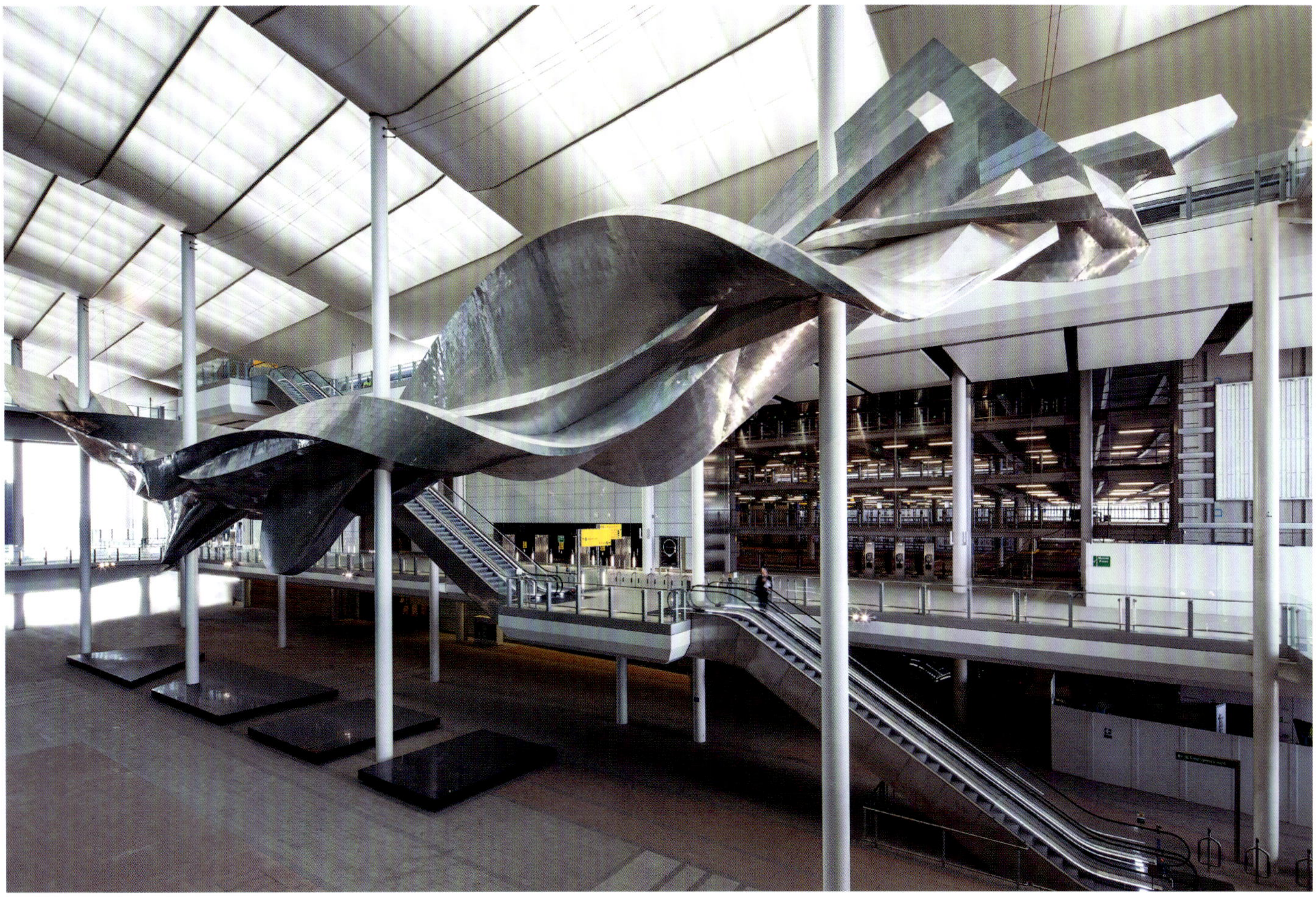

IC: *Slipstream* was a Heathrow Airport commission involving an extensive multi-disciplinary team. It's over 70 metres (230 feet) long, around 77 tonnes (85 tons) in weight and held together by approximately 47,000 rivets. How did this project develop?

RW: I first went to see Paul Bonhomme, the champion pilot, and photographed his aeroplane. Then I had a model made by the same builders in Utah – a faceted model that can be put into a computer and thrown virtually. It tumbles, then it's up and away, and this caught the clients' imagination. In a fictitious world, I'd fill Tate's Turbine Hall with clay, throw an aeroplane to roll through the clay, then tip the hall up vertically and fill it with plaster. When set, I'd remove the hall and the clay. That's the shape I wanted.

Originally, it was going to be twice as long, but the budget disintegrated when we had to make the work bomb-proof. We had to design laterally loaded bearings so, if a bomb ever went off in the terminal, the sculpture would take the blast and sway sideways. Each aluminium panel of *Slipstream* is a bespoke shape, as is the cladding. The sections travelled down from Hull: 22 journeys, with a police escort, as there was only a 2–4 a.m. window to cross the airport runway. *Slipstream* unfurls in front of your eyes as you move along the walkway, like a drill-bit twisting on a horizontal axis. It's an unusual movement for a form in space.

IC: *Butterfly* (2003), an earlier project at Wapping Hydraulic Power Station in London, also utilized an aeroplane. How did you use film to capture time and process in this work?

RW: Sculpture is good at describing volume and material, but not time, and I wanted time, along with volume and mass, to tell a story about process. Film deals with time very well. One day, I pulled a fiver from my pocket, which had been in the washing machine. While unfurling it I thought, 'I've got an idea. I'm going to crush something and pull it out again.' It's the purest of creative acts: flat, to ball, to flat; object to wreck, back to part-object. I then built and crushed several aeroplane models and, once I'd had enough of the mental gymnastics, I acquired a surplus Cessna aircraft. I cleaned the paintwork off, so it glistened, then it was crushed, brought into the space as a ball and hung for the private view.

With students from the University of East London, where I was research professor, I bored holes into it and inserted hydraulic equipment to pump it back out. During this unfurling process a camera clicked every five minutes, day and night. I'm fastidious about process – action to product – as it feeds other ideas. The camera fed to a computer and, every night, I downloaded hundreds of images. In the process of pulling out the volume, I realized I could compress time and turn it into a movie. At the end, I cut all the coloured straps and the plane crashed to the ground, all broken again. We then built a screen on one of the wings to fire projections of the unfurling plane. It was called *Butterfly* because of its metamorphosis from pupa to flying object. We all wore orange hard hats and high-visibility vests, so it became a palette of colour, movement and sound.

IC: *Set North for Japan* (2000) is a full-scale reconstruction of your London house, stripped to its skeletal core. Why is it located in Nakasato, Japan?

RW: *Set North for Japan* was an invitation from my dear friend the art director Fram Kitagawa. It was a project on the west coast of Japan, the theme being that I had to have a relationship to the region in some way. I thought, 'This is difficult; it's a rural setting and I don't work outdoors.' However, there was a site I liked at the back of Nakasato Junior High School: a big, flat site with a lovely temple gateway and picturesque mountain. As I flew from their late night-time into morning, the sun was behind me, and I caught the curvature of the earth. Suddenly, a light-bulb moment occurred in my head. When that happens, I totally mistrust it, which meant I had to take the idea on a journey. I teased and tested it for six months, but kept thinking, 'It's beautiful, so simple, let's do it'.

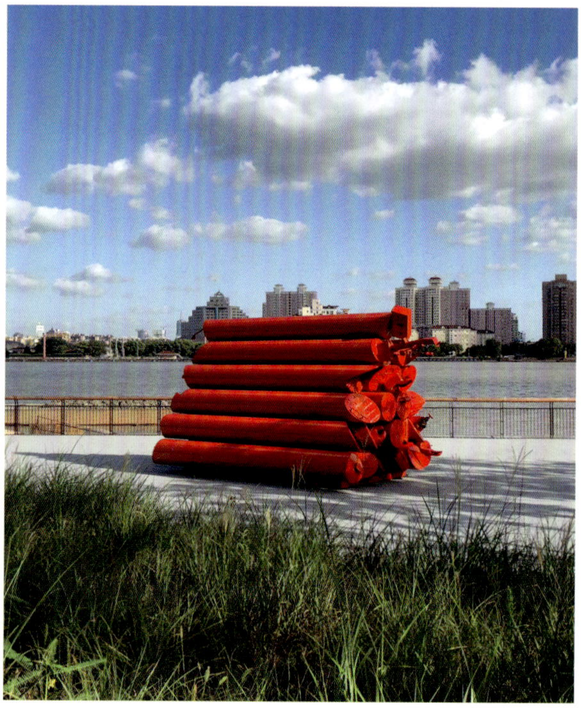

Richard Wilson
Huangpu Hold, 2019
Cut ship's shell plate, steel pipes, industrial paint
500 × 307.8 × 329.8 cm
(16 ft 4⅞ in × 10 ft 1⅛ in × 10 ft 9⅞ in)
Installation view:
Huangpu Riverfront as part of the Shanghai Urban Space Art Season (SUSAS) 2019

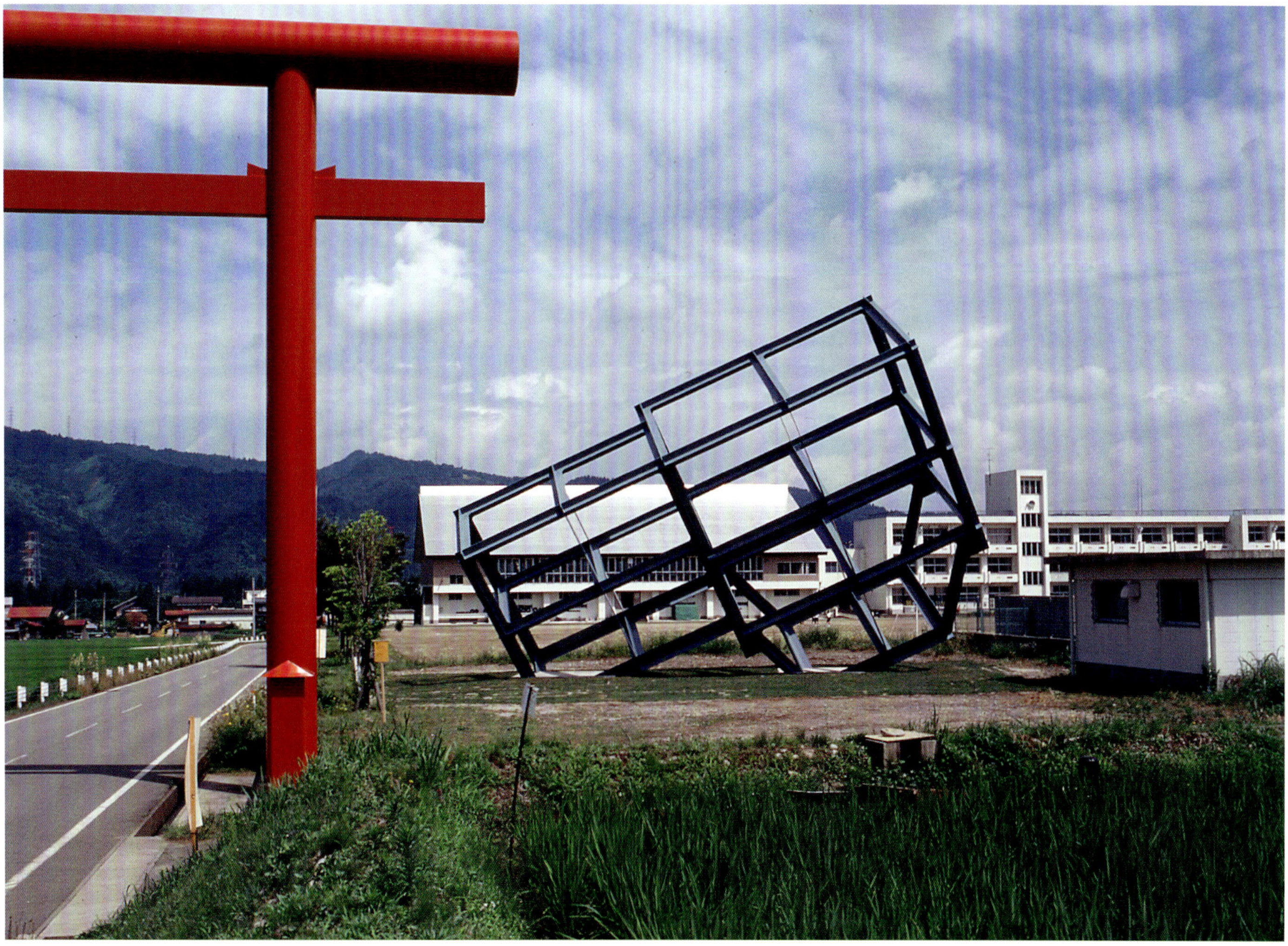

Richard Wilson
Set North for Japan (74°33' 2"), 2000
Painted steel, concrete base
14 × 8.8 × 4.6 m
(45 ft 11 ⅛ in × 28 ft 10½ in × 15 ft 1⅛ in)
Installation view:
Nakasato Junior High School,
Japan, 2000

The idea was to put my house in Nakasato, but at the exact angle it stands in Rotherhithe, London SE16. My house was then measured off the North Star and the angles of culmination sent to engineers in Japan. Five angles were sent – four to make sure we got it, and a fifth just to confirm – and they calculated those off the North Star in their region. The house ended up slightly crooked, upside down, as if it had been pushed straight through to Nakasato Junior High School playground. And that was my relationship to the region. There are now two houses at exactly the same angle on the planet. It's like a linear drawing of my house standing upside down in Japan, because it's standing at the same angles it does in Rotherhithe.

IC: *Hang on a Minute Lads, I've got a Great Idea* (2012) was a full-size replica coach, perched on the edge of the roof of De La Warr Pavilion in East Sussex and inspired by the last scene in the 1969 film *The Italian Job*. You've often spoken about edges, but why was this so important here?

RW: *Hang on a Minute Lads* was exhibited during our 2012 Olympics, as the second rooftop commission for the Pavilion. Antony Gormley had the first, but I wanted to use the edges rather than the terrace, as he had done, because the curvatures and straight lines are very beautiful. A rocking coach on the roof became about success and failure, which paralleled our Olympians as they were going for gold medals. The movie, *The Italian Job*, was also about going for gold, as was I in making a work on an iconic building referencing an iconic movie. The building became the plinth for a replica coach that rekindled British nostalgia – a kind of end-of-the-pier ride. The coach was designed on a shoestring, using plywood and fibreglass, and weighed approximately the same as a real coach. It functioned hydraulically, rocking backwards and forwards, but I couldn't put any weight on the roof, so it sat on two steel bridging beams with all the hydraulics anchored to them. Everything was cantilevered off two vertical brick walls to avoid touching the roof in any way, like bridge building. *Hang on a Minute Lads* was later shown on the seventh floor of the Peninsula Hotel in Hong Kong (2015), and at Artissima in Turin (2019).

Richard Wilson
Hang on a Minute Lads, I've got a Great Idea, 2012
Steel, aluminium, plastic, hydraulics, electrical timer
11 × 2.5 × 2.5 m
(36 ft 1⅛ in × 8 ft 2⅜ in × 8 ft 2⅜ in)
Installation view:
De La Warr Pavilion, Bexhill-on-Sea, East Sussex, 2012

IC: Much of your practice alludes to Britain's heritage. *Hang on a Minute Lads* was a flag-waving work for the Olympics; *Slice of Reality* (2000), a sliced section of an ocean-going sand dredger on the River Thames; and *Meter's Running* (2006), an iconic London taxi.

RW: Context and history are vital. A project needs validation to happen. *Hang on a Minute Lads* was about the red, white and blue coach colours as a flag, so it was very British in that respect. The actual flag was taken down from De La Warr's flagpole, and the coach became our Union Jack instead. *Slice of Reality* tampers with maritime architecture by slicing the dredger and

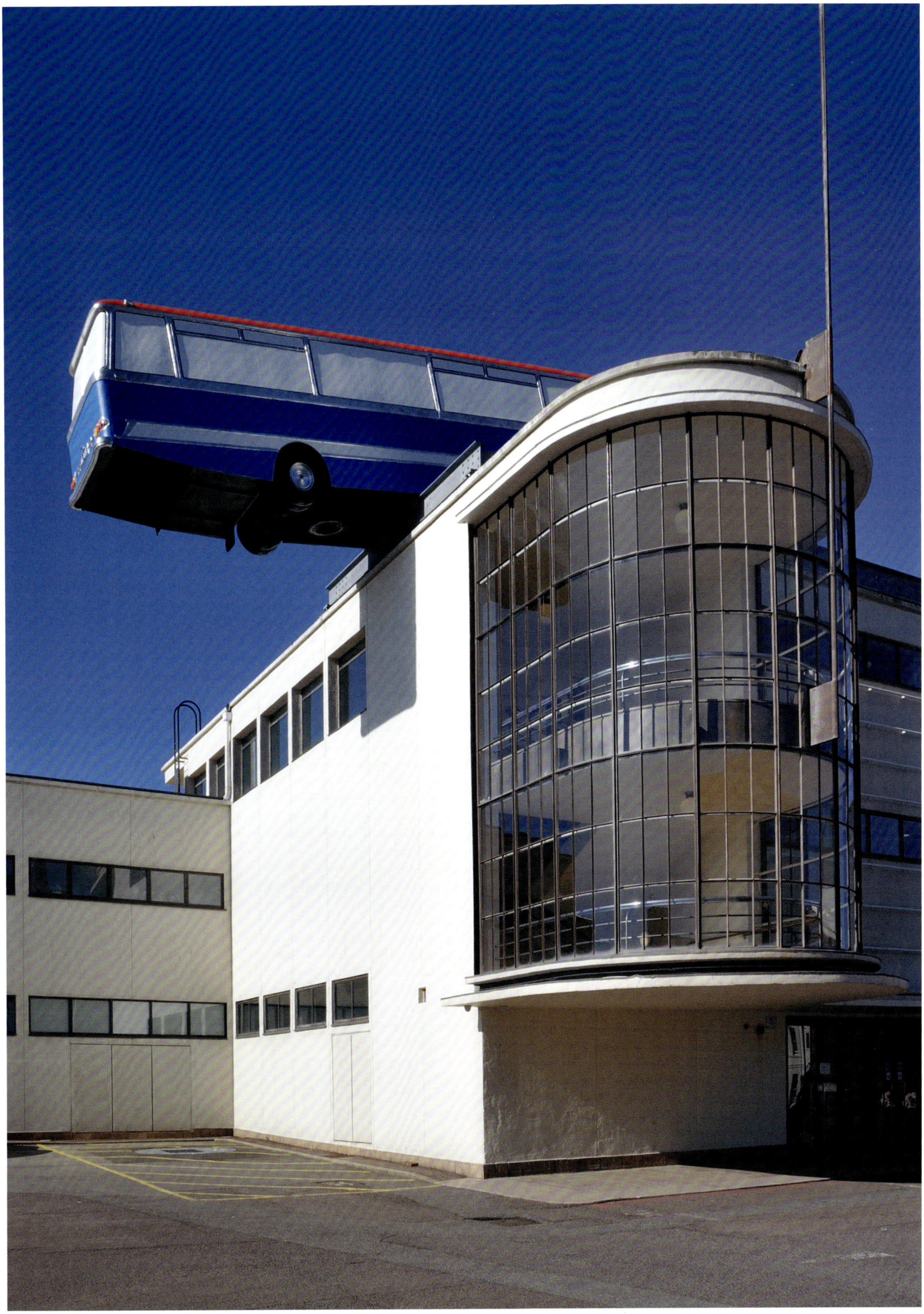

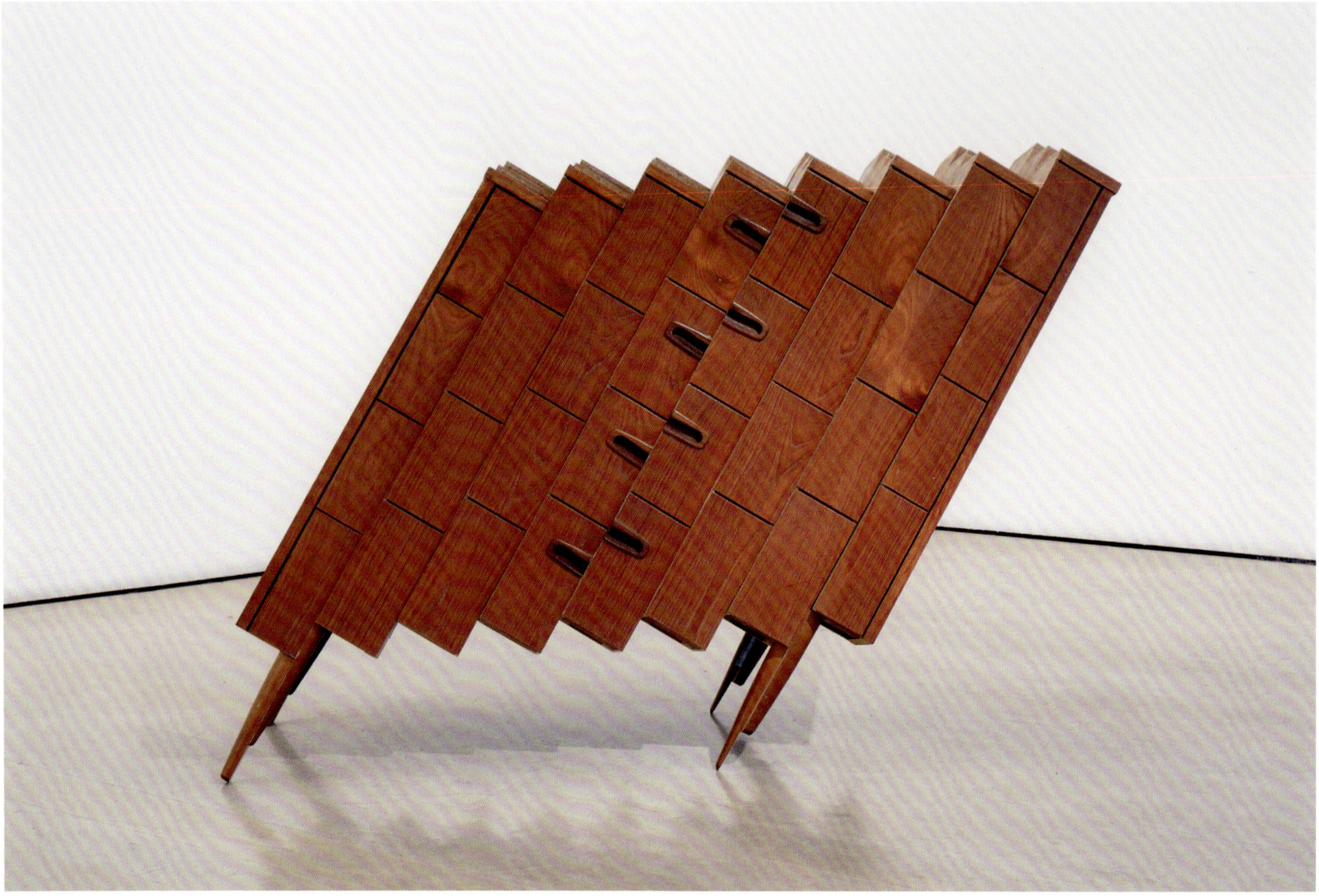

using just one section. I took a moment, a bit of its past, to create a suggestion of absence. Thousands of ships came onto the Thames when we had an Empire, but that was, by then, probably the only bit of ship left.

There's also a sense of humour in these things. In *Meter's Running*, I took a crazy journey through a taxi, and the metaphor was played out as a *double entendre*. Normally, one takes a journey using the car, but here I went into the car, through the engine at the front and out of the boot. My journey was filmed by cameras inserted into drilled holes as I smashed my way through with a jackhammer. When I cut a car or ship to the point of instability and collapse, I'm left with an elegant linear shape where form and function no longer relate. A bit of the form's history is left, but not its function.

IC: The performative and subversive feature strongly in your work. You've said it's important to absorb continually, to keep ideas fresh, and cite your influences as being the noise of a moving city and all the materials it harnesses.

RW: In order to come up with new ideas, I tamper with the rules of our ordered world. This is fundamental to my practice. I'm trying to carve my own path and play my hand against the conservatism abundant in the art world. If I can change peoples' perception of the world, I'm winning as a sculptor. How better to do that than with objects we think we know, and which I can get from scrapyards, as they're so quickly obsolete. The ergonomics of my body are designed to understand the world I'm in, and, being a sculptor, my world is tactile. I thrive on actions and coincidences. I'm never still; I've found the value of getting up with the sun.

Interviewed in 2019

←
Richard Wilson
Blocka Flats, 2017
Reconfigured furniture
123 × 77 × 48.5 cm
(48⅜ × 30¼ × 19⅛ in)
Installation view:
Annely Juda Fine Art,
London, 2017

↓
Richard Wilson
Butterfly, 2003
Cessna Aircraft, projection screen,
DVD and projector
6.6 × 5.8 × 2 m
(21 ft 7⅞ in × 19 ft ⅜ in × 6 ft 6¾ in)
Installation view:
The Wapping Project,
London, 2003

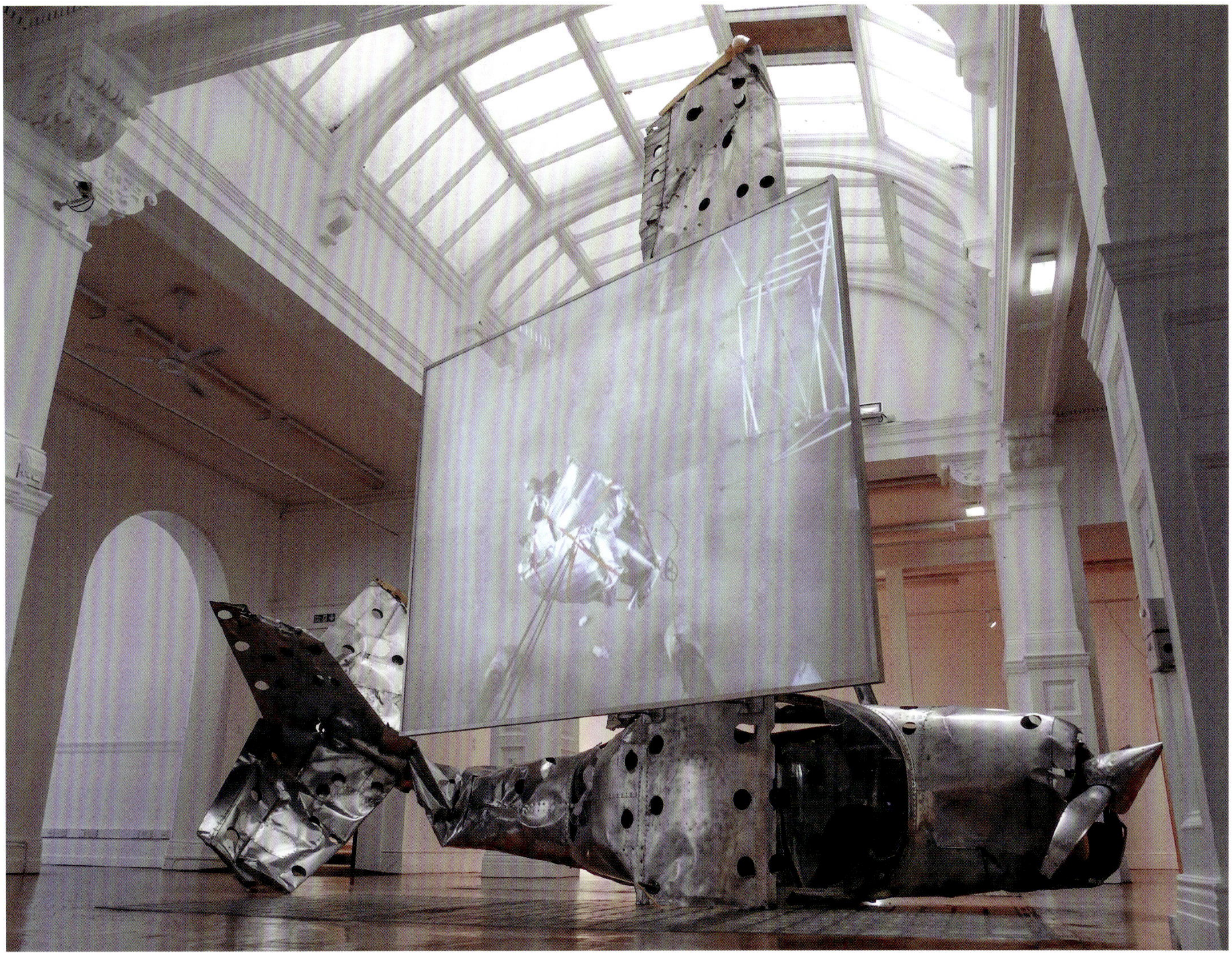

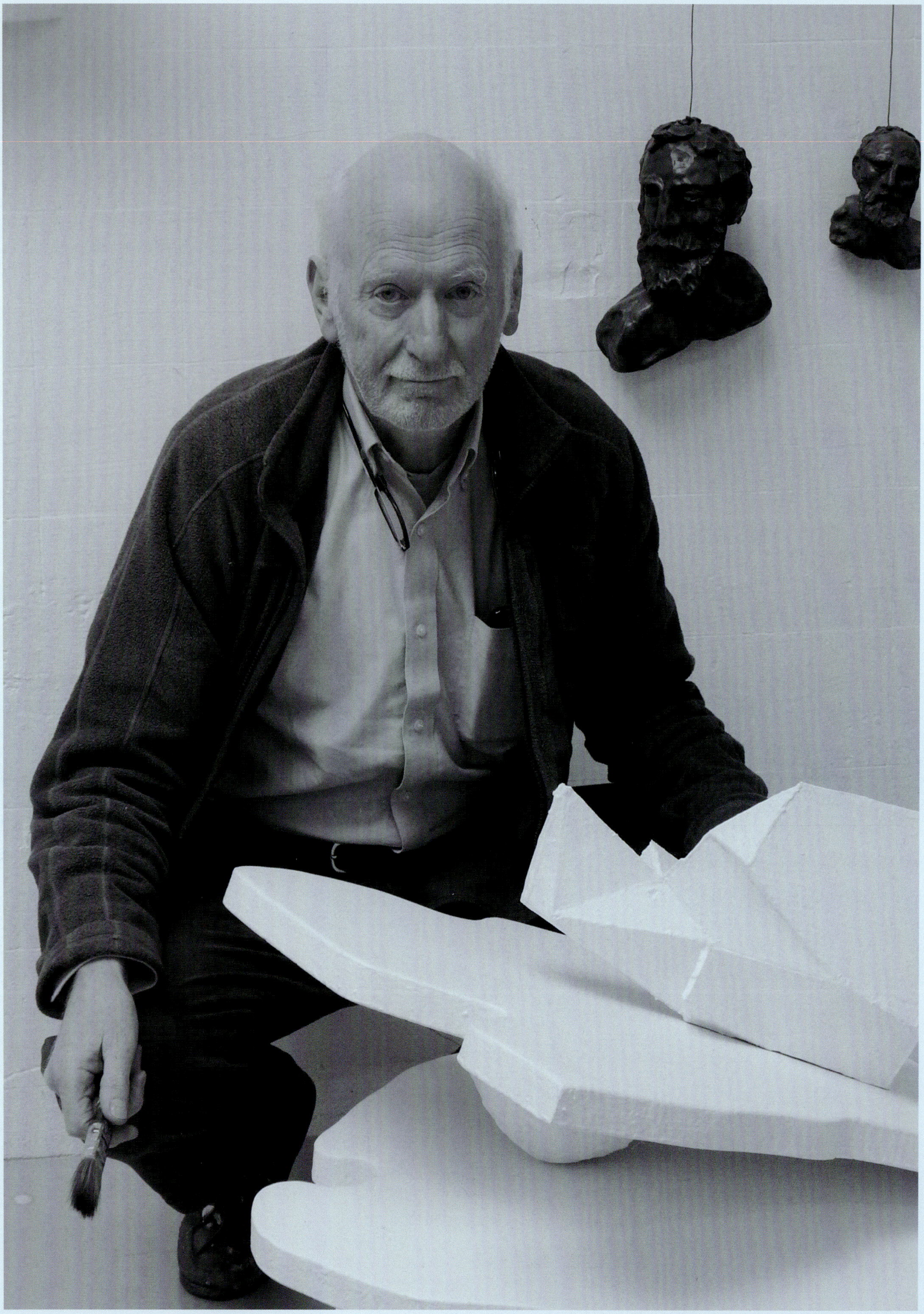

BILL WOODROW

Born 1948, Henley, Oxfordshire

Bill Woodrow's early work was made from discarded utilitarian objects, fossilized, cut and morphed into implausible ensembles that simultaneously quell their function and question society's relationship to its consumerist world. This manner of sourcing raw materials is not only opportunistic, it lends the final piece an unpredictability, thereby enhancing its dynamism. Woodrow's method of transforming context and form gave rise to a narrative element, which continued with sculptures made from welded steel and cast bronze. He habitually re-evaluates idea, form and technique, and this has culminated in an unparalleled repertoire of inventive and audacious configurations in which meaning remains elliptical, bestowing the work with a poetic and surrealist illusoriness. Later projects have taken Woodrow around the world in an exploration of indigenous cultures. This has resulted in arrangements of people and animals engrossed in the activities of survival within austere and icy terrain, as epitomized by *Settlements, Black and White 1–8* and *The Ledge*.

Ina Cole: In the 1960s, your immediate forerunners – New Generation Sculpture – sought to free the practice from its traditional heritage through an experimental use of material and form. At the time, narrative was largely rejected, yet it's an element that often reoccurs within your repertoire.

Bill Woodrow: Narrative was dismissed when I was a student in the 1960s, but I was interested in it even then. The work I became known for in the late 1970s and early 1980s, had a large element of narrative. I wouldn't set out to make a sculpture with a particular story, though; rather than being planned in a linear way, the narrative arose through the making. I find the whole abstract-versus-figurative question interesting. My work has always picked up on my life, so, in that sense, it's not abstract. However, when I did make abstract pieces just to do with form, there always came a point when it wasn't enough for me. On the other hand, some of my favourite artists are abstract artists – Sol LeWitt, early Frank Stella – whom I discovered as a student.

Bill Woodrow
Car Door, Ironing Board and Twin-Tub with North American Indian Head-Dress, 1981

Car door, ironing board, washing machine, enamel paint
186.5 × 283 × 157 cm
(73⅜ in × 9 ft 3⅜ in × 61¾ in)

IC: Initially, you fossilized domestic items by embedding them in plaster and concrete. Then, in the late 1970s, you went on to dismantle their constituent parts, as seen in *Tape Recorder* and *Hoover Breakdown*, two radical works from 1979, in which the objects' innards are seemingly unravelled. Was this an investigation into the function of components, or a more subversive gesture?

BW: I've not thought of it as subversive, but I guess it is in a way. As a child, when I was given a watch or torch for Christmas it would soon be in bits, because of curiosity about what's inside. The fossilized pieces came from looking at vitrines full of wonderful fossils at the Natural History Museum in London, and, one day in the studio, I wondered if I could make a contemporary fossil. I'd been collecting stuff off the streets and embedded those objects into plaster or concrete, totally covering them. When they set, I cut them back, like an archaeologist, revealing just enough information on what they were. That gave rise to a series of embedded utilitarian and domestic objects

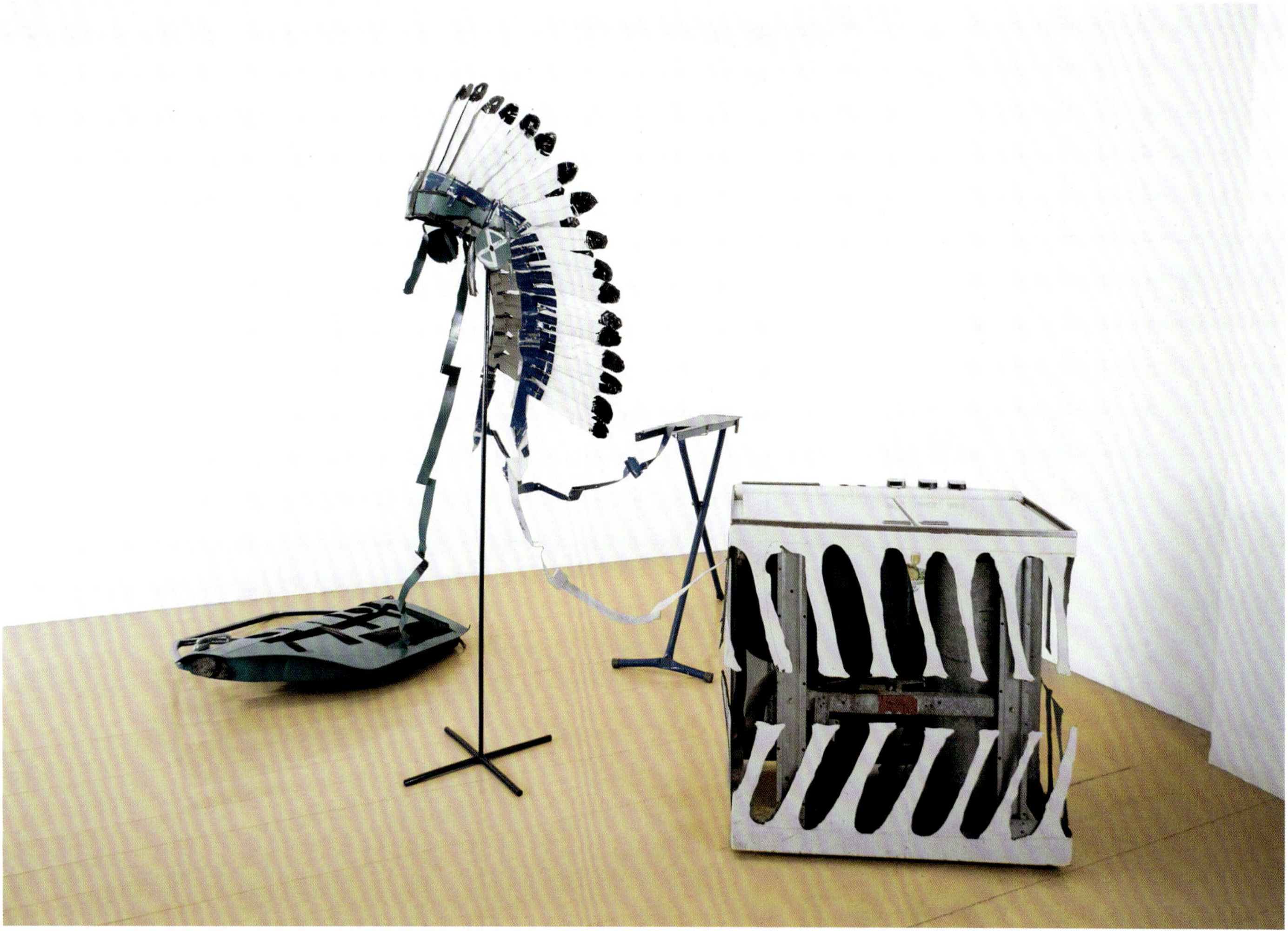

– hairdryers, telephones, record players, clothes irons, brooms and brushes.

This cutting-away eventually changed to working with the object alone, producing new work, like *Tape Recorder*, in which all the bits were removed and laid out, in order to display the contents under a cosmetic surface that you're not supposed to go beyond. In *Hoover Breakdown*, I dismantled an upright vacuum cleaner down to its smallest component and made a replica of it from wood, sacking and thick roofing paint. It was difficult to tell the two apart, and they're arranged so that the replica looks like it's functioning, sucking all the other original bits up.

IC: You then cut, twisted and morphed objects, as well – for example, *Spin Dryer with Bicycle Frame Including Handlebars*; *Twin-Tub with Guitar*; and *Car Door, Ironing Board and Twin-Tub with North American Indian Head-Dress*, all from 1981. In these sculptures, a new work is formed by peeling back the outer skin of a host object.

BW: The first cut-out pieces developed from the previous work. I had a bicycle frame and didn't want to replicate or embed it as a fossil. Instead, the frame was cut in such a way that it could be unfolded into one long, unbroken line. Then, in *Spin Dryer with Bicycle Frame Including Handlebars*, I wanted to remake a bicycle frame and did so by cutting into the surface material of a spin dryer, leaving the two connected. So that's how the first cut-out works came about. In *Twin-Tub with Guitar*, a guitar was cut from a 1950s twin-tub, as the tub's creamy colour reminded me of Eddie Cochran's guitar.

At this point, an interesting relationship was beginning to develop between the made and the host object. The idea for *Car Door, Ironing Board and Twin-Tub with North American Indian Head-Dress* came from

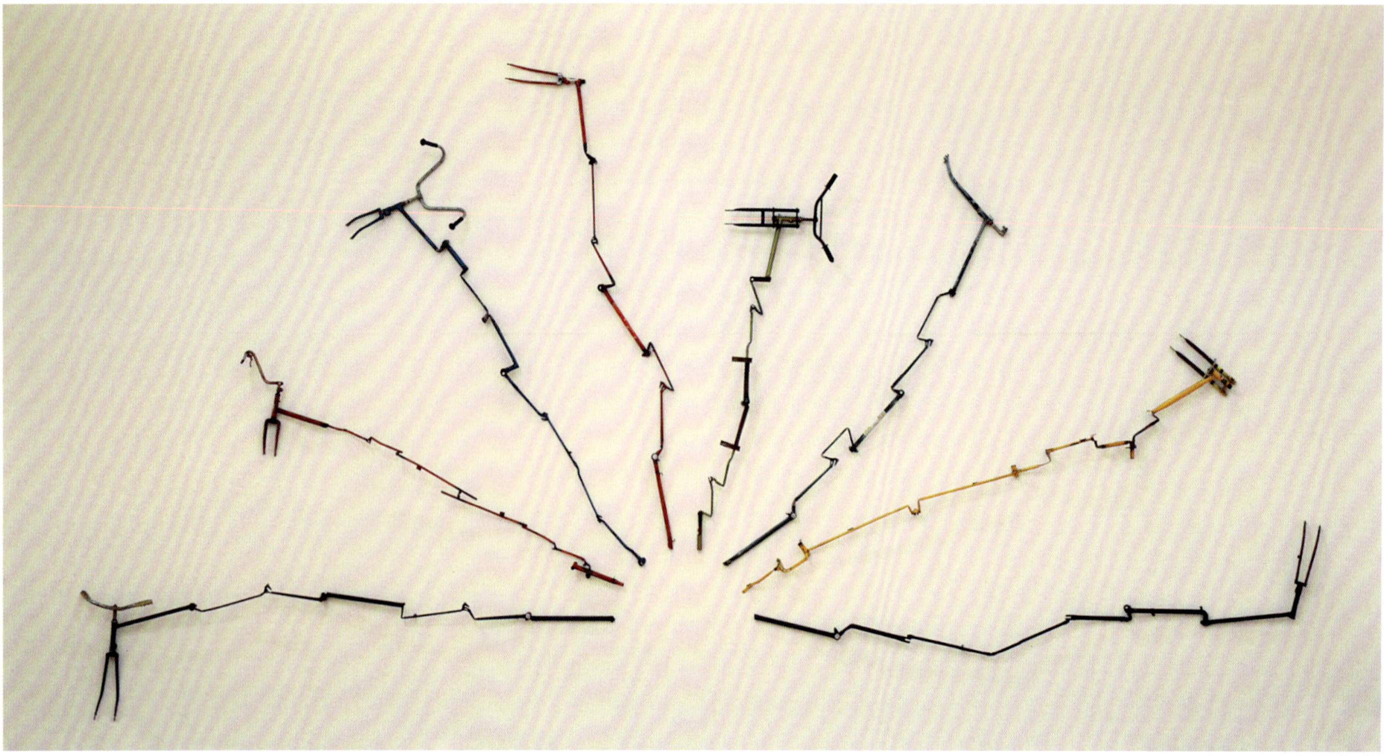

my kid's toy box, which contained a plastic head-dress with chicken feathers. I was curious about the distance it had travelled from the original object – time-wise, conceptually and metaphorically. The sculpture was presented as if it were a museum piece connected to the twentieth-century objects it was made from. This prompted me to look at other aboriginal or native artefacts, and the way they had been appropriated by different cultures, including ours.

IC: In these early pieces, the most unlikely combinations are assembled to create a new kind of hybrid. When merging a utilitarian item with another, totally unrelated, form, our association with it is challenged. It's as if a metamorphosis is taking place, conjuring a feeling of uncanniness. Was this sinister undercurrent intentional, or was your aim more playful, related to how different shapes activate each other?

BW: The term 'witty', or 'humorous', has also been used, but that was never my intention – it was a by-product. There's one sculpture in particular I call a hybrid, *Five Objects* (1980), as the fifth object looks like it's functioning, but it isn't, because it's made from bits of the others. The sinister, or uncanny, was quite deliberate, because it became apparent that, by combining different figurative elements, a certain ambience could be created, which allowed me to comment on things. Some of my views were pretty sinister, in terms of what was going on in the world. It was an exciting place, but grim – like being able to hear the IRA bombings in London. Also, I could walk the streets and pick up used stuff that had been thrown away. There was no organized recycling; things were just dumped for the rag-and-bone man to pick up.

However, making so many of these early works meant that explorative interest became lost, which is when I decided to use sheets of thin steel to construct *The Last Fruit (The Tree of Idleness)* (1988), the first in a new series

←
Bill Woodrow
Eight Bicycle Frames, 1980
Eight bicycle frames
600 × 1200 × 40 cm
(19 ft 8¼ in × 39 ft 4½ in × 15¾ in)

↓
Bill Woodrow
First Chair, 1989
Bronze
126 × 62 × 58 cm
(49⅝ × 24⅜ × 22⅞ in)

→→
Bill Woodrow
The Last Fruit (The Tree of Idleness), 1988
Steel, television, gold leaf, varnish
222 × 820 × 690 cm
(7 ft 3⅜ in × 26 ft 10⅞ in × 22 ft 7⅝ in)

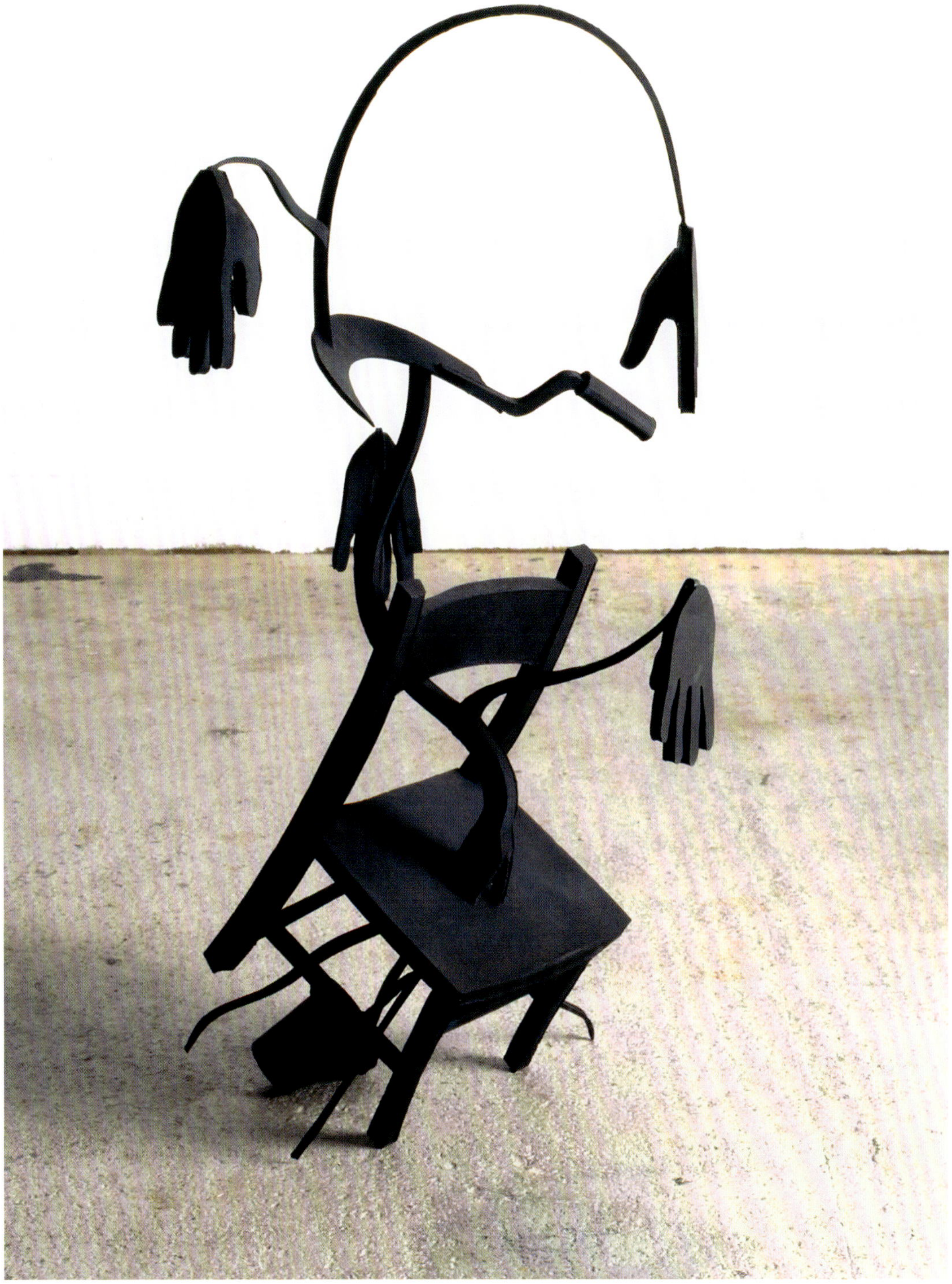

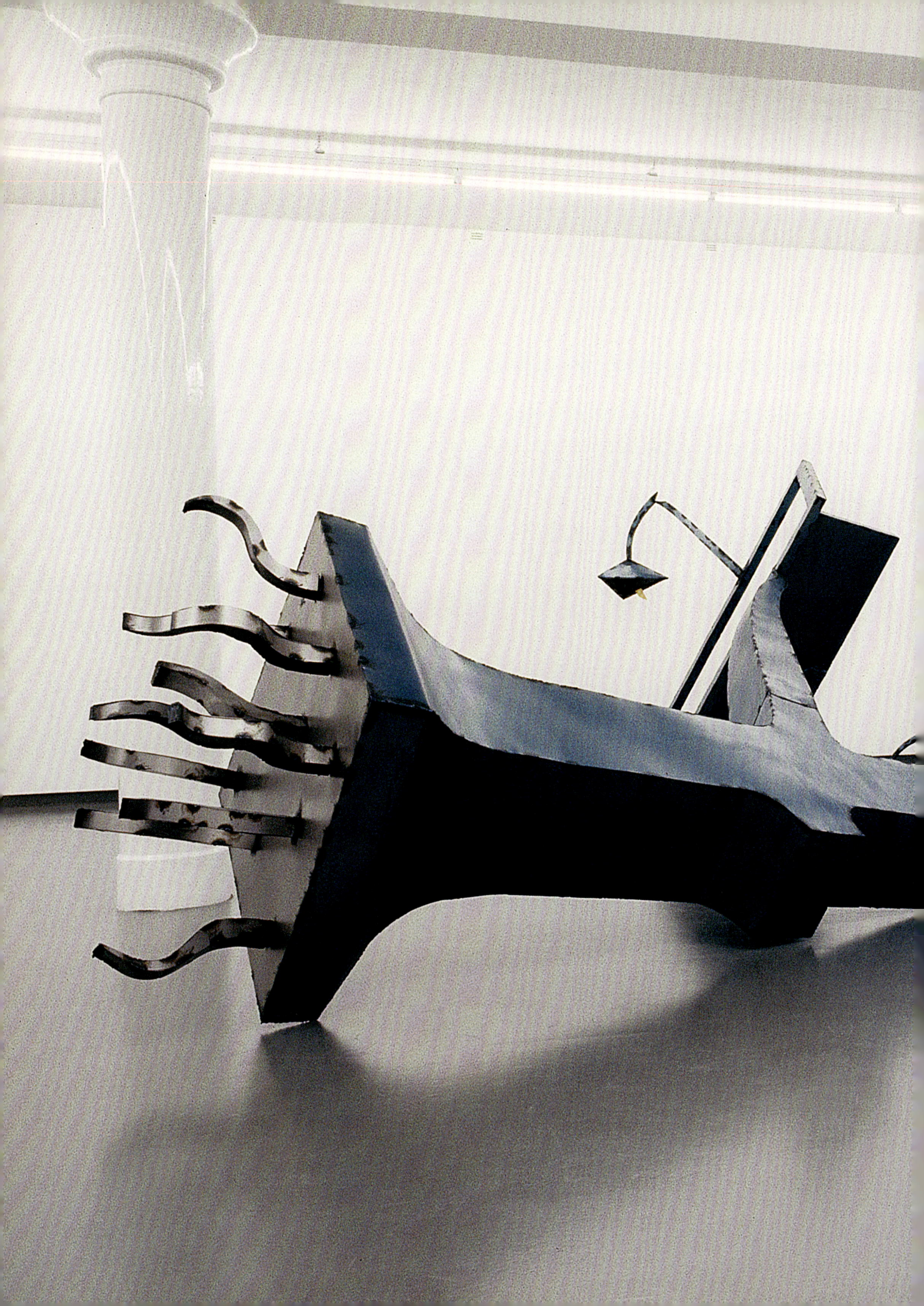

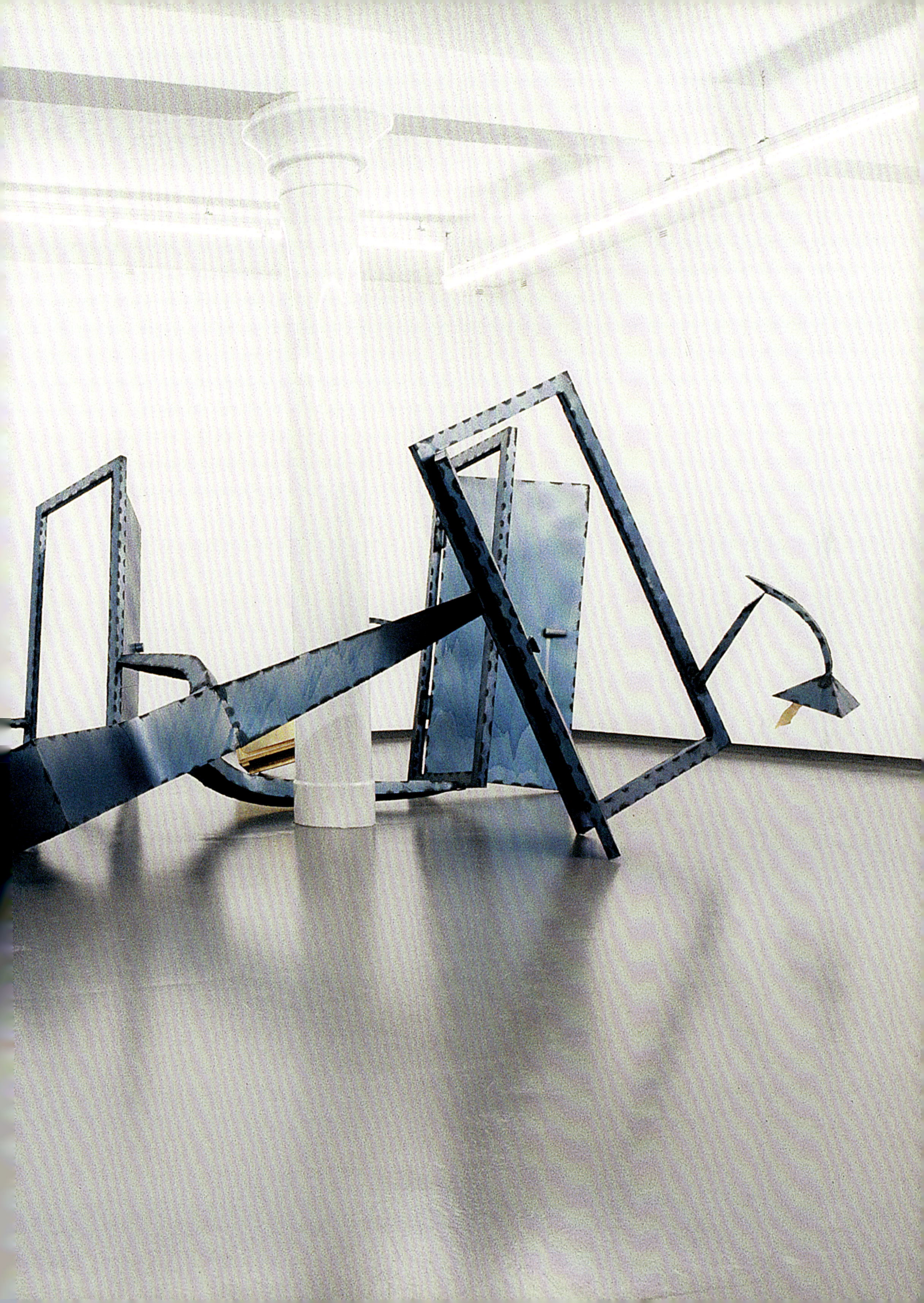

of welded forms. Another, *Eye of the Needle* (1988), is a landscape with different objects, including a horse and a flag, fitting together like a jigsaw puzzle, with a needle suspended over the top, like a moon. *Island* (1988) is an island, but in the shape of a face, surrounded by sea with battleships and fish. Others, like *The Glass Oar* (1989), included text within the composition. Sculpturally, I wanted to deal with space and shape, but there is a dialogue going on, even though you might not be immediately conscious of it.

IC: In many ways the Thatcher era was a politically negative time, yet the 1980s also saw massive achievement in British sculpture, with the emergence of New British Sculpture – a group, including yourself, which drew upon the decaying urban environment. How have times changed, and what impact is this having on sculptors practising today?

BW: The art world has changed, hugely. Artists are now household names, and art is viewed and spoken about all the time. However, the conditions for students are currently far worse, in terms of education, studios and the money they have to find. In the late 1960s, when I was a student, art was still seen as slightly rebellious, but it was easier in that art schools had more spaces available in which to make work. Nowadays, you're lucky if you get a studio at all. The more acceptable it all becomes, the more difficult it seems to be, which is odd. I think it's very hard to be radical today; everything has become so plural that you can do anything, and it's accepted. Earlier, you could clearly see what you were rebelling against, whereas there isn't a mainstream now. But I think you just have to get on with it. My work has become far worldlier; it's not as honed down and focused on specifics as in the 1980s. If I'm interested in something, I'll just do it. It could be anything, and I don't set any rules because I think it's more honest that way.

IC: In *First Chair* (1989) you relinquished the use of sheet metal and turned to bronze casting. Maybe this decision was directed by the theme, but did you also feel your artistic autonomy might be at stake if you didn't keep on the move?

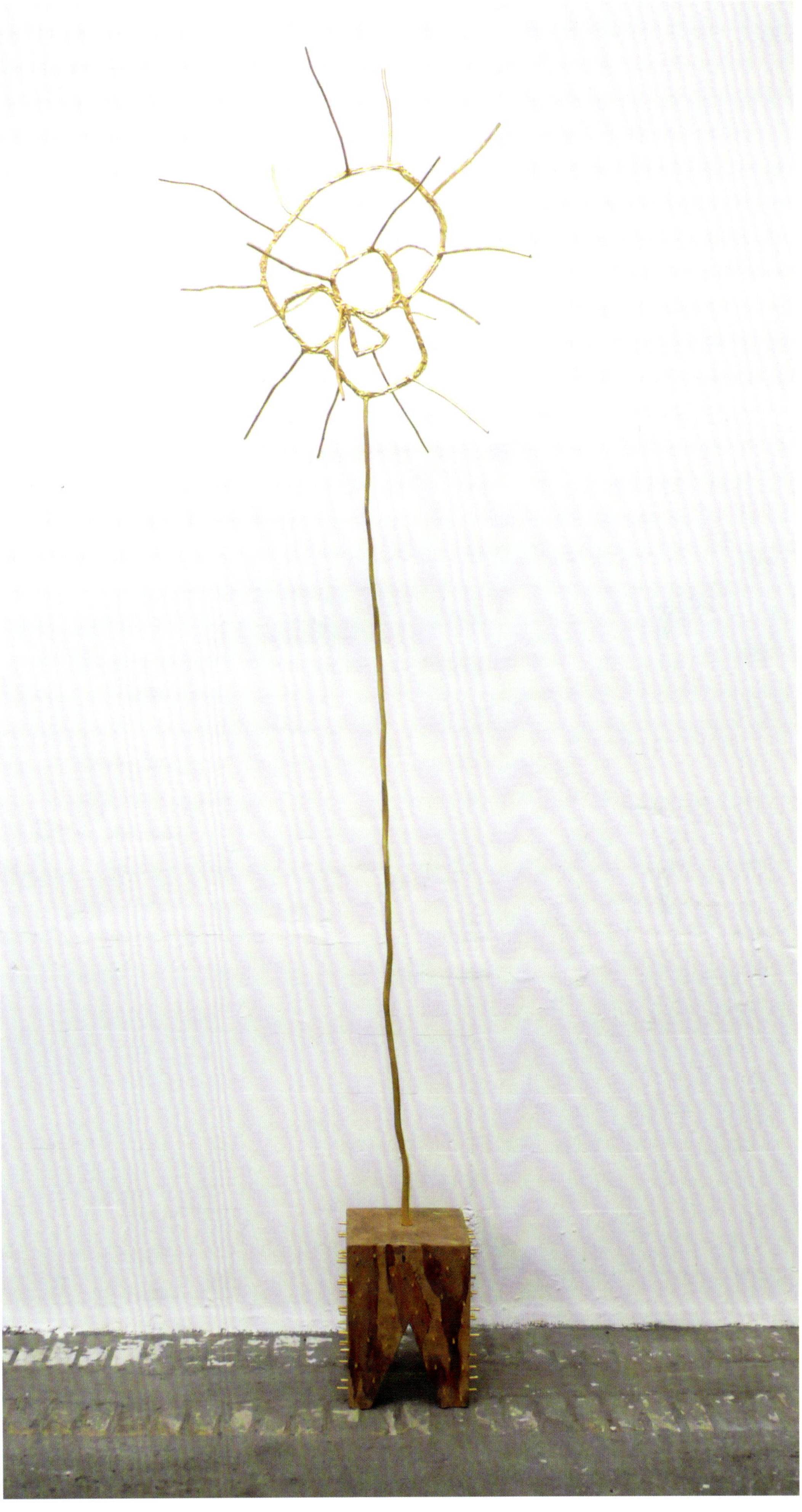

Bill Woodrow
Self Portrait in the Year 2089, 2013
Wood, gold leaf
317 × 90 × 50 cm
(10 ft 4¾ in × 35⅜ in × 19¾ in)

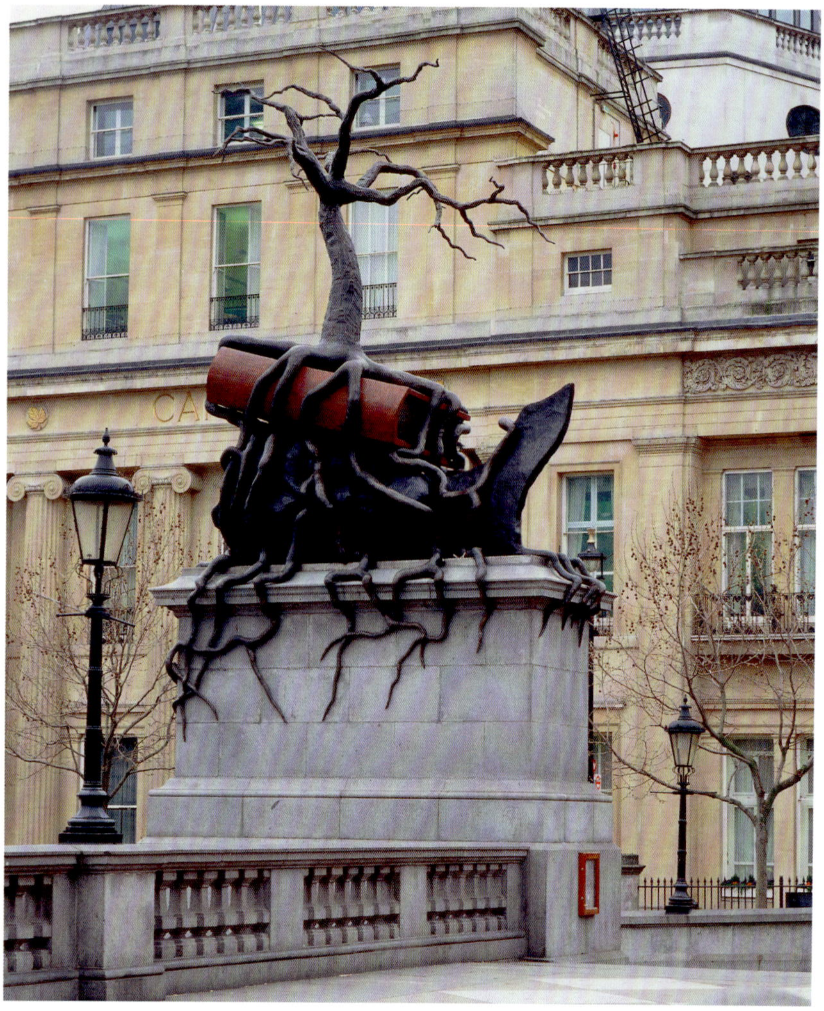

Bill Woodrow
Regardless of History,
2000

Bronze
5.6 × 5.4 × 2.45 m
(18 ft 4½ in × 17 ft 8⅝ in × 8 ft)
approx
Installation view:
Fourth Plinth, Trafalgar Square,
London, 2000

BW: Definitely, yet there's a strong heritage I can trace through my works; they're not a total break from each other. Changes come about because I simply get bored with making variations on the same theme. With the cut-out work of the 1980s, there came a point when the only way for it to become more interesting was to increase its complexity, but when that drowned the sculptural qualities there was little reason to continue.

First Chair was made for an exhibition at the Imperial War Museum in London (1989–90). After working with welded sheet steel, I used cardboard to make a full-size maquette of *First Chair*, as it's a quick, light and manoeuvrable material. However, it's somewhat delicate and, therefore, had to be changed into something more permanent. I hadn't used bronze before, because of the baggage of art history, which many young artists of the time felt. Still, I had the maquette cast in bronze, as one of a series of sculptures that responded to the machines and artefacts in the Imperial War Museum. *First Chair* is a child's chair, so it's as if a parent is looking back to their son or daughter lost in the conflict of war. The hands are like fruit and the sickle is obvious. Another sculpture, *Point of Entry* (1989), also the title of the show, is a formalized figure with guts spilling from it, named after the term given to where a bullet enters the body. The series is literal and straightforward.

IC: In the late 1990s, you developed a large group of thematically linked pieces on 'The Beekeeper'. The range is particularly diverse, revolving around the figure of a marionette, with sculptures of pupae, swarms and bee hives. You now keep bees, so they've become more than only subject matter. How did it all begin?

BW: In a fallow period following an exhibition in Tate Britain's Duveen Galleries in London (1996), I wanted to work on a new theme. One day in the studio, the word

Bill Woodrow
Celloswarm, 2002

Bronze, stone, gold leaf
82 × 92 × 208 cm
(32¼ × 36¼ × 81⅞ in)

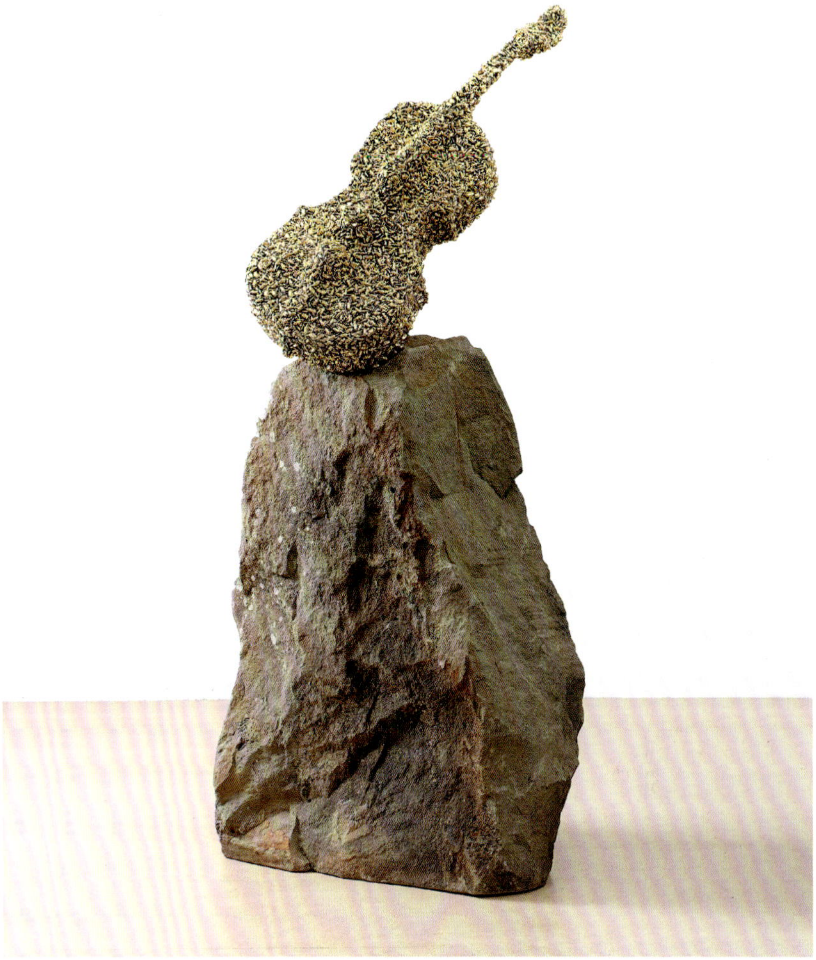

'beekeeper' popped into my head. I don't know where it came from, but realized it was conceptually and visually very rich, so started making sculpture from my limited knowledge of beekeeping. Later, I took a beekeeping course, which led to more work on the subject. When I moved out of London, everything dropped into place. It was life imitating art, rather than the other way around. I started keeping bees and it's fascinating. Bees have a symbiotic relationship with humans. We give them shelter, they give us products; not just honey, as they're essential to agriculture the world over. They've been farmed and used as a food source since prehistoric times. Structurally, their physical make-up is amazing and they organize themselves really thoroughly. People are generally frightened of them, but, if you have a swarm hanging from your arm, it feels very gentle. I particularly like that they're extremely small and can defy gravity – not totally, but in a way we can't.

IC: You've created a number of self-portraits, such as *Self-Portrait in the Year 2089* (2013), and *Self-Portrait as a Painter in the Year 2090* (2015). However, they're all pared-down and skeletal, utilizing a skull as the central element. Is this because bone can remain intact for the time span indicated in the title?

BW: Absolutely, although I hadn't thought of it in that way. Skulls can be dug up from a million years ago; it's one bit of you that can last, given the right conditions. Every now and then, throughout my career, I've made a self-portrait. They're a subversion of the classical self-portrait, where an artist paints a likeness by looking at themselves in the mirror. I thought it would be interesting to make one so far in the future that I'll be dead and buried, and the skull is the most natural object to represent that. With *Self-Portrait as a Painter in the Year 2090*, I wanted to animate this classical symbol of death, give it some sort of life, and therefore added extensions, like roots or branches; whereas *Self-Portrait in the Year 2089* looks more like a sunflower, growing.

IC: In *Regardless of History* (2000), a book is bound shut by tree roots and, in *Listening to History* (1995), it's bound to a head by twine. Can you expand on your recurring fascination with the closed book?

BW: In sculptural terms, there's a visual difference between a closed and an opened book. Books are amazing. Once made, they're very independent objects and, at the most basic level, they can be written by hand. They're one of the earliest ways of passing knowledge, and continue to this day, thank goodness. In *Listening to History*, the book is bound to the ear. Although the ear is listening, the eyes are blinded by the book's binding. You can hear, but not see; it's a reference to not learning from our mistakes.

Regardless of History was made for the Fourth Plinth in Trafalgar Square, London (2000), and I was keen for the plinth to become part of the sculpture. The head was taken from images rife in the media of fallen dictator's heads, such as Saddam Hussein's. So, the fallen head with the book on top references the accumulated knowledge of the world, while the tree roots hold everything together, including the plinth – a classical object presenting wonderful things of importance. My fascination with roots came from looking at photographs in which jungles had taken over, leaving old temples barely visible. There's a cyclical element to the way humans try to control cultures and environments, which just disappear when jungles thrive. Nature deals with it, and we're all part of that system.

IC: You've undertaken several visits to Arctic Norway, resulting in *Settlements* (2007) and *Black and White 1–8* (2012) – groupings arranged on plinth-like structures, which focus on indigenous civilizations and their predicaments.

BW: The figurative elements in my earlier work were surreal rather than reflecting the outer world, whereas a series called *Settlements*, developed from these trips to Norway, directly reflects my experience of seeing how people populate that landscape, with its high plateaus. Every now and then, I saw a small hut belonging to the reindeer-herding Sami people; further on were more huts and, eventually, a village or small town, then a city. Yet the huts are always next to an important feature of the landscape. However, I didn't have a fixed plan; whether something appeals to me visually always takes precedence.

The *Settlements* works led me to look at archive images of Inuit life, resulting in me making small-scale wax models of Inuit activities – hunting seals, sitting around a shared meal, waiting at an ice hole – and these models were the first components for new sculpture. The next stage was more formal. As the scenes take place on ice floes, I wanted to make a landscape resembling an iceberg, and used the most immediate material: cardboard boxes cut to raise the wax scenes off the ground. They're part of the work but separate the sculptures from their immediate surroundings. The boxes resembled modernist architectural icebergs, but, as cardboard and wax aren't durable, they were cast into bronze and painted white. Then, they needed a boundary to exist within. In order to reference oil exploration and the exploitation of the Arctic, I used thick industrial rubber, which has a connection with oil, as it's a natural, extracted material. *Black and White 1–8* arose through all those different stages.

The original culture of the Inuit probably still survives in certain areas, with the help of modern technology – phones, Ski-Doos, and so on. Many have given up the nomadic way of life over the past hundred years, but certain groups still want to hold on to it, and I hope these sculptures don't undermine that.

IC: This enquiry into indigenous cultures can be traced through your practice. *The Ledge* (2017) features an Inuit and a seal, and was created for Folkestone Triennial, in Kent, in 2017. Is it a continuation of ideas expressed in *Black and White 1–8*?

BW: Yes, *The Ledge* is actually an enlarged version of one of the *Black and White* series, but placed in a fantastic location right next to the sea. I've always had an interest in indigenous cultures, and other ways of living. It's not an easy interest, as I'm aware that the

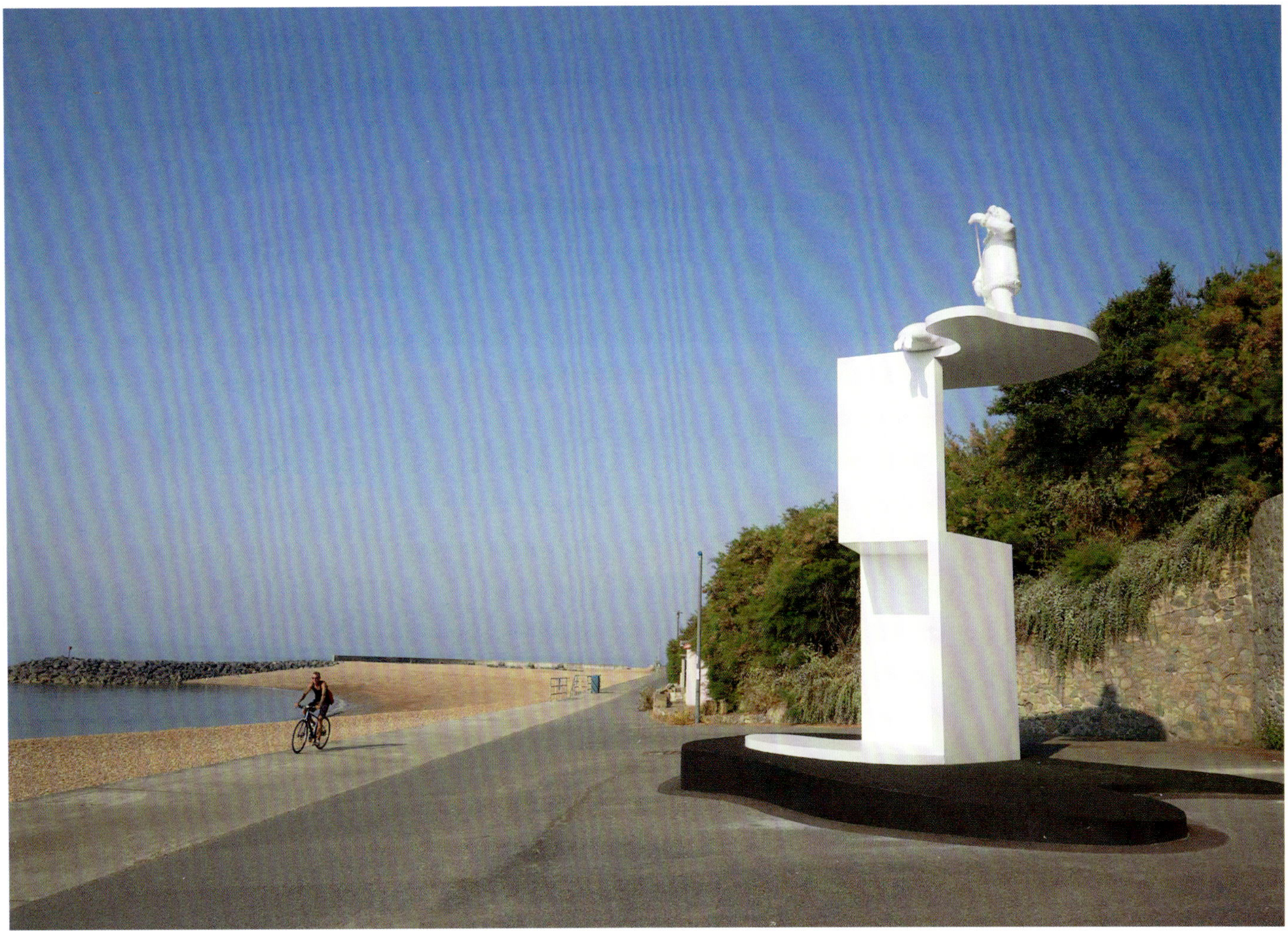

Bill Woodrow
The Ledge, 2017

Fibreglass, stainless steel, concrete, rubber, paint
Approx. 7 × 3 × 4 m
(22 ft 11⅝ in × 9 ft 10⅛ in × 13 ft)
Installation view:
Lower Leas Coastal Promenade, Folkestone, Kent, 2017

notion of romanticizing or exoticizing has a long history in the West. The history of the Inuit and Europe is pretty horrendous actually; how they were caught by early travellers, brought back and shown like circus acts. All this definitely informs the way I live and view the West. Cultures other than our own, in their original form, are much more self-reliant and balanced. I think they have a lot to teach us, particularly in how to respond to the Earth. Every natural system is made up of little individual systems, which have ways of regulating each other. The further we progress, the more we have the means to eliminate ourselves. It's part of the natural process, but I hope it doesn't come to that. The problem for artists is how to look at these other cultures without exploiting them.

Interviewed in 2014 and 2019

INDEX

Page numbers in *italics* refer to illustration captions

IMAGE CREDITS

FIONA BANNER

p.11 *1066*, 2010 (detail); photo: Steve White; © The artist; courtesy the artist and Frith Street Gallery, London; **p.12** *Buoys Boys*, 2016; © The artist; courtesy the artist and Frith Street Gallery, London; **p.13** *The Man and Mistah Kurtz*, 2018; © The artist; courtesy the artist and Frith Street Gallery, London; **p.13** *Falcon 59400 pt*, 2019; photo: Steve White; © The artist; courtesy the artist and Frith Street Gallery, London; **p.15** *1909-2011*, 2010; © The artist; courtesy the artist and Frith Street Gallery, London; **p.16** *Harrier*, 2010; photo: © Tate, Andrew Dunkley and Sam Drake; © The artist; courtesy the artist and Frith Street Gallery, London; **p.17** *Parade*, 2006; photo: Rafael Goldchain; collection: Pentti Kouri, New York; courtesy Tracy Williams Ltd., New York; © The artist; courtesy the artist and Frith Street Gallery, London; **p.19** *Tornado*, 2010; © The artist; courtesy the artist and Frith Street Gallery, London

PHYLLIDA BARLOW

p.23 *untitled (series of 10)*, 1965; © Phyllida Barlow; courtesy the artist and Hauser & Wirth; **p.24** *TIP*, 2013; 2013 Carnegie International, Pittsburg PA, 2013–14; © Phyllida Barlow; courtesy the artist, Hauser & Wirth and Carnegie Museum of Art, Pittsburgh; **p.25** *tryst*, 2015; photo: Kevin Todora; © Phyllida Barlow; courtesy Nasher Sculpture Center, Dallas; **pp.26–7** *untitled: dock: emptystaircasehoarding*, 2014; Duveen Commission, Tate Britain, London, 2014; photo: Alex Delfanne; © Phyllida Barlow; courtesy the artist and Hauser & Wirth; **p.29** *folly*, 2017; photo: Ruth Clark; © British Council; British Pavilion, 57th Venice Biennale, Italy, 2017; © Phyllida Barlow; courtesy the artist and Hauser & Wirth; **p.30** *untitled: dancer; 2018*, 2018; photo: Alex Delfanne; © Phyllida Barlow; courtesy the artist and Hauser & Wirth; **p.31** *untitled: spree (green); 2018*, 2018; photo: Alex Delfanne; © Phyllida Barlow; courtesy the artist and Hauser & Wirth; **p.32** *untitled: lintelshadow; 2018-2019*, 2018-19; *cul-de-sac*, Royal Academy of Arts, London, 2019; photo: Damian Griffiths; © Royal Academy of Arts, London; © Phyllida Barlow; courtesy the artist and Hauser & Wirth

ANTHONY CARO

p.37 *Sun Feast*, 1969–1970; photo: John Riddy; © Barford Sculptures Ltd.; **p.38** *Early One Morning*, 1962; photo: John Riddy; Tate Collection, London; © Barford Sculptures Ltd.; **pp.40–1** *Chapel of Light*, 2001–08; photo: John Riddy; © Barford Sculptures Ltd.; **pp.42–3** *The Last Judgement: Trumpeter 1, 2, 3, 4* and *Gate of Heaven*, 1996–9; photo: David Buckland; © Barford Sculptures Ltd.; **p.44** *Child's Tower Room*, 1983–4; photo: Mike Bruce; © Barford Sculptures Ltd. and Gagosian Gallery; **p.45** *The Barbarians*, 1999–2002; photo: John Riddy; © Barford Sculptures Ltd.; **p.47** *Achilles (The Trojan War)*, 1993–4; photo: David Buckland; © Barford Sculptures Ltd.; **p.47** *Paper Sculpture No.5 – Blackbird*, 1993; photo: David Evans; © Barford Sculptures Ltd.

RICHARD DEACON

p.51 *The Eye Has It*, 1984; photo: Anna Arca, 2014; Arts Council Collection, London; © Richard Deacon; courtesy the artist; **p.52** *Tall Tree in the Ear*, 1984; photo: John Riddy; © Richard Deacon; courtesy the artist; **p.55** *Laocoon*, 1996; photo: John Riddy; © Richard Deacon; courtesy the artist; **p.56** *Flat 27*, 2016; photo: Mareike Tocha; © Richard Deacon; courtesy the artist; **p.57** *Infinity #30*, 2006; © Richard Deacon; courtesy the artist; **p.59** *New Alphabet ABC*, 2018; photo: Yang Chao Studio; © Richard Deacon; courtesy the artist; **pp.60–1** *Out of Order*, 2003; photo: Dave Morgan; © Richard Deacon; courtesy the artist; **p.62** *Under The Weather #2*, 2016; photo: Ken Adlard; © Richard Deacon; courtesy the artist

LAURA FORD

p.67 *Giraffe*, 2013; photo: Müller-Naumann, Heidelberg; © Laura Ford; courtesy Galerie Scheffel, Germany; **p.69** *Three Bears* (Maquette), 2017; © Laura Ford; courtesy Galerie Scheffel, Germany and the artist; **p.69** *Rag and Bone with Blanket*, 2007; © Laura Ford; courtesy Galerie Scheffel, Germany and the artist; **p.71** *Dancing Clog Girls*, 2013 (detail); © Laura Ford; courtesy Kunstsammlungen und Museen Augsburg; **pp.72–3** *Weeping Girl 5*, 2009; photo: Allan Pollok Morris; © Laura Ford; courtesy Jupiter Artland; **p.74** *Espaliered Girl*, 2007; photo: Archive Galerie Scheffel; © Laura Ford; courtesy Galerie Scheffel, Germany; **p.75** *Days of Judgment*, 2012; © Laura Ford; courtesy New Art Centre, Roche Court Sculpture Park, Wiltshire; **p.77** *Headthinker VIII*, 2012; photo: Archive Galerie Scheffel; © Laura Ford; courtesy Galerie Scheffel, Germany

ANTONY GORMLEY

p.81 *Field for the British Isles*, 1993; Arts Council Collection, London; © Antony Gormley; **p.82** *Angel of the North*, 1995–8; photo: Sally Ann Norman; commissioned by Gateshead Metropolitan Borough Council, Gateshead; © Antony Gormley; **p.85** *Domain Field*, 2003; photo: Jerry Hardman-Jones, Leeds; commission for BALTIC, Centre for Contemporary Art, Gateshead; © Antony Gormley; **pp.86–7** *Critical Mass II*, 1995; photo: Oak Taylor-Smith; © Antony Gormley; **p.89** *Expansion Field*, 2014; photo: Dominique Uldry; © Antony Gormley; **p.90** *Inside Australia*, 2003; photo: Ashley de Prazer, Perth, Western Australia; commission for 50th Perth International Arts Festival, Western Australia, 2003; © Antony Gormley; **p.93** *Stream*, 2018; photo: Hyun Jin Park; © Antony Gormley; **p.93** *Shore*, 2012; photo: Oak Taylor-Smith; © Antony Gormley

MONA HATOUM

p.97 *Measures of Distance*, 1988; © Mona Hatoum; courtesy the artist; **p.99** *Hot Spot III*, 2009; photo: Agostino Osio; © Mona Hatoum; courtesy Fondazione Querini Stampalia Onlus, Venice; **p.100** *Current Disturbance*, 1996; photo: Ben Blackwell; © Mona Hatoum; courtesy the artist; **p.101** *Homebound*, 2000 (detail); photo: Fredrik Nilsen; © Mona Hatoum; courtesy The Menil Collection, Houston; **p.103** *Electrified (variable II)*, 2014; photo: © White Cube (George Darrell); © Mona Hatoum; **pp.104–5** *Remains of the Day*, 2017; photo: Ken Kusakari; © Mona Hatoum; courtesy Hiroshima City Museum of Contemporary Art; **p.106** *Cells*, 2014 (detail); photo: Joerg Lohse; © Mona Hatoum; courtesy Alexander and Bonin, New York; **p.107** *Bunker*, 2011; photo: Hugo Glendinning; © Mona Hatoum; courtesy White Cube

SUSAN HILLER

p.111 *Hand Grenades*, 1972 (from paintings made in 1969); photo: Todd-White Art Photography; © The Estate of Susan Hiller; **p.112** *An Entertainment*, 1990; photo: Edward Woodman; © The Estate of Susan Hiller; **p.113** *Belshazzar's Feast / The Writing on Your Wall*, 1983-4; photo: Todd-White Art Photography; © The Estate of Susan Hiller; **pp.114–15** *Witness*, 2000; photo: Parisa Taghizadeh; © The Estate of Susan Hiller; **pp.116–17** *Die Gedanken sind frei* (Thoughts are Free), 2012; photo: Anders Sune Berg; Documenta 13, Kassel, 2012; © The Estate of Susan Hiller; **p.118** *From the Freud Museum*, 1991–6 (detail); photo: Edward Woodman; © The Estate of Susan Hiller; **p.119** *Home Nursing: Homage to Joseph Beuys*, 1969–2011; photo: Todd-White Art Photography; © The Estate of Susan Hiller; **p.121** *Lucidity and Intuition: Homage to Gertrude Stein*, 2011; photo: Todd-White Art Photography; © The Estate of Susan Hiller

ANISH KAPOOR

p.125 *Sky Mirror*, 2006; photo: Seong Kwon Photography; © Anish Kapoor; all rights reserved DACS, 2020; **p.126** *Cloud Gate*, 2004; photo: Peter.J.Schluz; © Anish Kapoor; all rights reserved DACS, 2020; **p.127** *White Sand, Red Millet, Many Flowers*, 1982; Arts Council Collection, London; © Anish Kapoor; all rights reserved DACS, 2020; **p.128** *Void Pavilion VI*, 2018; photo: Nobutada Omote; © Anish Kapoor; all rights reserved DACS, 2020; **p.129** *ArcelorMittal Orbit*, 2012; photo: Dave Morgan; © Anish Kapoor; all rights reserved DACS, 2020; **p.130** *Shooting into the Corner*, 2008–09; photo: Dave Morgan; © Anish Kapoor; all rights reserved DACS, 2020; **p.131** *Blood Relations*, 2006; photo: Dave Morgan; A collaboration with Salman Rushdie; © Anish Kapoor; all rights reserved DACS, 2020; **p.133** *Leviathan*, 2011; photo: Dave Morgan; © Anish Kapoor; all rights reserved DACS, 2020

TANIA KOVATS

p.136 *Virgin in a Condom*, 1992; Arts Council Collection, London; © Tania Kovats; **p.139** *Meadow*, 2006; © Tania Kovats; **p.140** *Tide*, 2015; commission for the National Trust, UK; © Tania Kovats; **p.142** *Tree*, 2009; permanent commission for the Natural History Museum, London; © Tania Kovats; **p.143** *Colony*, 2012; © Tania Kovats; **p.144** *All the Seas*, 2012-14; © Tania Kovats; **p.145** *Rivers*, 2012; photo: Keith Hunter; © Tania Kovats; courtesy Jupiter Artland

RICHARD LONG

p.148 *Boyhood Line*, 2015; photo: © Max McClure; © Richard Long; courtesy the artist and Arnolfini; **p.150** *Circle to Circle*, 2018; © Richard Long; courtesy Lisson Gallery; **p.151** *Circle for Sally*, 2016; photo: José Luis Gutiérrez; © Richard Long; courtesy CAC Málaga; **p.153** *Camp-Site Stones*, 1985; © Richard Long; courtesy the artist; **pp.154–5** *Sunset Circles*, 2006; © Richard Long; courtesy the artist;

p.157 *Popocatépetl Line*, 2020; photo: Sebastiano Pellion di Persano; © Richard Long; courtesy Lisson Gallery; **p.159** *Heaven (Portrait of Carl Andre)*, 2011; © Richard Long; courtesy Sperone Westwater, New York; **p.159** *Stones/Years*, 2015; © Richard Long; courtesy the artist and Konrad Fischer Galerie

DAVID NASH

p.163 *Wooden Boulder*, 1978 (image from 2014); photo: © David Nash; courtesy David Nash; **pp.164–5** *Capel Rhiw* (interior), 2018; photo: © Jonty Wilde; courtesy David Nash; **p.166** *Black Sphere*, 2010; photo: © Jonty Wilde; courtesy David Nash and Yorkshire Sculpture Park; **p.168** *Red Column*, 2010; photo: © Jonty Wilde; courtesy David Nash and Yorkshire Sculpture Park; **p.169** *Ash Dome*, 1977 (image from 2009, matured); photo: © Jonty Wilde; courtesy David Nash; **p.171** *Two Ubus*, 1988; photo: Rob Harris; © Towner Eastbourne; courtesy David Nash and Towner Eastbourne; **p.171** *Oculus Block*, 2010; photo: © Jonty Wilde; courtesy David Nash and Yorkshire Sculpture Park; **p.172** *Millennium Book*, 2000; photo: © Jonty Wilde; courtesy David Nash and Yorkshire Sculpture Park; **p.173** *Crack and Warp Column*, 1989; photo: © David Nash; courtesy David Nash

CORNELIA PARKER

p.177 *Thirty Pieces of Silver*, 1988–9; photo: Anna Kučera; © Cornelia Parker; courtesy the artist; Museum of Contemporary Art, Australia; and Frith Street Gallery, London; **p.178** *Breathless*, 2001; permanent commission for the V&A Museum, London (collection V&A Museum, London); © Cornelia Parker; courtesy Frith Street Gallery, London and the artist; **p.179** *Cold Dark Matter: An Exploded View*, 1991; photo: Hugo Glendinning; Tate Collection, London; © Cornelia Parker; courtesy the artist and Frith Street Gallery, London; **pp.180–1** *Subconscious of a Monument*, 2003; photo: Anna Kučera; © Cornelia Parker; courtesy the artist; Museum of Contemporary Art, Australia; and Frith Street Gallery, London; **p.182** *Brontëan Abstract (Emily Brontë's quill pen nib)*, 2006; commissioned by the Brontë Parsonage Museum, Haworth; © Cornelia Parker; courtesy the artist and Frith Street Gallery, London; **p.183** *Transitional Object (PsychoBarn)*, 2016; The Roof Garden Commission, The Metropolitan Museum of Art; photo: Hyla Skopitz, The Photograph Studio, The Metropolitan Museum of Art, © 2016; © Cornelia Parker; courtesy Frith Street Gallery, London and the artist; **p.185** *Sawn Up Sawn Off Shotgun*, 2015; photo: The Whitworth (M. Pollard); with thanks to Greater Manchester Police; © Cornelia Parker; courtesy Frith Street Gallery, London and the artist; **p.186** *Left, Right & Centre*, 2017; production photography by Joseph Turp in the House of Commons Chamber, Palace of Westminster, London by kind permission of the Speaker of the House of Commons, Rt Hon John Bercow MP; commissioned by the Speaker's Advisory Committee on Works of Art, chaired by Alison McGovern MP; © Cornelia Parker; courtesy Frith Street Gallery, London and the artist

MARC QUINN

p.190 *Self*, 1991; © Marc Quinn; courtesy Marc Quinn studio; **p.191** *100 Heads (Adiam Yemane)*, 2020; photo: Marc Quinn studio; © Marc Quinn; courtesy Marc Quinn studio; **p.192** *Emotional Detox, The Seven Deadly Sins IV*, 1995; © Marc Quinn; courtesy Marc Quinn studio; **p.194** *Alison Lapper Pregnant*, 2005; © Marc Quinn; courtesy Marc Quinn studio; **pp.196–7** *Garden*, 2000; photo: Attilio Maranzano; © Marc Quinn; courtesy Marc Quinn studio and Fondazione Prada; **p.199** *Evolution VIII*, 2005; photo: Todd-White Art Photography; © Marc Quinn; courtesy White Cube; **p.200** *Waiting for Godot*, 2006; photo: Stephen White; © Marc Quinn; courtesy White Cube; **p.201** *All About Love (Breathe)*, 2016; photo: Todd-White Art Photography; © Marc Quinn; courtesy Marc Quinn studio

PETER RANDALL-PAGE

p.205 *Wayside Carving III*, 1986; photo: courtesy the artist; © Peter Randall-Page; **p.207** *Clay Bodies*, 2009; photo: courtesy the artist; © Peter Randall-Page; **p.208** *After Bessie Smith*, 1995; photo: courtesy the artist; © Peter Randall-Page; **p.209** *Fructus* and *Corpus*, 2009; photo: Jonty Wilde; © Peter Randall-Page; **pp.210–11** *Rocks in my Bed*, 2005; photo: Sally-Ann Norman; © Peter Randall-Page; **p.213** *Seed*, 2007; photo: Marc Hill; © Peter Randall-Page; **p.214** *Playing God I and II*, 2018; photo: Heiner Grieder; © Peter Randall-Page; **p.215** *Shapes in the Clouds IV*, 2014; photo: Kevin Deery; © Peter Randall-Page

EVA ROTHSCHILD

p.219 *Actualisation*, 1998; © Eva Rothschild; **p.221** *The Inside of Your Head*, 2007; photo: Andy Keate; © Eva Rothschild; **p.222** *The Leanover*, 2018; photo: Robert Glowacki; © Eva Rothschild; courtesy Stuart Shave/Modern Art; **p.223** *An Array*, 2016; photo: Robert Glowacki; © Eva Rothschild; **p.225** *Technical Support*, 2018; photo: Andrew Curtis; © Eva Rothschild; courtesy Stuart Shave/Modern Art; **p.226** *Us Women (New York)*, 2011; © Eva Rothschild; courtesy 303 Gallery, New York; **pp.228–9** *Amphi*, 2019; photo: Robert Glowacki; © Eva Rothschild; courtesy Ireland at Venice; **p.231** *My World and Your World*, 2020; photo: John Sturrock; © Eva Rothschild

RICHARD WENTWORTH

p.235 *Mode - Module - Modular*, 2004; © Richard Wentworth; courtesy Lisson Gallery; **p.237** *Ifs and Buts*, 2005; © Richard Wentworth; courtesy Lisson Gallery; **p.238** *Marginalia*, 2019; photo: Roberto Ruiz; © Richard Wentworth; courtesy Nogueras Blanchard, Barcelona/Madrid; **p.239** *False Ceiling*, 1995; © Richard Wentworth; courtesy Lisson Gallery; **p.241** *A Room Full of Lovers*, 2013; photo: Ken Adlard; © Richard Wentworth; courtesy Lisson Gallery; **p.242** *14 Rooms Upended*, 2005; © Richard Wentworth; courtesy Lisson Gallery; **p.243** *Stile*, 1991; © Richard Wentworth; courtesy Lisson Gallery; **p.243** *Foglio/Foglia*, 1997; © Richard Wentworth; courtesy Lisson Gallery

RACHEL WHITEREAD

p.247 *Untitled (Fire Escape)*, 2002; photo: Lamay Photo © Rachel Whiteread; courtesy the artist; Luhring Augustine, New York; Galleria Lorcan O'Neill, Rome; and Gagosian Gallery, London; **p.248** *Untitled (Pink Torso)*, 1991; © Rachel Whiteread; courtesy the artist; Luhring Augustine, New York; Galleria Lorcan O'Neill, Rome; and Gagosian Gallery, London; **p.249** *Untitled (House)*, 1993; photo: Sue Omerod; commissioned by Artangel; sponsored by Beck's; © Rachel Whiteread; courtesy the artist; Luhring Augustine, New York; Galleria Lorcan O'Neill, Rome; and Gagosian Gallery, London; **p.249** *Cabin*, 2015; photo: Tim Schenck; © Rachel Whiteread; courtesy the artist; the Trust for Governors Island; Luhring Augustine, New York; Galleria Lorcan O'Neill, Rome; and Gagosian Gallery, London; **p.250** *Holocaust Memorial*, 1995–2000; photo: © Werner Kaligofsky; © Rachel Whiteread; courtesy the artist; Luhring Augustine, New York; Galleria Lorcan O'Neill, Rome; and Gagosian Gallery, London; **p.253** *Ghost*, 1990; © Rachel Whiteread; courtesy the artist; Luhring Augustine, New York; Galleria Lorcan O'Neill, Rome; and Gagosian Gallery, London; **p.255** *Look, Look, Look*, 2012; photo: Mike Bruce; © Rachel Whiteread; courtesy the artist; Luhring Augustine, New York; Galleria Lorcan O'Neill, Rome; and Gagosian Gallery, London; **p.255** *Monument*, 2001; © Rachel Whiteread; courtesy the artist; Luhring Augustine, New York; Galleria Lorcan O'Neill, Rome; and Gagosian Gallery, London

RICHARD WILSON

p.259 *20:50*, 1991; photo: Antony Oliver; © Richard Wilson; **p.260** *Turning the Place Over*, 2008; photo: Tony Wilson; © Richard Wilson; **p.263** *Slipstream*, 2014; photo: David Levene; © Richard Wilson; **p.264** *Huangpu Hold*, 2019; photo: Shanghai Urban Space Art Season Executive Team; © Richard Wilson; **p.265** *Set North for Japan (74°33' 2")*, 2000; photo: Shigeo Anzai © Richard Wilson; **p.267** *Hang on a Minute Lads, I've got a Great Idea*, 2012; photo: Nigel Green; © Richard Wilson; **p.268** *Blocka Flats*, 2017; photo: Miyako Narita; © Richard Wilson; **p.269** *Butterfly*, 2003; photo: R Wilson; © Richard Wilson

BILL WOODROW

p.273 *Car Door, Ironing Board and Twin-Tub with North American Indian Head-Dress*, 1981; © Bill Woodrow; **p.274** *Eight Bicycle Frames*, 1980; © Bill Woodrow; **p.275** *First Chair*, 1989; © Bill Woodrow; **pp.276–7** *The Last Fruit (The Tree of Idleness)*, 1988; non extant © Bill Woodrow; **p.279** *Self Portrait in the Year 2089*, 2013; © Bill Woodrow; **p.280** *Regardless of History*, 2000; photo: Jerry Young, London © Bill Woodrow; **p.281** *Celloswarm*, 2002; photo: Prudence Cumings Associates; © Bill Woodrow; **p.283** *The Ledge*, 2017; photo: Manuel Vason; © Bill Woodrow

PORTRAITS

p.8 Fiona Banner: Photography Misha Haller; **p.20** Phyllida Barlow: Photography Cat Garcia; **p.34** Anthony Caro: Courtesy The Anthony Caro Centre; **p.48** Richard Deacon: Photography Ken Adlard; **p.64** Laura Ford: Photography Yu Scheffel; **p.78** Antony Gormley: Photography Oak Taylor-Smith; **p.94** Mona Hatoum: Photography Mizuho Miyazaki and The Japan Art Association/The Sankei Shimbun; **p.108** Susan Hiller: Photography Carla Borel; **p.122** Anish Kapoor: Photography Gautier Deblonde; **p.134** Tania Kovats: Photography Robin Mills; **p.146** Richard Long: Photography Jack Hems; **p.160** David Nash: Photography Jonty Wilde; **p.174** Cornelia Parker: Photography Sam Lane; **p.188** Marc Quinn: Courtesy Marc Quinn studio; **p.202** Peter Randall-Page: Photography Mike Smallcombe; **p.216** Eva Rothschild: Photography Anne Purkiss; **p.232** Richard Wentworth: Photography Thilo Hoffmann; **p.244** Rachel Whiteread: Photography Anita Corbin; **p.256** Richard Wilson: Courtesy Richard Wilson; **p.270** Bill Woodrow: Courtesy Bill Woodrow

ACKNOWLEDGEMENTS

I am immensely grateful to the artists who have contributed to this project, without whom the publication could not have been possible: Fiona Banner, Phyllida Barlow, Anthony Caro, Richard Deacon, Laura Ford, Antony Gormley, Mona Hatoum, Susan Hiller, Anish Kapoor, Tania Kovats, Richard Long, David Nash, Cornelia Parker, Marc Quinn, Peter Randall-Page, Eva Rothschild, Richard Wentworth, Rachel Whiteread, Richard Wilson and Bill Woodrow.

I would also like to express my gratitude to all artists' studios, galleries and estates that assisted with the project.

My thanks go to the team at Laurence King Publishing Ltd, for commissioning the publication, and for their commitment and enthusiasm throughout.

I am eternally indebted to my parents, Roy and Maria Cole, who instilled in me an awareness of the life-affirming power of the arts from a very young age.

Ina Cole

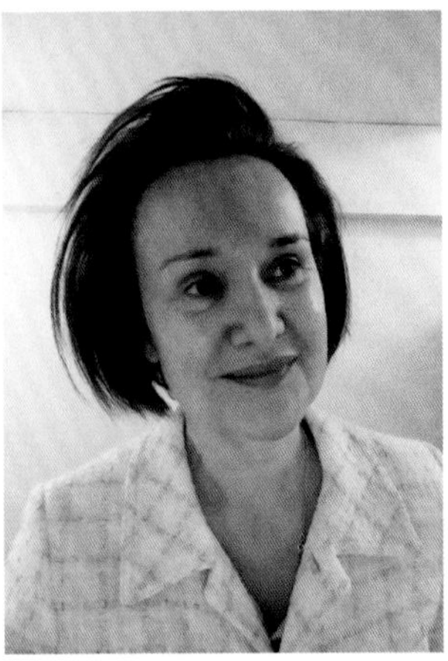

INA COLE has written widely on twentieth-century and contemporary art, publishing articles, artist interviews, essays and exhibition catalogues. She is UK contributing editor for *Sculpture*; a publication affiliated to the International Sculpture Center in the US. Following 10 years at Tate St Ives and the Barbara Hepworth Museum, she held several positions within culture and higher education, and has facilitated many live debates with artists. Ina has an MA in the History of Modern Art and Design from Falmouth University, Cornwall.